POLICY CHOICES AND PUBLIC ACTION

POLICY CHOICES
AND PUBLIC ACTION

Charles F. Bonser

Eugene B. McGregor, Jr.

Clinton V. Oster, Jr.

School of Public and Environmental Affairs
Indiana University

Prentice Hall
Upper Saddle River, New Jersey 07458

Library of Congress Cataloging-in-Publication Data
Bonser, Charles F.
    Policy choices and public action / Charles F. Bonser, Eugene B.
McGregor, Jr., Clinton V. Oster, Jr.
        p. cm.
    Includes bibliographical references and index.
    ISBN 0-13-442591-X
    1. Policy sciences.   2. Policy sciences—United States.
I. McGregor, Eugene B.   II. Oster, Clinton V.   III. Title.
H97.B66   1995
320'.6—dc20   95-34003
                                                                        CIP

Acquisitions editor: Jennie Katsaros
Editorial/production supervision
    and interior design: Mary McDonald
Copy editor: Ann Farkas
Cover design: Bruce Kenselaar
Buyer: Bob Anderson

© 1996 by Prentice-Hall, Inc.
Simon & Schuster/A Viacom Company
Upper Saddle River, New Jersey 07458

Printed in the United States of America
10 9 8 7 6 5 4 3 2 1

ISBN 0-13-442591-X

Prentice-Hall International (UK) Limited, *London*
Prentice-Hall of Australia Pty. Limited, *Sydney*
Prentice-Hall Canada Inc., *Toronto*
Prentice-Hall Hispanoamericana, S.A., *Mexico*
Prentice-Hall of India Private Limited, *New Delhi*
Prentice-Hall of Japan, Inc., *Tokyo*
Simon & Schuster Asia Pte. Ltd., *Singapore*
Editora Prentice-Hall do Brasil, Ltda., *Rio de Janeiro*

Contents

Preface   vii

PART I   THE FRAMEWORK FOR AMERICAN PUBLIC POLICY MAKING

1   What Does Government Do?   1

2   The Process of Public Policy Development   36

PART II   GOVERNMENT AND THE ECONOMY

3   Government Regulation   55

4   Financing Government Activities   74

5   Economic Policy: Stabilization and Growth   96

6   International Economic Policy   128

PART III   POLICY ISSUES

7   Poverty and the Welfare Problem   162

8   The Health Security Dilemma   191

v

9   Transportation Policy   215

10   Education and Training in the New Economy   245

11   Environmental Policy   278

12   Crime and Punishment in the United States   317

13   Agriculture Policy   338

14   Foreign and National Security Policy   361

PART IV   IMPLEMENTING PUBLIC POLICY

15   Governmental Reform: A Work in Progress   403

16   Managing Government in the 21st Century   425

Appendix: A Quick Guide to Public Affairs Information   456

Glossary   474

Index   485

Preface

Policy Choices and Public Action presents a framework for debate and discussion of the critical policy problems confronting American public affairs decision makers as one century closes and another opens. The aim is to stimulate intelligent analysis of substantive public choices. We place the reader in the context of complex issues that occupy the public affairs agenda and invite consideration of possible solutions. Our procedure, therefore, is to examine both the choices and the public action that real-world decision making requires and ask a simple question: In the end, do the available policy choices and actions advance the public interest and enhance the lives of citizens?

As authors, our job is complex, but manageable. Our ambition is *not* to pronounce correct answers to the many questions we pose. It is, rather, to help readers frame issues for themselves based on a public record that documents the history and context of many of our most significant policy struggles. We try to enhance the discussion by suggesting a range of policy options available to public decision makers, notwithstanding the many uncertainties and conflicts embedded in all public choices. We also endeavor to suggest that there are well-established criteria by which public choices and actions can be judged and, furthermore, that there are standards of analysis by which decision making can be informed. Finally, we provide full documentation so that readers may verify for themselves the truth or falsehood of competing policy claims and even independently update the data presented that rapidly become old.

In the end, we seek to convince readers that American public problems are not insurmountable ills defying understanding and solution. Rather, it is our thesis that careful study reveals a rich array of public choices and action options available to those who would understand and shoulder public responsibility. Our argument is presented in four parts. Part I presents a general framework explaining the many possible roles that can be played by government. We introduce an account of the public problem solving process, concentrating particularly on the way in which issues come to public attention and are framed for action by government. Part II examines the role that government plays in the larger market economy, with emphasis on government regulation, public finance, macroeconomic stabilization and growth policy, and international economic policy.

Part III provides substantive analysis of a variety of contemporary public policy issues, including poverty and welfare, health, transportation, education and workforce training, environmental policy, crime and punishment, agriculture, and foreign and national security policy. Finally, Part IV addresses managerial issues associated with implementing public policy, including public ethics, privatization, total quality management, and recent efforts to reinvent government and transform public management. An appendix provides supporting material to help those attempting to conduct their own investigations into public affairs issues. We include many of the universal resource locators (URLs) that are the internet addresses used to move information, previously buried in government document repositories, into a global and electronically mediated conversation.

Our focus is middle-range problem solving. We avoid the broadest philosophical debates, such as whether First Amendment rights should exist, and the most narrow gauge framing of current public issues, such as whether the federal government should assume responsibility for child immunization. The former problems are endlessly complex and hard to approach and define, let alone resolve; the latter approach would tie the book to issues better approached through the news media and recent documents than through formal textbook treatment. In the middle, however, are a large number of deeply structured and relatively stable issues confronting the American public. They are amenable to coherent definition and do not fade in and out with each change of political season and media whim.

Balances must be struck between simplicity and complexity and between description and recommendations for public action. Each problem in this volume addresses a major policy issue currently commanding public and government attention. Each is enormously complex and has been the subject of much analysis and many recommendations. In addition, each issue is action-forcing in the sense that there is general agreement that something must be done about the problem even as debate rages about the critical details. Indeed, to reject public action is itself a significant policy choice.

A basic logic unifies what would otherwise be scattered discussion of unrelated problems. Each chapter raises a key policy question begging public attention. Next, questions and problems are placed in context, and essential background information is provided. Third, available action alternatives are considered. Finally, the reader is invited to add his or her own creative instincts to the discussion and to test comparative strengths and weaknesses of policy choices that could contribute to national problem solving. In this way, a public policy logic is presented and reinforced through repeated application to several issues.

An attitude of intellectual humility and tolerance for debate is fundamental to understanding policy issues. The great issues of public policy and public management are great precisely because they represent complex problems that do *not* have simple technical solutions, for if solutions to enduring problems were simple and clear, they would have been discovered and embraced long ago. The facts of public life are that all of the issues here involve clashes of views, interests, and values surrounding collective choice. Furthermore, an increasingly well understood principle of effective government is that modern public policy issues cannot be captured effectively by a single academic discipline. Problems of poverty, national security, health, crime, and so forth, are not inherently sociological, economic, or political (or the property of any other discipline, for that matter). It is perhaps more accurate to say that public problems can be ground in all disciplinary mills, each of which can tell interesting and plausible stories about root causes of problems and the most desirable policy choices. Thus, sociologists remind us of the importance of social structure and process in the design of social action. Economists have developed a sophisticated understanding of the role of incentives—both costs and prices—and the power of markets to override even the best intentions of government. Political scientists have a keen sense of the significance of the inherent struggle for power implied by the existence of human interests that often clash when collectively binding policy choices are at issue. In our book, as in the School of Public and Environmental Affairs (SPEA) where we are faculty, the approach adopted is an interdisciplinary one. Each of us comes from a different academic background, but each of us also has spent over two decades in interdisciplinary academic environments and has had first-hand experience working in government. We draw upon these experiences as well as the perspectives of our SPEA colleagues in preparing this book.

The structure and organization of the book accommodate a variety of teaching styles and course objectives. The policy issue chapters are written to stand alone as substantive treatments of selected problem topics. However, should an instructor wish to address a smaller set of issues in greater depth, the chapters are designed to provide a foundation on which more detailed treatments can be built. We hope, in addition, that extensive citations, references, and the "quick guide" appendix provide a jump start for students preparing policy memos, longer paper assignments, debates, presentations, or other exercises associated with public affairs learning. The book can also be integrated with current sources of public affairs information such as *The New York Times, The Washington Post National Weekly Edition, U.S. News and World Report,* or other leading periodical magazines. The result is a framework by which an educated citizenry can track and understand the great debates.

Our acknowledgments are many, even as we take full responsibility for all aspects of the final product. Most recently, we must include the people directly involved in preparing the final manuscript, including secretarial support from Nancy Croker and Betty Fiscus; Cynthia Morehead Mahigian in graphic design; and research assistance from Denise Kaiser, Scott Burgins, Melissa Lenn, and Kellie Monroe. Many thanks are also owed to our reviewers, including H. George Frederickson, Edwin O. Sterne Distinguished Professor of Public Administration at the University of Kansas, who read and commented on earlier versions of the manuscript; to our teaching and research assistants Seth Tyler, George Candler, Kirk Emerson, Shawn McDuff, Laura Mears, Anne Marie Thompson, Cecil Autrey, and Karen Jewell; and to A. James Barnes, Dean of the School of Public and Environmental Affairs, for his enthusiastic support and encouragement.

Finally, acknowledgment and thanks are due to the thousands of Indiana

University undergraduates with whom, since the school was founded in 1972, the SPEA faculty has engaged the issues presented in V170, "Introduction to Public Affairs." Our gratitude to our students taking the class over the past three years is particularly great, for their questions, comments, and patience gave us the chance to test the materials presented herein.

Charles F. Bonser
Eugene B. McGregor, Jr.
Clinton V. Oster, Jr.

Bloomington, Indiana

POLICY CHOICES
AND PUBLIC ACTION

1

What Does Government Do?

Americans have always been in a boil about government. On the one hand, they agree with the rhetorical proposition that "that government is best which governs least." On the other hand, the record of government growth and involvement in every facet of American life is clear: government decisions and actions now touch directly every sector of society. As we shall see, despite all the railing, American government is big business!

Furthermore, for all the criticisms leveled at its performance, U.S. government works and, in many cases, works extremely well. The political scientist James Q. Wilson succinctly states the representative evidence.

> We live in a country that . . . still makes it possible to get drinkable water instantly, put through a telephone call in seconds, deliver a letter in a day, and obtain a passport in a week. Our Social Security checks arrive on time. Some state prisons, and most of the federal ones, are reasonably decent and humane institutions. The great majority of Americans, cursing all the while, pay their taxes. One can stand on the deck of an aircraft carrier during night flight operations and watch two thousand nineteen-year-old boys faultlessly operate one of the most complex organizational systems ever created. There are not many places where all this happens. It is astonishing it can be made to happen at all.[1]

This opinion is shared by a substantial number of political scientists and policy analysts embracing a variety of ideological persuasions.[2] The phrase "Good enough for government work" is a popular expression expressing a disdain for government's alleged malfunctions. It is, however, misapplied to programs and agencies whose tolerance for error is very low and whose requirement for precision is very high. Agencies like the National Aeronautics and Space Administration (NASA), the Federal Aviation Administration (FAA), the U.S. Navy, and the Internal Revenue Service (IRS) cannot afford to indulge, respectively, in the repetitive failures of badly designed rocket booster seals, slow and inaccurate traffic-collision-avoidance systems, sloppy carrier takeoff and landing procedures, and computer hardware and sofware breakdowns.

Demonstration of the many accomplishments of government has not squelched vigorous debate. The political reality is that myths and strongly held views persist. Perhaps the most recently vocal have been skeptics who delight in enshrining perceived government idiocies in verse and song. The rousing rendition of "That Dad Gummed Guv'ment" in the musical *Big River* summarizes a popular frustration many people have felt. So shaky can public confidence in government become that many recent political campaigns for public office have been based on the proposition that the candidate would, if elected, "Clean up the mess in [name the capital city or city hall of choice]." In essence, the public often entertains and even elects candidates who offer a dose of public philosophy that runs against government, a curious position in a democracy which, by definition, means self-government.

Irate skepticism is often met with painfully earnest defenses of the uses to which a complex set of institutions collected under the *government* label might be put. Thus, one of the notable features of U.S. public opinion is the simultaneous embrace of two seemingly contradictory principles: on the one hand, people generally agree with the ideological proposition that large government is undesirable, but on the other hand, they like the idea of having public services. Lloyd A. Free and Hadley Cantril, students of U.S. public opinion, have assessed the seeming contradiction in the following way:

> For a large proportion of the American people, there is clearly not only a separation in but conflict between their attitudes toward practical Governmental [*sic*] operations and programs, on the one hand, and their ideological ideas and abstract concepts about government and society, on the other. This conflict is resolved in a typically pragmatic American fashion: the practical is given precedence over the theoretical. At the operational level of government, the great majority of Americans are more concerned about practical problems than they are about abstract conceptions on the ideological level. They want government to work.[3]

How can these ideas be reconciled in the present? The beginning is to recognize that there is a debate about government and what it is, what it does, and what it ought to do. Clues about the debate abound. Consider one of the signature phrases from the farewell address of The Great Communicator, President Ronald Reagan:

> I hope we have once again reminded people that man is not free unless government is limited. There's a clear cause and effect here that is as neat and predictable as a law of physics: as government expands, liberty contracts.[4]

Contrast this argument with the 1993 address delivered by newly inaugurated President Bill Clinton:

> Let us resolve to make our government a place for what Franklin Roosevelt called "bold, persistent experimentation," a government for our tomorrows, not our yesterdays.[5]

Clearly, we are not of one mind about government.

A typical example of public sector ferment is found in the 1994 mid-term congressional elections maneuvering. In February 1994, House Republicans convened a conference on Maryland's Eastern Shore to develop a strategy that would reverse four decades of minority party existence. The result was *Contract with America*, publicly unveiled on September 27, 1994, on the steps of the U.S. Capitol and signed by 367 Republican candidates for House seats. A similar covenant with state voters was pledged on October 4 by candidates for state legislatures who stood on the steps of state capitols and repeated their commitment to the *Contract*. The pledge was again repeated on October 11 by local government candidates who stood on the steps of county courthouses and city halls.

The *Contract* was cast as a binding agreement, shown below, between voters and aspiring Republican candidates committed, if elected, to deliver action early in the 104th Congress with the promise: "If we break the contract, throw us out."

Contract with America

Congressional reforms to be passed on the first day of the 104th Congress: changes in congressional procedure designed to apply laws equally to the Congress, which has always enjoyed special perquisites and privileges; cut the number of House committees and staff by one-third; limit terms of committee chairs; audit the House's books with an independent firm, and require a three-fifths majority vote to pass a tax increase.

Bills to be brought to a House vote within 100 days:
1. **The Fiscal Responsibility Act:** pass a balanced budget amendment to the U.S. Constitution and line-item veto power for the president.
2. **The Taking Back Our Streets Act:** stop violent criminals by means of longer prison sentences; relax rules of evidence in trials, including "good faith" exclusionary rule exemptions; strengthen the death penalty; and convert resources previously allocated to police and crime programs into more money for prison construction.
3. **The Personal Responsibility Act:** discourage illegitimacy and teen pregnancy by prohibiting welfare benefits to minor mothers; deny increased benefits for additional children born to mothers on welfare; cut spending for welfare programs; terminate welfare benefits after two years; add work requirements for all welfare recipients.
4. **The Family Reinforcement Act:** require stronger enforcement of child support payment, tax incentives for adoptions, stronger parental control of their children's education, stronger child pornography laws, and elderly dependent care tax credits.
5. **The American Dream Restoration Act:** provide a $500 per child tax credit; repeal marriage penalty in tax code.
6. **The National Security Restoration Act:** prohibit U.N. command of U.S. troops; increase funding for "essential parts" of national security funding such as antimissile defenses.
7. **The Senior Citizens Fairness Act:** raise the Social Security earnings limit; repeal the 1993 tax increases on Social Security benefits; provide tax incentives for private long-term care insurance.
8. **The Job Creation and Wage Enhancement Act:** Enact small business incentives; cut and index capital gains taxes to inflation; require risk assessment and cost-benefit analysis as a basis for rolling back government regulation of the private

sector; reform unfunded mandates by which the federal government passes on responsibilities unmatched with funds with which to implement required programs.

9. **The Common Sense Legal Reform Act:** Enact "loser pays" laws; set reasonable limits on punitive damages in civil law suits; reform product liability laws, all designed to curtail excessive litigation.

10. **The Citizen Legislature Act:** For the first time on the floor of the House, bring to a vote term limits legislation designed to replace career politicians with citizen legislators by Constitutional amendment limiting senators to two terms and House members to six terms.

In one stroke, the race for political control of the House began and the 1996 presidential election season opened![6]

How can such action be understood? Display of the vaunted American problem solving genius? Political chicanery? Partisan political action designed to wrest policy leadership from an increasingly confident president threatening success in the 1996 elections? Decisive national debate about new directions for American civilization? All of the above? None of the above? Defenders of the *Contract* argued that bold "moves" were needed to "restore the fabric of trust between the American people and their officeholders" and "to renew the American Dream" through "a detailed agenda for national renewal, a written commitment with no fine print." The result would be "the end of government that is too big, too intrusive, and too easy with the public's money."[7]

Critics reveled in the *Contract*'s obvious problems and inconsistencies. How was it possible to correct the chronic federal budget deficit and reduce the national debt with tax cuts and further promises of increased spending on such programs as prisons and national security? Indeed, quick inspection of the *Contract* reveals an enormous number of questions and issues for public affairs discussion, many of which are the sorts of issues discussed in this text. The following merely illustrate the breadth of public affairs discussion (with text chapters included in parenthesis for the benefit of readers who wish to read ahead):

1. What does government have to do with producing any of the results proclaimed as desirable by the *Contract* (Chapters 1, 15, and 16)? Does government help or is it a hindrance?

2. Why is government so expensive? Will balanced budget amendments and line-item vetoes really produce fiscal responsibility (Chapters 4 and 13)?

3. Are stiffer penalties and more prisons anything more than an expensive "end-of-the-pipe" treatment of a problem for which the better solution lies in "front-end" investments in people and crime prevention rather than "hind-end" warehouse construction for criminals (Chapter 12)?

4. How do proposed cuts in welfare spending solve the long standing problems of poverty, health and welfare in the U.S. (Chapters 7 and 8)?

5. How could a $500 per child tax credit possibly dent the massive human capital investment requirements necessary to restore the American dream of growing, high-wage prosperity for all in a competitive global economy (Chapters 5, 6, 9 and 10)?

6. How does one limit litigation in a society in which regulation and rule of law are strategic public policy instruments (Chapter 3)?

7. Finally, how can constitutional term limits do anything but undermine public problem solving by populating government with amateurs who are constitutionally barred from office at the point that they begin to become reasonably expert and productive?

The real world of public problem solving involves more than simply finding correct answers to complex problems, however. Public relations people—"spin doctors"—also lay hands on problems in order to interpret (often creatively) "what is really going on." Not surprisingly, critics of the *Contract* condemned the plan as a "contract on America," a product of dark forces foisting self-inflicted wounds on an unsuspecting nation. For example, how could a national entitlement such as child nutrition, guaranteed since 1946 under uniform national nutrition standards, be protected when federal money used to subsidize school lunches for more than 25 million children each day (more than four billion meals per year) is lumped together with school breakfasts, day-care meals, and other programs and handed over to states in the form of a discretionary block grant? Forecasts of starving children, deepening poverty, and despair were rife.[8]

The *Contract* was clearly more than just a blueprint for policy choice. It was also a political action document aimed at generating an operating majority as the basis for policy choice. Thus, the strategy was to focus public debate on critical issues defined by a contractual rhetoric cast in simple language, carry a majority of like-minded congressmen and women into office, and hammer out legislation with the new majority. If the initial proposals were wrong, corrections could be negotiated. In any event, constitutional checks and balances would prevent the passage of legislation unacceptable to the public interest. For example, in the case of balanced budget and term limits amendments to the Constitution, two-thirds majorities in both houses would be required to produce an amendment requiring in turn, ratification by three-fourths of the states.

The political checks are real. Within the first 100 days of the 104th congress, the Senate defeated a Constitutional amendment requiring a balanced budget by the year 2002 and the House defeated a term limits amendment. Subsequently, the Supreme Court headed off attempts to legislate constitutional amendments, such as term limits, in its 5–4 decision finding against the attempts of state legislatures to impose term limits in the absence of a Constitutional amendment.[9]

The November electoral results were stunning! Republican majorities emerged *both* in the U.S. House of Representatives, where 224 of *Contract* signatories were elected, and in the U.S. Senate. The forty year old Democratic congressional dominance had been broken! In the bargain, a sitting Speaker of the House—representative Thomas Foley of Washington—was defeated for the first time in over 130 years. Moreover, not a single *incumbent* Republican congressman, senator, or governor was defeated. Clearly, the voters were sending a strong message. The country wanted action and it was prepared to turn to a new team to get results.

Whether the *Contract* was itself a precipitating event or whether it merely "caught a wave" of voter frustration with government's seeming inability to confront the current great issues will remain a lively topic of scholarly debate and research. This text is concerned less with explaining and predicting political outcomes and concentrates instead on substantive issues. The lesson of the *Contract* is clear, however: public choice and public action go together; one does not occur without the other.

WHAT GOVERNMENT IS

There are many myths and misunderstandings about government's size and its growth over time. It is important to recognize that government is indeed big business as measured by the the amount of money all governments spend, and in the number of people our governments employ. If one merely looks at the federal government, for instance, one is looking at an enterprise that in 1991 employed 2.8 million civilians and 2.5 million uniformed military personnel. It spent around $1.2 trillion, roughly 24 percent of the U.S. gross national product. The national effort is currently funneled through 13 line departments, each of which represents a complex conglomerate of bureau-level *firms* covering 350 to 400 agencies such as the Federal Bureau of Investigation (FBI), the IRS, the Social Security Administration, the Forest Service, and the Secret Service, to name only a few of the major federal agencies. Lying outside departmental structure are more than 60 independent agencies, public corporations chartered as publicly owned businesses, and regulatory boards and commissions. This enumeration does not include numerous federally sponsored corporations—mostly financial instruments such as public banks and insurance corporations—chartered since 1960.

But that is only part of the story. A review of the data about U.S. government reveals the creative and varied uses to which government is put, for not only do we find a large and complicated national government lumped under the *federal* heading but also 50 smaller and equally complex state governments that have recently become active members of the U.S. federal system. In addition, states have authorized the creation of an enormous number of local governments, including general-purpose towns, townships, cities, and counties to which have been added a large number of special-purpose school districts and numerous special districts each with specified duties and access to the public treasury. Indeed, Table 1–1 indicates that despite a dramatic consolidation of school districts from over 67,000 school districts in 1952 to well under 15,000 public school districts in 1992, there was an equally dramatic increase in the use of narrowly conceived special districts that numbered slightly more than 8,000 in 1942 and over 33,000 in 1992.

In addition, the scale and scope of public affairs in the United States has been marked by several developments. First, there has been a growth in government

TABLE 1–1 Number of General and Special Governments, 1952–1992

Year	Total	Federal	State	General Purpose Local*	Special Districts**	School Districts
1952	116,807	1	50	37,061	12,340	67,355
1957	102,392	1	50	37,465	14,424	50,454
1962	91,237	1	50	38,184	18,323	34,678
1967	81,229	1	50	38,202	21,264	21,782
1972	78,269	1	50	38,552	23,885	15,781
1977	79,913	1	50	38,726	25,962	15,174
1982	81,831	1	50	38,851	28,078	14,851
1987	83,237	1	50	38,933	29,532	14,721
1992*	86,743	1	50	39,005	33,131	14,556

*County, Municipal, and Townships. Does not include Special Districts.

**Special Districts are independent, limited-purpose governmental units (other than School Districts). They include libraries, airports, parks, and so forth.

Source: Census of Governments (Washington, D.C.: U.S. Department of Commerce, U.S. Census Bureau, quinquennial census).

responsibilities at all levels as reflected in the steady growth of government employment and revenue shown in Tables 1–2 and 1–3, respectively. All governments in 1991 employed 15 percent of a national labor force approaching 130 million persons. Second, the recent dramatic growth in government *revenue* has been in federal government while the *employment* growth has occurred at state and local levels, a clue about some of the different government functions. For example, the federal government manages to spend and redistribute nearly one-fourth of the gross national product of the United States with a workforce that has grown very little over three decades, while state and local governments might be characterized as the labor-intensive end of government. Students can profitably spend some time sorting out why this might be the case. (Hint: Think of the kinds of things government does that result in large outlays of cash managed by few people and, conversely, the sorts of services that are more labor intensive.)

TABLE 1–2   Government Employment as Percent of National Labor Force, 1960–1992

Year	Total	Federal	State	Local	NLF	% of NLF
1960	8,808	2,421	1,527	4,795	71,489	12%
1961	9,100	2,484	1,627	4,990	74,175	12%
1962	9,388	2,535	1,680	5,169	74,682	13%
1963	9,736	2,548	1,775	5,413	74,571	13%
1964	10,064	2,528	1,873	5,663	75,830	13%
1965	10,589	2,588	2,028	5,973	77,178	14%
1966	11,479	2,861	2,211	6,407	78,893	15%
1967	11,867	2,993	2,335	6,539	80,793	15%
1968	12,342	2,984	2,495	6,864	82,272	15%
1969	12,691	2,975	2,614	7,102	84,239	15%
1970	13,028	2,881	2,755	7,392	84,889	15%
1971	13,316	2,872	2,832	7,612	86,929	15%
1972	13,604	2,795	2,937	7,872	88,991	15%
1973	14,139	2,786	3,013	8,339	91,756	15%
1974	14,628	2,874	3,155	8,599	94,179	16%
1975	14,973	2,890	3,271	8,813	95,453	16%
1976	15,012	2,843	3,343	8,826	98,302	15%
1977	15,613	2,848	3,491	9,274	101,142	15%
1978	15,628	2,885	3,539	9,204	104,368	15%
1979	15,971	2,869	3,699	9,403	107,050	15%
1980	16,213	2,898	3,753	9,562	108,544	15%
1981	15,968	2,865	3,726	9,377	110,315	14%
1982	15,918	2,848	3,747	9,324	111,872	14%
1983	16,034	2,875	3,816	9,344	113,226	14%
1984	16,436	2,942	3,898	9,595	115,241	14%
1985	16,690	3,021	3,984	9,685	117,167	14%
1986	16,933	3,019	4,068	9,846	119,540	14%
1987	17,212	3,091	4,116	10,005	121,602	14%
1988	17,588	3,112	4,236	10,240	123,378	14%
1989	17,879	3,114	4,365	10,400	125,557	14%
1990	18,369	3,105	4,503	10,760	126,424	15%
1991	18,554	3,103	4,521	10,930	126,867	15%
1992	18,745	3,047	4,595	11,103	128,548	15%

Source: U.S. Department of Commerce, U.S. Statistical Abstract (Washington, D.C., Bureau of Census), annual editions.

TABLE 1–3 Total Government Revenue from Own Sources, 1960–1990

Year	Total*	Federal*	State*	Local*
1960	154,042	100,739	26,093	27,210
1961	158,741	101,341	27,821	29,579
1962	168,157	106,441	30,117	31,599
1963	181,152	114,557	32,750	33,845
1964	192,410	120,959	35,703	35,748
1965	202,587	125,837	38,507	38,243
1966	225,632	141,142	43,000	41,490
1967	253,070	161,350	46,739	44,981
1968	265,640	165,239	52,525	47,876
1969	312,638	199,637	59,809	53,192
1970	333,805	205,562	68,691	59,552
1971	342,488	202,544	73,424	66,520
1972	381,850	223,378	84,328	74,144
1973	426,173	247,849	97,108	81,216
1974	484,646	288,560	107,645	88,441
1975	517,174	302,613	116,805	97,756
1976	572,615	323,527	140,496	108,592
1977	657,321	382,149	155,799	119,373
1978	731,737	429,722	171,550	130,465
1979	829,372	499,601	189,918	139,853
1980	932,199	563,690	212,636	155,873
1981	1,075,388	658,955	240,042	176,391
1982	1,144,786	685,835	261,783	197,168
1983	1,181,421	677,817	284,933	218,671
1984	1,307,482	752,421	315,637	239,424
1985	1,418,370	804,877	349,032	264,461
1986	1,515,473	845,378	382,600	287,495
1987	1,677,736	950,144	414,560	313,032
1988	1,776,399	1,009,484	434,584	332,331
1989	1,917,451	1,089,757	470,922	356,772
1990	2,028,549	1,151,685	505,843	371,021
1991	2,124,211	1,197,448	516,414	410,349

*Millions of dollars. Duplicative intergovernmental transactions are excluded.

Source: Government Finance Series, annual reports.

A third conclusion suggested by the data is that over time the *rate of growth* in the government share of the total economy is beginning to moderate, despite the fact that the absolute numbers sound large. For example, as Figure 1–1 shows, the absolute number of employees has been growing as a result of state and local government hiring, and much of the hiring has involved street-level bureaucrats—the police officers, fire fighters, social service workers, teachers, park and recreation personnel, and public works construction and maintenance needed to keep nearly 87,000 government units functioning. Nevertheless, the share of the national labor force claimed by government has not in the 1990s exceeded the 1974–5 peak-load civilian employment total of 16 percent of the national labor force. Moreover, contrary to popular myth, the federal government portion of total U.S. government has not involved a burgeoning bureaucracy growing out of control. Indeed, at this writing it is a shrinking bureaucracy, undergoing much of the same restructuring

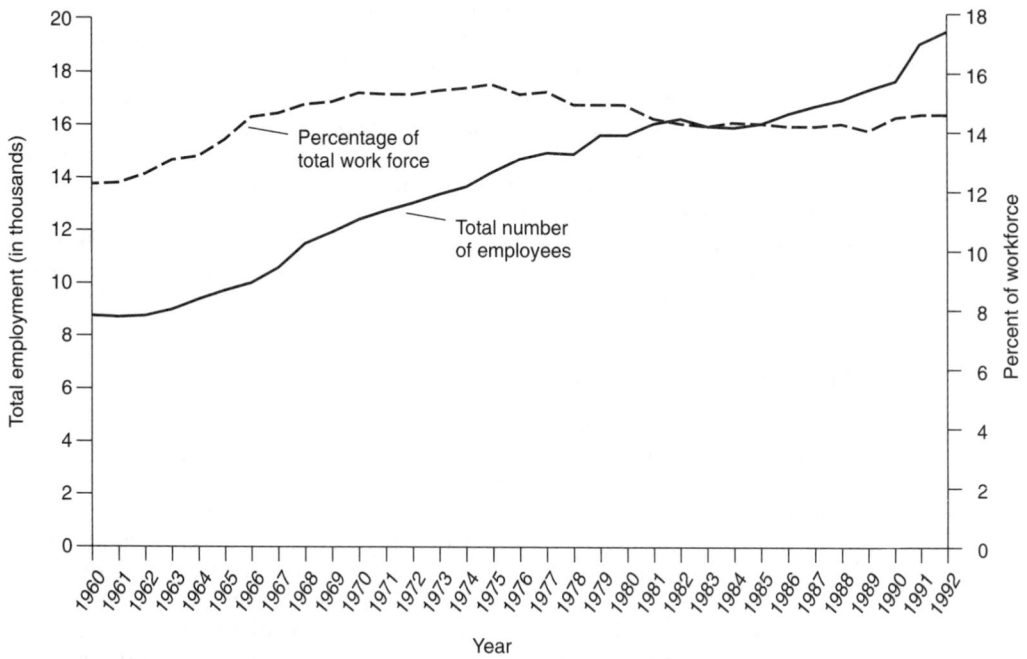

Figure 1–1   Government employment totals and percent of total workforce employed by all governments: 1960–92

Source: U.S. Department of Commerce, *U.S. Statistical Abstract* (Washington, D.C., Bureau of Census), annual editions.

and "reinvention" occurring throughout the economy. Chapters 15 and 16 examine many of these changes.

A fourth conclusion is that trends in government employment and spending follow closely the public affairs challenges of the past six decades. From the Great Depression through World War II and the regional wars in Korea and Vietnam, a strong hand was dealt the federal government to promote economic and national security aims requiring industrial productivity at home and global discipline abroad. With the decline of the wartime agendas and the rise of productivity growth and economic development concerns, however, the shape of public affairs has changed. The productivity agenda has left state and local governments with active responsibilities for education, industrial development, infrastructure and transportation, social services, housing, community development, health, and all the other details that require state and community deliberation rather than national management and control.

Finally, government is not static. The nation has always been engaged in a continuous debate about the future size and shape of its government. As the data show, U.S. government is multilayered and complex. Furthermore, there is constant change as new challenges and constraints are met and resolved. For instance, Federal financial assistance to state and local government peaked in 1978, leaving state and local governments scrambling for resources to replace the lack of growth in national government support. State and local governments, in turn, have had to be enormously clever and creative in adapting to the public demand for natural resource preservation, fresh water, fire protection, sewage disposal, electric power and other utilities, libraries, hospitals, community development, ports, and transportation facilities. States and localities have done this partly through the creation of special-purpose instruments of government—each with its own powers, authorities, and access to revenue and bond markets for financial support. Thus, complexity and change, rather than fossilized simplicity, characterize the uses U.S. government has made of the many instruments of public affairs. Few countries exceed the United States in its engineered governmental complexity, although some would say that the system has become too complex, too fragmented, and too unaccountable to public opinion.

Many Opinions

The reasons for American ambivalence toward government lie deep within our political history. As a nation founded on expansion into the new space of an open frontier, glorification of individual freedom and entrepreneurship has remained one of the defining characteristics of American character and public life. Less prominent, perhaps, but still present, are the voices extolling public responsibility and self-restraint in our individual claims to freedom by the requirements of living with other people in towns, cities, states, and nations, all of which coexist on an increasingly crowded planet. Thus, while the former group argues that there can be no freedom *with* government, the latter responds that there can be no freedom *without* government. The issue here is perhaps less the question of whether one view is right and the other wrong but, more significantly, the extent to which the two views capture some measure of truth. Students should develop their own opinions about this debate.

The many voices taking conflicting positions in public affairs can be found in the news media, some of which appear in the examples of print media displayed in Figure 1–2. The public affairs airplane is only faintly designed to help sort out public policy positions—such as right wing, left wing, and center—that have popularly been fastened to the many periodicals available to students of public issues. Serious students should peruse the periodical literature and compare their views with those of leading writers and columnists. Which views are most persuasive? What mix of newspapers and magazines seems to provide the best coverage of public affairs?

Debates about government were not recently invented. During the nation's founding era, there was great discussion of whether the weak Articles of Confederation should be supplanted by strengthening the organs of central national government. *The Federalist Papers*,[10] published in the newspapers of New York City from October 1787 through March 1788, were a series of 85 letters to the public, written under the pseudonym *Publius*, to advocate ratification of the proposed Constitution that had been produced during the summer and signed on September 17, 1787, by delegates to the Philadelphia convention. The propagandist aim was to convince the public that the proposed Constitution was a good idea and that the agrarian and small-town fears about tyranny from a strengthened national government could be overcome by a careful account of the advantages to commerce, defense, and social welfare offered by the compound federal republic.

The stakes were high. Approval of nine of the thirteen states was required, but opposition in critical states such as New York was strong, and a clear vote of dis-

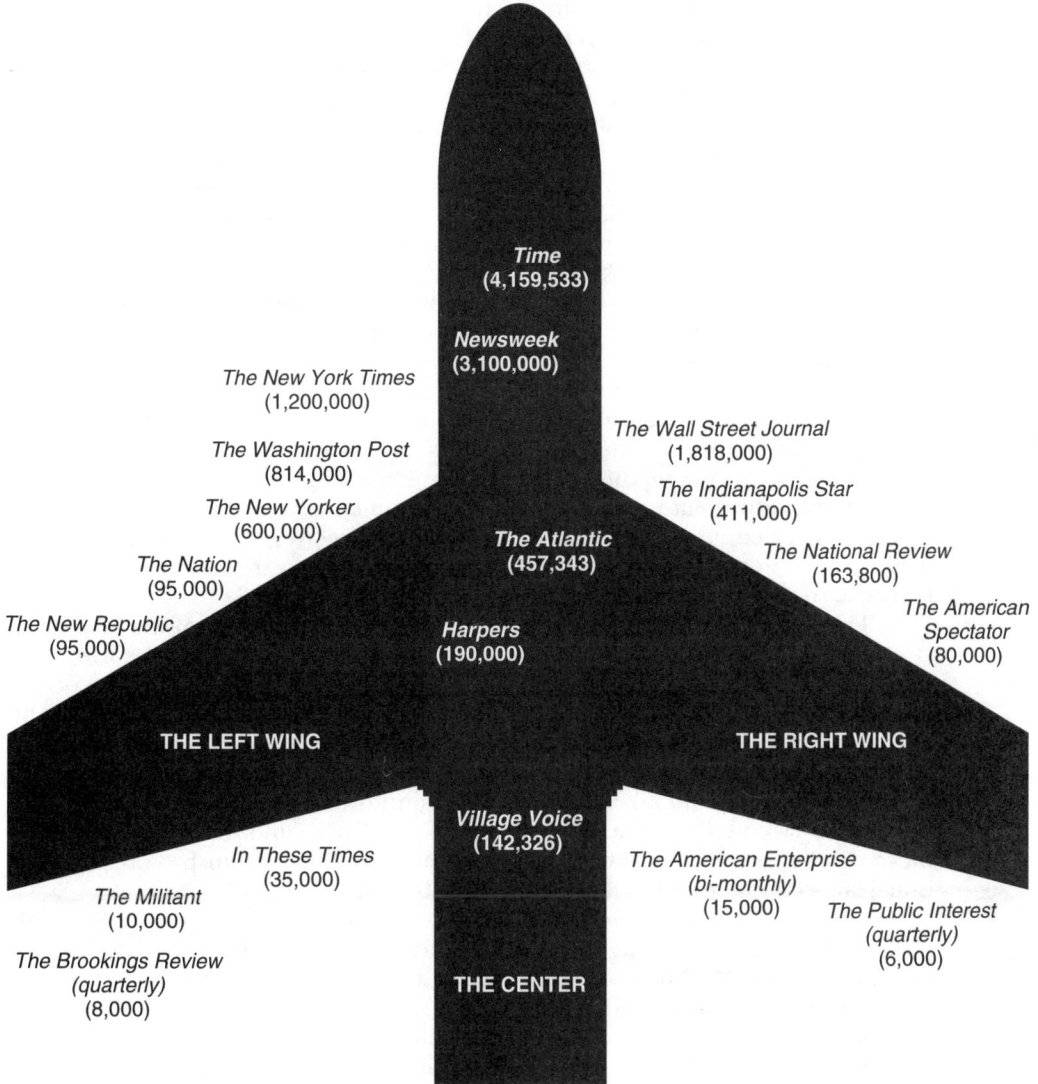

Time
(4,159,533)

Newsweek
(3,100,000)

The New York Times
(1,200,000)

The Wall Street Journal
(1,818,000)

The Washington Post
(814,000)

The Indianapolis Star
(411,000)

The New Yorker
(600,000)

The Atlantic
(457,343)

The National Review
(163,800)

The Nation
(95,000)

The American
Spectator
(80,000)

The New Republic
(95,000)

Harpers
(190,000)

THE LEFT WING

THE RIGHT WING

Village Voice
(142,326)

In These Times
(35,000)

The American Enterprise
(bi-monthly)
(15,000)

The Militant
(10,000)

The Public Interest
(quarterly)
(6,000)

The Brookings Review
(quarterly)
(8,000)

THE CENTER

Figure 1–2   Intuitive map of public affairs periodicals ordered by ideology and circulation numbers

Source: John Rowen, SPEA MPA Student, 1977; modified by Scott Burgins, 1993.)

approval in any one of four key states such as Massachusetts, New York, Pennsylvania, and Virginia would be sufficient to weaken seriously the democratic enterprise.

This was not the last time a fundamental clash of ideas about government would be heard. For example, Thomas Jefferson initially fumed about the creation of the First Bank of the United States—a *public* bank with branches in many states empowered to collect deposits and issue currency—and the fuming was resolved only when the Supreme Court under Chief Justice John Marshall refused the state of Maryland in *McCulloch v. Maryland* (1819) the power to tax (and thus to destroy) an agent of the federal government. Andrew Jackson was also frustrated by his initial inability to terminate the Second Bank, a bank he believed to be a federal affront to the sovereign powers of states to create and destroy banks.

The greatest constitutional crisis passed with the decisive outcome of the Civil War of 1860–1865 that resolved the question of state secession in favor of an indivisible union. But the post-Civil War era was loaded with ferment. For example, the Progressive Era at the end of the 19th and the beginning of the 20th centuries represented another great clash of ideas about government. The era was characterized by great expansion of territory, commerce, and industrial conglomerates that required large bureaucracies for administration as well as substantial public and private sector entrepreneurship. Yet, for every William Graham Sumner at Yale University preaching the doctrines of social Darwinism[11] and extolling the virtues of the extant social order "fixed by the laws of nature" (and therefore unyielding to social engineering), there was a Brown University sociologist Lester Frank Ward preaching the need for social responsibility to contain the evils of unconstrained individualism and to shape environmental forces to suit the designs and needs of people. In the Ward view, social engineering was both possible and desirable and not at all a fatal conceit doomed to failure by the natural laws of marketplace, society, and politics.

The debates have continued through the Great Depression of the 1930s, the Great Society days of the Kennedy-Johnson years in the 1960s, and the turbulent 1970s and 1980s. The stakes have always been high when issues of war and peace, economic well-being, and national social and economic purpose are involved. The debates are precisely what was intended in the system we know as U.S. government. Through it all, the question has never been whether or not to have government but what form it should take and how power authorized by it should be exercised. Students are warned that the following discussion is brief and is not a substitute for more detailed explorations of U.S. government, public administration, constitutional law, economics, and all the other possible subjects.

By definition, *government* is big business. Its root verb form, *to govern*, simply refers to the act of installing and using the rules of authority that members of a community have agreed to obey. Thus, the concept *govern* involves at its Greek (i.e., *Kybernan*) root and Latin (i.e., *Gubernare*) the exercise of political power. The metaphor is not unlike that of *steering*, thereby invoking the notion of a hand on the tiller that guides the ship. This does not mean that government is limited only to steering but simply that the steering of the collective whole remains the core task of all governments. The task, of course, is to achieve the goal on terms perceived as legitimate by those who are governed.

Government is therefore an extraordinarily powerful social institution. The concept of an institution is empowered to make authoritative decisions for a whole society or community—whether organized as nation, state, region, or municipality—takes some explaining. Part of the explanation pertains to the scale of government: government makes decisions and takes action with respect to a *collective whole*—the public. Theoretically, it does so by attempting to discover the *public interest* that compels public action or studied inaction. Realistically, however, government must also attend to *private interests* that make up a public and while it is accurate to say that government has sometimes been made the tool of private interests, but one does not begin the discussion of government's purpose by assuming that private use of the public interest is the primary aim. If anything, the purpose of government is quite the reverse—namely, the public use of the private interest.

But defining a public interest is difficult, partly because of the complexity of attempting to harmonize the interests of a whole community with the naturally diverse interests of the members of that community. Part of the difficulty most certainly lies in our inability to know with certainty precisely how, if at all, government actions produce public good. Unfortunately, government is often most appreciated by its absence. The inability of a community to constitute and maintain a collective steering mechanism alerts us to a grim fate visited on people unable to decide what holds their communities together. The world currently offers many examples of chaos, confusion, and even mass genocide that result when a collectivity of people is unable to establish and hold government in place. The independent states of the former Soviet Union, the republics of the former Yugoslavia, and Somalia are only a few recent examples.

All of this merely underscores one introductory point: the foundation of governments and publics is not something that occurs naturally. Government is a deliberate act of a community of people. Public institutions are acts of human design. But what design?

The Form of Government

Government is an official agent that acts on behalf of the public. There are, however, many ways to define a public and therefore many ways to define the governmental entity that serves public interests. The Greek concepts of *kratos,* referring to power, and of *arkhein,* meaning "to rule," fix the core concept of governmental authority. But what form shall the "-archy" and "-cracy" take? The following are among the many:

Monarchy: Rule by the *monos,* a single person, such as a king or emperor (the latter if the power is supreme and the territorial claim, often acquired by conquest, is vast);
Oligarchy: Rule by the *oligos,* the few, such as a ruling class or collection of first families, landowners, or businesspeople;
Democracy: Rule by the *demos,* the people, which implies ultimately that elections are held to determine the popular will;
Anarchy: The absence of *arkhein,* or rules or supreme law; in essence, government is held to be unnecessary for the maintenance of good order.

Even these simple designations are too general, for there are many variations on each theme. For example, monarchies can take many forms. Some of the earliest forms were absolute, or despotic, as seen in absolutist claims to divine authority, where the concept of the divine right of kings was invoked to command absolute obedience from subjects. There are, however, many other types of monarchies, as *constitutional monarchies,* representing a combination of hereditary and elective rule, as is found in Great Britain and modern Spain, in which constitutional law is supreme but a monarch serves as head of state, the official public representative. There is also *elective monarchy* such as existed in Poland for hundreds of years; *hereditary monarchy,* where bloodlines establish lines of succession; and *limited monarchy,* where supreme power resides in laws and where the administration of laws is vested in a single person and checked by elected assemblies of representatives, nobility, or both.

While it is conventional to say that the United States has the world's oldest surviving and continually functioning constitutional democracy, it is also important to recognize two things. First, democracy is really a very old idea, first tried in ancient Greece in 507 B.C. when the Athenian Cleisthenes gave the Assembly of the people the right to make decisions for the city-state of Athens. Thus, it is really more precise to say that the United States is the oldest of the *currently functioning* democracies. Second, ours is a *republican* (small *r*) form of government, meaning that the body of citizens does not rule itself directly; citizens rule only through officers and representatives chosen by citizens. Only in town meeting situations, where all citizens assemble, deliberate, and decide issues, can a true direct democracy be said to exist.

Stripped of all details, all democratic forms derive from resolving three problems of government existence. The first involves the definition of membership and deciding who *we* citizens really are. The second problem involves the selection of agents, or officials, who act on behalf of the citizenry. The third problem involves the rules of the game that codify who does what, to whom, and in the name of what principle. These problems are referred to, respectively, as problems of citizenship, officialdom, and constitution and are briefly discussed now.

Citizens, Officials, and Constitutions in Operation

All governments are based on a set of relationships between *citizens* who are the members of the community, or body politic, and *officials* who are authorized to act on behalf of the community through the rules (either written or understood) that govern the entire community. The essential logic of the democratic formulation is *self-government:* people are in charge of themselves and choose officials who act as agents, working on behalf of the people, the principals to be obeyed. Thus, in the democratic logic no *one* is in charge; hence we *all* are in charge.

There are many variations in the democratic recipe, however, yet all democratic formulations consist of at least the following six attributes:

1. **Equality in voting:** Each citizen is equally empowered to the extent that each vote is counted the same as his or her neighbor's in determining the outcomes of elections; thus, there is a one-person, one-vote rule among citizens.
2. **Competition for public office:** No one party or faction has a monopoly of power; voters have at least one other electoral choice such that they always have the option of "turning the rascals out" by replacing people in power with those who are not in power.
3. **Majorities and pluralities rule:** In decision situations where there are differences of opinion, majorities beat minorities; thus, candidates with the most votes take public office, and resolutions with a majority of aye votes are adopted for the whole public body.
4. **Freedom of expression:** The right to think, speak, write, publish, and assemble in groups for the purpose of political expression protects public opinion from being managed by either government officials or private interests. Citizens therefore need not fear reprisals for their opinions.
5. **Wide distribution of political resources:** There is no monopoly of the money, time, and information required to make intelligent choices; rather, political resources are widely distributed throughout the population.
6. **Protection of minority rights:** Those factions, interests, parties, and coalitions not large enough to form winning majorities are not destroyed; instead, their rights are protected and they live to "fight another day."

The principles seem simple enough until one contemplates what they really mean in operation. In a subsequent section we consider the paradox that emerges when one tries to combine majority rule principles with one-person, one-vote procedures to create a logical public choice.

There are, however, no more complex questions than the ones that arise under the freedom of expression rule. The Constitution is very clear on the need for free expression, as stated in the First Amendment:

> Congress shall make no law respecting an establishment of religion, or prohibiting the free exercise thereof; or abridging the freedom of speech, or of the press; or the right of the people peaceably to assemble, and to petition the government for a redress of grievances.

The reason is obvious. Self-government depends on a free exchange of views among citizens and on freedom of conscience as well as of expression. In short, democracy depends upon maintaining a lot of public chatter by which ideas can be offered, attacked, defended, and compared. Only in this manner can the truth emerge and be understood by a public opinion empowered to govern itself. This guarantee of freedom of speech and press remains, according to Carl Becker, the great gamble of democracy:

> Since primitive times virtually all religious or social systems have attempted to maintain themselves by forbidding free criticism and analysis either of existing institutions or of the doctrine that sustains them; of democracy alone is it the cardinal principle that free criticism and analysis by all and sundry is the highest virtue. In its inception modern democracy was, therefore, a stupendous gamble for the highest stakes. It offered long odds on the capacity and integrity of the human mind. It wagered all it had that the freest exercise of the human reason would never disprove the proposition that only by the freest exercise of the human reason can a tolerably just and rational society ever be created.[12]

So far so good. How far do we allow this free speech business to go? Pamphleteering? Certainly. Muckraking journalism? No question. Investigative reporting by the media? Yes. Antagonistic cross-examination (veritable roasting!) of presidents, governors, and mayors at press conferences? Absolutely! Meetings, parades, and demonstrations? Clearly.

Is there no limit beyond which freedom cannot go? Do we simply accept Voltaire's famous argument that "I disapprove of what you say, but I will defend to the death your right to say it?"[13] The argument for placing no limit on freedom of speech and expression was perhaps most compellingly explained by John Stuart Mill in his famous essay, *On Liberty* (1859).[14] He reasoned that if the thoughts expressed were wrong, people would be more appreciative of the truths they already held. If, in contrast, explanations and arguments captured some measure of truth, then people could exchange the error of their ways for newly discovered insights. Either way, public opinion was usefully informed. Thus, there was (and is) never a defense for limiting free speech, including all forms of communication and expression. Free speech supplies its own correction against error, if one simply assumes that ordinary people are basically rational and want to know truth and be guided by it.

The Americanization of Mill's notion is that the protection of free speech forces ideas to compete, as Supreme Court Justice Oliver Wendell Holmes put it, in the "free trade of ideas." Interestingly, Justice Holmes framed his eloquent defense of the earlier Mill argument in the famous case *Abrams v. United States.*[15] This case arose during World War I when the publication and distribution of two leaflets protesting U.S. conduct of the war—one of which urged a stop to U.S. intervention against the Russian Revolution—were deemed a violation of the Espionage Act of 1918. On this occasion in 1919, Justice Holmes rose to the occasion in his minority defense of the proposition that: " . . . the best test of truth is the power of thought to get itself accepted in the competition of the market. . . . "[16] He was joined in his opinion by Mr. Justice Brandeis.

The broad defense of civil liberties has not gone unchallenged in the nation's history. The question of limiting free speech appears most often during times of turbulence and confrontation—in short, during times of national insecurity. Thus, Thomas Jefferson proposed the Alien and Sedition Acts of 1798 as a means (he thought) of reducing internal dissension that would expose national weakness to the European powers that were carefully watching developments in the new republic. More recently, famous confrontations have occurred over the question of whether the public right to know is protected to the point that newspapers such as the *New York Times* have a right to publish papers—such as the Pentagon papers[17]—claimed by the Department of Defense to be secret documents about the historical conduct of the war in Vietnam.

However, a host of seemingly less dramatic questions surround the free speech question. For example, does the First Amendment protect only the exchange of ideas or does it also protect all expression whether informed or not? Can there ever be prior restraint placed on free speech? Does free speech extend to include that which is distasteful and abusive, notwithstanding that slanderous speech that injures others is punishable under the law? What restraints shall be placed on expression alleged to be obscene in speech, art, film, and print? Remembering that juicy but opinionated and somewhat exaggerated stories about public figures can help ratings and sell newspapers and magazines, what limits may properly be placed on a press corps that might otherwise be tempted to commit libel? The list goes on and on and involves issues beyond the scope of this chapter. Yet coming to grips with such questions lies at the heart of understanding democratic freedom of expression. Equally complex questions surround the other five democratic attributes.

WHAT GOVERNMENT DOES

It is difficult to overestimate the stakes of the government game. In democracies, when people make decisions through a polling of the majority will—more precisely, when representatives of a public will cast their votes behind a proposition that carries the day—the result is binding on the collective whole. Thus, once a public decides that taxes are required, then government or its designee is empowered to collect revenues. When government determines that external threats to public security exist, government is empowered to raise armed forces for which conscription may be a requirement. When public needs for roads, bridges, conduits and water mains, and waste disposal mandate construction, government can be empowered to claim land and buildings as well as to engage in large-scale projects to supply needed infrastructure. Thus, decisions of government are decisions that matter. Indeed, the power of democratic government is often overlooked by scholars and students who have construed democratic self-government to be an undisciplined exercise that does not really matter and whose results are not really binding on citizens. Political philosopher and university president Alexander Mieklejohn put the proposition this way:

Political freedom does not mean freedom from control. It means self-control. If, for example, a nation becomes involved in war, the government must decide who shall be drafted to leave his family and home, to risk his life, his health, his sanity, upon the battlefield. The government must also levy and collect and expend taxes. In general, it must determine how far and in what ways the customs and privileges of peace are to be swept aside. In all these cases it may be taken for granted that, in a self-governing society, minorities will disagree with the decisions which are made. May a man [*sic*], then, by appeal to the principle of "consent," refuse to submit to military control? May he evade payment of taxes which he thinks unwise or unjust? May he say, "I did not approve of this measure; therefore, as a self-governing man, I claim the right to disobey it"?

Certainly not! At the bottom of every plan of self-government is a basic agreement, in which all citizens have joined, that all matters of public policy shall be decided by corporate action, that such decisions shall be equally binding on all citizens, whether they agree with them or not, and that, if need be, they shall, by due legal procedure, be enforced upon anyone who refuses to conform to them. The man who rejects that agreement is not objecting to tyranny or despotism. He is objecting to political freedom. He is not a democrat. He is [an] anarchist. . . . Self-government is nonsense unless the "self" which governs is able and determined to make its will effective.[18]

One way to appreciate the power and authority of government is to review some of the muckraking accounts of the misuse of government. Accounts of greed mongering by special private interests that lobby government for the favors only government can bestow are offered simply to make a simple point: public policy is not a mere analytic exercise controlled by the disinterested analysts and civil servants empowered to manage public affairs for the public good. Public policy—defined as public choice, action, and impact—is also accomplished in the presence of many stakeholders whose private interests are heavily leveraged by the direction and course of public choice. The following vignettes are offered to illustrate the many channels of influence that play on policy choices and public action

1. **S & L Scandal:** The U.S. League of Savings Institutions has a strategic interest in the deposit guarantees provided by government. Thus, if the Federal Savings and Loan Insurance Corporation (FSLIC) could be authorized to increase the ceiling on deposit guarantees to a healthy level—say, $100,000 per account—deposits would flow into riskless savings and loan associations offering respectable rates of interest. At stake in such a decision is the survival of an entire sector of the banking industry.[19]
2. **The Protectionist Game:** Manufacturers and labor unions unable or unwilling to meet the rigors of international economic competition have gone to extraordinary lengths to influence trade negotiations. They have a great stake in seeing high tariffs placed on serious competitors in the name of fairness and other high-sounding aims. Thus, import-beleaguered domestic industries include autos, steel and machine tools, electronics, shoes, textiles and apparel, motorcycles and bicycles, tires, watches, and uranium producers along with rubber, plastics, coal, iron ore, machinery and fastener suppliers. Those opposing protectionist policies include consumers; producers of agricultural products, aircraft, construction machinery, telecommunications equipment, electric power machinery, computers, pharmaceuticals, photographic supplies, fertilizer and seeds, farm machinery, precious and semiprecious metals; and insurance companies and cargo companies.[20]
3. **Farm Subsidies:** The big-four farm organizations—the American Farm Bureau Federation, the National Grange, the National Farmers Union, and the National Farmers Organization—together with associations of individual commodity producers work very hard to insure that farm subsidies remain substantial and locked in place. Thus, dairy owners, peanut farmers, sugar cane companies, tobacco growers, and producers of every com-

modity from rice and wheat to corn and soybeans will work and spend to influence government commodity price supports and tariff policies. Their interests are further augmented by farm cooperatives and agribusiness firms including producers of farm inputs such as herbicides, pesticides, and fertilizer; manufacturers of farm equipment; and distribution and marketing businesses involved in storage, transportation, packaging, marketing, and exporting. Thus, while farmers constitute less than 2.5 percent of the U.S. population, the *effects* of farm policy go far beyond the farm.[21] This is discussed again in Chapter 13.

4. **Electric Utility Regulation:** The rates that public utilities—power, phone, and cable companies—can charge consumers is one of the critical public-private-sector interactions by state governments rather than the federal government, although "the feds" are involved with safety and standards licensing but not with the rates that producers may charge *consumers*. The interests of energy *producers* who require enormous capital resources for further development, clearly diverge from the interests of *consumers* who typically instruct their lobbyists to press for rate suppression. Striking a balance among the many interests is a task of the public service commissions in each of the states, a task that cannot be easily and happily discharged.

5. **The Weapons Sweepstakes:** Weapons systems research, development, and production are no longer merely functions of the military-industrial complex (MIC), about whose power President Eisenhower warned in his 1959 farewell address. They are functions of what is more accurately characterized as a military-industrial-bureaucratic-trade association-labor union-university intellectual-technical-service club-political complex whose dimensions are almost infinite.[22] Thus, debates about defense and national security strategy are not simply theoretical exercises in war and peace; they involve practical questions about how to manage the MIC that in reality has become a MIBTALUUITSCPC (a prize to the student who can convincingly pronounce this acronym).

It is clear from these illustrations that government decision making is not only analytically complex but intensely political, involving many powerful interests and convictions that do not disappear no matter how convincing rational analyses of problems and policy options might appear.

Even without the confusion of political interests, merely deciding what is theoretically desirable is difficult. If communities are necessarily comprised of individual citizens organized in groups, factions, and interests, how is it possible to discover the interests of the unified whole? We shall refer to this as the *e pluribus unum problem:* how can a coherent view be created from the many voices, opinions, and constituencies comprising a public? The problem is more complicated than it might at first appear, because an initial reaction to the question might be to say that one can derive a technically correct decision about public good simply by aggregating the wishes of the citizens into some summary judgment. That democracy in its definition frustrates such an outcome was mathematically demonstrated by the Nobel Prize–winning economist Kenneth Arrow, whose paradox consisted of the discovery and proof of an inherent contradiction in determining the will of the majority.[23]

As an illustration of Arrow's paradox, imagine a simple situation in which a collective decision must be made about how to allocate budget cuts or increases among different policy areas. For purposes of notation, we will term these marginal expenditure options X, Y, and Z. Where should government spend its money? The problem is trivial if everyone agrees on the answer or if there is a technically correct answer that can solve the problem. If, however, the political reality is that sane people of good will do not agree, then a problem exists in discovering what to do. Theoretically, democratic rules ought to help with the decision. Thus,

TABLE 1–4   Arrow's Paradox

	X Infrastructure	*Y* Prisons	*Z* Public Education
Person A	1	2	3
Person B	3	1	2
Person C	2	3	1

if everyone's vote counts the same and majority votes carry the issue, we should be able to rely on democratic procedures to derive a logically correct answer.

Herein lies the problem. Suppose there are three people or factions—A, B, and C—who have different preference orderings for the three decision options—X, Y and, Z—as shown in Table 1–4. For purposes of illustration, the three options shall refer to the problem of where to spend extra funds in the amount of $1 billion. The first option is to spend an additional $1 billion on infrastructure—streets, roads, bridges, conduits, transportation terminals—and will be termed option X. Option Y refers to spending an additional $1 billion on prisons, including prison construction and prisoner education programs. Option Z refers to spending the additional $1 billion on public education, meaning K-12 schools including programs, buildings, and facilities. As money becomes available, what is the order in which the spending should occur?

This hypothetical community of three people has a problem. Clearly, person A prefers infrastructure over prisons and prisons over schools; the position can be rationalized in a number of ways based on the idea that infrastructure spending is really an investment, while spending money on overcrowded prisons is both spending and an investment in public safety and security. By contrast, the same person might reason that spending more money on mediocre public schools is simply throwing money down the drain. The point, however, is that B and C have very different views about the order in which resources should be allocated, and there are credible ways to explain the ranking of the preferences shown in Table 1–4. How does the collective body arrive at a binding decision for a community of three? Of course, in reality, problems are much more complex because there are many more issues being ranked simultaneously by many more people and factions.

The democratic logic, discussed earlier, has an answer to the dilemma: the community should vote for its preferences under the conditions that each vote counts the same and majorities carry the day. A rational collective decision should be forthcoming from merely aggregating the preferences of rational individuals. But here is the problem: an intellectual gridlock derives from the voting because of the following:

1. A majority—A and C—can be mustered for the proposition that infrastructure spending is to be preferred to spending on prisons.
2. A majority—A and B—exists to support prison spending over public school spending.
3. The logical, or transitive, conclusion does not follow, for *there is no majority* to support the proposition that infrastructure spending is to be preferred to public school spending. To the contrary, a majority—B and C—reflects the conviction that spending on public school improvements is more publicly beneficial than increased infrastructure spending.

In short, there is no logically correct (i.e., transitive) preference ordering based on democratic rules. Thus, the paradox shows that intellectual gridlock is more than likely in complicated public policy decision situations. What then is to be done? Public action demands a solution to the gridlock so that decisions can be made. Arrow's paradox shows one of the principal strengths of some nondemocratic forms of government, for in cases where a single dictator rules, fragmentation and intellectual gridlock can be avoided provided the dictator knows what he or she wishes to do.

The solution to the dilemma is political rather than analytic, and democracies have plenty of options for breaking intellectual deadlocks. One strategy, for example, is to test the resolve of each of the factions to determine if one of the interests can persuade the others to accede to the wishes of the most determined faction. Another strategy is to form coalitions between and among factions, so that a winning coalition is formed possessing the votes necessary to achieve decision-making consensus. A third option is to devise a voting system such that majorities can be constructed from the diversity of policy preferences. Thus, there are many democratically founded political strategies available to break policy deadlocks.

THE U.S. FORMULA

As noted above, there is more than one way to design and run a democracy. The U.S. blend of idealism and pragmatism is unique. Among the world's nations, two general strategies are most often followed in democratic design. One strategy creates a parliamentary system. The other installs a presidential system. The parliamentary system is the most popular. It is one in which elections are held for seats in the legislature—the parliament—after which the head of the winning party or a coalition, which would be formed because no one party of a multiparty system received an absolute majority of parliamentary seats, is asked to assume the office of prime minister or premier and form a government of officials to run the bureaucracy that executes the policies passed by parliament. The United Kingdom, Germany, most European countries, and Japan are prime examples of parliamentary systems. Parliamentary systems are driven by the strength of political party power, where a majority parliamentary party governs as long as it enjoys the confidence of the parliament or until a term limit expires, at which time new elections are called. This has the effect of encouraging party discipline, since the selection of representatives serving constituent districts also results in the selection of the government's chief executive. In essence, party leaders and followers rise and fall together.

Presidential systems, by contrast, separate the legislative and executive functions by institutionalizing an administrative office whose tenure is held separately from an elected legislature. Different versions of this system can be found in France and the United States, for example. Separation of powers occurs because the selection of a chief executive, such as a president, occurs as a result of regularly occurring national elections whose practical effect is that the president enjoys a base of electoral support independent of the legislature. Thus, a legislature exists as an elected representative body that represents in its individual members the interests of constituents and districts—the pieces rather than the whole public—

while the president is assigned the role of representing the unified whole of the public. Institutionalized political conflict is built into the separate roles and power bases assigned the different parts of government.

While it is correct to say that the United States follows the presidential model, it has actually developed a unique system replicated in no other country. Three particular characteristics distinguish U.S. governance as founded in a Constitution formulated in Philadelphia in 1787, approved in 1789 (unanimous approval was gained in 1790), and placed in operation with the inauguration of President George Washington in 1789. Since the actual contents of convention proceedings were secret and no minutes of business conducted were kept, we are left with two sources of authoritative information about the Constitutional Convention. The first consists of the papers of John Adams written up from notes kept during the meetings. The second consists of the pamphleteering conducted after the convention to convince the thirteen colonies that a new arrangement was required to replace the practically ineffective Articles of Confederation. Thus, *The Federalist Papers,* referred to earlier, stands next to the Declaration of Independence and the Constitution itself as perhaps the clearest defense of U.S. constitutional democracy available. Review of the papers indicates that many of the tensions and conflicts presently found in U.S. government are not accidents of politics but institutional confrontations negotiated by the founding intellects.

By all accounts, James Madison played the pivotal role in designing the constitutional package that emerged from the Philadelphia convention. Students are still well advised to undertake serious study of the proceedings. In *The Federalist Papers* 10 and 51, the essential dilemma was posed: how to form a more vigorous and effective national government at the same time that the abuse of political power is curbed. The essential problem lay in human nature and the tendency to form factions by which Madison meant (*Federalist* 10):

> [A] number of citizens, whether amounting to a majority or minority of the whole, who are united and actuated by some common impulse of passion, or of interest, adverse to the rights of other citizens, or to the permanent and aggregate interests of the community.

Since the formation of zealous and privately held interests—such as religious, economic, social class, or regional pressure groups—is part of human nature (even human nature that is enlightened and well meaning), control of factional power and influence is a prime concern of government design. How could one simultaneously achieve vigorous and effective government at the same time that the effects of factional interest are directed in publicly useful directions?

The founders' answer to this puzzle can be simply formulated. First, national government should be a large, compound republic rather than a simple, direct democracy. Thus, public opinion would be laundered through elected representatives who, in turn, would be forced to interact and balance the many competing interests to arrive at decisions about the public interest. Second, government itself would be subject to three basic design principles.

1. **Separation of powers:** Legislative, executive, and judicial branches would be independently tenured, and each would be given explicit power separate from the other two branches. Furthermore, the Congress would be further subdivided such that every two years the House of Representatives would be up for renewal while only one-third of the

Senate would be. The quadrennial election of a president would mean that executive and legislative tenure would be independent, and further, the phenomenon of the off-year election (congressional elections in the middle of a presidential term) would ensure continuous public referendum on government activity. Thus, it is inconceivable that one faction could control all branches of government simultaneously and were such an extraordinary majority to be created, the views represented must be considered a legitimate concurrent majority.

2. **Checks and balances:** Each of the branches of government is empowered to meddle in the affairs of the other branches. Thus, for example, presidents have legislative and judicial power. They propose legislation and can veto congressional legislation. Presidents appoint judges who must be confirmed by the Senate. Courts—especially after the case of *McCulloch v. Maryland* (1803)—can declare presidential acts and congressional laws unconstitutional. Congress has control over executive affairs in its powers of the purse, appointment, and oversight. In this way according to *Federalist* 51, "Ambition must be made to counteract ambition."

3. **Division of powers:** Government power is divided between national government and independently chartered state governments that cannot be abolished by national government. Thus, in our *federal* system, two levels of government compete to serve citizens, with federal government having precedence on national matters and state governments having all remaining powers (Tenth Amendment), including the power to fix the terms of existence of local governments, which serve as instruments of a state. The strategic position of states is further anchored in the apportionment of Senate seats—two per state regardless of size—and in the electoral college whose vote total is fixed by the total number of senators and representatives to the Congress and whose winner-take-all voting rule means that presidential electoral coalitions must be put together on a state-by-state basis.

The significance of the Constitution in public policy can hardly be overstated. The Constitution establishes the procedures by which decisions are made binding on the entire citizenry. The Constitution institutionalizes the internal competition among political actors who must achieve substantial consensus before action can be taken . Thus, the loyalty of appointed officials and civil servants is to the Constitution rather than to the wishes of particular officials. Indeed, the oath of office taken by the president of the United States is constitutionally mandated and seals the commitment of a president to "preserve, protect and defend the Constitution of the United States." In the end, the object of loyalty in government is not some particular official or bureaucratic office; it is the principles of the Constitution as written in a very short document that has been amended only 27 times since 1789—17 times since the Bill of Rights was passed in 1791—and interpreted by the courts for over 200 years.

Federalism

The constitutional prescription for preserving state government power along with federal power contains enormous and not often appreciated potential for promoting dynamic change. Federalism multiplies the number of governments simultaneously laying hands on public problems. State governments can create their own local government instruments to do public work, and the federal government is also granted specific powers. Federalism is protected by limiting national government power in several ways. First, for example, the federal government is denied the power to tax interstate commerce. Second, the Constitution establishes the requirement that the Bill of Rights may not be violated by *any* government. Third, the federal government's power to change state boundaries is denied. Similarly, state governments are constitutionally limited; for instance, states cannot tax imports and exports, coin money, enter into treaties, impair obligations of contracts, or abridge the privileges or immunities of citizens.

Specific powers are also granted to both national and state governments. For example, the federal government is empowered to coin money, conduct foreign relations, regulate interstate commerce, regulate commerce among nations, provide an army and a navy, declare war, establish federal courts, establish post offices, and make laws necessary to carry out federal powers. State governments are empowered to establish local governments, regulate commerce within a state, conduct elections, ratify amendments to the Constitution, and take measures deemed necessary for public health, safety, and morals. In addition, both levels of government are empowered to tax, to borrow money, to establish courts, to make and enforce laws, to charter banks and corporations, to spend money for the general welfare, and to take private property for public purposes (with just compensation, of course).

Finally, the Tenth Amendment permits states to exert powers the Constitution does not delegate to the national government or prohibit the states from using. U.S. federalism would, at first glance, appear to be a layered cake with powers and duties unique to each level of government. While there is perhaps some truth to the layer cake metaphor, loosely defined to mean that each level of government carries a standard portfolio of duties and responsibilities, the reality is much more complex. For example, a description of the chief duties of each layer might include the following:

Federal	*State*	*Local*
Defense	Roads and highways	Police and fire
Diplomacy	Universities and schools	Public schools
The Mint	Health and welfare	Public assistance
Taxes	Highway patrol and state police	Public libraries
Interstate commerce	State parks	Parks and recreation
Science and technology	State prisons	Health clinics
Social insurance	Mental health facilities	Planning and zoning
Census	Occupational licensing	Sanitation
Forests, parks, and lands	Public utility regulation	Public works

Notwithstanding the seeming separation among the levels of government, the operating reality is that there is now a jumble of interactions rather than a neat layering of responsibilities. First, most functions of government are found throughout government, such that all levels are engaged in public works, welfare, health, transportation, police, prisons, and the like. It is even the case that while states and cities do not conduct foreign policy, they do maintain elaborate networks of representatives and offices overseas to service the economic requirements of recently expanding global trade.[24] In short, there is an enormous amount of redundancy and overlap throughout the federal system.

Second, it is extremely rare that one level of government delivers a class of service by itself. The implementation of national policy usually requires the cooperation of state and local governments. Even defense and national security depend to no small degree on the services and support that are provided by the many bases and facilities spread across states and localities and on the infrastructure that permits movement of troops and materials with ease. Or, to take another example, the provision of welfare or employment services is achieved through an intergovernmental cooperation whereby funds from one government are targeted toward categories of problems for which precise direction and interventions are defined and managed by state and local governments.

Finally, it is no longer the case that the states and localities are the junior partners in the current efforts to improve U.S. government. During periods of national crisis—wars and economic depression being prime examples—it is, indeed, the national government that takes the lead. National government also takes the lead in instances where state and local governments appear unwilling or unable to address large national problems. However, the more than 86,000 units of state and local government also provide an experimental test bed for solving problems whose characteristics are tied to distinctly local conditions. In this sense, state governments and their instrumentalities constitute, as David Osborne put it, laboratories of democracy.[25] Nor is it the case that state and local governments follow the lead of the federal government as they once did during the Great Depression of the 1930s or the Great Society days of the 1960s. Indeed, some analysts place states, in particular, in the forefront of national problem solving:

> The states have long been the "hands and feet" of federal policy. The states, moreover, have long been the nation's hothouses of policy innovation. Since the end of World War II, virtually every major domestic policy innovation in the United States has involved state and local governments. From transportation to environmental clean-up, from welfare to housing, the partnerships of American federalism have been the administrative engines of the nation's domestic policy. Federal programs have succeeded only to the degree that these partnerships have been nourished and energized.[26]

American Complexities

For all the originality, the U.S. formula does contain its sources of difficulties and concern to government reformers. First, the staggering of presidential and congressional elections makes political party discipline difficult, if not impossible. The result is that labels such as Democrat and Republican do not stand for coherent and disciplined party platforms in which party leadership and regular candidates for Congress march to the beat of the same drummer in nationally financed campaigns, as might be the case the in the United Kingdom. Parties are built and financed more narrowly around individual candidates and state and local constituencies. The result is that voters send a lot of independent actors to national and state capitals, who must then engage in the process of forming a governing coalition that usually, but not always, follows party lines. Party lines are themselves an amalgam of widely divergent views such that liberals in *different* parties may have more policy positions in common than both liberals and conservatives within the *same* party.

A second practical consequence of joining separations and divisions of power to checks and balances is that the execution of public policy can appear (and actually be) confused and fragmented. This is particularly apparent when chief executives appear to be placed in charge of vast bureaucracies that must carry out government programs. While business theory might suggest that presidents, governors, and mayors run public businesses just like chief executives in the mythical private sector corporation, the reality is otherwise. In truth, career civil servants charged with program execution certainly respond to the directions and requirements of chief executives, but they also respond attentively to the legislatures that oversee—sometimes in minute detail—the authorization, goals, directions, funding, and execution of public programs.

So tight are the linkages between the permanent bureaucracy, legislative committees, and the relevant interest groups affected by government action that it has sometimes been fashionable to speak of the *iron triangles* of subgovernment that determine, in the end, precisely what government will actually do. More recent formulations modify the metaphor from iron triangle to *policy networks,* which include the views and influence of the mass media, think tanks, university professors, professional groups, and other thoughtful and influential citizens constituting the attentive public of public policy discussions. Regardless of metaphor, however, the effect is that democratic political power is often marshalled in directions not desired and controlled by chief executives and their appointees formally charged and theoretically empowered to run the government machinery.

A third feature of democracy à la U.S. federal republicanism is the extent of competition built into the internal workings of government itself. For example, the president and the Congress are each charged with developing solutions to public problems, while the courts stand by to referee the public brawl. States compete with the federal government to provide the services required by citizens; states, in turn, compete with subsidiary local units to cover public needs. Indeed, the phenomenon of one level of government—governors, state legislators, mayors, police chiefs, city managers, and so forth—lobbying other governments for funding, authorization, and assistance is common. The result is a kind of competitive laboratory in which different teams of officials and citizens work to develop solutions to problems that, if successful, can be adopted and diffused through the rest of the nation. Agencies and governments that are unresponsive and even injurious can be held in check while new players are brought on line to fill the breach. Moreover, the experimental babble is continuously encouraged by the staggering of public referenda on officials and propositions that guide government action; thus, if a popular candidate for the U.S. Senate loses an off-year electoral bid to a candidate who promises to do something about health care, the message is quickly picked up by others that one ignores the health issue at his or her peril. The result is that *health* quickly moves to the government decision agenda for consideration. Thus, there is constant churning in the U.S. system.

This discussion does not mean to convey that U.S. democracy is without flaws and difficulties. In the most general sense, democracies work best when there is time for much debate, study, discussion, negotiation, and compromise. Conversely, notwithstanding the recent experience of Operation Desert Storm, democracies are severely tested when situations require either quick reactions and shrewd judgments or purposeful and sustained effort maintained over time at great cost and uncertain benefit. Winston Churchill is thought to have characterized an exasperation with democratic government in the following way: "Democracy is the worst government imaginable, with the possible exception of all the other forms."

Political practice in the United States adds another layer of complexity to democracy in action. Even defenders of the U.S. system of fragmented power are made nervous by the gridlock that can occur when different factions control different parts of government, and absent a governing coalition, the government appears to do nothing in times of crisis. Furthermore, even supporters of experimental ferment in government would agree that the price of ferment is often a cacophony that can make coherent policy look contradictory and even nonexistent at times.

HOW GOVERNMENT DOES IT

At rock bottom, two primary tasks confront all governments. First, governments are empowered to make authoritative decisions for a whole public; this lies at the core of government's definition. Second, governments are constituted to enhance public welfare, meaning that government existence is predicated on its ability to remove the collective ills that plague a public and to improve the stock of public good.

Precisely *how* these goals can be achieved is not always clear. Indeed, it has been suggested more than once by thinkers on the political stump that the absence of government is precisely what is required to arrive at collective choice and to produce public good. A leading advocate for this limited conception of government is management analyst Peter Drucker:

> The purpose of government is to make fundamental decisions and to make them effectively. The purpose of government is to focus the political energies of society. It is to dramatize issues. It is to present fundamental choices. The purpose of government, in other words, is to govern. This, we have learned in other institutions, is incompatible with *doing*. Any attempt to combine governing with doing on a large scale paralyzes government's decision-making capacity.[27]

The reader will have to draw his or her own conclusions about the Drucker position.

Obviously, government cannot merely sit around just making authoritative decisions. Governments exist to promote the public interest and create conditions of public good that they vote for. In short, governments must implement their policies. The much-quoted preamble to the U.S. Constitution is perhaps unrivaled as a statement that explains why governments exist and what they do:

> WE THE PEOPLE of the United States, in Order to form a more perfect Union, establish Justice, insure domestic Tranquility, provide for the common defence, promote the general Welfare, and secure the Blessings of Liberty to ourselves and our Posterity, do ordain and establish this Constitution for the United States of America.

What does it mean to provide for the "common defence" and "promote the general Welfare"? There are some powerful implications in these statements.

The concept of public good may be loosely thought of as a desired condition of existence available to all (i.e., the public) in which one person's enjoyment of the good or service does not diminish another person's enjoyment of the same good or service. A variation on the idea is to think of the removal of public bad—insecurity, poverty, ill health, and pollution—that plagues a community. So far, so good. Public goods are not private goods, but are there only public and private goods? What precisely distinguishes the different sorts of goods and services produced in the world? These are complicated questions that require at least brief consideration here because the answers reveal much about how to approach the government question. Case examples are provided in subsequent chapters.

The most efficient way to envision the possibilities is to review Table 1–5, which represents two critical characteristics of all goods and services.[28] One characteristic is determined by whether potential users of the good can be denied access because it can be locked up, fenced off, or otherwise denied those who either are not entitled to or have not paid for the right to use the good. This dimension is referred to as the property of *exclusion,* where the feasibility or infeasibility of exclusion defines a property right or ticket of admission that prevents people from consuming the good unless they possess the required property right.

The second dimension is fixed by the pattern of *consumption,* where some goods are individually consumed and others are jointly consumed, the latter meaning that one person's consumption of a good or service does not remove its availability for another consumer. This characteristic may be described as the presence or absence of *rivalness.* Rival consumption occurs in cases where consumption of a good removes its availability for another to consume the same good. Nonrival consumption, by contrast, means that one person's consumption does not remove its availability for another. Whether rivalness exists is largely a function of the character of the good and the extent to which a good or service is divisible or not; for example, if a good is divisible, then one person's consumption removes the item from circulation, while consumption of an indivisible good does not remove the good from consumption by another. The result is a two-way diagram, shown in Table 1–5, that sorts goods and services according to key features of excludability and consumption and provides examples as illustrations.

The classification scheme presented in Figure 1–3 only identifies the public policy problem. Once we define the public good desired, how do we in fact produce it? The remainder of this book deals with precisely this question. A few comments will suffice to set the stage, for in the end, our answers derive from our views about who the public really is and what we should all do for ourselves and each other. At polar extremes, there are two contrasting views. One view—call it the *communitarian* perspective—is holistic and unitary and conceives of a corporate public served by a vigorous government and bureaucracy that actively work on behalf of the entire community. One summary of communitarianism is expressed as a public ideology that defines the individual as an inseparable part of a community in which civic rights and duties are determined by the needs of the common good. In this concept, government plays a pivotal role as the planner and implementer of community needs. Two analysts express the communitarian ideal this way:

> Individual fulfillment and self-respect are the result of one's place in an organic social process; we "get our kicks" by being part of a group. A well-designed group makes full use of our individual capacities. Property rights are less important than the rights derived from membership in the community or a group—for example, rights to income, health, and education. The uses of property are best regulated according to the community's need, which often differs from individual consumer desires. Government must set the community's goals and coordinate their implementation. The perception of reality requires an awareness of whole systems and of the interrelationships between and among the wholes.[29]

Another contrasting view—call it the *individualistic* view—begins with a practical operating reality that communities and publics are, in fact, composed of many publics and many different kinds of governments and administrative agencies having specific functions tailored to the particular circumstances of production and consumption. This notion that a public is really built as an aggregation of individual contracts was enunciated by philosopher John Locke over 300 years ago. It forms the nucleus of what many observers regard as the American way, an ideology

Feasible Exclusion	Private Goods	Toll Goods
(Property Rights)	– Kentucky Fried Chicken	– Movies
	– Cars	– Cable TV
	– Candy bars	– Toll bridges
	– Books	– Telephones
Infeasible Exclusion	Common Pool Goods	Public Goods
(No Property Rights)	– Water from an aquifer	– National security
	– Fish from the lake or stream	– Clean air (outdoors)
	– Trees in the forest	– Open-air concerts
		– Public TV
	Individual Consumption	Joint Consumption
	(Rivalness)	(Nonrivalness)

☐ = Public Domain Goods

Figure 1–3   Classification of goods and services

Source: Adapted from Vincent Ostrom, *The Meaning of American Federalism* (San Francisco: Institute for Contemporary Studies, 1991), pp. 164–172.

that extolls the values of individualism, private property, free competition in an open marketplace, and limited government. One summary of this position puts the proposition in the following way:

> The community is no more than the sum of the individuals in it. Self-respect and ful-fillment result from an essentially lonely struggle in which initiative and hard work pay off. The fit survive and if you don't survive, you are probably unfit. Property rights are a sacred guarantor of individual rights, and the uses of property are best controlled by competition to satisfy consumer desires in an open market. The least government is the best.[30]

The differences between the two ideologies are clear and dramatic. The communitarian view finds it easier to justify action by government in the name of the whole community. The individualistic view is more cautious in recommending government intervention, since if a public is really made up of many constituent pieces of interests, publics, and governments, it is logical to conclude that self-correcting mechanisms exist such that grass roots adaptation will solve problems at the local level.

The conclusion of this discussion is that the reader will simply have to make up his or her own mind about what a public really is. There is no technically correct answer. Communitarians will defend their view that government is an energetic agent of the whole community, while the individualists will advocate limited government activity based on the argument that there are many publics and government should act only when the many interests individually converge on the conclusion that something needs to be done about a problem. Thus, the core debate is about whether publicness should arise directly, visibly, and coherently from a general-purpose agent—government—of the public or whether publicness and public good can best arise indirectly as a by-product of local, private problem-solving behavior by the constituents of the whole. Each position must be prepared to develop and defend its approach bearing in mind that the policy decision that results is a contested one, based on a competitive defense of policy ideas and positions. These points are reinforced in the chapters that follow.

As we ponder our own and our colleagues' positions on this debate, let us acknowledge a few of the realities about government developed in this chapter. First, while government is a powerful concept, it is not in its definition inherently simple and dumb. Government has many attributes and, as shown, may be designed with specific purposes and functions in mind. Second, government can be made to do whatever public opinion and the representatives of that opinion want it to do; thus, the history of government in the United States is a chronicle of creating and managing the many governments, authorities, corporations, compacts and agreements, and agencies authorized and managed with some public purpose in mind.

Third, it follows that much of the problem of thinking about government is not that government cannot be properly arranged to do public work but that the public is unclear about precisely what it wishes to do. The dilemma, in short, is not that government can do too little. The problem is that government can be empowered to do too much of the wrong thing and too little of the right thing! Yet deciding what is right and what is wrong for government *to do*, rather than debating the inherent properties of government, is the key issue. Surprisingly, our current democratic system is designed to perform this fundamental task of finding out what the public wants of its government. Editorial commentator and political pundit H. L. Mencken is alleged to have put the issue succinctly: "Democracy is all about finding out what the people want and then giving it to them . . . good and hard."

Finally, it should be noted that the very idea of government contains a broad range of action options available to public policy. As we will discover in subsequent chapters, the public is not stuck with a limited set of action options. On the contrary, government and public policy can choose from an extensive menu, as suggested in the following three summaries.

Laissez-faire

One option is that government can decide to leave things alone. This seeming indifference to problems has many variations, but all stem from the view that problems will, if let alone, solve themselves. Thus, people do not need direct assistance from so powerful an instrument as government and can be self-reliant in dealing with the matters at hand. Those who believe in self-reliance or who see natural self-correcting forces at work on public problems also believe that government meddling will only make things worse. Some of the possibilities include:

1. *Benign neglect:* Government can face a horrible problem that appears either to compel public action but conclude that there is no timely intervention available because of a lack of instruments, because it does not know how to solve the problem, or because it believes the problem will of its own nature resolve itself over time.
2. *Self-service:* Government can encourage citizens to serve themselves by encouraging, or at least not discouraging, voluntary associations and self-service arrangements to provide human needs such as housing, food distribution, and child care. Another variation on the theme is that government can provide the information—such as report cards and factual information—on the basis of which informed and targeted service production and consumption are enhanced by individual citizens.
3. *Private philanthropy:* Government can rely on private corporations, charitable associations, and wealthy individuals to supply services that public policy requires, such as housing, poor relief, job training, and health coverage.
4. *Private markets:* Public policy can rely on private markets to supply services that it requires. Thus, citizens can be required to contract privately for their own garbage disposal, automotive emission control, innoculations, and landscaping, while government's role is merely to designate the outcome to be achieved, not how the services are to be arranged and produced.
5. *Nonprofit organizations:* Public policy can rely on nonprofit organizations, associations, and corporations to provide essential services. The world of museums, repertory theaters, hospitals, symphony orchestras, and foundations is heavily populated with private corporations whose existence depends on a service charter that precludes profits and distribution of surplus revenues to shareholders. Service provision occurs through a mix of paid and unpaid volunteer staff.

Direct Government Action

A second possibility is that numerous problem conditions requiring government intervention can occur. They clearly include situations that will not improve with benign neglect and require powerful and swift intervention to achieve an effective social result. Examples include market failures, discussed in Chapter 3, which prevent the effective operation of voluntary exchanges between buyers and sellers; external and internal threats to the political and social order; catastrophes, both natural and manmade; and perceived opportunities to improve the collective well-being of a public. Among the most powerful instruments are the following:

1. *Regulation:* Government can apply rules and regulations to private and even public (i.e., mandates to other governments) behavior and by altering private behavior to solve public problems such as unsanitary practices in food preparation, predatory business practices, wage and price inflation, unseemly land use, and waste of natural resources. Regulation generally operates through negative injunction—for example, "Do not discriminate in hiring practices"—through systems of permissions or licenses, or through procedural prescription that causes costs to be absorbed by the persons or entities being regulated. Regulation therefore appears as a small charge to a government budget since it is administered largely by legal staffs and inspectors even though its private costs are calculated in altered behavior.
2. *Service provision:* Government can authorize, pay for, and actually produce services. At one time or another government has probably provided most of the services that are also provided by the private economy—health, transportation, food service—as well as many that are not—coining money, issuing travel visas, protecting natural preserves, waging wars.
3. *Grants:* Governments can simply give money, land, and equipment to enable producers to provide goods and services that one level of government cannot produce by itself.

Grants, then, are producer subsidies organized either in narrow categories or broad blocks of responsibility.

4. *Intergovernmental agreements:* Governments can use other governments as instruments to be brought on line to provide required services. This can be done in a variety of ways, including the use of intergovernmental agreements, treaties, alliances, partnerships, and outright grants.

5. *Government authorities and corporations:* Government can create wholly or partly owned enterprises to provide services by collecting fees and revenues that pay the operating costs of an enterprise whose capitalization depended on the public treasury.

6. *Government takings:* Government can tax and acquire what it needs to operate. It can claim land (at a fair price) required by community need, such as is recognized in government's eminent domain proceedings. It can require services of citizens as seen in drafts of personnel and the commandeering of equipment required to perform public functions. Government can also influence public goods creation by *failing to tax,* meaning that socially productive behavior is rewarded through systems of exemptions, tax credits, and deductions, which become loopholes in the tax code.

Market-Based Instruments

A third general strategy is for public policy to use private sector institutions and private incentives for public purpose. This is done by having government either use or create markets to which clients and customers can bring resources with which to acquire the precise services they require at prices they are willing to pay. These instruments are used in instances where achieving an efficient use of resources is critical and where excellence in customer service requires expression of personal preference by the consumer. Among the action possibilities are:

1. *Contracts, franchises, and vouchers:* Government can engage the services of the private sector. For example, government can enter into legal agreement by which a contracting party is paid to produce goods or services. Alternatively, it can grant monopoly producer privilege to a franchised producer who is allowed to run concessions for food, dispense licenses, or harvest natural resources. Finally, government can subsidize consumers of goods and services with vouchers that can take the form of stamps, certificates, and entitlements enabling recipients to shop for goods and services deemed by public policy to be meritorious.

2. *Transfer payments:* Government can merely act as a cash transfer mechanism that collects money and then disburses cash to citizens entitled to pensions, unemployment compensation, child support, and supplemental income to provide treatment for disabilities, child nutrition, and heat for homes during cold weather. In these cases, government does no work, but merely transfers resources. The policy instrument is really the individual person who converts the resources into a desired (it is hoped) public result.

3. *Government-sponsored enterprise:* Government can create enterprises necessary to carry out public work in cases where no provider of services can be found in the operating economy through the creation of public authorities and corporations. It can also create enterprises in the private and not-for-profit sector through multiple systems of authorization and financing. Enterprises can be based on various strategies that blend fee income with public subsidy in cases where enterprise goals are either strictly commercial or public goods creating, such as health clinics or public banks.

4. *Partnerships:* Government can enter into ventures that share costs, risks, and responsibilities through cooperative agreements, discretionary grants, manipulations of the tax code, or other rules of conduct through which public results are jointly produced by government and its partners.

5. *Risk insurance:* Public policy can do work by underwriting the risks that stand in the way of desired social action. Thus, guaranteeing loans against default can reduce the risk as-

sociated with making loans available to needy students or those unable to purchase homes. Similarly, insurance against institutional failure can induce private investment in banks and trading relationships that benefit a whole society.

Clearly, government has many instruments through which it can arrange the production, payment, delivery, and consumption of public services. Just as clearly, the choice of action instrument is a contentious one that is therefore almost always inherently political at the authorizing stage. Thus, public management and administration are not merely about the dull, technical details of paper pushing, for management is the discipline that decides in the end whether and how public services are to be delivered. Students should note that there are other issues that impinge on the choice of action instruments, such as:

1. The mix of resources that must be extracted and expended in the name of public productivity.
2. The extent to which other institutions are undermined or supported by public policy.
3. The nature of the problem situation, including the *problem* to be solved, the *resource constraints* in place at the time a problem requires action, and who is *trusted* to promote the collective values of the community.

Whom do we trust? The answer determines the shape of government both now and in the future. If we believe that government is needed to promote the collective values of the community and that government agencies are capable of producing results, then resources will flow to and through the collective instruments of society. If the public concludes that government cannot be trusted or is the inappropriate instrument to use, then other means are readily at hand. Questions about how government should operate cannot be answered in the abstract, however, unless the reader has a tolerance for endless academic debate. Real answers arise at the level of government action, where problems are faced and the details of problem-solving activity are contemplated. Readers are invited to read further and become immersed in some of the strategic details of policy choices and public action.

SUMMARY

Government has two basic functions. The first is to govern or steer the public ship by making authoritative collective choices; in this regard, government is society's largest and most powerful decision making agent and action instrument. The second is to provide for the production of public goods and the elimination of threats to public welfare. Since American government has confronted growing demands for public service spanning the entire twentieth century, it is not surprising to find that the government business has grown, especially since the Great Depression of the 1930's and World War II. Growth in federal responsibility dominated the period 1932 to 1980. Marked growth of state and local responsibilities characterizes American government since 1980.

American government is distinctive both in its decision format and manner of public goods production. On the decision making side, the dominant pattern involves simultaneous use of three constitutional principles by which political power is shared among several competing institutions. The principle of *separation of powers* distributes the power of government among three independently tenured branches of government, whereas *checks and balances* provides a constitutional basis for each branch's oversight of the other branches. Third, *federalism* ensures a division of power between the federal government and the states. The result is a level of complexity not easily understood by casual observers, but a government system with both strengths and weaknesses.

On the public goods production side, the historic pattern has been one of increasing governmental involvement in the private economy. The pattern parallels the growth of government decision making responsibility and is marked by more than 86,000 units of governments that employ directly roughly one-sixth of the U.S. labor force and spend 35 percent of the gross domestic product. Thus, the burdens of actually producing public goods are broadly shared and distributed throughout the public and private sectors. Notwithstanding the broad array of production options available to public decision makers, a lively debate exists about whether and on what grounds government intervention in the production of public goods is desirable.

DISCUSSION QUESTIONS

1. Assess the strengths and weaknesses of the American democratic formula. What works particularly well? What works less well?
2. What specific government reforms come to mind as appropriate for making American government work even better?
3. As a general rule, do you agree with Peter Drucker's notion that the business of government is not doing, but steering and deciding? What does your position lead you to conclude about the kinds of strategies available to government for getting work done?
4. How common do you think the Arrow's paradox is in public affairs? Illustrate your conclusion with as many applications of Arrow's dilemma as come quickly to mind. Choose one example and work through the problem, considering how in the end the issue might be resolved? (Hint: working through a problem in a small group helps in this exercise.)

SUGGESTIONS FOR FURTHER READING

Nancy Burns, *The Formation of American Local Governments: Private Values in Public Institutions* (New York: Oxford University Press, 1994).

James Fallows, *Looking at the Sun: The Rise of the New East Asian Economic and Political System* (New York: Pantheon Books, 1994).

Donald F. Kettl. *Sharing Power* (Washington, D. C.: The Brookings Institution, 1993).

John W. Kingdon, *Agendas, Alternatives, and Public Policies* (Boston: Little, Brown, 1984).

John Kohut, *Stupid Government Tricks: Outrageous (But True) Stories of Bureaucratic Bungling and Washington Waste* (New York: Plume, 1995).

David Osborne, *Laboratories of Democracy: A New Breed of Governor Creates Models for National Growth* (Boston: Harvard Business School Press, 1988).

Alice M. Rivlin, *Reviving the American Dream: The Economy, the States and the Federal Government* (Washington, D. C.: The Brookings Institution, 1992).

Hedrick Smith, *Rethinking America* (New York: Random House, 1995).

James L. Sundquist, *Constitutional Reform and Effective Government* (Washington, D.C.: The Brookings Institution, 1986).

James Q. Wilson, *Bureaucracy: What Government Agencies Do and Why They Do It* (New York: Basic Books, 1989).

NOTES

1. James Q. Wilson, *Bureaucracy: What Government Agencies Do and Why They Do It* (New York: Basic Books, 1989), 378.
2. Charles T. Goodsell, *The Case for Bureaucracy: A Public Administration Polemic,* 3rd ed. (Chatham, N.J.: Chatham House Publishers, Inc., 1994); John E. Schwarz, *America's Hidden Success: A Reassessment of Public Policy from Kennedy to Reagan,* rev. ed. (New York: W.W. Norton, 1988).
3. Lloyd A. Free and Hadley Cantril, *The Political Beliefs of Americans* (New Brunswick, N.J.: Rutgers University Press, 1967), 51.
4. *New York Times,* Thursday, 12 January, 1989, p. 8, national edition.
5. Delivered on Inaugural Day, 20 January, 1993.
6. Ed Gillespie and Bob Schellhas, eds. *Contract with America: The Bold Plan by Rep. Newt Gingrich, Rep. Dick Armey and the House Republicans to Change the Nation* (New York: Times Books, 1994), 13.
7. Ibid., 5–7.
8. Robert Pear, "G.O.P. Finds It Difficult to Deflect Attacks on the School Lunch Proposals," *The New York Times* National Edition (Sunday, April 9, 1995), 11.
9. *U.S. Term Limits, Inc., et al., v. Thornton, et al.* 93–1456, 93–1828 (1995). Argued November 29, 1994. Decided May 22, 1995.
10. Alexander Hamilton, James Madison, and John Jay, *The Federalist Papers* (New York: The New American Library of World Literature, Inc., 1961), contains an introduction, table of contents, and index of ideas by Clinton Rossiter.
11. That is, the doctrine of the survival of the fittest and the corollary that if one has survived and become prosperous, then one is, indeed, fit.
12. Carl L. Becker, *Freedom and Responsibility in the American Way of Life* (New York: Vintage Books, 1945), 37.
13. Attributed to François Marie Arouet Voltaire in S. G. Tallentyre, *The Friends of Voltaire* (London: Smith Elder & Co., 1906).
14. John Stuart Mill, *On Liberty,* ed. and with introduction by Currin V. Shields (New York: Liberal Arts Press, 1956).
15. *Abrams v. United States,* 250 U.S. 616 (1919).
16. Henry Steele Commager, *Documents of American History,* Volume II 7th ed. (New York: Appleton-Century-Crofts, 1963), 149.
17. *The Pentagon Papers, as Published by The New York Times* (New York: Bantam Books, 1971). The often-quoted portion of the concurring opinion of Justice Hugo L. Black (p. 663), taken from *The New York Times* case, presents the essential conclusion of the Court, which released its 6-to-3 decision on 30 June, 1971:

    Only a free and unrestrained press can effectively expose deception in government. And paramount among the responsibilities of a free press is the duty to prevent any part of the Government from deceiving the people and sending them off to distant lands to die of foreign fevers and foreign shot and shell. In my view, far from deserving condemnation for their courageous reporting, *The New York Times,* the *Washington Post* and other newspapers should be commended for serving the purpose that the Founding Fathers saw so clearly. In revealing the working of government that led to the Vietnam war, the newspapers nobly did precisely that which the founders hoped and trusted they would do.

18. Alexander Mieklejohn, *Political Freedom: The Constitutional Powers of the People* (New York: Harper & Row, 1960), 13–14.
19. James Ring Adams, *The Big Fix: Inside the S & L Scandal* (New York: John Wiley & Sons, Inc., 1990).
20. Peter Navarro, *The Policy Game: How Special Interests and Ideologues Are Stealing America* (Lexington, Mass: D.C. Heath and Company, 1984).

21. Navarro, 1984, chap. 6.
22. Navarro, 1984, p. 245; taken from a quotation by Senator William Proxmire.
23. Kenneth Arrow, *Individual Values and Social Choice* (Cambridge, Mass: Harvard University Press, 1953); this is the publication of Arrow's doctoral dissertation.
24. Jerry Levine and Fabienne Vandenbrande, "American State Offices in Europe: Activities and Connections," *Intergovernmental Perspective* (fall 1993–winter 1994): 43–46. Vol. 20, No. 1.
25. David Osborne, *Laboratories of Democracy: A New Breed of Governor Creates Models for National Growth* (Boston: Harvard Business School Press, 1988). The title refers to the famous 1932 dissenting opinion of Supreme Court Justice Louis Brandeis in *New State Ice Co. v. Liebmann:* "There must be power in the States and the Nation to remould, through experimentation, our economic practices and institutions to meet changing social and economic needs. . . . Denial of the right to experiment may be fraught with serious consequences to the Nation. It is one of the happy incidents of the federal system that a single courageous State may, if its citizens choose, serve as a laboratory; and try novel social and economic experiments without risk to the rest of the country."
26. John L. DiIulio, Jr., Donald F. Kettl, and Richard P. Nathan, *Making Health Reform Work: Implementation, Management and Federalism,* CPM Report 94–1, April 8, 1994. (Washington, D. C.: Brookings Institution, 1994), 6–7.
27. Peter Drucker, *The Age of Discontinuity* (New York: Harper & Row, 1968), 233.
28. Vincent Ostrom, *The Meaning of American Federalism* (San Francisco: Institute for Contemporary Studies, 1991), 164–172.
29. William F. Martin and George Cabot Lodge, "Our Society in 1985–Business May Not Like It," *Harvard Business Review,* 53(6) (November–December 1975): 143–152.
30. Martin and Lodge, 1975.

2

The Process of Public Policy Development

There is nothing mysterious or particularly complicated about the public policy process. When we speak of public policy, we are simply referring to the series of actions taken by the government as it carries out its functions and to the intentions behind those actions. When the federal government decides to spend money on our space program, the nation's policymakers—the president and the Congress—have determined that space exploration is in the country's best interests, and they take the legislative, budgetary, and administrative steps necessary to implement their decision. When a state government develops and supports a new university program, the policymakers of the state—the governor and legislators—are making public policy with the intention of improving the general welfare of the state. When a city establishes zoning regulations for the use of land within its boundaries, the mayor and the city council are setting public policy that restricts the rights of individual landowners in favor of the broader welfare rights of the community.

The public policy framework within which our federal governmental system operates was originally set forth at the founding of our nation. We noted in Chapter 1 that the preamble to the U.S. Constitution listed the principal public concerns of government as being to "establish Justice, insure domestic Tranquility, provide for the common defence, promote the general Welfare, and secure the Blessings of Liberty to ourselves and our Posterity." The federal government was given quite specific responsibilities, as well as the power to levy and collect taxes. The Tenth Amendment to the Constitution stated that "all powers not delegated to the United States by the Constitution, nor prohibited by it to the States, are reserved to the States respectively, or to the people." This constitutional authorization was eventually interpreted to include basic governmental functions such as the following:

1. Social and physical infrastructure provision: This responsibility was primarily assigned to state and local governments. It includes policy and delivery systems for the provision of physical infrastructure (roads, utilities, public facilities) and for general social welfare responsibilities such as the maintenance of law and order, education, and public health.
2. The guaranty and protection of individual rights: This policy responsibility mainly lies with our courts. It includes our basic constitutional freedoms: for example, the right of free speech, freedom of religion, the right of assembly, the right of habeas corpus (a person cannot be detained without a court hearing), and the right to form militia and bear arms.
3. Federal government domestic responsibilities: The domestic responsibilities of the national government were quite limited at the founding of the nation. The principal policy activities were to provide for a common defense of the republic and to regulate commerce and promote economic stability.
4. Federal government international responsibilities: The Constitution clearly gave to the national government the responsibility to conduct foreign policy. This function was defined to mean the establishment of relations with other nations, the support of international commerce, and the protection of the international rights of U.S. citizens and their interests.

Since the adoption of the Constitution, the powers granted by the people to the government have been interpreted by all three branches of government to include an almost limitless array of issues, resulting in serious policy debates about government's role in society.

There are essentially three reasons for this evolution of the public policy role of our government:[1] (1) the increased demand for governmental services by the citizens of the country; (2) the vested interests of individuals and institutions, both within and outside government, in the supply of more public services; and (3) inefficiency in the provision of government services. Each of these topics is discussed in the following sections.

INCREASED DEMAND FOR GOVERNMENT SERVICES

The more important reasons for the increased demand for government services include the following:

Demographic Change. Changes in both the structure and the absolute size of the population can result in increased demand for certain types of government services. For instance, consider a structural change in the population that involves the same total population size but a higher proportion of older persons as a percentage of the total. This change would likely lead to increased health care costs and higher Social Security payments.

Conversely, a higher proportion of children in the population results in higher expenditures for education and expanded needs for other youth-focused public policy activities. Changing ethnic mixes in communities can also lead to different expectations of the role of government in society and new problems and demands for the government to provide new services. For example, new language demands on the schools and other public service providers can be one result of rapid waves of immigration such as those experienced by southern Florida during the Cuban exodus of the late 1970s. The legitimacy of this new need for bilingual public services was established as public policy by the Dade County Council (Miami) in May 1993.

Growing Populations. Growth of the population also directly leads to a higher demand for services. This effect goes beyond the simple one-to-one impact of more people on the use of community resources. As cities grow and become more crowded, the complexities that result because of the higher population density lead to a greater than proportionate increase in the need for police and fire services; traffic problems multiply exponentially; and there is a greater strain on community health and other public facilities.

Income Growth. Higher per capita income usually results in more demand for improved quality and expanded government services. For example, wealthy communities want more spent on schools, parks, libraries, and other cultural amenities. They are also more likely to demand a more active role for government in community planning, as they seek to protect the value invested in higher-priced homes and neighborhoods.

Income Redistribution. Programs to alleviate poverty all need government agencies to administer the programs and consequently result in more government services being provided. For example, a graduated income tax is much more complicated to administer and monitor than a simple payroll or sales tax. Programs such as Aid to Families with Dependent Children (AFDC) require such complex tasks as monitoring and counseling, in addition to the routine administrative activities. Medicaid, which provides health care to those with low income, is extremely expensive to administer and requires a sizable investment in people and other resources by the government.

Risk Aversion. Government risk aversion programs such as federal flood insurance, federal farm subsidies, federal mortgage insurance for low-income households, and the federal guaranty of individual bank and savings institution deposits all add to the continuing growth of government. They have all experienced sizable growth since the 1930s, and government institutions designed to administer the programs, such as the Federal Emergency Management Agency (FEMA) or the Federal Deposit Insurance Corporation (FDIC), have become increasingly important components of the federal government establishment.

VESTED INTERESTS OF INDIVIDUALS AND INSTITUTIONS

The vested interests of individuals and institutions, both within and outside government, have led to growth of government in the following ways:

Pork Barrel Projects. These projects usually require more government activity. By *pork barrel* projects, we mean those special-purpose actions of the government that result from a public official's (elected or appointed) interest in supplying some special benefit to his or her constituents. For example, Senator Jesse Helms continues to be able to deliver a farm subsidy to North Carolina tobacco growers, in spite of other government policies designed to reduce smoking. During the Reagan administration, Secretary of the Navy John Lehman was accused of *home porking* (rather than *home porting*) in the location of naval bases in the districts of important members of Congress. President Bush, with the support of the Department of Defense, routinely removed the vertical-takeoff Osprey aircraft from his defense budgets, and Congress members from districts where the plane would be produced continued to put it back into the budget. (The Clinton administration reinserted the Osprey into its first defense budget.)

Bureaucratic Interests.   These groups, in protecting and expanding their own governmental programs, provide a natural source of support for the growth of government. One of the toughest tasks in any government is to terminate an existing program. The program directors are typically supported by those both above and below them in the organizational hierarchy and often by relevant legislative committees. These inside interests are also usually reinforced by constituencies and beneficiaries of the program and sometimes by the special interests of those seeking government employment or government contracts.

Public-Interest Groups.   Often known as lobbyists, public-interest groups have a major impact on the expansion of government activity. For example, farming interests are successful in maintaining, if not expanding, federal programs for agricultural assistance. Lobbyists for the space and defense interests help maintain and expand the government departments responsible for those programs. The labor unions support various programs of the Department of Labor, and the National Association of Cities and Towns supports the establishment and expansion of various programs in the Department of Housing and Urban Development (HUD) that are concerned with issues relevant to city problems. Public schools and universities both are active in lobbying for federal, state, and local programs affecting their responsibilities. Usually the result of success by the interest groups is an expansion of government activity.

Monopoly Power.   Some government organizations provide an agency with the ability to take actions and levy charges without the constraints of competition. This monopoly power can either be exercised by the government agency itself or be granted to a private firm on a contract basis. Its result is often an expansion of the supply of public services, either by the agency (e.g., a government-owned water company) or by an expansion of government as a result of the need to regulate legal monopolies. A monopoly granted to a company by a local government is always subject to abuse and requires monitoring. A recent example concerns the cable TV companies. With guaranteed local monopolies, many have been accused of increasing their programming beyond what is needed to generate higher fees. The result was a move in 1994 by government to regulate the activities of the cable companies as well as an effort to allow the regional telephone companies to compete with the cable industry for television viewers. Other examples of organizations with monopoly power in government include public safety organizations, certain health providers, and publicly owned corporations.

INEFFICIENCY IN THE PROVISION OF GOVERNMENT SERVICES

Inefficiencies in the delivery of public services result from many factors: poorly conceived government programs, insufficient or excessive program funding, poor management practices, unqualified personnel, or turf competition among agencies leading to waste and duplication.

These factors all have a direct influence on the conflicts that exist in our society about the policy agenda and scope of government activities. Additional forces that also come into play and expand the policy debate and conflict include the following:

The separation of powers in our government between the Congress, the courts, the president, and the states introduces multiple actors into the policy debate and generates natural differences of opinion and policy conflict. The Congress and the president have had substantial differences of opinion over the years about who has the power to do what—especially when the executive and the legislative branches of government have been held by opposing parties.

For instance, during the Nixon administration a number of conflicts arose about the rights of presidential privilege to protect certain documents and information during the Watergate affair. But even within the Clinton administration, with the Democrats controlling both branches of government in the first two years of the administration, there were differences of opinion about fundamental policy issues such as taxes and expenditure policy and whether the president should have the right to veto specific items in the federal budget (*the line-item veto*) or must accept or reject the budget passed by Congress in its entirety.

There have also been conflicts between the federal courts and the Congress over policy issues. On occasion the Congress has taken action to change the law as a result of a difference of opinion with the Supreme Court. And of course there are frequent disputes between the states and the federal government over a variety of policy issues: for instance, civil rights matters and the right of a woman to have an abortion.

Philosophical differences about limits to individual freedom have also contributed to basic policy conflict: for example, the current differences between the Republican and the Democratic platforms on the issues of gun control and individual choice in abortion.

The ongoing philosophical debate about whether or not particular issues should even be on the public agenda can slow down the policy process somewhat. This debate often goes to the heart of the differences between the liberal and the conservative views of the role of government in our society. On the one hand, a liberal view might be that government has the right and the ability to intervene economically, socially, and even culturally to accomplish goals and objectives that elected officials determine to be desirable. A conservative, on the other hand, would argue that the government that governs least, governs best.

Differences in how a particular problem or issue should be framed, or where it fits in a scale of priority, can lead to great policy differences. Early in his term, President Clinton proposed to Congress and argued for an economic stimulus program that included expanded expenditures for public works, extended unemployment benefits, and a new youth summer-jobs program. His frame of reference was that the economy was weak and needed this stimulation to speed its recovery from the 1991–1992 recession. The Republican minority in the Senate, however, successfully argued that the economy was recovering from the recession without this stimulus and that these expenditures were too little and too late to do any real good and would weaken the economy by unnecessarily expanding the federal deficit.

President Clinton also encountered a conflict in public policy priority setting by arguing for more aid to Russia, while others argued that domestic problems in the United States should take precedence in our funding priorities.

Differences of opinion about how and by whom implementation of public programs should be accomplished further complicate the public policy conversation. Some of this is simply the result of bureaucratic rivalries within the government. For instance, whether the State Department, the Department of Commerce, or the Department of the Treasury is the key actor in the policy development and administration of programs to expand U.S. international trade probably is immaterial, except to those agencies involved. Other bureaucratic debates can be more substantive. Should the Navy or the Air Force have the primary mission of rapid response to regional conflicts? The debates also carry over into which levels of government should control the implementation of government programs. If the funds to support a particular program at the local level are from the federal or state governments, should the operation of the program be left to the city governments? The issues involve both accountability and effectiveness.

Differences in party platforms in presidential campaigns highlight the intensifying debates and conflicts that can occur when philosophical disputes about public policy issues are confronted. For instance, in 1992 there were the following differences between the Democrats and Republicans:

Economy

Democrats: Launch a national program of public investment in infrastructure, transportation, training, science, and technology.
Republicans: Stimulate the economy by cutting taxes and reducing government spending and regulation.

Taxes

Democrats: Increase tax equity by raising taxes on the rich and lowering taxes on the middle class. Reduce capital gains taxes (a tax on the profit of asset sales) only on long-term investments in new businesses and technologies.
Republicans: Oppose further tax increases and seek ultimately to repeal the 1990 tax agreement with Congress that raised the top tax rate from 28 percent to 33 percent. Reduce the tax on capital gains from 28 percent to 15 percent, and to 0 percent in urban enterprise zones.

Health Care

Democrats: Begin a pay or play plan, requiring employers to provide private health insurance for their employees or contribute to a publicly sponsored health care program.
Republicans: Continue to rely on private insurance for most health care. Provide tax credits and deductions to low- and middle-income people to help them buy health insurance.

Abortion

Democrats: Support the right of every woman to choose to have an abortion, consistent with the U.S. Supreme Court decision in *Rowe v. Wade.*
Republicans: Support a constitutional amendment banning abortion for any reason.

Federal Regulations

Democrats: Increase government regulation of employer-employee relations, environmental affairs, and financial institutions.
Republicans: Impose a 90-day moratorium on new regulations; examine all federal regulations on a cost-benefit basis; allow more rapid approval of new biotech products; generally limit the imposition of new regulations.

THE POLICY IMPLEMENTATION DEBATE

As if the differences of opinion about public policy directions were not enough, even if there is agreement on the necessity for action, there are still wide differences between the Democrats and the Republicans, as well as among conservatives, liberals, and various interest groups, about how a particular public policy should be implemented and by whom.

In his book *The New Economic Role of the States,* Scott Fosler discusses how the states have begun to replace the federal government as the key mover in the economic development of the nation.[2] Neal Pierce's recent book, *Citistates,*[3] goes further when he argues that the principal focus of getting the people's business done is shifting from both the national and the state governments to what he describes as Citistates—geographic clusters of related industries, supported by networks of local world-class research institutes, specialized business services, a workforce with specialized skills, and demanding and knowledgeable local consumers who set the pace for global markets.

Emmanuel Savas, in his book on privatization, describes the forces behind the movement of the delivery of public services from the government to the private sector.[4] He suggests this implementation shift results from the desire for more efficiency and cost-effective public services; from ideological arguments that government is too large; from an interest in strengthening private companies; and from the populist view that people should have more choices in their consumption of public services.

David Osborne and Ted Gaebler, in their widely acclaimed book *Reinventing Government,* argue for entrepreneurial, decentralized government. They suggest: "For the last 50 years, political debate has centered on the questions of ends: what government should do, and for whom. We believe such debates are secondary today, because we simply do not have the means to achieve the new ends we seek. . . . The central failure of government today is one of means, not ends."[5]

Thus, the debate in which the United States is involved today is one of ends and means, a far cry from the public policy issues of only 40 years ago. In one of his syndicated columns in the summer of 1992, David Broder, a prominent and respected political columnist, suggested that 12-year political gridlock resulted from the Democrats controlling the Congress while the Republicans occupied the White House. This problem needs to be overcome if the country is to begin to deal with the substantive problems of education, health, post-Cold War defense strategy, and other key issues.[6] The differences between the Democrats and the Republicans on a range of issues are clearly wide and fundamentally different. Broder argued that the 1992 campaign needed to illuminate these differences on the issues and help voters understand the economic, social, and political values that underlie them.

Columnist William Raspberry raised the same question when he asked, "How have we come to a point where we prefer inconclusive political warfare to peace based on compromise?"[7] He cited several examples of "battles that have divided the country in recent years: affirmative action, taxes, abortion, drug trafficking, gun control, school choice." As a result, he argues, "It isn't so much that common ground is hard to find as that nobody seems interested in looking for it." A large share of the blame for this situation, Raspberry implies, lies with those special-purpose interest groups who own particular issues and whose power comes not from truce and compromise but from continued fighting for their point of view. Their interest is in highlighting disagreement, not in minimizing it.

We have thus moved from a point in U.S. history when the key issues were how to protect our citizens from government, and how to limit government's involvement in our society, to a situation today where it is difficult to identify any aspect of our lives that is not touched by government in one way or another. With this increasing involvement of the public sector in our culture has come increasing divisiveness about the issues of the day. The public policy gridlock in which our government found itself at least until the 1992 elections (and perhaps after the 1994 congressional elections) is symptomatic of the complexity of the issues, of the diversity of our population, and of the difficulty in achieving consensus on almost any issue.

Is there a more rational way to approach public policy issues? Are we condemned to letting special interests frame the issues of the day for us? Can the public agenda be set only on the basis of political strength? Is there a more rational framework that we can use as we begin to deal with the policy problems of our society? We now turn our attention to these matters.

THE PUBLIC POLICY PROCESS

First, let us recognize what most observers agree are the three stages of policy development.[8]

1. Pre-policy development: Problem definition or issue formulation, policy demands, and agenda formulation.
2. Policy adoption: The culmination of a debate involving interest groups, government officials, experts, and constituents. The results are laws, executive orders, and regulations.
3. Policy implementation: The action instruments that bring into being the purposes of the policy. They include constitutions, laws, court decisions, administrative actions, regulations, budgets, treaties, informal agreements, executive orders, and legislative precedent.

In addition, another stage of the policy process is recognized by most policy experts.

This is:

4. Policy evaluation: The evaluation stage is concerned with assessing what actually happened as a result of the policy created and its implementation. It asks questions about whether the purposes of the policy were met and how implementation might be improved. In some cases, the evaluation might result in the policy's being changed or even abandoned.

At all of these stages, substantive policy disagreements can exist among the concerned interest groups, the involved governmental agencies, and the political parties; they also exist within the parties.

Pre-Policy Development.[9]   At this stage, the primary questions with which we are concerned are:

1. How do issues get on the public agenda?
2. What are the factors that affect the timing of an issue that is moving to the forefront of public attention?
3. Once an issue reaches the point where it is ready for serious consideration and, we hope, resolution, what kind of process or framework can we use to try to reach rational conclusions about the matter?

We turn first to how issues appear on the public agenda. William Johnson suggests that there are two kinds of policy agendas: the popular agenda and the institutional agenda.[10]

The popular agenda is the list of issues the public is interested in at any particular time. They arise from old problems, radically redefined problems, and new problems. Issues rise and fall on this agenda for many reasons. Some issues have a definite "time in the sun" and soon fade from the public's attention, whether or not they are resolved. In 1991, for example, dealing with Saddam Hussein and the Iraqi invasion of Kuwait was very much on the front burner. Today, the Iraqi dictator surfaces only periodically as an old problem, as he did in the fall of 1994 when Iraqi troops again moved close to the Kuwaiti border.

Johnson's popular agenda is developed from what has been referred to as an *issue attention cycle.*[11] This cycle has four phases:

1. *Alarmed discovery.* For example, the public became very concerned with the regulation of the lending policies of the savings and loan institutions when several of them incurred huge losses and had to be bailed out by the federal government. Other examples of an alarmed discovery of an issue by the public occurred in the early 1960s when the Soviets succeeded in launching their Sputnik—the first satellite—into space. As a result of that jolt out of our complacency, the United States set new priorities for science and technology in education and in research. Other examples include the heightened awareness of the acquired immune deficiency syndrome (AIDS) epidemic when actor Rock Hudson died of the disease and later when the Los Angeles Lakers' Earvin "Magic" Johnson announced he had tested positive for HIV.

   More recently, the 1993 Los Angeles riots, following the jury acquittal of the police involved in the Rodney King arrest and beating, increased the public awareness of the need to do more in our inner cities. Hurricane Andrew and the flooding of the Mississippi and Missouri Rivers similarly raised numerous public policy questions, such as how we respond to natural disasters, where we locate our military bases, and the logic of providing federally subsidized flood insurance in regions susceptible to hurricanes and floods. The 1995 bombing of the Federal Building in Oklahoma City focused the Clinton administration on the need to change police powers.

2. *Enthusiasm* for the issue, based on the belief that it will be solved. Several of the previous examples qualify here (particularly the Sputnik reaction). One is also particularly reminded of the first Earth Day in 1970. There was a crusade-like enthusiasm that pervaded the college campuses of the nation and a whole new public policy initiative in Washington that led to the establishment of the Environmental Protection Agency (EPA) in 1971. But the environmental enthusiasm faded for several years before reemerging even higher on the public agenda.

3. *The dilemma of conflicting policy issues* comes into play when the public has to confront the fact that sometimes choices must be made between competing and conflicting policies. For example, there is a major push at this writing to build a four-lane highway between Indianapolis, Indiana (in the center of the state), south to Evansville, Indiana, on the Ohio River. There would be obvious economic and safety benefits from such a highway. In order to build the new road, however, it may be necessary to intrude on environmentally sensitive areas. So, which policy—economic development or environmental protection—should take precedence? The same situation occurred when the Alaskan pipeline was built over areas of fragile permafrost in Alaska in the 1970s.

4. *An appreciation of the costs of significant progress* occurs when citizens realize the economic reality that "there is no such thing as a free lunch." Wish lists have to be pared, and priorities must be set. If we want energy independence from foreign oil, for example, oil prices will increase for the American consumer. If the public wants fewer auto emissions of lethal chemicals, cars will have to be more expensive. If we want to decrease acid rain resulting from Midwest power companies using soft coal to generate electricity, then higher electric bills in the Midwest for businesses and consumers will be the result. If we want more education or public support programs, they may have to be paid for by higher taxes. These realities have an obviously dampening effect on the consideration of what at first may seem like desirable public policy changes.

The effect of these considerations on potential new policies is that many lose support and retreat from the public agenda. Only a limited number of the issues from the public agenda make it to what Johnson calls the institutional agenda.

The institutional (or decision) agenda is made up of the decisions that are to be addressed now. These decisions arrive on this agenda because they have been ranked as high priority by public officials. They are brought into the decision loop by the appropriate action agency: for example, a legislative committee or the policymaking process of a governmental agency.

The institutional agenda occasionally reflects the same sort of alarmed discovery as does the popular agenda. In fact, sometimes the public agenda instigates the institutional agenda. But the issues included on the institutional agenda are those for which it has been determined that some agreement is possible. If there appears to be only a low probability of resolution of the issue, it is not taken seriously by the policymaking system.

Issues elevated to the institutional agenda also derive from the internal agendas of the relevant agencies. Federal agencies such as the EPA, Departments of Transportation (DOT) and HUD all have their own internal policy agendas. For example, HUD, under its former secretary Jack Kemp, was very interested in promoting tax-free enclaves for urban business development (*enterprise zones*). The policy agendas of governmental units at different levels (state, local, and federal) also sometimes interlock in areas such as crime, environmental protection, and housing.

Admission to the institutional agenda is controlled by *gatekeepers* who must come to an agreement if the issue is to reach the point where it is under serious consideration. Examples of gatekeepers include leaders and committee chairpersons of legislative bodies, who are able to keep an issue from being considered by a legislative committee; chief executives of government agencies; presidential or gubernatorial staff (e.g., the president's Office of Management and Budget (OMB) and the state budget agencies) and dominant personalities both within and outside government. The politics of the electoral process also acts as an important filter of policy agenda possibilities.

A number of factors affect the timing of a particular policy issue's entry into the institutional agenda. These include the following:

1. Political timing, which is influenced by factors such as:

    Expert consensus: One of the reasons why the North American Free Trade Agreement (NAFTA) between the United States, Canada, and Mexico reached the institutional agenda in 1992 was that most economists, business financial experts, and foreign policy specialists agreed that it would be in the best long-run economic interests of the United States. The aggressive success of the European Union's now 15 member trading bloc no doubt also played a role.

    Public hearings: These are typically held when an issue reaches the institutional agenda. The hearings add information to the debate and give proponents and opponents the opportunity to test the political waters to ascertain the acceptability of various solutions. For example, at the local level of government, hearings are usually held by the planning officials to obtain reactions to the proposed characteristics of a long-range physical plan for the community. Hearings of this type are also a useful way to add to the public understanding of the issue.

    Legislative readiness: Another key to the advancement of a public policy is the willingness of the relevant legislative body to consider the policy being proposed. This involves the body's both understanding the issue and making sure an adequate number of alternative solutions are considered. It also has to do with making sure the general public has reached a point at which it is ready to accept a new policy: for example, a new state lottery or tax. Sometimes a bill is introduced in several legislative sessions before it is eventually passed by the legislative body.

Intergovernmental acceptance: Many public policy initiatives affect more than one level of government. For instance, environmental laws and most entitlements have an impact on both the federal government and the states. Therefore, for such complicated issues, the need to reach a consensus within the intergovernmental system when the timing is right for an issue to be resolved lowers its chances of reaching the institutional agenda.

2. Leadership push can be a key factor that affects when an issue reaches the institutional agenda. For example, when Dr. Otis Bowen was appointed secretary of the U.S. Department of Health and Human Services (HHS) during the second Reagan administration, his experience both as a former family doctor and as the governor of Indiana led to his having several policy issues with which he was well acquainted and personally interested. These included the problems of long-term disability insurance, medical liability, and the problem of teenage pregnancies (as he put it, "babies having babies"). As a result of these interests, when he became HHS secretary, he was able to and did move these policy issues to the top of the internal agenda of the department. He was also able to convince President Reagan to support him on elevating several of these matters to the institutional agenda of the White House.

3. Issue coalitions are an extremely important factor in moving an issue to the institutional agenda and in seeing the issue through to resolution. An issue coalition is a group of organizations and or individuals that is formed to focus on one particular policy issue. Its membership does not necessarily have anything to do with political parties or even political philosophies. For example, one of Secretary Bowen's allies in enacting new legislation on long-term disability coverage was Senator Edward Kennedy. Other parts of the coalition included the American Association of Retired Persons (AARP) and some of the health care public interest groups.

   When the state sales and income taxes were first introduced in Indiana in 1963, the coalition that designed and moved the legislation to enactment included the State Chamber of Commerce, the Indiana Farm Bureau, the AFL-CIO, the state's public universities, and the Indiana State Teachers' Association.

4. Process factors can also have an effect on the elevation of an issue to the institutional agenda. For example, changes of administration following an election will result in changed policy priorities. Public opinion changes, membership changes in bodies relevant to the issue, or simply power shifts within or between key organizations can affect the policy priority action list. A prime example of the latter occurred when the *Class of 1974* was elected to the U.S. House of Representatives following the Watergate scandal. This group of new Congress members eventually succeeded in overhauling the seniority and committee system of the House of Representatives. As a result of these changes, they were able to have an important effect on which policy issues received attention by the House. The 1994 Republican takeover of the Congress had the same result.

   Special task force reports can also have an impact. For example, look at two recent reports: the first was the Packard Commission Report (early 1980s), which recommended a very different approach to the management of the government. In the Department of Defense, the entire weapons-acquisition system was eventually overhauled. The second report was by the Goldwater-Nichols Commission, which recommended numerous changes in the structure and operation of our armed forces. In Indiana, from early 1960s through the late 1970's, the Commission on State Tax and Financing Policy research reports had a major impact on which tax policy matters were considered by the legislature. They also affected the range of policy alternatives considered.

5. The media, as we suggested earlier, also have a significant effect on the issues when they elevate issues to the point where they attract the attention of those able to make decisions about them. The recent conflict in the former Yugoslavia between the Serbs, the Croats, and the Muslims is a classic example of how media attention can attract government policy attention at a time when other problem areas around the world may go unnoticed.

ACTION ON THE INSTITUTIONAL AGENDA

Once an issue is elevated to the institutional agenda, what happens next? First, we shall look at the management of the issue. Earlier we alluded to the fact that many policy issues are managed by nonpolitical party coalitions. In fact, most issues fall outside the dominance and certainly the management of the two political parties. The main reason for this is the sheer mass and complexity of government activity today. Another reason is that the political parties have relatively little influence over a particular legislator or even a member of the executive branch once they have been elected to their jobs. Increasingly these individuals have their own power base independent of their political party. (This is quite different from those countries with a parliamentary system of government. In those cases the party is much more able to control who runs for office and who is chosen for administrative roles in the government. The members of the parliament are therefore less independent than the typical U.S. legislator.)

So if the political parties are not the driving force behind most policy issues, who is? The answer is the issue coalitions referred to earlier. These coalitions, or networks, are groups that share a body of knowledge that is relevant to the issue. Sometimes they are ad hoc, fluid, and short-lived, and sometimes they are more or less permanent. They typically include persons and agencies from the executive branch; members of Congress and congressional staff from both parties; specialists from both inside and outside the government; public policy think tanks (e.g., the American Enterprise Institute or the Brookings Institution); topical experts on the issue (e.g., defense, telecommunications, health); and special interest groups with a particular concern about the topic (e.g., the U.S. Chamber of Commerce and the AFL–CIO were on opposite sides of the policy debate surrounding the NAFTA). The coalitions interact, keep each other informed, agree on strategy, and sometimes lobby for their solution. They are capable of either promoting or killing a policy proposal.

A particular type of issue coalition that is relatively permanent is known as an *iron triangle*. This coalition is relatively fixed in its focus and its membership. For example, President Eisenhower, in his departing speech to the nation, warned of the iron triangle of the military-industrial complex, a coalition of military officers, defense industries, and members of Congress focused on expanding the military and its associated industries.

In fact, however, the issue politics of today is primarily made up of networks of the shifting variety. The style of the U.S. Congress, as an example, requires avoiding personal attacks on fellow members about differences on issues because last week's opponent may be next week's ally.

Are issue networks good or bad for the rational resolution of public policy problems? The answer is both. On the one hand, they can link the Congress and the executive branches in ways that the political parties cannot. They therefore are able to help avoid gridlock on many issues. They also can track an issue over time, maintain the *institutional memory* for the issue, and bring expert analysis to an issue because of the specialization of many of the members of the coalition.

On the other hand, issue networks can make it difficult for an elected or appointed official to act without the network's cooperation. In that sense, the democratic legitimacy and accountability of the network come into question. As an example, a major priority of the Clinton administration has been to reform the nation's health care system. The issue networks involved in this policy area are complex and powerful. They include representatives of the health care providers such as: the hospitals, the doctors, and the associated health care professionals; representatives of the health care recipients such as the American Association of Retired Persons and the various civil rights organizations; the health care insurers; and business associations such as the U.S. Chamber of Commerce and the American Manufacturing Association who represent the employers who pay a large share of the health care costs of their employees. On some particulars of the reform proposal the interest groups are in agreement. On others they are in opposition. All are politically important, and as such, they can reward supportive members of Congress or exact a toll from those opposed to their position on policy changes. The result is that the final policy choices represent not necessarily the optimum health policy mix for the country as a whole but a compromise among the various interested parties.

Now let us assume that an issue has made it to the action stage. What happens next? Assume you are the executive or legislator in charge. What do you do when an important, complicated policy issue lands on your desk? The rational decision maker lays out the goals and uses logical processes to explore the best way to reach them.

A FRAMEWORK FOR MAKING POLICY CHOICES

There are several alternative ways in which one can go about analyzing policy options and making rational decisions. They are all quite similar but each uses different key words to describe their particular framework and each goes into varying amounts of detail. The framework proposed here is a hybrid. It draws from several approaches in one way or another, while perhaps placing different emphasis on some categories and attempting to integrate different but related concepts.[12] The approach uses an iterative process consisting of eight parts.

Establish the Context

What exactly is the issue? What is the environmental paradigm that is relevant to the issue? What categories of our population are affected by the issue? What are the political interests involved? How does the issue fit in the cultural framework of our society? Are there conflicting goals involved, and if so, what are they? Are there currently issue networks involved in this policy discussion? Who has primary control of action on the issue (the states, the federal government, Congress, the president)? Does the problem have the possibility of an acceptable solution?

Formulate the Problem

This step is critical to the process. It deals with such questions as: What are the source and background of the underlying problem? What are the objectives to be accomplished? How can the problem be clarified and constrained? How can we make sure the problem has been differentiated from the symptoms?[13]

Additional questions to ask in the problem formulation stage include the following: How did the situation arise? Why is it a problem? Who are the people who believe it is a problem? What should a solution look like? What sort of solution is likely to be acceptable to the issue networks and other interested parties? Are there competing views about what should be done? What is the basis for assumptions upon which these views are based? Are there data to test the assumptions? Have we identified the right problem or merely a part of a deeper problem? Given what is known, does it seem sensible to use analytical resources on this problem?

Specify Project Objectives

What is it exactly that a policy change can hope to accomplish? Is there more than one objective of the change? What criteria can be used to help develop more precise objectives?

Explore Alternative Solutions to the Problem

The policy analyst needs to be careful to avoid starting with a preconceived idea of the preferred alternatives. It is necessary to consider a variety of factors when one begins the search for possible solutions to a public policy problem. Some of the questions that should be asked are: What further information is necessary to begin to consider relevant alternatives? Are adequate data and other important information about the problem on hand?

A useful sequence of analyst activities is:

Identify, design, and screen the alternatives. At this point the analyst needs to think broadly and creatively about all possible approaches to solving the problem at hand. No potential solution should be ruled out because it seems impractical for one reason or another.

Predict the consequences of each alternative. This is the point at which the analyst begins to reduce the alternative solutions to a manageable, practical set of options. The nature of the problem and the information available about it determine just how this analysis is carried out. In some cases a simple logical assessment about impact is all that is possible. In others, the analyst may utilize a variety of analytical tools to include statistical forecasting approaches or theoretical modeling of the problem. Models are simply abstractions of reality that assist the analyst in predicting and comparing the impact of alternative policy interventions on the policy paradigm. The models can be simple, descriptive statements about the problem that allow the development and testing of alternative scenarios, or they can be highly sophisticated statistical or mathematical models of the problem. Various types of models can also be used in combination with each other.

The purpose of the modeling exercise is to develop answers to a variety of questions about the feasibility and difficulty of the several alternative policy approaches under consideration. For example, to the extent that the model can offer information about who benefits and who pays under the proposed alternatives, the analyst is in a better position to predict both the equity impact and the political acceptability of the alternatives. Other important information can be developed from modeling the problem, including the following: The effect of the alternative solutions on the government's budget—for example, does the solution add to or reduce, or is it neutral on, government revenues and expenditures? In the impact of the alternatives over time, for example, are there differences in the short- and long-term effects? What impact do the proposed solutions have on future generations? What are the opportunity costs of the various solutions to the problem? (What other opportunities are we forgoing by choosing this solution?)

Determine the externalities. What are the unintended side effects of a particular action? Does the proposed solution to the policy problem have related effects on other public policy issues? For example: A policy designed to enhance the economic development of a particular region of the country (e.g., the timber industry in the Northwest) may have negative effects on endangered wildlife species (e.g., the spotted owl) or unintended effects on tourism. The policy of the former West German government to pay for the absorption of the former East Germany by borrowing, rather than levying taxes, resulted in higher interest rates and higher unemployment throughout Western Europe. Some argue that raising the federally legislated minimum wage has resulted in higher teenage unemployment and the use of illegal aliens in our workforce. Secondary impacts of the federal government's Clean Air Act have been to cause unemployment among U.S. coal miners, as well as increased imports of foreign oil and higher prices for automobiles. In all these cases, conflicting public interests come into play and must be resolved before a proposed solution to a public policy problem can be considered viable.

Control the number and types of alternatives. This step is considered by some to be the essence of the political game. The issue coalition or interest group that can make sure its preferred alternative is on the list of options, and that alternatives to which it is opposed are not, has a good chance of winning the debate.

Synthesis—compare and rank the alternatives. When the analysis of several alternatives has been completed, the policy analyst begins to synthesize the results. The process requires more than just listing the results of the analysis. Moving toward a solution to the problem under consideration will require ranking the alternatives according to criteria chosen by the analyst or his or her responsible authority. Two approaches to analysis are useful at this stage, particularly if the problem under consideration is straightforward, such as a choice between alternative military weapon systems or modes of transportation: (1) the cost-effectiveness approach and (2) the fixed budget approach.[14] The cost-effectiveness approach fixes the level of effectiveness sought by the analyst and then tries to determine the alternative that is most likely to achieve this level of effectiveness or to solve the policy problem at the lowest cost. The fixed budget approach sets a certain cost level or budget to be used to attain the objective of the analysis. The alternatives are then ranked on the basis of their ability to come closest to meeting this criterion.

Obviously, actual policy analysis is seldom as neat and specific as implied by this process. The real world of public policy is messy, and it is not usually possible to assemble all of the information that one would like in order to prepare a complete assessment of all conceivable policy options. Most inquiries are under time and financial pressures and suffer from incomplete or inadequate data. Analysts are seldom completely satisfied that they have answered all of the questions about the problem and its possible solutions. In some cases, a real understanding of the impact of an alternative will not be reached until it is actually implemented. That is one reason why test cases (e.g., implementing new approaches to problems such as health care cost containment in one state) are considered particularly valuable before adopting the approach at the national level. Unfortunately, experimentation is not usually possible in public policy analysis, although simulation models can be a helpful substitute for some decisions.

Set the Policy

To be effective, policy analysis must not only find the proper course of action, its findings must be accepted and incorporated into a decision. This stage can involve a number of different levels of approval. In the simplest case, a particular government agency can make a decision on its own about a specific public policy issue and proceed to implement the decision. In other cases, a decision may require the department to submit the proposed policy to a higher level in the executive branch of government (e.g., the White House OMB), work with the Congress to enact a new law, and ultimately have the decision reviewed by the judicial process before it can actually be implemented.

Develop an Implementation Plan

When the policy decision has been made by the relevant parties, the policy is still only an intention; at this point the decision must be made operational before this intention can be converted to the purpose for which the policy was created. In its simplest form, the implementation stage involves assigning the program to an agency and giving it the money and authority to hire personnel and make other operational decisions about tasks to be performed and procedures by which the program will be operated.

As we suggested earlier, however, there are often differences of opinion between various interested parties about how an agreed-upon policy decision should be implemented. For example, two of the important recent public issues facing the United States are the changes needed in both our health care system and our welfare system. When decisions have finally been made about the nature of the changes in both of these policy areas, the implementation of the new policies will be crucial to their success. In both cases there will be disagreement about the respective implementation roles of the national government, the states, and the major metropolitan regions of the country (the Citistates). There will also be differences about the role to be played in the reform effort by the private sector and the responsibilities of the beneficiaries of the programs. The public policy analyst must therefore carefully consider possible implementation approaches both from the standpoint of their effectiveness in the accomplishment of the goals of the policy and the political acceptability of the approach to the parties most involved.

Monitor and Evaluate

This stage can be regarded as both the end and the beginning of the policy process. It is the end in that it follows all of the previous steps that led to the adoption and implementation of the new policy. The purpose is to evaluate the success of the new policy to determine whether it accomplished the goals for which it was intended. Program evaluation requires a systematic, objective framework if it is to avoid the natural bias of those responsible for the program. This means that the evaluation design should be prepared well in advance of the implementation of the policy in order to include the collection of the necessary data and other information in the implementation plan. It cannot be properly done as an afterthought to implementation.

The evaluation stage can also be thought of as a beginning in that, properly accomplished, the information gained from the evaluation sets the stage for beginning the policy process anew. It can result in fine-tuning the existing policy or in the conclusion that an entirely new policy approach is needed. Some states have passed *sunset* legislation to ensure that public programs do indeed receive periodic evaluation. These laws specify that, after a set number of years, the law establishing a particular public program automatically expires—and the program is ended—unless it is positively reviewed and reauthorized by the state legislature.

Recycle the Process

Figure 2–1 illustrates the iterative nature of public policy process. The untidy world of public policy requires that those responsible for the policy process understand that no solution to a public problem is likely to be perfect, nor is the first attempt to solve a public problem likely to be completely successful. Even if effective when instituted, the policy solution will undoubtedly prove less than satisfactory as our population, culture, and other circumstances change with the passage of time.

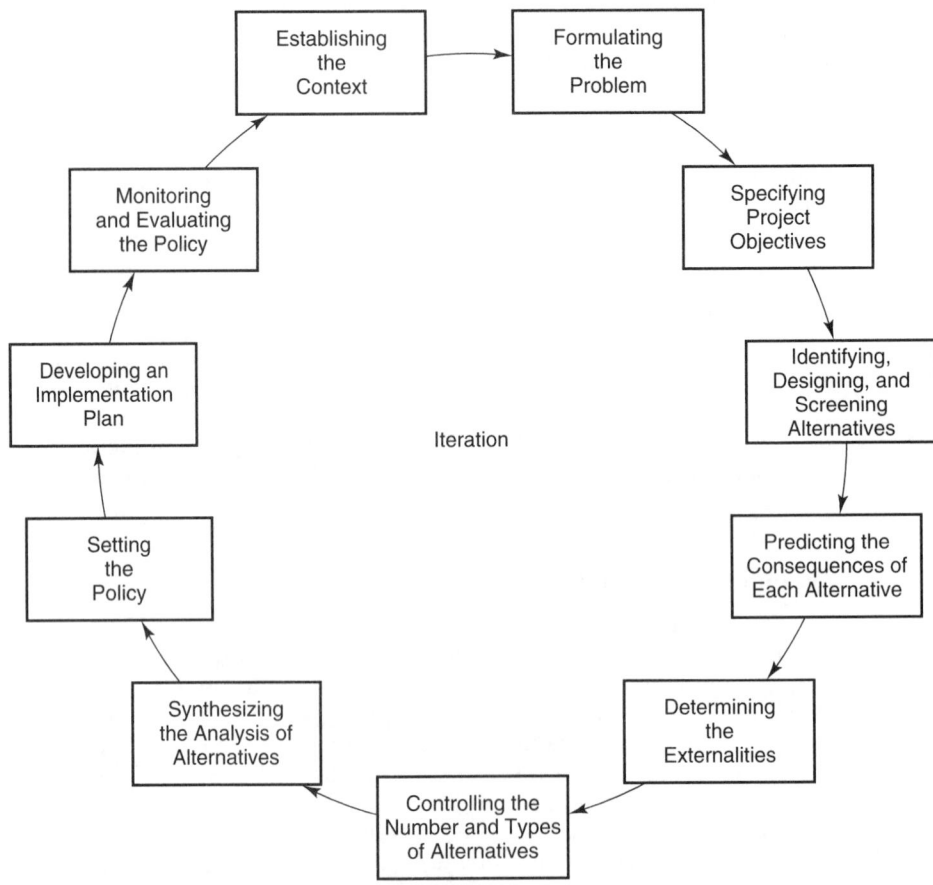

Figure 2–1   The iterative framework for policy analysis

This fact of life requires viewing the policy process as a circular phenomenon that needs to be kept in a constant state of reassessment.

Therefore, the next step after the results of the policy's implementation have been evaluated is to return to the context of the issue to see what, if anything, in the environmental paradigm may be different than originally determined; to redefine, if necessary, the problem under consideration; to reconsider the project objectives; to reexamine the alternative solutions to the problem; to determine if a revision in the earlier selected policy is necessary; to reconsider the implementation plan; and once again, to prepare to evaluate any changes that may be made in the original policy action.

SUMMARY

The purpose of this chapter has been to demystify the public policy process as it operates in the United States at all levels of government. The first section of the chapter discussed the origins and evolution of U.S. public policy. Reasons for the increase in both the supply and demand for public services were explored, and we also reviewed some of the major factors adding to and influencing the public policy debate in this country.

The second section reviewed what most observers agree are the four stages of the public policy process: pre-policy development, policy adoption, policy implementation, and policy evaluation.

In the final section of the chapter, we set out a framework for making policy choices that can be used to assist policy analysts in their task of reviewing public policy problems and trying to reach sensible solutions. In the chapters that follow, in which we will discuss several issues and problems on the contemporary U.S. public policy scene, the framework presented in this chapter will be at least implicitly followed and should be kept in mind as various policy proposals surface for consideration.

DISCUSSION QUESTIONS

1. How does the unique form of democracy found in the United States affect the nation's ability to make meaningful public policy?
2. Using the policy analysis framework found in this chapter, describe the problems with and possible solutions to a societal issue of your choice. (e.g., homelessness, teen-age pregnancies, juvenile crime.)
3. Discuss, using examples of your choice, the factors affecting the timing of when a public policy issue reaches public agenda and the action agenda.

SUGGESTED READINGS

B. Guy Peters, *American Public Policy: Promise and Performance,* Chatham House Publishers, Inc., Chatham, N.J. 1993.

Henry J. Aaron and Charles L. Schultze, (Eds.), *Setting Domestic Priorities: What Can Government Do?,* The Brookings Institution, Washington, D.C., 1992.

David L. Weimer and Aidan R. Vining, *Policy Analysis: Concepts and Practice,* Prentice Hall, Englewood Cliffs, N.J., 1992.

James E. Anderson, *Public Policy Making,* Houghton Mifflin Company, 222 Berkley Street, Boston, Mass., 1994.

NOTES

1. Emanuel S. Savas, *Privatization: The Key to Better Government* (Chatham, N.J.: Chatham House Publishers, Inc., 1987); Clark E. Cochran, Lawrence C. Mayer, T. R. Carr, and N. Joseph Cayer, *American Public Policy: An Introduction* (New York: St. Martin's, 1990), for a more complete discussion of this evolution of the public policy dimension of government.
2. R. Scott Fosler, *The New Economic Role of American States: Strategies in a Competitive World Economy* (New York: Oxford University Press, 1988).
3. Neal R. Pierce, *Citistates: How Urban America Can Prosper in a Competitive World* (Washington, D.C.: Seven Locks Press, 1993), chap. 1.
4. Savas, 1987.
5. David Osborne and Ted Gaebler, *Reinventing Government: How the Entrepreneurial Spirits Are Transforming the Public Sector* (Reading, Mass: Addisson-Wesley Publishing Co., 1992), xxi.
6. David Broder, "Olympic Antidote for Government Gridlock," *Washington Post,* 12, August 1992, p. 21.
7. William Raspberry, "An Interest in Failure," *Washington Post,* 5, November 1993, p. 27.
8. Cochran et al., 1990.
9. We draw primarily on William C. Johnson, "The Sources of Public Policy," *Public Administration* (Guilford, Conn.: Duskin Publishing Group, 1992), chap. 5, 149–182.
10. Johnson, 1992.
11. This concept was developed by Professor Anthony Downs. For more information, see Anthony Downs, "Up and Down with Ecology: The Issue Attention Cycle," *Public Interest* 32 (summer 1972): 38–50.
12. The key words, but not the detail, are from a book by Edith Stokey and Richard Zeckhauser, *A Primer for Policy Analysis* (New York: W. W. Norton, 1978), chap. 15, 320–329.
13. E. S. Quade, "Initiating the Analytic Process," *Analysis for Public Decisions,* in ed. Grace M. Carter (New York: North Holland, 1989).
14. Quade, 1989.

3

Government Regulation

A basic way in which the government changes the behavior of businesses is to issue regulations governing private-sector actions. The use of regulatory power has grown in the United States, particularly in recent decades. Government regulation of private economic activity, however, is as old as human history. Restrictions on lending are mentioned in the Old Testament. The Babylonian code of Hammurabi established uniform weights and measures and limited the rate of interest. Thus, while the origins of regulation are not new, the extent and nature of regulation have changed markedly in the past few decades.

This chapter begins by charting the growth of government regulation from the first major federal regulation, aimed at the railroad industry in 1887, to the surge in social regulation in the 1970s. (The initial moves toward regulatory reform in the late 1970s and early 1980s began in the transportation industries and are discussed in Chapter 9.) This chapter next examines the kinds of private-sector behavior that lead to calls for government regulation. Next, the Iron Law of regulation is described and explored. The Iron Law states that any regulatory change creates winners and losers within the regulated industry. As will be seen, understanding the Iron Law is critical to understanding the effects of government regulation and how regulated companies respond. The chapter next turns to the most important rationales for regulation, namely control of monopoly, externalities such as environmental pollution, and inadequate information. Finally, two of the more common problems in designing and implementing government regulation are discussed.

THE GROWTH OF REGULATION

In the United States, regulatory activities began on a small scale with the individual states. In *Munn v. Illinois* in 1876, the Supreme Court ruled that the Illinois legislature could set a maximum charge for storing grain in warehouses, stating that "when private property is devoted to a public use, it is subject to public regulation."

In 1887, Congress established the Interstate Commerce Commission, the first federal rulemaking agency, to regulate railroad rates and routes. The legal authority for federal regulation is contained in the commerce clause of the Constitution (Article 1, Section 8), which gives Congress the authority to regulate commerce with "foreign Nations, and among the several States. . . . "

At first, the growth of federal regulatory activity was slow. Following the establishment of the Interstate Commerce Commission, the Antitrust Division of the Justice Department was set up in 1903 to prosecute violators of the Sherman Act. The Federal Reserve System was established in 1913 to oversee the commercial banking system. The Federal Trade Commission (FTC) was created in 1914 to carry out the Clayton Act which was designed to promote competitive behavior. The Federal Power Commission (now the Federal Energy Regulatory Commission) was established in 1920, covering the interstate transmission of electricity and other forms of energy. These early regulatory agencies were concerned primarily with preventing abuses of monopoly power.

The Depression in the 1930s caused many policymakers to question whether a market economy should be given free reign and led to a burst of new government agencies, such as the Securities and Exchange Commission (SEC), the Federal Deposit Insurance Corporation (FDIC), the Federal Home Loan Bank Board, the Federal Maritime Commission, the Federal Communications Commission (FCC), the National Labor Relations Board (NLRB), and the Civil Aeronautics Board (CAB). In addition, existing agencies were given expanded regulatory powers. For example, the Interstate Commerce Commission's regulatory authority over the railroads was extended to the intercity bus industry and the trucking industry. These regulatory agencies were each focused on a single industry or narrow sector of the economy. They tended to look after a wide range of issues within that industry but had no focus at all outside that industry. In some cases, the regulatory agency had a dual mandate both to regulate the industry and to promote its growth and development.

Following a lull in new regulatory activity during and after World War II, government intervention in economic activity expanded rapidly in the 1960s and 1970s. Examples of the newer regulatory agencies include the Environmental Protection Agency (EPA), the Consumer Product Safety Commission (CPSC), the Occupational Safety and Health Administration (OSHA), and the Equal Employment Opportunity Commission (EEOC). Unlike the earlier agencies, these did not focus on a single industry, but on a single set of problems across a wide array of industries.

WHY IS THERE ALL THIS REGULATION?

What is the reason for all this regulation? The government regulates in cases where without government intervention, some business or some person would do something that is judged not to be in the best interests of society. In the absence of environmental regulation, for example, some businesses dumped their waste products in rivers, thereby polluting the water. In the absence of antitrust regulation, some large companies lowered prices to below costs on their products and drove smaller competitors out of business. Once their competitors were gone, these companies then raised their prices to very high levels, and consumers suffered.

Why do companies take such actions? Is the world full of callous people who enjoy inflicting harm on others? Some people may be that way, but most are not. However, companies, and the people who manage them, have goals, such as making profits, and have to compete with other companies that are also trying to make profits by selling the same goods or services. If a company can lower its costs, it may be able to continue to sell its product at the same price and make higher profits. Or, with lower costs, it may be able to lower its price and take sales away from its competitors, again making higher profits. This is the *carrot* in a market economy: if you can lower your costs, good things will happen to you. There is also a *stick* in a market economy: if you do not lower your costs and one of your competitors does, you may lose business to that competitor and even go out of business.

Thus, companies have a strong incentive to keep their costs as low as possible. If they do not keep their costs low, they may go out of business. If there is nothing to prevent them from simply dumping their waste in the river and if that is the cheapest way to dispose of that waste, they have an incentive to dump it. If they have an opportunity to force a competitor out of business before that competitor becomes a threat to their business, they have an incentive to do so. When those incentives lead them to do something detrimental to society, they are likely to do so. Will the people who make these decisions feel bad about them? Perhaps, but perhaps they are only dumping a little waste into a big river and perhaps so many others have done the same that they believe it will not really matter. They may also believe that if they do not take this action, their competitors will. They thus feel forced to take the action even if they would prefer not to.

The company is simply responding to the incentives it faces. The problem, from society's perspective, is that these incentives lead to an undesired action. The first important point in considering regulation is that if society wants to change the actions of people or companies, society must change the incentives it faces. Most of the failures of regulatory policy in the United States stem from a failure to consider the incentives. The goal of regulation is to change behavior, and the most effective way to change behavior is to change the incentives that guide that behavior.

THE IRON LAW

There is an unfortunate tendency in considering the impacts of government regulation to view industries as monolithic, perhaps because it is easy to think that all companies in an industry are pretty much alike. If that were true, then it is logical to expect that they must all be affected in essentially the same way by a new government regulation or policy. In reality, however, various individual companies in an industry usually differ in important ways. In manufacturing, factories may have been constructed at different times and employ slightly different technologies. Some factories may use more energy per unit of output while others may use more labor. Some factories may be located where raw materials are less expensive, while others may be located closer to their markets so that their transportation costs are reduced, and still others may be located in regions where wages are generally low.

For a wide variety of reasons, companies in the same industry will differ from one another in their cost characteristics. Industries are not monolithic. A regulation imposed on an industry will not affect each company in the industry the same way. This simple observation leads to the so-called Iron Law that states that any government action creates winners and losers within the competitive sector of the economy and within the same industry. To be sure, a government regulation may affect one industry more than another, thereby changing competition between those industries. For example, a regulation that restricts logging on land where the spotted owl is found will increase costs for the lumber and wood products industry while it will not change the costs of other building materials that can be substituted for wood. This increase in price as a result of a regulation can be thought of as a level effect; that is, one impact of regulation is to change the level of prices charged in the industry. As a result of prices increasing, consumers will reduce their consumption of the good, and industry output will be reduced. As a result, some jobs will likely be lost in that industry, and in some cases, companies may be forced from business.

Often overlooked and often more important is the effect on the structure of costs that a regulation will have on an industry. In the case of the spotted owl, the same regulation will increase the costs of those companies that relied on trees from forests where spotted owls are found while having no adverse impact on those companies who got their trees from other lands. On the one hand, the more a company relies on trees from the restricted area, the less it will be able to produce, or if it must find an alternate source of trees, the higher its costs will be. On the other hand, the less a company relies on trees from the restricted area, the less its output level and costs will be affected. If the price of lumber and wood products increases because of the reduced supply, then a company that did not rely heavily on trees from the restricted area will see the price at which it can sell its products increase while its costs are affected far less or not at all. The result is higher profits for this fortunate company. Thus, because regulation affects the structure of costs, some companies that find themselves with higher costs from a regulation will also find themselves with higher profits if the price they can charge increases more than their costs to produce the product.

Recognizing the cost structure effect is a critical point in considering the effects of government regulation. If only the price level effect is recognized, the conclusion will usually be that a regulation will hurt an industry and that companies in the industry will or should oppose the regulation. By recognizing the cost structure effect, however, the conclusion will be that while the regulation will hurt some companies in the industry and may even put some out of business, it will help other companies in the industry by increasing their profits. Thus, while some companies in the industry may understandably oppose the regulation, others will, or should, support it, even though it will increase their costs. Suppose, for example, the price of a product increases by $1.00 because of a certain regulation. Company A is severely affected by the regulation and its costs go up by $1.10. Company B, however, is less affected and its costs go up by only $.90. Company A has clearly been hurt by the regulation, but Company B is better off even though its costs increased.

This point is based on the economic principle of comparative advantage. Under comparative advantage, it is not the absolute advantage or changes to the absolute advantage that matter; it is the relative or comparative advantage that is important. The issue is not how a regulation alters costs in absolute terms, but how it alters costs compared to the costs of the other companies in the industry. If one company's costs go up less than another's, the first company's comparative advantage in costs has improved even though its costs have gone up in absolute terms. The same can work in reverse. If one company's costs fall, but the costs of other competitors fall by a greater amount, the first company's comparative advantage has worsened even though its costs have dropped.

Understanding the Iron Law of government regulation can help both in understanding public policy decisions and in improving public- and private-sector decision making. Consider the example of the development of the Corporate Average Fuel Economy (CAFE) standard. In the wake of the Arab oil embargo of 1973–1974, there was public concern about U.S. dependence on imported oil. In response, Congress decided that an improvement in the fuel consumption of automobiles driven in this country would reduce oil imports and lessen this dependence. Two alternatives were considered: (1) setting a minimum standard of fuel consumption for autos sold in the United States with a tax or fine levied on those cars not meeting the standard, or (2) requiring a corporation to attain a set fuel economy average on its cars sold in the United States with a tax or fine levied if this average is not met.

At first glance, it is easy to understand the first alternative and hard to see how the second one would even have been devised. The first alternative is simple and direct whereas the second is a bit convoluted. By considering both the price level and the cost structure effects of the Iron Law however, the differences between the two policies become clear, and the economic and political reasons for the eventual adoption of the second alternative are easily understood.

Consider the alternative of simply setting a minimum fuel economy standard. Who would win from such a policy and who would lose? The clear losers would be the producers of cars that did not meet the standard—large cars or high-performance cars. Their cars would be subject to a fine, thereby either increasing the price to consumers and reducing the number of such cars sold or, if the manufacturer did not pass the fine along to the consumer, decreasing the profit earned on the sale of each car. Who were the producers of large and high-performance cars? In part, they were European producers such as Jaguar, Mercedes, and Ferrari. In part, they were also U.S. producers such as General Motors (which produced Cadillac, Buick, Oldsmobile, Pontiac, and Chevrolet) and Ford (which produced Lincoln and large Ford and Mercury sedans). The winners would be producers of small, fuel-efficient cars, which at the time were Japanese manufacturers and German makers of the Volkswagen. U.S. manufacturers would also be partial winners since they produced some small, fuel-efficient cars. On net, then, some foreign producers would be big losers, U.S. producers would win a little and lose a little, and some foreign producers would be big winners.

Consider now the CAFE alternative. The key point is to recognize that fuel-inefficient cars tend to be larger and more expensive and, most important, tend to earn the companies that make them higher profits per car sold. Fuel-efficient cars tend to be smaller and cheaper and earn their manufacturers less profit per car. Clearly, a company would prefer to earn higher profits on each car sold. The problem is that the gas mileage of the large cars is worse than the CAFE standard. To sell a large car without incurring a fine for violating that average, you also need to sell a small car that gets better mileage than the standard. So the way to think about a small car under the CAFE standard is that by selling a small car, you earn the right to sell a large car without exceeding the standard. In other words, selling a small, low-profit car is a license to sell a large, high-profit car. Indeed, under this scheme, it might well be worth lowering the price of small cars to earn more of these high-profit licenses.

Under the CAFE standard, the winners and losers are different from those under a minimum fuel economy standard in important ways. The advantage goes to those with broad product lines that include both small, fuel-efficient cars and large, high-profit cars. These companies are large U.S. manufacturers, particularly General Motors and Ford, which produce broad product lines to take advantage of this regulation. European producers of large cars are still losers under this policy, but their losses are even higher. Now they have to pay the fine while the producers of large U.S. cars can avoid the fine through the sale of their small cars. Under this policy, Volkswagen and the Japanese producers are also losers. They produce only small, fuel-efficient cars so they do not have to pay the fine, but they also do not have any high-profit cars to sell. Under CAFE, the U.S. producers can lower the price of U.S. small cars to increase their sales. Foreign small-car producers will see the prices consumers are willing to pay for their cars pulled down by this U.S. action. But whereas the U.S. producers can make up for reduced profit on small-car sales with high profits on large-car sales, the foreign producers with narrow lines of fuel-efficient cars cannot compensate for lower prices. Thus, under CAFE, U.S. producers win while foreign producers of both large and small cars lose.

The comparative advantage of U.S. automakers was their broad product line, and the policy the U.S. government adopted emphasized that comparative advantage. As part of the Energy Policy and Conservation Act of 1975, companies producing more than 10,000 cars per year must meet the average fuel economy standard for their fleet. General Motors at that time made about 4 million cars per year. The initial standard was to be 18 miles per gallon in 1978, increasing to 27.5 miles per gallon by 1985. Failure to meet the standard was to result in a fine of $5 per 10th of a mile per gallon by which the standard was not achieved for each car sold. Companies that exceeded the standard in some years could build credits for use in future years. Similarly, the law allowed companies to *borrow* from future years' performance if they could convince the National Highway Traffic Safety Administration that their performance would improve. The act also separated domestic production of autos from foreign production. This provision discouraged U.S. automakers from shifting production abroad or from acquiring existing foreign small-car production capabilities. Under this provision, shifting small-car production abroad would lower the CAFE. This provision did not help consumers, but it benefitted the United Auto Workers (UAW) by preserving jobs in the United States.

A second energy conservation measure was imposed on the auto industry as part of the Energy Tax Act of 1978. Cars that achieved less than a stated fuel economy were charged a gas-guzzler tax. Initially this tax ranged from $500 on a 20-to 21-miles-per-gallon car to $2,650 on a car achieving fewer than 13 miles per gallon. The maximum tax increased to $3,850 in 1985. The direct effect of this tax was to increase the price of luxury cars such as Rolls-Royce and some models of Mercedes. An indirect effect was to create an incentive for U.S. manufacturers to make large cars smaller (to downsize them) or to eliminate some of the largest cars. Within the U.S. auto industry, the losers were Ford and General Motors, who previously had a comparative advantage in producing large cars. American Motors was a winner because its most successful models were smaller cars; indeed, they had never produced a successful large car. Chrysler was also a winner because by that time they had committed their corporate strategy to front-wheel-drive cars with fuel-efficient four-cylinder engines.

Consider another government policy toward the auto industry, the voluntary import-restraint agreement between the U.S. and Japanese auto manufacturers. Under the program, Japanese manufacturers agreed to limit their imports of autos into the United States. From the U.S. perspective, the policy was in response to an increasing share of Japanese autos sold in the United States. The rationale behind the restraints was to give the U.S. auto industry a chance to adjust to the new demand by consumers for fuel-efficient cars, in other words, to give the U.S. auto industry the chance to get back on its feet. While the short-run effects of this policy may have benefitted the U.S. manufacturers, the long-run effects almost certainly hurt them.

The short-run effect is driven by the simple notion that if the supply of something people want is reduced, the price goes up. These import restraints, by reducing the supply of small cars, raised their price. Another way to raise the prices and reduced the sales of imported small cars would be to impose an import tax. One way to think of these import restraints is as an import tax where the Japanese manufacturers get to keep the tax proceeds instead of the U.S. government. Thus, this approach probably increased the profits of the Japanese manufacturers. This is hardly surprising. After all, they agreed to the program voluntarily. The program also probably raised profits for U.S. manufacturers by allowing them to sell their small cars at higher prices. Recall that the impact of the CAFE standards had been to reduce prices on small cars. Thus, in the short run, the policy probably helped the U.S. auto industry, although at the expense of consumers and without hurting the Japanese manufacturers.

The long-run effects, however, were not nearly so favorable. Before this program, the U.S. manufacturers had to compete with the Japanese for small-car sales, but they faced no competition from Japan, and only limited competition from Europe, for large- and luxury-car sales. Because the CAFE increased the comparative advantage of companies with broad product lines, it provided some inducement for the Japanese to consider broadening their line beyond small, inexpensive, fuel-efficient cars. The voluntary import-restraint program, however, made such a strategy so attractive as to be almost required. By limiting the number of autos sold, the incentive is to increase the profit per auto sold. Thus, this program gave the Japanese a very strong incentive to increase the profit per car by moving into progressively more expensive, more luxurious, higher-performance, larger cars. Indeed, during the first four years of import restraints, while the number of cars was being limited, the Japanese increased the dollar volume of auto sales by 50 percent. This program brought the Japanese manufacturers into the last bastion of the U.S. auto industry. Before the program, the United States had to compete with the Japanese in only one segment of the market, whereas after the program the auto industry faced Japanese competition in virtually all segments.

Another example of the Iron Law is the Reagan administration's attempt to relax the regulatory restrictions on lead in gasoline. Adding lead (actually a lead compound called tetraethyl lead) to gasoline is a relatively inexpensive way to improve its quality (increase its octane rating). Unfortunately, however, lead interferes with the catalytic converters used by most automobiles to reduce pollution. Furthermore, lead in engine exhaust creates a pollution hazard. Reducing the amount of lead permitted in gasoline had increased gasoline costs. The Reagan administration came into office with a philosophy of reducing unnecessary regulation and "getting government off the backs of business."

Anne Gorsuch, Reagan's newly appointed administrator of the Environmental Protection Agency (EPA), took this philosophy seriously and proposed to relax restrictions on lead in gasoline. Permitting more lead should save oil refiners money, and the oil industry was expected to support the move. Instead, to the surprise of the EPA, both Mobil and Exxon came out actively against the proposed regulations. Why did two major refiners come out against a regulatory change that would have reduced their costs? Allowing more lead in gasoline would have given a comparative advantage to small blenders of gasoline, who could have more easily produced high-octane gasoline without costly refinery capacity. Also, reducing lead would have increased the refinery capacity of the industry by allowing more gasoline to be made from a barrel of oil at a time when there was a glut of capacity. So despite reducing these large companies' costs, this regulation would have benefitted their competitors more and reduced refinery profits. Under pressure from these companies and under more visible pressure from environmentalists, the EPA actually reversed itself and tightened the standard, permitting less lead in gasoline. The environmental community thought it had won a victory, and it had pushed for this change to improve air quality. But it was not the victory over large oil interests that many believed. Rather the large oil companies had been the environmentalists' hidden allies, but for different reasons.

RATIONALE FOR REGULATION

To understand the impacts of regulation and, therefore, to assess whether regulation is achieving its goals, it is critical to consider the competitive consequences both between industries and especially within an industry. With this in mind, consider what regulation is trying to accomplish.

Why do governments become involved in regulating private industry? Competitive markets, under the right circumstances, result in an efficient allocation of resources. In theory and in the long run, companies competing in such markets produce only those goods and services that consumers value most highly, in quantities consumers are willing to purchase, by methods that minimize the costs of production and that sell at prices consumers are willing to pay. In such a world, society's resources are being used to respond to what people want and are being used with a minimum of waste. In practice, however, the right circumstances do not always occur, companies do not always behave this way, and markets are sometimes regarded as having failed. There are a wide variety of types of market failure and an even wider variety of reasons for government intervention in the market. Most regulation, however, is in response to one of three major problems: (1) monopoly, (2) externalities, and (3) inadequate information.

Monopoly

Monopoly behavior was behind the first major federal regulation in the United States, the Act to Regulate Commerce of 1887. This act, which gave rise to the Interstate Commerce Commission, was in response to monopoly practices of the railroads. In a monopoly, a single company is the sole supplier of the good or service in the market. If the company decides to raise its prices, customers must choose between either paying the higher price or not buying the good, or at least buying less of it. In a competitive market, by contrast, if a company tries to raise prices, other companies can keep their prices low. The customer has the option of switching and buying the good from a different company. Because the monopolist does not have to worry about competition, it can raise prices at will. In response to higher prices, some consumers will simply stop buying the good, so the monopolist will lose some business, but other consumers will still buy some at the higher price. If the monopolist charges too high a price, too many consumers will stop buying the good, and the monopolist will make less money. The trick for a monopolist is to know how much to raise the price to increase profits and at what point raising the price further will actually lower profits. It turns out that by applying some simple economics and a bit of experimentation, monopolists can figure out how much to raise prices so as to maximize profits. In general then, in a monopoly, the monopolist will charge higher prices and sell a bit less. Consumers will be worse off by having to pay higher prices or by buying less of a good they wanted than if they had the choice of buying from several different companies.

There are two distinctly different types of monopoly situations that require different regulatory approaches: a natural monopoly and an artificial monopoly. In a natural monopoly, a single company has substantial economies of scale; as it produces more, its average cost of production falls—thus a big factory is more efficient than a little factory. Many companies find scale economies up to a point. Often, moving from a very small plant to a medium-size plant can result in lower average costs of production. Usually, however, these economies of scale are exhausted at fairly low levels of production.

If these economies of scale are such that the company finds its average costs continuing to fall at an output level that satisfies total market demand, then a natural monopoly occurs. Typically, local telephone and electric companies find it progressively cheaper to serve additional people. Once the basic telephone or electrical network is in place, adding another household or business to it is pretty cheap. With a natural monopoly, one company can provide the service more cheaply than two or more companies. If the government were to break up the monopoly to stimulate competition, the result would be a higher cost of providing that service. If the government does nothing, then the natural monopolist is free to charge higher prices, even though its costs are lower.

Government's typical approach when faced with a natural monopoly has been to grant the company the right to be the sole supplier of the good or service but to regulate the price by imposing a ceiling that serves as a maximum price at which the good or service is sold. The goal is to prevent the monopolist from charging too high a price while retaining the benefits of low costs of the scale economies of a single company. If the price ceiling is set properly, prices can be kept down for consumers and still allow the monopolist sufficient profits to remain in business. If the ceiling is set too high, the monopolist will still be able to earn some additional profits. If the ceiling is set too low, the monopolist will either be forced out of business or will take steps to lower the quality of the product in line with the low price. Setting these regulated prices is complicated, in large part because to set the prices the regulators must rely on the regulated industry to get the necessary information about the company's costs. The regulated industry has an incentive to provide information that would lead to a high price. In addition, regulators need information about consumers' demand for the product, which is also difficult to get.

One problem the government faces in deciding whether to grant and regulate a natural monopoly is that changing technology can weaken or even eliminate the scale economies that create the natural monopoly in the first place. For example, the advent of cellular phones has weakened the scale economies of local telephone service. Cellular phones seem able to compete effectively with hard-wired networks, and one can even imagine that multiple cellular phone companies could jointly serve the same area if they could arrange to connect with one another. Similarly, the scale economies that have led to cable-television monopolies are not present with satellite dish technologies. Thus, the case for natural monopoly should be reviewed periodically in light of technological development.

Given the opportunity for a monopolist to make higher profits by charging higher prices, it is easy to understand why a company might want to create a monopoly by forcing competitors out of business and by creating barriers to entry for new companies into the industry. An artificial monopoly is one where there is a single company not because of scale economies, but rather because that company is able to keep other companies from entering into competition with it. Whereas in the case of a natural monopoly, having a single company supply the entire market can lower costs, in the case of an artificially created monopoly, costs as well as prices are likely to be higher.

A company might try to create a monopoly by driving out a smaller competitor through predatory pricing, which means that the company would lower prices to below the costs of a smaller competitor. The smaller company would either have to give up virtually all sales or to match the lower prices and sell at a loss. After a prolonged period of selling at a loss, the smaller company would go out of business. Once competitors had been driven from business, the remaining company would be free to raise prices to monopoly levels. To be sure, the larger company might incur losses during the price war, but it would hope to recoup those losses through monopoly pricing later on.

Predatory pricing is illegal, but it is also very difficult to prove. Small companies that find their prices undercut by larger ones are often quick to claim that they are victims of predatory pricing. The large companies usually claim, to the contrary, that they simply have lower costs and are pricing accordingly. Wal-Mart, the national discount store chain, has frequently been accused of offering intentionally low prices to drive smaller competitors out of business. Wal-Mart typically counters that their prices are lower because their costs are lower. Several airlines have also accused competitors of predatory pricing in an attempt to drive them from business. The companies accusing their competitors have usually had a difficult time proving their contention in the courts.

It is clear that more competition in a market results in lower prices. In the airline industry, for example, fares in markets served by two airlines are generally about 4 percent lower than in comparable markets served by only a single carrier. Similarly, markets served by three carriers are about 14 percent lower than comparable single-carrier markets. Thus, a major concern in public policy is trying to encourage competition in the marketplace.

One of the more difficult public policy choices concerns a proposed merger of two companies. The usual argument in favor of merger is that the merged company will be able to enjoy lower costs from economies of scale and, as a result, will be able to offer customers lower prices. The usual argument against a merger is that it will result in one less competitor in the market and that less competition will lead to higher prices. When two companies seek to merge, they must seek approval from the U.S. Department of Justice. Merger applications are decided on a case-by-case basis and are often hotly contested.

One concern with all monopolies, natural or otherwise, is that the monopoly may not have as strong an incentive to seek means of lowering costs. With a company in a competitive industry, the company has both the carrot and the stick incentive to lower costs. The carrot incentive is that if a company lowers its costs, it will be able to earn higher profits. It can either continue to sell the same amount at the same price and just earn more per unit sold, or more likely, it can use part of its cost advantage to lower its price and take business away from its competitors. The carrot incentive applies both to companies in competitive industries and to a monopoly. With a monopoly, there are no other competing companies from which to take business away, but the company can use its lower costs to earn more per unit sold. If the monopoly is regulated, however, the regulators may simply use the monopolist's lowered costs to lower prices to the consumers without any benefit to the regulated company. In this case, the regulators have removed the incentive to seek lower costs. Most regulators realize, however, that removing cost-reducing incentives is not in the long-term interests of consumers. Thus, the monopolist has much the same carrot incentive as the competitive company.

A competitive company, however, also has a stick incentive. The stick is the unpleasant part of not seeking cost reductions. If a company in a competitive industry does not seek ways to lower its costs and one of its competitors does, that competitor can use the lowered costs to drive the company out of business. In a competitive industry, the penalty for failing to lower costs can be the survival of the company itself. For a monopolist, however, there is no competitor to provide the pressure to lower costs. A monopolist who does not seek lowered costs will not be punished by its competitors because there are none. Thus, while monopolists have the carrot incentive to lower costs, albeit one dulled by regulators, they do not have the stick incentive so that they may not pursue cost-reducing strategies as aggressively.

Externalities

A second major reason for government regulation is the presence of externalities. An externality is when one person's or company's activity confers an unintended and uncompensated effect on another person or company. As an example, consider that neighbors in the next room or apartment like to play music. If the music is played loud enough or the walls are thin enough, you can hear that music whether you want to or not. The neighbors have conferred an externality on you. If you like the music and it is played at a time you want to listen to music, then you benefit from it and you have experienced a positive externality. In that case, perhaps they should have played the music a little louder so you could have heard it better. Conversely, if you do not like the music and you do not want to listen to music, then you have experienced a negative externality. In that case, they should have played the music more softly or perhaps compensated you for having to put up with it.

The externalities that most often bring government into the marketplace are environmental problems. When you travel by car, that car emits pollution into the air that degrades the air quality for others. Your intention is not to degrade the air quality but to go from one place to another, yet in doing so you have created a negative externality. Prior to the mid-1960s, the externalities created by automobile exhaust were not considered serious enough to require government intervention. Starting in the mid-1960s in California and spreading to the rest of the United States by the late 1960s, auto air pollution was considered enough of a problem to begin requiring cars to emit less. By the 1990s, automobile exhaust was considerably cleaner than it was 30 years earlier. However, by the 1990s, there were also far more cars so that automobile exhaust is still a major source of air pollution in many urban areas.

Another environmental externality is generated by electric generation plants that use coal as a source of fuel. When coal is burned, it releases a chemical called sulfur dioxide. As it is released in the exhaust stack, sulfur dioxide combines with the air to make sulfuric acid, which eventually falls to the earth as acid rain. Often this acid rain falls to earth hundreds of miles from the power plant that generated it. Although it is not the electric company's intent to make acid rain, a pollution problem is created nonetheless. To combat this pollution problem, the government has implemented regulations to require electric power plants to take steps to reduce the sulfur dioxide emissions either by installing devices called scrubbers that remove the sulfur dioxide from the exhaust or by switching to fuel that contains less sulfur. Most pollution problems fall into the category of externalities. Environmental externalities will be discussed in greater detail in Chapter 10.

Inadequate Information

For a market economy to function well, consumers must have enough information about the goods and services they buy to make choices that best serve their interests. If consumers make choices based on inaccurate information, these choices are unlikely to make them happy. The problem with getting enough information to make good decisions is that information, like many other things, is not free. Getting information takes time and effort and may also require considerable out-of-pocket expenditures. As a result, consumers rarely have complete information on which to base a decision. Do students have complete information when they selecte a college or a particular course?

Often, not having complete information may not be a very serious problem. On the one hand, when someone goes to a restaurant, they may not know what everything tastes like. If they order something that turns out not to be as good as they had hoped they will know to try something else next time. On the other hand, if the kitchen is not storing and preparing food in a sanitary way and they get sick as a result, then the lack of information is serious enough to call for government intervention. Similarly, when someone visits a doctor, they are not likely to have any means of telling if that doctor was properly trained. When someone buys medicine, they may not be able to tell if it really will do what the manufacturer claims or even if it is safe to take. When someone takes a trip via airplane, they are not likely to be able to tell if the plane has been properly designed and maintained or if the pilot is qualified to fly the plane safely. In cases like these, not having enough information can be a serious, or even deadly, problem.

To combat the problem of consumers making choices with too little information, one approach the government can take is to test the claims of manufacturers to be sure, first, that the product is safe to use and, second, that it will do what it claims. Most of the activities of the Food and Drug Administration (FDA) are of this nature. Another approach is for the government to license people to offer certain types of services. Doctors, dentists, nurses, lawyers, and airline pilots must meet certain training standards and have government licenses to provide these services. As a result, a consumer knows when using the services of one of these people that they have met at least the minimum standards for licensing. Another approach is to require labeling the product to inform consumers of the ingredients. Cosmetics and some foods have such labeling requirements. Still another approach is for the government simply to ban an option that it determines consumers should not be permitted to have. The FDA, for example, forbids the use of certain drugs even if patients want them. OSHA forbids certain hazardous working conditions even if workers are willing to subject themselves to them in exchange for higher pay. In essence, this approach is a paternalistic one that says that the government will impose a choice on consumers that it is convinced consumers would make if they only knew as much as government specialists. Finally, the government can simply be in the position of provider of information to consumers through various education campaigns.

REGULATORY ISSUES

In considering specific areas of government regulation, two regulatory issues come up repeatedly: first, how to regulate a monopolist, and second, the problems faced in actually setting regulatory standards.

Regulating a Monopolist

There is a long history and considerable experience in the problems of regulating a government-sanctioned monopolist. In the United States, various levels of government have wrestled with this problem since the late 1880s, in connection with the railroads, and throughout the 20th century, with other transportation industries, the telephone industry, and the electric power industry, to name a few. The problems of monopoly regulation would warrant inclusion in this book just due to their prevalence, if nothing else. However, these problems are beginning to emerge in a wide variety of new circumstances as federal, state, and especially local governments look to privatize services they had previously provided directly themselves. In most instances, proposals to privatize government services amount to granting a monopoly to a private-sector company. Before rushing headlong into such arrangements, governments must consider how to regulate these new monopolists.

The traditional approach is known as cost-of-service rate making, because it sets rates for the regulated monopolist based on the costs of providing the service. This type of rate making has its origins in regulated monopolies such as electricity, natural gas, and telephone service. It would be equally applicable in regulating newly privatized garbage collection, airports, custodial services, or bus services. The problems cost-of-service rate making confront will occur anywhere the government contracts with a private company for a service and where sufficient economies of scale exist that it is most efficient for only one company to be given the contract.

The basic problem with a monopoly is that the monopolist has the incentive to sell less of the good or service and charge a higher price. The goal of the regulator is to place a ceiling on that price to encourage the monopolist to sell more at a lower price. The regulator wishes to keep the monopolist in business by allowing prices to cover costs plus a *reasonable* profit while at the same time preventing excess profits from prices that are too high. Cost-of-service rate making is the administrative mechanism by which those prices are set.

The basic approach is to select a base year for which the rates will be calculated. The regulator then adds the operating costs, taxes, and depreciation, which is an allowance for the fact that the monopolist's equipment wears out gradually over time and must be replaced eventually. To this amount is added a reasonable profit. That profit is usually calculated by taking the amount of money the monopolist has invested in the business, subtracting the allowances for depreciation, and applying an allowed rate of return to that *rate base*. The rationale behind this approach is that private, unregulated companies will only invest in plant and equipment if they believe they can earn a reasonable rate of profit on their investment. The rate of return times rate base approach tries to mirror this private-sector investment approach.

This amount of money—operating costs, taxes, depreciation, and profit—is called the revenue requirement, in other words, the amount of revenue the monopolist is required to earn. The regulator then sets the monopolist's prices to generate the amount of revenue. To set these prices, of course, requires some knowledge of how the quantity sold will change in responses to increases or decreases in the price.

So far, this procedure sounds pretty simple. Where are the problems? There are several. One, to return to an earlier theme of this chapter, is that the incentives this system creates for the monopolist are not ideal. Consider the monopolist's investment incentives. If someone had the opportunity to borrow money at 5 percent annual interest and immediately invest that money in a risk-free account at 6 percent annual rate of interest, how much money would they borrow? The answer is that under those conditions they would borrow as much as they could because the more they borrowed and invested, the more they would make. If the monopolist is allowed a rate of return that is greater than the cost of borrowing, the incentive is the same as this person, to borrow and invest as much as possible. After all, the larger the rate base, the larger the profits.

This effect, called the Averch-Johnson effect after the two economists who first studied it, creates problems for regulators. When the allowed rate of return is greater than the cost of borrowing, the monopolist will try to invest as heavily as possible. By investing heavily, the monopolist will increase the rate base, which will in turn increase the profits. If the investment is not needed, then consumers will be forced to pay more than necessary.

How can you tell, as a regulator, if the investments are necessary? The monopolist will not be so obvious as to make totally unwarranted investments simply to increase the rate base. Rather, investments will be made to increase the reliability of the service or to improve the quality. At what point is the quality or reliability being pursued beyond what is needed or beyond what consumers are willing to pay for? These are some of the questions that inevitably come up in cost-of-service rate making.

While there are problems with a situation where the rate of return is greater than the cost of borrowing, there are also problems if the rate of return is below the cost of borrowing. The situation is analogous to being able to borrow money at 6 percent but being able to invest it at only 5 percent. Under these circumstances, borrowers lose money by borrowing and investing, and the more they borrow the more they lose. Their incentive is not to borrow at all. Similarly, if the rate of return allowed the monopolist is below the cost of borrowing money, the monopolist will not wish to borrow. When investment is needed to provide the service, the monopolist has no incentive to make that investment, and the quality and reliability of the service will suffer.

Thus as a regulator, setting rates of return that are either too high or too low have different but equally undesirable consequences. Hitting the right rate of return is all the more complicated by changes in the cost of borrowing. As interests rates change, the incentives of the monopolist can change even if the rate of return is left alone.

Standard Setting

In the United States, setting standards to govern behavior is the most common approach for a wide variety of problems, particularly in the environmental, health, and safety areas. For many of these problems, particularly in the environmental area, there are other approaches such as taxes on pollution that have been used successfully on a limited basis or in other parts of the world. The choice between standards and taxes will be examined in more detail in Chapter 11. For now, the focus is on standard setting and some of the issues that are raised when regulators are faced with the actual task of setting a standard.

Ideally, standards would be set by a process that started by defining the adverse effect that was to be reduced or prevented. An analysis would be conducted that would seek to assess the damage caused by this effect and balance that damage against the cost of reducing or eliminating that damage. It is not necessarily the case that it makes sense to totally eliminate the problem. It would be hard to justify spending $1,000 to eliminate a problem causing $500 worth of damage. On the other hand, if that $500 of damage could be eliminated at a cost of $250, one would reach a much different conclusion. Once it was decided how much of the damage to eliminate or prevent, a standard would be selected to accomplish the reduction. After implementing the standard, it would be reviewed periodically to see if it was working as intended or if it needed to be revised.

In practice, of course, standards are rarely if ever set in this sort of analytical manner. Instead, because of procedures that give ample public notice and opportunity for comment, standards are usually set through lengthy processes of adversarial negotiation and appeal. The process is often complicated by the need to go to the industry for which the standard will apply to get the information necessary to evaluate alternatives and to set the standard.

In other cases, standards may be set very quickly when Congress reacts strongly to a problem it has just discovered. For example, in 1970, Congress passed the Occupational Safety and Health Act in response to concerns about the health and safety conditions in many workplaces. A new agency, the Occupational Safety and Health Administration (OSHA), was formed and given very little time to set a wide array of workplace safety and health standards. Conducting careful analysis and developing new standards was impossible with the congressional time deadline, so OSHA adopted industry guidelines from a wide variety of organizations. The problem is that these had been voluntary guidelines. While they had been set with the best of intentions, some were badly out-of-date for modern workplace conditions, some sets of guidelines had proven ill-advised, and some sets were in conflict with other sets. Because the guidelines had been voluntary, industries had little incentives to keep the guidelines up-to-date or even internally consistent. If a guideline proved ill-advised, the companies would simply not follow it because it was voluntary. Once the former guidelines became the law, however, the problems emerged quickly and created considerable havoc.

When there are time and opportunity to formulate a standard, several other issues emerge. One is whether to aim the standard directly at the evil you are concerned with or to aim it at some substitute or surrogate. In some cases a surrogate may be easier to enforce or administratively simpler. For example, in the wake of energy shortages, one of the steps taken was to impose a national speed limit of 55 miles per hour. Although such a speed limit may have saved some fuel, there were other ways to conserve fuel, many of which could have been far more effective. The problem with using surrogates is that they can easily take on a life of their own even after the original reason for using them is gone. In the case of the 55-mile-per-hour speed limit, once the oil crisis had passed, the speed limit measure became increasingly defended because of its alleged highway safety benefits. Here again, had the original goal been to reduce highway fatalities, there were far more effective ways available. Eventually the 55-mile-per-hour speed limit was repealed in most areas without any evidence that its repeal either increased fuel consumption or cost lives.

A second issue is the degree of specificity in the standard. Here the question is often how much discretion to give those who enforce the standard. More specific standards allow greater control and involvement by the agency while more general standards lead to administrative simplicity and greater flexibility. In setting standards for the transport of dangerous cargo, should each shipment be licensed, should each permissible route be specified, or should there be a set of guidelines about how to select acceptable routes?

A third issue is whether the standard should be a design standard or a performance standard. A design standard specifies precisely how a machine must be built whereas a performance standard specifies how that machine must perform. Design standards are easier to enforce, but may retard innovation and prevent the development of more effective and less expensive approaches. A performance standard allows flexibility and encourages innovation, but is likely to be more difficult, time consuming, and expensive to enforce. In practice, design and performance standards may converge, at least in the short run. Performance standards may be written so that only one design can meet them. In the short run, then, there is little meaningful difference. However, a performance standard is more likely to encourage experimentation and research and development, so that in the long run even a performance standard originally written to be met by a specific machine may encourage more innovation.

A final question is whether the agency should adopt a standard that cannot immediately be met with existing technology in the hope that by doing so, the agency can force the regulated industry to develop new technology. The agency may distrust the industry and not believe its claims about what is and is not possible. The major difficulty is that the agency rarely if ever has the knowledge or technical expertise to know whether the industry will actually be able to comply. And if the industry does not comply, was it because the agency was wrong about what the industry could do, or did the industry just call the agency's bluff?

This possibility points to the broader problem that the agency rarely has the knowledge needed to set standards. It often must rely on the industry for information, but the industry may not have an incentive to provide complete, unbiased information. Since the information it provides can, in a sense, be used against it, there is an incentive to hold back. Specifically, there is an incentive to withhold information in a strategic sense and use it to counter standards once they are proposed.

Given the obvious problems with the industry to be regulated as a source of information, where can the agency turn? One possibility is an outside expert, either a consulting firm or an academic researcher. Here the problem is that outside experts rarely have their own independent source of up-to-date information. They too must rely on the industry. Moreover, while many consultants provide important information, others are better at getting consulting contracts than at delivering a useful product.

Another possibility is to use consumer or public-interest groups. Here, the problem of lack of information is often compounded by an anti-industry bias that can get in the way of careful analysis. Such groups also rely heavily on volunteer and part-time labor. As a result, the credibility of such groups may be in question.

None of the questions that need to be raised in setting standards are unanswerable, and none of the problems in getting the needed information are insoluble. They are, however, important questions and difficult problems, and they must not be ignored when standards are contemplated as a form of regulatory control.

VOLUNTARY STANDARDS AND THIRD-PARTY CERTIFIERS

Government regulatory agencies are not the only source of standards. Indeed, in the United States, almost half of all standards are set by the private sector as part of a voluntary consensus process involving all of the key players, including the government. The United States has a long history of private-sector participation in standard setting dating back to the 19th century. These standards-development organizations first emerged in response to specific needs and concerns and took a variety of forms. The first American standards organization was the U.S. Pharmacopoeial Convention, which was established in 1829 to set up uniform standards for drugs. The American Iron and Steel Institute was established in 1855 and was the first trade association to develop standards. The American Society of Civil Engineers was formed in 1852 and was the first scientific society involved in standards development. As an example of these early activities, in response to an average of 1,400 boiler explosions per year, the American Society of Mechanical Engineers developed a boiler code in 1910. With the adoption of this code by states and cities, such explosions virtually stopped.

Within the U.S. standards community today, there are approximately 400 organizations involved in standards development. These groups are organized and function independently of one another. There are essentially five different types: trade associations, professional societies, general membership organizations, consortia, and third-party certifiers. All of these organizations are private-sector, voluntary organizations that arrive at decisions through a process of consensus, and all have mechanisms for participation, comment, and appeal. Of particular interest are third-party certifiers, and their range of activities can be illustrated by looking at three of the major companies: Underwriters Laboratories, Inc. (UL), American Society for Testing and Materials (ASTM), and NSF International.

Underwriters Laboratories (UL) is an independent, not-for-profit, third-party testing and certification organization that was formed in 1894. By the mid-1990s, UL has developed over 665 standards to help promote public safety. The UL mark on a product means that samples of the product have been tested to UL's standards and found to be reasonably free from foreseeable risk of fire, electric shock, and related hazards. The computer upon which much of this textbook was written carries the UL mark. UL standards are developed under procedures that provide for participation, review, and comment from industry, government, insurance groups, consumers, other interested parties, and the general public. These procedures take into consideration the needs and opinions of a wide variety of interests concerned with the subject of the standard and afford the opportunity to comment to all those who will be affected by the standard.

The American Society for Testing and Materials (ASTM) was organized in 1898 and is also a not-for-profit organization. ASTM relies on volunteer work by 33,000 ASTM members, who organize their work around 134 standards-writing committees. ASTM publishes over 8,500 standards each year regarding testing methods, specifications, practices, guides, classifications, and terminology. ASTM's standards-development activities encompass metals, paints, plastics, textiles, petroleum, construction, energy, medical services, computerized systems, and many other areas.

NSF International was formed in 1944 to specialize in public health and environmental sciences. NSF provides a range of services including development of consensus standards, voluntary product testing and certification, education and training, and research and demonstration. Areas in which NSF has certification programs include food processing and serving equipment, drinking-water-treatment chemicals and water contact products, plastic piping-system components for drinking water, and on-site recycle-and-reuse wastewater treatment plants and devices.

SUMMARY

Regulation is one of the most powerful policy tools of the government and also one of the least thoroughly understood. As will be seen in later chapters, the United States seems to go through cycles of government regulation with periods where stricter regulation is seen as needed to protect the public welfare followed by periods where there is growing belief that many regulations have gone too far and need to be reconsidered, revised, or even done away with altogether. In part, these cycles are because technological change can remove the need for regulation in some areas while other technological change can create the need for new regulations in other areas. In part, these cycles are also because policy makers have an imperfect understanding of the eventual effects of the regulations they put in place. To improve that understanding, a proposed regulation must be examined from several perspectives, with particular attention paid to how the regulated company is likely to respond. The Iron Law can be of great help in guiding us to this improved understanding. It is also important to understand the principal rationales for regulation and how changing technology can change the need to respond to these rationales. Regulation will be discussed as a policy tool throughout much of the rest of this book. This chapter has tried to lay the foundation for these later discussions.

DISCUSSION QUESTIONS

1. What are the principal categories of justifications for government regulation? Which are the most important in terms of providing justification for the greatest amount of current government regulatory activity? Describe examples of government regulation and activity in each of these three areas.
2. How can government regulation create winners and losers within an industry? From the perspective of an individual company, how might a regulation that increases your costs also increase your profits? Why is it important to understand this from the perspective of government regulators? from the perspective of businesses?
3. Compare the Corporate Average Fuel Economy (CAFE) with the alternative of setting a minimum fuel economy standard in the auto industry. Who would be the winners and losers under each alternative?
4. Explain how and why changing technology can create problems for government regulation. Compare the role of changing technology in putting pressure on regulation of telecommunications and on banking regulation. How might changing technology make antitrust enforcement more difficult in the airline industry?

SUGGESTED READINGS

Stephen Breyer, *Breaking the Vicious Circle* (Cambridge, MA: Harvard University Press, 1993).

Murray L. Weidenbaum, *Business, Government, and the Public,* Fourth Edition (Englewood Cliffs, NJ: Prentice Hall, 1990).

Alfred E. Kahn, *The Economics of Regulation: Principles and Institutions* (Cambridge, MA: MIT Press, 1988).

Robert A. Leone, *Who Profits: Winners, Losers, and Government Regulation* (New York: Basic Books, 1986).

Stephen Breyer, *Regulation and Its Reform* (Cambridge, MA: Harvard University Press, 1982).

4

Financing Government Activities

In 1993, government expenditures at the federal, state, and local levels in the United States totaled nearly $2.2 trillion dollars, which amounted to nearly $8,500 per capita per year. Government expenditures as a percent of gross domestic product (GDP) amounted to 34.4 percent—a little over a third. U.S. government expenditures as a share of GDP have been roughly one-third since the mid-1970s. Before that, they were lower: in 1970, expenditures were about one-fourth of GDP; in 1960, they were roughly one-fifth; and in 1929, they were roughly one-tenth.

Some argue that a public sector that has grown to about one-third of the U.S. economy is too large and that government needs to be made smaller. Although there may be some validity to that argument, the United States is not alone by international standards in having a large public sector nor does it even have the largest among developed countries. For example, both Japan and Australia have government outlays that, like the United States, are about one-third of GDP; both Germany and the United Kingdom have larger public sectors with above 37 percent; both Canada and France are above 43 percent; and Sweden has government outlays that are over 60 percent of GDP.

Where does the government get all this money? The government gets most of its money from taxes, of course, but which taxes are most important and how do they work? Table 4–1 shows government revenue by source and level of government for 1990–1991. The government gets most of its money from general revenue taxes, but it also gets some from other sources. Some of its revenue is tied to special programs such as Social Security and unemployment compensation. The largest tax category is individual income tax, which accounts for about 49 percent of all government tax revenues. While primarily a federal tax, the individual income tax is also levied in most states and in many localities. As the table shows, however, while the individual income tax accounts for over 72 percent

TABLE 4–1 Governmental Revenue in the United States, by Source and Level of Government 1990–1991 (Millions of Dollars)

	All	*Federal*	*State*	*Local*
Total general revenue	$1,905,813	$812,339	$551,722	$541,752
Intergovernmental revenue[1]	$345,367	$0	$143,534	$201,833
From federal	$154,099	$0	$134,926	$19,173
From state	$182,660	$0	$0	$182,660
From local	$8,607	$0	$8,607	$0
General revenue, own sources	$1,557,213	$809,105	$408,188	$339,920
Taxes	$1,167,337	$641,982	$310,561	$214,794
Property	$168,000	$0	$6,228	$161,772
Individual income	$577,168	$467,827	$99,279	$10,062
Corporation income	$120,329	$98,086	$20,357	$1,886
Customs duties	$16,034	$16,034	$0	$0
General sales gross receipts	$125,448	$0	$103,165	$22,283
Selective sales gross receipts	$42,461	$42,461	$50,369	$9,752
Motor vehicle and operators' licenses	$20,226	$0	$19,419	$807
Death and gift	$15,449	$11,138	$4,284	$27
All other	$22,102	$6,436	$7,461	$8,205
Current charges	$211,527	$86,292	$47,334	$77,901
Miscellaneous general revenue	$80,831	$80,831	$50,293	$47,225
Special revenue	$566,998	$388,343	$108,226	$70,429
Utility revenue	$57,165	$0	$3,460	$53,705
Liquor store revenue	$3,571	$0	$3,013	$558
Insurance trust revenue[2]	$506,262	$388,343	$101,752	$16,167

[1]Duplicative intergovernmental transactions are excluded.

[2]Includes Social Security and medicare insurances, unemployment compensation, employee retirement, and other insurance trust expenditures.

Source: U.S. Bureau of the Census, *Governmental Finances, 1987–1991, and Preliminary 1992* (Washington, D.C.: U.S. Government Printing Office, 1994).

of federal tax revenue, it accounts for about 32 percent of state tax revenue and less than five percent of local tax revenue. The corporate income tax is also primarily a federal tax but is levied in some states and localities. It accounts for about 10 percent of all government tax revenues. The property tax is primarily a local tax, although some states also have property taxes. The property tax accounts for 14 percent of total government tax revenues, but at the local level it accounts for over 75 percent of local tax revenues. The general sales tax is primarily a state and to a lesser extent a local tax and accounts for nearly 11 percent of total government tax revenues. Selective sales taxes are levied at federal, state, and local levels, but mostly at the state and federal levels. They account for less than 4 percent of total government tax revenues. Each of these taxes will be discussed in more detail later in the chapter.

What does all of this money get spent on? As is evident throughout this book, government expenditures go for a great many things. When all levels of government are considered together, the patterns may not be the same as in newspaper reports or politicians' television speeches. Table 4–2 summarizes government expenditures in some of the major categories in 1990–1991. As expected, national defense and international programs together are one of the largest categories of

TABLE4–2   U. S. Governmental Expenditures by Source and Level of Government 1990–1991 (Millions of Dollars)

	All	*Federal*	*State*	*Local*
Direct General Expenditure	$1,804,005	$899,363	$368,360	$536,282
Selected federal programs	$0			
National defense and int'l programs	$366,112	$366,112	$0	$0
Postal service	$43,102	$43,102	$0	$0
Space research and techonology	$13,514	$13,514	$0	$0
Other nondefense	$0			
Education and libraries[1]	$334,334	$20,589	$80,750	$232,995
Transportation[2]	$84,048	$8,639	$40,340	$35,069
Public welfare[3]	$167,680	$40,716	$100,114	$26,850
Hospitals, health[4]	$130,173	$45,656	$41,899	$42,618
Public safety [5]	$88,043	$8,111	$26,459	$53,473
Sewerage, sanitation	$31,014	$0	$1,994	$29,020
Parks, recreation, natural resources	$74,668	$46,162	$12,468	$16,038
Housing, community development	$33,345	$16,698	$1,759	$14,888
Administration[6]	$64,181	$15,720	$18,943	$29,518
Interest on general debt	$247,376	$195,142	$23,393	$28,841
Other general expenditure	$126,416	$79,202	$20,241	$26,973
Insurance trust expenditures [7]	$494,160	$420,001	$64,214	$9,945
Utility expenditure [8]	$155,997	$0	$14,434	$141,563
Liquor store expenditure	$3,005	$0	$2,504	$501

[1]Includes elementary and secondary education, higher education, other education, and libraries.

[2]Includes highways, air transportation, parking facilities, water transport and terminals, transit subsidies.

[3]Includes cash assistance payments, vendor payments, welfare institutions, other public welfare.

[4]Includes hospitals, health, employment security administration, veterans' services.

[5]Includes police protection, fire protection, correction, protective inspection and regulation.

[6]Includes financial adm., judicial and legal, general public buildings, other govt. adm.

[7]Includes Social Security and Medicare insurances, unemployment compensation, employee retirement, railroad retirement, veteran's life compensation.

[8]Includes water supply, electric power, gas supply.

Source: U.S. Bureau of the Census, *Governmental Finances, 1987–1991, and Preliminary 1992* (Washington, D.C.: U.S. Government Printing Office, 1994).

government expenditures at the federal level. What is surprising, however, is that when expenditures at all levels of government are taken together, the United States spends almost as much on education and libraries as on national defense. But for education and libraries, expenditures come mostly at the local level where they constitute by far the largest category of expenditures. What is most surprising to many people is that insurance trust expenditures, for such things as Social Security, Medicare, unemployment compensation, and public employee retirement are far larger than either national defense or education expenditure.

BENEFITS VERSUS ABILITY TO PAY

Of the taxes listed in Table 14–1, which is *best?* Which is most *fair?* These questions arise all the time in discussions of tax policy and public finance. If the government needs to raise money, how should the burden of providing this money be distributed among the citizens? In making this decision, two basic standards can be applied. Taxes can be levied by the benefit principle, according to the benefits taxpayers receive from the public service provided with the tax revenue, or taxes can be levied by the ability-to-pay principle, according to the taxpayers' ability to pay or to bear the financial burden. The first approach is very much in line with the philosophy of a private market whereas the second approach recognizes that many of the goods provided by the government are fundamentally different from those provided by the private sector.

The benefit principle relies on the logic of a private market. Ideally in a private market, people must pay for a good or service in order to consume it, and the amount that they pay covers the full cost of providing that good or service. If a person chooses not to pay for the good or service, he or she gets no benefits from that good or service. Consumers' willingness to pay for the good sends a clear signal to producers about how much to produce so that there is neither a sustained shortage–or a sustained oversupply. If that general principle were extended to goods and services provided by the government, then taxpayers would pay in proportion to the benefits received. A taxpayer who received 1 percent of the benefits would pay 1 percent of the costs. There would be no cross-subsidy among taxpayers: users who received benefits would pay, and those who did not receive benefits would not pay.

A good example of taxing according to the benefit principle is the use of the gasoline tax to pay for highway construction and maintenance. The more people use the highways, the more gasoline they use, and the more gasoline tax they pay. The match between gasoline consumption and highway use is not perfect—there is variation in fuel efficiency among cars and trucks, for example—but it is pretty close. Even the variation in fuel efficiency works in the right general direction. One of the reasons that some vehicles are less fuel efficient is that they are heavier. A heavier vehicle that gets poorer mileage will pay more tax per vehicle mile than a lighter vehicle. But a heavier vehicle also does slightly more damage to a highway per vehicle mile and causes higher maintenance expenditures, so paying more seems appropriate.

However attractive and fair it may appear to some, the benefit principle has limitations. First, much government activity lies in the provision of public goods, such as national defense, where there is no way to allocate benefits among taxpayers, nor is there a way to exclude those who do not pay from receiving the benefits. The benefit principle cannot be applied in such situations. Second, some government activity, such as public education, results in benefits to the recipients but also brings to nonrecipients benefits that can be thought of as externalities. All people benefit from the education of others as well as from their own education. Third, some government activity, such as the various welfare programs, is directed explicitly at redistributing income or benefits from one group to another. The cross-subsidies that the benefit principle avoids are often an explicit goal of some government programs. In these kinds of situations, the market exchange philosophy of the benefit principle is simply inappropriate.

The ability-to-pay principle does not follow market exchange principles, but separates the government's decision to provide goods and services from its decision about how to finance these provisions. Under this principle, those who are better able to pay must bear a greater portion of the burden of financing government activities. In practice, using the ability-to-pay approach involves making two separate decisions: first, what determines the ability to pay and how is it measured, and second, how should the tax burden vary with the ability to pay? In determining how to measure the ability to pay, the question often revolves around focusing on current income or on accumulated wealth. In determining how the tax burden should vary with ability to pay, the question is whether someone with twice the ability to pay, however that might be measured, should pay twice the taxes, less than twice the taxes, or more than twice the taxes. Neither of these questions has a clear, widely agreed upon answer.

HORIZONTAL AND VERTICAL EQUITY

How does government assess whether a tax is fair? What is meant by *equity* in taxation? There are two main dimensions to equity and fairness in taxation: horizontal equity and vertical equity. Horizontal equity addresses the widely held belief that people who are in like circumstances should be treated alike. More specifically, a tax system has horizontal equity when two taxpaying units equivalent in all the relevant aspects pay the same tax. The principle of horizontal equity is simple and intuitive and appeals to most people's sense of fairness. In practice, however, it is not always easy to agree on whether a tax is horizontally equitable. For one thing, what is the appropriate taxpaying unit? Is it the individual or the household? Is it the corporation or the stockholder in the corporation? When are two taxpaying units equivalent? Is equity based on annual income or wealth? Should expenses be taken into account in considering annual income and if so, which ones?

Horizontal equity is concerned with the relative taxes paid by people with the same capacity to pay, and vertical equity is concerned with the relative taxes paid by people with different capacities to pay. Horizontal equity tries to consider the relative treatment of equals whereas vertical equity tries to consider the relative treatment among unequals; it asks how much more those with greater capacity should pay or indeed whether they should pay more at all. The question of vertical equity is usually addressed by looking at tax incidence asking whether a tax is *progressive, proportional, or regressive.* Asking questions of tax incidence requires considering the effective tax rate, which is the tax paid divided by the measure of capacity to pay (usually income). The capacity to pay is as a rule measured in terms of current income. A tax is considered *regressive* if the effective tax rate is lower among groups with higher ability to pay (higher income). A tax is considered *proportional* if the effective tax rate is the same across all income groups. A tax is considered *progressive* if the effective tax rate is higher in higher-income groups.

Figuring out whether a new tax, or a change to an existing tax, is regressive, proportional, or progressive can be difficult in practice. One problem is that the ultimate burden of the tax may be shifted by how people behave in response to the tax. For example, Social Security is financed by a payroll tax that has two components: one paid by the employee and one paid by the employer. In assessing tax incidence, clearly the portion paid by the employee should be counted, but what about the portion paid by the employer? Some analysts argue that in the absence of the tax, most or perhaps all of the money paid by the employer would have been paid to the employee in the form of higher wages. Thus, even though part of the payroll tax appears to be paid by the employer, the true tax burden falls on the employee.

A second problem is that taxes may not be levied on true taxing capacity but instead may be levied in a manner that is convenient and simple to collect. Consider a sales tax on consumption goods. The same statutory rate applies to purchases no matter what the characteristics of the household making the purchase. Thus a sales tax would appear to be proportional. However, studies of consumption patterns indicate that the proportion of income spent on consumption goods declines with increasing income. In other words, a household with a $50,000 annual income will not spend twice as much on consumption goods as a household with a $25,000 annual income. Thus, while the statutory tax rate appears proportional, the effective tax rate, defined in this case as the tax paid divided by income, declines as income increases, making the tax regressive.

In assessing tax incidence, other things need to be kept in mind. A frequent area of confusion surrounds taxes that are levied on corporations. In many respects, the legal system treats a corporation as if it were a person. While this is a convenient fiction for many purposes, it creates confusion in assessing tax incidence. From the perspective of public finance and tax incidence, corporations cannot bear taxes; only people can. A tax levied on a corporation is ultimately borne by people: by employees of the corporation in the form of lower wages, by stockholders in the corporation in the form of lower profits, by customers of the corporation in the form of higher prices for the goods or services sold, by landlords of the land and buildings used by the corporations in the form of lower rents, and so forth. Although tax revenues are collected from corporations, ultimately the burden of those taxes is borne by people. Taxes are ultimately paid by people even though they may be collected through institutions.

Both the sources and the uses of income should be considered in assessing incidence, for example, the tax levied on expensive boats in 1991. Proponents of the tax, by focusing on income uses, argued that it would be progressive as these boats were purchased primarily by high-income households. Others argued that the tax would decrease the purchase of such boats, thereby reducing employment and harming those who manufactured and maintained these boats. Because most employees of these manufacturing and service facilities had moderate to low incomes, the tax could be regressive when all its effects were considered. This issue was never fully resolved, but the tax was repealed in 1993.

Finally, the full incidence of a tax depends not only on the tax itself but on how the money raised by the tax is spent. Expenditures on hot lunches for school children are likely to have much different distributional consequences from expenditures for research on heart disease or for agricultural subsidies. It can be difficult or even impossible in practice to tie changes in tax revenues to changes in expenditures on specific programs, but expenditures have incidence implications just as taxes do.

TYPES OF TAXES

The revenue from any tax is the product of the tax rate applied to the tax base. Taxes are categorized by the base to which they are applied. The most common bases for taxes are income, consumption, and property or wealth. Taxes on income or consumption are applied to current transactions whereas taxes on property or wealth are on the value of accumulated holdings.

Personal Income Tax

The federal income tax is the largest single source of revenue for the federal government and perhaps the tax that fills the average taxpayer with the greatest sense of dread. Each year on or before April 15, millions file their federal personal income tax returns that compute their previous year's tax liability. Computing federal income tax liability can be quite complicated, depending on the circumstances of a particular household, and many people hire specialists to help them in filing their returns. These federal returns also serve as the basis for state income tax returns in many states.

While determining federal income tax liability can be complex in its details, the basic approach can be described fairly simply. The first step is to compute adjusted gross income (AGI), which is considered to be income from taxable sources such as wages, salaries, interest, stock dividends, business and farm profits, rents, royalties, and prizes. Interestingly, the tax law provides no definition of what constitutes income. Instead, the constitutional amendment that introduced the income tax says, "The Congress shall have power to lay and collect taxes on incomes, from whatever source derived." Rather than define income, the tax statutes list the transactions that produce income for tax purposes.

Specialists in public finance often define income as the money value of the net increase to an individual's power to consume. According to this definition, income is not just the sum of money received from the kinds of sources listed above. Rather, for income to represent a measure of tax-bearing capacity or ability to pay, some of the expenses incurred in earning that income should be subtracted. This concept of income, however, is not a perfect guide to income tax. Some sources of money income, which might be included because they represent an increase in the power to consume, are not included in AGI. For example, interest earned by individuals on bonds issued by states and localities is not subject to federal income tax. Also, employer contributions to employee retirement funds are not subject to tax, nor are employer contributions to health insurance. Similarly, some employee retirement savings are not taxed. Within limits, gifts and inheritances are also not subject to tax. Thus in practice, the federal income tax version of AGI comes close to measuring the increase in the ability to consume, but still contains some omissions.

Once AGI is calculated, only some of it is subject to income tax. The next step is to subtract various amounts, exemptions and deductions, from AGI to calculate taxable income. A family is allowed an exemption for each of its members. The exemption was $2,450 in 1994, and it is adjusted annually for inflation. Thus, in 1994, a family with two adults and two dependent children received an exemption of $9,800. (For incomes above certain levels, these exemptions are less.) Some argue that the purpose of these exemptions is to adjust the ability to pay for the costs associated with children, although as most parents know, the amount falls far short of the costs of the typical child. Others argue that these exemptions are a way of providing some tax relief for low-income families, as they are phased out at higher-income levels.

Another form of subtraction from AGI, the deduction, has two types: the standard deduction, a fixed amount available without documentation to all taxpayers, and the itemized deductions, subtractions for specific expenditures cited in the tax statutes. Taxpayers may choose either the standard deduction or itemized deductions, whichever results in the lowest taxes they must pay. The standard deduction in 1994 was $6,350 for joint filers (married adults) and $3,800 for singles and is adjusted for inflation. About 72 percent of tax returns use the standard deduction.

Alternatively, taxpayers may elect to use itemized deductions, which must be listed separately on the tax return. If audited by the Internal Revenue Service, taxpayers must be able to prove that these expenditures have been made. There are many different possible deductions, which are a complex area of the personal income tax. Personal deductions may change the tax's horizontal and vertical equity by allowing individuals with such deductions to lower their taxable income. Personal deductions may also encourage taxpayers to do things they might not otherwise do because of the tax savings that may result.

For some itemized personal deductions, a taxpayer may pay a reduced tax compared to people with similar incomes. For example, deductions are allowed for medical and dental expenses above 7.5 percent of AGI, for losses from casualty or theft above 10 percent of AGI (less $100), and for state and local income and property taxes. Presumably through little fault of their own, individuals must bear these special financial burdens, which more fortunate individuals do not incur. Thus an adjustment in tax-bearing capacity is permitted.

Other expenditures are deductible because the federal government has decided that private spending in those areas is meritorious and should be encouraged by reducing their after-tax cost. Interest paid on home mortgages (for both first and second homes) is deductible to encourage home ownership. The tax deductibility of mortgage interest substantially reduces the price of owning a home compared to the price of renting. Interest payments on consumer loans such as credit card charges or car loans are not deductible. Charitable contributions are also directly deductible even though they are voluntary, because the government seeks to encourage private contributions.

Finally, some expenditures are deductible because of the philosophy that tax applies to net income as much as possible. Thus, expenses associated with moving to a new job are deductible as are some job-related expenses such as union dues, education needed to maintain or improve job skills, and research costs for college professors.

After all of the exemptions and deductions have been subtracted from the AGI, the income that remains is called taxable income; it is this amount that is subject to the income tax. A tax rate is applied to the taxable income to determine the tax that must be paid. The tax rates are structured in a series of increasing steps. For example, in 1994 a single taxpayer with a taxable income of between $0 and $22,750 paid a tax of 15 percent on taxable income. If the taxable income was greater than $22,750, a tax of 15 percent was paid on $22,750, and a tax of 28 percent was paid on taxable income between $22,751 and $55,100. These tax rates are called marginal tax rates because they are applied to income above a certain level. The 1994 marginal tax rate for taxable income between $55,101 and $115,000 was 31 percent, and the marginal tax rate for taxable income between $115,001 and $250,000 was 36 percent. The highest marginal tax rate in 1994 was 39.6 percent on taxable income over $250,001.

These tax rates and the way the tax is calculated have some interesting implications for taxpayer behavior. Consider a charitable contribution for a person with a taxable income of $22,000, and therefore a marginal tax rate of 15 percent: a $100 charitable contribution would really cost only $85 because the deduction would lower taxable income by $100 and reduce the federal income tax by $15. If taxable income was $100,000, the marginal tax rate would be 31 percent, and that same $100 deduction would reduce taxes by $31 so that the real cost would be only $69. Two things should be clear from this example. First, the deductibility of certain activities for income tax purposes can encourage people to undertake those activities by lowering the price. A $100 charitable contribution does not cost the donor $100 if it is tax deductible. Second, because of the tax rate structure of increasing marginal rates, the same deduction is worth more in terms of reduced taxes to a higher-income person than to a lower-income person. The same $100 deduction costs a rich person less (after taking taxes into account) than it does a poor person.

Over the history of the federal personal income tax, these marginal rates have varied quite a bit. When the income tax was introduced in 1913, the lowest marginal rate was 1 percent, and the highest rate was only 7 percent. Throughout the 1950s, the lowest marginal rate was generally around 20 percent while the highest marginal rate was 91 or 92 percent. The rates dropped in the mid-1960s, with the lowest rates around 14 percent and the highest rates around 70 percent. In 1982, the highest tax rate dropped to 50 percent; in 1987 it dropped to 38.5 percent, and in 1988 it dropped again to 33 percent. Throughout this period, the lowest rate was between 11 and 15 percent.

Corporate Income Tax

In 1993, 53 percent of GDP originated in nonfinancial corporations. A corporation is a form of business organization created by a specific state's approval of its corporate charter. The charter is filed with the state by the founders of the corporation, and the corporation is owned by its stockholders, with ownership usually represented by transferable stock certificates. The stockholders have limited liability for the acts of the corporation; thus the stockholders' liability is limited to the amount they have invested in the corporation.

A corporation is a separate legal entity that can make contracts, hold property, incur debt, sue, and be sued. Corporations are often referred to as separate legal persons. As with individuals, corporations pay taxes. One immediate question, though, is whether it makes sense from an economic standpoint to tax corporations. As stated earlier, ultimately only people pay taxes. Why then is it not sufficient to tax the incomes of the owners of corporations? The government is taxing the same income twice with a corporate income tax. Under the current system, when a corporation makes a profit, that money is taxed via the corporate income tax. When those profits are paid to the owners of the corporation in the form of stock dividends, those dividends are counted as income to the people receiving them, and the money is taxed again via the personal income tax. Indeed, most public finance economists argue that a separate corporate income tax makes little sense and that it constitutes a double tax on dividends and almost certainly reduces the rates of savings and investment. Low rates of savings and investment harm the United States' ability to compete in a global economy.

The corporate income tax is widely criticized by public finance economists, but several justifications for a separate corporate income tax have been proposed. One view offered in defense of the corporate tax is that large corporations have thousands of stockholders who exert very little control over the managers of the corporation so that there is a separation of ownership and control in the corporation. Although true for many large corporations, the separation of ownership and control does not provide a justification for a separate tax. Another view is that society provides special privileges to a corporation, chief among which is the limited liability for the owners. The corporate tax is thus viewed as a user fee for these privileges. The tax is structured however, so that there is little reason to believe the revenues paid approximate the benefits received.

There are differing views on the appropriateness of taxing corporate income separately, and most economists dislike the corporate tax. Yet it seems unlikely that the corporate income tax will be abolished in the near future. For one thing, it is the third-largest source of federal revenue, and that revenue would be difficult to replace from other sources. The *relative* importance of the federal corporate tax has lessened in recent years, however. In 1950, the tax accounted for nearly 28 percent of all federal tax collections, whereas in 1993, this figure had dropped to just over 10 percent.

The corporate tax rate structure is graduated, with the lowest bracket having a rate of 15 percent and the highest bracket having a rate of 35 percent. The highest bracket starts at $10 million of taxable income, and most corporate income is taxed at that rate. Thus in practice, it is not too much of a simplification to think of the corporate income tax as a flat rate tax with a rate of 35 percent. This rate has dropped in recent years. Before the Tax Reform Act of 1986, the rate was 46 percent, the act lowered the rate to 34 percent, and the rate was raised to 35 percent in 1993.

As with the personal income tax, there are deductions for the costs of earning income. Wages paid to labor, for example, are excluded from taxable income. Similarly, when a corporation borrows money, the interest paid on the loan is excluded from taxable income. The costs of raw materials and supplies are also deducted. Durable goods and equipment that last many years are treated differently. Rather than allow the deduction of the full cost of a machine in the year that it is purchased, the cost is apportioned over a number of years, its tax life, and the amount apportioned for that year is deducted. This process, known as depreciation, attempts to reflect the fact that machines wear out gradually and eventually have to be replaced. There are different ways of calculating this depreciation, and the treatment of depreciation is often a target of those who wish to change the tax law. Allowing an item to be depreciated more quickly than it had been creates a greater incentive to invest in new equipment, although there is disagreement as to how big this incentive really is over the long run.

Sales and Excise Taxes

Whereas income taxes can be thought of as taxes on potential consumption, sales and excise taxes are taxes on actual consumption. A general sales tax applies the same tax rate to all transactions, typically at the retail level. Some items such as food purchases are not usually subject to general sales taxes. A selective sales tax, or excise tax, applies only to specific goods, such as gasoline. Sales taxes can be either unit taxes, where a specific amount, such as a certain number of cents per gallon of gasoline, is paid for each unit purchase, or *ad valorem* taxes, where the tax is computed as a percentage of the purchase price.

Sales and excise taxes are only the fourth-largest source of revenue at the federal level, largely because the federal government does not levy a general sales tax. Moreover, several of the federal government's selective excise taxes are earmarked for funds that can be used only for specific purposes. For example, the federal gasoline tax supports the Highway Trust Fund; the federal tax on airline tickets supports the Airport and Airways Trust Fund; and the federal hazardous waste tax supports hazardous waste cleanups through the Superfund. At the state and local levels, however, sales taxes assume much greater importance, with almost all states and many localities levying general sales taxes. At the state level, sales taxes are the single largest source of tax revenue and provide almost half of total state tax revenue.

Sales taxes are relatively easy to administer. There are fewer taxing units with a sales tax levied at the retail level than with a tax like the personal income tax. All that is required is a record of the amount of goods sold at each retailer. This makes a sales tax particularly attractive in a developing country where record keeping can be a problem.

In the United States, most general sales taxes exempt some items. The most frequently exempted items are food for consumption at home and prescription drugs. Purchases of these items usually constitute a higher percentage of the income of low-income households than of higher-income households. If these items were taxed, the sales tax would be strongly regressive, whereas exempting them makes it much less regressive. Some states have also exempted clothing purchases, although these expenditures are less concentrated among low-income households. Exemptions and taxes targeted at specific commodities certainly have the potential to change the regressivity of the tax or to achieve certain other goals, but they can also add to the administrative burden of the tax. In California, for example, *snacks* are subject to a special sales tax but *food* is not. What is a snack and what is food? In California, some crackers are subject to tax while others are not, wrapped slices of pie are taxed, but pie served on a plate is not. Similarly, in Massachusetts, athletic gear is taxed, but regular clothing is not; the distinction is not always clear and unambiguous. A few states use a tax credit or rebate as an alternative to exemptions to control sales tax regressivity. The rebate may be set at the amount of the sales tax a low-income family would pay on such necessities as food purchases. The rebate does not increase as income increases, thereby concentrating the assistance where it is most needed and simplifying record keeping on the part of retail establishments.

The federal government, as well as many state and local governments, levies selective excise taxes on specific goods and services, including such items as gasoline, hotel and motel lodging, restaurant meals, alcoholic beverages, and tobacco. These selective excise taxes raise revenue, but their principal purpose often lies elsewhere. For example, luxury excise taxes are applied to commodities whose purchase is believed to reflect extraordinary ability to pay. These taxes attempt to distribute the cost of government to those who can afford to pay and to increase the progressivity of the tax system. One problem with such an approach is that the tax distributes the burden according to the preferences of the individuals rather than strictly according to their ability to pay. Another problem is in defining luxury goods. Jewelry has often been considered a luxury and subjected to a luxury tax. Is a watch jewelry, and should watches be included? Finally, as pointed out earlier, if a luxury tax reduces consumption of that good, as will almost certainly happen to some degree, then production of that good will fall, and part of the effect will be on those who produce the good.

Some selective excise taxes are designed specifically to discourage consumption by raising prices to consumers. Taxes on tobacco products and alcoholic beverages fall into this category and are some of the oldest taxes in the United States.

Some argue for these taxes on the grounds that consumption of these goods creates costs to society that would not otherwise be borne by the purchaser. Others argue for the taxes on moral grounds. No matter what the justification, these taxes raise revenue, and revenue concerns may well temper how high the rates are raised. The taxes are ostensibly to discourage consumption, but most public officials are aware that if consumption is discouraged too much, too little revenue may be generated from the tax. As a revenue-raising device, these taxes have shortcomings. As with luxury taxes, they are based on people's preferences rather than on ability to pay. A rich person who does not drink will pay less alcohol tax than a poor person who does. Indeed, there is a general concern that the burden of these taxes falls proportionately more heavily on the poor than on the rich.

Some excise taxes, such as the gasoline tax and the tax on airline tickets, are intended to be benefit based, and the revenues from these taxes are earmarked for special funds for specific purposes. Gasoline taxes, for example, are intended to serve as user fees. The reasoning is that highway use is related, at least approximately, to gasoline consumption and that it is administratively easier to tax gasoline than to set up and administer a system of toll and user fees for street and highway construction and maintenance. The gasoline tax, of course, is not a perfect benefit tax, and questions remain unresolved about how much of the tax should be paid by cars versus trucks and about how much, if any, of the gasoline tax should go to support mass transit.

A concern both with general sales taxes and with selective excise taxes is tax-avoiding or tax-reducing behavior by consumers. As these taxes are often at the state or local level, a consumer can reduce the amount of tax paid by making purchases in a nearby jurisdiction where the taxes are lower. Many consumers also avoid state and local taxes by purchasing items through catalogues from companies in other states. Recently with the growth of mail-order catalog sales, some states have become increasingly concerned about tax revenue loss from these sales and have begun to take steps to recover some of the lost revenue. Canada has substantially higher taxes than the United States, and cross-border smuggling of goods taxed more heavily in Canada than in the United States has been a growing concern.

Value-Added Tax (VAT)

A value-added tax (VAT) is another form of tax on consumption. It is common in Europe and in Canada and, although not used in the United States, is often discussed as an option. A value-added tax recognizes that goods are usually produced in several stages. Consider a simplified version of how a pad of notebook paper is made. A tree farm grows trees and sells them to a paper mill. The paper mill produces large rolls of paper and sells them to another company, which forms paper into sheets with printed lines on them and makes the pads. That company then sells the pads to bookstores, which then sell them to students. A value-added tax is a percentage tax on the value added in each stage of production. For example, the paper mill would pay tax on the difference between what it sells the paper for and what it pays for the trees used to make the paper. The company that makes the pads would pay the tax on the difference between what it sells the pads for and what it pays for the paper. The bookstore would pay the tax on the difference between what it sells the pads to students for and what it pays to the pad manufacturer. In essence, a VAT is an alternative way of collecting a sales tax on the consumption of the pads.

In Europe, the tax is collected using the invoice method. Each company is liable for the tax levied on the basis of its sales, but it can claim credit for the tax already paid by its suppliers. This credit, however, is allowed only if supported by invoices provided by the suppliers. Such a system provides a strong incentive for producers to police themselves against tax evasion. If a business buys materials from a supplier who has not paid the VAT, the business is liable for both its tax and the supplier's. Thus, there is a strong incentive to buy only from producers who have paid the tax and who have documentation to prove it.

Proposals for a value-added tax in the United States are usually based on having this tax replace another tax, such as the corporate income tax, or to have the tax become a new way to fund Social Security. Some fear a value-added tax will increase the size of the government sector. A value-added tax collected by businesses might be concealed in the total price paid by consumers and therefore not clearly perceived as a tax burden. Perhaps coincidentally or perhaps not, in virtually all European countries with a VAT, the rate has increased over time as has the share of the GDP devoted to taxes.

Property Tax

The personal income tax, corporate income tax, sales tax, selective excise tax, and value-added tax are all taxes on transactions or flows of money. In each case, there is a transaction where money changes hands, and tax is levied on that transaction. Property taxes, on the other hand, are levied not on a flow but on accumulated wealth or stocks of wealth. Property taxes can be levied on either real property— land and improvements, including soil and things permanently fixed to it by nature (trees, crops, grass, water, minerals) or by people (buildings, fences)—or personal property, which includes everything that can be owned that is not real property, such as machinery and equipment, jewelry, cars, household furnishings, and stocks and bonds. The distinction between real and personal property is not always clear, nor is what makes up personal property. As a result, government units that tax property often use lists of how property is to be classified and what is to be included. Property taxes are a form of wealth tax, but in the United States they are not comprehensive net wealth taxes. They typically omit some forms of wealth (in many cases personal property is not taxed), and they apply to gross and not net wealth. The value of the house or car will be taxed, but no allowance will be made for the debt owed against that property (mortgage or car loan).

With income, sales, and excise taxes, the base to which the tax rate is applied is easily measured because there is a transaction or series of transactions to observe. The base of the property tax, however, is the accumulated value of the asset rather than an easily observed transaction. The core of the property tax is the process to establish a base, called the assessed value, to which the tax rate is applied. Local governments commonly set the property tax rate by first determining how much money must be raised from the property tax and then dividing that by the total assessed value in that jurisdiction. The process by which the assessed value is determined will determine the distribution of tax burdens among the property holders in the jurisdiction.

Two principal issues regarding property assessment are how the assessment is done and how often the property is reassessed. Assessment is a technical process, and each system as applied in each jurisdiction has differences. There are, however, three general approaches to estimating real property values. The techniques are (1) the market-data or comparable-sales approach, (2) the cost approach, and (3) the income approach.

The market-data or comparable-sales approach uses evidence from real estate transactions to estimate values of particular properties. Sales of similar properties are used to gauge buyer and seller attitudes to determine what the value of the property would be if it were to be sold. This approach works reasonably well for residential property, but special characteristics can make the approach more problematic for commercial or industrial properties.

The cost approach estimates the cost to reproduce a particular structure and then subtracts estimated depreciation since the building was built. The approach typically determines the cost of constructing a standard-grade structure at a particular date with the labor and materials prices of that time, in the size of the subject property, and with the prevailing technology. That cost is adjusted to nonstandard construction materials and workmanship, either higher or lower than standard. To that cost will be added extra features not in the standard unit such as fireplaces, central air conditioning, and so forth. The final cost will then be adjusted for depreciation to allow for the fact that the structure is not new—physical, technological, and economic forces have influenced its current value. This approach is suitable for buildings and structures, but does not apply to land valuation.

The income approach is most applicable to estimating the value of income-producing properties such as apartment buildings, retail stores, offices, and agricultural land. The method estimates the sustainable net income flow from the property and capitalizes that income at an appropriate interest rate, taking account of the risk of the investment. The resulting value approximates the amount a willing, knowledgeable buyer would pay for a property yielding that income flow.

With any of these approaches, a problem in assessment is how to treat a property that is not being used in its most economically beneficial manner. For example, how should a farm located at the edge of a metropolitan area be treated? Should the valuation be based on the income earned from farming, or should it be treated for what the land would be worth if it were converted to housing or commercial property? In a sense, the best measure of wealth is what someone else is willing to pay for the property, but if it is valued that way, the result may be to force the farm to be converted to another use just to pay the taxes. As with other areas of public finance, there is no universally accepted answer to this question.

Governments have varied policies about how often properties are assessed, but they can be grouped into three general approaches: mass cyclical assessment, segmental assessment, and annual assessment. Under mass cyclical assessment, all properties in a taxing jurisdiction are valued for tax purposes in a particular year, and that value does not change until the next scheduled mass assessment. The decision of the length of the cycle between assessments is left up to the states and typically ranges from two to ten years. Segmental assessment is a procedure by which a specified fraction of real property parcels in a jurisdiction is reassessed each year in a particular sequence. If a three-year cycle is used, one-third of the parcels are reassessed each year. The final system is annual reassessment, which tries to update values for each parcel each year. Re-evaluation with actual physical inspections and inventories of properties is not normally done under annual assessment. Rather, the annual valuation will use the physical characteristics of properties as identified in the most recent periodic inventories and apply different values to those characteristics. For example, a fireplace might add $1,200 to the value of a house in one year, and that might be increased to $1,600 in the next year. If no values are changed from one year to the next, then there is not any reassessment. Such a system is possible only with computerized records of property characteristics.

Property tax systems usually include provisions that exclude or exempt a portion of the assessed value from taxation. These exemptions reduce the tax base but are not a direct credit against the tax owed. Exemptions may be granted to certain individuals or institutions or may be granted to certain types of property. Exemptions may be granted to certain properties to promote certain activities such as for economic development, pollution control, or keeping land in undeveloped natural state. Exemptions may also be granted to government-owned property (such as airports) or to property held by religious, educational, nonprofit, or charitable organizations. Individuals may be granted exemptions, such as homestead, veterans', and seniors' exemptions. Homestead exemptions allow homeowners a given assessed value base before any property tax is levied against the property. Veterans' and seniors' exemptions provide similar partial exemptions from the tax. Nationwide, partial exemptions reduce gross assessed value by a little over 4 percent. In some cases, however, exemptions can be dramatic. Homestead exemptions claim over 25 percent of gross assessed value in Louisiana and nearly 16 percent in Florida.

Exemptions are politically popular, but they may not be very good public policy. For one thing, they do not focus property tax relief on the neediest. All people falling into an exemption category, such as homeowners, veterans, or seniors, qualify regardless of their specific needs or their income. Although not all homeowners are equally well off, homeowners are still generally better off than are renters for a variety of reasons such as the income tax deduction for mortgage interest. Nevertheless, renters are the target of few if any widespread exemption programs. In addition, if an exemption program applies to a large portion of property taxpayers, it creates more the illusion of an exemption than a real exemption. A widespread exemption program may cost the local government enough that property tax rates are raised to make up the revenue shortfall. Thus an exemption can lower the tax base, but the end result may be a higher tax rate and about the same amount of total tax paid.

Because property tax exemptions do not target tax relief to those most in need, in some states, residential property tax circuit breakers are used for this purpose. Circuit breakers try to alleviate property tax overload, which is defined in terms of the ratio of property tax payment to current household income. A circuit breaker typically uses the state income tax as a vehicle to consider the burden of the local property tax. With this approach, a taxpayer reports the amount of property tax paid on his or her state income tax return. If the ratio of the property tax paid to current household income is too high (as defined by the state's circuit breaker law), then it is considered a property tax overload, and a portion of the property tax is returned to the taxpayer in the form of a state income tax refund. The effects of circuit breakers depend on how they are designed and how they treat such characteristics of the taxpayer as age, income, and their status as owners or renters. Circuit breakers are often limited to seniors because the tax bill on the property they have accumulated during their working lives does not fall as may their incomes after retirement.

Property tax relief can also be given through deferral of taxes. Individuals whose property has increased substantially in value and whose income has not kept pace are allowed to continue to pay property taxes at the old rate. Records are kept of the difference between the taxes paid at the old rate and the full taxes that are owed. This difference is not forgiven but is deferred to a later time, usually when the property is sold or in the case of seniors when the estate is settled.

Exemptions and deferrals try to compensate for two of the problems with property taxes. As the tax is on wealth rather than on current income, the property tax liability may not be well matched to the ability to pay from current income. In principal, a person can convert part of the wealth into income to pay the tax, but such expectations are extremely unpopular politically. Exemptions and deferrals can address that problem. Another problem property taxes can deal with is assessing the value of property that is not in its most productive use. For example, if a farm lies at the fringe of a metropolitan area, how should it be valued? Should it be valued as farmland, or should it be valued at the price someone who intends to build houses or commercial property would pay? Some argue the land should be valued and taxed at its highest and best use, in this case as a housing or commercial development. Such valuation, however, would likely force the landowner to convert it to that use, even if the household wished to retain the land as a farm. Deferrals are a means of allowing the land to remain in farming while still taxing it according to its most productive use.

Other Revenue Sources

In addition to taxes, governments obtain revenue from other sources such as user charges, license fees, state-run monopoly revenues, utility revenues, and state lotteries. Compared to taxes, these revenue sources are not major sources of government funding, but they can nevertheless be important, particularly at the local level. These sources usually involve the sale of a good or service by the government that is voluntarily purchased by the individual.

User charges can involve things such as fees at municipal parking lots, tolls for roads or bridges, and tuition for optional education services. Such charges have the political advantage of raising revenue while not adding to the general tax burden. User charges can also improve the government provision of services by sending a clear signal to the government about which services people value and how much they value those services. To apply user charges, it must be clear who benefits from the activity, and it must be possible to levy the charges in an economical fashion. It would seem foolish, for example, to impose a user fee when the cost of collecting the fee exceeds the revenue from the fee.

Licensing and the associated fees cover a variety of situations. In some cases, the license is imposed to regulate specific activities such as hunting and fishing and the operation of motor vehicles. Without a license, the activity is forbidden so that the license is a necessary condition for the activity, but no specific government service is provided. In some cases, fishing licenses for example, the license fees may be used to support fish-stocking programs so that a service is provided. An indication of the importance of the regulatory function of a license activity may be the extent to which there are inspections or qualifications associated with obtaining the license.

Governments can also obtain revenue from the sale of goods or services available only from the government. Although the United States relies much more heavily on private ownership than do many other developed countries, in some localities the government may still be the sole provider of services such as water and mass transit. In some states, alcoholic beverages can be purchased only from government-owned and -operated stores.

Another nontax source of state revenue is the state lottery. In 1964, New Hampshire initiated the first state lottery in the 20th century. By 1990, at least 32 states operated state lotteries. As lotteries have grown and become more widespread, states have become more aggressive at marketing and promoting their lotteries. Lotteries appear to be a painless supplement to government finances, but they have come under criticism. One drawback is that low-income families spend a higher percentage of their income on lotteries than do high-income families, making the burden of this activity regressive. It may be a voluntary burden, but the regressivity is a concern nevertheless. Lotteries may also be an unstable source of revenue for states, making it difficult to forecast revenue and plan accordingly.

INTERGOVERNMENTAL GRANTS AND MANDATES

In the United States, the federal, state, and local governments provide public services and finance them. Each level of government is distinct and separate from the others, and each has its own powers and authority. Each is selected by its own electorate, and no government level operates as a department or branch of another. Although the various levels of government have considerable political independence, there would be serious problems if they all operated totally independently.

One problem, and a reason for intergovernmental grants, involves spillovers of government activity. Consider an example of a town, located on a river, which must decide how much to spend on sewage treatment. The town's decision will largely be made by comparing the costs incurred in constructing a sewage-treatment plant with the benefits received from the operation of that plant. Unfortunately, many of the benefits of the town's sewage-treatment expenditures accrue to other towns downstream rather than to the town constructing the plant. More rigorous sewage treatment may well be worth the cost from society's standpoint, but not from the perspective of the town. Here it makes sense for the federal government to finance a large share of the project to account for the large share of benefits going to people downstream of the town.

Intergovernmental grants may also redress a fiscal imbalance among units of government. There is wide variation in the tax-bearing capability of communities throughout the country. For communities with less tax-bearing capability to provide the same level of service as richer communities, for things like elementary education, requires a much higher tax rate than that of the richer communities. This mismatch between the need for government service and the capacity to finance services has prompted state and federal governments to provide fiscal assistance.

A common form of such assistance is grants, which transfer spending power from one government to another. Such grants have become an important part of state and local government finance. The federal grant system has included three types of grant assistance: (1) categorical grants, (2) block grants, and (3) general revenue sharing.

Categorical grants provide assistance for a particular purpose or program and limit spending for certain activities. Their intention is to provide an incentive for the receiving government to behave the way the federal government wants by lowering the *price* of certain government activities. The award of categorical grants can be either at an agency's discretion or on the basis of a formula developed by an agency or a legislature. Most categorical grants are at the discretion of the granting agency. Categorical grants create a conflict or divergence of interest between the recipient and the donor. From the donor's perspective, the whole point is to cause the recipient to undertake an activity it otherwise would not have. For the recipient, however, the goal would be to get the grant to finance an activity that was going to be done anyway, thereby freeing resources for other uses.

Block grants are usually distributed to governments according to a formula to finance activities in broad functional areas such as mass transportation, community development, education, health, job training, and criminal justice. Block grants are usually not expected to stimulate new initiatives and are directed at activities for which a broad consensus already exists. They are not designed to bend local choices in a direction more consistent with national interest or to cause local governments to change their operating methods. They have often been used as a means of consolidating a much larger number of specialized categorical grants.

General revenue sharing started in 1972 and ran through the mid-1980s. It provided funds distributed via a formula that included population, percentage urban population, tax effort, and per capita income. There were few if any restrictions on the use of these funds. Revenue sharing can strengthen local spending power and reduce disparities in fiscal capacity across communities, but it does not reshape local priorities or provide a particularly effective way to target aid to people who are disadvantaged.

In a sense, mandates are the other side of grants. A mandate is a constitutional provision, statute, administrative regulation, or judicial ruling that places an expenditure requirement on a government. Mandates are much like the operating restrictions that governments place on private industry to regulate workplace safety, environmental quality, and equal employment opportunities. As with regulation and the private sector, mandates seek to cause governments to behave in some manner other than the way they would ordinarily behave. Most of the concern about mandates comes at the local level because the small size of these governments can make accommodating mandates difficult. Recently, federal government mandates to state governments have become a large political issue as well. Under prodding from Congress, federal mandates to state and local governments were reduced in 1995.

The case for mandates rests on two arguments. First, a state or local government action, or lack of action, may have spillover effects on other government units. An action by one government unit can reduce that unit's expenditures, but can also increase the costs of surrounding units or harm the residents of surrounding jurisdictions. A mandate can be used to prevent this. Second, a higher unit of government, or the judiciary, may view uniformity of the provision of some service as essential. Thus, the requirement of the same expenditure per unit for schools or other services may be mandated to prevent individuals from having low service levels simply because of their place of residence.

There are also at least three strong arguments against mandates. First, as the government unit imposing the mandate is not responsible for funding it, mandates can become a political tool for the higher government unit while the lower unit is stuck with financing. Separating the decision to provide a service from the responsibility of funding that provision is unlikely to lead to carefully considered decisions. Second, mandates can threaten other government programs. If local governments are limited in their capacity to raise revenues, then mandates can threaten the provision of other services. Third, mandates are often enacted by the higher government without a careful consideration of the costs. Even if a goal is desirable, the benefits of that goal must be weighed against the costs. With mandates, and particularly judicially imposed mandates, such balancing of costs and benefits is rarely done.

TAX REFORM

Dissatisfaction with the tax system is nothing new, but as the United States moves into the second half of the 1990s, there seems to be growing pressure for tax reform at the federal level. The principal complaints about the tax code are that it is far too complex, difficult to understand, and expensive to administer; and the tax system discourages savings and investment thereby hampering gains in productivity. Intermingled with these two criticisms are also concerns that taxes in general are too high and place too great a burden on taxpayers and that marginal tax rates are too high.

A wide variety of proposals have been put forth to address these issues; most seem to focus on reducing the tax burden and removing disincentives for savings and investment. For example, the House Republicans, as part of their Contract with America, have proposed a $500 tax credit per child for families with incomes under $200,000 and children under 18; elimination of the so-called marriage penalty by raising the personal credit for married couples to equal the personal credit for nonmarried individuals; a new type of savings account for retirement with reduced taxes; a 50 percent exclusion of net capital gain from gross income for any taxable year; and indexing to inflation the capital gains of assets held longer than one year. The Clinton administration has made similar proposals that include a $500 tax credit per child for families with children under 13; a new tax deduction of up to $10,000 per year for higher-education tuition for families with incomes below $120,000 a year; and a variety of provisions to reduce the taxes paid on savings accounts for retirement. In varying degrees, these proposals reduce the disincentives for savings and investment and reduce the tax burden, but they may add further complications to the tax code rather than simplify it.

Flat Tax

A proposal aimed primarily at tax simplification and also at tax reduction is that of Representative Dick Armey (R, Texas) to replace the current individual income and corporate income tax with a flat tax—a single tax rate applied to all households and companies. Under this plan the tax rate would be set at 20 percent for the first three years and then drop to 17 percent. While a single tax rate would be applied, the effective tax rate (the tax paid divided by total income) would still be progressive under this proposal. Households would be allowed both a personal allowance and dependent deductions; some of a household's income would be free of taxes, but that amount would not grow as household income grew. Beyond these, all other exemptions and deductions would be dropped. The flat tax concept has fairly broad-based appeal in both political parties. House Minority Leader Richard Gephardt (D, Missouri) has also indicated that he is drafting a flat tax proposal, and several other flat tax type proposals have been developed. These proposals differ in details. Some allow a few of the more popular deductions, but all allow few if any deductions and apply a single tax rate to all taxed income. Still other proposals are similar in concept but allow two or three different tax rates. The appeal of these proposals is based largely on their simple and straightforward nature compared to the overwhelming complexity of the current personal and corporate income taxes. Indeed, the tax code has become so byzantine that the cost of compliance for individuals and corporations in the United States has been estimated at about $75 billion a year, including the sums citizens pay lawyers and accountants for tax services, the hours taxpayers spend dealing with tax matters, and the budget of the Internal Revenue Service.

Consumption Tax

Another tax reform approach gaining increasing attention is replacing the corporate income tax with a consumption tax. Under this approach, companies would subtract their purchases of goods and services from their gross income and pay a tax, often proposed at around 10 percent, on that amount. The big difference in this approach is that expenditures on capital equipment, inventories, and other large items would be written off in the year the expenditures occur, rather than being spread over several years as is currently the case. Such an approach would go a long way to encourage investment, which in turn would spur economic growth. This sort of proposal would be a dramatic change from the current system, and versions of it are being proposed by some of the most senior members of the Congress in both political parties, including a bill proposed by Senators David Boren (D, Oklahoma) and John Danforth (R, Missouri) and another bill proposed by Senators Pete Domenici (R, New Mexico) and Sam Nunn (D, Georgia).

SUMMARY

Table 4–3 lists the principal taxes discussed in this chapter, summarizes their basic characteristics, and indicates how much money they contributed to federal, state, and local governments in 1990–1991. As is evident in the table, these taxes play different roles in different levels of government. None of these taxes is clearly and unambiguously better than the others. All have their strengths and weaknesses.

In evaluating these or other taxes, several questions need to be asked. One is the principle according to which the tax is levied. Is the tax levied according to the ability of the taxpayer to pay or according to the benefits received? The benefit principle is patterned after the logic of the private market. In a market, people pay for the benefits they consume. Conversely, if people do not consume the goods or services, they do not have to pay for them. If that general principle were extended to goods and services provided by the government, then taxpayers would pay in proportion to the benefits received. A taxpayer who received 1 percent of the benefits would pay 1 percent of the costs. There would be no cross-subsidy among taxpayers; users who received benefits would pay, and those who did not receive benefits would not pay. User fees are an example of charging according to the benefit principle. Among taxes, the gasoline tax has benefit principle characteristics in that the more a person uses the highway system, the more gasoline that person consumes and the larger amount of gasoline tax is paid.

The ability-to-pay principle does not follow market exchange principles and separates the decision of the government to provide goods and services from the decision of how to finance this provision. Under this principle, those who are better able to pay should bear a greater portion of the burden of financing government activities. In practice, using the ability-to-pay approach involves making two separate decisions: first, what determines the ability to pay and how is it measured, and second, how should the tax burden vary with the ability to pay? Determining how to measure the ability to pay often requires focusing on either current income

TABLE 4-3 Summary of Tax Characteristics

Type of Tax	Base	Exemptions and Deductions	Most Common Rate Structure	Federal Revenue (Millions, 1990–1991)	State Revenue (Millions, 1990–1991)	Local Revenue (Millions, 1990–1991)
Personal Income	Income from wages, salaries, interest, dividends, etc.	Personal, business expenses, home mortgage interest	Graduated for federal, graduated or flat for state and local	$467,827	$99,279	$10,062
Corporate Income	Income from sales	Business expenses, wages, materials, interest	Graduated for federal, graduated or flat for state and local	$98,086	$20,357	$1,886
General Sales	All sales transactions except those exempted	Selected categories such as food for home consumption, prescription drugs	Flat rate	$0	$103,165	$22,283
Selective Excise	Specific sales transactions	NA	Flat rate or unit tax	$42,461	$50,369	$9,752
Value Added	Difference between the sales price and the cost of the input materials	NA	Flat rate	NA	NA	NA
Property	Assessed value of real property, in some cases personal property	No allowance is made for debt owed against the property	Flat rate	$0	$6,228	$161,772

NA = not available.

Sources: U.S. Bureau of the Census, *Governmental Finances, 1987–1991, and Preliminary 1992* (Washington, D.C.: U.S. Government Printing Office, 1994), and this chapter.

or accumulated wealth. The income tax, for example, focuses on current income whereas the property tax focuses on accumulated wealth.

Another set of questions addresses how fair a tax is by examining the horizontal and vertical equity. Horizontal equity addresses the widely held belief that people who are in like circumstances should be treated alike. Vertical equity is concerned with the relative taxes paid by people with different capacities to pay. Horizontal equity tries to consider the relative treatment of equals whereas vertical equity tries to consider the relative treatment among unequals to ask how much more those with greater capacity should pay or indeed whether they should pay more at all. The question of vertical equity is usually addressed by asking whether a tax is progressive, proportional, or regressive. Questions of progressivity are not easily answered and depend strongly on the specific details of how the tax is administered and what is included or excluded from the tax base.

Inevitably, taxes create dissatisfaction on the part of taxpayers and public policy analysts alike. Many taxes have become complicated, and concerns are growing that these taxes not only discourage savings and investment; they also discourage people from working as much as they otherwise might. As a result, calls for tax reform have grown in recent years, and proposals are emerging for new approaches to taxation, such as a flat income tax, a consumption tax, or a value-added tax.

DISCUSSION QUESTIONS

1. "In 1990, the top 10 percent of the taxpayers paid over 54 percent of all personal income taxes collected; the top 5 percent paid 43 percent. In addition, the proportion of taxes paid by the rich has risen during the past decade." What do these statements tell us about the progressivity or regressivity of the federal income tax? Explain. (Hint: what other information would you need to assess progressivity or regressivity more completely?)

2. Many analysts regard the retail sales tax as regressive. However, sales taxes vary from state to state with regard to their specific provisions. What features of a sales tax would make it less regressive? What features would make it more regressive?

3. Consider the following headline from *The New York Times:* "Corporations Have to Pay Fair Tax Share," (February 19, 1993, p. A26). What view of the corporation is implicit in this statement? Is this view accurate? Do corporations pay taxes or do people pay taxes? Explain. Why do you think the view implicit in this headline is so popular among politicians and journalists?

4. How does the corporate income tax result in double taxation? How do you think this double taxation might affect people's behavior? Is this good public policy?

SUGGESTED READINGS

Harvey S. Rosen, *Public Finance,* Fourth Edition (Chicago: Irwin, 1995).

John L. Mikesell, *Fiscal Administration: Analysis and Applications for the Public Sector,* Fourth Edition (Belmont, CA: Wadsworth, 1995).

Alan Altshuler and Jose A. Gomez-Ibanez with Arnold Howitt, *Regulation for Revenue: The Political Economy of Land Use Extractions* (Washington, DC/Cambridge MA: Brookings Institution/Lincoln Institute for Land Policy, 1993).

Joel Slemrod, editor, *Why People Pay Taxes: Tax Compliance and Enforcement* (Ann Arbor: University of Michigan Press, 1992).

Henry Aaron, *Who Pays the Property Tax? A New View* (Washington, DC: Brookings Institution, 1975).

5

Economic Policy:
Stabilization and Growth

The formulation and implementation of economic policy have been principal activities of our government since the founding of the country. The earliest disputes between the American colonists and the British Empire had to do with the commercial activities and rights of the colonists vis-à-vis the mother country. The 1776 Revolution was precipitated by the desire of the Americans to be free of British meddling in and restrictions on the colonial economy. As we discussed earlier, when the U.S. Constitution was written, it set forth a major responsibility of the new central government to be the promotion and regulation of commerce. But until the mid-nineteenth century, government's main economic activities were the establishment of tariffs and the creation of a banking and currency management system.

The Civil War had as much to do with economic conflicts between the North and South as it did with human rights. After the Civil War, the U.S. government became very active in opening up new lands in the West and in spurring economic development in this new territory through land grants and expansion of our transportation infrastructure. The end of the Civil War also saw a need for reconstruction in the South and a push for economic development throughout the entire country.

The American government, for the first time, thus became actively involved in all phases of the economic development of the nation. It encouraged immigration to expand our labor force, supported the movement of settlers to develop the West, established a system of land grant universities in the states, and issued bonds for the development of a rail system and other public infrastructure projects. In the later part of the nineteenth century, the federal government moved to curtail some of the abuses that had resulted from the almost unbridled efforts at national economic development. Chapter 15 discusses the evolution of the role of the American government in our society in more detail.

THE GOVERNMENT'S ROLE IN THE CONTEMPORARY ECONOMY

In the early days of this country, the predominant view was that government should have a minimal, or laissez-faire, involvement in the economic life of the nation. Adam Smith (1723–1790), the first of the great British economists, talked about the "invisible hand" in his famous treatise, *The Wealth of Nations*.[1] This theory essentially said that the best interests of society would be served if people were left alone to pursue their own selfish interests. In Smith's words: "Every man, as long as he does not violate the laws of justice, is left free to pursue his own interest his own way, and to bring his industry and capital into competition with those of any other man, or order of men. The sovereign is completely discharged from a duty, in the attempting to perform [that] which no human wisdom or knowledge could ever be sufficient; the duty of superintending the industry of private people, and of directing it towards the employment most suitable to the interests of society."[2] This view still drives the basic political philosophy of many politicians, who argue for less government interference in the economy in order to "unleash the creative power and ingenuity of the private sector."[3]

Indeed, modern-day laissez-faire has recently played a role in bringing economic prosperity to many regions of the world, as governments have retreated from such heavy-handed interference in their economies as investment and currency exchange controls, price controls, and import protection policies. The problems of a hands-off economic policy in the nineteenth century came from the side effects—the externalities—of unbridled laissez-faire. These side effects included exploitation of children and other workers, appalling social conditions, and the development of huge fortunes by monopolists and land speculators. Thus, one of the results of laissez-faire in this country in the late nineteenth century was the Theodore Roosevelt–Woodrow Wilson movement to break up monopolies, to enact fair trade laws, to set limits on the exploitation of the poor by passing laws against child labor, to allow unions to bargain collectively, and to undertake taxation and expenditure policy to even the distribution of income in the country.

We have also increasingly recognized that the invisible hand of the market system cannot perform all of the functions required in a modern economy. For a variety of economic activities, it is necessary for government to intervene if the economic system is to perform smoothly. Some have described this need for government to intervene in the private economy as resulting from market failures that "violate the basic assumptions of the idealized competitive economy and therefore interfere with efficiency in production or consumption."[4] These market failures result in undesirable externalities (e.g., air pollution); natural monopolies in some industries; a lack of consumer information; and the need for government provision of some goods and services.

This necessity for some public action in the marketplace is what led prominent public-finance theorist Richard Musgrave to comment, "The proper size of the public sector is, to a significant degree, a technical rather than an ideological issue."[5] Among the more important reasons for this fact are the following:

1. The government needs to create and enforce the legal structure necessary for contractual arrangements and the conduct of commerce.
2. Certain types of social goods necessary to society cannot be provided by the private sector.
3. Social values, and the stability of the social system, may require adjustments in the distribution of income that can be provided only by the government.
4. In a modern industrialized economy, a market system, left to operate by itself, will not

necessarily lead to price stability, a socially accepted level of employment, and a desired rate of economic growth.

Drawing on Musgrave's terminology, the three major economic functions that only the government can effectively perform in our society are described in the following sections.

The Allocation Function

As discussed in Chapter 1, certain goods cannot be provided by the market system. These are characterized as social or public goods, as distinct from private goods. For example, when an individual purchases a television set, he or she alone receives the benefits of that TV, unless he or she decides to share it with another person. The TV is obviously a private good. On the other hand, social goods are those goods that one individual cannot exclude others from enjoying. For example, when the government reduces air pollution, everyone can enjoy the benefits of that reduction, whether or not he or she helped pay the costs of providing the cleaner air. This is a clear characteristic of a social good. Another classic example of a social good is national defense. If one of us is protected by the nation's system of national security, we are all protected. Similarly, the management of fiscal and monetary policy by the government benefits all persons and businesses in our country.

There is a second type of public good, known as a *merit good*, that results in direct benefits to some individuals and indirect benefits to others. These are goods for which the choice of public production has been made because an inadequate amount of the good—in terms of societal benefits—would be produced if payment were left only to those receiving direct benefits. For example, in the early days of this country, only individuals purchasing a *firebrand* had their houses protected by the local fire department. We subsequently decided that the entire community benefitted from fire protection, and the decision was made to offer it by the government as a merit good. Similarly, education directly benefits the individual receiving the education. At the same time, the whole nation benefits because of the positive effect on national economic productivity of having an educated labor force. Therefore, the society as a whole also benefits—in a nonexcludable manner—from one of its members receiving an education. We therefore have chosen to provide education as a public good and pay for it through our public tax system, rather than through individual user charges. The decisions to offer these social goods are made through the political consensus process.

A third type of public good is offered by government to prevent private monopoly of an essential good and to control the pricing of those goods. For example, we have chosen to have our highway system provided by the government, even though it could be delivered by the private sector. In the early days of this country, people commonly owned roads they had privately constructed, and they charged travelers a fee for using the roads. We have therefore created a public monopoly for the provision and maintenance of our highway, road, and street systems.

The Distribution Function

When a society makes the policy decision, through its political process, to change in some manner the distribution of income in the society, the only way that function can be carried out is by the government. Government accomplishes this redistribution of income through the provision of welfare and other entitlement programs (such as public-health benefits); through regional transfers of income and expenditures from wealthier parts of the nation to the lower-income regions; and through the use of progressive tax structures to alter the distribution of disposable personal income.

The Stabilization and Economic Growth Function

Modern governments use fiscal policy (taxes and expenditures) and monetary policy (interest rates and changes in the money supply) to influence the level of employment and price stability in the country because these goals are not necessarily met without such government intervention. As John Maynard Keynes demonstrated in the 1930s, economies can stabilize at a low level of employment. As we have seen in many parts of the world, nations can also endure long periods of price instability. Neither employment nor inflation will necessarily restore itself to acceptable levels automatically. Governments therefore use *stabilization policy* because it is the only way of affecting these economic variables.

As we discuss in Chapter 15, the Great Depression and the administration of President Franklin D. Roosevelt (FDR) moved the government to a new level of economic involvement that has carried over to the present. After World War II, the Congress declared the stabilization and growth of the U.S. economy to be top priorities of the government. Congress set this in public policy by enacting the Full Employment Act of 1946. The act stated:

> The government should use all practicable means to achieve maximum employment, production, and purchasing power.

The act also created the Council of Economic Advisors within the Office of the President for the purpose of advising the president about economic policy. Before we discuss how the government is supposed to influence economic activity in the country, we shall review a few of the basics about the economy.

THE STRUCTURE AND MEASUREMENT OF THE ECONOMY

How do we measure the economy so we know how we are doing? Let us first look at some definitions that we will need to discuss economic policy.

The National Income Accounts

The federal government compiles statistics to measure national output and income. Two of the most important sets of statistics are *gross domestic product* and *gross domestic income.* It is important to recognize that these measures include only purchases and incomes created by production. They do not include resales, transfer payments among taxpayers, or exchanges of assets. For example, a purchase of common stock by a consumer is not included as a new investment.

Gross Domestic Product.   Gross Domestic Product (GDP) is the most comprehensive measure of national output. It is a measure of the value of all goods and services produced annually in the nation. One should think of GDP as a flow: it is an amount of production of goods and services measured in dollars per unit of time.

GDP is prepared and published by the U.S. Department of Commerce. It is a compilation of expenditure data from all sectors of our economy, and it is divided into four components. These four components are classified by the type of use of the output.

1. Consumption expenditures on all goods and services by individuals.
2. Gross private domestic-investment expenditures, a measure of the capital additions to the real productive assets of the country. It includes investments in plant and equipment by businesses, private investment in residential construction, and the change in business inventories (inventory investment).
3. Government purchases of goods and services, including expenditures by all three levels of government.
4. Net exports, positive or negative depending on whether the nation exports or imports more goods and services during a particular time period.

The sum of these expenditure categories in a period equals GDP.

We mentioned earlier that GDP is usually measured on an annual basis. When you read in the news that GDP for the third quarter of the year was $X,XXX, this figure is actually quarterly expenditures converted to an annual rate, that is, multiplied by four. It is also "seasonally adjusted," and given in "real" dollars. In other words, we are interested in the real growth of GDP during a particular time period so we can see how the economy is doing compared to other periods. To find that out, the effects of both seasonal expenditure patterns within the year (e.g., Christmas retail sales) and inflation (price changes in goods and services from period to period) are removed from the figure. With these adjustments to the current dollar GDP estimate, it is possible to see the real change in GDP over time. For example, recent reports of the Department of Commerce express GDP from 1987 to 1995 in 1987 dollars. This allows the reader to see the real economic change over that period, unobscured by price level changes. Figure 5–1 shows the growth of real GDP over the past several years.

It is necessary to point out one other definition before moving on. Most news reports about economic growth now use the term GDP rather than the previous measure, gross national product (GNP). The only difference between the two numbers is that GDP excludes economic activity by U.S. citizens or companies that occurs outside of the United States. The purpose of this change is to obtain a better measure of actual U.S. production. (Under GNP, as long as the labor and property are supplied by U.S. residents, they may be located either in the United States or abroad.) To give the reader an idea of the actual differences between the numbers, during the second quarter of 1992, GNP was $5913.2 billion, while GDP was $5893.6 billion. Thus, GDP represented 99.6 percent of GNP. For our discussions, unless indicated otherwise, we will be referring to GDP.

Gross Domestic Income.   If you stop to think about it, you realize that one person's expenditure is another person's income. The same thing is true in the national income accounts. The income that represents the opposite side of the GDP ledger is categorized by the type of income that is created by the expenditures included in GDP.

The categories are the following:

1. Wages and salaries,
2. Interest income,
3. Rental income,

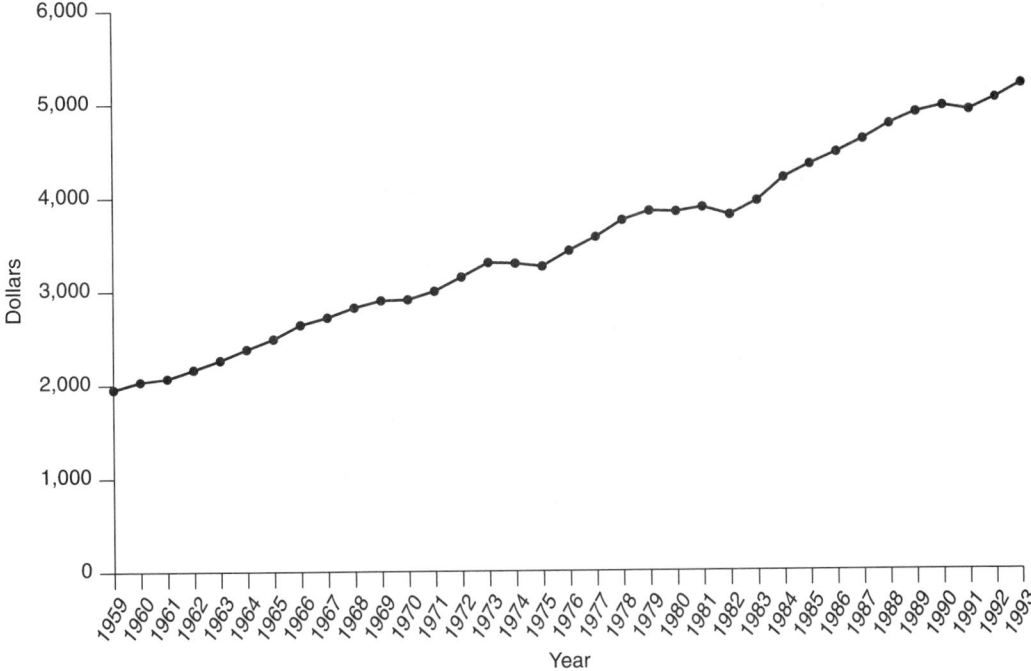

Figure 5–1   Gross Domestic Product in 1987 dollars

Source: Economic Report of the President, 1994.

4. Corporate profits,
5. Unincorporated business income,
6. Depreciation, and
7. Other incomes (mostly local property and sales taxes that are not included in incomes but that do show up in government expenditures on the GDP side of the national income accounts).

The total of these income categories is called gross domestic income (GDI).

It should be apparent to the reader that the two figures must be equal: GDP must equal GDI; the sum of all incomes created in production must exactly equal the value of the output. In fact, as is shown in Figure 5–2, the two measures of economic performance interact with each other in a circular manner, each generating the other. Production creates income, income creates expenditures, expenditures call forth production. There is no beginning and no end to this circular flow. The forces that produce fluctuations in the economy result from this relationship between production, income, and expenditures.

So when we see in the news that GDP went up or down, one of the relevant questions we need to ask is: Which components of GDP changed and how? When we hear that national income went up or down, we want to know how those various components have changed. The change in the GDP components tells us something about what is going on in the economy, an essential before policy action can be taken. Of course, that is where fiscal and monetary policy, the government's tools for dealing with economic problems that occur as a re-

The Flow of Production, Spending, and Income

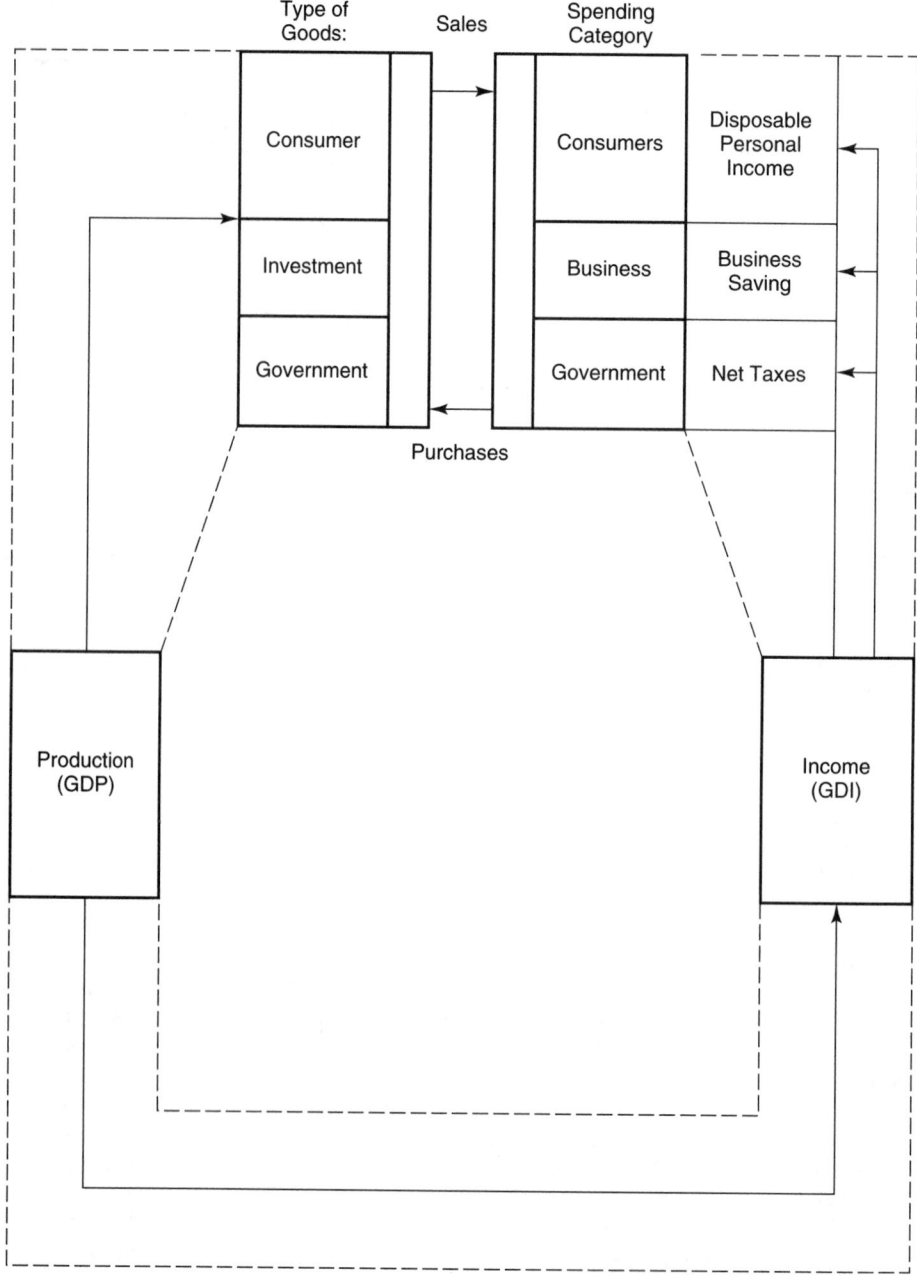

Figure 5–2   The flow of the three spending categories

sult of disruptions in the production-income-expenditure relationships, comes in.

Given these definitions, let us now ask how can we gauge the health of the economy.

MEASURING THE LONG-TERM GROWTH OF THE ECONOMY

Knowing a particular level of GDP or GDI does not necessarily tell you much about how the economy is doing. The relevant question always is, compared to what? The most important factor in assessing how the economy is doing is comparing how it is doing in relation to its potential. What do we mean by economic potential? Essentially, using available physical and human resources, how much output can the economy produce at any particular point in time? But how do we determine this potential?

The U.S. Department of Commerce provides estimates of the economy's *productivity* over time. Productivity is simply the amount of output per labor-hour worked in the economy. Productivity, or output per labor-hour, is calculated by dividing real (actual adjusted for inflation) dollar GDP (or output) during a particular period by the number of labor-hours worked in the same period. During most of the years since the end of World War II, output per labor-hour grew at about 2.5 to 3 percent per year. In recent years it has slowed to an annual rate of growth of 1.5 to 2.5 percent. In the eight quarters following the bottom of the 1991 recession, nonfarm productivity grew at an average annual rate of 2.3 percent. In 1992, it grew 3 percent. During 1993, productivity for the year as a whole grew at a reduced rate of 1.7 percent, but at the end of that year was growing at a much faster rate—in excess of 4 percent.

Thus, to determine GDP potential for any period, we need only to multiply our estimate of output per labor-hour (based on historic patterns and actual recent figures) by the total number of labor-force hours available to be worked in that period. The number of labor-force hours available in the economy at any particular time is determined by taking the size of the labor force, which is typically defined as the number of people between the ages of 14 and 65 who are seeking work, and multiplying that number by the average number of hours worked per year per employee. This yields the number of labor-hours available to be worked during the period in question.

But one final adjustment is necessary before calculating potential GDP. Because of the nature of the country's workforce, all potential workers are not available to work at all times for the following reasons:

1. Some people are always between jobs. This category of the labor force is known as the frictionally unemployed.
2. Other members of our labor force have no skills that can be used by employers. This category of the labor force is known as the structurally unemployed. No matter how well the economy is doing, it is unlikely that the structurally unemployed can find work.

Taken together, these two categories currently account for approximately 5.5 to 6 percent of the labor force. So, for example, if we have 7 percent of the labor force unemployed at a particular time, let's assume roughly 5.5 percentage points of that 7 percent figure represent those either frictionally or structurally unemployed and not truly available to work. That 5.5 percent of the labor force, therefore, should not be included as part of the full employment GDP potential.

The result of this situation is that our working definition of full employment is the point at which approximately 5.5 percent of the labor force is unemployed. Therefore, to summarize the calculations:

Total labor-hours available	=	total labor force (assumes 94.5 % employable)	×	average hours worked per year per employee
Output per labor-hour (productivity)	=	total GDP	÷	total labor-hours worked
Full employment potential GDP	=	output per labor-hour	×	total labor-hours available to be worked

In summary, then, potential GDP is the amount of output the economy could produce at a given time under conditions of reasonably full employment of the labor force and normal utilization of plant capacity. Comparing actual GDP with potential GDP at any time provides us with a yardstick to assess how well the economy is doing. As the Indiana University basketball coach Bobby Knight says, we are not just interested in how well we are performing; we are interested in how well we are performing compared to our potential. Using the reported statistics on both actual and potential GDP gives us that measure.[6] Figure 5–3 offers an estimate of actual GDP versus potential GDP since 1965.

An example of the usefulness of this concept in economic analysis is the direct relationship between both the rates of unemployment and inflation and the closeness of the fit between actual and potential GDP.

1. If there is a significant gap between actual and potential GDP, the excess plant and human capacity represented by that gap will be reflected in a rate of unemployment higher than 5.5 percent (our assumed full employment level of GDP).

Figure 5–3   Actual GDP v. potential GDP

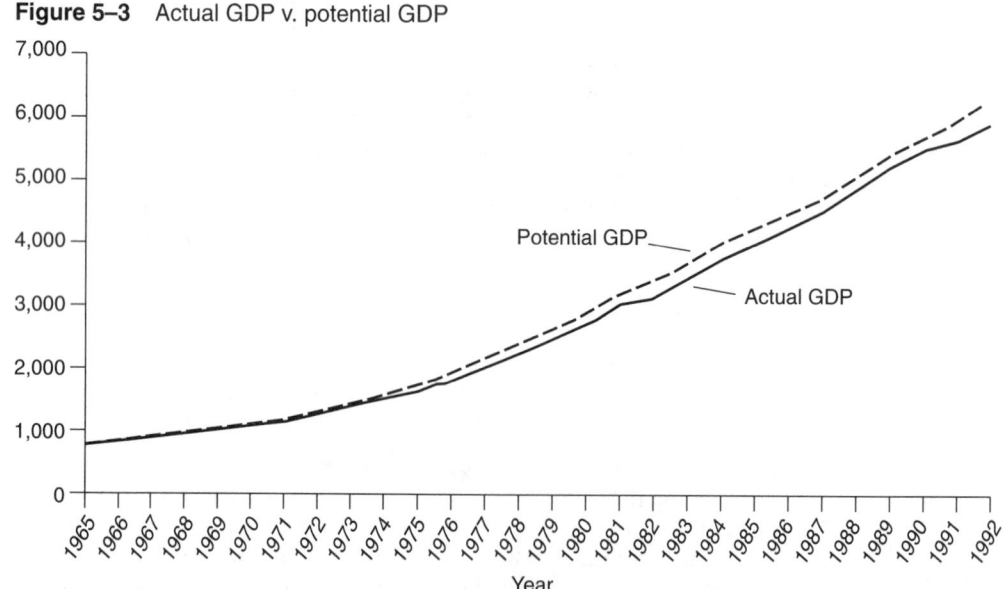

Source: Economic Report of the President, 1994, U.S. Government Printing Office.

2. If actual GDP and potential GDP are very close, prices may begin to rise to reflect the pressure on physical and human resources.

But before moving on we need to point out that, while this concept is very useful to an understanding of the dynamics of our domestic economy, unfortunately things are not so precise as implied by the above discussion. In the first place, there is no consensus on the rate of unemployment that represents full (or natural) employment.[7] These different estimates of full employment, of course, also result in different estimates of potential GDP and the amount of gap that exists between actual and potential output at any time. Furthermore, an analysis reported by the Federal Reserve Bank of St. Louis suggests that potential GDP can vary during a given period due to shifts in such economic forces as labor force growth or capital formation.[8] For example, one model showed potential growth ranging from a 3.3 percent rate in 1986 to a 1.2 percent rate in 1993–1994.

There is some evidence that the Federal Reserve Board (FRB; commonly *the Fed*) is conducting monetary policy (discussed below) on the assumption that potential GDP is growing at about 2.5 percent per year and that unemployment cannot fall much below 6 percent without accelerating inflation. Yet in 1994—due largely to higher productivity growth resulting from the restructuring of American industry—the rate of potential growth was at least 3 percent.

There is also disagreement about the effect of the gap—whatever its size—on inflation. Those more sanguine argue that other factors in today's economy suggest that inflation will remain low in spite of the closeness between actual and potential GDP. These factors include changing technology, the decline in the power of unions, and growing international competition from both developed and developing countries, which in effect expands the capacity of domestic industry by forcing down prices of domestically produced goods and keeping wages from rising.

Now that we have covered some of the basics, we turn our attention to the economic problems and policy issues of today. We are particularly interested in what seem to be the points of debate about economic policy and what appear to be the alternative policies that can be pursued to improve the performance of the nation's economy.

THE OBJECTIVES OF ECONOMIC POLICY

The economic policy objectives of today are the same objectives as those legislated by the Congress in the Employment Act of 1946 and the Full Employment and Balanced Growth Act of 1978: achieving maximum employment, production, and purchasing power and, by doing so, improving the economic well-being of our citizens.

In keeping with these objectives, the economic policy actions of the government are designed to achieve the following:

1. Improve the long-term growth and performance of our economy.
2. Reduce as much as possible the short-term economic fluctuations and instability (such as recessions) that have characterized industrialized economies since the early nineteenth century.
3. Maintain reasonable price stability.

We will now take up each of these policy objectives.

Long-Term Economic Growth

Obviously, the maximum amount an economy can grow over time is limited by its full employment potential GDP. To increase long-term growth, we therefore need to increase potential GDP.

Again, potential GDP in an economy is determined by its productivity (output/labor-hour), the size of its labor force willing and able to work, and the average hours worked per member of the labor force. So if we are interested in increasing our potential GDP, one or more of these variables must increase. The economic policy issues for the government, then, have to do with what alternatives the government possesses to affect these variables.

Let us look first at the government's options available to affect the size of the labor force. The size of the labor force is determined by:

1. The size of our population of working age (14 to 65 years).
2. The labor-force participation rate—that is, the percentage of the population of working age able and choosing to work.

Figure 5–4 shows U.S. Department of Labor projections for labor-force participation rates to the year 2050. The changing age structure of the population is the primary factor affecting the projected participation rates.

If we wish to increase the number of labor-force hours available to be worked in the economy at any given time, some of the ways in which we might try to accomplish this could be, first, increasing the size of our working-age population. One way is to expand immigration. Another might be to encourage people to work beyond age 65. In some countries, for example, Singapore, the approach is to try to expand the size of the population by encouraging larger families.

Recent U.S. policy has recognized that, because of low birth rates in the years

Figure 5–4   Population and employment

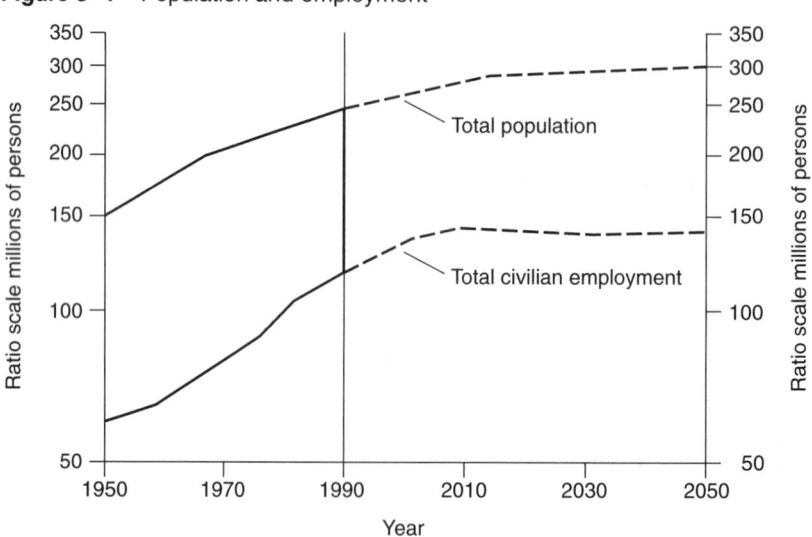

Source: U.S. Department of Labor.

ahead, we will be facing a reduced number of working-age people in our population. We have therefore indeed been encouraging immigration as one way to expand the size of our labor force.[9] Early retirement programs are also being re-evaluated in both the private and public sectors with a view to encouraging people to remain longer in active employment.

Another way to expand the number of working hours available in the labor force might be to try to reduce the number of people at any time who are classified as frictionally unemployed (between jobs). This could be accomplished by, for example, providing better information and counseling systems for job placement.

Third, an expanded effort to provide education and training to the structurally unemployed could also help reduce the category of unemployables and expand the number of labor-force hours available in the economy.

Improving Productivity.   Most analysts regard the other component of potential GDP, output per labor-hour, or productivity, to be even more important than expanding the size of the labor force. The reason is that high productivity translates directly to higher per capita income and higher living standards for our people. If output grows only as fast as labor input and if labor productivity stays unchanged, then real income per worker is "doomed to remain constant."[10] (If only the size of the labor force were important, India and China would be the richest countries in the world.)

So how do we increase productivity? This can be a complicated topic, but in simple terms, we do it by increasing investment in technology that enables one worker working one hour to produce more output. We also do it by improving the worker's ability to produce more output in one hour by improving his or her education and training.

What can the government do to increase business investment in capital goods and technology? That is where the policy arguments begin. Basically, government can act to increase the amount of personal and business savings available for investment, and government can make sure that its tax structure and other government policies (e.g., regulatory and industrial policy-incentive systems) encourage—or at least do not discourage—business and personal investment (which for these purposes is defined as additions to or replacements of *real productive assets*).

What about improving our workers' productivity? Clearly, education is one of government's primary responsibilities. In order for our workers to be able to compete in the new global economy of which the United States is a part—we need to make substantial progress in the basic skills of our work force. Much of that progress is the responsibility of our system of public education. Government can also encourage training and education by our private sector through the provision of specially designed tax deductions and credits for work-force educational programs.

What are some of the other factors inhibiting the nation's ability to improve its long-term rate of growth? One of the major issues is the size of the federal budget deficits that have built up over the past several years. In the 1970s the federal budget deficit averaged 2.1 percent of GDP. By 1983 it had shot up to 6.3 percent of GDP. Throughout the 1980s, the deficit averaged 4.1 percent of GDP. While in fiscal 1994–1995 it declined to about 3 percent, it is still high by historical standards. The trend in the deficit, in dollars, is shown in Figure 5–5.

A majority of economists believe there are a number of reasons to reduce

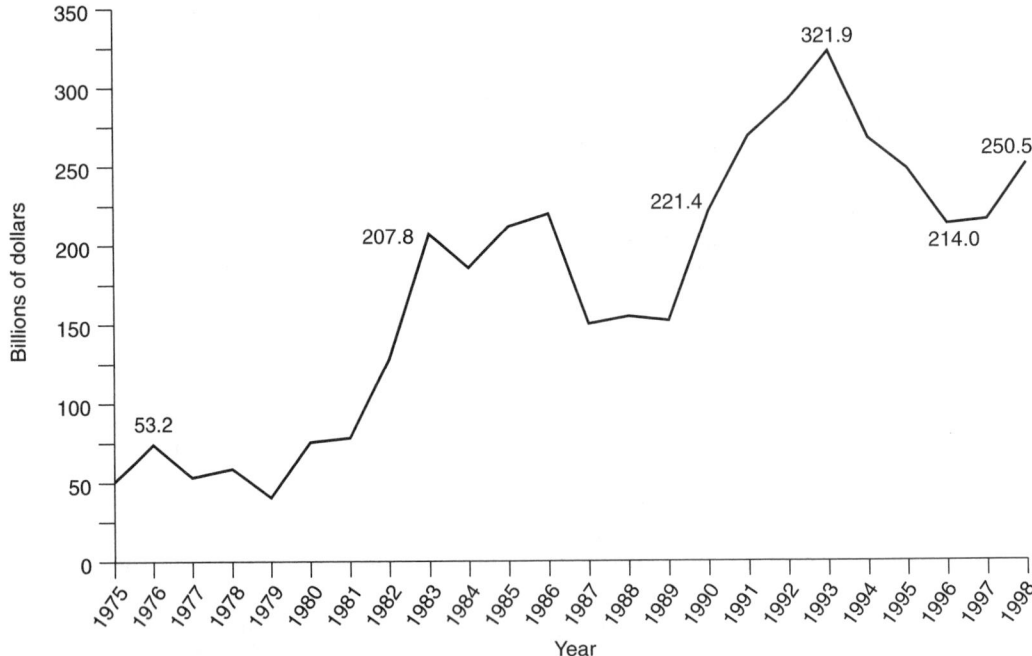

Figure 5–5 The budget deficit 1975–1998

Source: U.S. Office of Management and Budget.

or even eliminate the budget deficit. First, the government's need to finance such a large deficit requires it to borrow heavily from private investors. In 1987, the federal government borrowed only 20 percent of the total credit available for investment in the economy. In 1991, it accounted for some 60 percent of all U.S. credit. This huge demand for federal borrowing to finance the federal government deficit has the effect of soaking up savings that could otherwise be used to invest in private-sector plant and equipment. This investment would improve productivity (and therefore potential GDP) and long-term economic growth.

By way of documentation for this concern, the Federal Reserve Bank of New York released a study that quantified the effect of large deficits on the economy. The study estimated that by 1989, low private saving had cost the U.S. economy 15 percent of its capital stock and about 5 percent of its potential GDP. By the turn of the century, the accumulated loss could grow to 28 percent and 10 percent, respectively. These are sizable numbers, particularly when coupled with the expanding world demand for capital.

A second argument is that, because of the necessity to attract more money from the private sector to finance the large federal deficit, interest rates need to be higher than would otherwise be the case. Higher interest rates also act to reduce private long-term investment by making it more expensive. In support of this argument, even though inflation dropped to about 3.2 percent and short-term interest rates declined to about 3.5 percent in 1992, long-term interest rates had decreased only one percentage point from early 1991 to a level of 7.25 percent. Long-term rates did recede somewhat in 1993, but there was still a considerable spread between long-term and short-term rates. Some analysts argue that this spread results from long-term investors being concerned about the prospects of future inflation driven by continuing large federal deficits. They therefore still demand higher long-term interest rates to hedge this risk.

Third, the interest we need to pay annually on the federal debt (approaching $4 trillion in 1994) has reached about $200 billion per year. Aside from its affect on reducing funds available for other government priorities, this debt is an increasingly large burden to pass on to future generations. It is also true that while a number of years ago the argument would have been "not to worry" because "we owe it to ourselves," today, in fact, a substantial share (12 percent, or $467 billion) of the U.S. government debt is owed to foreigners. Unless the holders of these government securities reinvest their interest income in the United States or use it to purchase U.S. goods, the income has left our economy.

Another problem that worries many analysts is that if foreign holders of U.S. debt became reluctant to reinvest in U.S. securities when their obligations become due, the federal government would have to raise interest rates to attract the investment necessary to finance the debt. This could have a dampening effect on the economy at an inconvenient time.

All analysts do not agree on the importance of reducing the budget deficit, however, and some suggest that it really does not matter. Their argument goes something like this:[11]

1. A large share of the deficit in 1991–1992—some $70 billion—was needed to bail out the savings and loan industry during its crisis. This bailout did not affect consumer behavior because consumers never really thought they had lost the money they had invested in the savings and loan institutions.
2. The Joint Economic Committee of Congress estimated in 1993 that the 1991–1992 recession and the subsequent slow rate of growth in the economy were responsible for an increase of $100 to $110 billion in the deficit. Deficit *doves* argue that the economic recovery of 1994–1995 eliminated this effect, and we will eventually be able to grow our way out of the deficit.
3. The result, according to this argument, is that the deficit was actually only about $200 billion in 1993.
4. The low interest rates the nation enjoyed in the early 1990s should cut $16 to $24 billion from the deficit in future years.
5. Compared to some of our trading partners, the U.S. deficit is not so large in relation to GDP.

The result, this argument goes, is that we need not panic about reducing the size of the federal deficit. Instead, we should opt for a gradual reduction in the deficit over the next few years.

But without major changes in taxes or in entitlement programs such as Medicare-Medicaid and Social Security, the U.S. Office of Management and Budget (OMB) estimated in 1993 that the deficit could reach $600 billion by 2005 if there is no change in government programs or taxes (see Figure 5–6). As a percent of GDP, under this scenario, the deficit would drop from 3.9 percent of GDP in 1993 to 3.2 percent in 1996. It then would again gradually increase, reaching over 4 percent of GDP in 2002.

Of course one needs to recognize that these forecasts are no more than estimates based on a variety of assumptions about factors such as the rate of economic

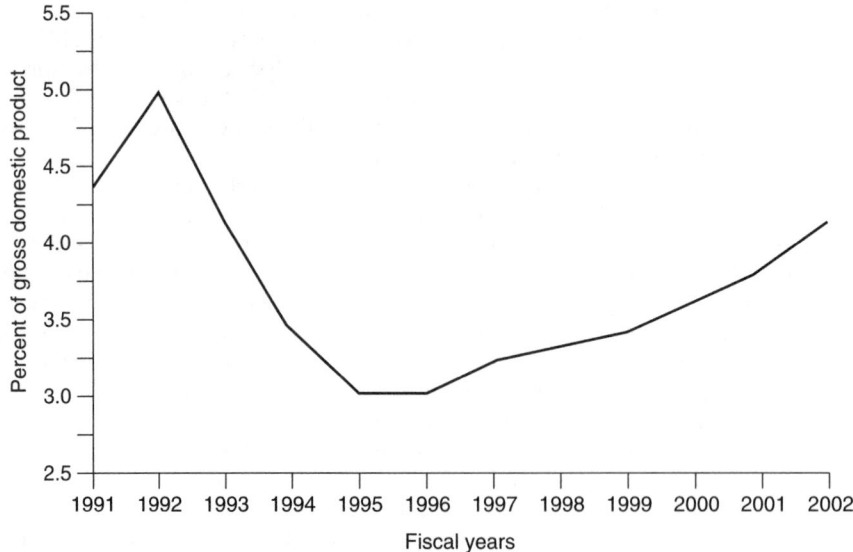

Figure 5–6 Long-term deficit projection[a] (as a percentage of GDP)

Assumes: Discretionary spending consistent with BEA through 1995, constant thereafter. Tax revenues and mandatory spending based on current law.

[a]Excludes Deposit Insurance and Desert Storm contributions.

Source: U.S. Office of Management and Budget.

growth in the nation. They are therefore really more useful for pointing out trends for policy analysis purposes than as actual forecasts of probable events.

But if one accepts the conclusions suggested by this scenario—namely, the need to take further action to reduce the federal budget deficit—then we need to ask what the options are for cutting the deficit. Some suggestions (none of them very good) and their approximate values in 1993 dollars are as follows:

1. The easy cuts have been made in national defense expenditures. Fortunately, the end of the Cold War has permitted significant reductions in defense without seriously impairing our national security. Defense expenditures in fiscal 1995 were about $264 billion. However, even a 30 percent cut over the succeeding five years would still free up only $90 billion for deficit reduction purposes. Although some policy makers argue for a 50 percent cut in defense, cuts of this magnitude seem unlikely at present. Even if such cuts were achieved, though, the savings would be only $140 billion.
2. Cutting out foreign aid would yield about $20 billion. The two major recipients of U.S. aid have been Egypt and Israel. We are now adding Russia and Eastern Europe to that list. Most responsible policy makers believe cuts in these programs would be untimely, unwise, and unlikely.
3. Increasing taxes on upper-income taxpayers could yield about $14 billion, some analysts say.
4. Cutting off entitlements (e.g., Social Security) to wealthy people could yield about $20+ billion.
5. An increase in general taxes would help, but is an unlikely possibility.
6. Enacting a national value-added tax (a form of broad-based sales tax) would be politically difficult and unlikely.

Figure 5–7 was constructed before the passage of President Clinton's first budget, but the amounts have not changed much. The figure shows federal spending, revenues, and deficits. It projects the budget to 1998, assuming no major program changes. Observe that in the future, the major dollars in the budget are going into the domestic programs such as Social Security and Medicare-Medicaid. These categories of the budget are regarded by many to be politically untouchable. If so, it will be very hard to cut the deficit in the years ahead.

During the 1992 presidential campaign, the two major party candidates, President George Bush and Governor Bill Clinton, both spoke about how they would deal with the budget deficit. Their proposals were as follows:

President Bush:

1. Allow taxpayers to indicate that up to 10 percent of their annual income tax payment should be used for deficit reduction. However, under the U.S. Constitution, such a designation can only be advisory to the Congress. If it had gone into effect, it would have saved $50 billion in 1993 and more in future years.
2. Place a rate of growth benefit cap on all government entitlement programs to force reductions of $293 billion over five years. The cap would have included Medicare-Medicaid, farm price supports, veterans' benefits, and other unspecified programs (not Social Security).

Governor Clinton:

1. Cut the deficit in half to $140 billion by 1996. Increase taxes on people earning over $175,000.

In fact, neither candidate proposed a viable strategy for cutting the deficit during the campaign. Independent estimates of the costs of the budget programs found that both were some $300 billion or more short of their deficit goal.

The Current Budget Situation.   The Clinton administration's major initiative to reduce the federal budget deficit in the summer of 1993 included increases in income taxes on the wealthy and gasoline taxes (four cents per gallon) on the rest of the taxpayers. The initiative also extended the percentage of Social Security payments subject to income taxation from 50 percent to 85 percent. Total

Figure 5–7   Federal spending, revenues, and deficits: FY 1992–1998 ($ in billions)

	Actual 1992	1993	1994	1995	1996	1997	1998
National Defense	302.6	292.1	277.7	272.8	265.2	249.3	252.8
International Affairs	19.2	21.9	21.3	21.8	21.3	21.4	21.4
Domestic Programs	214.2	239.7	251.1	262.3	273.2	283.3	293.1
Total Discretionary	536.0	553.7	550.1	556.9	559.7	554.0	567.3
Mandatory Programs	645.4	712.4	753.1	789.6	821.4	878.6	941.5
Net Interest	199.4	201.5	212.1	227.6	243.5	257.6	272.3
Total Outlays	1,380.8	1,467.6	1,515.3	1,574.1	1,624.6	1,690.2	1,781.1
Revenues	1,090.5	1,145.7	1,251.3	1,327.7	1,412.9	1,476.1	1,530.5
Deficit	−290.3	−321.9	−264.0	−246.4	−211.7	−214.1	−250.6
Memo:							
Deposit Insurance	2.6	2.8	7.5	−1.3	−13.2	−11.0	−7.4

Source: U.S. Office of Management and Budget.

taxes raised per year under this program were estimated at approximately $30 billion.

The budget cuts, assuming eventual congressional action, were estimated to average $30 billion per year (most in later years). It should be recognized, however, that the cuts are in fact only reductions in what spending levels would be without legislative changes, not cuts from current levels of expenditures. In other words, it was a reduction in the rate of increase, not the absolute level, of federal expenditures. The overall plan was to cut the deficit over five years by $500 billion from what it would have been without the tax and budget changes.

Thanks to lower interest rates and more rapid than expected economic growth, the fiscal 1994 budget deficit dipped to about $170 billion. But it was expected to reach $207 billion in fiscal 1995 and hover around the $180+ level until it again begins to increase later in the decade. Of course the 1995 Republican congressional proposals to cut government expenditures and reduce income taxes on the middle class lend a degree of uncertainty to the shape of the federal budget deficit as we approach the 21st century.

Long-Range Options.   Two process suggestions that were proposed during the 1992 campaign as possible ways of helping to alleviate the nation's budget problems are the following:

1. Enact a balanced budget amendment to the Constitution that would require the Congress to balance federal revenues and expenditures each year. Although there was support for this proposal, enthusiasm for the idea fell off, and the Senate failed to support a resolution on the issue in March 1994. The proposal, however, was resurrected in the Republican Contract with America in the 1994 congressional campaign, and was introduced in Congress when it convened in January 1995. A change in the Constitution is never politically easy to effectuate, and many are concerned that such an amendment would unduly limit the ability of the government to set priorities, to stabilize the economy in times of economic troubles, and to act in the case of national security or other budget emergencies.

   Another of the Contract process proposals designed to cut unnecessary federal spending—the line-item veto for the president—has much broader support and is more likely to actually have an effect on spending.

2. Set up a so-called blue ribbon commission with broad powers to reduce the budget deficit. However, this recommendation flies in the face of what is one of the principal constitutional responsibilities of Congress. It is only a remote possibility that Congress would agree to such a power-sharing arrangement. In short, such a plan would be hard to sell, and it would be hard to implement any recommendations that resulted from such an approach.

Karl O'Lessker, a scholar of the federal budget, suggests three propositions that emerge from a consideration of the political-economic problems associated with reducing the budget deficit:[12]

1. Nibbling around the edges—cutting a program here or there—while worth doing for other reasons will not have a significant impact on aggregate spending.
2. Only the biggest programs—national defense, Social Security, Medicare, net interest— offer any real opportunity for making substantial cuts in spending growth. But most of this growth is driven by demography, and real program cuts will not be easy.
3. The least-painful way to control spending is not to let it start in the first place—to resist new programs with an iron will. But even this, in some instances, may not make good policy sense.

As a result, O'Lessker argues that the only real options are to increase taxes or to impose caps on all mandatory entitlement programs and to retain the existing system of caps on discretionary programs. This same conclusion was reached by the bipartisan Commission on Entitlements, headed by Senators John Kerr and John C. Danforth, in their fall 1994 report.

Industrial Policy

Another debate affecting long-term growth concerns the direct role of the government in influencing the development of specific industries. This approach to economic development is known as industrial policy.

Briefly, industrial policy involves the government's identifying those domestic industries that it believes has or will have an important role in world trade and assisting in the development of those industries. This is done through the use of tax incentives, direct assistance, research support, or various other forms of subsidies. For instance, in the fall of 1993, President Clinton announced that the U.S. government was entering a joint effort with General Motors, Ford, and Chrysler to develop a state-of-the-art, low-energy-using automobile for the next century. In essence, if the United States actually adopts this public policy approach, government would play a much more active role in industrial planning than at any time in our history.

Industrial policy is also periodically linked with other public policy issues facing the country. For example, some observers have argued that we need an urban industrial policy to restore the economies of our old urban centers. Others argue for an industrial policy to counter the effects of downsizing the defense industry or to compensate for jobs anticipated to be lost with the expansion of free trade policies such as the North American Free Trade Agreement (NAFTA) and the General Agreement on Tariffs and Trade (GATT).

Critics believe that industrial policy will not work in the United States because it is impossible to pick the winners and losers in industrial competition. Even if correct choices could be made, they argue that it would be against U.S. tradition, would waste valuable public resources, and would have more undesirable long-term effects for the country than positive benefits. As might be expected, industrial policy traditionally has been more supported by the Democratic party, while Republicans have been opposed to using this type of intervention in the market system.

Another long-term economic policy debate concerns what government can do in an indirect way to encourage business investment and, therefore, improve productivity. The Republican party has been trying for several years to convince Congress to enact a cut in the tax on capital gains (the gain achieved when a business or individual sells an asset that has appreciated in value). President Bush made this proposal a key component of his 1992 re-election campaign. He argued that by reducing the tax on such capital gains, long-term investments would become more profitable and therefore lead to the kind of investment expansion that the country needs to improve productivity and become more competitive in world markets. An expansion in business investment would also, he suggested, jump-start the economy and return it to a viable, long-term growth path.

Governor Clinton did not support a general cut in the capital gains tax but did propose a capital gains cut for small businesses. He was also in favor of tax credits for some research and development expenditures, and he included a $10 billion per year investment tax credit in his suggested economic program. In 1995 the Republican Congress reintroduced the idea of cutting the tax on capital gains from its current level of 28 percent to 21 percent.

SUMMARY

In summary, the long-term growth objectives of our economy require a focus on increasing our capacity for growth. This means expanding potential GDP. We can do this by (1) increasing the size of our labor force or (2) increasing productivity (output per labor-hour) or both. Policy debates about the long-term growth of our economy concern how these two changes will be carried out. Ongoing issues in the debate include:

1. What to do about the federal deficit, which many believe is doing serious damage to the long-term growth objectives of the U.S. economy.
2. How active the government should be in industrial planning in our society.
3. Which tax and other incentives should be used to encourage more savings and business investment.

Short-Term Economic Stabilization

The second major objective of the nation's economic policy is to reduce short-term economic instability. So far we have discussed only increasing our potential GDP to expand the opportunity for long-term growth. But what about the nation's ability to meet its potential GDP and to maintain short-term economic stability?

As we pointed out earlier in this chapter, the forces that produce fluctuations are found in the relationship between production, income, and spending. Simply stated, economic instability occurs because business and consumer purchases are too low to provide a market for potential output—a certain level of income does not guarantee an equal level of spending.

In the United States, the years 1872, 1882, 1893, 1907, 1920, and 1929 all marked the beginning of a major downturn in production and employment in the nation. There have also been numerous smaller recessions. In all of these years actual GDP was substantially below potential GDP. As we discuss in Chapter 15, the result of this disparity during the Great Depression of the 1930s was that the rate of unemployment exceeded 15 percent each year from 1930 to 1939. Short-term instability was becoming a long-term trend, a very dangerous situation to say the least. While this near collapse of the economic system has not been repeated, we have still had several recessions since the end of World War II, the most recent being 1980, when unemployment rose to 11 percent, and in 1991–1992, when the rate of unemployment in the country reached more than 7.5 percent.

The questions arise, then, why has actual GDP differed from potential GDP at various times in our history, and what can public policy do to bring them more closely together? The reader will have to wait for a course in macroeconomics to get a thorough understanding of this phenomenon, but let us explore a shorthand version.

First, as described earlier, even though output generates an equal amount of income (GDP = GDI), that does not necessarily mean that the income will guarantee an equal amount of *spending:* demand, not income, determines production.

Demand is what drives actual GDP. A number of things can cause demand to be less than would be expected by a certain level of income, for example:

1. Reductions in business spending in the form of:

    -   inventory cutbacks because of concern about future demand or mistakes resulting in overproduction,
    -   reduced investments for a variety of reasons (e.g., taxes, high interest rates, uncertainty about economic or political situations, or international shocks).

2. Cutbacks in demand for residential housing resulting from:

    -   demographic changes,
    -   high interest rates or a reduced supply of money in the economy (for a variety of reasons).

3. Reduced government purchases because of:

    -   a political decision to retire debt,
    -   the end of the cold war,
    -   a desire to balance the governmental budget after a period of deficit financing.

4. Consumer purchasing cutbacks that are a result of:

    -   a loss of confidence in the economy, resulting in decisions to save more and retire personal debt,
    -   demographic changes that affect consumer-purchasing requirements,
    -   tax increases that are not counterbalanced by more government expenditures,
    -   reduced consumer-expendable income due to external factors (e.g., much higher prices of imported oil).

If such cutbacks in demand do occur and actual GDP is significantly lower than potential GDP, what can government do to increase demand in the economy and bring actual output back in line with potential?

This is where fiscal and monetary policy come in. They are much less complicated than they may appear at first blush.

Fiscal Policy. The term *fiscal policy* refers to the tax and spending actions of government. Government can stimulate demand, for example, if it is sluggish and if actual GDP is below potential GDP. It can do this by cutting taxes, thereby putting more spendable money in the hands of consumers and businesses. If government does not change its own spending in reaction to the lower taxes, then overall spending in the economy will increase, thereby moving actual GDP toward potential GDP and beginning to reduce unemployment.

Government can also increase demand by borrowing and increasing its own spending. The result is similar to a tax cut. The expansion of government expenditures puts more money in the hands of consumers and businesses, which they can use to expand their own demand for goods and services. This was President Franklin Roosevelt's strategy to pull the country out of the 1930s Depression. President Clinton also proposed new expenditures for public infrastructure early in his term as part of his economic recovery program. However, the plan was not successful in gaining the support of the Congress.

If actual GDP and potential GDP are very close and the federal government is concerned about the possibility of inflation, it can also reduce demand by increasing taxes without increasing spending or by reducing spending without cutting taxes.

Monetary Policy.   The term *monetary policy* refers to the federal government's management of money and debt. The government's actions are designed to change the level of interest rates and the amount of money in circulation in the economy for both stabilization and long-term growth purposes.[13] If rates are cut and the money supply is increased, more new investments become cheaper, and expanded investment expenditures will eventually occur on the part of businesses and consumers. If rates are increased and the money supply is reduced, businesses and consumers will cut back on expenditures.

Monetary policy is controlled in the federal government by the Federal Reserve System (FRS). The seven-member Federal Reserve Board (FRB; usually referred to as the Fed) is the decision-making body of the system. It is composed of rotating representatives of the 12 banks that make up the system (the New York Federal Reserve Bank has a permanent seat) and of presidential appointments. The appointees are chosen (with Senate confirmation) for 14-year terms, with the chairman (currently Alan Greenspan) being appointed for a 4-year term. The most recent policy directive to the Federal Reserve Board for the conduct of monetary policy is contained in the Humphrey-Hawkins Act of 1978. The act requires the Fed to "maintain long-run growth of the monetary and credit aggregates commensurate with the economy's long-run potential to increase production, so as to promote effectively the goals of maximum employment, stable prices, and moderate long-term interest rates."

The Fed conducts monetary policy through the following major tools to influence the level of interest rates and the amount of money in the economic system:

1. The reserve requirements commercial banks must maintain as a percentage of their outstanding loans are set by the Fed. This affects the amount of credit available in the economy and, hence, the level of business and consumer expenditures.
2. The Fed fixes the maximum interest rates that banks can pay on savings deposits. These rates have an effect on the willingness of individuals to save or spend money.
3. The Fed also controls the level of the discount rate, the interest rate at which banks can borrow short-term money from the FRS, and it sets the federal funds rate—the rate that commercial banks pay when they borrow overnight. These changes in turn affect the level of interest rates and the amount of money available for commercial bank loans to consumers and businesses. In recent years, when there are reports that the Fed has changed interest rates, it is the federal funds rate that is usually cited.
4. A major power possessed by the Fed is its ability to control the size of the nation's money supply by its open-market operations. The FRS maintains very large amounts of U.S. government securities in its own portfolio. The Fed conducts open-market operations by buying and selling these U.S. government securities on the open market. When it buys securities, it puts new money into circulation in the economy; when it sells U.S. government securities, it takes money out of circulation. This in turn expands or contracts bank reserves and affects the amount of money that banks have to lend.

An increase in the money supply decreases interest rates, and a decrease in the money supply increases interest rates. This is a simple function of the supply and demand for money (an interest rate is the price of borrowing money). Open-market operations, therefore, also have an effect on investment through their impact on interest rates.

Federal Reserve Policy Issues.   Federal Reserve Board members may not be removed over policy disagreements. They are therefore virtually independent in their policy actions, and the Fed is arguably the most powerful organization in the

U.S. economic policy-making system. One of the continuing debates about monetary policy in the United States has to do with whether the Fed should remain independent or be brought more closely under the political control of the White House or the Congress.

In 1993, House Banking Committee Chairman Henry G. Gonzalez introduced a bill in Congress that would require the 12 Federal Reserve regional bank presidents to be selected by the president, rather than by local banks' boards of directors. The bill would also force more frequent public release of Fed policy actions and provide greater congressional oversight of the Fed's budget.

Alan Greenspan, chairman of the Federal Reserve Board, rejected the move to make the Fed more politically accountable, calling the efforts "assaults" that could lead to economic instability and recession.[14] He went on to say that the current structure has stood the test of time in giving the country a central bank that can pursue anti-inflationary policies that might cause temporary unemployment without fear of political interference. At this writing the matter remains unresolved, but a Greenspan *win* on the issue looks likely.

Other critics of the Fed worry about its penchant for what they regard as attempts to fine-tune the economy through the use of interest rate changes. The Nobel Prize-winning economist Milton Friedman, for example, criticized the Fed for its focus on the federal funds rate:

> Established in 1914, the Fed presided over a more than doubling of the price level during World War I; generated a major contraction from 1920 to 1921; converted a garden-variety recession in 1929–1930 into a catastrophic depression; produced a serious recession in 1937–1938, when the economy was recovering from the depression; presided again over a more than doubling of the price level during World War II; and produced a disastrous cumulative inflation during the 1970's whose consequences we are still living with. Hardly a record justifying the continued use of the federal funds rate as the Fed's principal operating instrument. Yet pegging the Federal Funds rate is strictly peripheral to the Fed's real task, which is to ensure that the quantity of money behaves in such a way as to produce a stable price level.[15]

Maintaining Price Stability

The third major objective of our economic policy is to maintain reasonable price stability. Price inflation can be measured in several ways. The most useful measures for economic analysis are:

- The consumer price index (CPI), which measures the price of a fixed market basket of goods and services in seven major categories purchased by consumers.
- The wholesale price index (WPI), which measures the average prices charged by wholesalers to their retail customers.
- The producers' price index (PPI), which measures average changes in selling pries received by domestic producers of goods.
- The implicit GDP price deflator, which measures average price changes for all goods and services produced in the United States, including investment goods and goods produced for export.

The United States, like most other countries, has experienced periods of severe inflation during its history. Inflation can be as destabilizing to an economy (and a government) as high levels of unemployment. Rapid inflation causes an arbitrary redistribution of wealth between borrowers and lenders; hurts those living on fixed incomes; and discourages savings and investment by creating uncertainty about future prices, thus causing inefficiencies in the distribution of resources and harming productivity and economic growth. Hyperinflation can also be politically destabilizing, as was the case with Germany in the 1930s and several other countries after World War II.

Price inflation can occur in an economy for several reasons. First, actual GDP can crowd potential GDP when the economy reaches capacity production in both physical and human resources. This can be caused by low interest rates and a substantial increase in the money supply in the face of high consumer and business demand; by tax cuts, resulting in more spendable income, during a period of high demand; or by an expansion in government spending without corresponding tax increases, during a period of high demand and full employment of resources (this occurred in the United States during the Vietnam War). Since the economy cannot physically produce more than its potential, prices simply rise to reflect the fact that consumer and business demand for goods and services is greater than the supply.

External shocks can also stimulate the short-term rate of inflation. For example, in 1974 the world economy was strained by an oil embargo by Middle Eastern oil producers. This sudden cutoff in the supply of imported oil drove up U.S. prices for oil. These price increases then filtered through the economy raising the prices of other commodities and services. The same thing can happen when the agricultural sector suffers a poor harvest and agricultural prices increase to reflect the change in the relationship between supply and demand.

Fluctuations in the international value of a nation's currency can stimulate changes in its rate of inflation. The reason is that the country, particularly if it relies heavily on imported goods, will need to pay more for those goods if their currency loses value vis-à-vis other currencies. This in turn will lead to increases in the prices of many domestic goods. The smaller the nation, the more vulnerable it is to such inflation-causing currency value swings. Mexico experienced this situation in 1995 when the peso was devalued by almost one-third.

Inflation can become embedded in an economy through a wage-price spiral. This type of situation can result from labor contracts that link wages and salaries to increasing prices but do not allow them to decrease when prices decline. Increasing wages then result in higher demand for goods and services, and if the economy is operating near its potential or capacity production level, prices simply increase to reflect the increased demand and to ration the available goods and services to the highest bidder. Once a wage-price spiral begins, it is very hard to stop. This was the situation the United States faced in the late 1970s, and it took a severe recession in 1982, with high unemployment, to end the spiral. During that period the nation suffered from stagflation—both high inflation and high unemployment.

There is now fairly well documented evidence that the primary culprit in instigating and sustaining inflation is a too-rapid rate of growth in the money supply (quite often induced by government deficits), that is, a rate of money growth inconsistent with the rate of growth in the capacity or potential of the economy. In fact, the rise in inflation in this country from the mid-1960s through 1980 was associated with an upward drift in the rate of growth in the money supply.[16] The annual average rate of growth in the money supply more than doubled from 3.5 percent per year during the five-year period 1961–1965 to 8.6 percent in the five years ending in 1980. Inflation soared to double digits in the late 1970s.

In October 1979, the Federal Reserve Board reversed its policy. The trend rate in the money supply fell from 8.4 percent in late 1979 to 6.3 percent in 1982. The rate of inflation fell to less than half of the 1980 rate, and by 1983 it had been reduced to less than one-fourth the 1980 rate. This monetary policy change set the stage for an almost unparalleled term of expansion in the rate of economic growth in the nation for the balance of the 1980s. The low interest rate policy continued into early 1994, before the Fed made its move to raise interest rates in response to its perception that the economy was expanding so rapidly that inflation might be rekindled. Thus, the rate increase was in the category of a pre-emptive strike. Whether it was the right move remains to be seen. One of its effects was a tumble in both the bond and stock markets. By the summer of 1995, however, both markets had recovered and the stock market set new record highs.

Assessing Economic Performance

One of the most difficult economic policy tasks that faces U.S. government leaders is trying to assess what is actually going on in the economy and using this information to attempt to determine the economic outlook for both the short and long term. Without a reasonably accurate assessment of current and future economic performance, policy officials are in the dark with regard to the policy actions that need to be taken.

The situation faced by the president's economic advisors and the Federal Reserve Board shortly after President Clinton assumed office in January 1993 is a case in point. Many observers would agree that the beginning of the end of the economic expansion of the 1980s came in the 12-month period ending in the summer of 1990. At this time several factors came into play. The expansion, already the longest period of uninterrupted growth since the end of World War II, began to run out of steam. In addition, the Fed, in response to a concern about the growing federal deficit and the possibility of accelerating inflation, cut the rate of growth in the money supply.

The charts in Figures 5–8, 5–9, 5–10, 5–11, 5–12, and 5–13 tell the story of the results. The country entered a recession in the second half of 1990 that continued through the 1st quarter of 1991 and continued sluggish growth the rest of the year. The recession was successful in heading off a return to inflationary times. However, instead of the economy's rebounding at a more rapid rate of growth when the recession ended, as it has done many times, growth continued to be slow through the first half of 1992. The timing could not have been worse for the re-election campaign of President Bush in 1992 (see Figure 5–14).

When President Clinton took office in January 1993, there was still concern that steps needed to be taken to stimulate the economy. Unfortunately (or fortunately as it turned out), the federal government did not have many opportunities to use fiscal policy to expand consumer and business demand. The federal budget deficit was already too high to allow more federal expenditures, and tax cuts also seemed inadvisable given the budgetary situation. The fiscal policy constraints were essentially the reason for Congress's negative reaction to President Clinton's proposed economic stimulus package shortly after he took office. The president's economic summit that followed was designed to reduce the budget deficit, in the hope that long-term interest rates would come down and thereby increase demand in the economy. (The resulting tax and budget changes were discussed in this chapter's section on the budget deficit).

(Text continues on page 123)

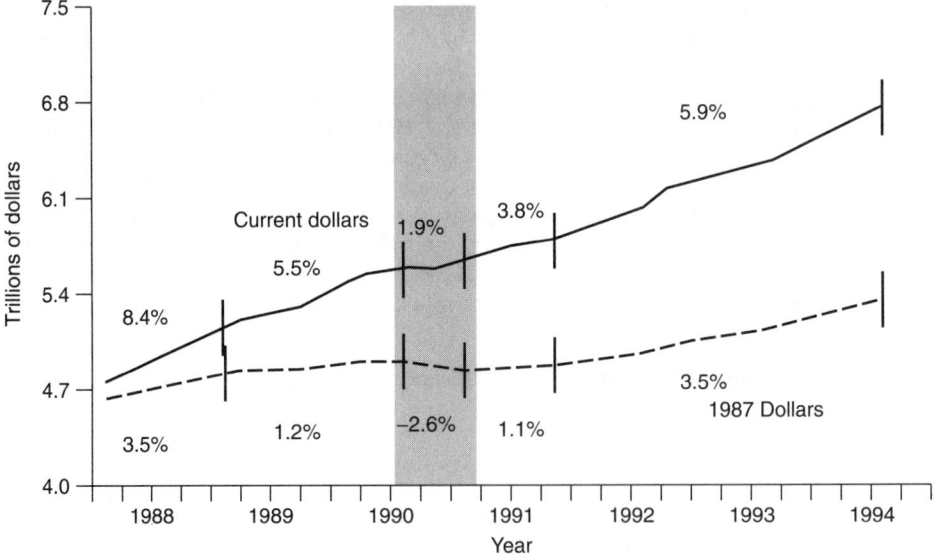

Figure 5–8 Gross Domestic Product (seasonally adjusted)

Shaded area represents a period of business recession. Percentages are annual rates of change for periods indicated.

Prepared by Federal Reserve Bank of St. Louis.

Figure 5–9 Retail sales (seasonally adjusted)

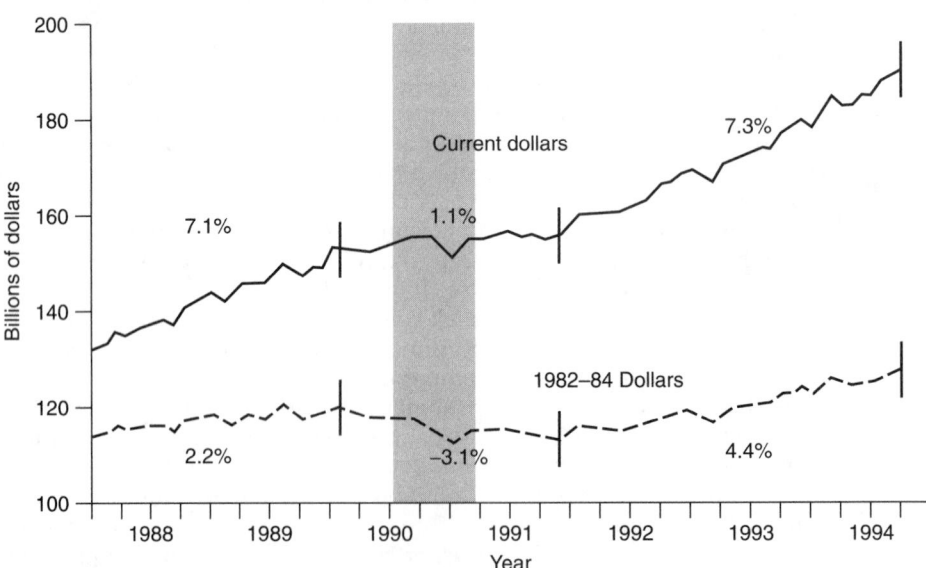

Shaded area represents a period of business recession. The CPI is used to deflate retail sales data. Percentages are annual rates of change for periods indicated.

Prepared by Federal Reserve Bank of St. Louis.

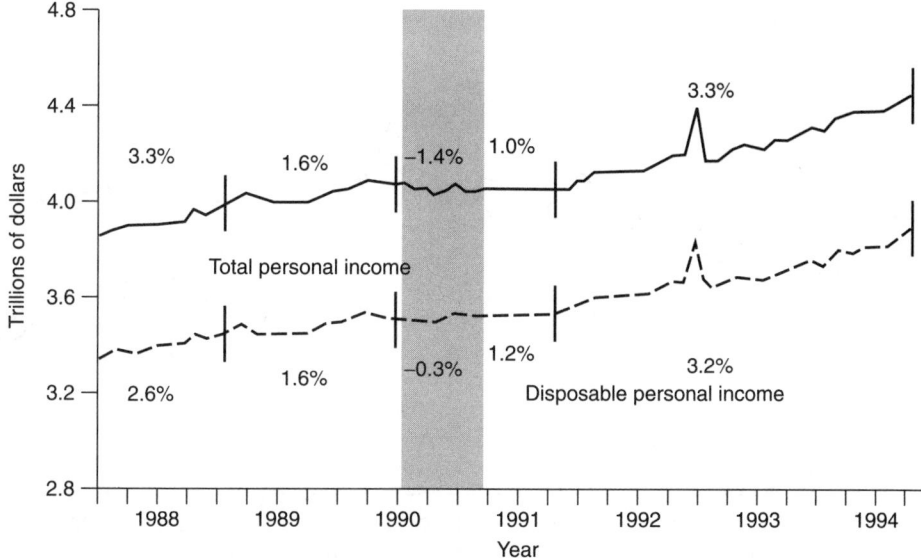

Figure 5–10   Personal income in 1987 dollars (seasonally adjusted)

The personal consumption expenditures deflator is used to calculate real personal income. Shaded area represents a period of business recession. Percentages are annual rates of change for periods indicated.

Prepared by Federal Reserve Bank of St. Louis.

Figure 5–11   Civilian employment and unemployment rate (seasonally adjusted)

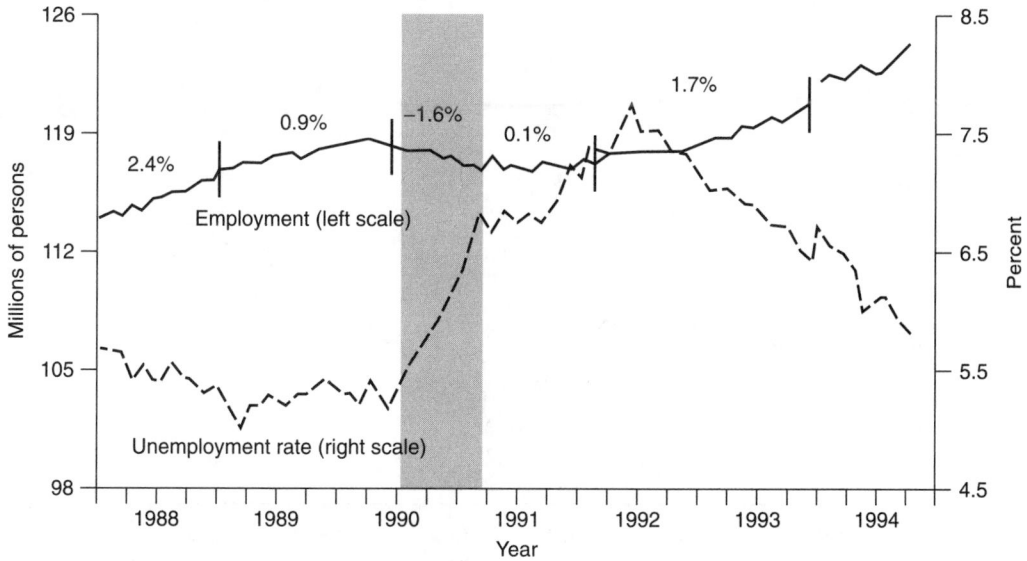

Shaded area represents a period of business recession. Percentages are annual rates of change for periods indicated. January 1994 figures reflect revised data collection procedures and are not directly comparable with previous data.

Prepared by Federal Reserve Bank of St. Louis.

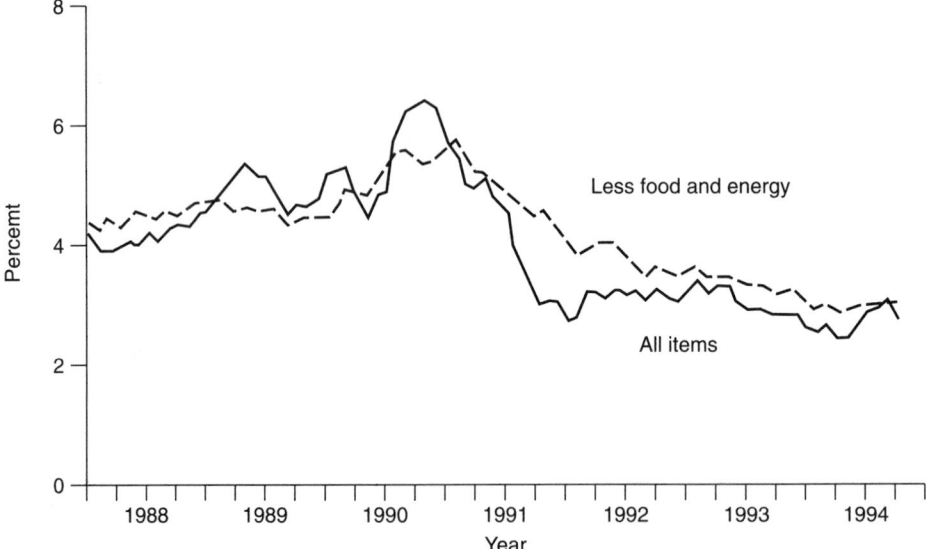

Figure 5–12 Consumer price index—All urban consumers (percent change from previous year, seasonally adjusted)

Prepared by Federal Reserve Bank of St. Louis.

Figure 5–13 Industrial production (seasonally adjusted)

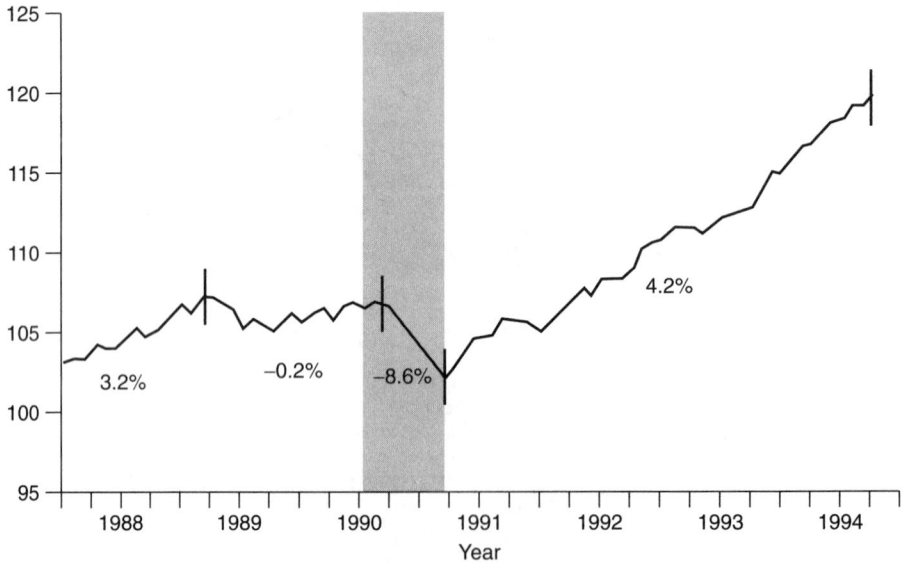

Shaded area represents a period of business recession. Percentages are annual rates of change for periods indicated.

Prepared by Federal Reserve Bank of St. Louis

TALL IN THE SADDLE

Figure 5–14

Source: Chicago Tribune. Reprinted by permission: Tribune Media Services.

The Fed continued easing interest rates and increasing the money supply to try to stimulate demand throughout 1993. In early 1993, short-term rates were seven percentage points below their peak in 1989, but although there were increasing signs that the economy was reacting positively to the monetary stimulus, the initial response was small. Then industrial production began to expand in the second quarter of 1993. The rate of unemployment dropped to less than 7 percent for the first time since the recession began, and short- and long-term interest rates were at their lowest levels in over 20 years. GDP grew more than 7 percent in the fourth quarter of 1993. In February 1994, the Fed reversed its course and began increasing interest rates again to try to slow down the rate of growth in the economy. It increased rates five more times that year, and at year end, rates were up by 2.5 percentage points.

GDP expanded at an annual rate of about 3.5 percent for all of 1994, and by the end of the year the rate of unemployment had dipped to 5.4 percent, its lowest level since 1990. Since the Fed had apparently adopted a *natural* rate of unemployment of 6.25 percent as the full-employment benchmark, more rate hikes were predicted as the chairman, Alan Greenspan, and his colleagues struggled to keep the expansion under control and noninflationary.

The 1992–1994 situation exemplifies the tight rope the Fed tries to walk as it uses the rough tools of monetary policy to meet its statutory responsibilities. And of course its policies continue to generate criticism from those who believe the Fed is over-reacting to a nonexistent inflation bogeyman and unnecessarily slowing down the economy. For purposes of steady, long-term growth that would permit more rational planning by both businesses and households, one can only hope that the Fed is eventually able to develop a monetary policy strategy that is more consistent and excludes the kind of nasty surprises that investors and home buyers have experienced over the past several years.

Long-Term Policy Issues

As the nation enters the last presidential term of this century, a number of unresolved economic policy issues vie for attention by the Congress and the president. In no particular order of priority, they seem to us to include the following:

1. The United States continues to generate less savings than required for investments in a healthy long-term economy. During the period of 1947–1973, U.S. net national savings averaged 8.5 percent of national income per year. For the next six years they averaged 6.9 percent. But since 1986 the yearly savings average has been 3 percent or less. This is by far the lowest savings rate of any industrial power. Capital gains tax changes initiated by the Republican Congress in the second half of the Clinton administration and the proposals by the president to allow new deductions for individual retirement annuities (IRAs) were designed to offer more personal and business savings incentives and are a step in the right direction.

    But as we discussed earlier in this chapter, the total amount of savings available for investment in the economy is equal to private savings plus the government's budget surplus or minus the government deficit. Therefore it is obvious that future national savings are also threatened by the looming increase in the federal deficit as the baby boom generation approaches retirement age and begins to make significant demands on government expenditures for entitlements. Barring some change, our present method of deficit financing trades social programs for economic growth—an outcome not even in the interests of people whose incomes are at the lowest level.

2. The first two years of the Clinton administration saw major strides in the world economy. Receiving bipartisan support in the Congress, President Clinton led enactment of the North American Free Trade Agreement (NAFTA) and the ratification of the agreements of the Uruguay round of the General Agreement on Tariffs and Trade (GATT). Both sets of treaties offer major market opportunities for American business and industry and need to be capitalized on by both our public and private sectors if the United States is to compete effectively in the newly opened world economy. Another challenge for the future will be extending the NAFTA to other nations in Latin America and the Caribbean Region as quickly as their economies are ready. The first steps in this direction were taken when President Clinton hosted a meeting of Latin American leaders in Miami in November 1994, and all committed to move in the direction of freer trade by early in the next century. We discuss the topic of international trade in more detail in Chapter 5.

3. The restructuring of many large U.S. corporations that was well underway in 1993 and 1994 has caused both blue- and white-collar unemployment and anxiety among the nation's workforce. These fundamental structural changes are meant to improve productivity and the international competitiveness of the companies and should have positive long-term results. Furthermore, as market position and profitability improve, new opportunities for skilled workers should expand. However, looking to the long-term benefit is difficult for those caught in the restructuring process, and one is inclined to hope that American companies would be competent enough to practice gradual pruning as a means of keeping their cost structures competitive, rather than undergoing the kind of traumatic restructuring we have seen in recent years.

    These structural changes in American industry are also coming at a time when the U.S. defense industry is being reduced significantly as a result of the end of the Cold War. As a report of the Council of Great Lakes Governors suggested: "The year 1993 marked a significant year of transition. No longer can national security dominate federal spending priorities, nor can defense spending artificially bolster industries concentrated in the Sunbelt on both coasts. New approaches must create an environment where U.S. corporations can meet the test of international competition and move to high performance."[17] The policy problem for government is to help ease the transition from defense to civilian-related employment for the communities and the thousands of individuals caught in this transition. This challenge has yet to be adequately met.

In an article in the *Atlantic Monthly* in 1991, Robert Reich, later secretary of labor under President Clinton, argued for a shift in government priorities that would address these kinds of productivity concerns and make major government investments in both public infrastructure and in human capital.[18] Reich argued: "Herein the new logic of economic nationalism: the skills and insights of a nation's work force, and the quality of its transportation and communications links to the world (its infrastructure), are what make it unique, and uniquely attractive, in the new world economy. Increasingly, educated brainpower—along with roads, airports, computers, and fiber-optic cables connecting it up—determines a nation's standard of living." His message then to the politicians: "Stop fighting over how much money government is taking from the wealthy and redistributing to everyone else. Start worrying about the capacity of Americans to add value to the emerging world economy."[19]

Whether or not one agrees totally with Reich's prescription, it is apparent that the American economy is not making full use of its available human capital, and the only solution on the horizon that seems capable of making a difference is the type of large-scale investment in education and training (and perhaps physical capital as well) that will begin to allow the nation to compete with the other industrial powers in the high tech world of the 21st century. This investment in education seems to be the only way to bring down the high level of structural unemployment that begins to strain our productive capacity at a level of unemployment too high to solve many of our social problems. In addition, if the United States is to take advantage of the more than $100-billion-per-year GDP increase forecasters expect from passage of the GATT, we will need an overall increase in the skill levels of our labor force.

4. A related problem of increasing concern to many is the nation's growing gap in the distribution of income among income classes. The Census Bureau's most recent statistics reveal the widest gap between the rich and the poor since they began to keep these statistics in 1947. The share of the nation's income received by the richest 5 percent of American families rose from 18.6 percent in 1977 to 24.5 percent in 1990, while the share of the poorest 20 percent fell from 5.7 percent to 4.3 percent. In real terms, wages at the bottom of the distribution fell, while wages at the top rose.[20]

Some of the reasons blamed for this situation, besides the Reagan administration's tax and social program changes in the 1980s, include the decline in the number of well-paying, low-skill jobs in today's economy, the growth in the number of single-parent families, and the increase in the number of low-skilled immigrants, particularly in the south and southwest regions of the country. It is unlikely that the middle-class tax cuts initiated in the second half of the Clinton administration will have much, if any, affect on this income disparity. In addition to the inequity and the fertile ground for social instability this situation creates for the country, it also results in a very real reduction in our productivity and rate of economic growth.

SUMMARY

This chapter has surveyed the major economic policy issues facing our national government and has discussed the institutions and mechanisms available for policy action. We reviewed the evolution of the federal government's involvement in economic policy, noting that in the early days of the Republic the role of the government was quite limited. The first major expansion of the federal government's role in the economy came in the mid-nineteenth century following the end of the Civil

War. This expanded role included both promoting the economic development of the nation and developing a regulatory function and instruments to prevent the abuses of unbridled economic power.

In the 1930s, with the onset of the Great Depression, President Roosevelt moved the involvement of the government in the economic and social life of the nation to a new level. Traditions and patterns initiated by FDR during that period continue to influence U.S. economic policy as we head toward the 21st century.

The chapter also reviewed the philosophical basis for the current view of the role of government in our society and described its actualization into the following primary economic policy goals of:

1. Creating and enforcing a legal framework for the conduct of commerce.

2. Supplying those social goods to our citizens that the private sector is either unable or unwilling to supply.
3. Ensuring equity in the distribution of income in our society.
4. Promoting price stability, acceptable levels of employment, and the maximum possible rate of long-term economic growth.

We then explained the national income-accounting system that is used to assess the performance of the economy, and we reviewed how economic problems occur. Finally, we examined the fiscal and monetary tools at the disposal of the government to address these problems and reflected on the economic status of the nation as we move toward the last half of the 1990s. Many of the long-term issues raised at the conclusion of the chapter are dealt with under other headings in this book. Economic policy does not operate in a vacuum, but is inevitably integrated with the social, educational, cultural, and physical components of our society.

DISCUSSION QUESTIONS

1. Discuss the minimum economic functions that must be performed by the government and why this is the case.
2. Discuss the purpose and tools of monetary and fiscal policy. In what circumstances is one approach likely to be preferred over another?
3. Why do modern economies experience periods of economic fluctuation and instability? What are the principle factors that can cause aggregate demand to be less than would be expected given a certain level of income?
4. How can we determine the health of the economy at any particular point in time? What are the principle factors inhibiting the long-term growth of the U.S. economy?
5. Why is the Federal Reserve System under attack by some members of Congress? Are the criticisms of the Fed justified?

SUGGESTED READINGS

The Economic Report of the President, Council of Economic Advisors, U.S. Government Printing Office, Washington D.C., (published every year).

Each of the Regional Banks in the Federal Reserve System publishes a monthly journal. These are often outstanding sources of information on both current and theoretical matters about economic stabilization and growth.

Richard T. Frayen, *Macroeconomics, Theories, and Policies*, Macmillan, New York, 1990.

Frederic S. Miskin, *Money, Banking, and Financial Markets*, Scott Foresman, Glenview, IL 1989.

NOTES

1. Adam Smith, *The Wealth of Nations* (New York: P.F. Collier & Son, 1905).
2. Smith, 1905, book 4, chap. 9.
3. A favorite slogan of former president Ronald Reagan.
4. David L. Weimer and Aidan R. Vining, *Policy Analysis: Concepts and Practice* (Englewood Cliffs, N.J.: Prentice Hall, 1992), 41.
5. Richard Musgrave, *The Theory of Public Finance: A Study in Public Economy* (New York: McGraw-Hill, 1959), 6–28.
6. For an excellent, more detailed explanation of the concept and measurement of full employment potential GDP, see Charles Schultze, *National Income Analysis* (Englewood Cliffs, N.J.: Prentice Hall, 1971).
7. Economist Stuart Weiner, of the Federal Reserve Bank of Kansas City, calculated the natural rate of unemployment at 6.25 percent in 1993; the Congressional Budget Office and the president's Council of Economic Advisors both estimated it to be 5.5 percent.
8. John Tatom, "Has Potential Economic Growth Declined?" in *National Economic Trends* (St. Louis: Federal Reserve Bank of St. Louis, September 1994).
9. For more detail on labor-force projections, see *Work Force 2000* (report prepared by the Hudson Institute [Indianapolis, Ind.] for the U.S. Department of Labor, 1988).
10. Schultze, 1971, 115.
11. For example, see Robert Kuttner, "Don't Worry So Much About The Budget Deficit," *Business Week*, 6 July 1992, 18.
12. Karl O'Lessker, "Sources of Growth in Federal Spending," *Public Budget and Finance*, 1, no. 4 (winter 1993).
13. Several definitions of money supply are used by economists. They differ in terms of what is included in the particular definition. For instance, one definition, M-1, includes currency in circulation plus demand deposits (checking accounts). M-2 includes M-1 plus personal savings deposits.
14. Congressional testimony by Federal Reserve Chairman Alan Greenspan, October 1993.
15. Milton Friedman, "End the Fed's Fine-tuning," *Wall Street Journal*, 15 September 1993, p. 22. The federal funds rate is the interest rate banks pay to each other for overnight borrowings.
16. See *Economic Report of the President* (Washington D.C.: U.S. Government Printing Office, 1986).
17. "Rebuilding America: Lessons From the Heartland" (H. John Heinz III School of Public Policy; Pittsburgh, Pa.: Carnegie Mellon University, 1992).
18. Robert B. Reich, "The Real Economy," *Atlantic Monthly*, February, 1991.
19. Reich, 1991, 52.
20. *Economic Report of the President* (Washington, D.C.: U.S. Government Printing Office, 1994), 25.

6

International Economic Policy

As we approach the end of the 20th century, it is clear that the international playing field on which the United States has operated for much of the post-World War II period has undergone enormous changes. For almost 40 years following the end of the war, the United States had the most powerful economy in the world, had few viable competitors in most industries, and was able to dictate the rules and prosper from this position. Today the U.S. economy is completely and irretrievably involved in a worldwide economy in which we are no longer always the major player; indeed, in many areas we find ourselves losing out to the competition. If we are to continue to improve the well-being of our citizens and lay the groundwork for the prosperity of the next generation, we must adjust to this new worldwide economic reality and become better than (or at least as good as) our international competitors at playing the game. It is therefore particularly important that both the U.S. public and our policy leaders begin to understand the realities of the international economic environment, support those policies that will establish the framework for our future prosperity, and eliminate outdated and mistaken views of economic cause and effect.

The role of international trade in the world economy has grown steadily since the 17th century. Between 1965 and 1990, *real* (actual, adjusted for inflation) merchandise exports grew by 439 percent, while world production grew only 136 percent. World trade, as a percentage of world gross domestic product, grew from 27 percent in 1970 to 40 percent in 1992.[1]

In the United States, merchandise exports during the same period grew from $92.1 billion to an annual rate of $375.3 billion by the end of the fourth quarter of 1990—an increase of 307 percent. Merchandise imports into the United States rose from $86.5 billion in 1965 to an annual rate of $452.7 billion in the fourth quarter of 1990 (see Figure 6–1). U.S. exports, as a percentage of gross domestic product (GDP), grew from less than 5 percent in 1965 to about 12 percent in 1994,

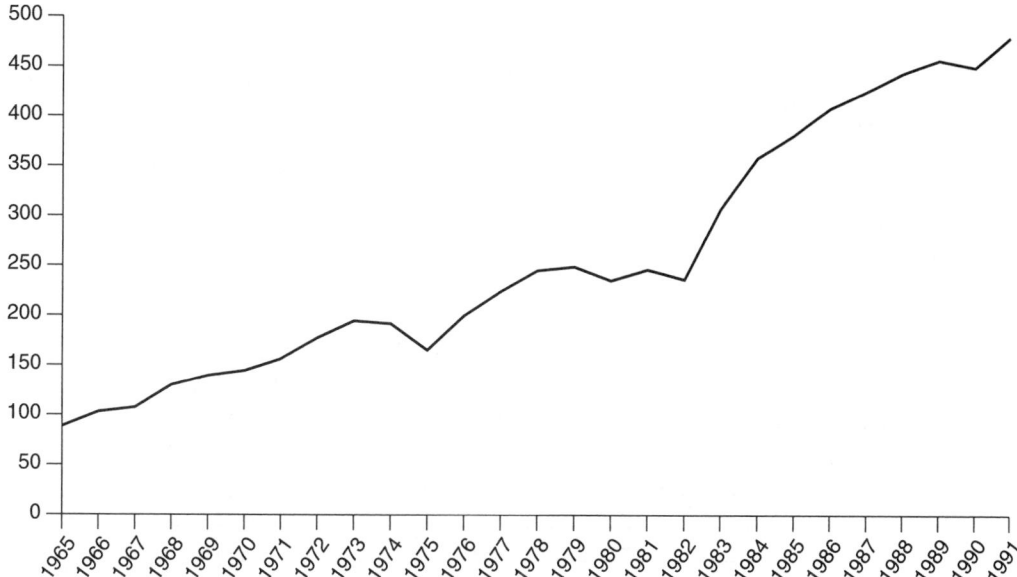

Figure 6–1   Merchandise imports of goods and services (Billions of 1987 Dollars)

Source: Economic Report of the President, January 1993.

while the import share of GDP increased to more than 13 percent (see Figure 6–2). When the indirect effects of trade are taken into account, roughly four-fifths of the increase in domestic production of manufacturers between 1987 and 1992 was accounted for by exports.[2] Obviously, international trade has become such an integral part of the U.S. economy (and indeed the economies of all industrial nations) that our economic success in the future will depend heavily on how well our businesses and industries compete in international markets.

It is not an exaggeration to say that, in the first two years of the Clinton administration, a number of crucial policy steps were taken that will be key to our future. These included ratification by Congress of the North American Free Trade Agreement (NAFTA), completion of and congressional concurrence in the trade expansion under the Uruguay Round of the General Agreement on Tariffs and Trade (GATT), and opening of discussions with both Asian and Latin American nations about future expansion of free trade.

The issues of international finance and economics are complex, and it is not easy to deal with them in any degree of depth in a limited amount of space. What we will try to do in this chapter is acquaint readers with the policy background, arguments, and alternatives for several of the key policy issues now on the action agenda of the United States. We hope this background will be sufficient to allow a rudimentary understanding of the issues so readers can follow the policy arguments as they unfold in the national media.

The topics we discuss include U.S. trade policy, past and present; forms of trade protectionism; arguments for and against free trade; the primary institutions involved in international trade policy development, including the World Bank, the International Monetary Fund (IMF), and the Group of Seven (G–7); the international

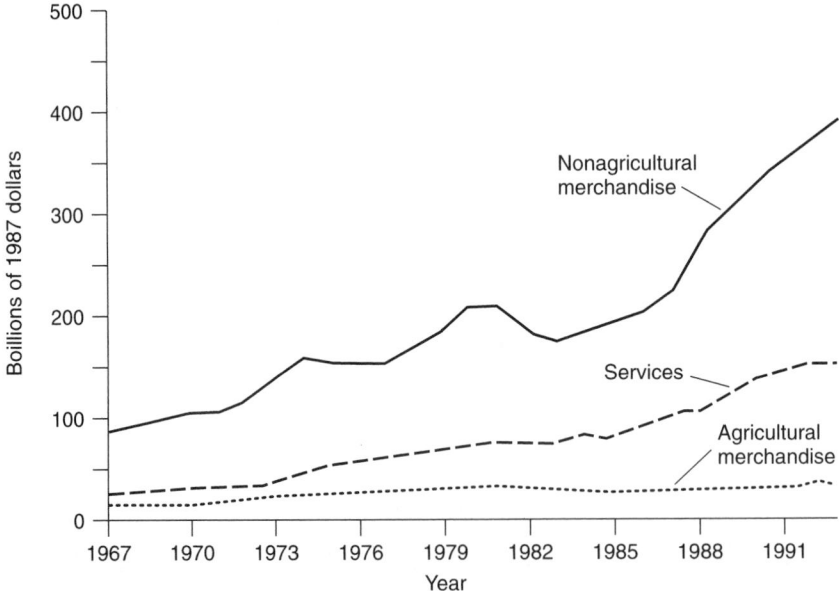

Figure 6–2 U.S. exports of goods and Services

Source: Economic Report of the President, January 1995.

trading environment: the GATT and its recently completed Uruguay Round; regional trading blocs such as the European Union (EU) and NAFTA; and finally the matter of currency exchange instability and its impact on the world economy.

U.S. INTERNATIONAL TRADING POLICY

If asked about U.S. trade policy, most people would probably respond that U.S. public policy supports free trade, and for the most part, they would be right. Following World War II, the United States dominated international trade for more than 20 years. In 1950, we supplied 20 percent of world exports, almost 30 percent of world manufacturers, and 50 percent or more of capital goods and other manufactured products. A major reason for this dominance in the early years after the war is the fact that Europe and many other regions of the world were still rebuilding their industrial economies.

As our trading partners and competitors strengthened their economies, the United States gradually slipped back to what many assumed would be a more sustainable share of international trade. But in 1980, our trade position began to collapse. An annual $1.8 billion current account trade balance became a $145.1 billion annual deficit by 1986.[3] Trade in manufactures fell from a surplus of $18.6 billion to a deficit of $133 billion. The U.S. share of world imports grew from 13.2 percent to 18.7 percent. This shift in world trade patterns is shown in Figure 6–3.

The change in the U.S. world trade situation in the 1980s was partly a result of the high real interest rates in the early 1980s that were engineered by the Federal Reserve Board (the Fed) to kill the double-digit inflation inherited by the Reagan administration in 1980. This monetary policy change by the Fed contributed to an appreciation of the dollar relative to the currencies of our major trading partners, making U.S. goods very expensive in international markets. The value of the dollar increased more than 50 percent between 1980 and 1985. Exports fell and imports—spurred by the strong dollar—ballooned. In addition, the United States was growing faster than most industrial countries in the 1980s, causing our imports to grow even more, while imports in these other countries declined.

A side effect of the changing import-export situation that would lead to future problems was the taste that people in the United States began to acquire for imported goods. For example, in 1992, imported beer sales to the United States were estimated at 19 million cases, up almost 10 percent from a year earlier. While that was only 2.4 percent of the total market, brewers in Japan and other countries were starting to compete more fiercely for a share of a market that had been owned for generations by U.S. producers.

Differences in the current account trade balance in the 1980s were also driven by the differences between the United States and its trading partners in savings and investment. The U.S. government has, as discussed in Chapter 5, been *dissaving*—that is, spending more than it receives in revenues. National saving (personal saving + business saving + government saving for all levels of government) declined from 17 percent of gross national product (GNP) in 1981 to 12.2 percent in 1987. One result of this situation is that the U.S. economy has demanded more goods and services than it is capable of producing, thus requiring more imports to satisfy domestic demand.

As the U.S. economy recovered from the 1981–1982 recession and gained momentum in the mid-1980s, the high real interest rates that persisted helped the value of the U.S. dollar increase significantly. It peaked against European currencies and then began to depreciate gradually in February 1985, following a decision by the G–7 that the dollar was too high and had to decline. The treasury secretary James Baker "talked down" the value of the dollar in the summer of 1985, which signaled to international currency traders that the United States would do all it could to drive down the value of the dollar further. The rate of decline picked up speed at that point and finally began to stabilize in the late 1980s. In May 1995, for example, the dollar was valued at 5 French francs versus a value of 10 francs to the dollar in February 1985, 8.9 francs in July 1985, and 7.8 francs in December 1985. The dollar followed a similar pattern vis-à-vis the Japanese yen in the 1980s, but has continued to decline, and was near an all-time low of 99 yen to the dollar at the beginning of 1995. Figure 6–4 shows the volatility of the relationship between the U.S. dollar and selected major world currencies over much of this period.

With the decline of the value of the dollar, U.S. manufacturers began to do a better job of competing in international markets. As a result, U.S. exports have improved considerably since the 1980s, and the trade deficit has declined. Table 6–1 shows the leading product exports and imports by the United States in 1991.

In June 1992, U.S. exports were at a record high level. Unfortunately, imports were also at a record high level. The two fastest-growing markets for U.S. goods were Latin America and the Pacific Rim countries. The slow rate of economic activity in Europe since 1991 has caused low export growth to Europe that continued into 1994. At the beginning of 1995, unemployment in the 15 countries of the European Union (EU) was still averaging more than 10 percent (more about the EU below). Figure 6–5 shows the growth in U.S. exports to our major trading partners over the period of 1973–1993. As can be seen from the graph, both the East Asian and Latin American markets have grown much more rapidly

Item	1983	1984	1985	1986	1987	1988	1989
Exports	201.8	219.9	215.9	223.3	250.2	320.2	362.1
Industrial countries	128.3	141	140.5	150.3	165.6	207.3	234.2
Canada	44.5	53	55.4	56.5	62	74.3	81.1
Japan	21.8	21.8	23.2	22.1	26.4	37.2	43.9
W. Europe[2]	55.4	56.9	56	60.4	68.6	86.4	98.4
Australia, N.Z., and S. Africa	6.6	7.8	7	7.1	7.4	9.4	10.9
Other Countries except E. Europe		74.6	71.9	71.0	82.3	109.1	122.2
OPEC[3]	15.3	13.8	11.4	10.4	10.7	13.8	13.3
Other[4]	55.2	60.8	60.5	60.6	71.6	95.3	108.9
Eastern Europe	3	4.3	3.2	2.1	2.3	3.8	5.5
Imports	268.9	332.4	338.1	368.4	409.8	447.2	477.4
Industrial countries	60.1	205.5	219.0	245.4	259.7	283.2	292.5
Canada	55.2	67.6	70.2	69.7	73.6	84.6	89.9
Japan	43.3	60.2	65.7	80.8	84.6	89.8	93.5
W. Europe[2]	56.2	72.1	77.5	89.0	96.1	102.6	102.4
Australia, N.Z., and S. Africa	5.4	5.6	5.6	5.9	5.4	6.2	6.6
Other countries except E. Europe	107.4	124.7	117.3	121.1	148.2	161.8	182.8
OPEC[3i]	24.9	26.9	22.8	18.9	24.4	23.0	30.7
Other[4i]	82.5	97.8	94.5	102.2	123.8	138.8	152.1
Eastern Europe	1.4	2.2	1.8	2.0	1.9	2.2	2.1
Balance (excess if Exports +)	−67.1	−112.5	−122.2	−145.1	−159.6	−127.0	−115.2
Industrial countries	−31.8	−64.5	−78.4	−95.1	−94.1	−75.9	−58.3
Canada	−10.7	−14.6	−14.8	−13.2	−11.6	−10.3	−8.9
Japan	−21.6	−37.0	−43.5	−54.4	−56.9	−52.6	−49.7
W. Europe[2]	−8.0	−15.2	−21.4	−28.6	−27.5	−16.2	−4.0
Australia, N.Z., and S. Africa	1.2	2.2	1.4	1.1	2.0	3.2	4.2
Other countries except E. Europe	−37.0	−50.1	−45.3	−50.1	−65.8	−52.7	−60.6
OPEC[3]	−9.7	−13.1	−11.4	−8.5	−13.7	−9.2	−17.4
Others[4]	−27.3	−37.0	−33.9	−41.6	−52.1	−43.5	−43.2
Eastern Europe	1.6	2.1	1.4	.1	.3	1.6	3.5

[1]Preliminarily seasonally adjusted.

[2]The former German Democratic Republic (East Germany) included in Western Europe beginning fourth quarter 1990 and in Eastern Europe before that time.

[3]Organization of Petroleum Exporting Countries: Algeria, Ecuador (through 1992), Gabon, Indonesia, Iran, Iraq, Kuwait, Libya, Nigeria, Qatar, Saudi Arabia, United Arab Emirates, and Venezuela.

[4]Latin America, other Western Hemisphere countries, and other countries in Asia and Africa, less members of OPEC.

Figure 6–3   U.S. merchandise exports and imports by area, 1983–1993 (Billions of Dollars)

Source: Economic Report of the President, January 1994.

1990	1991	1992	*1993 first 3 quarters at annual rate[1]*
389.3	416.9	440.1	448.7
253.8	261.3	264.9	267.2
83.5	85.9	91.1	99.4
47.8	47.2	46.9	47.2
111.4	116.8	114.5	109.2
11.2	11.4	12.4	11.4
130.6	150.4	169.5	175.8
13.4	18.5	20.7	18.7
117.2	131.9	148.8	157.1
4.3	4.8	5.6	5.7
498.3	490.7	536.3	582.0
299.9	294.2	316.2	342.2
93.1	93.0	100.9	112.5
90.4	92.3	97.4	105.2
109.2	101.9	111.3	118.0
7.3	7.0	6.6	6.5
196.1	194.8	218.1	236.6
38.2	33.4	33.7	35.0
157.8	161.4	184.4	201.7
2.3	1.8	2.0	3.2
−109.0	−73.8	−96.1	−133.3
−46.1	−32.8	−51.3	−75.0
−9.6	−7.1	−9.7	−13.0
−42.6	−45.0	−50.5	−58.0
2.2	14.9	3.2	−8.9
3.9	4.4	5.8	4.9
−65.6	−44.4	−48.6	−60.9
−24.8	−15.0	−13.0	−16.3
−40.7	−29.4	−35.6	−44.5
2.1	3.0	3.7	2.6

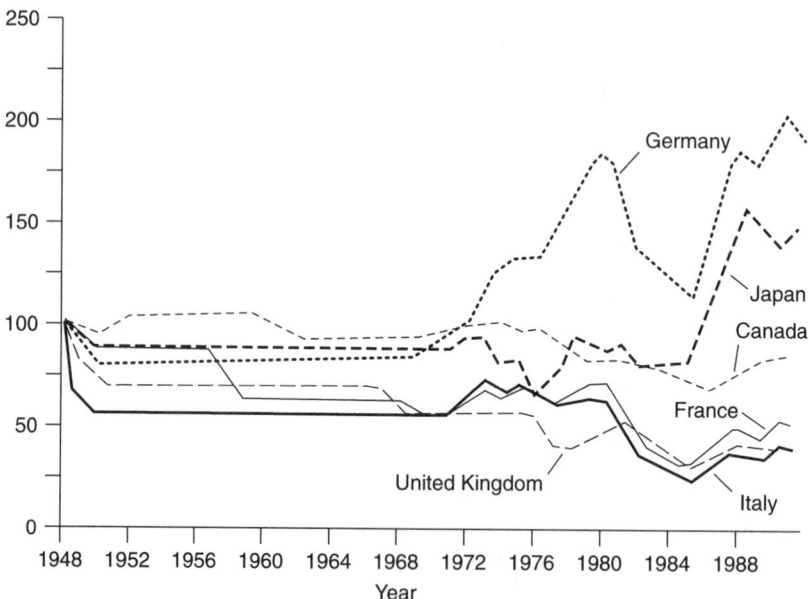

Figure 6–4   Exchange rates of major industrialized countries in terms of the dollar (Index, 1948 = 100)

Source: International Monetary Fund.

than our exports to the Organization for Economic Cooperation and Development (OECD: major industrial) nations since 1980. This more rapid rate of growth reflects both the much faster rate of population growth, as well as the expansion in GDP per capital, that has been occurring in these two regions, compared to the OECD nations.

The public's perception of the U.S. trade situation of the 1980s and early 1990s has revived interest in many quarters of the United States in a more protectionist trade policy. The term *revive* is used because protectionism has been very much a part of U.S. trade policy for most of our history. The Constitution had

TABLE 6–1   Leading U.S. Product Exports and Imports (1991)

Domestic Exports	*Millions of Dollars*
Electrical machinery	$29,935
Automatic data processing equipment, office machinery	25,953
Aircraft	24,158
General industrial machinery	17,107

General Imports	*Millions of Dollars*
Crude Oil	$37,153
Electrical machinery	35,103
Automatic Data Processing equipment, office machinery	30,065
Clothing	26,205

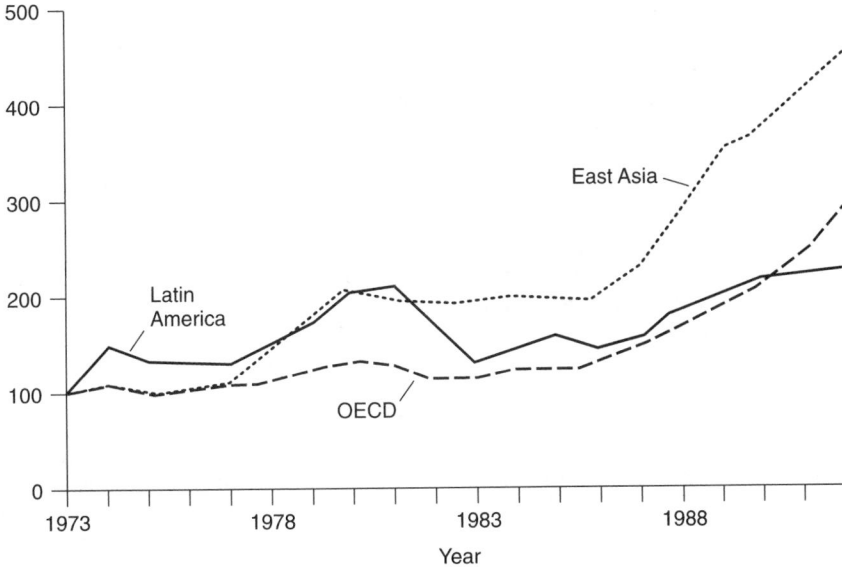

Figure 6–5   Growth of U.S. exports to selected trading partners (constant 1987 Dollars) (Index 1973 = 100)

Organization for Economic Cooperation and Development (OECD) nations are Australia, Austria, Belgium, Canada, Denmark, Finland, France, Germany, Greece, Iceland, Ireland, Japan, Luxembourg, Mexico, the Netherlands, New Zealand, Norway, Portugal, Spain, Sweden, Switzerland, Turkey, the United Kingdom, and the United States. (On 18 May, 1994, Mexico became a member of the OECD but would still be more accurately considered a developing nation and was not examined for the sample period. The United States is excluded.

Source: OECD

given Congress the power to control international trade, and Congress almost immediately erected high tariffs to protect the nation's young industries. Tariffs were also used to raise money to support the government. In fact, they were the main source of federal government revenue until early in the twentieth century, when the federal income tax was enacted.

In 1897, Congress gave the president the power to negotiate bilateral trade treaties and to impose countervailing duties to offset foreign export subsidies. But Congress retained the right to ratify treaties. Congress expanded the president's trade powers in 1933, following the disastrous experience with the Smoot-Hawley bill, which had raised tariffs to their highest level in history and helped aggravate the Great Depression by precipitating retaliation by our trading partners. World exports had dropped 50 percent between 1928 and 1932, and U.S. exports had dropped 66 percent.

The Reciprocal Trade Agreement Act of 1934 made protection of domestic markets from foreign exporters the exception rather than the rule. It allowed trade liberalization and selective protection to coexist. With the end of World War II in 1945, a consensus began to develop that free and open trade offered the best chance for economic growth throughout the world. In the United States, business and public opinion leaders concluded that it was in our best interests to have a trading system where U.S. products could compete as freely as possible. It was assumed that the nation would do well in such a system, and it did.

Even though the U.S. trade position weakened by the mid-1960s, the demand for protection was not strong. The United States was still running large trade surpluses with the rest of the world, and its main problem was trade barriers against its products, not competition within its continental market. In 1974, Congress gave the president more authority to liberalize trade and also made it easier for industries having problems to receive some protection from foreign competition. There began to be a revival of interest in trade protection that has continued to the present in some quarters.

During the 1992 presidential elections, both political parties supported a free trade philosophy, and President George Bush and Governor Bill Clinton stated they were in favor of free trade. There was somewhat of a debate about the details. Governor Clinton qualified his support for NAFTA and implied he would demand more concessions in opening foreign markets than had been the case under the two preceding Republican administrations.

After assuming office, President Clinton's foreign trade rhetoric was indeed tougher than had been the case under the Bush administration, but it is doubtful if there has really been a major policy shift toward a more aggressive protectionist posture vis-à-vis the trading partners of the United States. The first half of 1995 did see very aggressive moves by the United States to persuade the Japanese to open their markets, particularly in the automobile sector, and the administration threatened the use of trade sanctions against those nations they regarded as protecting their own markets against U.S. goods. The administration also acted aggressively in early 1995 to try to force the Chinese to close down copyright pirates of computer software and compact discs. But the bipartisan consensus in Washington supporting a free trade philosophy was also evidenced by the passage of NAFTA in 1993, the endorsement of the Uruguay Round changes to the GATT in November 1994, and the initiation in 1995 of talks to expand NAFTA to include Chile and possibly other Latin American countries.

FORMS OF PROTECTIONISM

Trade protection can be implemented in several ways.[4] All are intended to improve the position of domestic producers relative to foreign producers. Market protection can be accomplished by increasing the prices of foreign producers; decreasing the costs of domestic producers (e.g., farm subsidies); or restricting access of foreign producers to the home market. Following are the most common techniques of protection.

Tariffs

Tariffs are taxes imposed on goods that enter a domestic economy from a foreign country. They are politically popular because they appear to be taxes paid by foreigners, not citizens. In fact, their effect is to raise the prices of the imported goods to domestic consumers, and in that sense, they act as a hidden domestic tax. They also permit domestic producers to charge more for their goods than would be the case if they faced foreign competition. As discussed earlier, the United States has had a system of tariffs since its founding. U.S. tariffs peaked with the implementation of the Smoot-Hawley legislation in 1932.

Quotas

Quotas involve the placing of limits on the amount of goods importers can bring into a country. This form of protectionism causes prices of both imported and exported goods to rise, just as do tariffs (the difference being that tariffs also raise money for the government). Sometimes quotas are described as voluntary, although the true situation is more akin to someone voluntarily surrendering a wallet to another who is holding a gun to his or her head. In some cases, however, foreign producers benefit (they capture *quotas rents*) because they receive higher prices than they otherwise would receive in the absence of quotas. This is one reason why exporting countries are willing to negotiate quotas. In recent years, for example, the United States has had agreements with Japanese exporters of automobiles to voluntarily restrict the number of cars they export to the United States.

Regulatory Barriers

This type of trade barrier—sometimes known as a nontariff barrier—is more subtle than tariffs and quotas. The rationale typically given for regulatory barriers is that they protect the public health and safety of the importing nation. For example, both the United States and the European Union have product standards that require inspection and certification of foods, electrical equipment, products using hazardous chemicals that may come into consumer hands, and food processing equipment. Product quality assurance is also recently becoming a barrier as, led by the EU, importers of intermediate producer goods are requiring their suppliers to have their manufacturing systems and plants inspected and registered as being quality certified.[5]

In many cases, the regulatory requirements of a nation are justifiable on the stated grounds for which the regulation was imposed. There are numerous cases, however, where regulations and product standards are simply thinly veiled attempts to protect domestic producers of foods and manufactured products from foreign competition.

Much of the dispute over the congressional ratification of NAFTA was focused on what some would characterize as nontariff barriers designed to protect domestic industries. Some opponents of the legislation argued against ratification of the treaty on the grounds that the agreement violates the U.S. National Environmental Policy Act by, for example, raising the possibility that food grown with unacceptable levels of pesticides or fish caught by methods illegal in the United States may be able to enter the United States from Mexico. Labor unions also argued that products imported from Mexico are not subject to the same worker standards as those produced in the United States and would have an unfair advantage over U.S.-produced goods that would ultimately lead to U.S. jobs being relocated to Mexico.

Another issue that appeared in the GATT debates raised the matter of child labor in Asia, Africa, and Latin America. The argument was that the United States should bar the entry of goods from those countries that utilized child labor in their production. The counterargument was that barring those imports would leave the children and their families in even more desperate straits. Instead, the respondents argued, the way to abolish child labor is to raise the standard of living in those nations by giving them more access to cheaper goods and by allowing them to sell what they produce to the rest of the world.

Subsidies

Another way to protect domestic industries is to offer government subsidies to the home producers. This action in effect reduces the costs of the domestic producer and allows it to charge lower prices than it would otherwise be able to charge. It then is in a more favorable position in the marketplace relative to the competing foreign producer. This type of subsidy has been used by numerous countries in both domestic and foreign markets. The industries that have typically benefited include agriculture, shipping, arms production, and aircraft manufacturing. The EU subsidization of agriculture was a major stumbling block to completing the 1993 negotiations to liberalize world trade under GATT. The agriculture subsidies of the United States have also been criticized by its foreign competitors as unfairly aiding U.S. farm products in the world marketplace.

Currency Exchange Controls

The several trade barriers described here restrict the flow of goods. Exchange controls restrict access to the foreign money needed to *purchase* foreign goods. This type of trade barrier has typically been used by developing countries in pursuit of an import substitution form of trading policy. It was also used as policy by the former Soviet Union and its Eastern European allies to restrict access to foreign currency to force the purchase of Soviet bloc goods and services at prices set by the state. In some cases, nations have held exchange rates artificially low to keep domestic prices lower than the prices of imported goods.

Pros and Cons of Free Trade

Economic Theory and the Free Trade Logic.   In 1776, Adam Smith wrote in his *Wealth of Nations,* "If a country can supply us with a commodity cheaper than we ourselves can make it, better buy it of them with some part of the product of our own industry, employed in a way in which we have an advantage."[6] This idea became known as the principle of comparative advantage. The argument is that through imports, a country can acquire goods and services that it cannot produce at home or can produce at home only at a cost that is greater than the cost of obtaining them for the exports it produces.[7]

Economists have actively considered the benefits and costs of free trade since Smith's observation. In 1817, David Ricardo, one of the earliest classical economists, discussed the gains from free trade in his book *Principles of Political Economy and Taxation.* To illustrate the gains, he used an example involving trade between England and Portugal that demonstrated the concept of absolute advantage. This concept is based on the labor theory of value, which held that the prices of goods were proportional to their labor inputs.[8]

In the example, the two countries both produced the same goods: wine and cloth. To keep the example simple, he assumed that the only production costs involved for both countries were labor costs. The labor costs were measured in terms of how many labor-hours were required to produce one bottle of wine or one bolt of cloth in each country:

	Wine	*Cloth*
England	100	120
Portugal	90	80

In this example England is less efficient than Portugal, using more labor for both products. Portugal thus has an absolute advantage over England in the production of both wine and cloth. But even though this would seem to rule out trade between the two countries, it turns out that both countries can indeed benefit from trade. The reason for this anomaly is as follows:

- England could exchange one wine, costing 100 labor-hours, for one cloth, which would have cost it 120 hours to produce.
- Portugal can exchange one cloth, costing it 80 hours to produce, for one wine, which would have cost it 90 hours to produce.
- Thus, England saves 20 labor-hours in the transaction, and Portugal saves 10 labor-hours.

This example demonstrates that both parties can benefit from specialization and international trade and that there is a basis for specialization and exchange even if one party has an absolute cost advantage in both of the two products. Each country can gain from specializing in that product for which either its *relative efficiency* is greater or its *relative inefficiency* is less. This is the product in which it has a comparative advantage. Thus, the shift of labor between wine and cloth in the two countries can raise the total production of both products. This increase in output will be shared by both countries. The example illustrates that the consumption of the two goods and the wealth of both countries are increased by the specialization that results from international trade based on comparative advantage.

Over the years economists have tested Ricardo's example under various alternative assumptions. The results have, if anything, strengthened the case for free trade. Three additional sources of gain are identified:

1. As the *market* available to be served by producers expands from a national to an international market, gains result from declining costs per unit of production.
2. Gains result from decreased monopolistic power of domestic producers and increased competition from foreign producers, as domestic producers are forced to produce the output demanded by consumers at the lowest possible cost.
3. Consumers gain from the increased variety, quality, and lower prices resulting from the increased competition that comes with an open world market.

OTHER ARGUMENTS FOR AND AGAINST FREE TRADE

On a worldwide scale, the movement toward free trade has had the positive results one would predict from the theoretical analysis.[9] Most knowledgeable observers would agree that the reduction of worldwide tariffs and the gradual elimination of other protectionist measures that have accompanied the opening of the world economy over the past 50 years have been largely responsible for the great advances in prosperity enjoyed by most of the nations of the world since the end of World War II. The vision of a world economy in which all producers operate in an environment of free trade, however, has been losing ground in recent years. Protectionist pressures increased during the 1980s as a result of the negative balance of trade that the United States and some other industrialized countries experienced. The decline in worldwide economic growth has increased unemployment in many countries, and that decline has led to political pressure to protect domestic industries and jobs. The movement of low-skill jobs away from the developed nations and toward developing countries has also added to protectionist arguments.

Enlightened economic policy leaders in the United States and other nations see this drop-off in worldwide growth as evidence of the need to move forward with a continuing liberalization of trade within the framework of GATT. But the harder economic times also create a more friendly atmosphere for those who believe in protecting domestic markets. One of the difficulties in this situation is that most people do not understand the logic and benefits of an open world-trading environment, and their natural tendencies are to support more protectionism, particularly if they work in an industry that is facing aggressive foreign competition.

Another explanation for the support of protectionist trade policy is that many politicians gain from providing protectionist legislation, because even though the national economic costs of protectionism exceed the benefits, at a local level the politician may see different costs and benefits.[10] The gains from free trade nationally—although cumulatively quite large—may be difficult to measure for each consumer, while the local losses for a particular company or industry are much more focused and obvious.

The eventual outcome of this policy debate is extremely important to the future of the United States, and the facts of the situation warrant a careful examination by all citizens. Those who argue against a policy of free trade and who support increased U.S. government control over imports and exports typically do so on the basis of the following four arguments:

1. Import restrictions will decrease the nation's trade deficit because imported goods will be replaced by domestically produced goods.
2. The large trade deficits that the United States has been experiencing since 1980 have been responsible for massive job losses and a reduction in the nation's rate of economic growth.
3. The U.S. trade deficit is de-industrializing the U.S. economy and eliminating manufacturing jobs.
4. Other nations with which we trade are not playing fair. U.S. policy needs to ensure reciprocity between trading partners and a level playing field for all competitors.

Let us take them one at a time.

Protectionism and the U.S. Trade Deficit.   Some argue that if the U.S. trade deficit were eliminated and spending shifted to domestic goods through the imposition of a general tax (a tariff) on imports, the United States would benefit from expanding national economic output because consumers would purchase more domestically produced goods. Others claim that such a tax would lower the value of the dollar and would make our domestic goods more attractive both at home and abroad. These arguments are mistaken for several reasons. First, an import tax would reduce spending on imports, but in an international trading system with flexible currency exchange rates and unchanged savings and investment, the

U.S. dollar would *appreciate,* not *depreciate.* Because other nations would be exporting less to the United States, their currencies would depreciate vis-à-vis the U.S. dollar.

As a result, exports would decline because of the higher-value dollar, and imports would fail to decline as much as if exchange rates remained unchanged. The primary effect of the import tax would be to introduce inefficiencies into the domestic economy, which in turn would reduce productivity and national income. Companies producing goods for the domestic market would do better, and companies primarily involved in exporting to foreign markets would do worse. This situation would result in an unnatural shift of resources away from exporting industries and toward industries producing mainly for the domestic market. So, for example, imports of products such as steel, autos, and apparel would likely be reduced, making the domestically produced products more competitive. But exports of industries such as aircraft, chemicals, and machinery would also be reduced; their products would be more expensive in foreign markets because of the higher-value dollar.

In addition, for basic intermediary products such as steel, the higher prices the industry would receive as a result of an import tax would also be reflected in the products of the other industries that use the product in their production process. The products of these companies would therefore also be less competitive in international markets (e.g., steel used in automobiles). Second, because of these offsetting changes, the U.S. trade deficit would not likely improve. In fact, it is more likely that the situation would worsen because other countries would probably retaliate against the U.S. tax, further reducing the exports of U.S. industries. The most vulnerable U.S. producers, such as agriculture, would be tempting targets for retaliation. The third reason is that if the tax were directed at only a few countries, the result would be even less successful in reducing the trade deficit: the targeted countries would shift their exports to the exempt countries, and countries exempted from the U.S. tax would expand their exports to the United States.

The point is that a nation's trade balance is determined by macroeconomic factors such as relative interest rates, savings and investment, consumer preferences, and productivity. Protectionist measures such as import taxes are not likely to have much effect on reducing a trade deficit. In fact, a trade deficit is not necessarily a bad thing. Over time a nation's trade deficit must be followed by a trade surplus, or other countries would be willingly exporting to it without the hope of being repaid. The import of goods and services now must be paid for by the export of goods and services later.

Protectionism and Jobs. Some observers argue that protecting our industries from foreign competition would save jobs. The implication is that reductions in imports would lead to greater spending on domestic goods. This policy approach is known as *import substitution.* In fact, although protectionism may save jobs in the near term, the jobs saved are likely to be matched by jobs lost elsewhere in the economy. Protectionist countries also may find themselves injuring exporting industries to protect industries that are dying out or that are unable to compete with competitors in other countries because of some important advantage possessed by the foreign competitors.

Trade barriers ignore market signals that patterns of demand have shifted or that an industry's international competitiveness has declined. Other industries in the protected economy pay higher taxes than they would otherwise, and their cost of materials is inflated. They are therefore handicapped in their long-term growth.

The result is that the very goal of job preservation that the protectionist measures are designed to serve becomes even less obtainable than it was before the measures were adopted. A few examples will be useful to illustrate this point.

A classic case of a dying industry is the U.S. harness industry in the early 20th century. The introduction of the automobile marked the beginning of the end in the production of harnesses for horse-drawn carriages. Protectionist measures designed to reduce the import of harnesses by foreign producers into the United States would have helped the industry in the short run. However, the costs would have been the reduced exports by other U.S. industries and a misallocation of U.S. resources away from other investments that could help the long-term productivity and competitiveness of U.S. industry. Indeed, one could argue that even the harness industry would be harmed because it would delay its inevitable transition to new products that could be more in keeping with the needs of the 20th century economy.

Another example concerns the fruitlessness of trying to protect industries that are in a stage of geographic transition. The athletic shoe industry is an excellent case in point. Nike, a U.S. corporation, has built itself into one of the dominant powers in the athletic shoe industry by weaving together a network of subcontractors and international partners involved in the production of Nike products.[11] Because of the low tech, labor-intensive nature of footwear manufacturing, the industry has essentially moved offshore. Today, none of Nike's athletic shoes are produced in the United States. The principal producers are located in Taiwan, Korea, China, Thailand, and Indonesia. Only the high tech design part of the business is done in the United States, with the *partners* handling the actual production of various product lines. The geographic location of the shoe models' production shifts over time, reflecting changing wage structures and the technological abilities of the partners. The use of this international production network is the only way Nike could have survived and prospered in this industry, and it has worked very well for them, with worldwide sales of their shoes exceeding $1 billion.

Those countries that have adopted a trading policy of import substitution have all had serious economic problems as a result. Mexico, for example, conducted an economic policy of import substitution and protectionism for many years. Their reward was a sick economy that was not competitive with the rest of the world. Domestic products were shoddy, and both unemployment and inflation increased. Only when President Carlos Salinas de Gortari shifted to an export-oriented policy, reduced tariffs and other protectionist measures, and welcomed foreign investment did Mexico begin to boom economically. Of course we have seen the same situation in the Central European nations of Hungary, Czechoslovakia, and Poland as they have shifted from protected, planned economies to free market systems.

Protectionism and De-industrialization. The claim is made by protectionists that competition by importers into the United States has resulted in the de-industrialization of U.S. manufacturing. It is true that in some export- and import-competing industries, U.S. manufacturing employment has declined. It is also true that total employment in manufacturing is less than it was 10 years ago.

But if one looks at manufacturing *production* rather than *employment* it is clear that production by U.S. manufacturers has not declined. As Figure 6–6 shows, manufacturing output has grown steadily with the expansion of the U.S. economy. There has not been a radical shift away from U.S. manufactured goods. Manufacturing production's share of GNP has remained relatively constant for the past 20

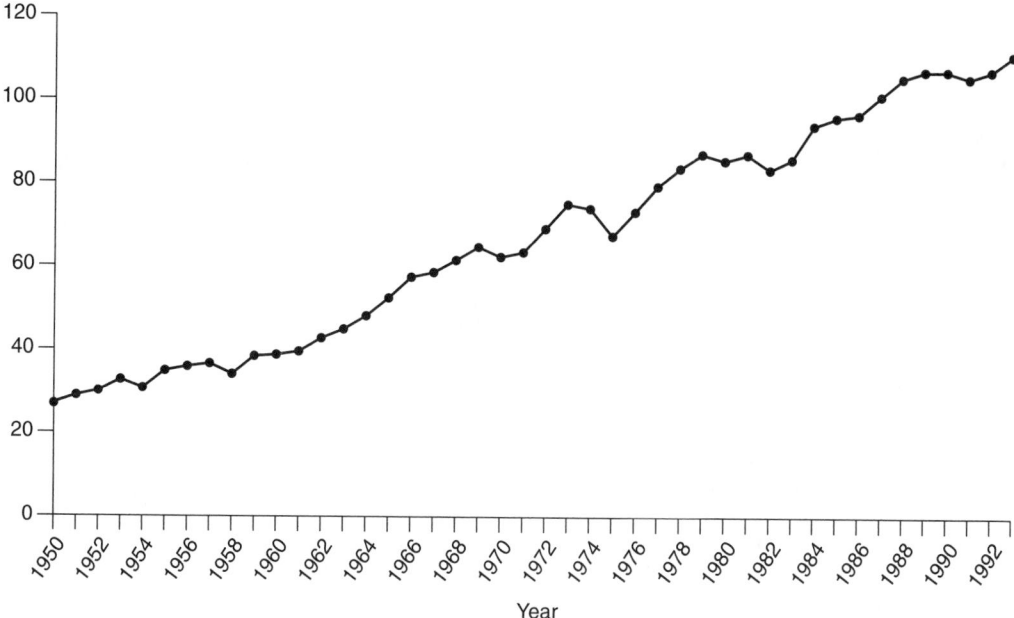

Figure 6–6 Production and business activity (Index 1987 = 100)

years. The reason for the manufacturing employment decline is not that we are producing less in the way of manufactured goods but that our productivity—our output per labor-hour—has improved. This improvement has allowed U.S. manufacturers to produce more goods with fewer workers. One reason for the improved productivity is that manufacturers have substituted capital for labor.

Enhanced productivity is a positive, not a negative. It is the reason why real per capita income and the economic well-being of a nation increase over time. U.S. manufacturing is going through a transformation similar to the one that our agricultural industry went through with the introduction of new farm machinery and farming techniques 70 or more years ago. In 1900, more than one-third of U.S. workers were employed in agriculture. Today, that figure is only about 2 percent. However, this 2 percent produces enough not only to feed 260 million Americans but also to export almost $40 billion worth of produce to other countries. The late 1990s will see a continuation of this industrial-restructuring process on a worldwide basis. The result will be improved product prices, quality and variety, and higher productivity with resulting improved per capita income for those nations that can successfully compete in the new global environment (Table 6–2).

The charge is also often made that, because of international competition, the United States is replacing good, skilled jobs for service *hamburger flippers*. In fact, this type of employment actually declined in the United States by 2 percent between 1982 and 1991. Table 5–2 shows where the major job shifts occurred during that decade. Service employment did indeed increase, but the big winners were in the professional or highly skilled service fields.

Between 1982 and 1991, the number of jobs in the United States increased by 16 million—a growth of 16 percent. Even in 1993, with a relatively slow recovery from the 1991–1992 recession, the number of jobs increased by about a million.

TABLE 6–2   Big Winners and Big Losers: Change in Employment by Sector (In Thousands)

Occupation	1982	1991	Percentage Change
Computer analysts	719	1,321	84
Data processing repair workers	98	152	55
Social workers	407	603	48
Airline pilots	69	101	46
Veterinarians	36	51	42
Police and detectives	645	870	35
Designers	393	527	34
Accountants and auditors	1,105	1,446	31
College teachers	606	773	28
Registered nurses	1,372	1,712	25
Food or short-order cooks	419	411	–2
Textile machine workers	806	676	–16
Timber cutting and logging workers	96	80	–17
Household workers and servants	512	403	–22
Farm workers	1,149	883	–23
Garage and service station workers	293	207	–29
Garbage collectors	63	43	–32
Typists	906	591	–35

Source: Bureau of Labor Statistics, U.S. Department of Labor. Published by the *Washington Post,* 8 October, 1993.

Reciprocity and a Level Playing Field.   A currently in vogue argument for protectionist legislation focuses on bilateral trading balances with specific countries (such as Japan). Proponents argue that retaliatory threats, combined with tariffs and quotas, provide protection for domestic industries and induce more open foreign markets. Two relatively recent examples involve conflicts over access of both the automotive and the construction industries to the markets of the United States and Japan and access to the telecommunications industry of the United States and the EU. In both cases the U.S. government has taken action to try to force access to foreign markets by threatening to close its domestic market to the industry in question.

Another mechanism some governments use to force fair trade is antidumping legislation. *Dumping* refers to instances where a company sells its product in a foreign market at below its average total costs or at a lower price than in its home market. In 1993 for example, the U.S. Department of Commerce found 19 foreign companies guilty of dumping steel on the U.S. market. In the United States, under Section 301 of the 1974 trade act and current GATT rules adopted in the Uruguay Round, antidumping actions do not require any evidence of intention to monopolize or to drive competitors out of business. When an antidumping decision is upheld, the penalty is to assess a duty equal to the amount by which the offender's price exceeds the U.S. competitor's price. Under extraordinary circumstances, with the power granted in the Super 301 provision of the 1988 trade act, the United States retains the right to impose punitive tariffs—an effective embargo—on the imports of those found guilty of unfair trade practices.[12]

Critics argue that fair trade is simply a euphemism for protectionism and that the escalation of trade barriers that results from this approach causes losses for the countries involved. Critics of the steel dumping case argue that the U.S. Department of Commerce cannot penalize foreign sellers without also harming American buyers, since many types of steel hit by the dumping duties are not produced in the U.S. in sufficient quality or quantity to satisfy the needs of American manufacturers.

Opponents of fair trade also argue that trade between two countries does not have to be in balance for the trade of both to be in global balance. Differing demands and production capabilities will cause a specific country to have trade deficits with some countries and trade surpluses with others at various times (see Figure 6–7). This situation is a normal result of countries' trading on the basis of comparative advantage. By focusing on a bilateral trade deficit, a nation can arrive at mistaken conclusions about fairness that lead it to policies designed to eliminate the bilateral trade deficits. This in turn can lead to an elimination of gains from a multilateral trading system.

The Costs of Protectionism

Estimates of the cost of trade protectionism, made in the mid-1980s by the Institute for International Economics (IIE), suggest that the U.S. tariffs and quotas on autos, textiles, steel, and sugar cost U.S. consumers over $13 billion annually in higher prices and reduced consumption opportunities. Another researcher estimated that trade restrictions on clothing, sugar, and automobiles cost those consumers $14 billion in 1984. The cost estimates also indicate that, because of family consumption patterns, low-income families are affected more by these trade restrictions than are high-income families.

Professor Gary Huffbauer of the Georgetown University Department of Political Science calculated that the cost per job saved by U.S. protectionist measures in 18 of 31 cases examined was $100,000 per year. In chemicals, steel, bolts, nuts, and screws, the cost per job exceeded $500,000 per year.

The bottom line for those supporting a system of free trade in the world economy is that protectionist legislation results in serving the goals of specific interest groups at the expense of the nation as a whole.

Figure 6–7   Trading places

Country	Year to Date
Canada	−4,304
Western Europe	+4,368
Britain	+2,330
France	+233
Germany	−2,846
Japan	−22,542
Mexico	+1,506
Taiwan	−3,139
Venezuela	−1,301
OPEC	−5,563
China	−7,500
Former U.S.S.R.	+837

The U.S. merchandise trade deficit or surplus with some of our major trading partners.

A negative number indicates the United States had a trade deficit with the partner while a positive number indicates the United States enjoyed a trade surplus.

Source: Associated Press, July 17, 1993.

INSTITUTIONS IN THE INTERNATIONAL TRADING ENVIRONMENT

The International Monetary Fund (IMF) and the World Bank were established when the Marshall Plan for the reconstruction of Europe was enacted following World War II. They were designed as instruments to assist with the redevelopment of European and other Post-war economies. Their duties were set out at a conference of the United States, Great Britain, and the other allies who had won the war. The conference was held at Bretton Woods, New Hampshire, in July 1944, and has colloquially become known as the Bretton Woods Conference.

The World Bank is essentially a publicly owned bank. It borrows funds by selling bonds and lends money for investments to countries needing funds for worthy purposes. The IMF is not a bank, but a club.[13] Member countries pay a subscription fee and agree to abide by a mutually advantageous code of economic conduct. The IMF lets members borrow briefly from the fund. The World Bank's task is to promote development, the IMF's to maintain order in the international monetary system. The two institutions work very closely together; they once occupied the same building in Washington, D.C.

Since the establishment of these two institutions, the international environment has changed, and both institutions have evolved somewhat in scope. But their missions have remained essentially the same, and they have succeeded in becoming an integral part of the environment responsible for the postwar development of the world economy. Obviously their clientele has changed over the years. At present, both the World Bank and the IMF are actively involved in aiding Russia and the other member-states of the former Soviet Union in their conversion to market economies.

The International Monetary Fund (IMF)

The IMF was initially given the mission of helping nations stabilize their balance-of-trade payments. Countries can, from time to time, normally be expected to import more goods and services than they export. When this happens, they need to pay the difference by either drawing on their reserves or borrowing to finance the deficit. However, if the deficit is a chronic problem, the country's options are more drastic. For example, they can (1) cut back on domestic demand for goods and services by reducing government spending or by raising taxes, (2) devalue their currency, thus making their exports cheaper and their imports more expensive, or (3) adopt protectionist or other trade restrictions to reduce domestic demand.

The IMF offers the additional option of aiding the country in covering its trade deficit without these more drastic steps. In the case of the nations with chronic financial problems, its policy has been to require the country to put its economic house in order to qualify for the loan. These conditions placed on the borrowing countries typically include such requirements as: a noninflationary monetary policy based on modest budget deficits; a trading system that is open to competition and foreign investment; and the use of the market system as a means of allocating resources in the subject economy. Today, the international capital markets have, for all practical purposes, replaced the IMF for industrialized nations. Its main clients now, therefore, are the nations of the developing world.

The World Bank

The World Bank complements the IMF by making long-term loans to nations for the purpose of economic development projects. The World Bank does not make a loan until the IMF has conducted a financial investigation of the applying country.

The bank's first mission was to help rebuild the European economies ravaged during World War II. As the U.S. Marshall Plan assumed more of that responsibility, the World Bank became more involved with economic aid to developing countries. In the 1950s it focused on the building of public physical infrastructure in these countries. In the 1960s it concentrated on issues such as the support of farming, education, population control, and urban development. Today the bank's priorities for lending are based on the following criteria for its client nations:

- *Sound macroeconomic policies:* This criterion requires governments to moderate public spending, raise adequate revenue, control government borrowing and the creation of money, and maintain a competitive exchange rate for their currency.
- *Measures promoting microeconomic efficiency:* For example, governments must eliminate price controls, allow free entry and exit of businesses, define private property rights, and invest in adequate public infrastructure.
- *Liberal trade:* This criterion promotes free trade within the country, eliminates protection for domestic industries, and opens up the country to imports and foreign investment.
- *Social investment:* This requirement ensures adequate public investments in social infrastructure services such as primary education and health care.

Both the IMF and the World Bank have been under the criticism that their purpose and methods of operation are out of date and in need of reform, and both have been conducting long-range planning reviews of their future directions. In 1994 a blue-ribbon commission headed by Paul Volker, a former Federal Reserve Board chairman, concluded that the IMF should be given a central role in persuading governments to achieve a greater economic convergence, with relative currency stability as a goal. Others have argued that the IMF is still needed to provide short-term financing to countries with current account debts and that its expertise is invaluable to those Eastern European nations trying to establish market economies. It has also been suggested that the IMF could serve as permanent staff to the G–7.

Harvard University Professor Jeffrey Sachs, writing a guest commentary for *The Economist,* suggested that the central task of the international economic institutions created by the Bretton Woods Agreement, along with the new World Trade Organization (WTO) established to replace the GATT bureaucracy, should be to further consolidate the integration of the world economies.[14] He argues that four tasks need to be accomplished by these institutions:

- Helping the ex-communist reformers, with the IMF playing the leading role. Here the IMF should combine fiscal restraint with "ample foreign loans, exchange rate stabilization, increasing central-bank independence, and debt relief, all designed to restore confidence in the currency and the government's ability to continue to provide essential services."
- Helping extremely poor countries, mainly in sub-Saharan Africa, with the World Bank supporting programs to combat disease, civil unrest, and collapsing infrastructure. The Bank should phase out "traditional project-financing operations" and redirect its resources to Africa's urgent needs, as well as promote and disseminate research on economic development approaches and techniques.

- Promoting good citizenship in international trade, with the new WTO playing the leading role to combat protectionism and encourage "even handed commitment to open trade for all."
- Extending the framework of international law to govern commercial relations. "The IMF should aim to create international responsibilities regarding capital movements, and so forestall another abrupt reversal in flows to developing countries of the kind that helped to trigger debt crisis." International rules are also needed for the capital flows of developed countries.

The Group of Seven (G–7)

The organization known as the Group of Seven (G–7) is composed of the heads of the seven major industrialized countries who meet periodically to coordinate their economic policy, including monetary policy, fiscal policy, trade policy, assistance to developing countries, and reactions to international emergencies. The countries composing the group are the United States, France, Germany, Great Britain, Canada, Italy, and Japan. Mikhail Sergeyevich Gorbachev, president of the former U.S.S.R., was invited to a meeting of the group in Houston before he left office, and Boris Nikolayevich Yeltsin, president of the Russian Federation, joined the meeting that was held in Tokyo in June 1993 and has routinely attended G–7 meetings since that time.

The World Trade Organization (formerly the General Agreement on Tariffs and Trade [GATT])

John Maynard Keynes (Lord Keynes of Tilton) was the British delegate to the Bretton Woods Conference of 1944.[15] Keynes argued for a separate institution to create and defend an open trading system.[16] He proposed the establishment of the International Trade Organization (ITO). However, the U.S. Congress did not support the proposal, and the idea was abandoned in 1950. A treaty-cum-institution was created to take the ITO's place; that organization was the GATT.

GATT, now the WTO, operates the general legal structure under which a large share of the world's trade is conducted. Over a hundred countries currently are signatories to the agreement. Most economists would agree that GATT was a primary reason for the substantial expansion of trade the world has enjoyed over the past 40 years. Real global output has risen at an average rate of 4.5 percent per year, and the real volume of international trade has grown 6.5 percent per year. GATT operates within the following four basic principles:

1. Members of the organization should work to lower trade barriers and eliminate quotas.
2. Any trade barrier should be applied on a nondiscriminatory basis to all member countries (the principle of the most-favored-nation treatment).
3. No tariff concession can be rescinded without compensation to affected trading partners.
4. Trade conflicts should be settled by consultation among the involved parties.

GATT has been extended progressively over its history. Each set of negotiations, which can last for a few years, is referred to by a name. For example, the Kennedy Round of GATT talks took place in the 1960s, the Tokyo Round in the 1970s (1973–1979). The most recently completed round of talks was known as the

Uruguay Round (December 1993), because it was initiated in Uruguay in 1986. The several GATT rounds since 1947, and the estimated value of trade involved in each, are listed in Figure 6–8.

The Uruguay Round of talks was the eighth round since World War II and the first since 1979. The U.S. goal for the round was to extend free trade further. Specific matters of interest to U.S. negotiators were the reduction of trade barriers to professional services and foreign investment and the protection of intellectual property rights. The United States also pressed the Europeans to reduce their subsidies to farmers and thereby create a more open market for agricultural products.

As the 16 December 1993 deadline for completing the agreement approached, the future of the Uruguay Round, and indeed of GATT itself, was in question, because the talks were deadlocked by the disagreement between the EU and the United States. The importance of a successful completion of the round was enhanced by the collapse of the Warsaw Pact and the need to include the struggling nations of Eastern and Central Europe in the world-trading environment. In addition, many observers believe the world-trading system is desperately in need of the boost that liberalized trade should offer.[17] The Uruguay Round was expected to reduce tariffs further, improve access to markets for merchandise goods, and open new trading opportunities in a wide range of business services such as banking and insurance. It was also scheduled to include a comprehensive agreement on intellectual property rights such as patents, copyrights, and trademarks and to take steps to improve the trade environment for problem sectors such as agriculture and textiles.

Both the World Bank and the OECD suggested that conservative estimates of the gains to the world economy from reforms contained in the Uruguay Round would amount to $213 to $274 billion per year. These figures do not include benefits from strengthening existing GATT rules and from liberalizing investment in trade in services.[18] Estimates of the economic benefit brought by Uruguay Round changes for the United States range from 0.4 percent to 1 percent of GDP.[19] Perhaps of even more concern than the monetary loss that would have resulted from a collapse of the round would be the reversion to protectionism that could have threatened the entire multilateral world-trading environment.

On 15 December 1993, President Clinton notified Congress that the negotiations on the GATT had been successfully completed. Congress ratified the treaty

Figure 6–8 GATT negotiating rounds

Round	Starting Date of Round	Number of Countries	Value of Trade Covered (Billions of U.S. Dollars)
Geneva	1947	23	10
Annecy	1949	33	NA
Torquay	1950	34	NA
Geneva	1956	22	2.5
Dillon	1961	45	4.9
Kennedy	1964	48	40
Tokyo	1973	99	155
Uruguay	1986	117	755

NA = Not available

Source: Economic Review (Federal Reserve Bank of Kansas City) (79, No. 3 third quarter, 1994).

by large majorities in both houses in a special session in late November 1994. In the final analysis, both the United States and the EU backed away from the brink and accepted a compromise solution. The overall cut in tariffs to which members agreed was 40 percent. Agriculture and textiles were brought into the agreement, and the EU agreed to liberalize its common agricultural policy. The Americans were successful in including intellectual property in the agreement, and the round allowed for payment of royalties and strengthened the security of patents, trademarks, and copyrights.[20] Disagreements over audio-visual trade were deferred, and the French were permitted to continue to discourage further market penetration by the U.S. television industry through taxes and through continuing to subsidize their own industry. The parties also agreed to continue talking about financial services and did not tighten antidumping laws. They also announced that the GATT bureaucracy that administers the agreement would be replaced by the WTO. Figure 6–9 summarizes the key changes in GATT that resulted from the Uruguay Round.

As the dust cleared from the conclusion of the GATT negotiations, there was speculation in some quarters that the Uruguay Round marked the end of omnibus multilateral trade negotiations—the last of the GATTs, so to speak. The concern was that such negotiations are simply too complicated and difficult. Others were concerned that the agreement failed to deal adequately with many pressing issues and focused too much on yesterday's, not tomorrow's, industries.[21] However, when the negotiators have recovered from the fatigue of their efforts, appraised their successes, and considered what remains to be done to advance international trade and ward off protectionist tendencies, a new round of talks will most likely be initiated. As we can see from Figure 6–10, the world-trade picture has been favorably affected by each round of GATT negotiations, and it is unlikely that these benefits will be foregone in the future.

Regional Trading Organizations

Recent years have seen the formation of several regional trading organizations. The two most prominent examples are the *European Union* (EU) and the new *North American Free Trade Agreement* (NAFTA). Many believe that the world is moving in the direction of the establishment of trading zones held together by bilateral arrangements or by a strong organizational framework like the EU. There is concern among those committed to free trade that these regional blocs will undermine GATT and other multilateral efforts to build an open world market. Others are more sanguine about the trading blocs, suggesting that trading blocs can focus on open trading within the blocs without necessarily opposing free trade outside the regions. In fact, some observers go so far as to suggest that regional trading blocs will make movement toward an open multilateral trading system easier because it will be simpler to conduct negotiations among three or four parties than with the 150 or so members of the GATT.

The EU. Until 1994, the organization was known as the European Community (EC). It consisted of 12 member nations: France, Germany, Great Britain, the Netherlands, Luxembourg, Italy, Denmark, Ireland, Belgium, Spain, Greece, and Portugal. Several countries made application to join the EU in 1992–1993. These included Finland, Sweden, Hungary, the Czech Republic, Austria, Norway, and Switzerland. Those that were accepted to membership, effective in January 1995,

Important Tariffs
Cut of more than 33% on thousands of products, including electronics, wood, and metals.

Textiles
Phaseout over ten years of quotas that protect industrialized countries from cheaper Third World imports.

Product Dumping
Tougher restrictions on exporting goods at below-cost prices. Among U.S. industries hurt in the past: steel, shipmaking, automakers.

Agriculture
Gradual cut of 36% on crop tariffs and crop export subsidies. Countries dependent on crop exports will benefit, but subsidized farmers in countries like France and Japan opposed change.

Intellectual Property
Clampdown on theft of copyrighted goods like bootlegged films and music. Tougher protection of patents. Stronger rules against counterfeit goods like fake designer wear.

Not Included, but to Be Negotiated Later

Entertainment
Import restrictions on American television shows and films in Europe will remain.

Financial Services
Restrictions preventing U.S. banks and securities firms from operating in Japan and other countries were left mostly intact.

Aircraft
Subsidies to the aircraft industry, such as those to the European consortium Airbus Industrie that have hurt U.S. manufacturers, were largely untouched.

Figure 6–9   GATT: The Uruguay Round results

were Finland, Austria, Norway, and Sweden. However, in a fall 1994 referendum, the Norwegian electorate voted not to affiliate with the EU, leaving the membership at 15 in 1995.

The EU was set up after World War II to bring political and economic stability to Western Europe. Known then as the European Iron and Coal Community, it was originally a free trade area for steel and coal and was gradually expanded to become a common market free of national boundaries. The EU currently is the single largest market in the world, having a population of about 350 million in 1995. The EU is much more than a regional trading organization and is therefore discussed in more detail in Chapter 13 on foreign policy and national security.

The European Free Trade Area (EFTA).   This organization was originally formed as an alternative to the EC. Its members included Sweden, Finland, Iceland, Switzerland, Austria, Norway, and, until its defection to the EC, Great Britain. With the movement of the EU toward a truly integrated economic, and perhaps in the future, political, system, the EFTA has begun to lose its position. As stated earlier, several members have now applied and been accepted for membership in the EU. EFTA has also been negotiating with the EU to create a European Economic Area. Whatever the details of the eventual resolution between EFTA and the EU, EFTA's days seem to be numbered.

The World Trade Picture

Total value of world exports and imports in trillions of U.S. dollars

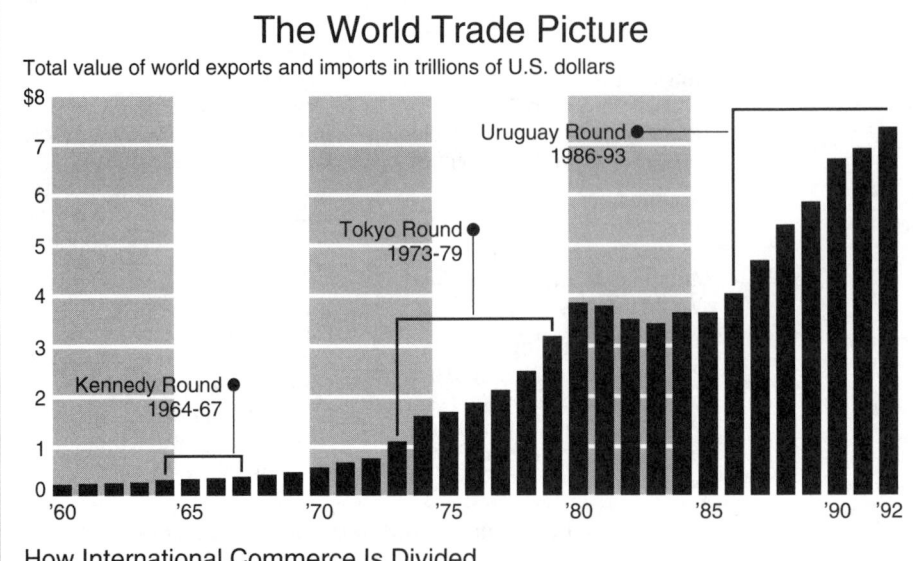

How International Commerce Is Divided
Percentage shares of world exports and imports in 1992 and 1960

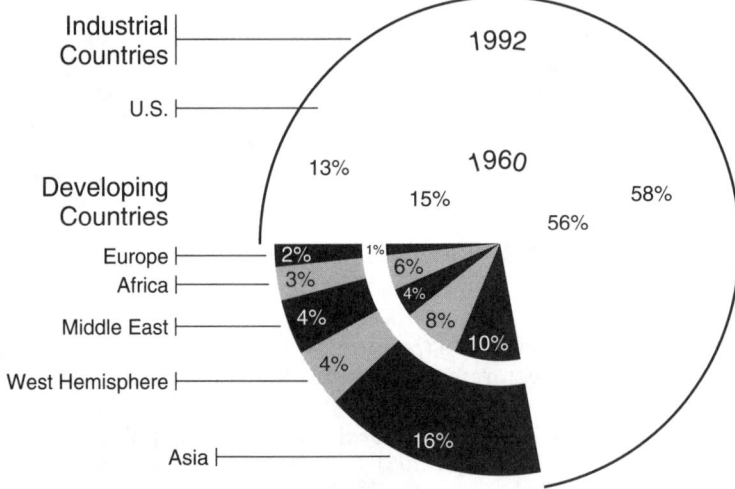

Summary Results of the Most Recent GATT Accords

- Kennedy Round (1964-67): Named for President John F. Kennedy who had urged the major industrial countries to undertake the negotiations. Key results included an average reduction of about 35% in tariffs on manufactured goods the introduction of rules against dumping.

- Tokyo Round (1973-79): These talks yielded further reductions in tariffs on industrial goods and made it harder for countries to use licenses, customs rules and technical standards to keep imports out.

- Uruguay Round (1986-93): Like past agreements, the latest accord is intended to cut tariffs on a wide variety of goods including, for the first time, a wide array of agricultural products. The pact also includes protections for patents and copyrights. In addition, the agreement calls for the creation of a new— and in some ways more powerful— Multilateral Trade Organization to replace GATT.

Figure 6–10   The World Trade Picture

Source: Wall Street Journal, Dec 16, 1993, p. A–12. Reprinted by permission of AP/Wide World Photos.

Asia-Pacific Region.   As we suggested earlier in this chapter, the Asian market for U.S. exports has been expanding quite rapidly since the early 1980s. Its share of U.S. exports almost doubled in 20 years—from 9 percent in 1972 to 17 percent in 1992. This region of the world will become even more important to the United States in the next 20 years.

At present there is no direct counterpart to either the EU or NAFTA in the Asia-Pacific region of the world. However, regional organizations offering collaborative programs that could eventually assume that role do exist there. One possibility is to convert the Association of Southeast Asian Nations (ASEAN) from what once was primarily a regional security organization to an economic trading bloc. The best candidate, however, is probably the Asian-Pacific Economic Cooperation (APEC) organization. This group was set up in 1989 to encourage economic cooperation in the region. At its 1994 meeting in Bogar, Indonesia, the APEC heads of state agreed to move toward free trade within the region in the first decade of the next century. The APEC membership embraces 18 countries, including the United States, Canada, Australia, New Zealand, Mexico, and Chile.[22] The 17 economies joining the United States in APEC now account for over half of all U.S. trade.

NAFTA.   The North American continent's answer to the EU is the North American Free Trade Agreement. This 1993 policy shift extended the U.S.-Canadian Free Trade Agreement to include Mexico and thereby developed an open trading market for the entire continent. It is one of the largest markets in the world, with a population of some 350 million people. President George Bush, Prime Minister Brian Mulrooney of Canada, and President Carlos Salinas of Mexico completed negotiations on the agreement before Mr. Bush's and Mr. Mulrooney's leaving office. The Clinton administration negotiated additional side agreements to NAFTA on both labor and environmental issues before agreeing to submit it to Congress. The treaty was ratified by both Mexico and Canada and was narrowly approved by the U.S. Congress in November 1993.

As alluded to earlier, there has been opposition to the agreement by those fearing a loss of U.S. and Canadian jobs to Mexico. While there will undoubtedly be short-term dislocations, most credible estimates suggest that the United States will gain overall—even in the short term—by creating such a large market. For the long run, the weight of opinion is that the United States could hardly afford not to proceed with the agreement. The transition, however, must be aided by providing retraining and other assistance to any U.S. workers displaced by manufacturing shifts that might take place.

Studies reported during the NAFTA debate estimated that the United States will lose about 150,000 low-skill jobs in the short run as a result of NAFTA. But 325,000 higher-skill jobs would be created—a net gain of 175,000 jobs. Mexico would gain a total of 609,000 new jobs and would increase exports to the United States by $7.7 billion. Some observers, however, believe that the major wage change would be on the Mexican side of the border, as wages increase with the improvement in productivity. They also argue that U.S. jobs in low-wage industries not lost to Mexico would eventually be lost to other low-wage countries in the world.

Another challenge to NAFTA came from environmentalists concerned that the agreement would reinforce Mexican development at the expense of the environment in both countries. But a study by the World Bank supported just the opposite conclusion.[23] The study concludes that fast-growing economies with liberal trade policies have experienced less pollution than closed economies.

Proponents of NAFTA argue that it is in our economic and political interests to help Mexico develop. An agreement like NAFTA is the only real possibility for Mexico to create growth and stability at home, and it is in the U.S. interest to have a stable, prosperous neighbor on its southern border. Among other benefits is the fact that Mexico has large, untapped oil deposits (estimates of 50 billion barrels) that, if they can be developed, would help reduce U.S. reliance on foreign oil. In addition, as Senator Richard Lugar put it during the NAFTA debate, "I don't deny that there will be jobs lost in NAFTA or in GATT. What I am certain of is that we do not have a free trade zone in our hemisphere. NAFTA is the critical link to Central and South America, to get a solid base. Without NAFTA our bargaining power with the EC or with the Pacific Rim is very suspect."[24]

The economic impact of NAFTA will not be determined for a few years. Yet, to date, the results have been encouraging for some industries, particularly autos, computers, telecommunications, and other high tech equipment. Some agricultural and retailing marketers have also shown sizable export gains. Overall, U.S. exports to Mexico grew by 22 percent in the first year of the agreement, and imports from Mexico grew 23 percent. The sizable job losses in the U.S. predicted by some NAFTA opponents have not materialized. Although there will undoubtedly be fluctuations in the import/export relationship, such as those created by the Mexican currency crisis in late 1994, so far the impact has been as predicted by the most reasonable proponents.

The next stage of hemispheric economic relations will be the eventual expansion of NAFTA to include other Latin American and Caribbean nations. Chile and the United States opened discussions about including these nations in NAFTA in 1995, and the leaders of 34 nations in the hemisphere (with only Fidel Castro absent), meeting in Miami in late 1994, agreed to work toward the creation of a free trade zone stretching from Alaska to Argentina by the year 2005. If successful, it would create a market of more than 850 million consumers.

In summary, trading blocs—be they benign or aggressive—seem to be the future. Both the Bush and the Clinton administrations supported ratification of NAFTA. The weight of professional opinion also appears to support the view that the United States would be ill advised to stick its head in the sand and ignore this worldwide trend. NAFTA will provide great bargaining strength to North America. It will also form a foundation upon which other Latin American and Caribbean countries can be brought into a hemispheric free trading zone.

The Special Problem of Japan

The problem of the persistent trade deficit that the United States runs with Japan will also require the continued attention of policymakers of both nations. In 1994 alone Japan accumulated a trade surplus with the U.S. of about $60 billion. This represents roughly 40 percent of U.S.'s trade deficit with the rest of the world. Particular problems with this imbalance are:[25]

- U.S. output and employment are transferred out of the country under conditions of less than full employment.
- Servicing the accumulated foreign debt requires additional transfers of U.S. resources abroad.

- The resulting continued depreciation of the dollar adversely affects the U.S. terms of trade and reduces our wealth and income. It also could eventually lead to higher inflation in the United States.
- The bilateral deficit with Japan generates pressures for protectionist measures that would inevitably reduce U.S.'s welfare and hurt other foreign policy objectives.

Evidence compiled by the International Institute of Economics (IIE) suggests that, although such macroeconomic factors as savings, investment, relative demand between the two nations, and currency exchange rate relationships clearly are primarily responsible for the trade deficits, a large share of the problem results from U.S. companies inability to gain access to Japanese markets.[26] In other words, an important aspect of the problem is not just our imports from Japan—it is our lack of export access to Japan. "Japanese market limitations have a large and disproportionate impact on the United States because of the sectoral composition of the two economies and the interaction of their governments' policies."[27]

Among the most important structural problems in Japan, according to the IIE, are the *keiretsu* system of linkages among Japanese companies and their suppliers and partners and the lack of an effective competition policy to counter their tendency to close markets to outsiders. Other problems are the Japanese approach to product liability and regulation; an inefficient product and service distribution system; the Japanese land use policy; and Japanese policies toward intellectual property rights. The international trade chapter of the 1994 *Economic Report of the President* suggested that "if Japan were to eliminate all formal and informal barriers to trade, U.S. exports to Japan would initially increase by somewhere in the range of $9 billion to $18 billion per year."

There is evidence that the U.S. and Japanese economies are converging at a fairly rapid pace. American exports to Japan have been growing at a more rapid rate than have Japanese exports to the United States. But the rate of convergence is not quick enough to solve the problems cited above. The IIE policy recommendations to begin to solve the problem have both macro- and microeconomic dimensions. At the macro level they suggest the following:[28]

- The United States should restore its underlying competitiveness and sharply reduce its budget deficit.
- Japan should stimulate its domestic demand sufficiently to restore sustained annual growth of $3\frac{1}{2}$ to 4 percent of GDP. This should be achieved through fiscal policy to avoid monetary easing that could weaken the yen.
- A system of target zones should be established to avoid renewed misalignments in the real exchange rate between the dollar and the yen.

At the micro level the IIE recommends that the United States should continue its efforts to improve its competitive situation. Steps should include reforming our educational system, increasing private savings through tax changes, and enhancing government support for private investment. Japan should give high-priority attention to antitrust policy, product liability law, patent policy, shareholder rights, and land use policy. "The goal should be to eliminate practices in either country that clearly impede trade with the other. In cases where only one or a very few American firms are competitive, an appropriate goal might be simply the acceptance of those firms into the cartel."[29]

The current U.S. policy toward Japan centers on the United States–Japan Framework for a New Economic Partnership, which was announced by President

Clinton in 1993. The framework calls for many of the reforms discussed above. Talks between the countries were organized into five areas:[30] government procurement, regulatory reform and competitiveness, other major sectors such as autos and auto parts, economic harmonization, and implementation of existing arrangements and measures. The framework establishes "objective criteria" to assess progress. It also raises the political profile of the talks by incorporating biannual meetings between the U.S. president and the Japanese prime minister to ensure that progress is made to resolve outstanding issues. It was the lack of progress in these talks that precipitated the punitive tariffs on Japanese autos announced by the United States in May 1995. Happily this crisis was resolved before the tariffs were actually levied.

CURRENCY EXCHANGE INSTABILITY

During the same post-World War II Bretton Woods Conference that established the World Bank and the IMF, a system of fixed, but adjustable, currency-exchange rates was also established. The values of the various currencies were fixed in terms of their relationship to the value of gold. These values could be altered, but only if the IMF certified that this was needed to correct a "fundamental disequilibrium."[31]

The Bretton Woods currency-exchange system worked quite well for several years. However, fixed exchange rates require that the countries of the world coordinate their monetary policies so that one country (or more) does not have a persistently higher rate of inflation than the others. If that occurred, its exports would be reduced (because its prices would increase), and its citizens would expand their imports. The result would be that the country would suffer a negative balance of trade.

During the 1960s, the United States began to incur a large trade deficit and higher inflation, making investors and governments in other countries leery about holding dollars. The increasing amount of dollars held by foreign central banks raised the specter that the United States might not be able to exchange the dollars for gold if demanded by the other central banks. The United States was unwilling to use fiscal or monetary policy to slow down the economy enough to permit it to meet the demands for converting dollars into gold at its committed price of $35 per ounce. Many countries began to face runs on their currencies. When the U.S. economy slowed in 1971 and the Fed relaxed its monetary policy, a run on the dollar started. President Richard Nixon suspended the convertibility of the dollar into gold and effectively ended the gold standard for the United States. The other countries of the world soon followed, marking the end of the fixed exchange rate system that had been used since the end of World War II. Today, most currencies float on international currency markets. A reading of daily newspapers provides the relative values of the various national currencies vis-à-vis the dollar, which has emerged as the benchmark currency for the international system of exchange rates.

The closest thing we have seen to a fixed-currency exchange system since the end of the Bretton Woods Agreement is the European Monetary System (the EMS), established by the EC in 1979. This system links, in a fixed but adjustable relationship, the currencies of several member nations of the EC to a range of values around the German mark. (The adjustable nature of this system has allowed a number of devaluations by individual member nations over the years.)

The EMS has been under considerable pressure since the merger of East and West Germany. In order to pay the costs of reunification without raising taxes or incurring inflation, the German government borrowed heavily on international capital markets. This borrowing drove up their real interest rates and increased unemployment and raised the value of the German mark on international currency markets. Since the other countries of the EMS needed to maintain their link to the mark (unless they took the formal step of devaluation), their interest rates, currency values, and unemployment also rose. The decline in economic activity throughout the EC nations worsened. In June 1993, unemployment rates in the EC countries averaged over 10 percent, with predictions that they would move above 12 percent in 1994.

In the fall of 1992, following major attempts to maintain their currencies' relationship with the mark, both Great Britain and Italy *temporarily* withdrew from the EMS. They cut interest rates, and the value of their currencies declined sharply (e.g., the British pound dropped from almost $2 per pound to about $1.50). Their economies also began to improve. The question now is whether the EMS can survive for the long term. Are the member nations willing to accept the same high interest rate low rate of economic growth that the Germans have chosen as the right policy for themselves (but that is magnified in the other economies)? At the beginning of 1995, unemployment rates were 8.3 percent in Germany, 12.6 percent in France, 14.6 percent in Belgium, 9.2 percent in Britain, 24.3 percent in Spain, and 11.6 percent in Italy. The comparable U.S. rate was about 5.9 percent (it dropped to 5.7 percent in May 1995). This situation also raises questions about how, and whether, the 1993 Maastricht agreement to adopt a common currency and monetary policy for the EU can or will be implemented by their target year of 1999 at the latest.

Some analysts still argue for a return to a gold (or other) fixed standard for currencies. They believe that the often-erratic movements of world currencies destabilize and inhibit the flow of commerce among countries because of the currencies' volatility, and damage economic policy coordination among the industrial powers. They are also concerned that floating exchange rates impede the ability of central banks to pursue domestic anti-inflationary policies.

Those who prefer the current system of floating exchange rates argue that fixed rates are never successful for very long; they eventually break down as nations pursue their own national economic priorities when they come in conflict with their fixed rate of currency exchange. In any case, a number of financial instruments now exist to allow the investor to hedge currency fluctuations.

Critics of fixed currency-exchange systems also point out that it is virtually impossible for a nation to stabilize the value of its currency at an unrealistically high level if its economic fundamentals do not support that value. Currency traders (mainly banks) channel money into countries with low inflation rates, trade surpluses, and high interest rates. It is unlikely that a country can counter that pressure. France, Italy, and Great Britain all tried to stabilize currency values in 1992 and 1993 by having their central banks buy their currencies on the open market. They had minimal success. The reason is that no country, or even group of countries, has the wherewithal to have much of an impact on currency values. Each day about $650 to $800 billion is traded in the currency exchange markets. The most these nations have at their disposal to trade is a fraction of that amount, less than 5 percent—not enough to make a dent.

In remarks typical of opponents of fixed exchange rates, Milton Friedman, a Nobel Laurate in economics, asked: "How many more fiascoes will it take before responsible people are finally convinced that a system of pegged exchange rates is not a satisfactory financial arrangement for a group of large countries with independent political systems and independent national policies?"[32]

SUMMARY AND FUTURE POLICY ISSUES

The environment in which world trade is conducted is in a rapid state of transition. The level of world trade has increased and has become a much more important component of national economic policy. At one time the United States had the twin luxuries of having its own large continental market to itself and having a lock on much of foreign trade elsewhere, but it now faces a situation where U.S. industries need to compete actively for both advantages. This change has come at a time when international markets will make the difference between a U.S. economy that thrives and one that stumbles along at a low rate of growth. Thanks to the end of the Cold War, the United States will be able to direct resources away from defense and toward economic development. The nation has the added advantage of emerging as the only true military superpower left in the world.[33] But with the disappearance of the Soviet threat, the value of the United States as a protective ally is diminished.

World markets have also changed in that we now not only compete for capital, markets, and new technology with the Europeans but find that many of our toughest competitors are Japan and the newly industrialized nations of Asia. Added to this new environment for international trade are the rise of regional trading blocs and the uncertainty of their eventual effects on efforts to expand free trade. Economic policymakers need to recognize that multinational corporations—in many cases forming strategic alliances with each other—have become major players in the world economy. These corporations have little loyalty to any nation. All the implications of this evolution of corporate control for governmental economic policy makers are unknown, but certainly they include the fact that those policy makers have less power over the levers of economic development than has been the case historically.

The Clinton administration arrived at a crucial time in international economic policy. There were both long-term and short-term policy issues that needed to be settled during President Clinton's first term that will have long-lasting implications. For the short term, it was important that the worldwide economic slowdown begun in 1991 be ended as quickly as possible. The recovery from recession occured in 1994 in most nations. Germany and Japan both must remain convinced that expansionary domestic policies on their part are required for the world trading system to function effectively. Japan must also be persuaded to play a mature role in world economic and political affairs and open its domestic markets to world competitors. It will continue to be important for all industrialized nations to do all within their means to assist Russia and the other former members of the Soviet bloc in developing their market economies as quickly as possible.

For the long term, the United States must ensure the successful implementation of the newly agreed-upon Uruguay Round of the GATT talks. The world economy is at a point where it needs the boost that would be provided by a further elimination of both tariff and nontariff barriers to trade. Most free traders would also agree that it is crucial that, with the congressional ratification of NAFTA and GATT completed, the United States should move as quickly as possible to extend the NAFTA agreement to its neighbors in South America and the Caribbean area. Within its own domestic economy, if the United States is to be competitive in the new world economy, the nation needs to make the investments in its physical, institutional, and human infrastructure that will make possible the productivity improvements that are necessary.

The administration, in cooperation with other nations, also needs to give attention to those institutions that serve the international community. Both the World Bank and the IMF are due for a reassessment of their purpose and manner of operation. The world environment has changed since they were created, and it would be unnatural if both did not require fine tuning. The next key priority of the industrial nations should be to aid those countries of the developing world that have not yet been brought into the worldwide economic expansion, paying particular attention to any developing countries suffering short-term problems as a result of the new GATT agreement. The World Bank and the IMF will be indispensable in that effort. As in the case of Eastern Europe, expansion of developing world economies is in both the political and economic interests of the United States and its trading partners.

DISCUSSION QUESTIONS

1. Discuss the various means a nation has at its disposal to restrict imports coming into its borders. Are these tools likely to be effective in improving a nation's balance of trade? Why or why not? What are the primary determinates of a nation's trade balance?
2. Discuss why or why not protectionist measures would or would not save jobs in the United States.
3. Should the United States move as quickly as possible to include several of the Latin American nations within the framework of the North American Free Trade Agreement? What would be the benefits/costs of such an expansion?
4. Prepare a position paper attacking or defending the current U.S. policy of promoting free trade.
5. The Japanese have been accused by the Clinton administration of purposely closing several of their markets to imports from the U.S. and other nations. Is this criticism justified? What can the U.S. do to improve its access to the Japanese markets?

SUGGESTED READINGS

Berhanu Abegaz, Patricia Dillon, David H. Feldman, Paul F. Whiteley, (eds.), *The Challenge of European Integration: Internal and External Problems of Trade and Money,* Westview Press (Boulder, Colo., 1994).

C. Fred Bergsten, *American in the World Economy,* Institute for International Economics (Washington, D.C., 1988).

Peter B. Kenen, (ed.), *Managing the World Economy: Fifty Years after Bretton Woods,* Institute for International Economics (Washington, D.C., 1994).

Paul R. Krugman and Paurice Obstfeld, *International Economics: Theories and Policy,* (3rd ed.), Harper Collins (New York, 1994).

Theodore H. Moran, *American Economic Policy and National Security*, Council on Foreign Relations Press (New York, 1993).

NOTES

1. David M. Gold and William C. Gruben, "GATT and the New Protectionism," *Economic Review* (Dallas, Tex.: Federal Reserve Bank of Dallas, 1994), (third quarter), 42.

2. *Economic Report of the President* (Washington, D.C.: U.S. Government Printing Office, 1994), 208.

3. Current account refers to the balance of exports and imports.

4. For more detail, see Cletus C. Coughlin, K. Alec Crystal, and Geoffrey E. Wood, "Protectionist Trade Policies," *Journal of the Federal Reserve Bank of St. Louis* (January–February, 1988).

5. The process and regulations under which quality systems are reviewed and certified were produced by the International Standards Organization (ISO). The set of procedures described for certification is known as ISO 9000.

6. Adam Smith, *The Wealth of Nations*.

7. The example used in this section is drawn from Holley H. Ulbrich, *International Trade and Finance: Theory and Policy* (Englewood Cliffs, N.J.: Prentice Hall, 1983), chap. 3.

8. David Ricardo, *Principles of Political Economy and Taxation* (London and New York: Dutton, 1911).

9. This section draws primarily from two sources: The *Economic Report of the President* (Washington, D.C.: U.S. Government Printing Office, 1986) and Coughlin, Crystal, and Wood, 1988.

10. Coughlin, Crystal, and Wood, 1988.

11. For a complete description of Nike's organization and method of production dispersion, see M. T. Donague and R. Barff, "Nike Just Did It," *Regional Studies* (1992).

12. For an excellent discussion of the dumping issue and its detailed status under the new GATT agreement, see Gold and Grubben, 1994.

13. This section draws on an excellent discussion of the current status of both the IMF and the World Bank contained in "Fine Art of Persuasion," *The Economist*, 12 October, 1991, p. S33(5).

14. "A New Blueprint," *The Economist*, 1 October, 1994, p. 23.

15. Council of Economic Advisors Jeffrey Sachs, Washington, D.C.: U.S. Government Printing Office, 1988).

16. *The Economist*, 12 October, 1991.

17. See, for example, Peter D. Sutherland, "If GATT Fails, We All Lose," *Wall Street Journal*, 19 October, 1993, p. 16.

18. "The Eleventh Hour," *The Economist*, 4 December, 1993, pp. 23–24.

19. *Economic Report of the President* (Washington, D.C.: U.S. Government Printing Office, 1994), p. 234.

20. For more detail on the specifics of the agreement, see "And Now for Something Completely Different," *The Economist*, 18 December, 1993, p. 59.

21. For example, see Douglas Harbrecht, "GATT: It's Yesterday's Agreement," *Business Week*, 27 December, 1993, 36.

22. The membership of APEC as of 1995 included: Australia, Brunei, Canada, Chile, China, Hong Kong, Indonesia, Japan, Malaysia, Mexico, New Zealand, Papua New Guinea, Philippines, Singapore, South Korea, Taiwan, Thailand, United States.

23. "International Trade and the Environment," *World Bank Policy Research Bulletin* (January–February 1993).

24. *Fiscal Policy Bulletin* (Indianapolis, Ind.: The Indiana Fiscal Policy Institute, October 1992).
25. C. Fred Bergsten and Marcus Nolad, *Reconcilable Differences? U.S.-Japan Economic Conflict* (Washington, D.C.: Institute for International Economics, 1993).
26. Bergsten and Nolad, 1993, 200.
27. Bergsten and Nolad, 1993.
28. Bergsten and Nolad, 1993, 207–232.
29. Bergsten and Nolad, 1993, 243.
30. *Economic Report of the President,* 1994, 220.
31. *The Economist,* 12 October, 1991.
32. Milton Friedman, "Deja Vu in Currency Markets," *Wall Street Journal,* 22 September, 1992, p. A24.
33. Germany and Japan certainly qualify as economic superpowers.

7

Poverty and the Welfare Problem

The faces and cases of poverty in the United States are both heartrending and disturbing. The vignettes below illustrate the face of the poverty issue, even if they cannot measure the size and shape of what we refer to in this chapter as *the welfare mess*.

Vignette 1:   Linda Baldwin lives in the South Side of Chicago. She is the mother of four young children and has no husband. She used to be on welfare, but now leaves for her $6-an-hour clerical job at 7:30 A.M. each morning. Her children remain behind with a patchwork of child care that sometimes works. She is feeling better about herself now that she is off welfare even if she is living in a desolate high-rise apartment building. There is only one problem: her low-paying job leaves her with $169 less each month than the welfare system had provided. She is falling behind $7.75 for every day she works at a paying job. She wonders if it is all worth it.

Vignette 2:   Thirty-three years old and a mother of three, Mary Ann Moore has a laundry list of the problems that can arise after a welfare recipient goes out to find work as now required under Illinois' attempt to reform welfare. She has landed and lost at least 11 jobs in the past five years and has gone through perhaps twice as many since receiving her first welfare check at age 19. She has driven trucks and peddled nuts, fried eggs and bathed invalids. She has strapped a revolver on her hip to guard the high-rise building complex where she was brought up. She no longer qualifies for food stamps or welfare. The facts of life are, however, that she remains only a sick child or an ailing $1,200 automobile away from disaster. She starts each new day at 3:30 A.M.

What does society do for the Linda Baldwins and Mary Ann Moores of the world? Is it reasonable to think that either person can be a true participant in the president's plan "to end welfare as we know it"?

These cases only illustrate the individual complexities of a problem that is afflicting millions of people who struggle, without much hope, against the odds. Why are there so many such people in the world's richest country? Foreign visitors to the United States frequently comment on one of public policy's more notable discontinuities: by its own definition, the world's richest nation tolerates a high level of poverty, in particular among its nonwhite citizens.[1] The argument has sometimes been dismissed by many people in the United States who like to point out that all countries have to deal with poverty. Thoughtful people, however, have recognized that the problem is more than just an embarrassment for a nation of plenty, founded on the idea of equality. The problem reflects the reality that a large number of its citizens are truly afflicted with an insufficiency of resources and that the effects of this insufficiency extend far beyond vignettes of private struggle and hardship.

Poverty is a term that must be handled carefully, for sloppy definitions lead to unworkable policy thinking. A beginning is to recognize that poverty is not a new condition but a problem as old as human society. To found recommendations for social action on the eradication of so old a condition is to tempt the patience of even the most tolerant reader, who might well wonder what solutions could be proposed to eliminate a condition that has never in history been solved and that, by definition, cannot be solved. The poor, as the Old Testament points out, have always been with us.

The current debate does not require that we begin with the start of recorded history. A historical perspective is required, however, because U.S. national policy efforts to deal with the most recent incidence of mass poverty began with the Great Depression of the 1930s. The Depression was a massive shock to U.S. public consciousness: persistent conditions of unemployment and negative income growth afflicted an unusually large proportion of the U.S. population. Before 1929, gross national product (GNP) (and gross domestic product, GDP) had grown at an average annual rate of 3.5 percent for over a generation, and normal unemployment involved only 1.5 to 2.2 million workers, or less than 5 percent of the workforce. The Roaring Twenties were, indeed, a time of excitement, change, and economic prosperity.

The four-year period following the stock market crash in October 1929 saw ever-deepening depression. Unemployment increased 10 times during the period from 1929 to 1932, and the GNP fell by over 10 percent per year, on average. Over the same period, some 11,000 banks failed—44 percent of the 1929 total number of banks—causing nearly $2 billion in deposits to disappear. In short,the economy had collapsed in what became a decade-long depression that ended only with the onset of World War II.[2] So deep and long was the Great Depression that massive government experimentation—most significantly federal experimentation—was required to invent new programs and responses to what had become not only a national but also a global economic and social disaster. New programs of social insurance, aid to families with dependent children, and unemployment insurance resulted from the Depression experiment.

As we shall see, however, the policy effects of the Great Depression are still with us. Thus, attempts to cope with the poverty and welfare issues of the 1990s include the logics, policies, and machinery of the 1930s as well as the War on Poverty of the 1960s and the experimental consolidation of poverty policy efforts during the 1970s and 1980s. As a result, the U.S. poverty and welfare problem has become increasingly complex over time and has only slightly diminished from the War on Poverty days that launched the last major attack on one of the nation's most serious problems.

This chapter examines four issues. First, a definition of what might be taken to be the original problem is presented with supporting data to show the length and breadth of the U.S. poverty problem. Second, the basic policies and programs designed to deal with poverty, measures that some would refer to as the *welfare mess,* are outlined. Third, an assessment of some of the leading proposals to deal with the combined problems of poverty and welfare is provided to set the stage for the fourth section, which presents some basic decision dilemmas readers might wish to keep in mind in formulating a judgment about future courses of public action.

DEFINING POVERTY

To appreciate the extent of poverty in the United States, clear definitions must be established, without which it would be impossible to say whether poverty is increasing or decreasing and who the people described as *poor* are. There are two basic approaches to defining poverty. One is to create an *absolute* definition of a standard of living below which is poverty. The second is to define poverty in terms *relative* to the general conditions found in society. Both approaches have their advantages and disadvantages. Absolute measures, if they can be created at all, provide a kind of benchmark to indicate the incidence of poverty in a particular community. Relative measures, by contrast, recognize that in the end the baseline for comparison is a moving target—the standard of living enjoyed by everyone else in a society—and that public policy must be defined in relation to that shifting standard. Thus, there is no perfect or correct measure. Absolute measures are very difficult to create but have the advantage of being useful to policy makers because they pose a target for action; policy discussions can address how to reduce the number of people living below an official poverty line. Relative measures are not as difficult to create, but they do not present a compelling policy target because, by definition, there will always be relative inequality; thus, it is simply not inherently clear how much relative inequality is desirable.

Definition is particularly difficult in a wealthy country like the United States. An absolute standard might propose, for example, a global subsistence definition of poverty, as this appears to be the de facto condition found in much of the world. Such a standard would say, in effect, that the poverty line would be set so that, if a person ate one less mouthful of food, that person would die. While such a definition literally describes conditions in some parts of the southern hemisphere, such a standard would clearly be inappropriate for the United States. Notwithstanding the fact that there is hunger in the United States, the number of people who are homeless, wear inadequate clothing, and have no transportation is very small. Where does one draw the line in a rich country?

Absolute Poverty

A standard answer to the question of measuring absolute poverty was developed by a Social Security Administration (SSA) economist named Mollie Orshansky in the 1960s.[3] The basis for a national measure of poverty was the then prevalent notion that the average U.S. family spent one-third of its cash income on food. Thus, Orshansky reasoned that if one multiplied a basic food budget by three and indexed the dollar amount for inflation, a constant real measure of the absolute level of U.S. poverty could be derived. The concept was compatible with the Department of Agriculture's research that defined an economy diet in terms of a market basket that would sustain people living in poverty. For over 30 years, the Orshansky poverty index has been calculated and reported. To illustrate, in 1960 the annual poverty income for a family of four was $3,022 by the SSA test, the retroactive base year of the measure. The poverty line definition was adjusted to suit the household size and further adjusted for annual inflation. The results are indicated in Table 7–1, which shows the poverty level for an illustrated family of four along with the proportion of the total U.S. population that fell below the poverty line, according to the SSA test.

It is important to recognize that the poverty line is only a statistical measure. It is not a policy measure in the sense that there is an official policy mandating that the money incomes of all citizens be brought up to meet the poverty line, although poverty data are used in some intergovernmental grants programs to determine eligibility for federal financial assistance to states and localities. The poverty line is simply a yardstick that tracks the nation's performance on a single definition of poverty—the annual money income acquired by a primary household. State and local governments have their own definitions of what constitutes poverty and, therefore, what levels of public assistance are required to ameliorate its effects. In many cases, state and local policy definitions fall well short of the national statistical definition.

The data from Table 7–1 show several things. First and most obvious is that some progress has been made in reducing the share of the population falling below the poverty line. The extent of the progress is revealed in Figure 7–1, which displays the proportion of the total population falling below the poverty line by the SSA's stringent test. By that test, nearly 20 percent of the U.S. population fell below the line in 1963. By 1992, the poverty line for a family of four had inflated to $14,335, and over 14 percent of the population, or nearly 37 million people, fell below the line. Thus, it is reasonable to conclude that the country has made some modest progress over a period of three decades. The progress is less heroic, however, if one considers that the result follows three decades of public policy aimed at eradicating poverty and that the nation has been backsliding since the War on Poverty of the Johnson and early Nixon administrations. Indeed, the period at the end of the Bush administration was marked by an upturn in levels of poverty.

The alert reader will perhaps note other points. Most dramatic is that when one realizes that the minimum wage is $4.25 per hour, then a single wage earner working 2,080 hours per year (no vacations, 40 hours per week times 52 weeks) can gross only $8,840! After payroll taxes, the worker would take home a prospective $8,164, meaning one gainfully employed person cannot even begin to push the family unit above the poverty line and two people working full time can only barely do it if the costs of child care and services required by an overworked family are not counted! Enormously wrenching choices and difficulties are associated with a

TABLE 7–1   U.S. Absolute Poverty: 1960–1991

Year	Household Median Income (Current Dollars)	Poverty Threshold Family of 4 (Current Dollars)	Percentage of Median Income (Percentage)	Total No. of Poor (Millions)	Percentage Below Poverty (Percentage)
	Poverty Line—Family of Four			*Total Population*	
1960		3,022		39.9	22.2
1961		3,054		39.6	21.9
1962		3,089		38.6	21.0
1963		3,128		36.4	19.5
1964		3,169		36.1	19.0
1965		3,229		33.2	17.3
1966		3,317		28.5	14.7
1967		3,410		27.8	14.2
1968		3,553		25.4	12.8
1969		3,743		24.1	12.1
1970	8,734	3,968	45.4	25.4	12.6
1971	9,028	4,137	45.8	25.6	12.5
1972	9,697	4,275	44.1	24.5	11.9
1973	10,512	4,540	43.2	23.0	11.1
1974	11,197	5,038	45.0	24.3	11.6
1975	11,800	5,500	46.6	25.9	12.3
1976	12,686	5,815	45.8	25.0	11.8
1977	13,572	6,191	45.6	24.7	11.6
1978	15,064	6,662	44.2	24.5	11.4
1979	16,461	7,412	45.0	26.1	11.7
1980	17,710	8,414	47.5	29.3	13.0
1981	19,074	9,287	48.7	31.8	14.0
1982	20,171	9,862	48.9	34.4	15.0
1983	21,018	10,178	48.4	35.3	15.2
1984	22,415	10,609	47.3	33.7	14.4
1985	23,618	10,989	46.5	33.1	14.0
1986	24,897	11,203	45.0	32.4	13.6
1987	26,061	11,611	44.6	32.2	13.4
1988	27,225	12,092	44.4	31.7	13.0
1989	28,906	12,674	43.8	31.5	12.8
1990	29,943	13,359	44.6	33.6	13.5
1991	30,126	13,924	46.2	35.7	14.2
1992	30,786	14,335	46.6	36.9	14.5

Source: U. S. Bureau of Census, *Current Population Reports*, pp. 60–184. Procedural changes in 1983 and 1987 make comparisons with prior years difficult.

fundamental fact that becomes more cruel in times of inflation without corresponding wage increases.

Second, while it is true that the poverty line remained unchanged as a proportion of median family income (i.e., the income level of the 50th percentile household), the conclusion may not be that poor people are relatively less poor. Another reading is that the average wage earner has become, over time, comparatively less well off during a period—namely, the 1970s and early 1980s—of comparatively high inflation. In short, a majority of American workers suffered a comparative drop in their standard of living, and the poverty line rose against a declining standard. This is a subject to which our discussion will return in subsequent chapters.

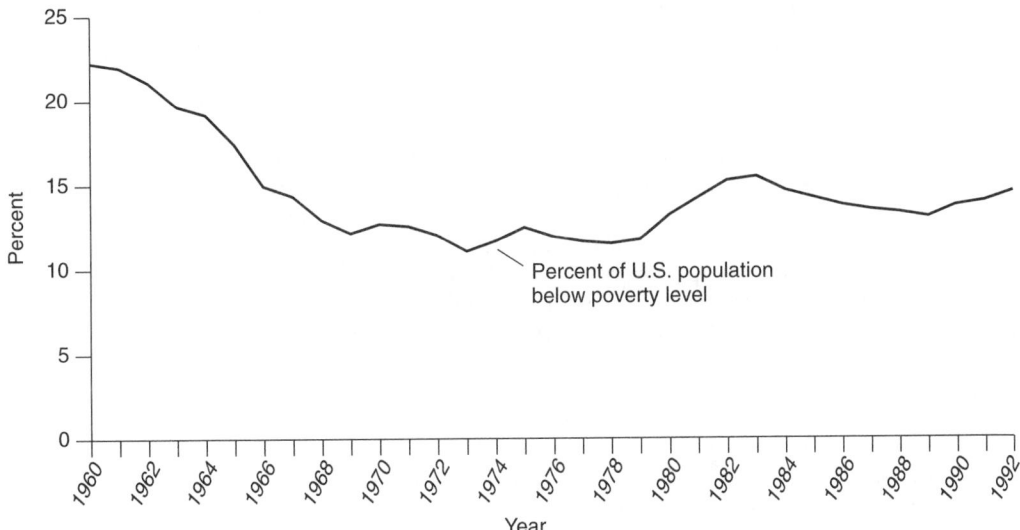

Figure 7–1   Percentage of U.S. population below poverty level, 1960–1992

Source: Current Population Reports P-60 No. 175.

A third point can be found on the right side of Table 7–1. In absolute numbers, there were only four million fewer poor in 1991 than there were in 1960. The magnitude of the problem should be riveting, however; after three decades of wrestling with the problem, at any given time 36 million people now endure conditions of poverty. The problem is even larger if the poverty definition is biased in the direction of underreporting or if one includes in the poverty category persons whose incomes are uncertain and who are hovering close to the poverty line.

This is not the whole story, however. It is critical to remember that as a poverty line merely measures a condition for purposes of tracking and not for driving public action, the line is not controlling. It does not require, for instance, that states whose populations fall below the line bring everyone up at least to the poverty line standard. Nor does it mean that public assistance and food payments must be indexed to inflation. Thus, it is not surprising to find that the actual amount of poverty, or welfare, spending falls well short of the amount required even by the theoretical poverty line. But how much short? The Orshansky measure is based on cash income before taxes. It does not include noncash income such as homegrown produce, fish from streams and lakes, and meat from the forest. Nor does it subtract taxes (since the poor pay taxes and thus have less disposable income than their gross money income indicates). Finally, the measure does not count the value of Medicaid, food stamps, housing allowances, and other benefits that define the complete income profile of a family.

When one attempts to measure the amount of poverty compared to a standard that counts the cash value of payments and services in addition to money income, clearly the amount of poverty is reduced. But how much? As Table 7–2 indicates, poverty is reduced, but not by any means eliminated. Indeed, that so much poverty should remain after so much is spent is one of the interesting findings about measuring absolute levels of poverty. We will discuss the mix of programs now on the books that provide public assistance in a later section. What Table 7–2 shows, however, is that the net effect on household money income is relatively slight. While 13.5 percent of the 1990 population was poor in money income before taxes (excluding appreciation of the value of any owned capital such as poverty), the after-tax income, including all transfers such as Social Security, Medicare, Medicaid, and unemployment compensation, reduced the poverty level to only 11 percent of the population. That means that current public policy activity and spending still leave over 27 million in the United States at a poverty level. This might be understandable and forgivable if the outlays for human welfare were small, because a simple argument could be made for increased expenditure as a simple solution to a complex problem. However, the reality is that public welfare outlays are large and increasing, yet many of them appear to fall short of even a poverty line standard.

We should note that all of these findings are compounded by evidence that the original poverty mark may be set too low. Observers argue that the measure is time bound and does not take into account modern standards of need. For example, since it appears that the actual portion of household income spent on food has sunk below 20 percent during the past 30 years, the use of the multiplier of three underreports the actual incidence of poverty. Moreover, if modern living standards now require that people have telephones, televisions, acceptable housing, child care, immunizations, energy, and transportation simply to have access to the possibilities of an advanced technological society, then the current absolute definition of poverty grossly understates the modern resource requirement to keep people alive and productive.[4] Indeed, so many questions have now been raised about the current poverty measurement system that Congress has mandated a National Academy of Sciences examination of the poverty line definition. Until the report is issued and action is taken, however, the old definition remains the dominant standard.

Relative Poverty

Because of the difficulties inherent in measuring absolute poverty in a rich and changing society, many analysts feel that *relative poverty* is a better approximation of the poverty condition. By the relativity test, there is no absolute definition of poverty. Poverty can only be indexed in terms of the well-being enjoyed by everyone else in the society. Thus, poverty in poor societies must be judged by different standards from those of rich societies.

What relative standard works for the United States? Shares of income

TABLE 7–2   Policy Impacts of Poverty Programs by Definition of Income: 1990

Income Definition	Number Below Poverty (Mil)	Percent Below Poverty (%)
1. Money Income (excluding capital gains) before Taxes	33.6	13.5
2. After Tax Money Income Plus All Nonmeans - Tested Government Transfers	35.5	14.3
3. After Tax Money Income Plus All Means- Tested Government Transfers	27.3	11.0

Source: Adapted from *Statistical Abstract of the United States 1992*, p. 460.

earned is one of the leading ways to measure relative poverty. Another is percentage of the median income. By either test, an examination of trend data reveals two very clear conclusions (Table 7–3). First, there is substantial inequality as revealed in the shares of total income earned by the rank-ordered quintiles of wage earners and by the top 5 percent of wage earners. In essence, the highest fifth of wage earners captured well over two-fifths of all income earned in the United States, while the lowest fifth of wage earners captured significantly less than 5 percent of all income. A further finding is that the top 5 percent of wage earners, who earned $102,358 per household or higher in 1990, captured not quite one-fifth of all income earned. The general pattern of relative income shares has been stable over several decades, reflecting the institutionalization of income inequity in U.S. society. Other societies, by contrast, do not show nearly the income inequality of the United States, although cross-national comparisons reveal a much more varied pattern in the distribution of wealth—the stock of land, buildings, securities, and equipment owned by a population—than is revealed in the analysis of income alone.

The second conclusion from Table 7–3 is that over the past two decades what was once a relatively stable pattern has begun to drift. As a result, during the 1970s and 1980s, an ever-increasing disparity has occurred between the top and bottom layers of income earners. In percentage terms, the drift may not appear large— 42.7 percent of all income for the highest fifth in 1967 and 46.4 percent in 1990— but the numbers are huge: 250 million people generating a greater than $5 trillion economy are steadily becoming more unequal in income! Similarly, the top 5 percent is also increasing its share of income, suggesting an elitist shift in the capture of income shares. Slowly but surely, the U.S. economy is pulling people apart in their relative economic standings: the rich have been getting richer, and the poor have been getting poorer. Why this is happening is subject to much analysis in later chapters about the structure of households and wage earnings and the comparative abilities of the population to capture advantages from the globalization of economic growth. But that the increasing disparity of earnings is occurring is both undeniable and worrisome to those who ponder the effects of economic and social trends on the general welfare of the population.

The reader should note that this discussion has concentrated thus far largely on the statistical dimension of an increasingly complex problem. Poverty in some quarters has been acquiring a much harder edge. One indicator is the rise in the number of homeless people concentrated largely in the cities. Estimates vary,[5] but most compelling are those suggesting at least a 40 percent national increase in homelessness during the 1980s with current estimates ranging from more than 500,000 to under 2 million people plagued by homelessness. The result is a condition of abject poverty—people literally without a dwelling, subject to the risks and meanness of life on the streets. John E. Schwarz summarizes the condition:

> Homelessness is in many ways at the vortex of impoverishment. It combines the many horrors of poverty. A tenement is gutted by fire, or is gentrified, and the tenants lose their homes, the jobless among them unable to find other affordable homes in a tight housing market. Or a textile worker loses his job, eventually becoming unable to pay his rent. He is evicted and no longer has the up-front money (both first and last month's rent plus deposit) to get another. Having no place to wash, no place to sleep, and no place to get messages, homeless people find it ever more difficult to land a new job. Virtually all who live on the streets are unemployed. One homeless person observed: "Can't get no job without a home, and you can't get a

TABLE 7–3 Relative Shares of Pre-tax Money Income Earned by U.S. Households: Rank-ordered Fifths and Top Five Percent 1967 to 1990

		1967	1971	1974	1977	1981	1984	1987	1990
Lowest Fifth	$	3,025	3,825	4,881	5,734	8,024	9,500	10,800	16,846
	%	4	4.1	4.4	4.1	4	4	3.8	3.9
Second Fifth	$	5,876	7,312	9,106	10,800	15,000	17,780	20,500	29,044
	%	11.1	10.7	10.6	10.2	10.1	9.9	9.6	9.6
Third Fifth	$	8,380	10,702	13,359	16,462	23,200	27,393	32,000	42,040
	%	17.6	17.3	17	16.9	16.7	16.3	16.1	16
Fourth Fifth	$	11,775	15,257	19,362	24,000	34,300	41,380	48,363	61,490
	%	24.6	24.5	24.5	24.7	24.8	24.6	24.3	24.1
Highest Fifth	$								
	%	42.7	43.4	43.5	44.1	44.4	45.2	46.2	46.4
Top 5%	$	18,432	24,197	30,796	38,000	55,200	68,500	80,928	102,358
	%	16.3	16.9	16.6	16.9	16.5	17.1	18.2	17.4

Source: U.S. Bureau of Census, *Current Population Reports*, P-60 Series.

home without a job. They take one and you lose both." Homelessness becomes self-perpetuating.[6]

Who Is Poor?

Increasingly worrisome is the discovery of who the poor really are. One way to see the pattern is to take a statistical snapshot in a recent year and examine the factors associated with poverty. Table 7–4 shows the poverty demographics. First, in absolute numbers the problem of poverty is a white problem, not a stereotypically black problem; there are more white poor persons than nonwhite poor persons. This derives from the fact that even though the incidence of poverty is higher among non-whites—32.7 percent for blacks and 17.6 percent for "other races"—African Americans constitute only 11 to 12 percent of the population and all persons of color taken together account only for about 22 percent of the population. What is so dramatic, however, is the relative burden of poverty carried by blacks as compared to whites; nearly three times the incidence of poverty occurs among blacks compared to whites. This phenomenon of black people enduring a doubling and tripling of white disabilities in income, employment, education, and health is strongly suggestive of a continuing racial disparity in U.S. society.

A second finding is that poverty is disproportionately visited on either the very young or the very old. Indeed, over 50 percent of all persons classified as poor (See Table 7–5) occur among those not normally counted as being available for full-time productive employment. Hence, another poverty myth needs to be dispelled: many of the poor in the United States are truly helpless people, too young, too old, disabled, or caught in family circumstances that make it unlikely that they can help themselves significantly. Public policy must consider what should be done for people who appear to have limited means to help themselves. The current incidence of poverty among children is particularly alarming and is shown clearly in Table 7–4. In essence, over one-fifth of each new generation is living under conditions of deprivation. In an economic environment where the development of capable workers is regarded as the key to future prosperity, the incidence of child poverty is perhaps a direct indicator of economic suicide.

TABLE 7–4   Incidence of Poverty by Groups in 1991

1991	Percentage of Population (Percent)	Total Number of Poor (Thousands)
All persons	14.2	35,708
By racial group		
White	11.3	23,747
Non-hispanic white	9.4	17,741
Black	32.7	10,242
Others	17.6	1,719
Hispanic	28.7	6,339
By age		
Children (under 18)	21.8	14,341
Seniors (65 and over)	12.4	3,781
By family		
Female-headed household	39.7	13,824

Source: U.S. Statistical Abstract, 1992.

TABLE 7–5   Distribution of Total Number of Poor Persons by Background: 1991

1991	Percentage of Poor (Percent)	Total Number of Poor (Thousands)
All persons	100	35,708
By racial group		
White	66.5	23,747
Non-hispanic white	4.9	17,741
Black	28.7	10,242
Others		1,719
Hispanic		6,339
By age		
Children (under 18)	40.2	14,341
Seniors (65 and over)	10.6	3,781
By family		
Female-headed household	38.7	13,824

Source: U.S. Statistical Abstract, 1992.

Also important are some of the findings about why people are poor. Table 7–6 confirms what one might suspect: family background and education have much to do with the economic conditions of households. Table 7–6 contains particularly worrisome data because the recent trend toward childbirth among young single women—an increase of 150 percent from the early 1970s to the late 1980s[7]—nearly guarantees poverty for both the mother and her children. A population trend toward out-of-wedlock births, observed from 1982 to 1992, contributes to the condition of poverty among children and creates an independent social effect. The soaring percentages of never-married women 18 to 44 years of age, who have children, have changed the definition of households, the conditions of child-rearing practices, and the structure of demand for public services.

Households headed by single women deserve further comment, for there are clearly mixed effects associated with out-of-wedlock births.[8] For example, unmarried women with either bachelor's degrees or graduate professional degrees, who have children, do not cause welfare problems to be dumped on the public policy doorstep, although out-of-wedlock births in this group increased dramatically from 1982 to 1992, rising from 3 and 2 percent respectively in 1982 to 6.4 percent and 4.1 percent in 1992. Thus, the mere fact of out-of-wedlock birth does not imply a major public welfare problem, although a rousing debate did erupt during the 1992 presidential campaign involving Vice President Dan Quayle's condemnation of television's Murphy Brown for deciding to have a child without a husband as a lifestyle choice. However, when women with less than a high school education show an already high incidence of out-of-wedlock births, rising from 35 percent in 1982 to over 48 percent in 1992, and unemployed women increase out-of-wedlock births from 29 percent to nearly 45 percent, the social implications of such trends go beyond personal lifestyle choices. In effect, large numbers of children are being born in materially unpromising circumstances that virtually guarantee difficult problems of health, education, and upbringing. Private decisions about family formation and childbearing are associated with placing large numbers of children at economic and social risk, with associated public effects.

TABLE 7–6   March 1987 Poverty Rates of Young Families, by Age, Family Type, and Education of Householder: Under 25 and 25–29 Years Old

Family Type	Householder Under 25 (Percentage)	Householder 25–29 (Percentage)
Married couple: College graduate head No children	3.5	0.0
Married couple: High school graduate head No children	3.5	2.0
Married couple: High school graduate head 1+ children	18.5	9.0
Married couple: High school dropout head 1+ children	36.5	24.7
Female-headed family: High school graduate head 1+ children	72.8	57.5
Female-headed family: High school dropout head 1+ children	92.6	81.5

Source: Adapted from *The Forgotten Half: Pathways to Success for America's Youth and Young Families* (Youth and America's Future; Washington, D.C.: The William T. Grant Commission on Work, Family, and Citizenship, November 1988).

THE WELFARE MESS

Thus far, we have discussed only the dimensions of what might be considered the original poverty problem. The present problem is even more complicated, however, for U.S. government and public policy have actively attempted to deal with the original problem for many years. The cumulative result has been a welter of policies and programs representing decades of public action and inaction. The result might be referred to as the "welfare mess," a very loose term designed to cover the whole collection of public actions aimed at poverty.

Welfare received its initial, narrow definition during the Great Depression when public policy first began to address the problem of alleviating mass poverty on a national scale. Three specific programs from the 1930s are particularly significant. The first program was designed to meet the cash needs of several categories of widows (and other women without husbands) and their dependent children, through Aid to Families with Dependent Children (AFDC), popularly known as welfare. The AFDC program was established as a matching federal-state contract designed and administered by states and operated through county welfare offices. Thus, the federal government issues the broad guidelines for program operations and normally matches at least 50 percent of the level of need determined by each state. One founding assumption was that the use of AFDC would be modest and limited to widows and children who had lost the economic support of the head of the family. The possibility that a large proportion of the dependent population might consist of remarried, divorced, and separated women with numerous children was not contemplated at the time the AFDC program began.

Second, cash needs of those involuntarily thrown out of work were addressed through the Unemployment Insurance (UI) Act. This program provides cash to unemployed workers and is paid through a trust fund fed by employer contributions matched with state and federal contributions. The fund is administered by the states and supervised by the federal government. The UI aim was modest: to provide temporary support during business cycle dips. Thus, the total benefit package has a typical time limit of 26 weeks, although Congress has occasionally extended the benefit period by an additional 26 weeks during periods of lengthy recession (depression is now generally removed from public policy discussion of economic downturns).

Third, income insecurity among older people was handled by a program originally authorized as the Old Age Survivors Disability Insurance (OASDI) system, commonly known as Social Security. The program was and is a misnomer, for it was never an insurance program. That is, OASDI was not designed as a self-financed risk pool whose payout, based on premiums collected from policyholders, sustains those who are unexpectedly and prematurely widowed, orphaned, or disabled, as well as those who retire from full-time paid employment. It is true that those who participate in the Social Security program do pay into a Social Security trust fund. What is paid out, however, is subject to constant congressional redefinition and is currently indexed to inflation. Thus, payout bears no necessary relationship to what individuals pay into the fund. In effect, given current life expectancies, the individual payout is many times the individual contribution to the fund.

Finally, Congress created a system of legal entitlements comprised of civic claims on the public treasury mandated in public law. In the case of OASDI, the productivity of the current labor force must generate the money that feeds the trust fund supporting retirees. Thus, one generation comes to depend on the talent and productivity of the next generation.

The policy logic of Depression-era entitlement programs is still with us. As a principal feature, benefits are defined by a *categorical logic*, whereby government action may be invoked when an accredited government agency finds that a client belongs to a category eligible for government service or assistance. Thus, if one is a poor woman with children and lives in a household lacking either income or anyone capable of providing support for the family, then benefits from the AFDC program may be used at a monthly rate determined by the state to meet the family need. In addition, AFDC qualification means that the household qualifies for Medicaid services. Alternatively, if a person is blind or permanently or totally disabled, then he or she qualifies for Supplemental Security Income (SSI), which since 1974 represents a federal consolidation of what was once over 1,000 state and local categorical programs directed at blind and permanently or totally disabled persons. Thus, AFDC is locally administered under a state-federal contract, while SSI is federally administered with uniform benefits for each of the qualifying categories. Hence a categorical logic results: to qualify for assistance, one must first fit the category, after which certification of need can occur and resources can be disbursed. There is no halfway position of being "slightly poor" in the case of AFDC; one either qualifies or does not, and thus one either receives aid or does not.

Another attribute of categorical logical is that the many programs taken together represent not a national solution to a national problem but separate and discrete actions applied locally to specific categories of persons who have disabilities, are unemployed, have insufficient cash income, or have children in a household with an insufficient means of support. The categorical logic requires that a person or family be "beached, burned, and belly-up" before seeking assistance, which kicks in after the categorical requirement is met. Not surprisingly, once a person qualifies for AFDC, Medicaid, food stamps, rent assistance, and so forth, the incentive is to remain qualified.

A final feature is that there are gaps in coverage that must occur when cases of categorical need do not fit available programs. For example, what do people with special needs for nutrition, housing, medical care, and job training do? Suppose a single, middle-aged, able-bodied man has no children, no income, and no place to call home? People do slip through the categorical cracks.

The unwieldy nature of public programs designed to deal with different aspects of poverty and economic insecurity is illustrated in Table 7–7, which lists the major forms of public assistance according to programs that are either means tested or not. In the former case, public assistance is triggered by a certification that the client is without adequate means. In the latter case, public assistance is forthcoming regardless of whether there is need (or means) or not, because the categorical screen is not money income. Thus, while Ross Perot would not qualify for AFDC, he is as legally entitled to receive indexed Social Security payments and Medicare as the meanest pauper in the United States!

Several conclusions can be drawn from the table. Students should form their own conclusions about a number of criteria for judging the adequacy of the current welfare system. Among the issues to consider are stigma, cost, coverage gaps, equity, and work incentive. Evidence has been accumulating for many years that the current system does not really begin to meet current needs (as Table 7–2 shows). The system is also very expensive, cumbersome, and messy, as Table 7–7 documents.

FORMULATING ALTERNATIVES

What can be done about this complex mess? Alert readers will note that the mess is really two messes: the original condition of poverty in the United States and the welter of costly programs designed to deal with some part of the original mess. While there is no consensus among policy analysts and politicians about precisely what to do, there is agreement that a mess exists and a willingness to debate alternative courses of action. Thus, how one evaluates President Bill Clinton's 1993 inaugural claim that "welfare as we know it will cease to exist" depends on an assessment of a number of issues, discussed below.

Competing Ideologies

Perhaps a first cut at the problem should note that policy choice and public action derive from an initial judgment about why people are poor and what the basis is for making people less poor. Not surprisingly, there is a ferocious division of opinion about this fundamental issue. At one extreme are the views that make the condition of poverty a matter of personal responsibility. In this view, poverty means individual failure under competitive conditions—whether it is a failure of character or ability,

TABLE 7-7 Public Assistance Program Characteristics

	Means-Tested
Program	*Basic Eligibility*
Aid to Families with Dependent Children (AFDC)—Assistance to needy, dependent children in the home	Needy children lacking parental support
Food stamps—Help persons and families with low incomes obtain a more nutritious diet	Persons with low incomes
Medicaid—Furnish medical assistance to needy families with dependent children or aged, blind, or disabled individuals	AFDC or SSI recipients or those designated medically needy by the state
Public housing—Provide safe, decent, sanitary housing and related facilities for low-income families	Families of low income
Section 8—To aid low-income families in obtaining decent, safe, and sanitary housing in private accommodations	Low- and very low-income families, 30 to 50 percent of local median income
Job Training Partnership Act (JTPA)—Employment training opportunities for disadvantaged, unemployed, or underemployed	Economically disadvantaged, unemployed, or underemployed
Women, Infants, and Children's (WIC) supplemental food program—Food for mothers, infants, and children judged to be at nutritional risk	Needy mothers and children up to age five who are nutritionally deficient
School lunch and breakfast—By providing cash and commodities, maintain health and proper physical development of American children	School-age children from low-income families
Basic Education Opportunity Grant—To assist qualified students to obtain post-secondary education	Student enrollment full or half time at eligible institution
Supplemental Security Income (SSI)—Provide income to persons age sixty-five and over, blind, or disabled	Low income, age sixty-five, blind, or disabled
Title XX Day Care (Social Security Act Amendment)—To enable states to provide day care services to public assistance and other low-income families	Public assistance mothers and selected low-income less 115 percent median income

	Related Entitlement Programs—
Program	*Basic Eligibility*
Medicare	Medical care for elderly
Old Age, Survivors, Disability Insurance (OASDI)	Social Security
Unemployment Insurance (UI)	Income support

Source: Adapted from the U.S. Senate, General Accounting Office, Report to the Honorable William V. Roth, "Public Assistance Benefits Vary Widely from State to State, But Generally Exceed The Poverty Line" (HRD-81-6, 14 November, 1980), appendix 17.

Programs

Financing	*Benefit—Administration*	*Federal 1992 Outlays ($bil)*
Open-ended federal appropriation for 50 to 83 percent of state payments	Cash—State or local administration	15.1
Open-ended federal appropriations pay all food costs	Medical—State administration	19.6
Open-ended federal appropriation for 50 to 83 percent of state payments for medical service	Medical—state administration	59.8
Federal subsidies to cover debt service requirements	Rent supplement—Public housing agencies	2.4
Federal assistance payments to private service requirements	Rent supplement—Public housing agencies	2.4
Federal assisance payments to private owners and public housing agencies	Rent supplement—Public housing agencies	6.7
Federal	Training allowances, training, jobs—Local organizations	3.1
Federal	Food vouchers—USDA through local health clinics	2.6
Federal and state matching	Meals—State educational agencies	3.7
Federal funds	Tuition and books—Office of Education and designated agencies	9.7
Federal with some state supplements	Cash—Social Security office	16.2
75 percent federal matching of state funds, with $2.5 billion ceiling	Day care services—State agencies	0.6

Non-Means Tested

Financing	*Benefit—Administration*	*Federal 1992 Outlays (bil)*
Federal funds, covered by Social Security	Medical—HCFA	$124 billion
Fedral funds	Social Security office	$286 billion
Employer—employee trust fund	Cash—State employment security	Varies by state

or is simple bad luck need not occupy us at this point. By definition, the policy choices must treat the individual circumstances of poverty, a tall order.

Perhaps the strongest defense of this *individualistic* notion can be found in the *survival of the fittest* views of Herbert Spencer (1820–1903), a 19th-century social Darwinist philosopher, who is alleged to have advanced the judgment (paraphrased here) that poverty is nature's way of letting us know we are in the wrong line of work. Freely translated, the point is that in human affairs some people fail while others succeed, but resolution of the question of success and failure can only come from competitive applications of individual effort under conditions in which real failure is possible. Government's destructive intervention by constraining and controlling the competitive process and eliminating the spur to excellence points out the real prospect of failure. Spencer's statement defends the proposition that one should not attempt to intervene in a natural process that makes some people poor and others rich; when individuals find themselves poor, they should redouble their efforts to make good individual choices of jobs, marriages (or not), educations, and careers. In short, individuals are responsible for getting themselves out of economically unpromising situations. Moreover, the fact of having attained economic success is itself a sign of a just reward in a competitive environment.

Rhetorical defense of the proposition that poverty is an individual condition is echoed in the recent policy literature. One example is a caricature drawn by Michael Harrington, a policy analyst, who makes his own, very different, point about poverty.

> The poor are that way because they are afraid of work. And anyway they all have big cars. If they were like me (or my father or my grandfather), they could pay their own way. But they prefer to live on the dole and cheat the taxpayers.[9]

Another variation on the same theme, however, fixes responsibility in the following way:

> The lower-class person lives from moment to moment, he is either unable or unwilling to take account of the future or to control his impulses. Improvidence and irresponsibility are direct consequences of this failure to take the future into account . . . and irresponsible, he is likely also to be unskilled, to move frequently from one dead-end job to another, to be a poor husband and father.[10]

The direction of the argument is that individual decisions and actions are the source of social problems. Therefore, poverty and welfare solutions must be designed with that reality in mind, and thus, government intervention in these areas can have only minimal results. If the causal agents in producing states of human well-being—namely, individual effort and simple dumb luck[11]—are beyond the direct reach of the social engineer, then elaborate public policy programming is problematic. Even something as powerful as government cannot reach far enough to manage poverty's root causes!

A very different response to poverty is welfare policy design that attempts to intervene in this social condition and break the cycles that leave people poor. The most famous exponent of the *structuralist* view is Michael Harrington who, as a Democratic congressman from Massachusetts, was for many years at the center of the national poverty debates.

> The real explanation of why the poor are where they are is that they made the mistake of being born to the wrong parents, in the wrong section of the country, in the wrong industry, or the wrong racial or ethnic group. Once that mistake has been made, they

could have been paragons of will and morality, but most of them would never even have had a chance to get out. . . . The poor are caught in a vicious circle. . . . a culture of poverty. . . . In a sense, one might define the contemporary poor in the United States as those who, for reasons beyond their control, cannot help themselves. All the most decisive factors making for opportunity and advancement are against them. They are born going downward, and most of them stay down. They are victims whose lives are endlessly blown round and round the other America.[12]

Clearly, Harrington's view of the original problem involves a fundamentally different causal mechanism from the first view. As the title of his book implies, Harrington thinks that there is a structure of poverty consisting of hidden cohorts of poor people tucked away in isolated and insulated corners of U.S. cities, rural areas, and Native American reservations.

Thus, public policy faces a dilemma: the kind of welfare policy one designs depends on the causal interventions that are required to deal with the problem. But which interventions? There is no way to prove which causal contention is correct. If social conditions arise merely as an aggregation of individual choices and actions, then the individual controls the outcome. If poverty outcomes are socially determined the individual can have only marginal impact on the outcome. But the policy implications of each model are clear and profound: individual case management (if that is possible) in the former case, as nothing else will penetrate to the core of the problem; in the latter case, restructuring of the environment and social milieu in which people live and work is required.

Finally, it is quite possible that both positions are in some degree correct and that the condition of poverty contains many different kinds of people simultaneously influenced by multiple forces. This is the most difficult possibility, challenging both our intellectual understanding of the problem and our public policy system by requiring it to adapt to an enormous diversity of possible circumstances. At the individual level, for example, many personal shortcomings and disabilities can make it difficult, if not impossible, for individuals to be economically successful: mental and physical disabilities top the list. Mental disabilities can include developmental problems that limit intelligence and ability to learn as well as mental illnesses that render the individual incapable of functioning effectively. Other difficulties include lack of appropriate family support, education, personal motivation, and character. At the structural level, an enormous number of socioeconomic elements conspire to advance or retard personal effort, including the physical surroundings of the home, neighborhood, and community; the existence or nonexistence of institutions such as schools, churches, community centers, and health and sports facilities; and the structure of school-to-work transitions. Proposing programs of government intervention based on the presumption that both theories of poverty are simultaneously true thus results in perhaps the most complex public policy exercise imaginable. Whether U.S. public policy is now capable of generating *smart policy*—case-specific (i.e., customer-oriented) interventions based on systematic assessments of the individual's circumstances—remains an open question.

Policy Options

At stake in the policy debate is more than mere academic bickering over the number of angels dancing on the head of a pin. If on the one hand, Edward Banfield and others are correct, then public policy must be limited in its aspiration for curing the poverty problem. Discussion must focus instead on alleviating the pain and suffering of people who through their own actions put themselves into dire straits and endanger the prospects of both themselves and their progeny. Policy must focus on rescuing children from unhealthy environments, on providing public assistance, and on managing aggregate economic growth so that opportunity awaits people with enough gumption to go after it. Further options could focus largely on tinkering with the current systems rather than planning a major overhaul of public services. Moreover, welfare aid and services must be targeted carefully because there are many ways to throw money at the slothful and merely subsidize a higher level of poverty, squandering more resources. In Banfield's view, some people were either born to be poor or will, for reasons of individual character, become poor no matter what government tries to do. Thus, public subsidy and support can only be a palliative: they can alleviate human pain and misery and provide avenues of escape for children born into unpromising circumstances through no fault of their own. But it is a fatal conceit to suppose that public policy can change or alter some of life's most depressing realities because the core problem lies beyond the reach of public policy.

If, on the other hand, Harrington's view is persuasive, then policy shifts to a different position. Government's aim must be to break the cycle of poverty, using interventions aimed at altering the key environmental conditions that keep people poor. The many structural policy options can be expensive. For example, housing close to vibrant economic centers must be made available. Child day care services and adequate nutrition are required. Education and training are needed, especially programs tailored to the circumstances of poor clients, so that work and study arrangements, work and child care combinations, and tuition vouchers can be combined as needed. Head start programs targeting early childhood development must be available to reduce initial learning and developmental disadvantages. Even the provision of access to legal services and to practical advice on home and household management is a useful intervention. In short, massive services are required to break the suffocating grip of a culture of poverty.

Finally, a true structural approach would create and sustain community organizations capable of playing an effective role in organizing and articulating the needs of normally inarticulate and nonparticipative poor people in the public councils where decisions affecting them are made. During the War on Poverty of the 1960s, for example, the idea of community action took hold, and Community Action Programs (CAP) were directed at changing the fact that poor people are their own worst enemies when it comes to putting thoughtful pressure on government and public policy for attention. CAPs aiming to develop centers of community leadership and civic participation in poor communities were set up during the 1960s, to encourage "maximum feasible participation" in planning, designing, and running programs, by the very people whose lives were most affected by poverty. That CAPs would become a political liability was perhaps inevitable, for newly aroused and politically active poor people could not be expected to behave in a nonpartisan manner.

Over time, the services-based strategy championed by President Lyndon Johnson during the middle 1960s proved too expensive for a federal budget tightened, first, by the demands of the Vietnam War and, second, by lackluster rates of economic growth beginning after 1973. During the 1970s, the programs constituting the War on Poverty were either killed outright—such as the Office of Economic Opportunity Projects—or, with few exceptions (such as the Head Start program), were slowly strangled or transformed into bloc grants (such as was the case with the Manpower Development Training Act of 1962 that evolved into the Comprehensive Employment and Training Act of 1973 and later the Job Training Partnership Act of 1982). Despite the dismantling of what some would say was the war that was never fought, the core philosophy behind the great poverty eradication experiment remains on the policy agenda and informs current debate about where next to take the poverty policy effort.

Future Directions

The future of poverty policy can be arrayed into four blocks of options. Minimal intervention involves laissez-faire policies limited to macroeconomic management and carefully restricted relief. The policy aim is to force individuals to find their own way to prosperity; this is the view that says, "A rising tide raises all boats and public policy's job is simply to manage the tidal flow." It is the responsibility of individuals to propel themselves toward prosperity. Thus, government can legitimately use monetary and fiscal policy to stimulate *aggregate* economic stability, growth of jobs, and overall productivity. In this view, government is on sound footing in the design of trade agreements that lower barriers to imports and exports and thereby increase global levels of economic activity. Government is also legitimately interested in ameliorating the harshest effects of hunger and homelessness, although such problems are, in the minimalist view, best handled on a voluntary basis by local township trustees and community kitchens rather than by nationally authorized entitlement and implementation. Micropolicy is therefore designed as short-term relief to get people through the occasional rough patch, after which they are again placed on their own to create the opportunities that a growing, dynamic economy makes available.

A second and slightly more interventionist approach would contemplate a national income maintenance policy, whereby a minimum cash income would be guaranteed. Whether cash income would be fixed by a family assistance plan proposed in the late 1960s, a negative income tax proposed in the 1970s, or an earned income tax credit as proposed by the Clinton administration is not as critical as the strategic rationale: the poor are poor because they have not got enough money. Therefore, solve the problem by the most direct means possible: give cash to the poor! Such proponents were strongly in favor of the recent legislative initiative that produced the 1993 Earned Income Tax Credit, discussed below. The aim of this second approach is to *cash out* the other competing programs in favor of a direct attack on the core problem of insufficient cash flows.

A third and even more interventionist position would add an elaborate array of targeted services to all of the proposals summarized in the first two positions. This position would agree that there is a need to manage monetary and fiscal policy such that a growing economy creates jobs and opportunities accessible to poor and unemployed persons. Advocates agree that there also is a need for emergency relief in the form of locally administered cash assistance, community kitchens, and shelters. In addition, there is agreement with the need to create a national income maintenance system that guarantees a minimum cash income to all citizens. Yet the structuralist position goes further to argue that cash assistance, by itself, would be the equivalent of pouring cash into a losing cause. Without services structured to meet the specific needs of poor people, cash subsidies simply finance more comfortable levels of poverty, even under conditions of aggressive macroeconomic growth. Thus, cash assistance and job creation are necessary but insufficient conditions for reducing poverty, and it is precisely this demand for targeted services, discussed earlier, that distinguishes the advocates of the War on Poverty from those holding competing policy perspectives.

There are interesting variations on the services theme. One variation is to expand the availability of services by regulation rather than by either government provision, production, or purchase of services. An example can be found in the Family and Medical Leave Act of 1993 (discussed below), which mandates employers to provide unpaid leave to employees with personal or family needs and emergencies. In this way, government regulation can be used to produce a noticeable impact while the costs of such a policy are privately internalized by employers and employees themselves.

Finally, there is a fourth strategy, perhaps the communitarian ideal. Some observers find it possible to defend the idea of a full-blown national welfare state with universal human services coverage—such as might be found in Sweden and the Netherlands—where subsidies, grants, and services cover all citizens from the proverbial cradle to the grave in the form of civic entitlement. In this policy formulation, enjoyment of a minimum level of economic well-being is a right of citizenship and an obligation of government to provide (at, of course, appropriately high levels of taxation and financing). Thus, families receive grants for raising children. Universal health coverage is provided, and education and training grants are universal. Employment security is provided through elaborate unemployment insurance schemes; pensions are provided at retirement. The welfare state represents a significant departure from the liberal safety net policies that predominate in the United Kingdom or Germany or the U.S. safety net with gaping holes through which many people now fall.

Family Support Act of 1988

One of the more significant of several recent policy shifts was passage of the Family Support Act of 1988. In conceptual terms, the act was designed to encourage responsibility in forming families and in having and bringing up children. A significant step (Title I) taken by the act was authorization of states to track down and attach the wages of so-called deadbeat dads, absentee fathers who owe child support. The legislation also required states to begin operating Job Opportunities and Basic Skills (JOBS) programs, education, training, and job placement services offered to welfare recipients. Another provision was the authorization given states to package training and education with child care and other social services. This provision offered single welfare parents—mostly mothers—of preschool and school-age children training over several months, after which they would seek jobs whose earnings would *not eliminate* the partial support provided by the AFDC and Medicaid programs. Thus, social service philosophy has begun to move toward a full service concept in which the complexity of individual welfare cases is recognized and multiple services are designed to encourage a gradual withdrawal from welfare support.

Some encouraging experiments have been started in several states to combine welfare support with gainful employment. Examples include the Employment and Training (ET) program in Massachusetts and the Greater Avenues for Independence (GAIN) program in California. Evaluations conducted by the Manpower Demonstration Research Corporation (MDRC) confirm that while programs such as GAIN will not end poverty overnight, they can serve to increase employment and reduce welfare costs. State-level programs have the added advantage that they can be tailored to suit the economies, requirements, and constraints of each state and region and, in this way, shape welfare policy to suit local policy need. Such a finding militates against national solutions to the poverty problem.

There are, however, limits to the reach of the Family Support Act. The act did not appropriate resources sufficient to provide the range of services required to meet the child care, education, and training needs of single parents burdened with the full-time care of dependent children. Nor did the act determine how a full service concept of case management might work. Finally, the act did not eliminate the work disincentive already built into the present system of categorical entitlements—namely, that the labor market for entry-level workers with low skills typically offers only low wages, job instability, less than full-time work, and few employee benefits. These realities make it unlikely that welfare recipients will quickly earn their way off the welfare rolls. Not surprisingly, studies show that the majority of women on public assistance leave welfare through marriage, not through employment.[13]

Thus, much remains to be done to deal with so massive and complex a problem as poverty in the United States. What is clear is that the structure of the Family Support Act makes state and local governments the primary actors, who must try to design sophisticated client service systems and provide the array of services required to move into the economic mainstream those who are under-employed, undereducated, and hobbled by poverty and unpromising family circumstances. A great deal of competitive experimentation among states remains to be done.

Family and Medical Leave Act of 1993

National policy has also moved to alleviate the pressures that build on families that must confront extensive health care emergencies and burdens. The Family and Medical Leave Act of 1993 is a regulatory measure designed to require all employers with 50 or more workers to guarantee unpaid leave to employees burdened by illness or family responsibilities. Any worker who has been employed for one year and for at least 25 hours a week can take up to 12 weeks of unpaid leave in any 12-month period for any of the following reasons: birth or adoption of a child; serious illness of a child, spouse, or parent; or a serious illness that prevents the worker from doing the job. Under the unpaid leave policy, an employee must be given back his or her old job or an equivalent position upon returning to work.

The act provides protections against employee abuse: for example, workers on leave cannot collect unemployment or other government compensation. Companies may deny leave to a salaried employee in the highest-paid 10 percent of its workforce, if letting the worker take leave would create "substantial and grievous injury" to the enterprise. Employers can also require medical certification of the need for leave. Employers must continue to provide health care benefits during the leave but are not required to pay the worker's salary and, in the event the employee does not return to work, can ask an employee to repay any health care premiums paid by the company during the leave.

What is the likely impact of the Family and Medical Leave Act? Clearly, the power of the act resides in its ability to leverage private behavior in the interest of creating a publicly useful outcome. In an age of large enterprises, this powerful measure would relieve burdens that might cripple some families. But in this era of massive industrial restructuring, where large companies are downsizing and productivity is driven increasingly by networks of small enterprises chained together in a global production system,[14] the act's intent may be diluted simply by the realities of current labor markets. For example, of the nearly 3.9 million companies last surveyed by the United States Census Bureau in 1987, only 4 percent of companies—around 142,000—employed more than 50 workers; 96 percent of companies—about 3.7 million—had fewer than 50 workers![15] The result is that only 66 percent of all employees would be covered by the act; roughly one-third would not. Clearly, the act is not aimed at eradicating the deep pockets of poverty but, instead, simply protects already employed and secure families whose inability to confront health emergencies would only add to the crushing burdens already carried by health and social service systems trying to assist persons and families that already have failed. Thus, public policy must look elsewhere to find direct solutions for the original poverty problem.

The 1993 Earned Income Tax Credit

Another recent legislative initiative is the expansion of the Earned Income Tax Credit (EITC), originally passed in 1975 as a means of providing dollar-for-dollar reductions in payroll taxes owed by people with little income. Over the years, amendments to the original EITC have expanded the credit—most recently, once under Ronald Reagan and once under George Bush. Thus, the 1986 Tax Reform Act raised the credit from 10 percent to 14 percent of payroll earnings. The credit was increased again in 1990, and a small adjustment for family size was added.

The 1993 Clinton economic package shifted the aims of the EITC toward making work pay by providing the working poor with a more generous tax credit. The latest amendment allows the credit to rise with earned income until a family of four, for example, achieves an earned income plateau of between $7,760 and $12,210 a year, after which the EITC is taxed away until the family unit reaches $23,070 a year, at which point the EITC is reduced to zero and the family is deemed self-supporting. Table 7–8 shows the practical effect of the plan in 1994, when a basic 1994 credit of 25 percent is given for families with two or more children.

The aim of the EITC resembles the aim of the Nixon proposal for a family assistance plan or negative income tax. The aim was, in Clinton's explanation, "a solemn, simple commitment" that ensures that "if you work 40 hours a week and you've got a child in the house, you will no longer be in poverty."[16] The result was a partial step in the direction of constructing incentives for simultaneously seeking work in order to escape public assistance and limiting family size among persons already poor. Thus, the focus was to design a tax credit that would raise a family of four or fewer persons above the poverty line. One effect was to cap the maximum EITC allowance at *families with two children,* leaving large families with no additional allowance (or credit) as a reflection of greater need. The practical effect was to leave millions of children from larger and needier families tied to poverty in the interest of controlling total program costs.

In addition, the program applies only to those who actually work and who apply for the credit. Those unable to find full-time employment or those who are unable to calculate the tax claim will not receive the tax credit. The net effect, then, is

TABLE 7–8 The 1994 Working Poor Worksheet: Calculating the Earned Income Tax Credit*

Income Source	Wage Rate ($/Hour)	Hours Worked	Total Income ($)
Earned income	$4.25	2080 hrs.= 40 hrs. /wk. × 52 wks.	$8,840
–Payroll taxes			-676
+Food stamps			+3,200
+EITC	25% credit	$7,760 plateau	+2,003
Net Total			$13,367
Poverty level (1994)			$15,192
Income required to reach poverty level			$1,825

*Family of four with one full-time wage earner and two children.

Source: Adapted from David S. Cloud, "Clinton Looking to Tax Credit to Rescue Working Poor," *Congressional Quarterly* 13 March, 1993, 583–585.

that only a small step toward moving working heads of households above the poverty line has been taken. As the Table 7–8 calculation for 1994 shows, a full-time working person heading a family of four would take home a gross earned income of $8,840, or a net income (after $676 in payroll taxes) of $8,164. Once the value of food stamps eligibility ($3,200) is added, the net family income rises to $11,364. Thus, even with an added 1994 EITC of $2,003, the family would still be $1,825 below the 1994 poverty line of $15,192!

One should note that even this outcome is theoretical. Whether in fact all eligible families will properly file for the credit is not known. Even more significant is whether wage earners at the lowest income level even know about an EITC option that allows them to incorporate the credit into their weekly paychecks, thereby reducing the anticipated withholding from take-home pay. Much depends on implementation of the tax credit program. But clearly, the EITC is a long way from the full-scale negative income tax that nearly passed the Senate Finance Committee during the first term of the Nixon administration.

DILEMMAS OF DECISION

In the end, the heart of the poverty and welfare issues involves fundamental questions about equity. Government clearly has the power and the instruments through which to distribute and redistribute the wealth and income generated by society. These issues are pursued again in Chapters 15 and 16. The question is not whether improvements in equity *can* be made, but whether adjustments *ought* to be made. Readers must think long and hard about public ethics.

At a basic level, poverty is a problem of justice and equality. There are some thorny issues about the interventions government can reasonably undertake and about the many definitions of equality and inequality, such as *vertical* and *horizontal equity*. Vertical equity requires that rich and poor, upper class and lower class, be treated equally and fairly. Horizontal equity seeks equality for people in similar circumstances; thus, people with the same level of need in similar circumstances should be treated roughly the same. In addition, government must consider the ancient debate about whether the goal of public policy is equity of condition or equity of opportunity. *Equity* is a noble-sounding policy goal, but one that is exceedingly difficult to define in policy-relevant terms.

The costs and benefits of poverty policy reform are also issues. These are less concerned with the public *duty* to increase equity by reducing poverty and more with *estimation of the consequences*—the costs and benefits—of public action. The costs clearly include direct program costs and the opportunity costs of alternative uses for public expenditures, including simply not spending public resources. The benefits include the social value of increasing the number of productive citizens gainfully employed in the business of earning their way and sustaining the families, neighborhoods, and communities that make public life possible. Benefit-cost analysis should also consider the external costs to society of not eliminating or reducing poverty.

A full accounting of costs and benefits is difficult, however. Part of the difficulty has to do with the substantive complexity of the problem, discussed throughout the chapter. Another part derives from the political reality of constituents who are not an asset but a liability in the sense that they are politically inarticulate citizens who do not register and vote and do not significantly influence electoral outcomes. Politicians who champion the cause of poor people know this and must deal with substantial risks; much volatile political imagery is attached to the problem. Furthermore, open and frank discussions about doing more or less for the poor, or even restructuring the allocation of already dedicated poverty resources, raise some of the ugliest charges of racial and ethnic discrimination. The popular image of welfare, for example, is one of squandering hard-earned tax dollars on the undeserving. It is difficult to make the case to the moderate political middle that it is good public policy to invest in people who, on the surface, do not help themselves.

Public opinion has been slow to understand that there are a large number of generous programs on the books that benefit comparatively comfortable people. These programs do not carry the welfare stigma. They are variously known by names such as mortgage interest deductions (welfare for homeowners and the construction industry), student loan guarantees (low-interest loan welfare for middle-class college and university students), Social Security and Medicare (non-means tested, free lunch for the middle class), and crop insurance and commodity price supports (benefits of disproportionate value to large farmers and agribusiness). The real welfare list is a long one, and clever readers can have fun adding their own nominations.

Finally, almost no one now defends the current system, which is no system. Liberals associated with the National Welfare Rights Organization (such as Chuck Willie and Jesse Jackson) see poor people as oppressed citizens denied their constitutional rights. Conservatives answer with arguments that judge the poor either as simply too lazy to do anything else (Ronald Reagan) or, more subtly, as victims of a welfare system that is an evil force seducing vulnerable people away from the industriousness and self-sufficiency that would otherwise encourage them to become self-supporting (Charles Murray).[17] Still other observers[18] focus on single facets of the problem; Daniel Patrick Moynihan, senator from New York, argues that poor people produce too many babies at too young an age; Jack Kemp, a former secretary of Housing and Urban Development, thinks that tax relief will cure problems of poverty.

Public discussion is now trying to comprehend the views of President Clinton whose stated aim of "eliminating welfare as we know it" is based on a conviction that the poor need our help to help themselves. The portrayal of the poverty problem has shifted as the nation calculates the costs of providing for that portion of the population that is malnourished, poorly brought up from childhood, ill educated, isolated from the economic mainstream , and increasingly incapable of competing in a global economic sweepstakes in which people inadequately prepared to meet global standards are the losers. How, and whether or not, this agenda will influence public policy thinking about poverty and welfare remain interesting questions.

At this writing, the Clinton administration is in the midst of defending its proposals to transform the welfare system into a system of job training and placement.[19] The cornerstone of the plan is placing a lifetime limit of 24 months for AFDC cash assistance for most adults on welfare in order to move welfare recipients into channels of education, job training, and job placement. Able-bodied adults, including minor mothers under the age of 18, who refuse to pursue education, training, and jobs, would be removed from the welfare system. In support of these broad aims, other proposals added to the package include:[20]

Requiring a minor mother to identify the father of each child.
Requiring unwed mothers younger than 18 to live at home with their parents.
Trying to collect more child support payments from deadbeat dads.
Giving states the freedom under AFDC guidelines to limit additional welfare benefits to
    women who give birth to children conceived while already receiving welfare.

Not surprisingly, the Clinton proposals are controversial. They combine seemingly harsh regulation with sudden expansion in the demand for sophisticated, targeted services aimed at job creation, education and training, and placement. Yet the proposed budget involves only modest federal grants to schools and neighborhoods to enhance service delivery capacity, while a great reliance is placed on the president's use of the bully pulpit to campaign for more "responsible" behavior by young teens and to enlist the help of the private and nonprofit sectors in discouraging teenage pregnancies. Ultimate disposal of this plan cannot now be forecast.

As a concluding note, income disparity and insufficiency are tied to other social policy issues. One of the most dramatic examples is the difference in health outcomes that express levels of physical and mental well-being separating rich and poor people in the United States. A recent study of factors associated with mortality rates concluded that the health gap between well-educated, high-income persons and poorly educated, low-income persons has greatly widened over the past three decades.[21] Thus, by 1986, Americans with family incomes of less than $9,000 a year confronted death rates over three times higher than persons with family incomes of $25,000 or more. Indeed, among people 25 to 64 years of age, white men in the lower-income category faced 16 deaths per thousand, while higher-income white men experienced only 2.4 deaths per thousand. African American men of similar ages and economic circumstances confronted 19.5 deaths and 3.6 deaths per thousand, respectively. Clearly, income and the education that qualifies people for higher-paying jobs are more powerful determinants of mortality rates than race, although some differential risk does appear to exist across the races. Just as clear, however, is the conclusion that poverty and welfare are related to education and health as well as to many other factors such as housing and employment. Thus, it happens that dealing with one problem has implications for dealing with other problems on the public policy plate.

SUMMARY

The essence of the U.S. poverty and welfare problems is the large cohort of people who, by the federal government's own definition, fall below the poverty line. In addition to the persistence of absolute poverty, the level of relative inequality among income earners is increasing, judging by the shares of income captured by the top and bottom of the income distribution. Furthermore, poverty is a condition that is visited disproportionately on single-parent families and children. Indeed, the United States is now raising between one-fifth and one-quarter of its children under conditions of poverty.

This poverty has given rise to a welter of means-tested and non-means-tested programs that, taken together, might be conventionally referred to as the welfare mess. Virtually all programs are based on a logic of categorical entitlement that reduces the incentive to trade welfare support for paying work, especially as earnings approach the U.S. minimum wage; when pooled, the value of program benefits substantially exceeds the earnings generated through minimum wage employment. Moreover, the current welfare system does not cover need, because the poverty line is really a statistical construct designed for analytic purposes and, with the exception of food stamps, is not a measure that determines levels of public assistance. Thus, states determine what level of need exists and then make their own determinations about what level of support they will offer. In addition to its rising cost, the system is marked by a lack of horizontal equity (i.e., people in different states with the same need do not receive the same support), and there are large gaps in coverage as seen most dramatically in the rise of homelessness.

Solutions have proved elusive to this date. For one thing, the disadvantages of inadequate education and training make easy solutions infeasible, since the low minimum wage does not allow even industrious workers to generate the incomes necessary to escape poverty. Furthermore, applying simple work ethic solutions affects only a small proportion of the able-bodied population since children and elderly persons and those with disabilities are not instances where dependent persons can simply work their way off the welfare rolls.

In spite of the many constraints, several choices exist. One general strategy emphasizes cash assistance with the direct aim of eliminating income poverty with the least amount of government interference. The second general approach emphasizes the provision of services. A third strategy is the mixed case of providing a combination of both cash and services. Many states are now experimenting with an overhaul of portions of the welfare system—principally the operation of AFDC and Medicaid—for purposes of merging categorical welfare support with employment and training goals. Meanwhile, the federal government contemplates revision of national strategy and programs, including redesigning the measures of poverty by which policy achievement can be gauged.

DISCUSSION QUESTIONS

1. Does current public policy take a realistic approach to defining poverty in the United States in the 1990's? What modifications in the definition should be considered?
2. In the arsenal of poverty policies, which are the most valuable? Which are the least valuable?
3. Develop a general strategy for dealing with the poverty and welfare mess. What princi-

ples would apply? What changes should be considered in the current system?

4. Do you agree with recent attempts to turn over federal responsibility for dealing with the poverty problem to state and local government? When, where and how does the national government make a contribution?

SUGGESTED READINGS

Barry Bluestone and Benjamin Harrison, *The Deindustrialization of America* (New York: Basic Books, 1982).

Martha Derthick, *Agency Under Stress: The Social Security Administration in American Government* (Washington, D. C.: The Brookings Institution, 1990).

Richard J. Herrnstein and Charles Murray, *The Bell Curve: Intelligence and Class Structure in American Life* (New York: Free Press, 1994).

Christopher Jencks, *Inequality: A Reassessment of the Effect of Family and Schooling in America* (New York: Basic Books, 1972).

Christopher Jencks, *Rethinking Social Policy: Race, Poverty, and the Underclass* (Cambridge, Mass.: Harvard University Press, 1992).

Frank Levy, *Dollars and Dreams: The Changing American Income Distribution* (New York: Russell Sage Foundation, 1987).

Paul E. Peterson and Mark C. Rom, *Welfare Magnets: A New Case for a National Standard* (Washington, D. C.: The Brookings Institution, 1990).

NOTES

1. The unseemly juxtaposition of affluence and poverty as a characteristic of U.S. life has a long history in scholarship. See, for example; Gunnar Myrdal, *Challenge to Affluence* (New York: Pantheon Books, 1963); John Kenneth Galbraith, *The Affluent Society* (New York: Mentor Books, 1958).

2. H. John Thorkelson, *The Encyclopedia Americana,* international ed., vol. 13 (Danbury, Conn.: Grolier Inc., 1981), 343–346.

3. Mollie Orshansky, "The Shape of Poverty in 1966," *Social Security Bulletin* (U.S. Department of Health, Education, and Welfare; Washington, D.C.: Social Security Administration, March 1966).

4. Guy Gugliotta, "Drawing the Line on Poverty," *Washington Post,* national weekly ed., 24–30 May 1993, p. 38.

5. Gordon Berlin and William McAllister, "Homelessness," in Henry J. Aaron and Charles L. Schultze, eds., *Setting Domestic Priorities: What Can Government Do?* (Washington, D.C.: Brookings Institution, 1992); John E. Schwarz, *America's Hidden Success* (New York: W.W. Norton, 1988), 155.

6. Schwarz, 1988, 155. Also see Joel Blau, *The Visible Poor: Homelessness in the United States* (New York: Oxford University Press, 1993).

7. Committee for Economic Development, *The Unfinished Agenda: A New Vision for Child Development and Education* (New York: Research and Policy Committee for the CED, 1991), 9.

8. Jean Seligmann and Kendall Hamilton, "Husbands No, Babies Yes," *Newsweek,* 26 July, 1993, 53.

9. Michael Harrington, *The Other America* (Baltimore: Penguin Books, 1963), 14.

10. Edward Banfield, *The Unheavenly City Revisited: The Nature and Future of Our Urban Crisis* (Boston: Little, Brown & Co., 1970), 54.

11. Herbert Kaufman (*Time, Chance, and Organizations: Natural Selection in a Perilous Environment* [Chatham, N.J.: Chatham House Publishers, Inc., 1985], p. v.) notes the role of chance in human affairs by citing the Bible: "[T]he race is not to the swift, nor the bat-

tle to the strong, nor bread to the wise, nor riches to the intelligent, nor favor to the men of skill; but time and chance happen to them all" (Ecclesiastes 9:11).

12. Harrington, 1963, 14–15.
13. William L. Hamilton et al., *The New York State Child Assistance Program: Program Impacts, Costs, and Benefits* (Cambridge, Mass.: Abt Associates, Inc., 1993), 2.
14. James Brian Quinn, *Intelligent Enterprise* (New York: Free Press, 1992).
15. Susan Chira, "Family Leave Is Law; Will Things Change?" *New York Times,* 15 August, 1993, Section 4, Page 3, Column 1.
16. David S. Cloud, "Clinton Looking to Tax Credit to Rescue Working Poor," *Congressional Quarterly,* 13 March 1993, 583.
17. Charles Murray, *Losing Ground: American Social Policy* (New York: Basic Books, 1984).
18. Jason DeParle, "An Unfinished Portrait of the Poor," *New York Times,* 26 December, 1993, Week in Review Section, p. E1.
19. Jason DeParle, "Clinton to Propose A Strategy to Curb Youth Pregnancies," *New York Times,* 10 June, 1994, pp. A1, A9.
20. De Parle 1994, p. A9.
21. Robert Pear, "Wide Health Gap, Linked to Income, Is Reported in U.S.," *New York Times,* 8 July, 1993, p. 1.

8

The Health Security Dilemma

Is health care in the United States in crisis or is it merely one of a large number of unresolved public problems facing the nation? No one disputes the reality that the United States manages to spend a large amount of wealth, with mediocre public health results. Even the most cursory comparison with other countries reveals that the United States has created an extravagant system of health care (see below). The result is built into a private provider, fee-for-service, third-party payment system that is high tech, curative (rather than preventive), and highly interventionist. For those who can pay, the system is truly a wonder!

There is, however, a public health side to the same system. For this other side, perhaps the analysis is best launched with a sampling of vignettes reflecting numerous instances of hardship, insecurity, pain, and suffering that have become common as the battle to reform U.S. health care services unfolds. Television interviews, meetings, and conferences with people afflicted with a litany of health care burdens provide graphic glimpses of a national dilemma. The following four examples, taken from the president's 1993 report to the American people on health care reform, illustrate the complexity of the problem.

Vignette 1: "My husband and I own and operate a small business. This year we will make our employees pay for any increase [*sic*] premiums and may drop [some benefits] altogether. Our company cannot shop around for lower cost health insurance because I am uninsurable."[1]

Vignette 2: "When my two sons were three and six, Spencer and Evan were diagnosed with cystic fibrosis. In the blink of an eye, my two beautiful, healthy boys became part of our worst nightmare. We had to face the fact that we could lose them to this dreadful disease. We live in constant fear of losing our medical coverage. . . . Without the drug coverage that we now have, it would cost us at least

$1,500 a month for their medicine alone. These little boys are virtually uninsurable. . . . As mothers we need to protect our children, and I don't want to feel frightened about this all my life."[2]

Vignette 3: "Six months ago, my sister-in-law, Pam, had a disabling stroke. Pam is only 39 years old, and she's a severe diabetic. Six months have passed, her short-term memory has deteriorated, her vision is leaving, and it looks as if my brother will either have to hire someone to come into their home full time to care for her, or put her in a nursing home, which his medical plan does not cover.

"My brother's attorney has advised him to divorce Pam so that her medical bills don't pull him into financial ruin. My brother has two young sons that he's caring for and in order to continue to provide for them, he is giving this consideration. A man who loves his wife must divorce her so that her misfortune (in sickness and in health) does not leave him with the inability to raise their family."[3]

Vignette 4:   "My husband and I are 59 and 63 years of age, so we are not yet eligible for Medicare to help us. . . . A brief summary of our health insurance costs over the last four years are:

1988—$3,578 with $500 deductible
1990—$4,607 with $2,500 deductible
1992—$10,500 with $2,000 deductible

I have a pre-existing condition so I have to pay a penalty on the rates. Neither my husband nor myself, fortunately, has ever had a claim of any kind. . . . We do not want a "free ride." We are more than willing to pay our share, but these amounts are just too excessive."[4]

Several conclusions are implied by these vignettes. First, large numbers of people lack basic health care coverage and cannot get insurance under any circumstances. They receive treatment only by throwing themselves on the mercies of overworked and inadequately available public health clinics or expensive, acute-care health providers, who underwrite the income losses attributable to nonpaying patients by shifting the costs to paying clients. The personal nightmare scenario occurs when a person is unemployed and cannot afford insurance, is employed by a company (typically, a small company) that cannot afford health insurance, or is rejected for health coverage because of personal medical history.[5]

Second, many people, who are currently covered by health insurance but who change jobs, risk losing coverage if insurance screening procedures suggest pre-existent conditions. This pattern has an economic impact as well as a health impact: the practical effect is to discourage job mobility that is beneficial in the long term. Thus, a population fearing change because of uncertainty over health care availability can, by refusing to shift out of declining economic sectors and into rising sectors, injure a whole society's prospects for long-term growth and development. The result ultimately undermines economic performance by stifling the flexibility and entrepreneurship required to sustain a fast-moving, innovative economy.

Third, even fully insured persons, who are unlucky enough to encounter unusual health problems, can face financial ruin as insurance coverage limits are reached and the price of attempting to pay for uninsured care exceeds personal income and assets. In the words of an anonymous resident of West Lafayette, Indiana, cited in President Bill Clinton's health security report (p. 3): "The way the system works now, even employed, insured people are just one major illness away from financial disaster."

A new reality looms. The advancing sophistication of modern U.S. medicine and health technology has redefined the nature of the public health problem now confronting the U.S. public. Absent mass warfare and pandemics such as influenza, polio, or tuberculosis, people enjoy long lives generally (but not always, as noted below) free from the plagues of earlier centuries. Yet the technologies and levels of medical practice that make longevity possible—all fed and nurtured by public policy and public money—have become extraordinarily expensive. Elderly people with chronic, continuous health care needs are most vulnerable; also vulnerable are their children and heirs who will be called upon to make difficult decisions about the conditions under which life is extended.

The picture is even more worrisome than the vignettes imply. Many people lack ready access to health care largely because they do not have the money to purchase insurance or they do not work at jobs providing health care insurance. For those people and their children, there is no backup system of checkups and inoculations, except that provided by the occasional public school or clinic. Furthermore, the business community now cites the rising cost of health care coverage for workers as a major factor retarding its ability to remain globally competitive (a condition partly mitigated by business's ability to deduct health care expenses from corporate taxes—roughly a $90 billion *tax expenditure*). Thus, an estimated 37 million people do not possess work-related insurance and do not qualify for either Medicaid (federal-state coverage for poor people) or Medicare (federal health care coverage for seniors); in short, they have no coverage. Furthermore, an additional 50 million people may be underinsured, including those on Medicaid, where state control of reimbursement levels means that many providers will not accept Medicaid patients.

Complexity characterizes the U.S. health care system. For instance, people without insurance do not actually receive no treatment. They simply go through the back door in such a way as to minimize the effectiveness of available health treatments, shifting the cost of treatment to insurance companies and paying customers in ways that inflate billing rates for all. The U.S. health care system shunts poor people into hospital emergency rooms after acute-care episodes have developed, many of which could have been prevented by quick diagnosis or by relatively inexpensive preventive procedures dispensed early by primary-care providers. Late, costly, and risky intervention by expensive secondary and tertiary specialists who provide heroic measures often fails to overcome the effects of poor prenatal care, premature birth, low birth weight babies, lack of immunization against standard childhood diseases, lack of regular dental care, and so forth.

There is also a dark side to uneven health care coverage. One example is the recent rise of tuberculosis (TB) among poor people in the United States, a classic indicator of the effects of poor public health. The disease is curable but highly infectious; it is treatable through universal inoculation. Yet the public health failure to continue preventive inoculation and screening permits the "white scourge" to flourish in resistant strains of bacteria, such as the W strain that does not now respond easily to treatment. Shortsighted budget cutting in the 1970s eliminated TB screening programs in precisely those sectors of society most susceptible to crowded and impoverished conditions—central cities, prisons, homeless shelters, and public health facilities. As a result, people were exposed to a disease that resists successful treatment. Further, middle-class workers in proximity to TB patients in hospitals, prisons, and welfare offices were placed at risk along with their patients. Once contracted, TB strain W incurs enormous treatment costs. A quarter of a million dollars may be spent to treat one case that, until cured, is a walking time bomb, yet a few thousand dollars invested in screening and treatment at early stages would have eliminated the disease.

The public has begun to grasp the full significance and immediacy of the health care issue. Seniors, increasingly organized into groups such as the Grey Panthers and the American Association of Retired Persons (AARP), confront major health problems. But their children, including middle-age baby boomers, face a double difficulty. First, they acquire responsibility for their parents' care. Second, they are at an age when they should be planning for their own retirement and insuring long-term access to care for themselves.

Politicians sense the rising significance of a national issue. In 1992, a relatively unknown Democratic candidate for the U.S. Senate seat from Pennsylvania—Harris Wofford, a former president of Bryn Mawr College—emerged from obscurity to defeat Richard Thornburgh, a popular, front-running contender, a former Pennsylvania governor and U.S. attorney general. The campaign emphasized reform of the whole U.S. health care system, and its political message was unmistakable. Otherwise popular candidates who ignore the health issue could be defeated, while candidates who address such issues effectively would at least be given a chance to show what they could do. Tackling something as large and complicated as the U.S. health care system is risky, but the issue is now, and will be for many years, a primary concern of U.S. policymaking.

CONTEXT

Health care problems are not adequately defined by saying that one is in favor of good health. The real problem is that several health goals simultaneously interact. Three goals are strategic: first, access to health care services; second, the *quality* of care; and third, the cost of care. These health care goals have an impact on other public and private aims, such as economic development. For example, the aggregate cost of care can become so dominant that economic development objectives are compromised, as they would be if the cost of health care to business prevented businesses from remaining competitive in the marketplace. On the private side, the threat of a financially ruinous illness or accident, or the prospect of becoming responsible for aging, medically costly parents and relatives, can produce powerful feelings of financial and psychological insecurity. When a whole population feels itself under the financial gun, it can be difficult for people to contemplate the changes, risks, and entrepreneurial behavior that drive a dynamic and productive economy.

Can health goals of access, quality, and cost be achieved simultaneously? This task looks daunting. For example, universal access to high-quality care is likely to be expensive. Attempts to cut costs by limiting access may threaten quality and ration access to physicians, hospitals, dentists, and other providers of choice. Thus, government must have realistic expectations about what public policy can hope to achieve in these three areas.

Some basic terminology bears brief discussion. *Access* to care is the availability of facilities, providers, and services. Access includes the notion of client choice about providers as well as services, such as tests and diagnostic procedures, preventive and curative measures, curative, acute and chronic treatments, and posttreatment observation and convalescence.

Quality of care refers to the maintenance and restoration of "health." The idea of quality is complex, defined by the extent to which patients generally in the health care system receive competent treatment by providers whose training and abilities are proficient and up-to-date. Like access, quality has many meanings associated with the outcomes of health care services rather than inputs such as the extent to which heroic and invasive procedures and technologies are used. All health care aims to preserve or produce a healthy condition and, at a minimum, to "do no harm." In addition, quality assumes that "best practice" is followed. Finally, the idea of quality contains the notion of "disinterested care," prescribed care dictated by the patient's requirements rather than by the provider's desire to perform procedures and dispense treatments.

Cost of care, covers resource expenditures to provide health care. Although the cost goal of health care policy is to constrain the cash outlays allocated to health care, the low-bidder rule is not necessarily desirable. The concept is perhaps best seen as the search for the lowest reasonable payment for services rendered and health outcomes achieved. Thus, to control costs, preventive substitutes for curative procedures can be used, generic drugs can be substitutes for name brands, and low-cost staffing can be used as a substitute for overusing acute-care specialists and facilities.

The goals of access, quality, and cost pull in different directions. First, if policy is intended to raise the quality of care in the sense of using the latest and best technologies, tests, and procedures, such improvements may be reasonably thought more costly than more conventional options (we do not attempt here to resolve the debate about whether simple and holistic health care practices may be superior to modern curative health care practice; we simply note that a lively discussion exists). Second, if government attempts to increase access to care in the sense that more people are able to demand and receive more care, this increased access will probably cost more money. Finally, in certain circumstances access to care and quality of care may well be negatively related, as seen when patients for whom care was not previously accessible can now demand and receive care and existing facilities and services cannot satisfy the expanded demand. Whatever the precise interactions among the three goals, health care policy aims at simultaneous achievement of accessibility, high quality, and low cost. This means that public health decisions are therefore at least partly political and not simply medical decisions. The public is competent to decide—indeed, it is required to decide—what it wants to pay for its healthcare and whether or not it is satisfied with the levels of access and quality that result.

Alarming Health Indicators

By these standards, how is the United States performing? First, those who enjoy full access to the benefits of modern U.S. medicine, are living longer, can have health defects corrected, are relatively free from disease, and enjoy the benefits of diagnostic sophistication unrivaled in the world. But the vignettes suggest a further reality: the nation that boasts the best system of health care also suffers some less attractive features, as Table 8–1 shows. Comparative measures of public health from the 1980s show that, taken in the aggregate, the United States achieves only an average showing among nations with whom it is logically compared. For example, U.S. average life expectancy of 82.5 years in the late 1980s was the same as Italy's and below the life expectancies of Japan, Sweden, Canada, and France.

Cross-national comparison also reveals a bleak side as measured by infant mortality. The U.S. rate of 9.7 deaths per 1,000 live births is over twice that of Japan's, nearly twice Sweden's, and substantially below all the other advanced European countries' rates. Infant mortality is a particularly strong public health signature: its rates are sensitive to the quality of prenatal care and nutrition that, in turn, are tied to presence or absence of poverty, particularly to malnutrition and substance abuse. Infant mortality is not the only alarming indicator; others include the premature birth of low-birth-weight babies whose survival prospects are slim or improved only at the great cost of intensive care. These outcomes are driven by poverty and a two-tiered system of health care in which poor people are deprived of many basic wellness-promoting services that can prevent complications and poor medical outcomes.

Such outcomes are not the result of modest expenditures on health care. The United States stands alone in the world as the big health spender in any recent year. As an illustration, at the end of the 1980s the United States spent nearly 12 percent of gross domestic product (GDP), while none of the other countries with which the United States is normally compared spent over 9 percent, and Japan and Great Britain spent under 7 percent. The United States currently spends over 14 percent—one-seventh of GDP—on the maintenance and repair of minds and bodies, while other countries spend less than 10 percent. Moreover, U.S. cost growth shows no signs of moderating significantly.

How has the United States managed to achieve such mediocre results? What might be done? Table 8–1 provides a hint of where the problem lies and what the points of leverage might be. Whereas nearly all other countries use public money—either direct public expenditure or health insurance funds—to pay for health care, the United States largely uses private-sector funds. Whereas 11.8 percent of GDP was spent on health costs in 1989, the public share (as of 1986, when data were available) was only 4.5 percent of GDP. Over 60 percent of funds consisted of privately controlled outlays in the form of insurance and directly billed fees. The public share of health expenditure has risen over time (as will be shown in Figure 8–1), but all U.S. governments taken together are still minority players in the health care industry. By implication, public reform efforts must concentrate on redirecting the private structure of health expenditure and service delivery.

For all of its technological sophistication, the U.S. health care system is not a system, but an agglomeration of disparate health care services patched together by consumer choice and diverse funding. The result is a series of policy problems in each of the three goal areas of cost, quality, and access. Health care is provided immediately only to those with the ability to pay. Those who cannot pay receive minimal, if any, care until an emergency condition sends them to public clinics and hospitals.

In a privately dominated model of service provision, where markets mediate the relationship between buyer and seller, services quite logically follow the money, and insurance companies act as third-party intermediaries, paying the bills generated by the marketplace. Thus, middle-income people with insurance can purchase the latest and best technology; indeed, for those living in cities, suburbs, and

TABLE 8–1   Comparative Health Expenditures and Outcomes: Late 1980s

	Health Expenditures			Health Outcomes	
	1986 Public Expenditures (Percent GDP)	*1989 Total Expenditures (Percent GDP)*	*($ Per Capita)*	*Infant Mortality (Per 1,000)*	*Life Expectancy (In Years)*
Japan	4.8	6.7	1,035	4.6	84.3
Sweden	8.3	8.8	1,361	5.8	83.4
Canada	6.5	8.7	1,683	7.2	83.2
France	6.7	8.7	1,274	7.5	83.7
Germany	6.3	8.2	1,232	7.5	81.9
Great Britain	5.3	5.8	836	8.4	81.2
Italy	5.2	7.6	1,050	8.9	82.4
United States	4.5	11.8	2,354	9.7	82.5

Source: Adapted from Richard Rose, *Lesson-Drawing in Public Policy* (Chatham, N.J.: Chatham House Publishers, Inc. 1993), 75; public expenditures normally date from 1986, total expenditures from 1989. Per capita dollar amounts are adjusted for purchasing power parity.

other prosperous communities there is an oversupply of health care. People living in rural areas and small towns and communities, however, have restricted access to care because their unprosperous communities have only limited ability to recruit doctors, nurses, and other providers.

In addition, those who qualify for Medicaid have access to care limited to providers who accept Medicaid patients; in instances where no regular care provider can be found, poor patients—even those "covered" by Medicaid—must use the emergency rooms of hospitals as primary-care facilities. The results are predictable. First, patients receive care without the providers having detailed knowledge of their medical history. Second, risks of complications are higher because patients have not received the normal range of preventive-care services such as immunizations, wellness checkups, and diagnostic screenings for typical maladies. Finally, the use of institutional acute-care facilities for ordinary primary health care problems represents a misallocation of resources.

Several other features of the current system make systematic reform of health care a daunting endeavor. First, a structure of care that traditionally has depended on third-party payment for the fee-for-service relationship between buyer and private health care seller produces the result that supply creates its own demand. The mere availability of procedures, diagnostic machines, and drugs brings an almost instant demand for their use, *whatever the cost.* So great is the pressure to provide the latest and best technology for the treatment of AIDS, coronary artery disease, and organ transplants, for example, that the ethics of withholding or rationing treatment has become a major quandry plaguing providers and managers alike.

Second, public policy pushes the state of the medical art with flows of federal funds to health research and development. For example, the Department of Health and Human Services supports an enormous research medical establishment in the many National Institutes of Health (NIH). A quick review reveals that nearly every major affliction and part of the body has its own institute passionately and expensively engaged in advancing the state of the art in diagnosis and treatment. The following is merely a partial list:

National Cancer Institute
National Heart, Lung, and Blood Institute
National Institute of Diabetes and Digestive and Kidney Diseases
National Institute of Allergy and Infectious Diseases
National Institute of Child Health and Human Development
National Institute on Deafness and Other Communication Disorders
National Institute of Dental Research
National Institute of Environmental Health Sciences
National Institute of General Medical Sciences
National Institute of Neurological Disorders and Stroke
National Eye Institute
National Institute on Aging
National Institute of Alcohol Abuse and Alcoholism
National Institute of Arthritis and Musculoskeletal and Skin Diseases
National Institute on Drug Abuse
National Institute of Mental Health
National Center for Human Genome Research

The most advanced federal research enterprise is the national genome project now engaged in mapping the structure, location, and composition of all known genes. The presence or absence of specific genetic material is now believed to underlie many maladies afflicting the human body. The implications are enormous: systematic modification of human genetic content is possible to prevent and to cure disease. Thus, gene therapy holds the prospect of finding cures for cases of chronically high cholesterol, Alzheimer's disease, Down's syndrome, and chronically weak immunization systems, to name only a few.

Third, the strong technological basis for U.S. medicine has tended to make health care highly interventionist and heroic. New medications, procedures, and diagnostic tools and machines have proliferated to such an extraordinary degree that health policy wags are fond of noting (as in this remark attributed to Uwe Reinhardt of Princeton University), "Whereas other countries regard death as inevitable, in the United States it is regarded as an option."

Not everyone regards the use of heroic procedures as contributing to high-quality health care outcomes. The obvious example occurs at the end of life when heroic measures to prolong life become inappropriate. The heart of the criticism of U.S. health care practice, however, comes from those who view health as being currently subject to overtreatment and overmedication for conditions to which the proper response would consist of a large component of behaviorally and educationally controlled habits and practices, including proper diet, plenty of exercise, and a life of moderation and avoidance of unusual risk. In this view, when treatment is required, the interventions should be as minimal and natural as possible and supplemented with vigorous attempts to use the body's natural mechanisms to fight disease and heal itself.

A different reaction to the question of heroic intervention points out the futility of attempts to provide cures for every disease found in nature.[6] This view points out that the natural adaptation of organisms frustrates the search for perfect and final cures: viruses and bacteria can adapt and develop resistant strains more difficult to kill. In turn, scientists develop ever more powerful interventions that are met with even more resistant strains and more lethal diseases; the weaker strains having been killed off, only the most powerful and stealthy ones remain, and so the battle goes. There becomes no logical end to the process, a conclusion that invites consideration of whether major investments in heroic intervention are justifiable.

Finally, regardless of the outcomes of debates about the proper definitions of health care access and quality, the current U.S. health care system has been nothing if not expensive. Normally expensive heroic procedures are made even more expensive by the very way the health business has been organized and run, partly because the treat-and-bill system is subject to abuse. Providers, whose income is derived from the number of treatments, discuss possibilities with insured patients, who do not directly pay even a small share of the treatment costs. Doctor and patient agree to abundant treatment, certified and privileged under a system of regulation dominated by grassroots organizations of professionals.

To this fundamental service structure are added several cost burdens. First, patients who demand treatment but who cannot pay eventually get treatment covered by so-called cost shifting. In such cases, the provider shifts the income losses to the paying customers whose billing statements reflect not only their own costs of procedures, equipment, and supplies but also an added amount—an x factor—used to cover nonpaying clients. A second burden is that insurance is provided by a large number of insurance companies. The result is a large paperwork bureaucracy whose cost is roughly and casually estimated by the media to be easily ten percent of the current $800 billion cost of health care in the United States. Thus, the annual cost of health care paperwork may be as high as eighty billion dollars. The prospective savings from reorganization could be sufficient to provide basic coverage for all persons not now covered by health care insurance.

A third burden is the vulnerability of an insurance-based, fee-for-service system to provider conflicts of interest, if not to outright fraud. The most egregious instance of provider fraud involves *Medicaid mills* in which poor people are recruited, enrolled, and provided few, if any, services, for which government is billed through the third-party billing system. Another source of billing abuse lies in opportunities for multipocket cost shifting by state and local governments hard pressed to cover the skyrocketing costs of health care. A recent illustration arose in the states' use of the Medicaid billing system to levy a special tax on providers who are then reimbursed by state governments at agreed levels sufficient to more than cover the special tax on services. This scheme worked as long as the federal government reimbursed states at a rate of 50 percent of state payments to providers, as required by the Medicaid contract. For example, if a budget-conscious state, such as New Hampshire, wanted to establish an "enhancement fund" for purposes of acquiring additional general revenues without raising new taxes, it could feed the fund from programs like Medicaid by agreeing to pay providers $106 for every $100 in provider taxes paid the state. The state would bill the federal government for $53 (half the $106 cost to the state, based on a 50-50 federal–state-sharing arrangement). The state's net cost would then be $47, and the state would not only cut its Medicaid costs but would also create a substantial pool of revenue available for balancing its budget and paying for its general services. In essence, by padding their payments to hospitals, states increase federal matching funds. In this illustration, a net of $6 for providers and $47 for the state treasury (i.e., the net of a gross receipt of $153 and a total payout of $106) is generated.[7] A federal-state program designed to operate on a 50–50 matching payment basis actually costs the state only 44 percent ($47/$106) of Medicaid outlays.

Finally, costs are built into the structure of health care service by providers' competing to offer the latest and best available technology and treatments. The bills for these services are paid, of course, not by price-conscious consumers who shop carefully for good deals but by third-party payers. The possibilities for conflicts of interest, with providers amortizing the cost of expensive equipment by running many tests in facilities in which providers have a financial interest, should not be surprising. While there are certainly reasons to send patients to one's own lab and radiological facility whose technicians' skills are known to be reliable, the frequency with which patients are referred for unnecessary tests remains a point of contention among health care planners and policymakers.

In summary the sheer magnitude and seemingly uncontrollable nature of health care costs have finally placed the overhaul of the health care industry on the public policy agenda. A gap exists between the costs of heroic medical interventions and the ability of people to pay for care when insurance coverage runs out or is unavailable. All but the wealthiest citizens confront the prospect of personal bankruptcy in the event of catastrophic illness or accident, and hence, the size, scope, and organization of the U.S. health care industry have become obstacles to health security.

ASSESSING THE HEALTH CARE INDUSTRY

It is critical for policy analysts to understand something of the size and complexity of the U.S. health care system. It is now conventional in the mid-1990s to say that the health care industry consumes roughly 14 percent, or one-seventh, of GDP. If that large a resource pool is claimed by the business of repairing minds and bodies, what is left for all of the other objectives of society? Another point is equally arresting: an already large health care industry will exert enormous pressure to make even greater claims on the economy; huge costs have already been incurred for a population that is comparatively (by global standards) healthy by reason of being generally well fed, clothed, housed, and cared for. Furthermore, the U.S. population is beginning to age as baby boomers approach 50 and assume responsibility, in some cases, for parents who are living longer as septuagenarians, octogengarians, nonagenarians, and even centenarians. Will the United States become an aging nation preoccupied only with its health care and nothing else?

The health care system is no system. It is not an evenly structured, carefully coordinated enterprise to which public policy can simply apply budgeting rules and regulations to control costs. On the contrary, the health care sector is a huge agglomeration of many different professions, providers, insurers, and regulators interacting in complicated ways. Health care is a complicated business becoming more and more complex by its very success. Treatments, drugs, procedures, and technologies are now combined with huge advances in science, technology, and workforce training, in which government and public policy have become investment partners. The result is a health care sector size and complexity defying description, let alone management.

This result is not a planned outcome of public policy making. It arose from the way rules of access, payment, and service provision have been allowed to develop. An effect, however, has been the development of large and powerful health care interests which, because of their common professional training, outlook, and revenue generation potential, can look after their own political interests. Furthermore, as the population of potential patients ages, this group's ability to engage the political process for partisan benefit appears likely to grow because seniors are much more politically active than are others. Moreover, they possess the time to invest in making their needs and interests known to policymakers, who are keenly aware that infants, children, and poor people do not vote. Contemplating reform of the health care sector is an extraordinarily complex matter, as the following discussion suggests.

The Organized Interests

The organized interests consist of the providers, payers, and consumers of health care.

Providers

Doctors and other professionals, including nurse practitioners, nurses, technicians, therapists, counselors, clinicians, pharmacists, chiropractors, clinical psychologists, and paramedic health workers, fall into one of three systems of health care:

Primary care. The first line of treatment encounters the original cases of disease and trauma. Among physicians, such specialties would include family practitioners (popularly known as general practitioners), obstetricians-gynecologists, internists, and emergency physicians.

Secondary care. The second line of treatment sees patients on referral, usually from primary-care practitioners. Physician specialties include surgeons of all types such as general, vascular, cardiac, neural, thoracic, orthopedic (who themselves often specialize in particular parts of the body), and plastic; anesthesiologists; radiologists; urologists; ophthalmologists; psychiatrists; oncologists; dermatologists; neurologists; and cardiologists, to mention only some of the largest specializations.

Tertiary care. The third line of treatment deals either with diagnostic issues (and hence is not directly associated with patient care) or with advanced-stage and experimental treatments for which cases are referred from primary and secondary treatment levels. Examples include pathologists, cytologists, experimental transplant teams and centers, and biomedical engineers.

Hospitals and inpatient clinics provide acute care ranging from emergency trauma treatment to major health interventions.

Community mental health centers (CMHCs) and health clinics provide nonacute outpatient treatments.

Nursing homes and convalescent centers provide long-term care for nonacute or chronic conditions.

Pharmaceutical companies research, develop, manufacture, and distribute drugs and chemicals used in health treatment.

Payers

Insurance companies pool the health risks of a selected population, collect premiums from companies and individuals covered by insurance, and pay certified providers for rendering authorized services.

Governments finance health care coverage in several ways at multiple government levels. The largest programs are Medicaid and Medicare, whose payments to providers are laundered through insurance companies. They are not the only systems for which government pays. Others include the Public Health Service, the Veterans Administration hospitals, and public hospitals such as Cook County Hospital in Chicago or Boston City Hospital.

Some businesses and individuals are *self-insured;* they are without third-party insurance coverage and instead pay directly for their own health care. Kaiser-Permanente is perhaps the best-known example of a health provider operating on a membership system, where care is dispensed either on a per-treatment basis or on a fixed-price plan covering all treatments for a fixed price per person (i.e., a capitation method of financing).

Consumers

Basically healthy people, who are occasionally ill or who have accidents requiring health treatment, are the vast majority of consumers. They and their employers, purchase health insurance and pay the price of cost-shifting for patients who cannot pay either for health care or insurance.

People with known disabilities or pre-existent conditions, who are at high risk, such as those who are disabled or susceptible to disease; those who are blind or permanently or partially disabled; or those who otherwise require specialized services, often on a permanent basis.

Seniors endure a range of illnesses and disabilities associated with aging. They differ from the other two groups in that they constitute a well-organized interest group with high levels of political participation, capable of making their policy views felt through organizations such as the AARP. There is no official definition of this group. The term can refer to retired persons who are nevertheless fit and capable of making productive contributions to society. But it can also refer to a person's functional inability to take care of him- or herself, in which case some assistance must be provided either in the home (e.g., meals-on-wheels, a visiting public-health nurse) or in a residential or institutional care facility.

In addition to the main cast of players is a large supporting cast. Most prominent are the accountants and business services designed to aid third-party payment for health services, the Medical Insurance Bureau, and many data banks. Next is a cadre of malpractice attorneys whose function is to enforce the tort laws governing liability for mistakes and failure to follow documentable best practices. The legal constraints placed on private provider practice have much to do with provider decisions about testing and treatment, especially excessive testing. Last is a large group of hospital workers, orderlies, clerks, and other nonprofessionals tied to the current structure of institutional delivery.

Institutional Arrangements

The operation of a health care system depends entirely on how the components are arranged and tied together. Theoretically, there are infinite ways that providers, payers, and consumers can be linked. Indeed, within the United States, the enormous variety of practices produces huge spending differences from state to state.[8] So great is the spending range that per capita cost variations within the United States exceed the variations between it and other countries, such as Canada or the United Kingdom. For example, the U.S. per capita spending in 1991, including hospital care, doctors' services, and prescription drugs, totaled $1,877, or 11.5 percent of per capita income. Yet top-spending states such as Massachusetts and New York spent $2,402 (i.e., 10.5 percent of per capita income) and $2,134 (i.e., 9.5 percent of per capita income), respectively. By contrast, low-spending states such as Idaho and Wyoming spent only $1,234 (i.e., 8 percent of per capita income) and $1,301 (i.e., 7.6 percent of per capita income), respectively, on the three major components of health care. Clearly, there are enormous differences in providing, paying for, and consuming health care.

Many factors can account for such wide variations in spending. Leading causes include personal income (richer populations buy more health care than poorer populations) and such factors as large numbers of secondary and tertiary specialists performing expensive procedures (supply creates its own demand) and high concentrations of seniors. Some factors are not easily controllable by public policy. Others, however, can be controlled, including the manner in which insurance coverage is provided, the regulation of fees and hospital costs, and the medical culture that may either promote or retard the excessive use of expensive procedures. A large number of naturally occurring health care experiments occur within the United States. Further, any attempt to reform the U.S. health sector confronts the reality of variance among states and the question of whether there can truly be a national system of health care or whether national policy will have to be adapted to the reality of divergent practices in states and communities.

If the public goal may be defined as achieving acceptable health results at an acceptable cost, the experimental patching and regulation of the current system have been tried and have failed. In a system dominated by private providers, third-party payers, and consumer choice expressed through the marketplace, the options left to public policy designers are either to provide health care directly through a public-health service or to regulate local conditions. A remaining option, in the case where government itself is a third-party payer, is to constrain the procedures, copayment (portions of fees paid for each office visit by the patient, often set to discourage nuisance visits to providers) limits, and deductibles. No plan has, to date, proved adequate at containing costs.

ALTERNATIVES TO THE CURRENT SYSTEM

Countries around the world are experimenting with providing health care, and much can be learned by examining the strategies they employ to solve the same puzzle.

- *Canada:* Famous for its national health system introduced in 1971, Canada provides universal access to health care paid by a *single third-party payer*—the government—which reimburses private providers based on negotiated fee schedules. The operating reality, however, is a little more complicated: the provincial government is actually the payer. It defines specific terms of coverage and pays the bills through its own tax levy supplemented by a federal government grant that covers less than 50 percent of costs. In the decentralized Canadian system, provincial government collects the taxes necessary to cover the government health account, disburses payment to providers, and regulates the distribution and overall availability of health facilities and services.

- *Japan:* Japan provides universal coverage through several categorical programs that since 1961 have provided some form of *health care insurance.* Thus, the ministry of health and welfare oversees eight different schemes providing group-by-group coverage. The schemes are divided into employer-based insurance for employed persons and community insurance for other regional residents. Universal coverage is further subdivided by place of work. In addition, there are regulatory requirements; for example, 14 weeks of maternity leave is a statutory requirement.

- *United Kingdom:* Great Britain, Scotland, Wales, and Northern Ireland combine to constitute the leading example of *public health service* delivered by public employees on the public payroll, with payment for health care disbursed from a tax-supported general government fund. Private, fee-for-service health care is relegated to providers outside the national health system, whose clients and patients are able to pay either the fees or private insurance premiums.

- *Germany: Social health insurance* in Germany was introduced in 1883 with over 1,200 insurance schemes administered by autonomous federal, regional, and local organizations. Wage earners and apprentices, salaried employees with low incomes, and social insurance pensioners are insured on a compulsory basis, with employers and employees sharing costs on a roughly 50–50 basis. Voluntary insurance is also available. In addition, there are regulatory requirements; for example, during the first six weeks of illness, the employer is legally required to pay the normal wage.

- *Netherlands and Sweden:* These two countries maintain *tax-supported national health insurance* funds providing universal coverage, combined with a system of managed care in which family practitioners—such as *huisarts*, general or family practitioner, in the Netherlands—give initial coverage and referral to specialists.

One basis for comparing the United States with other countries is shown on Table 8–2, which catalogues some of the major health care system design variables. Four design dimensions can be identified: *access* to health care, the *mechanism* by which care is delivered, the structure of health care *technology*, and the extent of *government planning and management*. Once the basic choices are made in each dimension, the remaining attributes of cost and quality of care can be identified.

Principles of Access

To date, traditional U.S. health care has espoused, not the right to care, but consumer choice. Access is therefore conceived as a specified level of care and service for which payment is provided for each service rendered. In addition, the patient or client enjoys the option of shopping around for an appropriate provider. In such an arrangement, access to care is generally, but not always, provided on a curative basis, meaning that a patient or client first becomes ill, injured, or impaired (or believes such a condition exists) and then seeks the consultations and treatments of professional health care providers. Payment is typically covered by employment-based insurance that offers clients a variable package of coverage. Less frequently found, but growing, are health care plans founded on prevention and education, where wellness examination, diagnosis, and information dissemination are offered as part of the package. The idea of foundation coverage that defines a national model of health care provision simply does not exist in the United States; each private insurance plan has its own package of benefits, exclusions, copayments, and deductibles (that threshold amount of expenditure borne by the policyholder after which insurance coverage picks up some or all of the costs).

Delivery Mechanism

Health care providers are largely unorganized by large bureaucracies, although patterns are changing. Providers—especially physicians—tend to be organized as private, independent providers, partnerships, and groups rather than as a corporation or government bureaucracy. There is a trend toward extended networks of providers affiliated with a large hospital or clinic located some distance from the primary provider, who then refers his or her patients through the network of associates. Payment is based on a fee-for-service system where payment follows treatment, the so-called treat-and-bill system of payment. Such a system stands in marked contrast to a capitation system of financing, where all treatments are prepaid on a per capita basis, following which all treatment for a specified period of time is covered by the provider. In capitation systems, a provider has a direct incentive both to keep patients healthy and to economize on treatment. Health care decisions directly affect the provider's bottom line; provider income does not expand with the number of treatments as in a fee-based system, and thus the provider assumes greater financial risk.

TABLE 8–2   Health Care Delivery Design Variables

Design Dimension	Traditional U.S. System		Alternative Principles
Access Principles	1.	Access as earned condition	Access as civic right
	2.	Curative	Preventive emphasis, education
	3.	Employment-based insurance	Government service provision, universal insurance, purchasing cooperatives (alliances)
	4.	Negotiated and variable scope of coverage, e.g.: • Acute versus chronic • Nonelective versus elective • Dental • Mental health, etc.	Foundation coverage: • Medical • Dental • Mental health • Convalescent • Long term
Delivery Mechanism	1.	Private independent providers, partnerships, or groups	Public-health service, corporation, network
	2.	Fee-for-service	Capitation financing
	3.	Third-party payment • Copayments • Deductibles	Government, patient pay • Copayments • Deductibles
	4.	Unmanaged care (patient as arranger)	Managed care (primary care provider as manager)
Technology	1.	Medical model (doctors preside)	Public-health model; behavior model
	2.	Research and development Intensive (supply creates demand)	Stable technology
	3.	Specialist dominant	Primary care dominant
Extent of Government Planning and Management	1.	Peer certification, state licensing, provider privileging	Government certification, licensing, privileging
	2.	Market-based, unsupervised care	Government funding (single payer), managed competition
	3.	Full provider liability	Limited provider liability

Another critical dimension of health care delivery, however, is that payment is handled by a third party, typically the private insurer. Thus discussions about treatment between patient and provider do not involve decisions about money. Not surprisingly, third-party pay incentives to economize on treatment are absent.

Finally, decisions about care are largely unmanaged. The patient arranges his or her own treatment and is free to shop for providers and to arrange consultations as he or she deems necessary. As a consequence, without a trained provider to serve as quarterback, health providers market their services directly to paying patients.

Structure of Technology

U.S. health care is clearly organized on a medical model in which doctors preside over the structures and decisions made about care. This is perhaps not surprising in view of the available, extraordinarily advanced technology that can support heroic medical interventions. A corollary of the extended use of advanced technology, equipment, procedures, diagnostic tests, and pharmaceuticals is that highly specialized practitioners dominate the decision making around patient treatment. Not surprisingly, in a fast-paced technological environment, the supply of care often creates its own demand; thus, the mere appearance of magnetic resonance imaging (MRI) machines, gamma knives, AIDS drugs, techniques of angioplasty, orthopedic reconstruction, or genetic treatment creates a nearly instantaneous demand for new, presumably superior tests, treatments, and procedures. Such technology is not static; it advances constantly, making it difficult for even primary-care providers to match patient requirements and diagnosis to the availability of care from the secondary and tertiary sector.

However difficult it is for primary-care providers to oversee the current multitiered system, it may now be nearly impossible for patients to manage their own care at any level beyond minimal coverage. One option, to slow down or freeze the pace of health care advancement to allow primary-care systems to catch up, is probably undesirable for many reasons. One is the obvious contradiction in slowing the pace of development in an area where the aim is to relieve suffering and misery. Another reason is economic: U.S. companies conduct an enormous international business in marketing technology.

Less explored but still viable are models of public health founded on the removal of threats to health in the form of environmental waste and toxic chemicals, management of water and air systems, and the promotion of social practices and conditions of community living and general hygiene. Still other options revolve around education and modifying behavior, so that people engage in informed, self-healing management of their minds and bodies. Thus, habits of eating, drinking, smoking, playing, exercising, and working can be powerful contributors to health risks and outcomes.

Extent of Government Planning and Management

For the most part, the United States is notable for its lack of government planning and management of health care delivery. In general, a system of grassroots control dominates. For instance, certification of professional and practical competence is done by licensed peers trained in the specialties. States issue the licenses allowing providers to open the doors of facilities and to practice. Facilities, clinics, and networks define for themselves the levels of privilege accorded practitioners or house staff. In other countries, by contrast, central governments operate the dominant certification, licensing, and privileging systems.

Furthermore, the locus of decision making about care is anchored to the health care marketplace, where the client or patient seeks out that source of care he or she thinks is available, affordable, and effective. Thus, health decisions are for the most part unsupervised and unrefereed by either primary-care provider or government-funding agent. Not surprisingly, the mechanism by which patients and clients seek a redress of grievances, especially in the instance of malpractice or wrongful injury, exposes providers to full liability unless they carry expensive insurance covering such risk. In systems where public or nonprofit corporations or government bureaucracies manage the delivery of care, providers are less vulnerable, either because of their ability to employ teams of corporate lawyers or because tort liability (i.e., wrongful act, damage, or injury subject to a civil suit in the courts) limits provider exposure to damage awards.

WHAT POLICIES WORK?

A national debate is now underway about the future of U.S. health care, and readers should join the debate by considering the policy options discussed here against the design options and problems discussed earlier. If nothing else, by convening a national health care task force chaired by Hillary Rodham Clinton and by submitting the Health Security Act of 1993, the Clinton administration placed the health care issue on the nation's agenda, for discussion, debate, and decision. Thus, the question before the country was not whether the original 1,367-page document compiled by the task force would be approved, but whether and how the issues raised by the proposed bill would be decided.

The centerpiece of this debate is the question of how to extend access to a sophisticated array of health care services to people not now directly covered and at the same time to control health care costs. In this respect, government has already contributed to the problems of access and cost through its subsidy of health care (Research and development—R & D): it finances R & D directly; it provides grants to principal investigators; and it provides tax incentives for R & D undertaken by biomedical engineering firms and pharmaceutical companies, which are allowed to write off their discovery costs. Government further assists R & D by protecting the intellectual property derived from it and the marketing of that property through patent and trademark protections; swift evaluation and certification by the Food and Drug Administration (FDA) both protects public safety and contributes to the marketing of new discoveries. Thus, public policy has contributed in no small way to improving health care by protecting the golden goose of advancing technology.

Advancing technology aggravates the problem of extending otherwise unavailable coverage to those confronting health treatment needs, but without the ability to pay. Because health care access policies have been developed independently of policies promoting improvements in treatment quality and cost containment, none of the programs of access involve restructuring health care delivery as a condition of program execution. The net result had been to feed more money into the health care system as the cost of increased access. Not surprisingly, the result of increased utilization has been cost growth since Medicaid and Medicare were established in 1965 and since the population has both aged and endured substantial rates of poverty.

Finally, public policy has had to wrestle with the problem of health care cost caused by feeding technology that redefines standards of care and then providing access to this higher level of care. The predictable result is higher costs. How, then, to contain costs without killing the golden goose that yields an unrivaled standard of medical care for those who can afford to pay? Those initiatives that have been tried must be judged failures if their objective was cost control. Figure 7–1, which charts U.S. cost growth from 1961 to 1991, shows that medical costs have never been less than the rate of inflation. In fact, health cost growth has roughly doubled the rate of inflation. The comparability of these data are arguable, however; both access and quality have been changing since 1961.

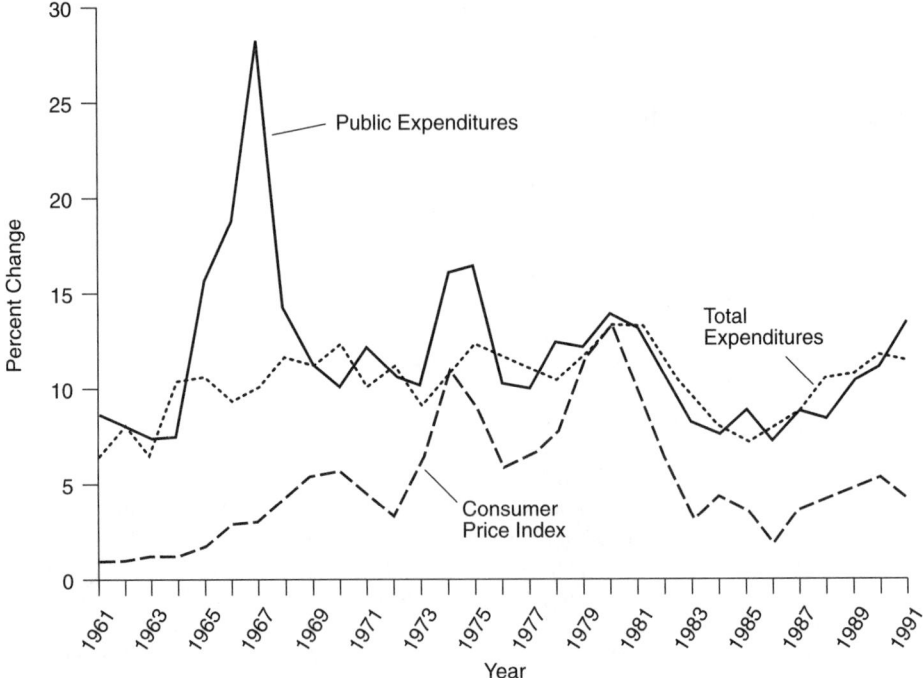

Figure 8–1 Annual percent change in health expenditures and inflation: 1961–1991

Source: U.S. Department of Commerce, *U.S. Statistical Abstract* (Washington, D.C.: Bureau of Census), annual editions.

Cost control initiatives have been defined largely by attempts at regulation. Virtually all regulatory options preserved the traditional health care system and sought to control strategic dimensions of care delivery. Among the points of leverage have been the following:

1. Control of the availability of facilities and equipment: the use of certificates of need as a requirement for receiving government-supported debt service for facilities construction and government grants to purchase capital equipment. A provider must convince a state health systems planner of the need for a facility or service on the basis of which an approval, or certificate, is issued.
2. Control of the use of procedures and interventions: the classic strategy for regulating excessive use of invasive procedures.
3. Control of prices charged by providers: policy can designate treatment parameters; number of hospital days per episode; allowable procedures within which a particular diagnosis is allowed. Thus, according to the diagnostically related groups (DRGs), begun in 1983, hospitals treating Medicare and Medicaid patients are reimbursed according to one of over 400 diagnostic groups (e.g., pneumonia) for which a specific sum is guaranteed. Beyond that amount, the hospital must absorb the cost or may pocket the surplus.

In the one attempt to control costs through subsidy of alternative institutions and program structures, the results have been mixed. The creation of health maintenance organizations (HMOs), founded on prepaid, capitation-based financing for which a comprehensive health care provider gives all care, retains unexpended funds when costs do not exceed earnings, and absorbs losses when costs exceed revenues, has been embroiled in controversy. Because HMOs have an incentive to keep patients healthy with vigorous preventive care, supporters argue that they deliver high-quality care at a lower price than does the fee-for-service option. Detractors argue that HMOs merely have an incentive to deny patients needed care.

WHAT TO DO NEXT?

Policymakers can choose from among many action options. We illustrate the range of policy choice here by sorting proposals according to fundamental issues anchoring the choices. Should health care, defined as the general standard of care available to a society (already established as very high in the United States), be considered a right? Does citizenship create an entitlement to health care regardless of ability to pay? If health care is not a right, is it an earned condition determined by the services required by the unique needs of people whose circumstances and budgets permit a range of care from which only the individual and the provider can choose? More than mere philosophy is at stake. Declaring health care a right requires government and public policy to determine how and when society delivers on its promises to all citizens. Declaring it an earned condition gives all citizens the right to choose the package that best suits their circumstances; government in this case must protect the market and allow it to respond to consumer demand.

.This latter presumption is the one under which U.S. health care policy has traditionally operated, as noted earlier. Notwithstanding the market-based heritage, however, the debates over the years have examined a continuum of policy options that try to blend the goals anchored by the rights-versus-choice debate. We categorize six basic policy options below, starting with minimal tinkering with current, market-based arrangements and moving toward increasingly interventionist actions aimed at securing a civic right to care. Regardless of legislation passed now and in the near future, public policy will be wrestling with these issues for many years.

Tinker with the Present System

A presumption of the market approach is that any notion of right to care is exceedingly difficult, if not impossible, to define. Do all otherwise healthy octogenarians have a right to triple coronary bypass surgery that would extend their lives by 10 to 15 years? Must an MRI be available to all communities for diagnosis of internal maladies? Must sufficient renal dialysis machinery and kidney transplant facilities and staff be created to cover everyone with degenerative kidney disease? The ethics of decision making under conditions of scarcity allocated by price pose some of the most difficult challenges conceivable.

This option recognizes the fundamental strength in a market-based system of consumer choice in which clients and patients seek and pay for the services they need, desire, and can afford. In health markets, there is an effective demand for service to which markets respond by allowing the flow of money to indicate where more and better treatments are desired. Concrete policies can render a market-based system of health care reasonably humane. First, public reimbursement policy can be tilted toward less expensive health care alternatives, such as the use of Medicaid and Medicare programs to pay for outpatient rather than in-patient care, home care rather than institutional care, and chronic care clinics rather than acute care (e.g., clinics rather than expensive emergency medical ser-vices for primary health care). Thus, health care practice can be nudged toward less costly and restrictive alternatives. Second , the use of generous grants and tu-ition forgiveness programs can encourage health care providers to establish their practices in underserved areas, such as rural communities and inner city areas that have difficulty attracting capable talent. Third, government grants can serve to set up health clinics and alternative health care delivery mechanisms. For ex-ample, government programs to establish more HMOs whose existence is based on preventive rather than curative practice, can provide grants and operating loss support until facilities and subscriptions are built up, and the HMO can be self-supporting.

Health systems tinkering can take many forms but always aims to preserve the current market-based, insured system while attempting to patch over market fail-ures and omissions of coverage. By computerizing and minimizing paperwork, de-veloping incentives for using cheaper forms of effective care, encouraging the extension of services to remote corners of society, and launching competitive ex-periments in alternative forms of health care provision, public policy tries to make the current system more productive, humane, and less costly.

Regulate the Current System

Another basic strategy uses law and regulation to correct many of the excesses of the traditional system. Most of the targets for regulation concern excessive cost and excessive use of medical procedures and tests. Some of the leading examples, promoted particularly in the 1970s, include the following:

Certificates of need: This instrument can be ignored by private providers, who conclude that their profit margins are sufficient and that they do not need government support.

Peer service review organizations (PSROs): While designed to review the excessive use of procedures billed through the fee-for-service system, this mechanism relies on peer con-trol to establish and enforce norms and standards of best practice; policymakers gener-ally regard it as a weak instrument of cost control, because *best practice* is often too expensive and based on prevailing fee schedules.

Regulating prices through DRGs: Limits to hospital stays, tests, and treatments constrain ex-penditures for each class of costs. Manipulation of diagnoses by physicians to provide ser-vices deemed necessary by expert providers appears eminently possible, leaving regulators with little basis for overruling attending physicians and risking lawsuits by ag-grieved patients.

Public policy also regulates insurers. An important issue concerns the extent to which insurers can be allowed to engage in cherry picking, making money by in-suring only persons who are healthy. Inasmuch as insurance companies are char-tered and regulated by state governments, however, limits can be placed on the current practice of weeding out policyholders based on preexistent conditions. An-other issue concerns the paperwork burden imposed on the health care system when a large number of unregulated insurers develop unique reporting systems and forms requiring special and costly paper-shuffling expertise. A corrective mea-sure here is a unified billing form used by all payers.

Catastrophic Health Insurance

The average citizens deepest fear about health care is the occurrence of a serious accident or a catastrophic illness leading to bankruptcy. A catastrophic insurance strategy insures everyone against this prospect. A catastrophic health insurance proposal (CHIP) requires people to supply their own private insurance as in the traditional system. Once some threshold level of family income has been spent on health care, however, a public CHIP would pick up the tab for charges exceeding, in one proposal from the 1980s, 10 percent of family income. This scheme does little to change current patterns of cost, quality, and access; even bankrupt patients can demand and receive basic care from all hospitals, which must absorb uncollected bills as income losses recovered from paying clients.

National Health Insurance

If health care is a right, full coverage, not catastrophic insurance, is needed. In this case, all persons and businesses pay into a risk pool of funds, based on a universal coverage principle and designed to cover all reasonable health expenditures. There are many variations on the national health insurance idea. Access may be universal or conditioned on meeting a criterion such as need, age, or infirmity; in its broadest variety, universal access gives a basic right to health care and in so doing sharply departs from the other approaches.

Deciding about the range of coverage, is very difficult: as technology changes, so does the practice of health care. Thus, any attempt to define the extent of coverage may become outdated. Presumably, no proponent of national health insurance would turn around and say, "In national health care there will be universal access only for nosebleeds, mumps, and broken bones; citizens must otherwise get their own private insurance, pay full costs for all other treatments, or do without until a medical emergency is declared." Oregon did develop a rank-ordered list of procedures for which the state health plan covers everyone, such as the first 600 of a list of 2,000 treatments, after which the budget is exhausted and people must on their own (as they are now) find health care treatment for the remaining afflictions.

Finally, government must determine whether and to what extent private insurance markets will be used in a national health care plan or whether only a consolidated insurance system will be used. This problem has at least two dimensions: the number of third-party payers chartered to handle billing and the ownership of the insurance scheme. At one extreme is the single-payer system, where the government is the insurer and pays health bills submitted by private providers according to fee schedules negotiated by the insurance authority. Other systems, such as those in the Netherlands and Sweden, use separate insurance funds to which wage earners and employers contribute, to which bills for service are submitted, and from which providers are paid; in both countries, nearly confiscatory tax laws (at upper income levels) and negotiated fee schedules limit the charges health care providers can and will submit to the insurance system. Still other countries, such as Germany, use an extensive array of private insurance instruments to provide universal coverage administered by autonomous federal, regional, and local organizations. Only the United States relies on independent private insurance companies to provide coverage and then supplements coverage for special categories of persons with government reimbursement.

Restructuring

A fundamental reform of the health care delivery system is envisioned by those who defend the right to care. Radical expansion of access to care without simultaneous adjustments in the structure of health care delivery produces an enormous potential expansion of costs. Thus, the Clinton health security strategy envisioned a simultaneous redefinition of a civic right to care and a restructuring of the provider system. Three concepts are critical.

First, to the extent that private insurance schemes would be used, a way must be found to provide coverage at reasonable cost for large numbers of people, some of whom may be uninsurable. Large pools of risk covering all citizens, who would enjoy the market power of a buyers' cooperative that can buy bulk health care, are a possibility. The concept of a "health alliance" was created in the proposed Health Security Act of 1993 to produce such a result.

Second, the heart of the managed-care concept is a complex system of health care provision requiring primary-care providers to engage in systematic case management of patients, including referrals of patients to secondary and tertiary parts of the system. This practice has been expanding rapidly.

Third, there is no basis for objectively knowing how much health care really costs. The answer must be competitively derived through a system of managed competition that pits the expertise of corporate health care experts and health alliance managers against providers' insider knowledge of costs and alternative schemes under which costs can be reduced. In this case, public policy's strategy is to encourage large-scale provider networks of managed care that then negotiate packages of coverage with health-purchasing alliances in a continuous, competitive search for acceptable packages of services and costs.

National Health Service

A final response to the conclusion that health care is a right rather than a privilege is a public agency's providing services directly to clients and patients. In the United States, Veterans Administration hospitals, the Indian Health Service, and public hospitals and clinics sponsored by state and local government offer such care. The national health service in the United Kingdom (U.K.) finances health care from general tax revenues, which cover the capital and operating costs of health care that is delivered directly through public institutions and providers. The great strength of the U.K.'s system is that health care is free, except for a minimal copayment. As the system is a service delivery system rather than a third-party insurance, the question of deductibles never arises.

In such a system, a great deal rides on the effectiveness with which public managers can allocate resources in the absence of a price mechanism by which patients and clients can signal how much service they want. Such a system may promote waste; providers are spending budgeted funds rather than money belonging to them, and hence the incentive to be highly productive is missing. This tendency can be (and is) partly corrected through incentive schemes that allocate fixed resources to providers if any money is left over at the end of the year; in essence, a kind of performance contract is developed between government and provider to encourage efficiency. A continuing debate can be expected, however, over whether such a system encourages a further rationing of already inadequate resources appropriated through government budgets to health care.

SUMMARY

We are now engaged in a great debate about the design of the U.S. health care system. Without an objectively correct answer about design, analysis requires both a clear view of current practice and conditions as well as a comparative examination of the options available to nations and regions of the world. In the end, however, the United States will have to design a system for itself; it is not like other countries either in the structure of its services or in the public-health problems that have resulted. Health care policy making revolves around the following set of questions that must be answered before the current system can be reformed.

1. Should access to health care be a right or an earned privilege?
2. Should coverage be financed through employer contributions, personal contributions, or general tax revenues?
3. Should a national plan preserve the principle of patient's choice of provider? How can the choices be institutionalized?

   - Budgets, either regional or national
   - Managed competition
   - Managed care
   - Direct price control
   - Single payer

4. Should health care reform occur on a national basis or on the basis of subnational regions, states, substate regions, or localities?
5. Should reform be accomplished in phases or as a set of sweeping changes? Over what time period will the changes be phased in? Clearly, phased rollout will reduce up-front costs of transition but will cause needy patients to wait for coverage.

The debate is animated by new imperatives driving health care choice. Nations are actively comparing strategies and results. In this comparison, U.S. practices are both criticized and admired. While the United States is unique among nations for its failure to provide universal health care as a matter of civic right, other nations are examining and copying U.S. technologies and initiatives.

DISCUSSION QUESTIONS

1. Why is the problem of health care in the U.S. not simply a medical question to be best decided by health providers, such as physicians?
2. If national policy were to focus on *one* public health problem, which one should be placed on the policy agenda? What would be second? Third?
3. Is U. S. health care a crisis or simply a problem? What are the policy implications of this decision?
4. If one were designing a national health care system, what features would the ideal system contain? What is the role of government in providing health care in your design?

SUGGESTED READINGS

Henry J. Aaron, *Serious and Unstable Condition: Financing America's Health Care* (Washington, D.C.: The Brookings Institution, 1991).

John J. DiIulio, Jr., and Richard R. Nathan, editors, *Making Health Reform Work: The View from the States* (Washington, D.C.: The Brookings Institution, 1994).

Theodore R. Marmor, *Understanding Health Care Reform* (New Haven: Yale University Press, 1994).

Vicente Navarro, *The Politics of Health Policy* (Cambridge, Mass.: Blackwell Publishers, 1994).

Marc A. Rodwin, *Medicine, Money, and Morals: Physicians' Conflicts of Interest* (New York: Oxford University, 1993).

Frank A. Sloan, Randall Bovbjerg, and Penny Githens, *Insuring Medical Malpractice* (New York: Oxford University Press, 1991).

Carol Wekesser, editor, *Health Care in America: Opposing Viewpoints* (San Diego, Calif.: Greenhaven Press, Inc., 1994).

NOTES

1. Health Security: The President's Report to the American People (Washington, D.C.: U.S. Government Printing Office, 1993), 4.
2. *Health Security,* 1993, 5.
3. *Health Security,* 1993, 33.
4. *Health Security,* 1993, 77.
5. The latter category of insurance exclusion derives from what is well known in the public hearings as a "preexistent condition," in which a previous history of cancer, heart disease, or AIDS, or even a family history of such conditions, becomes grounds for refusing insurance coverage. Readers should be aware that computers vastly increase the ease with which insurance companies can screen the medical histories of anyone who has had or who has applied for health insurance or life insurance and who has, as a result, allowed medical information and records to be released to insurers. A national data bank second in size only to the Medicare program recipient files is kept by the Medical Information Bureau for use by the insurance industry. See Lawrence G. Brewster and Michael Brown, *The Public Agenda: Issues in American Politics,* 3rd ed. (New York: St. Martin's, 1994), 121–122. The collateral issues associated with privacy and data use are not unlike those involving a bank's use of credit bureau information to assess customer credit worthiness.
6. René J. Dubos, *Mirage of Health: Utopias, Progress, and Biological Change* (Garden City, N.Y.: Doubleday, 1959).
7. Dan Morgan, "New Hampshire Cashes in on a Medicaid Loophole," *Washington Post,* national weekly ed., 8–14 March, 1993, p. 31.
8. *New York Times,* national ed., 7 October, 1993, p. A12.

9

Transportation Policy

Transportation is important throughout the world, in both developed and developing countries. Transportation has always played a particularly crucial role in the United States. Early in the country's development, transportation was crucial to unify the country, and throughout much of U.S. history, passenger transportation has been synonymous with communication. To move messages, people or physical documents had to move. Freight transportation was also critical to commerce, particularly to agriculture in an era when the primary agricultural lands were some distance from emerging population centers. Transportation continues to be important in the United States because of the country's geographic size and its relatively low population densities. Other countries, particularly in Europe, often adopt different transportation policies from those in the United States. In comparing these policies and in questioning why the United States relies more heavily than other countries on modes of transportation such as trucks and private automobiles, the country's size and its population density often explain the reasons.

Both freight and passenger transportation have changed over the past 50 years. The changes in the relative importance of freight modes can be seen in Table 9–1, which shows the intercity freight market share by mode over the period from 1940 to 1992. As can be seen in the table, railroads dominated in 1940, with over 60 percent of the ton miles. Rail share has declined steadily through 1985, however, but has slightly increased since then. Trucking, on the other hand, was not very important in 1940 but has increased steadily and now accounts for over 25 percent of ton miles. Pipeline share has also increased over the past 50 years, while water transport has declined slightly. Air cargo carries a very small portion of intercity freight in terms of ton miles partly because the goods shipped via air tend to be very lightweight.

Table 9–2 shows the share of intercity passenger travel by mode over the same period. Here the most noticeable feature is the dominant role of the automobile.

TABLE 9–1 Intercity Freight Market Share by Mode, 1940–1992 (Percentage* of Freight Ton Miles)†

	1940	1950	1960	1970	1980	1985	1992‡
Railroads	†61.3	56.1	44.1	39.8	37.5	36.4	37
Trucking	10	16.3	21.7	21.3	22.3	24.8	27.2
Oil pipeline	9.5	12.1	17.4	22.3	23.6	22.9	19.5
Water§	19.1	15.4	16.7	16.5	16.4	15.5	15.9
Air		0.03	0.07	0.17	0.21	0.27	0.37

*Percentages do not total to 100 percent due to rounding.
†Includes both for-hire and private carriers, mail and express.
‡Preliminary Results.
§Includes Great Lakes and rivers and canals.

Source: Transportation in America, 11th ed. (Lansdowne, Va.: Eno Transportation Foundation, Inc., 1993), p. 44. Figures for 1940 were taken from an earlier edition. The original sources for these data include: ICC's *Transport Economics*, the Corps of Engineers' *Waterborne Commerce*, the Department of Transportation's *Air Carrier Traffic Statistics,* and the Federal Highway Administration's *Highway Statistics.*

Although auto's share of passenger miles has declined from a high of over 90 percent in 1960, it remains over 80 percent today. Both rail and intercity bus shares have declined since the 1940s and 1950s. Airlines' share, however, has risen from under 1 percent of travel in 1940 to over 17 percent today. These changes in freight and passenger market shares result partly from technological change, but also from government policy.

In the past two decades, transportation policy in the United States has undergone a fundamental transformation. Throughout the development of railroads, trucking, intercity buses, and airline industries, government regulation has played a role almost as great as technological progress. In the 1970s, however, dissatisfaction with the effects of regulation began to grow, and many came to believe regulation had outlived its usefulness. By the late 1970s, the trend of increasing transportation regulation was quickly reversed across all modes. The results of this deregulation movement have been dramatic, bringing benefits to some and harm to others. Whether deregulation of transportation has been good or bad public policy is a complex and still debated question. What cannot be debated, however,

TABLE 9–2 Intercity Passenger Market Share by Mode (Percentage of Passenger Miles)

	1940	1950	1960	1970	1980	1985	1992
Automobiles	89	87	90.4	86.9	82.5	80.1	80.5
Airlines	0.4	1.8	4.1	9.3	13.9	17	17.1
Private Air	0.1	0.2	0.3	0.8	1	0.8	0.6
Buses	3.1	4.5	2.5	2.1	1.9	1.4	1.1
Railroads	7.5	6.5	2.8	0.9	0.7	0.7	0.7

Source: Transportation in America, 11th ed. (Lansdowne, Va.: Eno Transportation Foundation, Inc., 1993), p. 47. The original sources for these data include: ICC's *Transport Economics*, the Federal Highway Administration's *Highway Statistics*, and the Department of Transportation's *Air Carrier Traffic Statistics.*

are the great amount of change and the opportunity to learn about general public policy by looking closely at transportation policy. To understand those problems, it is first necessary to look briefly at the evolution of transportation policy in the United States.

EVOLUTION OF TRANSPORTATION POLICY

In the United States, government has been involved in transportation during four periods: (1) promotion, before 1887; (2) control of monopoly, from 1887 to about 1917; (3) ensurance of adequacy, from 1920 to the late 1960s; and (4) market competition, from the mid-1970s to the present. In each period, both the principal public policy challenges and the government responses were different.

Promotion

In the late 18th and early 19th centuries, the United States was much like a developing country. Its economy was based on self-sufficient agriculture, with little agricultural specialization and little recognizable manufacturing. As with many developing countries today, there was almost no internal transportation infrastructure; any agricultural surpluses were exported abroad. Aside from some intracoastal shipping, the primary focus was on export markets.

The country needed overland transportation in order for its economy to develop in areas away from the coast. The initial response to this need was the construction of turnpikes and private toll roads in the 1790s by the first U.S. corporations. When the War of 1812 began, there were 86 turnpike companies in Pennsylvania and 135 turnpike companies in New York.

Federal government involvement in overland transportation began in 1797 with the National Pike Project. The National Pike was to go from Cumberland, Maryland, to the western border, at that time St. Louis. The National Pike eventually became U.S. Route 40 and later Interstate 70. Congress appropriated about $6.8 million between 1806 and 1838 for the project, and by 1818, the road had been completed as far as Wheeling, West Virginia. In the early 1800s, a debate developed over the proper roles of federal and state governments in transportation infrastructure. Andrew Jackson's election in 1832 settled the debate in favor of strong state and weak federal roles, and the National Pike, which had reached Vandalia, Illinois, was abandoned as a federal project.

The decision to limit the federal role has set the pattern for much of U.S. transportation policy to this day. States owned and developed the highway system; federal involvement did not resume until 1916, and then in a matching funds arrangement. With a limited federal role, privately owned transportation companies became the rule. The Unites States is one of only a few countries without a system of federal government-owned transportation companies. There have been periods of federal ownership in the railroads, but private ownership dominated.

State governments' role in transportation development has varied over time. Although states seldom owned transportation companies, some states were heavily involved in ownership and development of canals between 1820 and 1850. Promoting transportation infrastructure was believed to promote economic development, but canals turned out to be not particularly good investments. In northern climates where they froze in winter, their use was seasonal, and canals lacked route flexibility because elevation changes could be accomplished only with locks. Thus, canals were confined to riverbeds and level terrain, and many were oriented in a north-south direction while most of the demand for freight movement was east-west. The economic depressions of 1837 and 1843 hit state finances hard, and most states got out of the canal business.

Railroads came to the United States in 1830 and eventually dominated the use of canals. Railroads had two critical advantages over canals: they could easily handle elevation changes, and they could carry east-west traffic. With the development of steel rails, railroads could carry heavy loads. Railroads were developed by the private sector but with heavy public-sector involvement. In order to encourage railroad development, particularly in the plains and western areas, the federal government gave the railroads land. In exchange for the land, a railroad had to be built and mail, government personnel, and government freight had to be given a discount for transport. In total, 130 million acres (200,000 square miles) were given to the railroads, an area equivalent to the combined areas of the states of Indiana, New Jersey, and California. The western routes tended to be monopolies, whereas the routes in the east tended to be competitive, with two or more parallel routes. The mid-1800s was a period of intense construction: over one-fourth of the present U.S. railway mileage was built between 1830 and 1870.

As the railroad industry developed, the public mood began to shift from promoting transportation to regulating it in response to a growing dissatisfaction with the industry's behavior. One problem was the growing revelation of fraudulent practices by the industry. With the public subsidy available in the form of land, some companies built the railroad as cheaply as possible, sold the land for a profit, and withdrew from the railroad business. A particularly prominent fraud was the Credit Mobilier scandal of the 1860s, where the directors of one railroad, the Union Pacific, owned a construction company and channeled the profits from their enterprise into this company at the government's expense.

A second problem was the high prices that the monopoly railroads in the western United States often charged, particularly for grain destined for eastern markets. Western farmers had little choice but to use the railroads for their crops. The high prices gave rise to the so-called Granger Movement: western farmers pushed for regulation to keep the costs of shipping grain low. A third problem was price discrimination: railroads charged different prices for the same service in different regions or different prices for different customers in the same region. They often gave favored customers hidden rebates or kickbacks. Prices were based not on the cost of providing the service but on the value of the goods being shipped. As a result of these practices, shippers often faced fluctuating transportation prices that made it difficult to plan their operations. A fourth problem was the price fixing engaged in by some railroads. Carriers who might potentially compete with one another for traffic instead chose to fix prices. In extreme cases, carriers pooled their revenues on a set of routes and divided them among themselves according to a previous arrangement.

In response to these concerns, state regulation was established in four states between 1871 and 1874 through the so-called Granger Laws. Although these laws proved ineffective, a U.S. Supreme Court ruling in 1877 upheld states' right to regulate "property affected with the public interest." This ruling helped pave the way for the transition from the promotional era to the regulated era in transportation policy. The promotional era, however, established four things: the pattern of private ownership of transportation companies; government withdrawal from ownership or operation of transportation companies, the concept of government aid to transportation infrastructure development, and the legal right to have public regulation of transportation.

Control of Monopoly

As state regulation of the railroads proved ineffective, pressure grew for federal regulation. The resulting regulation was patterned after British common law applied to stagecoach transportation as early as the 16th century. Here, the government granted an exclusive franchise to a private transportation company in exchange for the company's agreeing to meet four obligations. First, the carrier must agree that it would not refuse to serve a customer. Second, the carrier must serve customers at a reasonable price. Third, the carrier must serve all customers equally. Fourth, the carrier is responsible for the safe delivery of passengers or freight. These conditions were the origins of the notion of common carriage.

Congress passed the Act to Regulate Commerce in 1887. This act was patterned closely after the British Canals and Railways Act of 1854 and attempted to achieve consistent enforcement of the principles embedded in common law. The act established the Interstate Commerce Commission (ICC) to rule on the law and focused on preventing excessively high rates and curbing monopoly-pricing abuses. As might be expected in the first major regulatory act, the details contained many loopholes, not completely plugged until around 1910.

The act contained six major provisions (1) the rates charged must be just and reasonable; (2) all persons must be charged the same rates under similar circumstances and conditions; (3) rates and services cannot be unduly preferential or prejudicial; (4) rates must be the same or more for the long haul as for an included short haul; (5) pooling or concerted action is illegal; (6) the rates must be published and obeyed and notice must be given of changes. It is clear even from this brief description how this act was directed at the railroad practices of the time.

Adequacy

As monopoly abuses by the railroads were curbed by this regulation, a new concern began to emerge about whether the revenues allowed the railroads by the new regulation were adequate. Preventing high prices could easily go too far and leave the railroads with too little revenue to maintain their operation. The Transportation Act of 1920 addressed this concern by specifying that railroads be allowed to earn a "fair return on a fair value." The ICC was given the authority to set minimum rates. Less than 35 years after the landmark legislation to protect consumers from too-high prices, the government began to emphasize protecting the railroads from prices that were too low. Thus, the shift from regulating monopoly to protecting the railroad industry occurred.

This shift in emphasis is apparent in the passage of the next major piece of transportation legislation, the Motor Carrier Act of 1935. This act, intended as part two of the 1887 act, extended the pattern and philosophy of rail regulation to the trucking (or motor carrier) industry. Although trucking regulation was similar to railroad regulation, it evolved much differently. The demand for railroad regulation came from shippers concerned about high prices, but the demand for trucking regulation came from the trucking industry itself. Railroading had tremendous entry costs because of the need to lay tracks. Trucking, however, had very low entry costs because the government built the tracks in the form of highways. Thus, to enter the trucking industry, a person needed only a truck. With such low costs of entry, many trucking companies sprang up. The result was considerable downward pressure on prices and heavy turnover in the industry as businesses went bankrupt from intense competition. Some state regulation had evolved for the trucking industry, but there was little consistency across states.

Federal regulation was demanded by an unlikely coalition of interests. Companies already in trucking wanted protection from new entrants into the industry. Shippers liked the low prices that resulted from heavy competition, but they wanted stability in both prices and in the companies offering services. Finally, the railroad industry wanted trucking regulated to provide protection from the emerging competition. Thus, truck regulation focused on both maximum and minimum rates, like railroad regulation, but it also focused on controlling entry into the industry, which had not been an issue in the railroad case.

Government policy toward aviation and the airline industry evolved differently from policy toward trucking or railroads. The Wright brothers first flew a heavier-than-air craft in 1903 at Kitty Hawk, North Carolina. In 1916, the U.S. Post Office provided the first funds to aircraft operators to help cover the costs of carrying mail by air. In 1918, the U.S. Aerial Mail Service was established by the U.S. Post Office. Aircraft of the day, however, could fly only short distances, and this service eventually failed. In 1925, transcontinental mail routes were established, and airmail became successful. The key to its early success was night operation, which enabled aircraft operators to fly around the clock. (Early night operations were difficult, and the first night navigational devices were bonfires lit to help guide night flyers.) To put this development in perspective with the development of aviation, Charles Lindbergh's historic solo flight across the Atlantic Ocean was in 1927.

The first major legislation directed at aviation was the Kelly Act of 1925 governing mail contracts. In the tradition of common carriage, the routes were granted to airlines as monopolies. By 1933 four airlines had 94 percent of the mail contracts, which then totaled $19.4 million: American Airlines, United Airlines, Trans World Airlines (TWA), and Eastern Airlines. Through the late 1970s, these four airlines were the largest passenger airlines in the United States.

Three years after passage of the Motor Carrier Act of 1935, Congress passed the Civil Aeronautics Act of 1938, which was to serve as the basis for regulating the airline industry for the next 40 years. The act created the Civil Aeronautics Authority (reorganized as the Civil Aeronautics Board, or CAB, in 1940) and gave it the dual legislative mandate to regulate and to promote air transportation. Among the first actions under the new legislation was the grant of grandfather rights for the 16 carriers operating in 1938; these carriers became known as the trunk airlines, able to operate either nationally or over very large regions of the country. In essence, this action approved the airline structure that had been created by the U.S. Post Office in the awarding of mail contracts.

The focus of airline regulation was much like that of trucking regulation: preventing either too-high or too-low prices and controlling entry into the industry. Indeed, once the 16 airlines were granted grandfather rights, the CAB permitted no new trunk airlines to enter the industry after 1938 despite over 70 applications. Had it been up to the CAB, there would likely have been no new entry of any kind. In 1943, however, the CAB bowed to mounting political pressure and studied the prospect of allowing a limited form of feeder service. The result was the Local Service Airline Experiment; the CAB granted temporary operating authority to small local airlines that would operate 10-passenger aircraft in feeder service from small communities to larger communities where passengers could connect to trunk airline flights. Made permanent in 1955, the experiment gave rise to the Local Service Airlines (LSAs). These airlines gradually evolved to take on more and more of the characteristics of trunk airlines, although their service areas were much more geographically confined.

Another type of entrant into the industry was the supplemental carrier. These carriers were permitted to offer only nonscheduled charter flights to groups of travelers. Supplemental carriers were established by the CAB initially on an interim basis but were given permanent status in 1966. Many of the applications to become scheduled trunk airlines came from this group of supplemental carriers. Conversely, most of the trunk airlines conducted some charter operations.

The CAB regulated five important aspects of airline operations. First, they regulated entry into the industry. For an airline to offer services, it had to be issued a Certificate of Public Convenience and Necessity by the CAB. Carriers operating under these conditions were known as certificated carriers. To receive such a certificate the carrier had to be found at least "fit, willing, and able" to provide air service. Beyond demonstrating fitness, however, a prospective entrant had to demonstrate that its entry was required by the public convenience and necessity. As discussed earlier, the CAB was very difficult to convince. The only exception to the certificate requirements was commuter airlines, who were restricted to operating very small aircraft.

Second, the authority to issue certificates also allowed the CAB to control the route structure of each airline. Each certificate applied to a single route and specified both the pair of cities that were the end points of the route and the intermediate stops. The specification of intermediate stops was quite detailed and often included stops that had to be made, stops that could be made, and stops that could not be made. In addition, there were often restrictions on carrying passengers between intermediate stops. Through the use of these certificates, the CAB could control the route structure of each airline as well as the number of carriers permitted to compete in each city-pair market.

The CAB was only slightly more permissive about the entry of existing carriers into new city-pair markets than of new carriers into the industry. When a route was already served by a carrier, the CAB was reluctant to allow new entry if the incumbent objected that such entry would divert existing traffic and cause financial hardship. As further restrictions, route awards necessitated an application procedure and very lengthy, often expensive hearings.

Third, the CAB was able to use certificates to control exit, as a carrier could not stop serving a route without CAB approval. Some exit occurred, though, as the trunk airlines were permitted to turn over a few of their low-density, short-haul routes to local service airlines. To a much lesser extent, local service airlines were permitted to hand over some of their routes to commuter airlines (who fly regular schedules but use smaller planes).

A fourth critical aspect of CAB regulation was its authority over fares. Fare offerings generally were limited to coach and first-class fares based on mileage traveled. Although the CAB allowed limited experimentation with discount or promotional fares at various times (e.g., standby discount fares in the late 1960s), it could eliminate them at virtually a moment's notice. Fares typically were revised upward, though, to reflect increases in costs, and to allow airlines to pass on most or all cost increases to passengers. Perhaps more important, the CAB set the fare taper to be less steep than the cost taper.[1] This relationship between fares and costs created losses and disincentives for short-haul small town service, along with intense service rivalry and incentives to acquire wide-bodied aircraft for long hauls.

By suppressing virtually all fare competition, CAB procedures generally encouraged competition based on service rather than price. When combined with relatively rapid industry growth, such an environment did not breed an intense preoccupation with cost controls. For example, when faced with a labor dispute, the conventional managerial wisdom in the industry under CAB regulation was to settle a strike quickly rather than lose market share and growth from a prolonged shutdown. Furthermore, excessively generous labor settlements, or other managerial ineptitude, could usually be absorbed by some combination of market growth and technologically induced gains in productivity without asking the regulators for a fare increase. A major consequence was that consumers reaped fewer benefits from technological gains than they otherwise would. In essence, most of the substantial productivity improvements generated by rapid technological change in the industry were absorbed in rising labor and other costs.

Fifth, CAB approval was also necessary for airline companies to merge. In general, CAB took a restrictive view of mergers, granting approval only to maintain industry stability when one of the merger candidates was in serious financial trouble. Merger thus served mainly as a tool for averting bankruptcy.

Overall, the basic guiding principles of the CAB seemed to be equalizing the size of companies and avoiding bankruptcies to maintain stability in the industry. The CAB used its authority over entry, exit, route awards, and fares to maintain the financial viability of even the weakest carriers. Consequently, new route awards rarely went to the largest trunk lines. As a last resort to avoid an imminent bankruptcy, the CAB would also force mergers, often sweetened by access to new routes. As a reflection of these tendencies in CAB policies, regulation encouraged development and recruitment of management with legal and political skills, somewhat to the exclusion of skills in marketing and cost control.

Competition

In the 1950s, economists and others studying the U.S. transportation scene began to consider the possibility that the regulatory institutions then surrounding the industry had perhaps outlived their usefulness. In 1962, President John F. Kennedy set the tone for a move toward less regulation in a speech to Congress. By the late 1960s and early 1970s, the emergence of four factors led to moves to reform transportation regulation. One factor was a series of cost studies that pointed out how regulation caused transportation companies to behave inefficiently and make poor use of their resources. A second was the growing strength of the consumer movement. Consumer advocates began to realize that regulation had largely evolved into protecting the carriers from competition rather than protecting consumers from high prices. A third factor was the deteriorating condition of the railroads. The bankruptcy of the Penn Central Railroad, which threatened 20 percent of the nation's freight and passenger movement, was a pivotal event. A central justification for regulation was that it supposedly ensured adequate financial returns for the regulated companies to maintain operations, but regulation had clearly failed in this task with Penn Central. Fourth, the energy crisis of 1973–1974 called attention to some of the less efficient features of regulation. Trucks frequently ran without freight because ICC regulations prohibited them from carrying freight on their return trips (backhauls). Similarly, CAB regulations created strong incentives for airlines to fill only about 55 percent of their seats so that 45 percent were typically empty on flights. With gasoline available to motorists only after long waits, if at all, these regulation-induced inefficiencies attracted considerable attention.

Shortcomings in the regulation of all the modes—railroads, trucks, airlines, and intercity buses—were becoming increasingly apparent. It was most noticeable in the airlines because of the experience in Texas and California with intrastate airlines. The CAB did not have the authority to regulate airlines that operated entirely within a single state; only the states could provide economic regulation in these instances. In both Texas and California, there were major cities far enough apart to support service for intrastate carriers. In Texas, there was no fare regulation, so the intrastate carrier, Southwest Airlines, was able to offer fares without regulatory restrictions. In California, fares were regulated by the state, but they were based not on the average costs as was the practice of the CAB, but on the lowest-cost carrier. As a result, Southwest Airlines in Texas and Pacific Southwest Airlines and Air California in California offered intrastate jet service under a much different regulatory regime from that in the rest of the country. Intrastate service in both states offered low fares compared to those charged in similar markets under CAB regulation and offered still lower fares for service during off-peak hours. These airlines provided no-frills service and often served secondary airports that were located closer to the city centers. Such service patterns attracted many passengers, some diverted from auto travel and some making new trips stimulated by the low fares. The planes operated with a high percentage of their seats full (high load factors). Moreover, these intrastate airlines offering lower fares than their CAB-regulated counterparts were also more profitable than those airlines.

The stage for regulatory change in the airline industry was also set by two actions of the CAB. First was the route moratorium established in the early 1970s. The CAB wished to limit competition and protect the industry, so it decided to make very few new route awards. Those that would be made were to go to the smaller and financially weaker carriers. This action dampened opposition to deregulation by the larger and more prosperous carriers, who thought that the only way they could grow and add new routes was under deregulation. The second action was the capacity limitation agreements during the 1973–1974 oil embargo. Concerned about the large number of empty seats at a time of petroleum shortage, the CAB allowed the carriers serving the transcontinental markets to get together to form an agreement on those routes. Their goal was to reduce capacity and thereby increase the percentage of seats occupied (load factor). The carriers serving those routes were the larger ones; when they reduced capacity on the transcontinental routes, they put that freed-up capacity on other routes shared with some of the smaller carriers. As a result, the small carriers grew less opposed to deregulation.

In 1975, John Robson was named chairman of the CAB. Under his leadership, the CAB took two critical steps toward deregulation. It allowed some limited experimentation with discount fares and commissioned an internal study of regulatory reform that changed the opinion of many CAB staff members about less regulation. Before the study, the CAB's attitude had been what one might expect from a regulatory agency—wholehearted support for regulation. After the study, many became convinced that less restrictive regulation would benefit the public and the airlines alike. When Alfred Kahn was named chairman of the CAB in 1977, the change to less regulation accelerated. So great was the move away from the historic patterns of CAB regulations during the 1976 to 1978 period that this period is often referred to as "administrative deregulation." The CAB's actions toward less regulation, and particularly toward permitting airlines to offer lower fares, were not universally popular in the airline industry, and some groups began to challenge them.

On October 24, 1978, Congress passed the Airline Deregulation Act of 1978, which codified the previous actions of the CAB, ended the legal challenges to recent CAB actions, and removed the uncertainty of how far the reforms would go and how long they would last. One problem with administrative deregulation was that the CAB could revoke the liberalizations as quickly as they had been implemented, but the final form of the Airline Deregulation Act went beyond the initial CAB proposals and even scheduled the sunset of the agency.

The major provisions of the Airline Deregulation Act affected fares, route authority, and exit. The act initially instituted a zone of rate freedom for fares, allowing airlines to cut them up to 50 percent or to raise them between 5 and 10 percent without CAB approval. Later, the CAB gave up all control of fares on short-haul routes and, still later, gave up control of all fares. The act removed the provision specifying that new route entry was required by the public convenience and necessity but retained the provision that an applicant be fit, willing, and able. The act also provided for carriers to pick up route authority not used by the carrier possessing it and allowed a phased-in automatic entry on routes in a manner similar to an expansion draft in professional sports. Neither of these provisions turned out to be important, however, as the CAB chose simply to grant entry on any route to any qualified applicant.

The provisions regarding exit from serving a route were somewhat more complicated. A central concern with airline deregulation, and with the deregulation of trucking, railroads, and intercity buses, was whether small communities would still be served in a deregulated environment. Many observers argued that it was only regulatory restrictions that preserved any service to small communities. The Airline Deregulation Act addressed this concern with a provision that guaranteed Essential Air Service (EAS) for 10 years to any community that had been receiving air service by a certificated carrier (not commuters) at the time of passage of the act. Before deregulation, much of this small community service had been subsidized under legislative provisions originally intended to provide subsidy for mail service. In order to back up the EAS guarantee, the Airline Deregulation Act established a new subsidy program targeted specifically at small community passenger service.

Passenger airlines were the first to be deregulated. Both proponents and opponents of regulatory reform in trucking, rail, and intercity bus transportation looked to the early experiences of the airline industry as an indication of what might happen with these other modes. As these early experiences were being evaluated, Congress moved quickly to reduce regulation in the other modes. In 1980, the Staggers Rail Act removed regulatory restrictions on railroads, and the Motor Carrier Act largely deregulated the trucking industry. In 1982, the Bus Regulatory Reform Act removed restrictions on the intercity bus industry. None of these acts went quite as far as the Airline Deregulation Act, but all shared many of the same features. Thus, in the period between 1978 and 1982, the regulatory environment of all of the major intercity modes was dramatically changed. We now turn to an examination of these transportation industries during the transition to less regulation and in their current state.

AIRLINE INDUSTRY

When Congress committed to a path of deregulation for the airline industry, there was considerable uncertainty about what the eventual effects of this change would be. Would fares really drop, as might be expected from the experiences with intrastate airlines in Texas and California? Or would there be intense competition with low fares on high-density routes between large cities but little or no competition with high fares on low-density routes between small cities? Would the large carriers drive the small carriers out of business, with resulting monopoly behavior and high fares as seen in the railroad industry a century earlier? Would the carriers use their new route freedoms to construct rational, efficient networks, or would they all rush to the historically more profitable long routes and abandon small communities? Would the large carriers come to dominate the industry so that an oligopoly emerged? Would the EAS promote more efficiency in small community service through its use of commuter carriers, would subsidies mount to unacceptable levels, or would small community service erode despite the new program? Would airline deregulation lead to reduced safety as carriers tried to cut costs in a competitive environment?

While at first glance these questions appear straightforward, they are actually complicated. Comparing the post-deregulation industry with the pre-deregulation industry can shed considerable light on what has happened *since* deregulation, but it may tell little about what has happened *because of* deregulation. We can never know for sure what would have happened to the industry had regulation continued. Thus, in examining these questions, whether for airlines, trucking, or rail, it is important to keep the overall trends of the industry in mind and to consider how specifically deregulation might have altered these trends.

As background, Table 9–3 shows U.S. scheduled airline revenue passenger enplanements, revenue passenger miles, and cargo ton miles from 1961 through

TABLE 9–3   Passenger and Cargo Statistics, U.S. Scheduled Airlines, 1961–1992

Year	Revenue Passengers Enplaned (Thousands)	Revenue Passenger Miles (Millions)	Cargo Ton Miles (Thousands)
1961	63,012	39,831	1,093,343
1965	102,920	68,677	2,303,131
1970	169,922	131,710	4,984,197
1975	205,062	162,810	5,892,605
1980	296,749	254,180	7,188,610
1985	344,683	305,116	8,185,366
1986	418,946	366,546	9,071,136
1987	447,678	404,472	10,014,494
1988	454,614	423,302	11,469,193
1989	453,692	432,714	12,186,497
1990	465,557	457,915	12,603,656
1991	452,301	447,954	12,129,963
1992	473,305	478,081	13,053,681

Source: Air Transport, 1993 (Washington, D.C.: Air Transport Association, 1993), p. 2 and earlier editions.

1992. As is apparent, the industry grew strongly before as well as after deregulation. The effect of economic recessions can also be seen in the table: traffic was lower in 1991 than it had been in 1990, for example.

Fares

Perhaps the most basic question is whether deregulation caused passengers to pay higher or lower fares. If one looks simply in terms of current dollars, average fares are higher now than they were in 1977, but the same would be true of almost any cost. Adjusting for inflation and using the gross national product (GNP) deflator, however, we see that real average fares dropped nearly 25 percent between 1977 and 1989. Yet averages can conceal a great deal of variation.

Table 9–4 shows how fares have changed in markets of different characteristics. Two of the most important characteristics of a city-pair market are the distance between the cities and the density or number of passengers traveling in that market. As can be seen in the table, the fare experience differs significantly depending on these two characteristics. Trips over 1,000 miles in all density segments saw fares decrease, in most cases, substantially. Similarly, fares decreased in markets of between 750 and 999 miles where at least 400 passengers traveled per day. Fares also decreased in markets of less than 500 miles with more than 800 daily passengers. Fares increased in the remaining markets. In general, fares have decreased in long-haul markets and in high-density medium-haul markets and have increased in low-density, short- and medium-haul markets. By summing the share of trips in each cell in the table (the figures in italics), we see that markets in which fares dropped accounted for 80 percent of trips. Thus, most trips experienced lower fares in 1989 than in 1979, but in some markets, fares had gone up.

This pattern of fare increases and decreases is not surprising, considering

TABLE 9–4 Percentage Change in Average Real Fare per Mile by Market Distance and Density from 1979 to 1989

Passenger Trips per Day	*Market Distance (Miles)*					
	1–499	*500–749*	*750–999*	*1000–1499*	*1500–1999*	*2000+*
800+	-3.1%	10.4%	-2.0%	-10.7%	-17.2%	-18.2%
	28.3%	*10.2%*	*9.9%*	*11.3%*	*6.6%*	*10.6%*
400–799	31.6%	14.0%	-3.4%	-16.2%	-26.6%	-20.1%
	1.5%	*1.0%*	*1.3%*	*1.4%*	*0.9%*	*1.4%*
200–399	21.9%	16.0%	1.5%	-15.0%	-25.0%	-19.6%
	0.9%	*0.9%*	*0.9%*	*1.2%*	*0.8%*	*1.0%*
100–199	23.4%	18.5%	0.3%	-17.3%	-23.4%	-21.4%
	0.6%	*0.7%*	*0.6%*	*0.6%*	*0.6%*	*0.6%*
50–99	24.8%	17.1%	1.4%	-17.2%	-23.5%	-20.2%
	0.4%	*0.5%*	*0.5%*	*0.6%*	*0.4%*	*0.4%*
1–49	24.2%	16.3%	0.1%	-17.3%	-26.4%	-22.8%
	0.6%	*0.7%*	*0.6%*	*0.9%*	*0.5%*	*0.7%*

Note: The figures in italics are the percentage of total trips in that category in 1989.

Source: Author's calculation based on Department of Transportation data.

how the CAB had regulated fares. They had intentionally set fares in short markets below cost and had compensated the airlines for the losses in those markets by setting fares in long-haul markets well above cost. Furthermore, airlines often find it less costly to serve markets with a larger number of passengers because they can utilize their aircraft more efficiently than in smaller markets. Yet the CAB had never considered market density in its fare-setting process. The pattern in Table 9–4 shows fares moving away from those historically set by the CAB to a pattern that more accurately reflects the cost of serving those markets.

The other main feature of airline fares under deregulation was the advent and spread of discount fares. Under CAB regulation the only fares had been first class and coach. A limited experiment with discounted standby fares in the 1960s had been quickly abandoned. There were also some limited discounts for late night flights. Once the airlines had more fare freedom, they began instituting restricted discount fares. The restrictions varied, but usually involved some sort of advance purchase between seven and thirty days (generally fourteen days), and a stayover at the destination on Saturday night; the discount fares were available on only a limited number of seats on each flight.

The airlines' purpose in imposing these rather strange conditions is to try to segment the market into people traveling for business purposes and people traveling for leisure or vacation purposes. On the one hand, business travelers are willing to pay more for a ticket. In some cases their companies are paying for the trip; in most cases the cost of the trip is tax deductible. Leisure travelers, on the other hand, are not usually willing to pay as much for a ticket. The airlines would like to sell expensive tickets to business travelers and less expensive tickets to leisure travelers—that is, they would like to price discriminate. But how can they divide the market? Most business travelers do not like to spend weekends at their destinations, and business travel often comes up on short notice. The advance purchase and Saturday night stayover requirements do a good job of achieving this separation. The airlines also wish to avoid selling a seat for an inexpensive price if someone is willing to pay more. So they sell only a certain number of discount seats on each flight to save some seats for last minute business travel.

The rapid spread of discount fares can be seen in Table 9–5. Although the largest markets had more discount fares in 1976 than did the smaller markets, the depth of the discount was only about 20 percent. These were almost entirely late night discounts used by fewer than 20 percent of travelers. By 1981, discounts were

TABLE 9–5   Availability and Depth of Discount Fares

Market Rank	Percentage of Markets with Discount Fares			Average Discount Fare as a Percentage of Coach		
	1976	*1981*	*1984*	*1976*	*1981*	*1984*
Largest 50	69%	95%	96%	78%	63%	61%
51–100	60%	92%	90%	80%	67%	63%
101–150	36%	82%	84%	80%	70%	72%
151–200	39%	96%	80%	80%	72%	77%
Smaller markets	30%	81%	72%	80%	74%	76%

Source: Author's calculation based on Department of Transportation data.

much deeper and had spread to the overwhelming majority of markets. By the mid-1980s, well over three-quarters of passengers were using discount fares in the largest markets, and well over half were doing so in smaller markets.

Service

Airline service has improved since deregulation in the sense that more cities are being provided with more flights to more destinations than before. In addition, more city-pair markets are receiving competitive service from two or more carriers than they did before deregulation. Such competition is important for keeping fares low: competitive markets generally have lower fares than do markets with only a single carrier.

To provide this broad service, almost all airlines have adopted *hub and spoke* route networks. The principle behind such networks is the convergence of flights from a wide variety of destinations (the spoke cities) on a single airport (the hub) at about the same time. Such convergence is known as a connecting bank. A typical flight goes from a spoke city to the hub and then on to a second spoke city. A passenger from the first spoke city can either continue on to the second spoke city, thereby getting one-stop, single-plane service between the first and the second spoke cities; or, if the passengers destination is the hub, he or she gets nonstop service to it. Alternatively, the passenger can deboard the aircraft at the hub and connect to any of the other flights that had landed at the hub during that connecting bank. Thus, the passenger can get connecting service from the original spoke city to any of the other cities served by the connecting bank.

In principle, large connecting banks offer advantages over small connecting banks because a greater variety of destinations are available to passengers. Large connecting banks, however, also require passengers to walk longer distances between gates and need sufficient time for all the aircraft to land, take off, and incidentally create more airport congestion. Once the connecting banks become too large, passengers resist using them. Some airlines, having gone to very large connecting banks, have recently reduced the size of these banks.

Safety

Safety itself was not deregulated: safety regulation, the responsibility of the Federal Aviation Administration (FAA), was unchanged by the Airline Deregulation Act. Indeed, the act even stated that safety was not to be degraded by deregulation. The U.S. airline industry had amassed an excellent safety record, which no one wanted to see threatened.

Despite an undiminished role for the FAA, there were still concerns about whether deregulation and increased competition might lead to reduced airline safety. Initially, people thought that increased competition might lead to stronger pressures for cost reductions, resulting in maintenance shortcuts and reduced pilot and crew training. Because the airlines had long emphasized that their maintenance and training exceeded the FAA minimum requirements, some observers feared that the airlines might reduce service to the minimum. People also thought that rapid industry growth could lead to an influx of inexperienced pilots unable to fly as safely as before. As deregulation unfolded, other concerns were added. Would the hub and spoke systems lead to more air traffic control errors from higher workloads? Would there be a greater risk of midair collision? When new, in-experienced entrant jet airlines began operations, observers questioned whether they would be as safe as established companies. Questions about their historically poorer safety record arose as commuter airlines took over a greater role in service to small communities.

To assess what has happened to airline safety, we first need to consider how to measure it. In some transportation modes such as highway travel in private auto-mobiles, it is common to measure safety in terms of accidents per vehicle mile or fatalities per passenger mile. Such measures make sense in auto travel because each mile of travel on a trip poses roughly the same risk and longer trips are more dangerous (in total) than are shorter trips. In airline travel, however, such dis-tance-based measures do not reflect risk. Table 9–6 shows the percentage of fatal accidents for each portion of flight and the percent of flight time spent in each portion. All flights have to take off, climb to cruising altitude, descend from cruis-ing altitude, and land. The main difference between long flights and short flights is the time spent in cruise. As can be seen in the table, cruise is the safest portion of flight. On a typical flight, 60 percent of the time is spent in cruise, but only 7.7 percent of accidents happen there. In contrast, 22.9 percent of fatal accidents hap-pen during takeoff and initial climb, which occupy only about 2 percent of flight time; 24.2 percent of fatal accidents occur during final approach, which occupies only 3 percent of flight time. Because almost all of the risk in air travel is associated with takeoff and landing, and little of the risk is associated with cruise, the best type of measure for airline safety would be based on trips taken rather than miles traveled.

Did airline safety get better or worse following deregulation? Table 9–7 shows five measures of airline safety for the U.S. scheduled domestic jet airline industry for periods both before and after deregulation. All five measures improved notice-ably in the period following deregulation. At first glance, there is little cause for thinking that deregulation made safety worse. Indeed, one might be tempted to conclude that deregulation actually made the industry safer.

But such a conclusion is not be warranted by the data in this table: airline safety is a more complicated story than appears. Throughout the history of com-

TABLE 9–6   Percentage of Fatal Accidents by Portion of Flight

	Percentage of Fatal Accidents	Percentage of Flight Time
Loading and taxiing	2.7	
Takeoff and initial climb	22.9	2
Climb	8.4	13
Cruise	7.7	60
Initial descent	12.8	10
Initial approach	16.2	11
Final approach	24.2	3
Landing	5.1	1
TOTAL	100	100

Source: Communication with Boeing Commercial Aircraft Company.

TABLE 9–7   Safety of Scheduled Domestic Jet Service Before and After Deregulation

Safety Measure	1970–1978	1979–1985	1986–1987
Passenger fatalities per million enplanements	0.42	0.3	0.18
Passenger injuries per million enplanements	0.25	0.03	0.07
Fatal accidents per million aircraft departures	0.46	0.22	0.22
Injury accidents per million aircraft departures	1.92	0.83	1.12
Minor accidents per million aircraft departures	2.9	1.37	1.57

Source: Author's calculation based on Department of Transportation and National Transportation Safety Board data.

mercial aviation in the United States, safety has been getting progressively better, with remarkable improvements in aircraft, navigation, air traffic control, weather forecasting, pilot training, communications, and many other important features of airline operations. A great many people worked hard to improve safety before deregulation, and they have continued to do so after deregulation. It should not be surprising that safety has improved. The real question is not whether safety has changed following deregulation but rather would it have improved even more had economic regulation continued?

To consider deregulation's potential impact, one must turn to the specific fears about its effects and consider the specific causes of airline accidents. Table 9–8 categorizes the 323 accidents by domestic scheduled jet service between 1970 and 1988 into nine major causes. Such categorization is imperfect because almost all airline accidents have more than one cause. Consider, for example a situation

TABLE 9–8   Scheduled Jet Service Accidents by Cause (Accidents per One Million Departures)

	1970–1978	1979–1985	1986–1988
Equipment failure	1.49	0.43	0.67
Seatbelt not fastened	1.49	0.68	0.5
Environment	0.82	0.33	0.62
Pilot error	0.54	0.21	0.45
Air traffic control	0.26	0.11	0.11
Ground crew error	0.23	0.11	0.17
Other aircraft	0.1	0.04	0.11
Company operations	0	0	0.11
Other	0.39	0.5	0.17
TOTAL*	5.28	2.42	2.91
TOTAL ACCIDENTS	205	66	52

*Totals may not add due to rounding

Source: Author's calculation based on Department of Transportation and National Transportation Safety Board data.

where a plane suffers an engine failure during takeoff. Commercial jet aircraft operated by U.S. carriers are designed to be able to survive an engine failure during takeoff without crashing, but only if the pilot recognizes the situation and takes exactly the right action in a matter of seconds. If the pilot is slow to realize what has happened or makes a mistake, the cause of the accident is complex. In one sense, the cause is the equipment failure that started the sequence of events culminating in the accident. In another sense, the cause is pilot failure: with the correct action, the pilot could have prevented the accident. In Table 9–8, the cause is defined as the factor that started the sequence of events that led to the accident. In the case of our example, the cause would have been equipment failure.

Several things are apparent from Table 9–8. If deregulation had brought about shortcuts in maintenance practices, then one would expect to see more accidents initiated by equipment failure. In the table, however, the rate of equipment failure accidents is much lower following deregulation than it was before. If deregulation had brought about cutbacks in pilot training or an influx of inexperienced or unqualified pilots, then the rate of pilot error accidents would have been expected to increase. Yet, as the table shows, that rate also went down after deregulation. If air traffic control was overburdened because of the development of hub and spoke route systems, then the rate of air traffic control accidents should have increased, but as the table indicates, it too decreased. Indeed, comparing the rates by cause for 1970–1978 with those for 1979–1985, there was improvement in all categories of accidents. Thus, these specific fears about adverse safety effects accompanying deregulation do not seem to have been borne out. Similarly, an examination of the new entrant jet carriers does not show systematic safety differences between the new carriers and the established jet carriers.

Another feature of airline deregulation has been rapid growth in the commuter airline industry as commuters lines took over an increasing share of short-haul service to small communities. Commuter airlines operate propellor-driven aircraft with fewer than 60 seats. Commuters who flew aircraft with 19 or fewer seats had not been regulated by the CAB. With passage of the Airline Deregulation Act, commuters were permitted to fly larger aircraft with up to 60 seats and were also allowed to replace certificated carriers in serving small communities under the Essential Air Service Program. Both these replacements and the growing role of commuters gave rise to safety concerns because of the historically poorer safety record of the commuter industry.

Table 9–9 shows the safety record of the commuter industry broken down by industry segment in the periods before and after deregulation. Two important things are apparent in the table. First, the pre-deregulation safety record of the commuter industry, while worse than that of the jet carriers, varies dramatically by the size of the carriers. Among about 200 commuter airlines in the United States, the 20 largest carriers, carrying well over half of all commuter passengers, were far safer than the rest of the industry. Even the 30 next largest carriers, the rest of the top 50, were much safer than the remaining 150 or so commuter carriers. The top 50 carriers carried about 90 percent of all commuter passengers. Thus, in assessing the safety impact of commuter substitutions in small community service, it matters a great deal which commuter carriers are making those substitutions. In the overwhelming majority of cases, the substitutions were made by carriers in the top 20, the safest segment of the commuter industry.

Second, safety performance of the commuter industry was markedly better after 1978 than before 1978. It turns out that the FAA implemented a major revi-

TABLE 9–9   Safety Record of Commuter Carriers (Passenger Fatalities per Million Enplanements)

	1970–1978	*1979–1985*	*1986–1988*
Total industry	2.65	1.27	0.38
Top 20 carriers	0.69	0.67	0.12
Rest of the top 50	3.27	1.21	0.33
Rest of the industry	13.32	4.08	4.67

Source: Author's calculation based on Department of Transportation and National Transportation Safety Board data.

sion of commuter safety regulations in 1978. Although this was the same year that the Airline Deregulation Act was passed, the fact that the safety regulations were revised that year was coincidental; these safety revisions had been in the works for several years before passage. The largest safety improvements under the new regulations came among carriers smaller than the top 20. In essence, the safety regulation revisions sought to bring the safety practices of the smaller carriers more in line with those of the larger commuters. The combination of the good safety record of the larger commuters, the fact that it was these commuters who were doing most of the small community replacement service, and the improvements in commuter safety after 1978 alleviated much of the concern about the safety impacts of this feature of airline deregulation.

RAILROAD INDUSTRY

The fundamental characteristic of rail transportation in the United States since World War II has been overcapacity, specifically, too much capacity in terms of track miles. Table 9–10 shows the railroad mileage operating in the United States from the introduction of the railroads in 1830 through 1992. The period of heavy rail construction starting in the 1860s is evident. After 1910, however, rail construction slowed and almost no new rail was constructed after 1920. Railroad mileage peaked in 1930 and has declined steadily since then. Recall from Table 9–1 that rail's share of ton miles has declined steadily since 1940.

Excess capacity arose in part because of government policies during the promotion era. The federal government's promotion of railroads through donating large tracts of land, in exchange for the railroads' pushing west, was accompanied by state, county, and city governments' involvements. States used their powers of eminent domain to assemble rights-of-way to lay tracks. States, counties, and cities tried to influence track location decisions because of the expected economic development benefits from rail service. These attempts included loaning money to the railroads and guaranteeing loans, donating the land for rights-of-way, donating excess contiguous land, and exempting land from taxation. Indeed, these steps were similar to some of the steps these same government bodies use today to try to attract economic development. The result in the case of the railroads was that many lines were not economically justified, even at the time of construction.

The railroads probably had too much track shortly after the turn of the century. As competition grew from other modes and particularly from trucking, this overcapacity became a growing problem. The railroads, and their regulator the

TABLE 9–10   Railroad Mileage in the United States

Year	Miles of Road
1830	23
1840	2,818
1850	9,021
1860	30,626
1870	52,922
1880	93,262
1890	166,703
1900	192,556
1910	240,831
1920	259,941
1930	260,440
1940	233,670
1950	223,779
1960	217,552
1970	206,265
1975	191,520
1980	164,822
1985	145,764
1990	119,758
1991	116,626
1992	113,056

These figures represent the aggegate length of roadway, excluding yard tracks, sidings, and parallel lines.

Jointly used track is only counted once. If multiple main tracks, yard tracks, and sidings are included, total railroad track was 196,081 miles in 1991.

Source: Railroad Facts (Washington, D,C.: Association of American Railroads, 1993), p. 44.

ICC, aggravated that overcapacity through a practice called "value-of-service pricing." Value-of-service pricing allowed the railroads to price their service based not on the cost of providing it, but on the value of the goods being shipped. In practice, railroads charged low rates for low-value goods such as grain, coal, and iron ore; obviously, this practice was strongly supported by farmers and by the steel industry. The railroads then charged high rates to ship high-value goods, particularly manufactured goods. Thus revenues from high-value goods cross-subsidize the carriage of low-value goods. In a world without competition, profits can be enhanced by value-of-service pricing, and thus the ICC, whose concern was ensuring adequate revenues for the railroads, supported such a policy. Unfortunately, railroads were not without competition, and value-of-service pricing encouraged shippers of high-value goods to look for less expensive modes of travel. Because trucking is particularly suited to carrying high-value goods, it was the main beneficiary of this practice.

ICC regulation of the railroads had its major effects in three areas: rates, excess route mileage, and freight car utilization. Railroad rate regulation locked in value-of-service pricing for the railroads. As truck competition developed and the railroads began losing high-value freight to trucks, the railroads were not permitted to lower their rates in response. In many cases, the freight was likely to be carried by truck anyway because trucks offered far better service, particularly on relatively short hauls. In other cases, however, railroads were inherently more efficient and better suited to carry some goods, which went to trucks because of the ICC's unwillingness to allow the railroads to respond with lower prices. The ICC was also very reluctant to allow the railroads to abandon service on unprofitable routes. These routes were generally short ones carrying little traffic, in large part because they were the types of routes particularly well suited to trucks. Forcing the railroads to maintain such service imposed annual costs of between $500 million and $1 billion, a factor that contributed to the railroads' financial problems in the 1960s and 1970s.

ICC policies also contributed to low freight car utilization. Freight often has to be moved from an origin served by one railroad to a destination served by another. Rather than take the expensive step of transferring the freight from one freight car to another, the railroads *interlined* the freight cars themselves. To facilitate this, the ICC set up a system of car rental rates that lines can charge one another. The receiving railroad can use the car until it is convenient to return it rather than return the empty car immediately to the originating railroad. The rental rates consist of a mileage and per diem rental charge for cars in use and a *demurrage* charge for cars kept on a siding.

With an eye toward equalization and stabilization of the industry, the ICC set the rates too low, and railroads rich in cars cross-subsidized lines that were poor in cars. With rental rates so low, there was little incentive for poor railroads to buy cars. Shortages of cars sometimes arose when some lines hoarded cars for their needs during peak periods. Because demurrage charges were so low, some grain cars were used for storage when they were most needed for transport. Inefficient use of freight cars resulted from low penalties. Some estimated that this poor utilization cost society between $1.5 billion and $1.7 billion per year.

In response to these and other problems, Congress took the first step toward regulatory reform in 1976 with passage of the Railroad Revitalization and Regulatory Reform Act (the 4R Act). This act was intended to give railroads more commercial freedom in rates, abandonments, and mergers. These freedoms were limited, however, where the railroad was found to have market dominance. Although the act had features that held considerable promise, in practice it accomplished far less than hoped for. The ICC interpretations of the 4R Act rate provisions, which found market dominance everywhere, rendered the act virtually useless. As a result, the financial state of the railroads continued to deteriorate, and the initial evidence from the airline deregulation experience further suggested that transportation regulation was promoting inefficiency.

John Robson and Alfred Kahn were instrumental in moving the airline industry toward less administrative regulation. A similar pattern emerged in the Rail industry with the appointment of two pro-deregulation economists to the ICC, Darius Gaskins and Marcus Alexis. Under their leadership, the ICC removed control of rates on fresh produce, started granting more contract rates, and encouraged track abandonment in the case of bankruptcy of the Milwaukee and Rock Island Railroads. Gaskin and Alexis also took a more liberal view of abandonments elsewhere and took a strong pro-merger stance.

On October 14, 1980, Congress passed the Staggers Rail Act of 1980, which was a dramatic reversal of past regulatory policies. Its premise was that the railroad industry was no longer a monopoly requiring regulation, and the act contained provisions for less regulation and more reliance on the marketplace. The goals were to assist the industry in rehabilitation under private ownership, to reform federal regulatory policy to achieve an efficient, economical, and stable system, and to provide the regulation required to balance the needs of shippers, carriers, and the public. The act reduced the common carrier obligations to provide unprofitable service or profitable service at unprofitable prices.

A description of the complex provisions of the Staggers Act is beyond the scope of this chapter. In general, the act allowed railroads considerably more pricing freedom, including the right to cut rates as long as the rates did not fall below variable costs. To prevent weakening the act through interpretation, as had been the case with the 4R Act, market dominance was defined much more specifically. The ICC was given the power to exempt certain commodities from all rate regulation if there was sufficient intermodal competition, and the list of exempted agricultural commodities was expanded. Intermodal traffic such as trailer on flatcar (TOFC, or piggyback) and container on flatcar (COFC) was exempted from rate regulation. Abandonments became easier for railroads to get, and the process was speeded up with the imposition of a 255-day time limit on abandonment proceedings. Mergers were also speeded up with a 300-day time limit, and railroads were given expanded opportunities to own and operate trucking companies and barge lines.

In response to this new regulatory environment, the railroads have sought to broaden their traffic base through aggressive marketing and service innovations. Intermodal services such as TOFC, COFC, and double-stack container operations have enhanced the railroads' ability to compete for manufactured goods. In terms of ton miles, railroads carry more intercity freight than any other mode, and they carry more freight now than at any time in their history. Table 9–11 compares the average revenue per ton mile for intercity freight modes. For rail, the figure is lower in 1991 than it had been in 1980. Indeed, when adjusted for inflation, rail rates have fallen almost 30 percent between 1980 and 1992. Rail's traditional role as a long-distance carrier of low-value freight can be seen in these average figures.

TRUCKING

The trucking (or motor carrier) industry carries a little over a quarter of the ton miles of intercity freight but accounts for about three-quarters of the domestic freight transportation bill. Although rail carries the most freight, trucks provide relatively quick delivery of high-value freight and charge average rates nearly 10 times that for rail. Trucks also carry freight on substantially shorter distances than rail.

A critical feature in comparing the trucking industry to other freight modes is the trucking industry's cost structure. Whereas rail has heavy fixed costs because it must provide its own roadbed and right-of-way, trucking is a low fixed-cost, high variable-cost industry. Fixed costs, in the form of interest on loans, administrative overhead, and the like, account for less than 15 percent of typical trucking costs, whereas variable costs account for over 85 percent. The principal components in variable costs are the driver, who accounts for nearly 27 percent, and fuel, which accounts for over 21 percent. Other important components are maintenance and vehicle depreciation. With low fixed costs, entry into the industry is relatively easy, particularly for those who want to carry full truckloads of goods from a single origin to a single destination. Because of fears of excessive competition from too-easy

TABLE 9–11 Average Revenues per Ton Mile, Intercity Modes, 1960–1991 (in Cents)

Year	Rail*	Motor†	Barge	Oil Pipeline	Air‡
1960	1.4	6.31	NA	0.315	22.8
1965	1.27	6.46	0.346	0.279	20.46
1970	1.43	8.5	0.303	0.271	21.91
1975	2.04	11.6	0.518	0.368	28.22
1980	2.87	18	0.77	1.325	46.31
1985	3.04	22.9	0.8	1.565	48.62
1986	2.92	21.63	0.76	1.504	44.81
1987	2.73	22.48	0.733	1.453	43.47
1988	2.72	23.17	0.754	1.364	43.63
1989	2.67	23.91	0.769	1.327	48.57
1990	2.66	24.38	0.757	1.468	46.33
1991	2.59	24.86	0.778	1.398	44.45

*Class I freight railroads.

†Less-than-truckload rates of a sample of 27 general freight common carriers.

‡Scheduled air freight service, not including Federal Express. If all scheduled and nonscheduled air freight operations, including Federal Express and United Parcel Service, are included, the average revenue-per-ton-mile figure for air increases to $1.12.

Source: Transportation in America, 11th ed. Eno Transportation Foundation, Inc., Lansdowne, Va.: 1993), p. 49.

entry, the ICC focused much of its regulatory efforts on controlling entry not only into the trucking industry itself, but also entry into a new line of service by an existing trucking company.

Thus trucking evolved into a highly segmented industry with government-imposed barriers to entry into both the industry and into specific segments. Companies competed only with other companies in their segments. Restrictions drove up costs by frequently forcing empty backhauls even when freight, albeit freight from a different industry segment, was available to be carried. Such segmentation and regulatory restrictions increased the costs of trucking services and made it easier for unions to garner wage gains. The first step away from these restrictions came in a 1977 court case that reduced the emphasis on protecting established carriers on ICC entry decisions. Before the decision, the ICC's criteria were whether entry would serve a useful purpose; whether existing carriers could provide the service; and whether existing carriers would be harmed. The court decision eliminated the second of these criteria.

The main step in changing the regulatory environment in the trucking industry came with passage of the Motor Carrier Act of 1980. A major feature of the act was easing entry requirements by shifting the burden of proof. Before the act, the applicant had to show that entry was necessary for public convenience and necessity. Any entry determined to divert revenue from an incumbent company was typically denied. After the act, the burden of proof was shifted to opponents of entry, who had to show it was not useful to the public nor responsive to demand. The applicant had only to show that the proposed service was useful and the applicant itself was fit, willing, and able. The effect was to open entry up dramatically both for entirely new carriers and for existing carriers on new routes.

The act also opened up the industry by allowing greater freedom for fleets of trucks owned by manufacturing companies primarily to haul their own products. In other segments of the industry, restrictions on operating authority were removed. Previously, specific and often circuitous routes had been required between two points, and intermediate stops had often been prohibited. Round-trip authority was also granted to allow carriers to avoid empty backhauls. As with rail, merger procedures were speeded up, and restrictions on rail-truck intermodal operations were reduced. There were several provisions in the act about rates, including establishing a zone of rate freedom. The net effect of these provisions was to give the trucking industry nearly complete rate deregulation.

The Motor Carrier Act has dramatically altered the trucking industry. The number of new interstate trucking companies has grown substantially since passage of the act. In 1980, there were 17,721 interstate for-hire truckers; by 1987, the number was 37,627. The number of carriers competing for a shipper's business grew even more than these numbers suggest because existing carriers were able to expand their service offerings, in the type of service and the geographic region. As the number of carriers has increased, these companies have become more aggressive in competing for business.

Rates appear to have fallen substantially in the trucking industry, although with the increased ability under the act to enter into long-term contracts, it is difficult to be precise about rate changes. One study found that truckload rates fell about 25 percent between 1977 and 1983 and that less-than-truckload rates declined about 15 percent over the same period. It is not surprising that truckload rates would fall further because new entry is easiest in the truckload segment of the industry. Other studies have found similar rate declines.

Service in the industry has improved as a result of increased competition. While some shippers have responded in surveys that service has worsened, far more shippers have responded that service has improved. A particular concern in the case of trucking deregulation was the fear that small communities would not receive adequate service without regulation. When surveyed, shippers and receivers in small communities responded that both service availability and on-time performance are better following deregulation. It appears that whereas it had been easy for the CAB to hold airlines in small community service, the ICC had not had much effect on maintaining such service. Freeing restrictions on the trucking industry seemed to promote, rather than harm, small community service.

Although trucking deregulation has brought benefits to shippers from increased entry and more competition, many trucking companies have not been pleased at these developments. Without protection from competition by the ICC, the trucking industry has experienced a much higher rate of bankruptcies among those companies that have not responded well to the new environment. Most of the failed companies were small, but some were large, including the fifth-largest trucking company in the United States, McLean Trucking Company, which had sales of over $550 million in the year preceding bankruptcy. The great majority of new truckload carriers are small, nonunionized companies. In many cases their drivers are paid lower wages and have less restrictive work rules than Teamsters' Union drivers. According to some estimates, as many as 100,000 union truck drivers have lost their jobs as a result of deregulation, although even more nonunion truck drivers have found work as a result of the same deregulation.

URBAN TRANSPORTATION

Two forces came together in the early- to mid-1950s to force a change in urban transportation policy. The first was the cumulative effect of decentralization of places of employment and residences. As manufacturing continued its trend to assembly-line techniques, companies found horizontally organized factories to be more efficient. Such factories required large amounts of land, most easily available in suburban areas. Manufacturing companies considered these locations attractive in part because the growing trucking industry brought materials to the factory and transported finished goods to markets. With jobs in the suburbs, residences soon followed: people sought more residential space and a shorter journey to work. The second force changing urban transportation policy was increased auto ownership, in response to increased household income. Because of these two forces, streets and highways became overburdened, and traffic congestion worsened. The government's solution was to build more highways.

In 1956, Congress passed the Interstate and Defense Highway Act, which authorized 41,000 miles of interstate highway at a projected cost of $27 billion. Within those totals were 8,000 urban interstate miles at a projected cost of $15 billion. The federal government was to pay 90 percent of the costs of construction, financed via a federal gasoline tax, and this system was to be completed by 1972.

The interstate highway system has accomplished a great many things, but, disappointingly, it did not relieve traffic congestion. Among other reasons, the system was incomplete, and some of the incomplete portions created bottlenecks. These new facilities also had the effect of lowering the costs of travel, in terms of time costs, and in transportation as in other goods, when the price goes down, people consume more. In fairness, urban auto travel did improve as the average peak-period speed increased from about 25 mph to 35 mph. But this improvement was dwarfed by the off-peak increases from about 30 mph to 60 mph. When people traveled at these speeds in off-peak traffic, they expected to do the same during peak times. Nevertheless, the highway improvements enabled people to make longer trips. The average commuting time in a medium-size city remained at about 20 to 25 minutes, but the improved highway system allowed longer travel during this time. People were willing to trade a longer-distance commute for cheaper suburban housing.

Still, by the mid-1960s people had come to believe that the first attempted solution of building more highways had not worked. The next attempted solution in the mid-1960s was a move toward *balanced transportation,* promoting public transit ridership, which had been declining steadily since the late 1920s. In 1940, about 10.5 billion transit trips were taken, and during World War II, wartime restrictions pushed ridership up to about 15 billion by 1946. With wartime restrictions lifted, transit ridership resumed its decline. The argument behind balanced transportation was that the subsidy to highways meant the building of too many highways and, as a result, too little use of transit. Of course, highways were subsidized by a gasoline tax that highway users paid roughly in proportion to their highway use, but that argument was, and continues to be, overlooked by transit proponents. The move to provide subsidies to transit was largely supported on the grounds that its goal was congestion relief. As it turns out, people were quite eager for others to ride transit but not nearly so eager to ride themselves. By the mid-1960s, some inner cities were sites of unrest, and aid for transit was implicitly a way to aid these cities.

Heavy involvement by the federal government in promoting transit began with the Urban Mass Transportation Act of 1964. The act provided $100 million a year in aid in 1964 which grew to $1.5 billion per year by 1978. This aid was restricted to capital grants rather than to operating expenses. Thus, the money went to acquire rights-of-way, to construct rail roadbeds, to acquire rolling stock (buses and subway cars), and to purchase privately owned transit companies. Ironically, transit operating revenues had exceeded operating costs until about 1965. Thus, the government provided capital grants just when the need for operating subsidy emerged. Initially, the federal government paid two-thirds of capital costs, and the figure was increased to 80 percent after 1973.

The grants were restricted to capital for three reasons. First, such grants were thought to limit the federal role in what was essentially a local service. Second, many observers believed that capital assistance was less likely to be wasted. Concern arose that providing operating assistance would reduce transit management's incentives to control costs. And finally, the capital grants were to be a short-lived shot in the arm to break the "vicious cycle of decline." This cycle was believed to start with poor equipment, which in turn caused a reduction in ridership, which caused transit revenues to drop, which prevented purchasing the new equipment needed to attract riders.

Initially, the expenditures went largely to purchase private companies and new buses. The private companies purchased were usually financially weak, but by bringing together all transit in a metropolitan area under a single authority, transit would supposedly operate more efficiently and provide better service. In response to the capital grants, bus sales rose from about 2,200 per year before the program to 3,400 per year under the program, and the median bus age in the U.S. transit fleet dropped from 9.6 years to 8.3 years. By the beginning of the 1970s, most private companies were bought and most old buses replaced. The funds then began to go increasingly to rail transit systems. By the mid-1970s, about half of the capital grants went to build new rail systems or to extend existing rail systems. Also in the mid-1970s, the federal highway program was modified to divert gasoline tax receipts to transit.

We can evaluate this capital grants program based on three criteria: ridership, finances, and investment incentives. In terms of ridership, between the beginning of the program in 1965 and 1972, total transit ridership declined 23 percent. Bus ridership declined 25 percent, and heavy rail ridership declined 14 percent. Even in the few instances where ridership was up, very few new riders were drawn from cars, so there was little congestion reduction.

As disappointing as the ridership results were, the impacts on transit finances were even worse. Whereas operating revenues had roughly covered operating costs in 1965, they covered less than half of operating costs by 1978. When transit bought ailing private companies, it took on their losses. The hoped-for efficiency gains from consolidating transit in one organization rarely materialized. As transit extended service into low-density suburban areas, it found it could not compete with cars, and the losses increased. For example, in San Francisco's Bay Area Rapid Transit (BART) fare-box revenues were meant to cover both operating costs and the cost of rolling stock. By 1976, the average fare was $0.72, but the operating cost per rider was $1.96. Including rolling stock, the subsidy per rider was $3.76. However, only 35 percent of BART riders had previously been auto drivers. Thus, if the goal was to get people out of their cars, the subsidy per former auto driver was $10.74 per trip. And BART was about the most successful system at attracting former auto drivers. When Cleveland extended its rail line, it found only 8 percent of its riders were former auto users; the rest came from buses, airport limousines, and taxis. In Chicago, the rail extension also counted only 8 percent of riders as former auto users; 80 percent came from other transit lines and 6 percent from new trips. Indeed, all the extensions of rail rapid transit lines in the United States saw rail passengers drawn mostly from bus service rather than from auto use.

Grants restricted to capital also distorted investment incentives of transit operators. For example, as the federal government paid for 80 percent of new buses, but the transit agency paid entirely for maintenance, there was an incentive to retire a bus prematurely rather than spend money on maintenance and upkeep.

As operating deficits mounted, pressure grew for federal operating subsidies. The first federal funding of operating grants came in 1974 in response to pressure from cities too small for rail and thus increasingly missing out on capital grants and from cities whose rail transit construction had predated federal aid. Operating grants grew from $300 million in 1975 to $1.4 billion in 1978. Technically, the money from this program could be used for either capital or operating expenses, but only 6 percent of this unrestricted money went to capital.

The impact of this operating aid was disappointingly small. Part of the problem was that the aid was distributed by a formula biased toward small communities. Communities with populations between 50,000 and 100,000 accounted for only 4 percent of transit riders yet received 12 percent of operating aid. Another part of the problem was that the earlier fears about the potential for operating grants to weaken cost control incentives seem to have been justified. A large part of the grants went to increased wages of transit workers. Before operating aid, transit wages grew only at 83 percent of the wage growth rate of manufacturing workers. After operating aid, the rate jumped to 122 percent of manufacturing wage growth.

What is the state of the transit industry after all these programs? Table 9–12 shows quite modest growth in transit ridership from 1970 through 1991. Increases in 1979 and 1980 in response to sharply increased gas prices could not be sustained when gas prices fell. As a reference point, taxis carried about 2.4 billion passengers in the mid-1980s, more than heavy rail but less than buses. By 1991, buses carried about 66 percent of transit riders, and heavy rail carried about 25 percent. These shares have not changed dramatically since 1970.

This modest growth has been purchased at a high price. Table 9–13 shows that transit industry operating deficits, over the same 1970 to 1991 period, from $288 million in 1970 to almost $9.8 billion in 1991. These amounts are only operating deficits: if the transit industry has not collected enough to pay operating costs, it has obviously not covered capital costs either. Finally, Table 9–14 shows the sources of transit industry revenue for the period from 1976 through 1991. As can be seen in the right hand column, the share of revenue from passenger fares has fallen from 52 percent in 1976 to 36 percent in 1991.

SUMMARY

Both intercity and urban transportation provide excellent opportunities to see how public policy has evolved in response to changing economic conditions and to the experience gained under a previous policy. In intercity freight and passenger markets, the government became heavily involved in price regulation for the rail-

TABLE 9–12　Transit Passenger Trips, 1970–1991 (Millions)

Calendar Year	Light Rail	Heavy Rail	Commuter Rail	Trolley Bus and Other	Motor Bus	Total Passenger Rides or Trips*
1970	235	1,881	NA	182	5,034	7,332
1975	124	1,673	260	143	5,084	7,284
1976	112	1,632	260	142	5,247	7,393
1977	103	1,610	265	137	5,488	7,603
1978	104	1,706	267	137	5,721	7,935
1979	107	1,777	279	142	6,156	8,461
1980	133	2,108	280	209	5,837	8,567
1981	123	2,094	268	205	5,594	8,284
1982	136	2,115	259	218	5,324	8,052
1983	137	2,167	262	215	5,422	8,203
1984	135	2,231	267	288	5,908	8,829
1985	132	2,290	275	264	5,675	8,636
1986	130	2,333	306	255	5,753	8,777
1987	133	2,402	311	275	5,614	8,735
1988	154	2,308	325	289	5,590	8,666
1989	162	2,542	330	277	5,620	8,931
1990	175	2,346	328	273	5,677	8,799
1991P	186	2,167	324	280	5,686	8,643

P=preliminary.

Note: Total passenger rides from 1970 through 1979 based on individual transit data collection procedures. Unlinked transit passenger trips beginning in 1980 based on data collection procedures defined by Federal Transit Act, Section 15. Before 1984, excludes demand response and most rural and smaller systems. Series not contiguous between 1983 and 1984.

*Excludes commuter railroad, cable car, inclined plane, automated guideway, and urban ferry boat before 1975.

Source: 1992 Transit Fact Book (Washington, D.C.: American Public Transit Association, 1992), p. 64.

roads and in both price and entry regulation for trucks, buses, and airlines. In the case of the railroads, the initial motivation for such regulation was to protect consumers and shippers from excessively high prices. For the other modes, however, and eventually for the railroads, the motivation was to protect these industries from *excessive* competition and to nurture their growth. As the industries changed, such regulation was increasingly called into question. Beginning in the late 1970s and continuing into the 1980s, public policy shifted to rely less on government economic regulation and more on market competition. For the most part, this shift has been accompanied by lower prices for consumers and improved efficiency for the carriers.

For intercity passenger rail transportation and for urban mass transportation, the pattern has been somewhat different. With these modes, government involvement has grown throughout the 1970s and 1980s and continues high in the 1990s. Government subsidy rather than market competition has been the dominant factor. For intercity rail, however, questions are increasingly being asked about whether subsidies continue to be needed at such high levels. For urban mass transportation, questions are also being asked about the need for heavy capital and operating subsidies, although such questions are not asked as frequently or with as much political vigor. Nevertheless, with a growing emphasis, both in the United

TABLE 9–13   Transit Industry Operating Deficits, 1970–1991

Year	Deficit (Thousands)
1970	288,212
1971	411,400
1972	513,126
1973	738,499
1974	1,299,673
1975	1,703,526
1976	1,859,808
1977	2,024,791
1978	2,330,966
1979	2,707,497
1980	3,583,800
1981	4,240,576
1982	4,410,889
1983	4,451,900
1984	6,345,800
1985	7,104,400
1986	7,599,100
1987	8,040,300
1988	8,647,500
1989	8,715,700
1990	9,295,800
1991	9,767,200

*Calculated by subtracting total operating expenses from total operating revenues. Depreciation, amortization, and other reconciling items are not reflected. If they were, the industry's annual deficit would be considerably greater.

Source: American Public Transit Association, 1992 Transit Fact Book (Washington, D.C.: 1992), p 46, 51, and earlier editions.

States and throughout the world, on market forces and on a questioning of the need for government subsidy, it seems likely that urban mass transit will be subject to increasing policy scrutiny in the coming years.

Economic conditions will continue to change and we will continue to gain experience with the effects of current policies, both in the United States and abroad. As a result, transportation policy is almost certain to continue to evolve both here and elsewhere in the world.

DISCUSSION QUESTIONS

1. What were the four principal periods of government involvement in transportation policy in the United States? What was the major government objective during each period and what policies did the government use to pursue that objective? Toward the end of each of the first three periods, what factors caused the shift in government policy to the next period?

2. How and why have transportation policies evolved differently in the United States than in Europe? In comparing transportation policies in the United States and in other countries, what are the principal factors that must be kept in mind in explaining the differences?

TABLE 9–14 Sources of Transit Industry Revenues, 1976–1991 (Dollars)

Calendar Year	Operating Revenues			Operating Assistance				
	Passenger* (Millions)	Other (Millions)	Total (Millions)	Local & State (Millions)	Federal (Millions)	Total (Millions)	Total Revenue (Millions)	Passenger Share (Percentage)
1976	2025.6	210.5	2236.1	1244.5	442.9	1647.3	3883.4	52%
1977	2157.1	196.5	2353.6	1319.5	584.5	1904.1	4257.7	51%
1978	2271	178.9	2449.9	1542.1	689.5	2231.7	4681.5	49%
1979	2436.3	211.5	2647.8	2054.6	855.8	2910.4	5558.2	44%
1980	2556.8	248.3	2805.1	2611.2	1093.9	3705.1	6510.2	39%
1981	2701.4	343.8	3045.2	3225.7	1095.1	4320.8	7366	37%
1982	3077	380	3457	3582	1005.4	4587.4	8044.3	38%
1983	3171.6	332.5	3504.1	4194.6	827	5021.6	8525.7	37%
1984	4447.7	780.5	5228.2	5399.1	995.8	6394.9	11623.1	38%
1985	4574.7	701.8	5276.5	5978.5	939.6	6918.1	12194.6	38%
				Local / State				
1986	5113.1	737.3	5850.4	4244.5 / 2305.6	941.2	7491.3	13341.7	38%
1987	5114.1	776.6	5890.7	4680.6 / 2564.6	955.1	8200.3	14091	36%
1988	5224.6	840.7	6065.3	4893.1 / 2677.1	901.1	8471.3	14536.6	36%
1989	5419.9	836.7	6256.6	4995.4 / 2796.3	936.6	8728.3	14984.9	36%
1990	5890.8	895	6785.8	5326.8 / 2970.6	970	9267.4	16053.2	37%
1991P	6064	954.3	7018.3	5605.1 / 3241.8	945	9791.9	16810.2	36%

P = preliminary.

Note: Local operating assistance includes taxes levied directly by transit system and other subsidies from local government such as bridge and tunnel tolls and nontransit parking lot revenue. Excludes commuter railroad, automated guideway, urban ferry boat, demand response, and most rural and smaller systems before 1984. Scale not continuous between 1983 and 1984.

*Beginning 1984, includes fare revenue retained by contractors.

Source: 1992 Transit Fact Book (Washington, D.C.: American Public Transit Association, 1992), p. 51.

3. How have urban transportation commuting patterns changed in the past 20 years? What are the three basic reasons for these changes? What are the major factors behind metropolitan decentralization? Be specific and provide evidence in support of your answer.
4. In assessing aviation safety, are distance-based or flight-based safety measures more appropriate? Why?
5. In assessing airline deregulation's impacts on safety, what were the specific fears that lead some to worry that safety might degrade following deregulation? What is the evidence with regard to each of these specific fears?

SUGGESTED READINGS

Jose A. Gomez-Ibanez and John R. Meyer, *Going Private: The International Experience with Transport Privatization* (Washington, DC: The Brookings Institution, 1993).

John R. Meyer and Clinton V. Oster, Jr., *Deregulation and the Future of Intercity Passenger Travel* (Cambridge, MA: The MIT Press, 1987).

Clinton V. Oster, Jr., John S. Strong, and C. Kurt Zorn, *Why Airplanes Crash: Aviation Safety in a Changing World* (New York: Oxford University Press, 1992).

Roy J. Sampson, Martin T. Farris, and David L. Shrock, *Domestic Transportation: Practice, Theory, and Policy,* 5th ed. (Boston: Houghton Mifflin, 1985).

Transportation Research Board, *Winds of Change: Domestic Air Transport Since Deregulation,* Special Report 230 (Washington, DC: National Research Council, 1991).

NOTE

1. As used by the CAB, the taper is the relationship of the fare or cost per mile to the distance flown. The term *taper* is used because the cost or fare per mile starts high for short flights and tapers off to a lower level for longer flights.

10

Education and Training in the New Economy

A great debate surrounds U.S. public schools. Nearly everyone expresses some degree of unhappiness with the general condition of public schools, yet little agreement exists suggesting what should be done to improve public education, how soon, and at what cost. The rhetorical heat can be intense. An example is found in the 1983 report of the National Commission on Excellence in Education (The Carnegie Commission), which began its analysis with a blistering indictment of public education, quoted here at length because of the report's pivotal importance to the current debate.

> Our Nation is at risk. Our once unchallenged preeminence in commerce, industry, science, and technological innovation is being overtaken by competitors throughout the world. This report is concerned with only one of the many causes and dimensions of the problem, but it is the one that undergirds American prosperity, security, and civility. We report to the American people that while we can take justifiable pride in what our schools and colleges have historically accomplished and contributed to the United States and the well-being of its people, the educational foundations of our society are presently being eroded by a rising tide of mediocrity that threatens our very future as a Nation and a people. What was unimaginable a generation ago has begun to occur—others are matching and surpassing our educational attainments.
>
> If an unfriendly foreign power had attempted to impose on America the mediocre educational performance that exists today, we might well have viewed it as an act of war. As it stands, we have allowed this to happen to ourselves. We have even squandered the gains in student achievement made in the wake of the Sputnik challenge. Moreover, we have dismantled essential support systems which helped make those gains possible. We have, in effect, been committing an act of unthinking, unilateral educational disarmament.[1]

In one stroke, this rhetorically brilliant, but incomplete,[2] analysis accomplished two objectives. First, it placed public school improvement on the front burner of the U.S. public policy agenda. Second, it tied the fate and direction of public school reform to the nation's economic development and prosperity. A simple model and policy argument resulted: public school reform is integral to economic prosperity. Failure to achieve massive improvements in the performance of public education systems assures economic decline.

Over the last decade, public rhetoric about K–12 education has grown increasingly heated, and public education policy has become activist. Over 11 national commissions, forums, and task forces were convened to examine several aspects of the "nation at risk" issue.[3] Books continue to roll off the presses containing the same premise: "The schools are failing in their core academic mission."[4]

THE PROBLEM

By far, most current frustration derives from the newly understood significance that formal intellectual achievement has in the promotion of economic well-being. A short version of a long and complicated argument is to say that compared to an earlier industrial era, in which educated human labor was simply an industrial input to be combined with other resource inputs to produce manufactured products, postindustrial productivity depends on the knowledge, skills, and abilities of formally trained human intellects. The strategic importance of human resources exists because *products* produced by people have increasingly become complex manufactured goods based on the applications of formal theoretical knowledge to raw materials or nonroutine services rendered by trained professionals. Routine services and manufacturing tasks have been automated. Human resources have, as a result, become capital assets to be nurtured and grown rather than operational costs to be minimized (Drucker, 1968; see reading list at end of this chapter).

Evidence of economic transformation can be found in the traditional natural resource-dependent industries—such as textiles, shoes, paper, machine tools, papermaking, leather goods, and wood products—all of which have become highly automated and allow customization of products to market niche (Zuboff, 1988; see reading list at end of chapter). Transformation is also evidenced in the rise of research-based industries—such as petrochemicals, electronics, information-processing software, pharmaceuticals, and aircraft and satellite industries—where both final products and production processes are dependent on organized research from which are derived future inventions and process improvements. The result in nearly all cases has been the rise of an increasingly sophisticated economic order characterized by increasingly mechanized (i.e., computerized) industrial processes, product spin-offs from organized research and development (R & D), and an enormous increase in the array of services required to repair and maintain the information systems driving a knowledge-based economy.

By contrast, earlier industrial systems regarded human labor as a mere operational input to be combined with physical and monetary inputs in order to produce manufactured products. In such an economy, public schools were useful but not strategic to industrial development. Indeed, extended formal education made little economic sense except for the few who would compete for the professional and managerial positions at the industrial apex. Apprenticeship led to skill mastery in the crafts, although over time the autonomy of the skilled crafts would be replaced with automation and the routinization of work by industrial engineers.

Over time, large numbers of industrial jobs were *dumbed down* for efficiency purposes.

Not surprisingly, industrial-age schools became mirrors of the factory system of production that dominated the end of the 19th and most of the 20th centuries. Industrial workers became interchangeable parts for which low skills applied in large-scale enterprises generated high wages leveraged by collective bargaining. Entrance to advanced educational programs, universities, and elite professional training were governed by standardized aptitude and achievement tests whose *normal* distributions placed most *average* students in the middle of a scoring range in which only the bright few did very well and another few performed poorly and were deemed incapable of sustaining high academic achievement. The natural result was that industrial bureaucracies and public schools made few demands of, and invested comparatively little in, average students who would become front-line workers.

In public education, teachers were relegated to the role of ordinary factory worker—albeit a unionized worker with a college education. The teaching function was to supply "a steady stream of workers who had mastered the three R's, had some vocational skills, and were well disciplined."[5] The result was precisely the system of public education and worker training that business and industry had demanded—a compliant workforce able and willing to perform routine repetitive tasks for which economics of scale would pay relatively high wages to low-skill workers producing standardized products.

Stress, however, appeared. The flaws in the arrangement became apparent only as international competition forced business and society to confront head-on competition from businesses and societies whose strategies were based not simply on cost, but on product innovation and quality produced by formally educated front-line workers. From the middle 1950s onward, the structure of both U.S. business and the supporting educational system would confront periodic stress. One example appeared in 1957 when the U.S.S.R. space achievements—most notably the orbiting of the Sputnik satellite—served public notice that U.S. science and technology could be exceeded by others who invested carefully in advanced systems of education and programs of research and development. A flurry of U.S. educational activity immediately followed. One result was the National Defense Education Act, which attempted to shore up with loans and grants the development of scientific, technical, and linguistic talent in public schools and universities in order to meet the challenge.

A second stress point was more subtle and occurred in the aftershock of the energy crises of the 1970s that moved the center of oil pricing from Texas to the Persian Gulf. The Arab states together with other members of the Organization of Petroleum Exporting Countries (OPEC) attempted to limit the supply of cheap oil, and, in the wake of active U.S. intervention on the side of Israel in the 1973 Yom Kippur War, imposed an oil boycott on the United States and its allies in 1973 and again following the fall from power of the Shah of Iran in 1979. The immediate effect appeared in the price of crude oil that shot up from three dollars a barrel to over thirty dollars a barrel.

Nations dependent on the importation of petroleum as a strategic commodity were clearly vulnerable, and national economic adaptations to the price shocks were varied. For example, although the United States felt intense pressure, U.S. public policy was designed largely to ride out a perturbation rather than to redesign its infrastructure and retool an entire economy based on the assumption of severe constraints in energy supplies. More hard hit were the economies of western Europe and Japan.

In Japan, however, the effect of the oil shocks was transformational. Discussions in Japan took a different course from those in either the United States or Europe, for the entire basis of the Japanese industrial system was threatened. Because the key planning assumption was that Japan could no longer depend on predictable supplies of low-priced petroleum guaranteed by alliances and trade agreements, the country would either have to transform its economy or endure the continuous potential threat of interrupted energy supplies.

What policies would Japan pursue? Only a fundamental economic shift from mass-produced industrial production to an intelligent use of energy could work. Thus, products and production systems would have to be made increasingly smart by an intensive use of microprocessors and computers whose function was to reduce energy waste.[6] Not surprisingly, the shift in industrial strategy also changed the significance of education, for clearly it would take, as one ad for photocopiers put it, "smart people to produce smart products."

The reaction of the United States to the same global crisis was sluggish by comparison. Business pursued cost-cutting strategies, such as massive automation, to improve efficiency, sought protection from foreign competition in the form of tariffs and import quotas, and fought with only mixed success the growing regulation of business by government (Chapters 3 and 6 chart many of these developments). These reactions were incremental adaptations in a country rich in natural resources, such as forests, minerals, fossil fuels, and arable land. Little serious thought was given in the 1970s and early 1980s to reengineering U.S. economic foundations.

By the 1980s, however, a number of patterns were clear. First, the United States was confronting a serious problem of low productivity growth that worried nearly all economists who compared U.S. economic performance with that of other countries.[7] Second, other nations had confronted more severe challenges to conventional economic growth—fewer natural resources, more severe oil price shocks, more government regulation, stronger labor unions—and had nevertheless managed to outperform the United States in securing advantageous positions in a rapidly developing global economy. Popular, low-budget movies such as *Roger and Me*, which recounted the resistance to industrial change found in General Motors Corporation, depicted for all to see the resistance to transformational change afflicting many of the U.S.'s industrial giants.[8] Against this backdrop of mediocre economic performance, the Carnegie Commission produced *A Nation at Risk* in 1983. Hindsight shows that the report was broadly correct to emphasize the strategic importance of U.S. public schools. It was, however, misleading in several key details.

In the first place, the notion that public school performance could have brought the entire economy to its knees, as the introduction to this chapter implies, is a misreading of the evidence. Many more potent, noneducation factors contribute to economic development (or lack of it), including such obvious factors as business practices and work systems, technology applications, savings and investment, and monetary and fiscal policy. Indeed, to persist in the notion that school performance—a long-term human investment process—is a cause of short-term economic decline makes public schools scapegoats for economic failure and, in the bargain, tempts policy makers to seek quick fixes in the form of well-meaning and simple changes—such as merit pay for teachers or computers in the classroom—that by themselves will probably produce no measurable improvement.

A second problem in the report is the false presumption that public schools have failed and are getting worse. Recent evidence suggests that the overall quality of public education actually has been getting better rather than declining.[9] Moreover, there appears not to be one system of public education, but at least two or three.[10] For example, the top tier of perhaps 40 percent of the public school student population is fully competitive with the highest international standards, takes college preparatory courses, and moves on to postsecondary institutions where colleges and universities raise the accomplishments and achievements to an even higher level. The second tier captures perhaps 30 percent of the student population—the *mid-kids*—containing a heterogeneous mix of student achievement levels and interests in occupations and careers not requiring attendance at four-year postsecondary institutions. Mid-kids have typically been shortchanged by underdeveloped vocational education programs; they receive little or no investment in school-to-work transition information, counseling, and career preparation. They are potentially at risk, but not without hope.

A third and remaining student tier is worrisome both for its size and its low level of academic accomplishment. This tier typically displays an erratic record of academic achievement characterized by dropping out of school and *at risk* behaviors. Students are plagued by family instability, poverty, and abuse, all of which seriously interfere with education of any sort. These are the personal tragedies whose origins lie outside the public school system and about which public schools and even the most talented teachers can do little.

A third problem in the report is the notion that there was once a golden age of public education from which current institutions have fallen. The truth is nearer the conclusion suggested by Ray Marshall and Marc Tucker that America had no "golden era" in the sense that there were standards of mass classical education "once met" from which the current system had fallen. To be sure, many were well and classically educated in public schools, but the reality was more that a minimalist public education was dispensed with a strong dose of vocational education given out to students classified by educators as possessing low ranges of inherited ability and intelligence, as measured on standardized tests. Moreover, an average student could do well economically simply by completing a minimal education curriculum and joining the ranks of well-paid workers performing routine chores in a growing industrial economy that paid no attention to educational preparation.

Finally, it is simply the case that American education performance and industrial performance are both part of a national pattern by which the country developed over decades. Educational performance was not something foisted on an unsuspecting public by public educators who were out of step with the rest of society. On the contrary, the system has delivered precisely what the nation thought it wanted and deserved! As economic foundations shifted and as global economic standards pressed in on the comparatively rich U.S. economy, however, it was clear that something would have to be done. A fundamental mismatch had occurred between old-line industrial structures and educational systems and rapidly developing postindustrial standards found throughout the world. The observations of Lester Thurow, dean of the Sloan School of Management at the Massachusetts Institute of Technology, provide a convenient summary of the current comparative U.S. educational position.

> The rest of the world noticed the payoff from America's system of mass education, copied it, and upped the intensity level. Comparative international examinations re-

veal that Americans at all age levels know less than citizens abroad in other advanced industrial countries. The math test scores of the top 1 percent of America's high-school seniors would place them in the fiftieth percentile in Japan. The older the student, the larger the educational achievement gap. In science subjects Americans place eighth in a ranking of ten-year-olds from fifteen countries. By age 13 their position has slipped to thirteen. Not surprising, given that America has one of the shortest school years and school days to be found in the industrial world—180 days in the United States, versus 220–240 in Germany, 240 days in Japan, and 250 days in Korea [*sic*]. Combine a shorter school day and year with many fewer hours of homework, and less is learned. Top this off with a much lower high-school graduation rate (71 percent in the United States versus 94 percent in Japan and 91 percent in Germany), and the United States has a grossly undereducated work force."[11]

GAUGING THE CONDITION OF AMERICAN PUBLIC SCHOOLS

What has to be done to U.S. public schools to meet 21st century challenges? The magnitude of the question should not be lost on readers. By producing over 4 million children each year in recent years, the inhabitants of this country have ensured that the public education business will continue to grow from nearly 46 million students between 5 and 17 years of age in 1990 to over 48 million in 1995 and to nearly 49 million in the year 2000.[12] Public schools, defined as the K–12 system, represent a large and diverse set of nearly 15,000 quasi-independent, public school districts and corporations, over 83,000 public schools employing more than 4.2 million employees.[13] In addition to the public system, nearly 27,000 private, or independent, schools are engaged in teaching nearly 5.4 million students. Education was already big business before it confronted the demands of the economic development agenda!

Public education is also expensive, for it is a $210 billion business that has claimed over the past two decades ever larger shares of public spending. The facts of educational life are, however, that the main sources of financing and control of public schools come from the state education bureaucracies and the local districts supervised by state departments of education and *not* from the federal government. Whereas the federal government contributes little more than 6 percent of the total cost of education, states and localities carry over 93 percent of the burden. Sheer size and complexity create a practical problem for would-be reformers.

Public Policy and Public Education

What can and should public policy do? From the founding era of the United States, public education was seen as a liberating local force in our national political, social, and economic life. The high watermark of federal involvement in K–12 public education can be found in the Land Ordinance of 1785, passed by the U.S. Congress under the Articles of Confederation. This ordinance defined the surveying practices to govern western lands comprising the Northwest Territory (now the states of Ohio, Indiana, Illinois, Michigan, Wisconsin, and parts of Minnesota). The plan called for land to be surveyed into townships consisting of areas six miles square made up of 36 sections, each containing 640 acres. One section was reserved for the support of public schools. Because the Congress under the Articles had no power to raise taxes, land took the place of taxes.

Until 1965, however, federal involvement in public education in the 19th and 20th centuries has been largely limited to postsecondary rather than K–12 education. For example, the first major involvement of the federal government appeared in the form of the Morrill Act of 1860, which established land-grant colleges and universities for the purpose of bringing university research and technical assistance to family farmers. The result was an enormous expansion in the productivity of farms on which worked a majority of the U.S. population.

World War II saw a fundamental redirection of postsecondary education toward national objectives. The great research universities were thrown into the battle of prosecuting the war, seen most dramatically in the work of theoretical and applied physicists working to develop the theory and feasibility of nuclear fission for constructing the atomic bomb. As the war drew to a conclusion, a new massive involvement of national policy in postsecondary education began in the form of Public Law 346, the Serviceman's Readjustment Act of 1944, popularly known as the G.I. Bill, designed to give returning veterans a chance to receive a college education. The mechanism was simple: for each 90 days of service, military personnel were guaranteed one year of education, plus one month of education for each month of active duty up to a maximum of 48 months. Thus, tuition, fees, books, and supplies up to $500 per year would be paid directly to the college or university, and the government would pay a subsistence allowance of $50 a month for single veterans and $75 a month for married veterans.

Although only a handful of veterans were expected to take advantage of the opportunity, the results were unpredictably spectacular.[14] Out of 14 million eligible veterans, 2.2 million seized the opportunity, at a cost of $5.5 billion. The result was, according to one recent account, "450,000 engineers, 240,000 accountants, 238,000 teachers, 91,000 scientists, 67,000 doctors, 22,000 dentists, 17,000 writers and editors, and thousands of other professionals."[15] In short, the G.I. Bill produced on a massive scale the human capital required to power postwar economic expansion. It was a classic case of the government program that worked!

National policy again engaged the question of public education during the Cold War competition with the Soviet Union. Sputnik was orbited by the Soviet Union in 1957, creating a direct challenge to the widely advertised superiority of American science and technology. The result was shock and a new national resolve to strengthen prowess in science, mathematics, and foreign language instruction. Important legislation and programs followed immediately in the form of the National Defense Education Act (NDEA) of 1958. The NDEA established a system of direct loans to college students and a system of grants to universities and colleges to strengthen the three key areas.

Most recently, national policy engaged the question of the need of disadvantaged students for special services and support. The result was the Elementary and Secondary Education Act of 1965, of which Title I provides categorical federal grants to state departments of public instruction for ultimate distribution to local school districts. For the first time, the federal government got into the business of providing financial assistance to local schools for textbooks, libraries, and other instructional materials, as well as special instruction for disadvantaged students.

What has been the effect? Clearly, federal policy making has concentrated on colleges and universities, not on setting education standards or financing public education. The practical effect has been the creation of a postsecondary system second to none in the world, anchored by strong graduate research and education programs for which admission is sought from all parts of the globe. At the K–12 public school level, however, federal influence has been marginal, limited to narrow categories of financial assistance.

The absence of national policy making in public education is an anomaly when compared to other countries. As Table 10–1 illustrates, deep structural differences separate the United States and educational systems found in countries such as Japan. In a nutshell, Japanese public policy values public education much more than do the 50 U.S. states, as seen in the setting of standards, the allocation of resources, and the achievement of results.

The story of U.S. public schools is much more complex than a simple two-country comparison, however. Education systems change over time. As Figure 10–1 shows, the system is huge. U.S. production of babies declined from the 1946–1964 baby boom height of nearly 4.3 million births per year to a low in 1977 of only 3.2 million births, to be followed in turn by a boomlet from 1977 to the mid 1990s that peaked at just under 4.2 million in 1990 and has been slowly declining since 1990 while remaining over 4 million births per year.[16] The result is a K–12 elementary and secondary enrollment that exceeded 51 million students in 1970 as the 1946–1964 post-World War II baby boom *pig* passed through the python, bottomed out in 1984 at just under 45 million students, and rose again in response to rising birthrates toward the 50 million mark in the early 1990s.

The overall conclusion, then, is one of stability within which two additional comments should be made. First, since the private school share of enrollments stood steady during the 1970 to 1993 period—never dipping below 5 million nor rising above 5.7 million—the larger fluctuations in the K–12 system have been absorbed by the public K–12 system. The independent sector has remained largely fixed. Second, in the face of a cyclical rise, decline, and then rise in the K–12 pub-

TABLE 10–1 Public Education in the United States and Japan: 1987 Comparison

Educational Dimension	United States	Japan
Literacy rate	80%	99%
High school completion rate	73%	90%
Length of school year	180 days	240 days
Proportion of high school seniors spending less than five hours per week on homework	76%	35%
Financing of Education		
National	6.2%	47.3%
State	49.0%	28.1%
Local	44.8%	24.6%
Teacher salaries	Determined locally	By national law, must be paid 10% more than the top civil servants
Salary compared to other wage earners	Approximately average among all wage earners	In the top 10% of all wage earners

Source: Adapted from Mike Tharp, "High Schoolers in U.S. Lack Drive of Japan's but Show Spontaneity," *The Wall Street Journal* (March 10, 1987), p. 1.

lic school system, enrollments in postsecondary higher education have risen throughout the 23-year period depicted in Figure 10–1.

Clearly, a large portion of the population has been successful in moving beyond the K–12 system and has pursued higher education in massive numbers, an issue to which we return shortly. At the same time, a sizable proportion of students do not even finish high school. Even when the definition of completion is expanded to include 19- and 20-year-olds, the proportion of individuals who had completed 12 or more years of school only slightly exceeded 81 percent in 1991. This was an aggregate estimate of the number who eventually complete high school without first becoming a continuing-education adult. When the cohort is disaggregated, whites attained an 87 percent completion rate, while African Americans and Hispanics achieved rates of 72.5 and 55.4 percent, respectively.

On the input side, public schools are clearly becoming more expensive. Figure 10–2 shows the basis for some public policy concern. Expenditures per pupil in constant dollars have been increasing during the period from 1970 to 1992, calculated either as current operating expenditure or as total expenditures that include capital outlays and debt service. Substantial increases in school expenditures began in 1982 and only began to level off in the 1990s. At the end of the 1980s, expenditures on buildings and equipment have slowly begun to increase as operating expenditures for curriculum, teachers, and maintenance have leveled off slightly. Thus, the average total expenditure per child in 1992 exceeded $6,000.

Figure 10–1   Enrollment in Educational Institutions by Level: 1970 to 1993

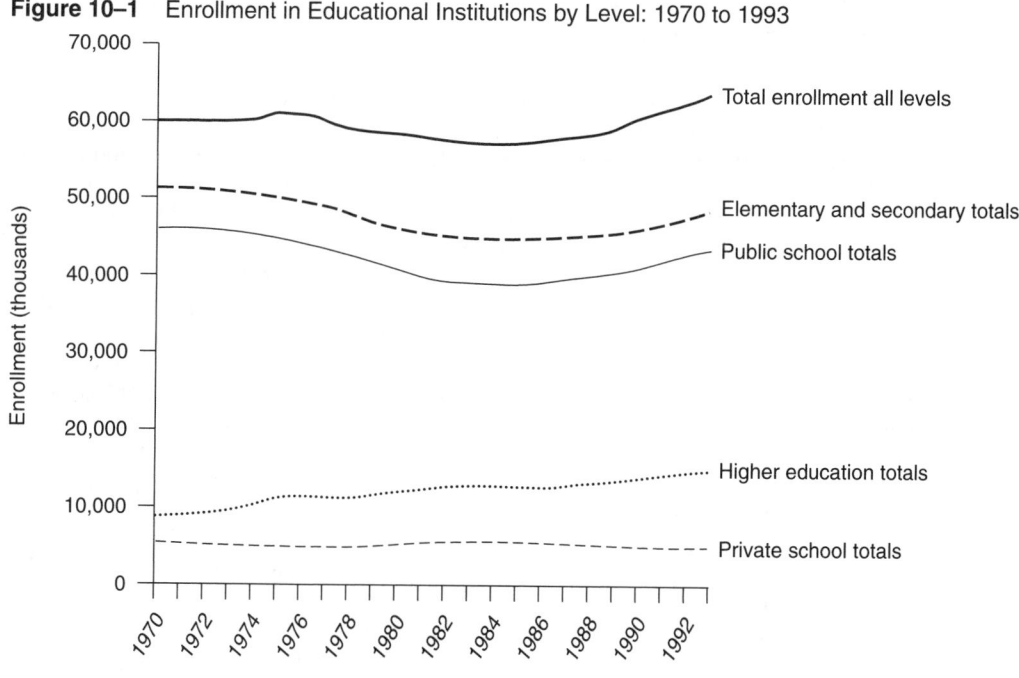

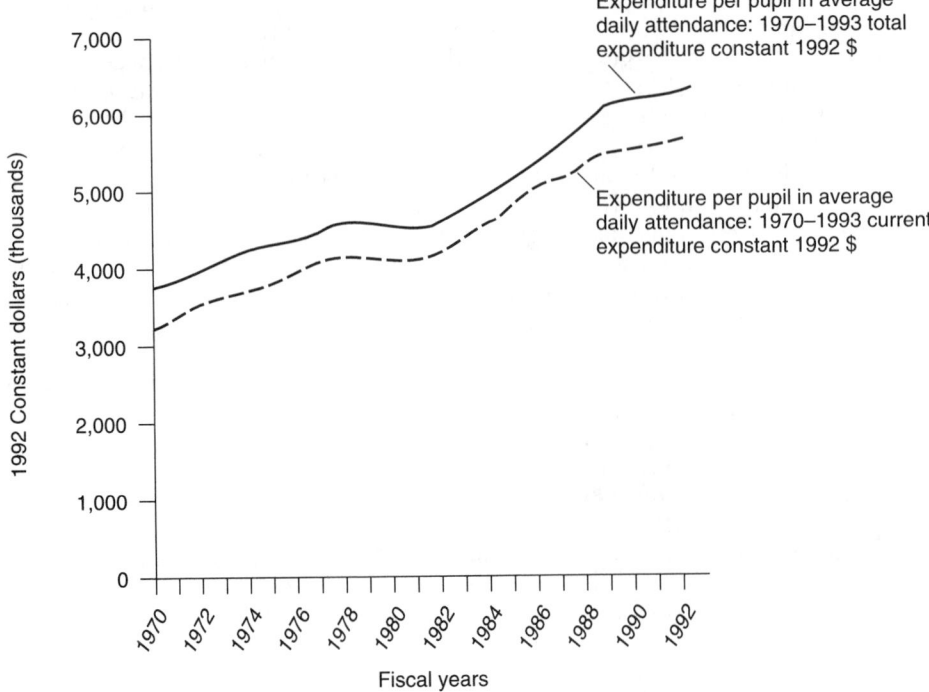

Figure 10–2   Total and Current Expenditures per Pupil in Public Elementary and Secondary Schools: 1970 to 1993

Even at that level, substantial additional expenditures would be required to implement major educational reforms, such as better pay for teachers or longer school years. Furthermore, recent reports indicate that many of the 80,000 public schools need over $112 billion in repairs and upgrades to the physical facilities. The reason for the spending requirement is not the age of the buildings, but the deferral of maintenance and repair due to shortages of funds![17]

The nature of public alarm about schools is clear when analysis turns to an assessment defined as academic achievement. Increasing costs applied to a stable and slightly rising population can be easily explained by significant rises in the measures of student performance. Thus, if it can be argued that more was being spent on student improvement, then at least a justification exists for significant increases in outlays. But examining the results of standardized tests, such as the Scholastic Aptitude Test (SAT) given to college-bound high school seniors, only heightens alarm because of the long-term decline. Figure 10–3 shows the basic pattern common to a large number of examinations, such as GREs, MCATs, LSATs, ACTs: all show dramatic declines in student scores on standardized exams beginning in the early 1970s, bottoming out in the early 1980s, only to show little net improvement over this past decade.[18]

The debate over the significance of the test score decline is substantial. The dark side of the debate contemplates that the nation pours increasing treasure down the drain of public education and gets in return only poor performance

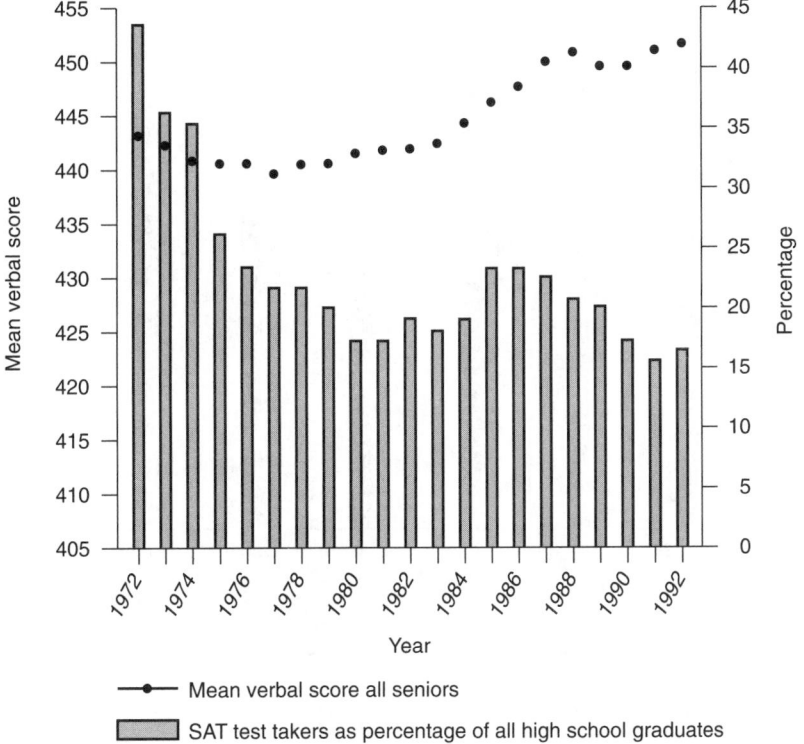

Mean verbal score all seniors

SAT test takers as percentage of all high school graduates

Figure 10–3   Mean Verbal Scholastic Aptitude Test Scores for Graduating Seniors: 1972 to 1992

which if continued for any length of time places the nation at risk. The more optimistic side of the debate sees some hope in the rising percentage of graduating seniors actually taking college-level aptitude tests. This increase, by definition, depresses aggregate scores but reflects a reality that a larger share of graduates plans for an advanced education, the precise requirement of modern secure employment. Thus, the facts that nearly 42 percent of graduating seniors now take the exam (Figure 10–3) and that postsecondary enrollments have shown steady increases since 1970 (Figure 10–1) are causes for hope, regardless of declining scores.

However hopeful public opinion might be about the direction in which the nation's schools are now headed, comparative assessment of educational performance reveals a cross-national dimension to the concern. When one compares the performance of 9-year-olds and 13-year-olds on international assessments of student facility in mathematics, science, and literacy, several conclusions can be drawn, as shown in Figure 10–4. First, by nine years of age, the average U.S. student is already less facile with formal academic subjects than are children in the other countries shown on the figure. Second, by age 13, the country differences are even more pronounced with the United States operating on a par with Spain rather than with advanced countries like Canada. Third, high variability in student performance is obvious. The U.S. interdecile range (i.e., the spread between the highest

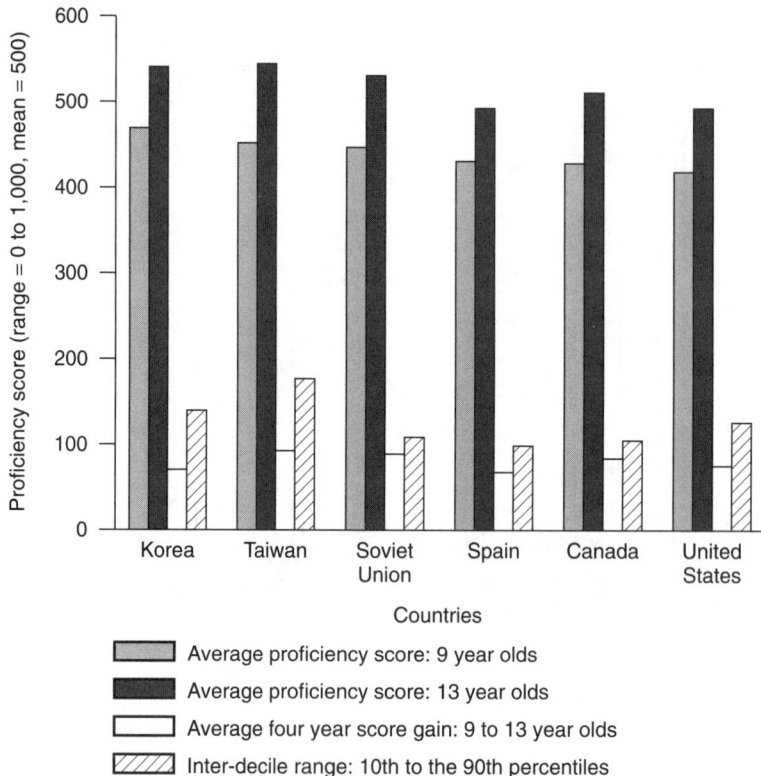

Figure 10–4   Proficiency Scores on International Mathematics Assessment, by Age and Country: 1991

and lowest 10ths of test takers) exceeds one hundred points: the bottom 10th lags far behind the pace set by the top students.

Such comparisons invite all sorts of reactions. One is to point out that international comparisons between U.S. public school children and European and Asian children are chancy at best. Student representatives of the U.S. comprehensive school plan will, of course, compare less favorably on standardized tests where the standards of comparison are the results of grammer school training, the object of which is precisely the kind of education and training that show well on standardized tests. Thus, some might regard the U.S. results as meaningless because schools are being held accountable to an unfair and unrealistic standard!

Perhaps. But over time sources of bias have been removed from cross-national comparisons. The assessments no longer compare average U.S. students with selected European and Asian elites attending selective grammar schools. More and more, the comparisons involve similar populations of students. In essence, when compared to peers of a similar age, *average* U.S. children know less than their foreign counterparts about matters requiring formal intellectual training. Readers may recall the earlier discussion about the averages being comprised of three different segments of the student population—well-educated elites, mid-kids, and at-risk children.)

STRATEGIES AND STANDARDS

Improving public schools depends on the goals and operating standards by which public school performance can be judged. The goals of public schools are nothing if not complex. Thomas Jefferson was perhaps the most systematic early thinker about the need for a "systematical plan of general education," whose aims included: "to diffuse knowledge more generally through the mass of the people," and to teach all students "how to work out their own greatest happiness, by showing them that it does not depend on the condition of life in which chance has placed them, but is always the result of a good conscience, good health, occupation, and freedom in all just pursuits."[19] Thus, Jefferson defended a system of mass education that would encourage a natural aristocracy of "virtue and talent" whose advancement would occur without regard to social and economic background.

From the beginning, U.S. public education has embraced multiple goals. For example, in addition to the goals of creating general literacy and numeracy, public schools also became instruments of socialization; they were the institutions that integrated immigrants into a democratic civic culture by bringing together the entire age cohort of a community. Schools were also instruments for fostering creativity and appreciation for the arts and culture and thus became a repository and preserver of national cultural tradition. They included organized sports in their sponsorship of activities and advanced the cause of physical education of the nation's youth. Finally, they provided rudimentary mechanical and vocational training to develop skills required by people who would become parents and workers. In sum, *public school* has meant more than simple attendance at an economic "brain farm."

In the past 30 years, public schools have acquired new functions as social service distribution centers. Economic pressures on families now typically require both parents to pursue full-time employment, with less parental time devoted to rearing and caring for children in the home. The economic reality is compounded by the stubborn persistence of high rates of poverty among children, as explained in Chapter 7, which has placed one-fifth to one-quarter of the nation's children at the mercies of inadequately funded social service programs and overloaded case workers. As the gap between the social service requirement and availability has grown and budget pressures mount, schools have been thrown into the breach, often supplying before- and after-school child care, a growing range of extracurricular activities, nutrition, social service counseling and therapy, and health checkups.

So pervasive has the public school become in children's lives that current public policy discussions envision major expansion in the noneducational services provided by public schools.[20] Some services are necessary simply to prepare children to learn, such as support services for children plagued by high risk behaviors, like early active sexuality, drug use, and criminal behavior. Other services aim to bring children with learning disabilities into the educational mainstream. Still other services forge firmer links between the school curriculum and a transition into the workforce, popularly known as the school-to-work transition, discussed below.

As if these demands were not enough, schools confront further public demands that both curriculum and student achievement match the requirements of a global marketplace that has been restructuring over the last several decades. The current economic reality is that telecommunications and strategic applications of information technology by multinational corporations have transformed the world's economic markets. American workers now compete in a global auction for talent in which work and enterprise flow to those workforces and parts of the globe where the greatest value-added contributions are made. Telecommunications technology makes possible the movement of manufacturing and even knowledge-intensive services to any part of the globe. Workers now compete based on the price of their knowledge and skill. The old industrial practice of paying high wages to low-skill unionized industrial workers was a first casualty in the rush to a competitive global economy.

Competition is not limited to a simple substitution of low-wage foreign labor for high-wage manufacturing jobs. High-end skills, products, and markets in both the manufacturing and service sectors are involved. Workforces around the world now perform tasks once associated only with elite research centers in Tokyo, Palo Alto, and Boston. In electronics, for example, Taipei, Edinburgh, Singapore, and Penang all compete as research and development hubs developing multimedia equipment from digital answering machines to interactive computers. Service providers, such as Citibank, employ workers in India, Hong Kong, Australia, and Singapore to manage data and develop financial products. High tech pioneers, such as Motorola, Hewlett-Packard, and Philips Electronics, have established global bases for product development, manufacturing, distribution, and servicing. High tech training quickly disseminates sophisticated skills around the globe with a speed that keeps pace with rapidly advancing technology.[21]

A long list of high-paying jobs—engineers, draftsmen, librarians, bookkeepers, software designers—once the exclusive domain of well-educated U.S. workers is now no longer secure from competition. When Taiwan is well stocked with computer circuit-board designers earning $25,000 per year and top Indian and Chinese Ph.D.s earn less than $10,000, it is easy to conclude that there are plenty of substitutes for California designers earning from $60,000 to $100,000 per year.[22] High U.S. salaries can be maintained only when U.S. workers stay ahead of the developmental pace and establish themselves in the value-added chain of economic activity that justifies high salaries. One key to the puzzle of creating and sustaining secure, high-paying jobs is the development of a workforce in which a high level of intellectual skill has been cultivated.

WHAT SHOULD BE DONE?

Should public schools take on the economic development challenge? The question is really not whether public schools should either avoid or embrace the challenge; the question is deciding how much of the challenge public schools should shoulder. Clearly, public schools by themselves cannot solve the problem of the intellectual preparation of the entire U.S. workforce. Just as clearly, global educational standards have been rising during the time that the debate about U.S. schools has been going on.

If public school performance should be measured by the economic development challenge, how much weight should our schools pull? It is arguable whether public schools should have their main purposes dominated by the newly emergent standard that they serve as brain farms supplying trained talent for the new economic order. Even if public schools exist to train workers for the modern workplace, which of the many educational standards should be met? How can public policy be arranged to deliver the required result? Because the structure and operation of American public school systems were designed for the needs of an earlier era, should experimental change proceed at a gentle, incremental pace? Or is radical, comprehensive reform the order of the day? If a complete transformation of public education is deemed necessary, what shall be the standards by which the results shall be judged? This is further amplified in the appendix.

Readers will note that by multiplying the number and difficulty of educational missions, schools will become more significant guardians of the nation's children. This expansion of school charter, in turn, has run into other long-simmering policy arguments. Do schools become custodians of values education, for longer school years and reduced parental involvement in rearing children conspire to deal a stronger responsibility to schools? If so, what are the values? To what extent shall religious values, variously nurtured in homes, communities, and places of worship, be incorporated into public schooling? If religious discussion is admitted, whose religion is included? Such issues could be dodged only when school days were comparatively short and the school year did not exceed half of the days of the year.

Reinventing Public Education

There are no simple, correct answers to the many questions posed above, but Public discussion has been actively examining the possibilities. For better or worse, the U.S. experimental urge to create something better has risen to the top of the public policy agenda, and both discussion and experimental action are under way. We consider some of the policy options, beginning with national initiatives in the area of educational reform and concluding with a discussion of further options for *reinventing* public education.

It must be noted at the outset that it is not correct to say that U.S. public school systems have no standards. There are many standards! For example, state government specifies the number of courses in particular subjects that students must take and pass to graduate. They designate the *seat time* students spend in school in terms of numbers of days and the length of the school day. States also regulate the licensing of teachers by specifying the courses teachers *must* take in order to be employed in full-time teaching.

School districts add a second layer of standards by regulating class sizes, selecting textbooks to be used throughout the district, and specifying the length of school periods. Thus, whether there shall be seven period days of which six are pre-empted by mandated academic subjects and one remaining for art or music is primarily a district judgment. Districts also specify the scope and sequence of instruction.

Finally, the federal government participates in a small way in the regulation of funding for special education and disadvantaged students. Federal intergovernmental grant programs specify the class sizes for students with disabilities, the distribution of financial aid to disadvantaged students, eligibility formulas for aid to illiterate adults, and other aspects of categorical grant program administration.[23] All these standards are input standards. They say nothing about how much students must learn or what they must be capable of doing once they have learned.

Indeed, the overspecification of *input* standards rather than performance standards means that responsibility for performance failure becomes easy to obscure. In the words of Marshall and Tucker:

> American schools operate on design standards set by legislatures, state school boards, chief state school officers, local school boards, superintendents of schools, and central office staffs. The standards are remarkably uniform, they stifle innovation, and because so many individuals and bodies set them, no one can be held responsible for the failure of the system to produce results.[24]

The inevitable result is the same as the shortcoming plaguing American industrial bureaucracies assaulted by competitive forces that concentrated on results rather than on adherence to prescribed process. As Theodore Sizer explains the compromise at his hypothetical Franklin High School:

> The curriculum does not help. Franklin High School has a statement of goals, but it is as vague as it is hortatory and conventional. The goals connect only rhetorically with the formal Course of Study. The latter is laid out by course and grade and is usually cast as a list of ideas, classics to be read, facts, skills, procedures, and qualities of character to be admired, opportunities to stock one's mind. Simply, the curriculum, however artfully described, is a listing of what the *teachers* will do, what "things" the kids will be "exposed" to. The students remain invisible, lumped in their age-graded cohorts, ready to watch the teachers' parade of things.[25]

Public policy seeks a way out of the hammerlock that input standards and bureaucratic procedure have placed on U.S. education for nearly a century.

Goals 2000

The Clinton administration's educational strategy has been to embrace the *America 2000* strategy of the Bush administration. Signed into law on March 31, 1994 as the *Goals 2000: Educate America Act*, the president and the Congress launched a strategy of education reform aiming to create a "world-class education for every child." Thus, an attempt to "reinvent our schools" was launched with an experimental initiative aimed at creating alternative routes toward achieving national goals. The goals now consist of the original six goals embraced by America 2000, the strategy initiated by executive order in the Bush administration, and two goals added in Goals 2000 legislation. The eight goals are as follows:

1. All children in the United States will start school ready to learn.
2. The high school graduation rate will increase to at least 90 percent.
3. All students will leave grades 4, 8, and 12 having demonstrated competency over challenging subject matter including english, mathematics, science, foreign languages, civics and government, economic, the arts, history, and geography, and every school in the United States will ensure that all students learn to use their minds well, so they may be prepared for responsible citizenship, further learning, and productive employment in our nation's modern economy.
4. U.S. students will be first in the world in mathematics and science achievement.
5. Every adult U.S. citizen will be literate and will possess the knowledge and skills necessary to compete in a global economy and exercise the rights and responsibilities of citizenship.
6. Every school in the United States will be free of drugs, violence, and the unauthorized presence of firearms and alcohol and will offer a disciplined environment conducive to learning.

7. The nation's teaching force will have access to programs for the continued improvement of their professional skills and the opportunity to acquire the knowledge and skills needed to instruct and prepare all U.S. students for the next century.
8. Every school will promote partnerships that increase parental involvement and participation in promoting the social, emotional, and academic growth of children.

How, then, can such ambitious goals be achieved? The Goals 2000 logic is the same as the America 2000 logic that preceded it. First, set high standards as embodied in the above goals. Second, develop a process, fed by a small amount of federal grant money and augmented by private-sector contributions, by which states and localities "buy into" the concept of being Goals 2000 states and schools, respectively. At this writing, 41 states have been recognized and funded as Goals 2000 states, and other applications are pending.

Third, finance competing models of education by distributing seed money raised through a partnership of public and private fundraising in an effort to create "break the mold schools." The original America 2000 plan was committed to creating 535 new schools—one in each congressional and senatorial district—to serve as competitive alternatives for delivering educational performance that meets national and international standards.

Fourth and critical, states and localities must allow students to transfer from more traditional models of public schooling to the new, improved models. (Indeed, it is assumed, but not guaranteed, that the "break the mold" experimental programs and schools will win in the competition for student business!) Competition among different models of public education would result, over time, in migrating students', and the per capita student funding they bring with them, feeding the successful models and starving the less productive models. Faced with starvation, discredited models of education would be forced either to improve or go out of business.

The Goals 2000 concept is driven by a venture capital notion of how to create and disseminate large-scale change without spending large dollars on old educational products that consume an infinity of resources without performing adequately. The essence of the idea is one of innovation and diffusion of results through organizational learning in a competitive marketplace. Implicit is that in a customer-driven marketplace, the customers know what they want and choose wisely when presented with good alternatives. Also implicit is that an immediate and direct expenditure of large sums of cash on existing systems would simply waste resources, by continuing to subsidize undeserving school systems that have failed in their central missions.

Finally, it is further assumed that governments can adequately oversee the competition among education providers to ensure that shortcuts are not taken by new competitors who may be tempted to "game the system" in order to achieve the appearance of gains at the expense of a resource-starved public school system made to look worse than it actually is. Thus, public schools may undeservingly lose the resource base necessary to educate those students left behind after more fortunate students have fled the old public schools, taking their talents and resources with them. The public policy nightmare scenario would be that new schools are built and equipped with new equipment and skim top student talent thereby creating the illusion of education excellence; on the basis of that illusion—documented by high test scores caused by self-selection rather than excellent teaching—more migration occurs, leaving behind the students whom public education most needs to help. In the postindustrial environment, when a segment of society gets left behind, the whole society loses from the lost productivity and problems that crowd around the lives of unproductive people.

Will the Goals 2000 program do the job? The concept is appealing, but there are problems. Funding is uncertain, for whether a small federal allotment can leverage private contributions in a program of national educational reform is not known at present. The public money appropriated is small, and the program's prospects are fixed partly with the ability of administrators to attract private funding with which to leverage change. The Goals 2000 model is driven by a research and development view toward education that assumes that the current system is broken, that the task of educating students to meet current international standards is not well understood and requires R & D to develop working prototypes, and that, once tested, successful experiments and prototypes will be adopted by communities wishing to upgrade their educational systems.

Numerous policy alternatives exist. One obvious course of action is to stay with the present timeworn pattern of comprehensive, publicly funded, publicly run public schools. There are, after all, many countries in which state-run schools provide excellent educations. Germany, several countries in Eastern Europe, and the Russian Federation all have educational systems whose graduates are considered very well educated. Indeed, in the United States there are already a number of highly regarded public schools, and the U.S. Department of Education's Blue Ribbon Awards Program has honored several hundred elementary, middle school, and high school exemplars. Thus, one might argue that public education excellence does not require the breaking of molds; plenty of path-breaking molds currently exist.

Human Resource Capitalism

Still other policy alternatives exist, however. One proposal that is much more optimistic than Goals 2000 about the prospects for direct government action on this problem is represented by those promoting *human resource capitalism* (HRC). The basis for the proposal, as stated by its leading proponents, Ray Marshall and Marc Tucker, lies with the conclusions drawn from a simple assumption:

> Let us assume for the moment that the average American student has the same innate abilities, the same generic capacity to learn, as students elsewhere in the world. Let us also assume that our teachers and school administrators are as intelligent and care as much about their students as teachers elsewhere. A visit to a school in any major foreign nation will show no major differences in curriculum or teaching techniques from the United States.[26]

What might explain the performance differences reported earlier? In the views of Marshall and Tucker, there are two primary roadblocks to student achievement: student motivation and poverty. Student motivation is a problem because of the lack of institutional demands made either by public schools or by workplace employers. Thus, in the analysis offered by Marshall and Tucker, "For the vast majority of American students, there is no incentive to do any more in school than simply show up and do just enough to get by."[27] The facts of life are that the United States has never defined what students need to know and be able to do to succeed. Nor have sanctions and predictable consequences for failing to perform in school been clearly stated.

What is the answer? In the Marshall-Tucker formulation, the policy required is not mysterious and does not require space-age, break-the-mold schools that experiment with new curricula and instructional technologies (although all of that cannot hurt). Human resource capitalism is built on two pillars: first, strategic use of performance standards to motivate excellence in learning and teaching; and, second, ameliorating the effects of poverty by strengthening family and community supports and institutions. The pillars support a direct multipronged attack on the central issue: systematic development of human capital required by the emerging economic order. At least five prongs can be identified: installing performance standards as the basis of public education; strengthening families as learning and development instruments; rebuilding the community fabric; building technical and professional education; and building the labor-market system by which the school-to-work transition is negotiated.

First, the Marshall-Tucker premise adopts a widely held judgment that performance standards are notably absent from most public school systems, not because people do not want standards, but because there are no institutional rewards or punishments for achievement or failure. Teachers and administrators get paid whether students learn or not. Students do not suffer workplace sanctions for poor performance, because their records do not follow them into the workplace. School systems therefore concentrate on *how things are done* rather than on what students learn and accomplish. The basic strategy for educational reform is multi-pronged: *teachers' standards* independent of the state regulatory machinery's requirements that teachers attend officially recognized teacher preparation institutions; *student achievement standards* divorced from intelligence and aptitude tests, standards designed to make students work hard and not be satisfied merely with being "bright"; and *certificates of mastery* that measure and authenticate levels of achievement for postsecondary admission and for awarding degrees.

Second, the Marshall-Tucker strategy involves strengthening families. Families, and also communities, have enormous leverage, in part because the allocation of formal education is typically constrained to six hours per day, 180 days a year, from kindergarten through 12th grade. In essence, as analysts are fond of pointing out, only 9 percent of a student's time on earth is spent "under the school roof. The other 91 percent is spent elsewhere."[28]

Families however, are, in trouble. Part of the reason is identified in Chapter 7: the incidence of poverty is substantial, and the problem of raising children is further compounded by the number of single-parent families. Two healthy, well-educated people who are married, securely employed, and staying together have a fighting chance to rear happy, healthy children—if they work at it. As the building blocks of secure family life are removed, however, problems multiply. One dramatic educational result—children typically get less attention from adults, 40 percent less than in 1965: 17 hours a week now, compared to 30 hours a week 30 years earlier.[29] As a cumulative effect, families are much less effective learning systems than they once were in the best of circumstances.

For many families, however, these are the worst of circumstances, and the effects on children are devastating. In the words of Marshall and Tucker:

> The main family problems are due to the fact that too many households have members who work full-time for wages below the poverty level, too many children are born into poor households,too many women have inadequate prenatal care for themselves and their babies, too many fathers do not support their children at all, too many children are born to unwed mothers who are unable to care for them, and too many mothers transmit drug addiction to their children. On all of these indicators, the American experience is much worse than that of any other major industrial country.[30]

The statement suggests the scale on which human resource capitalism must act in order to achieve the desired effect. The recommendations closely follow the recommendations of the National Commission on Children, including the following:[31]

1. Provide tax credits for raising and educating children and more generous personal tax exemptions for dependent children.
2. Fully fund the earned income tax credit (as was done in 1993, discussed at the end of Chapter 7).
3. Improve child-support enforcement and provide government-insured benefits when absent parents fail to meet their obligations.
4. Provide community-employment opportunities for parents who are willing and able to work.
5. Raise the minimum wage to bring a family of four with one wage earner up to the poverty line.

In short, the HRC argument is that child support policy should be changed from means-tested, categorical targeting to universal coverage and access. The reason is political: means-tested programs by definition benefit only a politically weak minority interest, and the country will not do what must be done for children until all children benefit.

Third, government must strengthen communities with grants, leadership development, and empowerment. A frequently quoted African proverb reinforces the point: "It takes a whole village to raise a child." Effectively functioning communities find ways to develop support systems for families in crisis on the assumption that keeping families together is vastly preferable to operating orphanages and foster-care systems. Communities are the places where problems with nutrition and threats to child health, such as lead poisoning, are eliminated. Communities generate part-time jobs matched with student need as a way of generating income required to keep children in school and families functioning. Finally, communities solve problems, build facilities, and maintain infrastructure required to operate recreation programs, run PTAs, operate scout troops, and maintain local delivery systems.

Fourth, government must strengthen technical and professional education. Vocational education has received little support in the United States by comparison to other countries, such as Germany, Japan, Denmark, and Sweden, all of which have made substantial investments in school-to-work transition programs for young people whose attendance at a university or college is neither an ambition nor a possibility. The problem faced in all countries is to integrate academic work done in school with training and education requirements found in high-performance workplaces paying high wages, by means of the development of certifiable academic standards and of cooperative educational programs permitting study and wage-earning work to proceed simultaneously.

Other developmental options include youth centers established to recover dropouts. Roughly one-quarter of each graduating class cohort fails to acquire even the high school diploma whose value has been depleted by the absence of high standards governing the promotion of students through K–12 grades and the award of the diploma. The instructional responsibilities of traditional four-year colleges and universities must be clarified as opposed to the high school feeder system and other vocational and technical institutions. Colleges and universities must not waste valuable time on remedial education; students must have constant access to advanced learning that is available to them without loss of time, money, and academic credit.

Fifth and last, HRC requires an effective labor market system so that students leave public school aware of, and having acquired, the necessary skills demanded in the workplace. The heart of this ambitious undertaking is an employment service with access to job information that can be relayed to prospective or unemployed job seekers, who can either apply or train for the opportunities indicated in the labor market information. The job-matching process must then trigger a packaging of public resources covering the costs of education, training, job, and income needs all designed to move workers up the scale of increasingly productive work.

Much admired by HRC advocates is the Swedish labor-market system, which makes use of sophisticated computer technology to generate job-matching information, which, in turn, results in the packaging of services tailored to the needs of the individual worker. The system is maintained by national and local labor-market boards that track changes in the demand and supply of labor and maintain the job-matching information system and counseling services required to serve worker needs. Local employment offices are then empowered to pay the costs and provide the services required to produce an employable worker, including:

1. The cost of travel to job interviews;
2. Moving costs if relocation is required;
3. Training costs, including all living costs for the trainee and his or her family.

Training is modularized, flexibly delivered, and conducted with state-of-the-art equipment. Finally, microlabor market policies are developed in response to macro policies, and a liberal use is made of relief work as a means of taking up the slack in labor markets with projects that pay wages, provide useful work, and offer an economic cushion to workers—often young workers—who need time and training to adjust to new market conditions.

The conclusion is not necessarily that the Swedish labor market system could or should be slavishly imitated in the United States. A complex U.S. federal-state patchwork of unemployment insurance, training and development grants, and labor-statistics gathering makes wholesale adoption impossible in the short term. The real point is that in virtually all advanced countries of the world, an enormous expenditure of money and time has been lavished on solving a problem that the United States has, until recently, ignored.

Vouchers and Choice

Not all policy makers agree that the education and training problem can be solved with a coordinated, comprehensive, government-led attack like the HRC strategy. For example, the aim of Goals 2000 (and its predecessor, America 2000) is strengthening private choice and mechanisms that force competition between public school monopolies and private-sector providers of the same *merit good*.

One mechanism that maximizes private choice is a *voucher*. Vouchers are *consumer subsidies* in which a claim on resources is given to a consumer who then exercises a preference for such things as food, housing, and even education. By taking the voucher to the provider of choice, consumers can acquire the mix of goods and services that best meets their needs. It is precisely the "beating of feet" in the educational marketplace—scrambling to get into those schools perceived as good and out of those schools perceived as bad—that leverages strategic change.

Vouchers are potentially powerful instruments. They rely on the wisdom of educational markets in which consumers can use government-financed vouchers to pay for education in the public or private school of their choosing.[32] The result is a withdrawal of authority from centrally controlling management institutions and a vesting of authority directly in schools, which must compete for student business. Thus, the direct democratic control of schools—exercised through state departments of public instruction, school boards, superintendents, and principals—would be eliminated. Authority would, instead, be vested in schools, parents, and students; schools would be legally autonomous, and parents and students would be empowered to choose among alternative teams of educators.

In the voucher approach to choice, state agencies set the criteria by which public schools could exist and compete for student business along with eligible private schools. The state would set up a Choice Office that would maintain a record of funding associated with each child to be assigned to the school chosen by the student. The Choice Office would also maintain comprehensive information about each school in the district on the basis of which parents could be informed and could judge the quality and appropriateness of the school for each child.

Once parents and students know their school preferences, applications would be filed with the desired schools. Schools would make admission decisions subject to nondiscrimination requirements and the further constraint that each student is guaranteed a school place. Schools would be free to set tuitition and to expel students or deny them readmission. Each school would be granted sole authority to determine its own governing structure, including being run entirely either by teachers or by a principal. Schools thus would be run by site-based management.

Government does not disappear from the scene. The democratic authority of the state is simply reassigned to a new institutional framework. The framework would break institutional monopolies now conferred on districts for both the governance and the provision of education. Government would still provide funding, approve applications for new schools, recognize the findings of certifying agencies to issue licenses to teach and run schools, administer the choice process, collect and disseminate information about schools, provide transportation to students, hold schools accountable to the law, and collect taxes in support of education. Government could even enter the competition for student business by operating its own system of schools.

Charter Schools and Choice

There is still another strategy for creating parent and student choice. In contrast to vouchers, which are consumer subsidies, an alternative institutional arrangement involves deregulating public schools by chartering competing *public* schools. Charter schools are therefore designed to break the monopoly power of educational authorities by allowing more than one organization to offer public education in the community. Charter schools are created by offering a written agreement—a charter—to a school, consisting of a group of teachers, to carry out an instructional program for a designated period of years under the goals, objectives, and responsibilities spelled out in the educational charter.[33]

A charter creates site-based management under law by creating a legal entity empowered to hire and fire employees, hold property, make legal agreements, and, in short, to organize and operate as the teachers see fit in order to achieve the objectives specified in the charter. The charter school is bound by the principles of public education. Religion is not taught; no tuition is charged; admission policies are open; schools may not deliberately reject the difficult cases. Discrimination is not allowed; health and safety standards are binding.

Several states have begun to see charter schools as a way to shift the emphasis of educational policy from process to performance. Minnesota led the way in 1991, followed by California in 1992. By the end of 1994, Georgia, New Mexico, Colorado, Massachusetts, and Wisconsin had approved charter legislation. Some states are proceeding cautiously on an experimental basis, as in the case of New Mexico. Other states emphasize creating charter schools in disadvantaged areas, such as in Massachusetts. Still other states have grown bolder; for example, Illinois in 1995 approved the creation of 45 charter schools and passed legislation allowing school districts to seek waivers from most state educational laws and rules.

The charter idea has yet to be fully implemented and evaluated. It remains an alternative to vouchers by creating other organizational routes to achieving public educational goals. Whereas vouchers are consumer subsidies and school accountability is therefore to parents, charters represent a performance contract with a school board or other public body that is dealt a strong hand in evaluating school performance according to the criteria of the charter. Vouchers, by contrast, allow parents to take their subsidies to alternative providers of educational service, including the private sector.

WHO WILL PAY?

Public schools of the future will be nothing if not expensive. The missions now contemplated for public education imply enormous increases in spending. New facilities will have to be built, and equipment and infrastructure will have to be installed. More sophisticated and expensive teachers will have to be brought on line to teach advanced subjects at a pace and complexity adequate to modern learning needs. The burgeoning service portfolio of schools will, in all liklihood, grow and claim more resources. Virtually all public policy discussions are at least partly driven by the mounting resource requirements of the U.S. human capital production system.

When bringing up and educating children is viewed in its modern context, what would have been considered in an earlier era as an "expenditure to be minimized" is probably better viewed as an investment in society's future security and well-being. Indeed, a clear trade-off is implied. Pay the required sums early and raise the human capital needed to drive a knowledge-based economy of the 21st century. Or pay a much larger sum later to build the social welfare programs, courts, and prisons that will be required to warehouse the casualties of the disharmony and dysfunctional behavior resulting from a population made useless by the gale forces of economic and social change at work in the world.

Once human capital is understood as an investment, it is unlikely that too much can be spent in view of the constantly rising standards referred to above and in the appendix. Moreover, a powerful new argument is made for generous investment in poor people, average students, and the frontline workforce on whom much productivity growth and a rising standard of living depend. The vision of generous and equitable educational investment collides with the operating reality of current inequality in funding public schools. With state and local control of education, the means for providing education are tied to local and state fiscal capacities and willingness to spend for public education. Therein lies a problem.

States and districts do not possess the same wealth or ability to pay for public education. Thus, great disparities in fiscal capacity exist among states and communities in the availability of economic resources to be taxed in order to raise revenue. Moreover, there are differences among the three levels of government in the source of taxation and thus in the fiscal capacity to support education. Chapter 4 discusses several complexities associated with the tax system, but it is the case that the federal government is funded primarily by taxes on personal income and thus enjoys a flexible fiscal capacity that grows as income grows. State and local governments depend on much less elastic sources. States base tax revenues largely on consumption taxes (i.e., sales taxes) and personal income taxes (with a few exceptions), and localities obtain revenue from real (i.e., land and buildings rather than securities or intellectual property) property taxes. As state governments currently provide more than 50 percent of school revenues and local governments provide an average of 44 percent of school revenues, public education is overwhelmingly dependent on state and local fund raising, although a long string of minor additional funding sources have been thrown into the pot including grants, gifts, tuition payments, fees, fines, licenses, forfeitures, lotteries, and so forth.

Herein lies a problem in any plan of public school reform. There are enormous disparities in the ability to pay for public education based on the different fiscal capacities of the states and communities in which students happen to reside. One 1983 study compared state personal income that stood behind school-age children and found the 48 contiguous states ranged from a high of Connecticut's $82,567 per child 5 to 17 years of age to Utah's low of $36,750 per school-age child.[34] The same study also examined patterns of assessed valuation (AV) per average daily membership in states. In Arizona, the 15 richest school districts reported between $113,171 to $2,441,675 of AV per child in public school whereas the 18 poorest districts reported between $6,403 and $823 of AV per child.[35] The disparity of fiscal capacity among school districts within states is repeated throughout the nation. Clearly the ability to pay varies widely among different parts of the nation!

Public policy decision making is required to reduce the naturally occurring inequities found among districts and states. Inasmuch as federal levers and responsibilities for public education are weak, it has remained for the state legislatures to act. Most states acknowledge their general responsibilities for public education as a part of their state constitutions. The federal power with regard to providing public education is weak, however, even though the U.S. Constitution does guarantee basic personal rights, such as the "due process" clause of the Fifth and Fourteenth Amendments, the First Amendment guarantees of individual right to free expression and religious liberty, and the "equal protection" clause of the Fourteenth Amendment.

The "equal protection of the laws" clause of the Fourteenth Amendment has loomed as the most potent federal weapon since the Supreme Court in *Brown v. Board of Education of Topeka* (1954) struck down *de jure* segregation, or segregation by law. This concept was held to be constitutionally acceptable since the 1896 *Plessy v. Ferguson* ruling that the "separate, but equal" doctrine was an acceptable basis for legal segregation of the races in public facilities. The court's unanimous ruling in *Brown* was stunning in its power and its recognition of the significance of public education in modern life.

Today, education is perhaps the most important function of state and local governments. Compulsory school attendance laws and the great expenditures for education both demonstrate our recognition of the importance of education to our democratic society. It is required in the performance of our most basic public responsibilities, even service in the armed forces. It is the very foundation of good citizenship. Today it is a principal instrument in awakening the child to cultural values, in preparing him for later professional training, and in helping him to adjust normally to his environment. In these days, it is doubtful that any child may reasonably be expected to succeed in life if he is denied the opportunity of an education. Such an opportunity, where the state has undertaken to provide it, is a right which must be made available to all on equal terms.

We come then to the question presented: Does segregation of children in public schools solely on the basis of race, even though the physical facilities and other "tangible" factors may be equal, deprive the children of the minority group of equal educational opportunities? We believe that it does. . . . We conclude that in the field of public education the doctrine of "separate but equal" has no place. Separate educational facilities are *inherently unequal* [emphasis added].[36]

So powerful was the concluding last sentence that *de facto* as well as *de jure* segregation was counted as contrary to the meaning and intent of the Fourteenth Amendment. Thus, racial separation that occurred simply in the sense of the physical separation of the races in communities was suspect and was a candidate for court remedies. Every urban system—north and south—fell under court guidance; for the 40 years since the *Brown* decision, massive redistricting and bussing have been part of the nation's attempt to deliver on the 1954 promise.

It has remained, however, for the courts to determine whether and how the Constitution and federal law apply in the area of school finance. Huge variations among states and localities occur in the actual funding of public schools even after redistricting and school consolidation were done in part to permit student access. Indeed, since 1970, over half of the states have been called upon by lawsuit to review their systems for funding public schools, and legal challenges have been lodged based either on equal protection guarantees in the federal and state constitutions or on a state constitutional guarantee to provide free public schools.

The results have been mixed, marked by a refusal of the U.S. Supreme Court in *San Antonio Independent School District v. Rodriguez* (1973) to construe the federal "equal protection of the laws" clause generously to cover state school finance plans. Thus, a bare majority of the court found the Texas "minimum foundation program" for school funding acceptable and declined to step into the arena of overseeing equity in state decisions about school finance. As a result, some states— such as California and New Jersey—have taken the lead in pressing for equity in per-pupil spending while others—such as Texas—have found reasons not to reduce inequity. The result is a patchwork of judgments and standards that establish no national pattern or policy.

In one dramatic case, Kentucky, the court not only returned a finding of unconstitutional inequality in 1989, but placed the state's entire education system into receivership and mandated a top-down overhaul of the entire structure of public education by the legislature in 1990. The result was KERA, the Kentucky Educational Reform Act of 1990, which appropriated $1.3 billion in new taxes to fund a new plan of education with much of the revenue going to property-poor districts. But the legislature also rewrote all the laws and regulations, establishing a new accountability structure, including the creation of school councils empowered to manage school budgets, personnel, and programs. The new state Council on

School Performance Standards, appointed by the governor, was created to oversee the measurement of school performance and the distribution of rewards to schools in proportion to the extent to which students were successful. Schools not successful would be designated "schools in crisis" and placed on probation with staff tenure suspended. In short, a detailed comprehensive plan of standards-driven education resulted.

Notwithstanding the Kentucky example, the predictable reality is that across the 50 states, substantial inequity in school finance is tolerated under current state interpretations of their own constitutional laws. Thus, in many states the spread between the richest and the poorest districts within a state will often be a factor of two or three. If the poorest district is guaranteed a foundation level of support of $2,000 per average daily attendance, the richest districts will often spend over $6,000 per pupil. Thus, the poor district that is determined to match the spending pace of public schools in richer districts must make an extraordinary level of tax effort and even then is unable to raise necessary funds to keep pace with current developments.

It is at precisely this point that educational restructuring, discussed above, looks good to policy makers seeking an equitable vehicle for providing educational services. In the traditional neighborhood-school model of raising property taxes to support community schools, children are locked into the portfolio of wealth and income that stand behind their *home* school system. Alternatives, such as vouchers and charter schools, break the dependence on wealth and thereby confer choices and options not now available to parents anxious to give their children the best education that money can buy.

In conclusion, it is not clear, however, that expenditure levels and academic achievement are strongly related.[37] Therefore, doubling or even tripling the financial input may not lead to a doubling or tripling of educational output. The linkage between spending and productivity is the basis for hot debate, with mixed evidence that appears to suggest that money itself does not buy very much. Yet, if money is cleverly used, resources that money can buy can be converted to educational advantages that reduce inequality. The common sense of this generalization is seen in the magnitude of the spending disparities found within many states. For example, if a class of 30 has only $3,000 to spend per pupil, then the budget of $90,000 will sustain one level of educational programming, while a doubling of expenditures raises an additional $90,000, whose uses are limited only by human imagination about what additional teaching personnel, computers, trips, and multimedia teaching aids might enrich the classroom.

Thus, the questions of education and training have been an ongoing debate for decades. Clearly, investment in public education, once vaguely and nearly unthinkingly supported as a good thing, is both a strategic decision and a gamble. It is a gamble in the sense that decisions are made under competitive conditions and the precise returns on the investment are difficult to specify and calculate. Yet it is precisely a sign of how interesting the times have become that the current debate is now focused on whether and how to "bet the farm" on the nation's economic and educational future.

SUMMARY

Public policy is engaged in a great debate over the future of American public education. The basis for the concern is the strategic significance of formal education in a postindustrial economy based on the intelligent management of knowledge and information under competitive conditions. The problem for public schools is not that they have not improved; they have. It is, rather, that the standard for judging the adequacy of a public education system has been changing. What was considered adequate decades ago now fails to meet the challenge posed by rapidly improving global standards.

The problem of upgrading public schools is particularly difficult in the United States because of the multiple missions embraced by public schools. Moreover, the public school mission has grown over time; adding more missions to the responsibilities of public schools can only increase their reforming and restructuring costs. Making decisions even more difficult is the further complexity that there are multiple educational standards from which to choose, each tied in part to different industrial strategies whose human capital requirements must be met.

What should public policy do? Four options were considered in this chapter: first, the Goals 2000 strategy of the Clinton administration; second, human resource capitalism; third, expanded use of education vouchers; fourth, vigorous use of charter schools. Each option seeks to improve public school performance at an acceptable cost, yet all four options raise profound questions about equity and accountability in addition to questions of performance and cost.

DISCUSSION QUESTIONS

1. Based on your reading of the evidence, do you think our nation is truly "at risk" because of the performance of our public schools?
2. How much economic development weight should our public schools pull in view of everything else they are required to do?
3. Will Goals 2000 do the job needed to improve public school performance?
4. Which of the four strategies best takes public schools to the next level of performance improvement?

SUGGESTED READINGS

Mortimer Adler, *The Paideia Proposal: An Educational Manifesto* (New York: Macmillan, 1982).

J. E. Chubb and Terry Moe, *What Price Democracy? Politics, Markets, and American Schools* (Washington, D. C.: Brookings Institution, 1990).

Peter Drucker, *The Age of Discontinuity* (New York: Harper & Row, 1968).

Chester E. Finn, Jr., *We Must Take Charge: Our Schools and Our Future* (New York: Free Press, 1991).

Edward B. Fiske, *Smart Schools, Smart Kids: Why Do Some Schools Work?* (New York: Simon & Schuster, 1991).

Paul Kennedy, *The Rise and Fall of the Great Powers: Economic Change and Military Conflict from 1500 to 2000* (New York: Random House, 1987).

Ray Marshall and Marc Tucker, *Thinking for a Living: Education and the Wealth of Nations* (New York: Basic Books, 1992).

National Commission on Excellence in Education, *A Nation at Risk: The Imperative for Educational Reform* (Washington, D. C.: U. S. Government Printing Office,1983).

Robert Reich, *The Work of Nations* (New York: Knopf, 1991).

Theodore Sizer, *Horace's Compromise: The Dilemma of the American High School* (Boston: Houghton Mifflin Co., 1984).

—— (1992). *Horace's School: Redesigning the American High School* (Boston: Houghton Mifflin Co.).

Thurow, Lester (1992). *Head to Head: The Coming Economic Battle among Japan, Europe, and America* (New York: William Morrow).

Zuboff, Shoshanna (1988). *In the Age of the Smart Machine: The Future of Work and Power* (New York: Basic Books).

APPENDIX TO CHAPTER 10

Note on Defining Educational Standards

If public schools take on the burden of preparing the workforce for economic development and productivity growth in a competitive world, the challenge will be great, for global intellectual standards are already high, and research suggests that educational standards can no longer be set too high! Indeed, one study reviewed the educational standards defined by more than 10 major commissions, forums, and task forces that have assessed U.S. educational policy since the *Nation at Risk* report and found not a single, stable strategy with a single educational standard attached; it found, instead, several strategies each requiring different educational standards.[38]

The *most basic* standard is founded on rudimentary business strategy aimed at winning competitive global position by focusing on *continuous improvements* in product quality and price. This strategy, in turn, sets an educational standard requiring a continuous upgrading of frontline workforce skills. In effect, lifelong learning has become part of the basic standard, and for this reason, the study termed this basic strategy-standard pair "the moving foundation," meaning that the level of acceptable business practice and skill attainment is continuously benchmarked against the performance of best practice among business companies and educational establishments. In the motto of one U.S. business corporation: "To be second is to lose."

Since the current expectation is that "best practice" will continue to improve and will require ever higher levels of skill on the part of *average* workers, there is no permanent test score or skill level that fixes the educational standard. There are, however, critical intellectual knowledge, skills, and abilities. Included on the list are the following:

- *Symbolic manipulation:* Advanced, abstract conceptual thinking of the sort required in advanced mathematics and computer-based problem solving;

- *Information management:* High-level communication skills, including oral presentation and writing skills and an ability to read and comprehend complex written materials; thus, the worker can teach himself or herself how to use new technologies and perform new tasks without formal instruction;

- *Problem-solving:* Ability to apply abstract thought to defining, designing, and implementing solutions to complex problems;

- *Teamwork:* Ability to function in group problem-solving contexts. This ability is critical as productivity is no longer achieved by lone individuals performing repetitive chores, but by teams with knowledge, skills, and abilities working and learning to solve constantly changing productivity problems.

Readers will note that the question of what to learn has surpassed rudimentary mastery of classic academic core subjects, such as English, mathematics, science, history, and geography. These subjects can be regarded only as gateway intellectual training to enable the development of the other, more sophisticated skills noted above. Such skills are expectations of *average* workers, placed in restructured workplaces and no longer operating under the direct supervision of elite, college-educated workers who instruct and direct dependent and ignorant industrial workers charged with performing repetitive tasks.

The practical result is a dramatic upgrading of the skill requirements of the frontline workforce, as shown in one evaluation:

> Bank tellers will have to know about the full line of the bank's products, from zero-coupon bonds to tax-deferred annuities and checking-account lines of credit, and be able to steer the customer to the right product. People who work on automobile assembly lines will have to know how to use flexible-automation systems, program computers, use the methods of statistical quality control, and do production scheduling. The salesperson in the carpet store will have to know not only the characteristics of the various synthetic and natural fibers from which carpets are made, the strengths and weaknesses of different fabrication and weaving methods, and the pros and cons of different stain-resisting treatments, but also the fundamentals of retail sales and marketing.[39]

Such requirements imply that educational systems will have to find ways to educate all students, especially the average and poor students who would have been marked for failure by the bell-shaped grading curve that once gave high grades for mastery to the few, average grades to the many in the middle of the curve, and low to failing grades to the few assigned to the bottom. Such practice was sustainable in an era when the average student did not need to worry about performance in school, and

the incentives for continuous striving were felt only by the good students competing for the few places in the professions and at the apex of the industrial hierarchy.

Educational standard setting does not end with the "moving foundation." More advanced business strategies make even greater demands on education. For example, in a "high-performance applications" strategy, the industrial aim focuses on the business need to identify and capture market niches quickly with customized products, develop new markets, create new production systems that compete on the basis of both time and customized customer service quality. Such strategic positions are attainable only if workers have mastered specific applications of knowledge and information to productivity goals and are able to function autonomously in teams without the traditional layers of expendable middle managers.

Virtually all high-performance strategies require the mastery of a long list of substantive skills, competencies, and personal qualities by frontline workers. In this case, the demands made of average workers and students are ratcheted up a notch from the moving foundation. One formulation of this high-performance workplace is found in the Secretary of Labor's Commission on Achieving Necessary Skills (SCANS),[40] which identified a series of SCANS skills defining the high-performance workplace competencies, including:

- *Manage resource portfolios:* Identify, organize, plan, and allocate resources including people, money, time, space, and equipment;

- *Engage in interdisciplinary collaboration:* Work in teams with people of *diverse* backgrounds through negotiation of agreements, exercise of leadership, and satisfaction of customer expectations;

- *Manage information:* Acquire, organize, and apply information and information technology to the tasks of decision making and communication;
- *Manage complexity:* Understand, monitor, and improve complex systems of activity; and
- *Apply technologies to specific tasks:* Select, apply, maintain, and update a portfolio of technologies useful in automating and performing work.

Clearly, high-performance applications demand an applications-oriented curriculum. Classrooms held to this standard would cease to be purely academic and theoretical developers of separate intellectual disciplines and would, instead, become arenas for team-based, integrative problem solving. Grades would be based, as in the moving foundation, on mastery rather than on a grading curve that expects and permits a large percentage of students to do poorly. Furthermore, evidence of student achievement becomes less a graded response to standardized tests and more the actual work sample presented in portfolio format. Obviously, an elaborate conversation between schools, workplace, and the community is required to create SCANS classrooms.

As if the foregoing were not enough, educational demands do not end with high-performance standards. The race continues for several reasons. The most obvious is that high-performance applications are always vulnerable to being superseded by experimental innovation that destroys old applications and creates new ones. As a result, production systems must be constantly redesigned. New products must be invented and moved into production, research must feed product development. The innovation process never ends.

The implications for education and workforce training are profound. "Innovative process" strategies require that workforces possess a mastery of un-

derlying principles (i.e., theory) as well as applications. Frontline workers must develop the intellectual capacity to learn complex subjects, conduct independent research, imagine rearrangements of production processes, discover and invent new products and processes, and conceive of transformation of whole systems. In short, the innovation process strategy requires continuous organizational and individual learning of a sort now found only in ambitious colleges and universities. Educational systems geared to implement the innovation process strategy must therefore develop curricula that move even faster and farther than the two preceding strategy-standard agendas imply because the workforce is required to:

- *Learn independently:* Workers must teach themselves new work methods, approaches to problem solving, and use of technologies;
- *Synthesize:* Workers must develop a capacity to reach new conclusions from findings and premises and generate job-related inferences from knowledge of basic facts and premises;
- *Do research:* Workers must conduct experiments and generate new knowledge by assembling relevant data in response to researchable questions;
- *Innovate:* Workers must invent new approaches, products, and ideas in response to situation needs and resource constraints;
- *Create:* Workers must generate original ideas and conceive of new forms based on leaps of imagination that depart significantly from previous patterns and achievements.

Clearly, such intellectual achievement adds yet another layer of complexity and challenge to the public school agenda. Ironically, subjects and activities traditionally thought to have little core education value and often cut in tight economic times may, in fact, make strategic contributions. For example, high-quality programs in art and music, far from being expensive luxuries, may have critical value in the sense that aesthetic appreciation, artistic understanding, and creativity form the essence of innovative processes that destroy old forms and orders and create new ones.

Several conclusions seem clearly implied by the above discussion. The principal conclusion is fixed by the policy environment. Absent national policy to protect U.S. workers, institutions, and schools from the forces of international competition (Chapter 6 has already discussed the reasons why such a move is both undesirable and unlikely) the policy choice is really quite simple: either meet and exceed a global standard of education, work, and productivity, or accept economic decline. In the latter choice, public policy would worry less about educational improvement, but would prepare the population for the growing absolute and relative impoverishment accompanying an inability to raise the human capital to keep up with the pace of postindustrial change.

The growth and decline of national economic fortunes operate according to different rules from earlier international economic contests. Earlier contests involved imperial and colonial struggles where control of territory, markets, and trade routes—often maintained by trading companies and strategic applications of military force—meant riches and economic prosperity for the winner and the loss of prizes for the loser.[41] This might be thought of as a zero-sum contest.

In the postindustrial era, human capital generates the new wealth. In economies rich in human capital, economic activity ceases to be determined by possession or domination of physical assets and territory. Productivity growth derives, instead, from know-how, being able to convert information and knowledge into a value-added product or outcome. Competitiveness gains by one economic factor do not necessarily come at the expense of the trading system, but instead can enhance the entire system's competitiveness and value.[42] In this sense, a rising tide of trade can theoretically raise all boats.

Paradoxically, however, the tidal metaphor does *not* mean that all societies and economies will rise equally. The economic result depends as much on the condition of the vessel as the tidal ebb and flow. Indeed, as explained in Chapter 7, some economic boats may sink in a rising economic tide when societies cling to old ways of doing business and refuse to develop systems of human capital production equal to global economic standards. The key to development lies *within* the boundaries of nations, states, regions, and communities. *Internal* social, economic, and political structures and processes, rather than external conquest and territorial domination, determine developmental outcomes. Thus, development depends on the capacity of a population to learn quickly the knowledge and skills required by constantly changing markets driven by an expanding and churning global economy.

NOTES

1. National Commission on Excellence in Education, *A Nation at Risk: The Imperative for Educational Reform*, A Report to the Nation and the Secretary of Education (Washington, D.C.: U.S. Government Printing Office, 1983), 5.
2. Ray Marshall and Marc Tucker, *Thinking for a Living: Education and the Wealth of Nations* (New York: Basic Books, 1992), chap. 6.
3. Eugene B. McGregor, Jr., "Economic Development and Public Education: Strategies and Standards," *Educational Policy* 8, no. 3 (September 1994): 252–271.
4. J. E. Chubb and T. Moe, *What Price Democracy? Politics, Markets, and American Schools* (Washington, D.C.: Brookings Institution, 1990), 1. See, also Chester E. Finn, Jr., *We Must Take Charge: Our Schools and Our Future* (New York: Free Press, 1991); E. B. Fiske, *Smart Schools, Smart Kids: Why Do Some Schools Work?* (New York: Simon & Schuster, 1991).
5. Marshall and Tucker, 1992, 20.
6. Daniel Yergin, *The Prize: The Epic Quest for Oil, Money, and Power* (New York: Simon & Schuster, 1991).
7. Edward F. Denison, *Trends in American Economic Growth, 1929–1982* (Washington, D.C.: Brookings Institution, 1985); Robert E. Litan, Robert Z. Lawrence, and Charles L. Schultze (eds.), *American Living Standards: Threats and Challenges* (Washington, D.C.: Brookings Institution, 1988).
8. Marshall and Tucker, 1992, chaps. 3 and 4.
9. Marshall and Tucker, 1992, 77.
10. Herbert Kiesling, "Reading the Report Cards: What Do "State of Achievement" Reports Tell Us about American Education?: Review Essay," *Economics of Education Review* 13, no. 2 (1994).
11. Lester Thurow, *Head to Head: The Coming Economic Battle among Japan, Europe, and America* (New York: William Morrow, 1992), 158–159.
12. U.S. Department of Commerce, *Statistical Abstract of the United States* (Washington, D.C.: Bureau of the Census, 1990), 16.
13. U.S. Department of Education, *Digest of Educational Statistics* (Washington, D.C.: U.S. Government Printing Office 1990), 14.
14. Edwin Kiester, Jr., "The G. I. Bill May Be the Best Deal Ever Made by Uncle Sam," *Smithsonian* 25, no. 8 (November 1994): 128–132.
15. Kiester, 1994, 130.
16. Trip Gabriel, "A Generation's Heritage: After the Boom, a Boomlet," *The New York Times* Sunday, 12 February, 1995, pp. 1, 15.
17. Michelle Healy, "Bill to Repair Schools Pegged at $112 Billion," *USA Today* Thursday, 2 February, 1995, p. 1.
18. John Bishop, "Is the Test Score Decline Responsible for the Productivity Growth Decline?" *American Economic Review* 79, no. 1 (1989); 178–197.
19. John Dewey (ed.), *The Living Thoughts of Thomas Jefferson* (New York: Fawcett World Library, 1940), 130–133.
20. National Commission on Aging, *Beyond Rhetoric: A New American Agenda for Children and Families*, Final Report (Washington, D.C.: U.S. Government Printing Office, 1991).
21. Pete Engardio et al., "High-Tech Jobs All Over the Map," *Business Week*, Special issue on 21st century capitalism, 21 January, 1995, pp. 112–119.
22. Engardio et al., 1995, 113.
23. Marshall and Tucker, 1992, 144.
24. Marshall and Tucker, 1992, 145.
25. Theodore Sizer, *Horace's School: Redesigning the American High School* (Boston: Houghton Mifflin Co., 1992), 6.
26. Marshall and Tucker, 1992, 143.
27. Marshall and Tucker, 1992, 143.

28. Chester E. Finn, Jr., "What to Do about Education," *Network News and Views* (Indianapolis, Ind.: Hudson Institute, November 1994), 61.
29. Marshall and Tucker, 1992, 176.
30. Marshall and Tucker, 1992, 168.
31. Marshall and Tucker, 1992, 172–174.
32. Chubb and Moe, 1990, 215–229.
33. Ray Budde, "Education by Charter," *Phi Delta Kappan* (March 1989), 518–520; Ted Kolderie, "Charter Schools: The States Begin to Withdraw the 'Exclusive,'" *Network News and Views* (Indianapolis, Ind.: Hudson Institute, February 1994), 103–108.
34. L. Dean Webb, Martha M. McCarthy, and Stephen B. Thomas, *Financing Elementary and Secondary Education* (Columbus, Ohio: Merrill, 1988), 108–109.
35. Webb et al., 1988, 120–121.
36. *Brown v. Board of Education of Topeka,* 347 US 483 (1954).
37. The originator of the debate was James Coleman et al., *Equality of Educational Opportunity* (Washington, D.C.: U.S. Government Printing Office, 1966); see also: Christopher Jencks, *Inequality: A Reassessment of the Effect of Family and Schooling in America* (New York: Basic Books, 1972).
38. Eugene B. McGregor, Jr., "Economic Development and Public Education: Strategies and Standards," *Educational Policy* 8, no. 3 (September 1994): 252–271.
39. Marshall and Tucker, 1992, 154.
40. Secretary of Labor's Commission on Achieving Necessary Skills, *Learning a Living: A Blueprint for High Performance* (Washington, D.C.: U.S. Department of Labor, 1992), 11–15.
41. Paul Kennedy, *The Rise and Fall of the Great Powers: Economic Change and Military Conflict from 1500 to 2000* (New York: Random House, 1987). Compare the concept of zero-sum and non-zero-sum competition in the works of Lester Thurow, 1992; and Robert Reich, *The Work of Nations* (New York: Knopf, 1991).
42. Robert D. Ebel and Laurence Marks, "American Competitiveness in the World Economy," *Intergovernmental Perspective* 16, no.1 (winter 1990); 5–9.

11

Environmental Policy

Environmental problems have been among the most pressing public policy issues during the past several decades, and they will almost certainly be among the most important for the next several decades as well. As we will see in this chapter, these problems are not really new in that we have always had environmental problems, but new technologies, new materials, and new consumer habits have changed the nature of the environmental problems we face. Moreover, while our initial approaches to environmental problems treated each of these problems separately, we have begun to realize the full extent to which these problems are interrelated. It does little good to "solve" an air pollution problem by converting it into a solid waste problem or to "solve" a hazardous waste problem by turning it into an air pollution problem. Rather we must take an integrated approach that recognizes that changing the form of a problem may not solve it.

The chapter begins by putting the current environmental problems in context by looking at early environmental problems. As we'll see in this examination, some of our environmental problems of an earlier era were far more serious than similar problems faced today. Indeed, while changing technology has created some of our current problems, it has also solved some of our past ones. We next turn to the basic problems posed by pollution and other environmental hazards and to the types of solutions we might consider. Next is a discussion of the role of science in environmental policy that focuses both on the necessity of incorporating science into policy making and on the limitations of science in helping to form policy. The remainder of the chapter then examines some of the principal environmental legislation in the United States and concludes with a more detailed examination of several diverse environmental problems to illustrate the range of problems we face.

EARLY ENVIRONMENTAL PROBLEMS

Virtually since humans appeared on earth, we have faced environmental problems of one sort or another. Air pollution, for instance, can be traced back to the time that humans began keeping fires in their huts. When researchers examined the bodies of primitive men preserved by freezing or mummification, they found lungs blackened by long exposure to smoke.[1]

Early recorded history also includes examples of pollution. The poet Horace mentioned that buildings in Rome were often blackened with soot. Ancient cities were small and suffered from overcrowding. As the availability of trees lessened, industries turned to coal. The smoke belched from the furnaces of bakers and brick-makers in medieval England, settling on nearby, densely packed inhabitants. One of the earliest recorded complaints about the health effects of air pollution was made in 1257 in Nottingham, England, when Queen Eleanor fled the area because she was worried that she might be harmed by the stench of coal.[2] In 1273, Parliament had passed a law prohibiting the burning of coal in London.[3] Further attempts at control occurred in 1307 when kilns were ordered to locate outside of London because officials worried that the air threatened Londoners' health. These and other attempts, however, were largely unsuccessful.

Water pollution problems were also noted. A viewer of the Thames in 1869 described it as: "Caked over with a thick scum of dirty froth, looking like a solid sooty crusted surface. Through the scum . . . heavy bursts of bubbles were continually breaking."[4] Of 56,000 river basins in England and Wales, 9,000 were listed as totally lifeless in 1890. The Industrial Revolution brought new industries and huge increases in factories and production. Science and laws could do little to stop the pollution onslaught, and by the turn of the century discouraged Victorians had almost accepted oppressive water and air pollution as inevitable by-products of civilization. Laundry could not be hung outside to dry because of the soot, and even fruit ripening on trees was affected. Smog was such an everyday part of life that it was featured in books of the time, such as Charles Dickens's *Bleak House*. Problems continued into modern times. In 1952, the smog in London (caused by fog and coal smoke) contributed to the deaths of 2,000 people. The ensuing public outcry led to the Clean Air Act of 1956.[5]

The United States was not without its problems. Citizens who spent a lot of time outdoors in heavily industrialized Pittsburgh had to take baths several times a day. Los Angeles' smog problems were a feature of popular novels in the 1930s and had a role in the movie *The Long Goodbye* (1949): "When you were in it you could taste it and smell it and it made your eyes smart. Everybody was griping about it."

In parts of the former East Germany, air pollution gets so thick that drivers turn their headlights on in the middle of the day to see. Visitors have been known to vomit after breathing. Residents were fleeing the contamination in Bohemia, a preview of Czechoslovakia, at such a rate that the government offered them financial incentives to stay. Other governments considered bans on growing vegetables because of heavy metals in the soil. Degradation in Eastern Europe has reached such gross proportions that it would seem almost a parody of pollution, except for the devastating health and environmental effects. Citizens of southern Poland find the air better 200 meters underground in a salt mine than they do on the surface.[6]

In 1988, the Polish government declared five villages unfit to live in because of the soil's heavy metals count. About 50 percent of Poland's water was so foul it was unfit even for *industrial* use. Ancient forests are withering, seaside resorts are empty because the water is too foul even to touch, and monuments are crumbling under the assault of acid rain. Reproductive rates and life expectancy are down in pockets of the region, and respiratory and cancer cases are up.

The extent of the problem became apparent after the Iron Curtain collapsed in 1989. There were outdated industries with no pollution controls and listless pursuit of cleaner methods, and these factories had sprung up after World War II when the new Communist governments rushed to industrialize the states. Researchers' attempts to measure the damage have been hampered by lack of equipment and poor record keeping. Residents angry at the former Communist regimes have also exaggerated pollution horror stories to near mythical proportions. One of the main problems is Eastern Europe's dependency on lignite, or brown coal. It is a poor fuel, and more of it has to be burned to generate power than is the case with other coal. Eastern Europe must use 50 to 100 percent more energy than the United States to produce a dollar of gross national product.[7] The region suffers from the same pollutants as does the United States, including sulfur dioxide, nitrogen oxides, and heavy metals, but in volumes that have not been seen in this country in decades, if at all. Czechoslovakia, for instance, has the highest average density of sulfur dioxide deposits in Europe—228 pounds per acre per year.[8]

Everywhere there are problems. Czechoslovakia's state-run radio had reported in 1982 that almost 30 percent of the nation's rivers—4,300 miles—had no fish life.[9] At the old East–West German border, there are mountain tops where not a single tree survives; all have been felled by acid deposition and logging. Environmentalists have estimated that a 95-mile stretch of the Danube is fed pollution from 1,700 industries, most of them unregulated.[10] This is worrisome because nearly all of the drinking water for river communities in both Czechoslovakia and Hungary comes from aquifers under and around the Danube. Heavy metals, cadmium, copper, and lead have been measured in dangerous levels at the delta of the Black Sea. Oxygen-starved waters have caused the collapse of fishing industries. Sturgeon catches, for instance, fell to 19 tons in 1989 from 191 tons in 1971.[11]

There are also alarming health statistics. A section of Bohemia has infant mortality rates 12 percent higher than the national average. In other regions of Czechoslovakia, women with newborn babies are given bottled water because tap water is considered a health hazard. In the Romanian city of Giurgiu, a chlorine and sodium plant emits pollution at levels 14 times greater than the nationally recognized safety level, and 88,000 children and 63,000 area adults were treated for lung disease in 1986.[12] Having recognized the problems, these countries now face the seemingly endless task of fixing them. Poland, which only recently adopted an environmental protection policy, estimates it will take $260 billion to repair the ecological damage.[13] Researchers in these countries are undertaking projects even though the nations are distracted by serious economic problems. They are further hampered by a lack of modern laboratories, monitoring equipment, and trained scientists. Environmental problems are neither new nor confined to developed countries nor confined to market economies. They are serious and pervasive and will be a critical focus of public policy throughout the world for years to come.

ENVIRONMENTAL PROBLEMS AND APPROACHES

The central concept in understanding environmental issues is externalities. An externality is when one person's action confers an unintended and uncompensated effect on another person. The key words in this definition are *unintended* and *uncompensated*. Consider, for example, a situation where one person does not like dandelions growing in the lawn. One way to get rid of dandelions is to spray a particular type of weed killer on the lawn. Even if the person doing the spraying is careful, some of the spray is likely to end up on a neighbor's lawn downwind, where it will also kill dandelions. An externality has just been created. The person's action, spraying the lawn with weed killer, has conferred an unintentional effect on a neighbor's lawn. Furthermore, there was no compensation for killing these dandelions.

Externalities can be either positive or negative. A positive externality is where the action confers a benefit on the second person. If the neighbor did not like dandelions, then having them killed is a positive externality. The neighbor benefited but did not compensate the person doing the spraying for this benefit. If, conversely, the neighbor liked dandelions, then having them killed is a negative externality. The neighbor suffered by having dandelions killed, and the person doing the spraying did not compensate the neighbor for the loss. This example could also contain a broader negative externality. If the person doing the spraying applies too much of the weed killer, there could be runoff of the chemical into nearby streams and rivers where it could do further damage. Here again is a negative externality. The person doing the spraying does not intend to kill plants beyond the yard or to pollute streams and rivers, and there is no compensation for these actions. There is a reciprocal nature to externalities illustrated in these examples. One person's action harms another. But to avoid that harm to the second person results in harm, in a sense, to the first person. To avoid killing the neighbor's dandelions, the person who wanted to spray must endure something unwanted, dandelions in the yard.

We encounter many externalities in our daily lives, some good and some bad. They are mostly minor and do not require intervention or regulation by the government. Environmental problems, however, are externalities that are often much more serious and do require intervention by the government. That pollution is an externality is fairly clear. Companies, or households for that matter, do not intend to produce pollution. Rather, it is just an unintentional by-product of their activities. They do not mean to impose harm on others, but they do not compensate them for that harm either. To avoid harming others would impose harm on the polluter, either in the form of the cost of pollution abatement equipment or of having to shut down the operation.

Economists call externalities a form of market failure. In most instances, the market economy of the United States produces the goods and services that people want in the quantities they want and uses efficient production techniques that result in low prices. In some cases, as discussed in Chapter 3, the market fails and the results are not what people want. Externalities from pollution are an example of such a market failure. The companies producing the pollution are not doing so intentionally. Pollution is a by-product that they would just as soon not have. To prevent that pollution would cost money, but most of the benefits of preventing the pollution would accrue to people in the surrounding area, not to the company itself. Thus, the company has little incentive to prevent the pollution. Market failures raise three issues: (1) when is the failure serious enough to require government intervention? (2) what is the right amount of intervention? and (3) how should the government intervene?

When Does Market Failure Justify Government Intervention?

Intervention, whether in the form of regulation or some other approach, is not costless. It takes time, effort, and money to design, implement, and enforce regulations. In addition to the government's costs, those regulations typically impose costs on businesses and households. Thus, unless the pollution externality is posing serious harm, it may not make sense for the government to intervene. In general, unless the benefits of intervention are greater than the costs to the government, to businesses, and to households, intervention probably is not wise. In the case of environmental problems, while the costs of intervention are often great, the costs of pollution are great as well, and intervention is usually justified.

What Is the Right Amount of Intervention?

When confronted with pollution, how much of the pollution should be prevented? It is tempting to say, "All of it, of course!" But is that really the right answer? Pollution can cause damage in a wide variety of forms. Beyond being unsightly, for example, it can harm or kill plants and animals, harm human health, and cause buildings and bridges to deteriorate more quickly. Does that mean that we should avoid all pollution regardless of the cost? Should we devote all of society's resources to pollution abatement, or should we save some for medical research, feeding the hungry, and housing the homeless? In pollution abatement, as in other programs, we need to balance the costs of our actions with the benefits that come from those actions. We would be happy to spend $500 to get $1,000 worth of benefits, but we should not spend $1,000 to get only $500 worth of benefits.

In the case of pollution abatement, the choice of how much pollution to prevent—that is, how much to abate—is difficult. When we look at the cost of pollution abatement, we usually find that the abatement cost goes up sharply the more we try to abate. To remove half the pollution from a factory may not be too costly, but to remove 75 percent may cost twice as much as removing half, and to remove 90 percent may cost twice as much as removing 75 percent. Against these rapidly increasing costs, we would like to weigh the benefits. Unfortunately, we know remarkably little about the benefits of pollution abatement. We know that there are benefits from abatement, and we believe that the greater the abatement, the greater the benefits. Beyond that, our knowledge of the benefits of preventing or abating pollution is unfortunately sparse. So instead of a precise trade-off of benefits versus costs, we try to make an approximate one.

How Should the Government Intervene?

Once you have made a decision about how much a particular industry or factory should reduce its pollution, how do you get the industry to do it? In the United States, the most common approach is to set a standard. Simply put, we say to the polluter, "You cannot pollute more than this amount. If you do, and if we catch you, we are going to make you pay a fine. If you pollute more than this amount repeatedly, we might even put some of you in jail." A pollution standard like this is called a *performance standard*. The polluter must meet a specific level of performance in pollution abatement, but the method used to achieve that performance is left to the polluter. Another approach is to tell the polluters they must use a particular pollution abatement device in their factory. A pollution standard like this is called a *design standard*. An advantage of standards is that they are easy to understand and relatively easy to enforce. A disadvantage is that once the polluter has met the standard, there is no incentive to reduce pollution below that.

Another approach would be to tax polluters according to how much they polluted. The polluter would face the choice of continuing to pollute and paying the tax or reducing pollution and paying a smaller tax. Presumably, polluters would compare the cost of the tax with the cost of pollution abatement and select the combination of abatement and tax that was cheapest in total. The higher the tax, the more worthwhile it is to install pollution abatement equipment and reduce pollution. In principle, either a tax or a standard could cause polluters to achieve the same level of pollution abatement. An advantage of a tax is that the more a polluter abates, the less tax must be paid. Disadvantages are that enforcement is more difficult than with a standard, and how such taxes work is difficult for many people to understand. For example, some people have argued that a problem with taxes is that rich companies will just pay the tax and not abate. This argument is not correct. Rich companies did not get rich by being foolish. Rich or poor companies will compare the tax with the abatement cost and choose the least total cost combination.

THE ROLE OF SCIENCE IN ENVIRONMENTAL POLICY

Developing sound environmental policies requires a careful blending of science and policy skills. First, an understanding of the natural trends and variability of environmental conditions is necessary to identify the additional effect of human activities. Because environmental policy is usually directed at human activities, it is critical to understand what portion of the environmental phenomena we observe is due to humans and what portion might have occurred naturally.

Second, we need an understanding of science and technology to monitor the environment and to interpret what we see properly. For example, one might think that a simple way to determine whether there is a trend of global warming would be to monitor the temperature at specific locations over a long period of time. While such an approach can give useful information, in some circumstances it can also be misleading. If, over the period of study, there has been increasing urbanization at or near some of the sites, those urban areas can act as so-called heat islands, and the average temperatures could rise at those sites even if overall global temperatures were not changing. Thus, it is important to understand this heat island effect to avoid misinterpreting the information.

Finally, it is necessary to have a thorough scientific understanding of the nature of the environmental problem and the effects of a policy change to be able to estimate the benefits of the policy. With environmental policy, as with other areas of human activity, we do not have enough resources to do all the things we would like. By assessing the benefits of our potential actions, we are able to set priorities and choose among them. If we do not have a scientific understanding of an environmental problem, we will not know how much of it we can change and what the benefits of that change would be.

Unfortunately, while science plays a critical role in environmental policy, it seldom gives neat, clear, or unequivocal answers to the policy maker's questions. There are usually several scientific views, and they are often in direct conflict. How can this be? Can scientific uncertainties about environmental problems not be resolved? Were environmental science like laboratory science, perhaps more of these uncertainties could be resolved. But environmental science is not like laboratory science. The environmental problems it confronts are not found in isolation in the laboratory; rather they exist in the world where, for example, pollutant in a stream can interact with a wide variety of other substances in complicated ways that are hard to disentangle. To study a complex system, it is usually necessary to make a simplified model of the system that ignores unimportant facts and interactions and concentrates only on the essential ones. The problem, of course, is how to tell the unimportant facts from the essential ones. In the course of environmental science research, factors previously thought to be unimportant become essential upon further investigation, and vice versa. Thus, scientific thought can evolve and change, a normal part of research but a troubling tendency for policy makers.

One example that illustrates the problems with environmental policy in the presence of uncertain science is our evolving thought on ozone destruction in the upper atmosphere. Ozone blocks the earth from harmful ultraviolet (UV) radiation. The concern is that depleting ozone in the upper atmosphere will allow more of this radiation to reach the surface, with a resulting increase in cancers and other problems. In the late 1960s, there was a policy debate about whether the U.S. government should support the development of a supersonic transport (SST) aircraft. Such an aircraft would fly much faster (and higher) than conventional jets and reduce travel times between the United States, Europe, and Asia. In March 1971, Congress finally killed the SST project, in part because the prevailing view was that the water vapor from the jet engines at high altitudes would deplete ozone by a few percent. Within a few weeks after the program was stopped, the prevailing scientific view changed to one that said water vapor was not a problem. Rather, the problem was oxides of nitrogen (NO_x), causing the ozone to be depleted not by a few percent, but by as much as 70 percent. By 1977, the opinion had changed again, and a fleet of SSTs was viewed as likely actually to enhance rather than deplete ozone. By 1979, the opinion had again changed. NO_x was again held to be the culprit, but the damage was felt to be minor rather than major. Still more recently, a view has emerged that NO_x was believed likely to mitigate the ozone-depleting effects of chlorofluorocarbons (CFCs) in the atmosphere, thus benefiting the ozone layer. Clearly, making sound policy in the face of such shifting scientific views is a nearly impossible task.

CFCs are now the focus of most of the concern about upper atmospheric ozone. The discovery of an apparent thinning of the ozone layer over the Antarctic prompted international concern that culminated in the negotiation of the Montreal Protocol in 1987. This agreement called for ratifying nations to freeze the production and consumption of several forms of CFCs and related compounds at 1986 levels, with an eventual 50 percent reduction by 1999. In the United States, CFCs have been removed from use in aerosol cans, and car manufacturers no longer use CFCs in automobile air conditioners. Companies are looking to find substitutes for CFCs in other products as well, such as plastic foam. Similarly, Western Europe has embarked on a substantial CFC reduction program.

At first glance, this appears to be a remarkably successful example of international cooperation to confront a serious environmental problem. A closer look, however, reveals a somewhat more complex picture. While the United States and Western Europe have embarked on CFC reduction programs, many developing countries, including China and India, have been unwilling to follow suit. Substitutes for CFCs are often more expensive and can result in inferior products. More important, the evidence on the role of CFCs in ozone depletion, and the evidence on ozone depletion itself, is not nearly as clear cut as some analysts would have us believe. The CFC-ozone theory on which the case for CFC reduction is based is regarded as inadequate even by its proponents. There are a great many factors thought to influence ozone levels other than CFCs, and these are poorly understood at best. This theory neither predicts the ozone hole in the Antarctic nor can it explain the changes in the hole. In addition, the health effects of a thinning of the ozone need to be put in perspective. A 5 percent reduction in the ozone layer, a fairly pessimistic prediction, would increase UV exposure to the same extent as moving about 60 miles south in the United States. An increase in altitude of about 1,000 feet would produce the same result.

Perhaps CFCs do, in fact, pose a threat to the ozone layer, and perhaps thinning of the ozone layer will result in substantial increases in the rate of skin cancer. If so, then the policies of the United States and Western Europe may be justified and should be followed worldwide. Perhaps, however, CFCs will eventually be found not to be a significant cause of ozone depletion, or ozone levels will be found to fluctuate on a long-term cyclical basis irrespective of CFC emissions. In that case, the policies of the United States and Western Europe will have put extra costs on consumers without any corresponding benefits. Which is it? At this point, one cannot be sure. Scientific uncertainty puts policy makers in just this sort of dilemma.

The following are some questions a policy maker should ask in making choices when faced with scientific uncertainty about a potentially serious environmental problem:

Are the effects of the problem likely to be serious?
Are the effects likely to be reversible?
What is the risk involved in postponing a decision to act?
How much worse will the delay make it?
What are the odds of gaining more scientific understanding as a result of the delay?
What is the time scale of the delay in relation to the time scale of the problem?
Are there some low-cost steps that can be taken even in the absence of conclusive scientific evidence?

These questions will not resolve the problem nor make the choice of policy easy. They may, however, help policy makers frame the choices and better understand their consequences.

PRINCIPAL ENVIRONMENTAL LAWS

In the United States, the principal environmental laws are organized around the type of pollution: the Clean Air Act is directed at air pollution, the Clean Water Act is directed at water pollution, the Resource Conservation and Recovery Act is directed at hazardous waste disposal, and the Comprehensive Environmental Response, Compensation, and Liability Act is directed at cleaning up hazards from past waste disposal practices. Each of these laws had predecessor laws, and each has been amended and modified since its initial passage. We now examine each of these major laws and then turn our attention to some specific environmental problems.

Clean Air Act

The Clean Air Act evolved from the 1967 Air Quality Act, which provided a set of principles to guide states in controlling air pollution through a series of detailed control requirements administered by the states but implemented by the federal government. The Clean Air Act was passed originally in 1970 and was amended in 1977 and 1990. The regulatory programs under this act fell into three categories, with a fourth added in 1990. First, the act subjects both existing and new sources of air pollution to ambient air quality regulations through source-specific emission limits contained in state implementation plans. The centerpiece of the Clean Air Act is the National Ambient Air Quality Standard program—NAAQS. These standards address pervasive pollution problems. They have been established for sulfur dioxide (SO_2), nitrogen oxides (NO_x), particulate matter, carbon monoxide (CO), ozone, and lead. For each of these pollutants, NAAQSs are set at a level intended to protect public health and promote public welfare. The NAAQSs are implemented through source-specific emission limitations established by the states. The Clean Air Act sets minimum criteria for the state plans, and approval depends on whether an area attains the level of air quality specified in the NAAQS.

Second, new sources are subject to more stringent control technology and permitting requirements than existing sources. In both the original act and the 1977 amendments, Congress expressed concern that the costs of retrofitting existing sources with state-of-the-art pollution control technologies could be prohibitively expensive. Congress believed that it would be better to require higher levels of technological performance at new sources because they have more flexibility as to location and design than do existing sources. Thus, new sources are subject to more stringent levels of control under the act than are existing sources. The Environmental Protection Agency (EPA) sets new source performance standards (NSPS) that reflect the degree of emission reduction achievable through technology that has been adequately demonstrated to be the best, taking in a variety of environmental impacts and energy requirements. These standards then serve as the minimum level of control that can be required at new or modified sources. Third, the act addresses specific pollution problems, including air toxic emissions, acid rain, visibility degradation, CFC emissions, and special concerns presented by mobile source emissions. Fourth, the act has a comprehensive operating permit program to focus in one place all of the act's requirements that apply to a given source of air pollution.

Figure 11–1 shows indices of air emissions for the principal air pollutants from 1940 through 1987. The indices are all calibrated so that they equal 100 in 1970, the year the Clean Air Act was passed. As the figure indicates, particulate matter had been declining steadily since 1950, although the rate of decline seems to have leveled off in the mid-1980s. For two of the other pollutants shown, sulfur oxides and volatile organic compounds, the emissions increased until 1970 and have decreased steadily since then. Lead and carbon monoxide are also shown on the figure, but data are only available beginning in 1970 for lead. Here again,

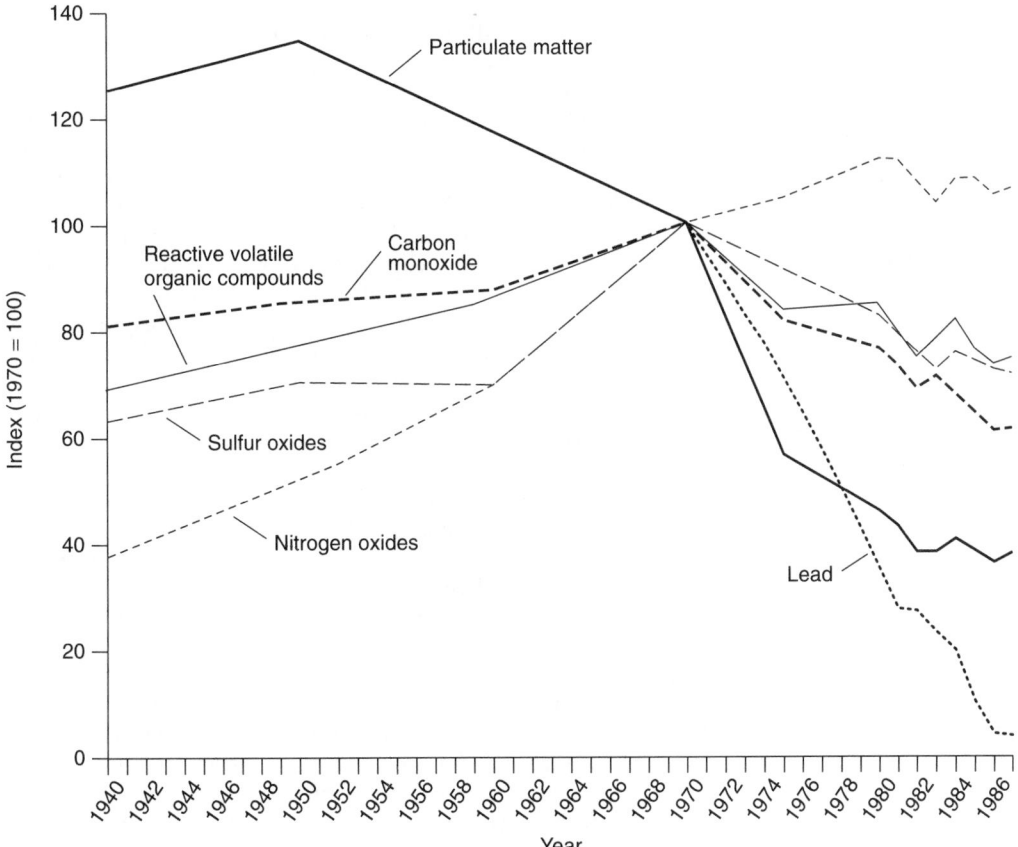

Figure 11–1   Indices of emissions for selected pollutants

there have been steady decreases since 1970, with particularly dramatic decreases for lead. Only nitrogen oxides have shown an increase since 1970, but even here, emissions dropped after 1980. Thus, in general, the Clean Air Act of 1970 and subsequent amendments seem to have made some important improvements in reducing air pollution in the United States.

Clean Water Act

Federal laws governing water pollution began with the Refuse Act of 1899. That early law focused on discharges into navigable waters, with the goal of protecting navigation rather than environmental protection. Efforts to improve water quality emerged in the late 1940s when public health concerns about bacterial contamination of drinking water led to federal programs to assist states in the construction and operation of waste treatment plants. The Water Quality Act of 1965 continued the approach of the federal government in assisting the states in setting water quality standards. Although a few states made this water quality approach work, it became clear by 1970 that a nationwide federal program based on minimum effluent criteria was needed. A comprehensive Clean Air Act was passed in 1970, but efforts at water pollution control ran into opposition.

In late 1972, Congress finally passed the Federal Water Pollution Control Act over a presidential veto. This statute made the EPA responsible for setting nationwide effluent standards on an industry-by-industry basis. The EPA was required to set such standards on the basis of both pollution control technologies and costs to the regulated industries. The Clean Water Act's stated objective was to "restore and maintain the chemical, physical and biological integrity of the nation's waters." The act established the national goal of achieving a level of water quality to provide for the protection and propagation of fish, shellfish, and wildlife and for recreation in and on the water. The basic framework for the act was established in 1972 and contained national effluent limitations, water quality standards, a permit program for effluent discharges, special provisions for oil spills and toxic substances, and a publicly owned treatment works construction grant program. Although the water pollution control legislation has been modified by subsequent amendments, the basic elements of the 1972 act remain in place today.

Initially, the EPA focused on oxygen-demanding materials that primarily affect aesthetics (algae growth) and wildlife and failed to emphasize toxic discharges that were perceived to threaten human health. Following a lawsuit brought by environmental groups, the EPA refocused on toxic control in 1976—an approach that was adopted into statutory law by the Clean Water Act amendments of 1977. In 1987, the act was amended again to tighten the focus on toxic discharges, to strengthen the enforcement mechanisms, and to attempt to resolve problems with efforts to regulate storm water runoff.

The Clean Water Act is a combined federal-state program: the federal government sets the mandatory minimum requirements, but the states are given flexibility as to the means of meeting the minimum and the freedom to impose requirements more stringent than those required by the federal government. Most states have assumed the permit function reducing the EPA's involvement to oversight, but the EPA watches over the state programs closely and makes its presence felt.

The central and most distinctive feature of the Clean Water Act is the National Pollutant Discharge Elimination System (NPDES). The act prohibits discharge of pollutants into navigable waters except in compliance with the act's permit requirements. The NPDES provides the requirements to obtain permits for the commencement or continuation of any discharge of pollutants into surface waters. To avoid violating the act, a prospective polluter must notify the state authority (or the EPA) of any anticipated discharge by filing a permit application. The authority issuing the permit can then notify the polluter of any limitations or conditions upon which the discharge will be permitted. The NPDES permit performs two important functions in the Clean Water Act process. First, it establishes specific levels of performance the discharger must maintain. Second, it requires the discharger to report failures to meet those levels to the appropriate regulatory agency. It also includes monitoring requirements intended to assure compliance.

Assessing the impacts of the Clean Water Act is much more difficult than for the Clean Air Act. Since 1972, taxpayers and the private sector have spent an estimated $540 billion on water pollution control in the form of end-of-the-pipe controls on both municipal and industrial discharges. However, the questions of whether as a result the water is cleaner than it otherwise might have been or whether the environmental benefits have been worth the costs have proved elusive to answer. The problem is an absence of conclusive information about existing water quality, as well as about the influence of current water pollution control measures. In 1981, the General Accounting Office (GAO) released a report that concluded that the federal government had no reliable method of measuring the environmental effects of spending $30 billion to construct municipal sewage treatment plants, a cornerstone of the Clean Water Act. The preponderance of evidence is based on case studies, subjective opinion surveys, and anecdotal information and seems to show that better municipal waste treatment has improved water quality in certain regions. There is little information on how much improvement there has been, however, and in some areas some indicators of water quality are worse despite improved treatment.

In 1993, scientists still could not provide reliable answers to basic questions such as what fraction of the nation's surface water fails to meet water quality standards for toxic substances and conventional pollutants. Part of the problem is that because of the vast array of toxic organic chemicals and other pollutants in the environment, it is highly impractical to monitor any but a relatively small number of pollutants on a regular basis. Another problem is that pollution measured at any point in a river is influenced by the whole array of activities upstream as well as the water flow at the time the measurement is taken. Much of the data is the result of state measuring programs that are often tailored for management of local water quality problems. They may be useful for these purposes, but there is little consistency among state monitoring programs so that aggregation of information to obtain a comprehensive national picture is impossible.

Resource Conservation and Recovery Act

The initial environmental concerns in the United States focused on the most visible air and water pollution problems, with little attention paid to disposal of solids and liquids on land. The federal government took small steps toward regulating waste management with the Solid Waste Disposal Act of 1965 and the Resource Recovery Act of 1970, but these acts were largely confined to promoting research and demonstration projects. The first major legislation was the Resource Conservation and Recovery Act of 1976 (RCRA). This legislation reflected a growing awareness that improper disposal of hazardous substances could result in serious and long-lived health hazards.

RCRA represented the first attempt to distinguish what constituted hazardous waste and focused on substances that resulted in increased mortality or illness or posed a threat to human health or the environment. While Congress laid out these general guidelines about what was a hazardous waste, EPA was left with the specific task of determining just which substances under what circumstances should be regulated. This was a difficult task, and EPA chose to use two parallel approaches. The first was to develop a set of characteristics that would identify a hazardous waste. A substance that had any one of these characteristics was considered a hazardous waste and fell under the regulatory authority of RCRA. The first of these characteristics was ignitability and was defined by a series of tests. The concern with ignitability was that these substances could pose a fire hazard during transport, storage, or disposal. The second characteristic was corrosivity, which is the ability of the material to corrode or degrade other materials. Again, specific tests were developed, including one that looked at the ability of the material to corrode steel. This standard was particularly important as many materials are stored in steel drums. The third characteristic was reactivity. A series of tests was developed that were related to the instability of the material and the potential of explosion. A particular concern was what happens when a material is mixed with water, a characteristic of added importance when materials are stored outside or buried where they might come in contact with groundwater. The final characteristic is toxicity, and specific tests were developed to test the potential of the material to leach hazardous concentrations into surrounding soils or groundwater.

Even with these tests, however, there was the possibility that a material that passed all of these tests could still have other characteristics that made it hazardous. No matter how comprehensive the tests, they cannot be expected to cover all possibilities. Thus, EPA also developed a list of specific materials that were to be considered hazardous even if they passed the tests. EPA also defined as hazardous any mixtures containing materials and wastes derived from treatment, storage, or disposal of a hazardous waste. Initially, 158 substances were identified as hazardous wastes. By the early 1990s, the list had grown to about 800.

A second critical element of RCRA was its adoption of a cradle-to-grave philosophy for tracking hazardous waste. One of the problems RCRA was trying to respond to was the large number of sites where hazardous wastes had been disposed of improperly in the past. In many cases, this improper disposal was unintentional in that the people disposing of the waste did it according to the laws and the beliefs about what was safe at the time. In other cases, however, the improper disposal was intentional. Materials were dumped along the roadside at night or intentionally mislabeled so that they would appear to be harmless. By the time such waste was discovered, it was often impossible to determine who was responsible. The companies who originally had generated the waste would claim that they had paid another company to dispose of it, and if that company had not done it properly, the initial company should not be held to blame. RCRA was designed to be sure that the companies who generated the waste could not escape responsibility for its disposal. By making sure they were ultimately held responsible for proper treatment, transportation, and disposal, the framers of the law thought that companies would have an incentive to be sure that they selected responsible companies to handle their waste or that they would handle it themselves.

The central element of this cradle-to-grave approach is a manifest system. A manifest is a document that identifies the generator of the waste, the transporter of the waste, and the facility where the waste is to be treated or stored. EPA gets a copy of this manifest and is informed when a shipment leaves and when it arrives at its destination. If the generator is not notified of the safe arrival of the shipment, it is the generator's responsibility to initiate a trace to find out what happened. Thus any shipment of hazardous waste can be tracked back to the generator, who is held responsible if anything goes wrong.

Comprehensive Environmental Response, Compensation, and Liability Act (CERCLA)

RCRA was designed to prevent the creation of hazardous waste sites and their accompanying health hazards. However, it did not address what to do with the hazardous waste sites that already existed. This issue was thrust to the forefront of public attention in 1978 with the discovery, at Love Canal in the Niagara Falls area of New York, that wastes had been buried where a school and housing tract were later built. Wastes were found to be leaking at the site and threatening the residents of the area. CERCLA was intended to help speed up the cleanup of these types of sites. CERCLA established an initial $1.6 billion fund for the remediation of old spills and storage sites. Because of the size of this fund, the law is commonly known as Superfund. The purpose of the fund was to speed cleanups by allowing EPA to choose the most expedient alternative to get the site cleaned up. The intent was that those responsible would pay for the cleanup. The fund allowed EPA to begin cleanup using money from this fund and then seek to get reimbursement from suspected polluters later. The initial funding proved inadequate, and Superfund was amended in 1986 with an additional $8.5 billion through a tax on chemical and oil companies.

Superfund has not been regarded as a successful effort to date. A great deal of money has been spent, but relatively few sites have been cleaned up. Several problems have emerged. For one thing, cleanup of these sites has been more expensive than originally anticipated. Part of the reason for higher costs is because mitigation has been more difficult than expected. Part of the reason is also because EPA tends to impose very strict, and therefore expensive, standards about how clean the sites must eventually be. Another problem is that the law provides that a company (or person) who contributes anything to the site can be held responsible for the cleanup of the entire site. This feature, known as joint and several liability, allows for the private sector to pay for the entire cleanup even if some of the companies that created the problems cannot be identified or no longer exist. The feature also means that a company that contributes only a little to the problem can be forced to pay for much more than its share of the cleanup. Not surprisingly, this feature has contributed to considerable litigation in Superfund cases. As a result, a very large share of Superfund moneys has been spent on legal fees rather than on cleaning up the sites.

We face a wide array of complex environmental problems that range in scale from local to global. In response to these problems, people have proposed an even wider array of prospective solutions. Although it would be comforting if a small number of universally accepted general policies would work for all of our environmental problems, the world is not quite so accommodating in practice. Virtually all of the environmental problems we face involve uncertainty, conflicting information and views, and difficult trade-offs about which honorable and well-intentioned people can differ. In the rest of this chapter, we will examine some specific environmental problems that represent an interesting cross-section of the challenges we face in developing environmental policy.

TOXIC CHEMICALS IN THE GREAT LAKES

The Great Lakes are a dominant geological feature in North America. Collectively, the Great Lakes are the largest body of fresh water on earth, containing 21 percent of the fresh water on the earth's surface. The Great Lakes drainage basin contains a population of over 28 million people in the United States and nearly 8 million in Canada. The basin contains 13,400 manufacturing and industrial plants and 28 cities with populations of more than 50,000 people.

As shown in Table 11–1, the Great Lakes are all very large, and all except Lake Erie are very deep. The lakes cover over 240,000 square kilometers, and they provide the drainage from over 520,000 square kilometers. All the Great Lakes

TABLE 11-1 Geological Features of the Great Lakes

	Maximum Depth (Meters)	Surface Area (Sq. Kilometers)	Drainage Area (Sq. Kilometers)	Volume (Cubic Kilometers)
Lake Superior	405	82,100	127,700	12,230
Lake Michigan	281	57,800	118,000	4,920
Lake Huron	229	59,600	134,100	3,540
Lake Erie	64	25,700	78,000	480
Lake Ontario	244	18,960	64,030	1,640
TOTAL	NA	244,160	521,830	22,810

Source: Toxic Chemicals in the Great Lakes (Toronto, Ontario: Environment Canada, 1991) pp. 3–7.

have rivers and streams that empty into them and water generally flows through the Great Lakes to the St. Lawrence River into the Atlantic Ocean. Water flows from Lake Superior and Lake Michigan into Lake Huron. From Lake Huron, it flows into Lake Erie and then into Lake Ontario. Thus Erie is downstream from three of the lakes, and Ontario is downstream from Erie. Because of the flow of water through the lakes, the water in the lakes is replaced eventually, but the volume of the lakes makes this a slow process. For example, the residence time—the time it takes to replace all the water in the lake from inflow—is 199 years for Lake Superior, 99 years for Lake Michigan, 22 years for Lake Huron, 2.6 years for Lake Erie, and 6 years for Lake Ontario. Once pollution is introduced into one of the lakes, it may eventually flush through the lake system, but very slowly. If the pollutants settle to the bottom, even the very slow flushing will not remove them.

As with other bodies of water, the Great Lakes have been used for waste disposal, both municipal sewage and industrial waste. Other pollutants entered from air pollution settling on the surface of the lakes and from agricultural runoff of fertilizers, herbicides, and pesticides. Toxic chemicals began to accumulate in the lakes, and processes of biomagnification began. Serious chemical contamination began after World War II and continued until the 1970s.

Even if chemical contaminants are present only in small concentrations in the Great Lakes, the effects can be much greater than one might expect because of biomagnification. Chemicals such as polychlorinated biphenyls (PCBs), dioxins, and organochlorine pesticides are absorbed from the water into microscopic plants and algae (phytoplankton). These organisms are eaten in turn by larger ones, and the contaminants are passed up the food chain to fish, aquatic birds, and mammals. Since many smaller organisms are eaten by a single predator, the total amount of contaminant in the predator is larger than that in its prey. Aquatic animals excrete these contaminants very slowly, or not at all, so that the concentrations can build up to dangerous levels. In Lake Ontario, the concentration of PCBs was measured at 5 parts per trillion in 1986. As can be seen in Table 11–2, the process of biomagnification results in concentrations in plankton of 0.01 part per million (10 parts per trillion); in smelt and sculpin, both forage fish, the concentration increases to 1.7 parts per million; in lake trout, the concentration increases further to 5.6 parts per million; and in herring gulls the concentration was 60 parts per million. As the table also indicates, a similar biomagnification process occurs for mercury. Moreover, when plankton die and decompose on the bottom, the re-

TABLE 11–2   Biomagnification

Species	PPM of PCB	PPM of Mercury
Herring gull	60	0.54
Lake trout	5.6	0.17
Smelt	1.7	0.09
Sculpin	1.7	0.07
Plankton	0.01	0.004

Note: PPM is parts per million by weight.

Source: Toxic Chemicals in the Great Lakes, (Toronto, Ontario: Environment Canada, 1991) p. 11.

sulting sediment can have concentrations 1,000 times higher than that found in the water. The contaminants are then absorbed by bottom-dwelling animals and again biomagnify up the food chain to bottom-feeding fish and waterfowl.

Problems from contamination were found as early as 1963 when studies of herring gulls in Lake Michigan revealed poor reproductive success and high levels of DDT. In 1968, high concentrations of mercury were found in the sediments of Lakes Ontario and Huron. In 1970, mercury was found in fish in several places throughout the Great Lakes, resulting in the closure of some commercial fisheries. By the mid-1970s, guidelines were issued for the amounts of various fish caught in some parts of the Great Lakes that could be safely consumed.

In response to these emerging problems, the governments of both Canada and the United States began acting to counter these threats. In 1978, for example, the Canada–United States Great Lakes Water Quality Agreement was revised to address contamination by persistent toxic substances with a philosophy and goal of zero discharge. The agreement was amended again in 1987 with a commitment to the cleanup of 42 severely polluted sites in the Great Lakes basin. By 1990, Canada and the United States agreed to develop a pollution prevention strategy for the Great Lakes.

By examining the concentrations of various chemicals in the lake bottom sediments, we can begin to picture how concentrations of pollutants have varied over time and space. Entry of nearly all the toxic chemicals and pesticides into the Great Lakes peaked in the 1960s and early 1970s. In general, the lakes have shown a downward trend since then, with lower contaminant concentrations in the 1980s than in the 1970s. Unfortunately, however, there has not been noticeable improvement since the mid-1980s. While some of the point sources of pollution can be controlled by these joint government programs, atmospheric deposition, which is air pollution settling on the lake surface or being pulled out of the air by rain and snow, can come from outside the region and is much harder to control and reduce.

This chemical pollution can pose health threats to both animals and humans. The concentration in fish varies across the different lakes. For lake trout in 1980, for example, the PCB concentration ranged from an average of 1 part per million in Lake Superior to 5 parts per million in Lake Ontario and 10 parts per million in Lake Michigan. By 1984, the average concentration in Lake Michigan fish had dropped to 5, but the concentration in Lake Ontario fish had risen to 6. A similar pattern was found for DDT concentrations. The size and species of the fish also affect the concentrations of chemical pollutants. As fish get older and larger, the concentrations tend to rise. For a 45-centimeter lake trout, the concentration averages 0.7 part per million, while for an older 85-centimeter fish, the concentration is 4.7

parts per million. At the same size, rainbow trout (steelhead) have only two-thirds the concentration of lake trout, while coho salmon and Chinook salmon have only about half the concentration. These fish are all from the same family and have similar feeding habits. Bottom-dwelling or bottom-feeding fish tend to have higher concentrations but are usually not fished for commercially. These sorts of findings have led the governments of Canada and the United States to issue advisories of how much of various types of fish from various locations humans should eat.

Animals, however, are issued no such advisories. These pollution levels have led to drastic declines in bald eagle populations in the Great Lakes Region. Because bald eagles eat some of the same fish and mammals that hunters and anglers eat, their health serves as an indicator of the potential risk to humans. Perhaps as a result of slight improvement in water quality, there is some early evidence of recovery of eagle populations in Ontario. When you recall the long residence times of water in these lakes, however, you begin to appreciate how long these pollution problems will be with us even after the inflow of pollutants is stopped.

GLOBAL WARMING

Air pollution has long been a concern in the United States and throughout the world. Until recently, however, the effects of pollution were thought to be largely confined to the region surrounding the source. With concerns about acid rain, we began to realize that the effects of air pollution could be felt a considerable distance away. The fear about global warming, however, is that the impacts of certain types of air pollution and other activities could affect the entire planet. Let's begin with what some people are saying about global warming.

> The world is warming. Climatic zones are shifting. Glaciers are melting. The warming, rapid now, may become even more rapid as a result of warming itself, and will continue into the indefinite future unless we take deliberate steps to slow or stop it.
>
> Richard Houghton, ecologist and senior scientist at Wood's Hole, and George M. Woodwell, ecologist and director of Wood's Hole, as reported in *Scientific American*, April 1989 Volume 260, Number 4, p. 18.

> But the theory of global warming will not be disproved, and the skeptics are vastly outnumbered by former skeptics who now accept the overwhelming weight of accumulated evidence.
>
> Senator Al Gore *Earth in the Balance* (New York: Houghton Mifflin, 1992) p. 39.

> There is no substantive basis for predicting a sizable global warming due to observed increases in minor greenhouse gases such as carbon dioxide, methane, and chlorofluorocarbons. . . . Rarely has such meager science provided such an outpouring of popularization by individuals who do not understand the subject in the first place.
>
> Richard Lindzen, professor of meteorology at Massachusetts Institute of Technology (in "Global Warming: The Origin and Nature of the Alleged Scientific Consensus," *Regulation* Spring 1992, p. 88).

With many other environmental problems, the evidence of degradation is clear. But with global warming, it is much more difficult to determine how serious the threat is or, indeed, if there is a threat at all. How do we make sense of the conflicting claims? We need to start by being clear about what the issue is with global warming. The issue is not just whether the earth is getting warmer or cooler. We have ample evidence that the earth's temperature has not been constant in the past. There have been ice ages when glaciers have extended into much of what is now the United States. There have been warm periods when average temperatures were much higher than at present. Thus, the earth's temperature has gone through cycles in the past, and there is little reason to believe that there may not again be cycles in the future.

The issues with global warming are whether there are temperature changes, whether these changes are being caused by human activities, and, more to the point, whether altering these human activities might after these temperature changes. These issues are more complicated questions than simply whether or not the earth is getting warmer and cannot be answered easily with a single piece of critical information. A whole series of questions must be asked and a range of issues investigated:

Is the earth's surface temperature changing in a systematic way?
Are these changes permanent or cyclical?
Is the earth's temperature inherently stable or inherently unstable?
Do temperature changes tend to be self-correcting?
What is the role of human activity in causing temperature change?
What other factors cause temperature change?
If there were no changes, how much would temperature change and how fast?
What would be the impacts of such changes?
How would humans adapt?
How would other species adapt?
Could changing human activities alter future temperatures?
What are the alternatives for changing such behavior?
How much would temperature change be affected?
What would be the impacts of such altered behavior?
How would lifestyles and standards of living change?
What would it cost?

We do not have nearly enough information or understanding to answer all these questions, but we can try to pull together the available information in a systematic way. The debate seems to center around broad issues:

Is the earth getting warmer?
What does human activity contribute to warming?
What would the effects of warming be?
How much consensus is there among scientists?

Let's look at the evidence on each of these issues presented by those observers who believe global warming is a problem. On the question of whether the earth is warming or not, several groups of researchers have found evidence that it is. For example, a group at NASA's Goddard Institute conducted an analysis of temperature records going back to 1860 and found evidence suggesting that the average global temperature has increased by 0.5 to 0.7 degrees Celsius over that period, with the greatest increase during the past decade. Another group of researchers at the University of East Anglia in England also found an increase in average global temperature, but the increase was not observed in all regions. Other researchers have pointed out that the average temperature of lakes in Canada has increased; the annual maximum extent of sea ice around the Antarctic and the Arctic appears to be declining; and glaciers in Europe and elsewhere have receded. The media frequently point out that the six warmest years on record were all in the 1980s. In contrast, however, analysis by a group at the National Oceanographic and Atmospheric Administration (NOAA) found no trend in temperature increase in the contiguous United States. Much of the popular and congressional concern about global warming emerged following the particularly warm summer of 1988, when there was a devastating drought in much of the United States and widespread forest fires in the western United States. Atmospheric scientists, however, note that there is often year-to-year variation in temperature and that one warm year is not, in itself, evidence of a long-term warming trend.

The difficulty in evaluating this type of direct evidence is that we simply do not have temperature records going back nearly far enough to determine whether the warming we seem to observe is a new phenomenon or part of a longer-term cycle. Thus, if we are going to try to shed some light on the second question, how much human activity is contributing to global warming, we need to examine the hypothesized mechanism by which this might occur.

The basis of concern about the role of human activity is the so-called greenhouse effect. In a glass greenhouse, sunlight passes through the glass to warm the insides, but the glass traps the radiant heat generated when the sun strikes the plants and other materials in the greenhouse. The earth's atmosphere does essentially the same thing. Sunlight passes through the atmosphere and strikes the earth, where some of the resulting radiant heat is trapped by that same atmosphere. Without this greenhouse effect on earth, the temperatures would be very low, and life as we know it would not exist. The balance of the natural greenhouse effect is critical. If too much heat is retained, global temperatures could increase and threaten life. If too little heat is retained, the earth's temperature could decrease with a similarly devastating effect.

The concern about global warming is that human activity is upsetting the earth's natural balance by generating additional gases that increase the greenhouse effect. The principal greenhouse gases are carbon dioxide (CO_2) and methane. These gasses are not present in large quantities. CO_2 makes up 0.03 percent of the earth's atmosphere, and methane makes up 100 times less than that. These are, however, the principal gases that give us the greenhouse effect. If human activities, or anything else, cause them to increase, the result could be more radiant heat trapped and an increase in global temperatures.

CO_2 and methane both occur naturally. Plants use CO_2 in photosynthesis and give up CO_2 in respiration. The CO_2 taken up in photosynthesis is given up again when the plants die and decay. Higher temperatures can alter this balance by increasing the rate of decay. Oceans absorb CO_2 and also give a little back. Methane is generated by biological phenomena in bogs, swamps, and moist soil. Human activities can affect CO_2 levels primarily through generating CO_2 by the burning of fossil fuels and by removing CO_2-absorbing plants through deforestation.

Sorting out all the effects of both natural and human activities is very complicated, and researchers have resorted to computer-based models called general circulation models (GCMs). These are large-scale climate models that attempt to trace the effects of both natural phenomena and human activities and predict changes in temperature by region. Many of these models are built by different groups of scientists. These models differ in their details, but virtually all of them predict global warming in varying extents. These models, however, are only as good as our understanding of the underlying phenomena. As our understanding changes, the models will change as well, and their predictions may also change.

These models are based largely on the theories of the role of greenhouse gases. What is the evidence about temperature change and greenhouse gases? An important piece of evidence comes from the Vostok ice core. A 2,000-meter-long ice core was drilled and extracted in the Antarctic. Because the ice in the Antarctic was deposited in layers, the sample contains ice dating back 160,000 years. The ice contains air bubbles trapped there as it formed, and these air bubbles can be analyzed to measure the CO_2 concentrations in the air at the time the ice was formed. Other measurements can give other information; notably, the ratio of certain isotopes of oxygen can provide information about the temperature changes over time. Thus, careful analysis of the Vostok ice core data can give us a picture of both temperature changes and changes in the concentration of a primary greenhouse gas over a 160,000-year time period.

In examining the Vostok ice core data, CO_2 concentrations were in fact found to be correlated with temperature—that is, in periods when CO_2 concentrations in the atmosphere were found to be high, the temperature was also found to be high. The question then is whether the CO_2 changes caused the temperature changes or whether the temperature changes caused the CO_2 changes. During periods of warming, the CO_2 and temperature seemed to move together. However, during periods of cooling, the CO_2 concentration lagged behind the temperature change. In other words, first it got colder, and then the CO_2 concentrations fell. In addition, the changes in temperature are between five and fourteen times greater than could be explained by the greenhouse properties of the concentrations of CO_2 observed. It would seem that in addition to CO_2, something else is going on that we do not yet understand.

More recent observations suggest that CO_2 concentrations have increased by 29 percent since 1800 but that the rate of increase has slowed since the early 1970s. Many of the early predictions of the increase in CO_2 concentrations have been revised downward. Moreover, CO_2 and methane are not the only factors in the greenhouse effect. Cloud cover and water vapor in the air are also important, yet the current GCMs do not do a very good job at modeling these effects nor do they typically include the effects of factors such as volcanic eruptions. The dust and ash from some past volcanic eruptions have reduced the sunlight reaching the earth with a resulting cooling. Thus, many scientists are convinced that global warming is occurring and that fossil fuel consumption and deforestation are important causes. Others, however, raise questions about the strength of the evidence and argue that there is too much we do not know to be sure global warming is happening and, if it is, whether or not it is a product of human activity. As these scientists point out, throughout much of the earth's history, CO_2 concentrations were higher than anticipated by those who are convinced global warming is a serious environmental hazard.

In deciding whether policies should be developed and implemented to reduce fossil fuel use, deforestation, or other activities that might contribute to global warming, one of the questions that must be raised is what the effects would be if the earth's temperature did rise as some fear. Many of the effects are uncertain, but a few impacts seem clear. One effect would be a rise in the sea level. Seas would rise in part because glaciers would melt and in part because as the oceans warmed, they would expand. With rising sea level, low-lying coastal land that is now dry would be under water. How much of a sea level rise could be expected is un-known. Some scientists have predicted an eventual rise of 4 to 5 meters. (Others have suggested a rise of 7.6 meters, but since that is the precise distance it would take to have the ocean reach the steps of the White House, one must wonder whether that estimate is more for dramatic effect than a serious view.) With warmer temperatures, the plants found growing in certain regions would likely change. If the temperature change were gradual, these plants might migrate natu-rally to regions where they were better suited. If, however, the changes were faster than natural plant migration could accommodate, many forests could die. In-creased CO_2 concentrations would also result in faster growth rates for many plants and harvested crops. Weather patterns would likely change with increased temper-ature. Some regions would become wetter and some drier, although it is difficult to predict the pattern of these changes with much confidence. The more rapid the changes, the more difficult it would be for the world's population to adapt; but with very gradual changes, adaptation would be less difficult.

RADON

Radon is a colorless, odorless, radioactive gas that was discovered in the early 1900s. Radon, or more precisely the radon-222 isotope, is the direct product of the radioactive decay of radium 226, which is the product of decay of uranium 238. Uranium 238 is found in varying concentrations throughout the earth's crust in virtually all forms of rock and soil. It is usually found in such low concentrations that it does not pose a risk. Radon itself neither readily interacts chemically with other elements nor lasts very long—it has a half-life of 3.82 days. As a result of that short half-life, only radon generated fairly close to the surface of the earth is likely to escape. Indeed, only about 10 percent of radon formed in the top meter of soil typically escapes into the air. The potential health risk is from radon *daughters,* which are products of radon decay. These daughters are particles that readily at-tach themselves to whatever they contact. Thus, they can be deposited in the lungs where they emit radiation in the form of alpha rays that can harm tissue.

The notion of a colorless, odorless, radioactive gas that can be found almost anywhere and that can harm people is frightening. Many people have become alarmed at the potential health risk:

> It is now widely recognized that indoor radon is the largest single source of exposure to ionizing radiation in the environment. The average effective radiation dose from radon is estimated to be greater than the dose from all other natural sources of radia-tion combined, greater than the dose from medical treatments including x-rays, and very much greater than the dose from industrial activities including nuclear power.
>
> David Bodansky, professor of physics,
> University of Washington, in *Indoor Radon and Its Hazards* (1987)

> Yet this radon, which emanates from soil and bedrock, from building materials, and even from water and air, is a major cause of lung cancer fatalities. In the United States alone, some 20,000 lung cancer fatalities due to indoor radon occur each year.
>
> Douglas Brookins, in *The Indoor Radon Problem* (1990)

Radon—the silent killer—is now recognized as a worldwide threat to health. The seriousness of long-term exposure to radon cannot be overstated.

Shyamal K. Majumdar, professor of biology,
Lafayette College, in *Environmental Radon:
Occurrence, Control, and Health Hazards* (1990)

How did we learn about radon and the risk from exposure? Not surprisingly, problems from radon exposure first came to light with miners, both in uranium mines and to a lesser extent in other mines. In the United States, for example, there were about 2,000 uranium mines in 1955. Conditions are much different today, but these mines used to be crude examples of mining. They were usually unventilated so that dust levels were very high, and the miners worked in cramped conditions. The dust contained uranium and its decay products. From this mining experience, we have some limited information on exposure to radon and can draw some tentative conclusions about the potential health effects. Exposure data are available only from a few of these mines, and much of that data may be unreliable. Even with these limitations, uranium workers were found to have a higher incidence of lung cancer, not only in the United States, but in similar studies in Canada, Sweden, and Czechoslovakia. In the U.S. studies in Utah and Colorado, there were both white and Native American miners, and white miners were found to have substantially higher rates of lung cancer. It was observed that white miners were much more likely to smoke cigarettes than Native American miners, suggesting that perhaps an interaction between cigarette smoking and radon exposure greatly increases the risk.

The current concern is not about miners but about people exposed to accumulations of radon in their homes. Radon can enter a house or building through the ground and through gaps in the building structure. It can also enter in small quantities through building materials, water, and natural gas. To the extent that structures are sealed against the outside air, radon can accumulate to higher concentrations within structures than found outside. As people have in recent years sealed their houses more carefully to conserve heating and cooling energy, the concern about radon exposures has grown. Indeed, in 1986, the EPA estimated that between 5,000 and 20,000 lung cancer deaths may have been attributed to radon exposure.

How can the risk of radon be assessed? One way is to try to extrapolate from the experience with miners. There are several difficulties with this approach, however. One is that the miners were exposed to much higher radon concentrations than are found in people's homes. How do we estimate the risk posed by exposure to low concentrations from information on the incidence of disease from high concentrations? We rely on a dose-response relationship that allows us to predict the response to a particular dose. In this case, we look for a relationship that predicts the incidence of lung cancer in response to a particular exposure to radon. The problem is that we do not really know what that dose-response relationship looks like, so we assume a particular shape of the dose-response curve.

In the case of radon, we assume it is linear—a population exposed to one-tenth the amount of radon that mine workers were experiences one-tenth the rate of lung cancer. We assume that zero exposure produces zero risk from radon; we look to the risk miners exposed to high concentrations experienced; and we draw a straight line between the two points. There is some uncertainty about how to do this because of the lack of controls for the effects of smoking among miners and the uncertainty about how the dusty environment in which they worked might have also affected their health. Besides a linear hypothesis, another possibility is that the relationship is not linear but that there is some sort of threshold exposure, below which there is no risk for most people. Still another possibility is that very low exposures might be good for you while much higher exposures might be harmful. We do not have much information on which to base a choice among these different dose-response possibilities. The linear hypothesis is the most conservative in that it predicts the largest number of lung cancers for a given low level of exposure and therefore provides the most basis for policies to reduce radon exposure.

Many scientists believe that a linear hypothesis is correct for radiation-related exposures, but some evidence calls this into question for radon. There have been some studies of miners exposed to low levels of radon. These studies produced wide variation in their assessment of the risk from low-level exposures. However, in general, U.S. miners exposed to low levels of radon had fewer deaths than would be predicted by the linear hypothesis. There have also been some epidemiological studies that compared the rates of lung cancer in areas of the country with high radon concentration to those in areas with low radon concentrations. If the linear hypothesis is correct, we would expect to observe higher rates of lung cancer in the high radon concentration areas. Instead, in areas with high radon concentrations, lung cancer rates are actually lower. In three states with the highest mean radon levels in homes, the lung cancer death rate averages 41 per 100,000, and in the three states with the lowest radon levels, that rate averages 66 per 100,000. More generally, in five states with twice the national average radon concentrations, the lung cancer rate is only 80 percent of the national average. Many things besides radon can cause lung cancer, and it is possible that these other factors are explaining these curious results. Similar results were found, however, in a study in the United Kingdom. A carefully controlled study in China compared 70,000 people in high radon concentration areas with a similar number in low concentration areas. The difference in exposure was a factor of three. The low-concentration group had more lung cancer and more cancers of other types. In Montana, Germany, and Yugoslavia, some high-radon-emitting areas have long been thought to have therapeutic qualities to cure a wide variety of ailments.

SOLID WASTE DISPOSAL

Solid waste disposal is an environmental problem that is often described in startling terms:

The United States represents 5 percent of the world's population, but generates 70 percent of its solid waste.

By the early 1980s, the U.S. population either directly or indirectly generated 108 pounds per person per day, or 20 tons per year, 15 times as much as the average person living in India.

Each year Californians alone produce enough trash to form a mound 100 feet wide and 30 feet high extending the entire length of the state.[14]

These are not new problems, and the magnitude of the problem is not unprecedented, even in the United States. During the first 20 years of this century, waste generation per capita in New York City was 17 percent higher than it is today.

Part of the earlier volume was ash disposal from coal furnaces, but food wastes then averaged 160 pounds per person annually, whereas they are only 106 pounds today. As late as 1939, annual per capita discards ran as much as 20 percent higher than in the late 1980s. The disposal methods then left much to be desired. Before 1872, much of New York City's garbage was just dumped in the East River. Even after that practice was stopped, most was disposed of by ocean dumping.

The municipal solid waste disposal problem today has been aggravated by changes in environmental regulations. Ocean dumping has been sharply curtailed. Open burning of trash and yard waste is no longer permitted in most communities. The small-scale incinerators that used to be a common feature in apartment buildings have been shut down. Open refuse dumps are no longer permitted. Sanitary landfill regulations have been tightened in a way that reduces landfill capacity. As a result, there has been added pressure on landfills at a time when people are increasingly reluctant to have a landfill sited near them—a phenomenon known as NIMBY (not in my backyard).

People in the United States do generate more municipal solid waste per capita than do people in other developed countries. As Table 11–3 indicates, however, the United States generates only about 10 percent more than the United Kingdom. The United States is not the world leader in solid waste generation. For example, citizens of Mexico City generate about 20 percent more waste per person, mostly due to greater food waste. Frequently, places such as Mexico City and other developing countries are credited with far less solid waste generation. The problem is that many of those figures first count the entire population, but then examine only the municipal collection, which is typically restricted to a limited number of residential districts. The solid waste generated by those living outside of the municipal system is not included. When all sources are included, as is the case with the Mexico City figures, per capita generation in the developing world is higher than is commonly recognized.

Solid waste generated per capita is not the only way to look at the problem. To the extent that landfilling remains an important means of waste disposal, then the size of the country in relation to the waste generated is another important dimension. The right-hand column in Table 11–3 shows daily pounds of solid waste generated per square mile of area in the country. By this measure, the United States generates far less solid waste than do the other countries in the table. For example, while Japan generates about 37 percent less solid waste per person, it generates 167 percent more solid waste per square mile. Thus, the issue is not just solid waste generation, but the capacity for disposal.

To extend the international comparison further, consider Minnesota. Minnesota is about the same geographic size as the United Kingdom, but the United

TABLE 11–3   Daily Municipal Solid Waste Generation

	Pounds per Person	*Pounds per Square Mile*
United States (48)	3.5	696.5
Japan	2.2	1863.4
United Kingdom	3.2	1062.4
West Germany	2.6	1695.2

Source: Authors' calculations based on data found in Judd H. Alexandar, *In Defense of Garbage* (Westport, CT: Praeger, 1993) p. 9

Kingdom has 14 times as many people. Despite the greater population in the same size area, the United Kingdom has less difficulty in disposing of solid waste. In the United Kingdom, the volume of waste to be disposed of is less than the volume of minerals extracted in mining operations, and the old mines are used for waste disposal. Minnesota is also a mining state, and the iron ore taken from the Hibbing area alone is more than 10 times the tonnage of all of Minnesota's solid waste generated since statehood. Indeed, in the United States, we extract six times more coal and thirteen times more gravel than we generate solid waste. In principle, we could use the same approach as in the United Kingdom and put our solid waste in old mines without coming near to using up all of these mines.

On a national basis, solid waste disposal problems do not appear as severe as they often do at local levels. In the United States, a single area 20 miles by 20 miles and 100 feet deep would hold all of the solid waste expected to be generated in the Unites States for the next 500 years. In the United Kingdom, the area devoted to landfills is only 1 percent of the area devoted to parking lots. Although it might appear that on a national level there would be ample disposal space, however, at the regional or local level the situation can often be quite different. Overall, the United States has a population density of 80 persons per square mile. In the mid-Atlantic region, however, the population density is 381 persons per square mile, and in New England, it is 199. Finding sites for sanitary landfills is clearly more difficult in these regions. In other regions, geological features can pose problems. In Florida, for example, high water tables make burying solid waste difficult.

One of the problems in assessing the solid waste disposal problems both in the United States and elsewhere is that it is difficult to get good information. There is no national source of consistent information. The first government estimate of solid waste disposal concluded that we disposed of 20 percent more paper annually than the combined amount that we produced and imported. That estimate was based on an extrapolation from a small sample, as are most current estimates. Such extrapolation can be difficult, particularly when different people are using slightly different definitions. It is important, for example, to distinguish between solid waste that is *generated* and that which is *discarded*. The generated category includes material that is recycled, whereas discarded does not. Nearly half of corrugated paper boxes are recycled, as are high proportions of aluminum. The media frequently quote the larger generated numbers as if they were discarded numbers. As a result, it is easy to get a misleading impression, particularly about packaging.

It can also be easy to draw seemingly logical but incorrect conclusions. Why does the United States produce more solid waste per capita than most other countries? Part of the reason is the higher standard of living in the United States. Our per capita GDP exceeds that for the European Community, Japan, and the former Soviet Union. From that, one might be tempted to conclude that within the United States, affluence is part of the problem and that high income households discarded more than low income households. In fact, within the United States, there is little difference by household based on income. Poor households are found to discard about as much as rich households. It is certainly true that the poor spend less on goods, but because of low income they tend to buy less durable goods that are more frequently disposed of. The rich discard more reading material and more yard waste (because they are more likely to have yards) than the poor.

Table 11–4 summarizes the contents of municipal solid waste in the United States. The top portion of the table breaks down municipal solid waste in terms of

TABLE 11–4   Contents of Municipal Solid Waste

Materials	Share
Paper and paperboard	34%
Yard wastes	20%
Food wastes	9%
Plastics	9%
Metals	8%
Glass	7%
Rubber, leather, textiles	5%
Wood	4%
Miscellaneous inorganic wastes	2%

Products	Share
Yard wastes	20%
Communications papers	15%
Durable goods	15%
Other nondurables	13%
Bottles and containers	10%
Food wastes	9%
Other packaging	9%
Shipping boxes	8%
Miscellaneous inorganic wastes	2%

Source: Based on data contained in Environmental Protection Agency, *Characterization of Municipal Solid Waste in the United States: 1990 Update.* Washington, D.C.: 1990.

materials, and the bottom shows the breakdown in terms of the products. These figures are based on weight. A better measure in terms of the landfill disposal burden would probably be compressed volume, but such measures are not available. In general, manufactured products tend to take up a larger share by volume than by weight, whereas food and yard wastes tend to take up less volume than suggested by weight. Containers and packaging make up about the same share by either weight or volume.

The top portion of the table shows the striking feature of the shares of paper and yard waste. Before the mid-1960s, much yard waste was disposed of by backyard burning. Then federal legislation prohibited the practice, and cities had the incentive to curtail burning to meet the Clear Air Act requirements. As a result, cities started picking up yard waste and landfilling it. Recently, some communities have addressed the yard waste portion of the solid waste stream by separating yard waste and composting it. Paper remains a large problem in all of these communities. It is also striking how little solid waste is plastic. The media have often portrayed discarded plastic as a major contributor to landfills, but it is far less important than paper products. Look next at the bottom portion of the table. Durable goods include major appliances, furniture, tires, car batteries. Nondurable goods include paper towels and plates, clothing, razors, and pens. In addition to these materials and products, most municipal landfills also accept construction and demolition debris. Indeed, these materials often make up as much as 21 percent of the material in landfills even though they are typically not part of municipally collected solid waste.

Table 11–5 shows how municipal solid waste discards have been changing throughout the 1970s and 1980s. During that period, U.S. population grew by 21 percent while municipal solid waste discards grew by 38 percent. The growth in these discards was not uniform. Food, yard waste, and containers and packaging grew more slowly than average, thereby decreasing their share of municipal solid waste. Reading materials, office and other paper, durable goods, and clothing and footwear grew more rapidly than average, thereby increasing their share.

Much of the growth in municipal solid waste has been in disposable products. Many question the necessity for such products and wonder whether consumers are likely to change their habits and return to reusable products. Consumer habits may change for some products, but many disposable products offer consumers more than simply convenience. Paper napkins, for example, are more energy efficient than reusable cloth napkins. The energy to produce and launder a cloth napkin over its life exceeds the energy to produce, distribute, and dispose of a corresponding amount of paper napkins by 40 percent. Disposable cups, plates, and flatware can offer considerable sanitation advantages over their reusable counterparts. A study of 21 facilities including restaurants, hospitals, nursing homes, motels, and school cafeterias found that reusable utensils had an average of 410 organisms per unit, whereas disposable utensils had an average of only 2 organisms. *Eschericia coli* bacteria were found at seven of the locations using reusable utensils.

Fast-food restaurants often come under considerable fire for the waste they generate. The U.S. population consumes 40 percent of meals away from home. At McDonald's, only 17 percent of waste is over the counter—that is, handed to customers. Another 4 percent of waste is newspapers that customers bring to the restaurant and leave there. The remainder is associated with the food as it is delivered, which is not packaged much differently from food delivered to grocery stores. Indeed, the average home-cooked meal generates more waste per person than a meal at McDonald's.

Foam plastic coffee cups are another product frequently cited as wasteful and environmentally unfriendly. Some critics argue that they should be phased out to avoid the release of CFCs into the atmosphere. A closer look reveals that while polyethylene plastic foam often used CFCs in production, plastic coffee cups are

TABLE 11–5 Population and Municipal Solid Waste, 1970–1988

	Percentage Growth: 1970–1988
Population	21%
Municipal solid waste discards	38%
Selected components:	
Food, yard, and miscellaneous inorganic	24%
Reading materials	44%
Durable goods	62%
Office and other paper	87%
Clothing and footwear	60%
Miscellaneous nondurable	475%
Containers and packaging	9%

Source: Based on data found in Judd H. Alexander, *In Defense of Garbage* (Westport, CT: Praeger, 1993) p. 18.

made of polystyrene and use pentane rather than CFCs. The pentane used in polystyrene foam production is recovered for use as fuel. These cups generate virtually no scrap in production and, because they are thermoplastic, can be remelted and recycled. At this point, they are not generally recycled because it is too costly to collect and separate them. Compared to paper cups, foam cups weigh only half as much, thereby reducing transportation cost to the landfill. When compacted in a landfill, they take up no more volume than paper cups and, because the plastic is inert, produce neither leachate nor air emissions in landfills. They are also cheaper than paper cups. Compared to reusable ceramic cups, plastic cups actually do less environmental damage than if the ceramic cups are washed after each use because the detergents and surfactants used to wash ceramic cups can cause water pollution problems. Sometimes with environmental problems, a closer look can reveal some surprises.

Another target of those concerned with solid waste is disposable diapers. These diapers, which end up in landfills, are used for 85 percent of infants in the United States and in over 90 percent of hospital maternity wards. Some communities have gone so far as to ban their disposal in landfills. Critics point out that a disposable diaper costs more per diaper than the cost of using a cloth diaper. However, cloth diaper users often put double diapers on an infant; thus they use an average of 79 percent more diapers so that cloth diapers are more costly overall. In addition, disposable diapers use half the energy, create half the air pollution, and create one-seventh the water pollution of cloth diapers. While they do end up in landfills, disposable diapers create only half the municipal solid waste of cat litter, yet there are few, if any, calls to ban cat litter. The point of this discussion is not to promote plastic cups or disposable diapers but to show that many public perceptions about environmental problems do not stand up under close scrutiny.

Packaging in general comes under close scrutiny in the solid waste stream, and many municipalities have developed ordinances to reduce the volume of packaging that enters landfills. Much packaging is already recycled. Over half of corrugated boxes are recycled, and about 80 percent of wooden pallets are reused. Overall, food and beverage packaging is responsible for about 59 percent of the packaging discarded into municipal solid waste. Most of the function of this packaging is to reduce damage and spoilage. Much of the packaging is never seen by the consumer but is used to transport the material to the retail site. Table 11–6

TABLE 11–6   Food and Beverage Share of Packaging Discards

Package	Total Discards (Million Tons)	Food and Beverage Share
Glass containers	9.9	98%
Steel	2.4	90%
Aluminum	1	98%
Shipping boxes	12.6	35%
Other paper packaging	9.3	46%
Plastic	5.5	63%
Wood	2.1	21%
Miscellaneous	0.2	15%

Source: Based on data found in Judd N. Alexander, *In Defense of Garbage* (Westport, CT: Praeger, 1993) pp. 66–67.

shows the volume of various categories of packaging discards and the food and beverage packaging share. For glass, steel, aluminum, and plastic, food and beverage accounts for well over half. One impact of sophisticated packaging is that this country devotes the lowest share of private consumption expenditures on food and beverages of any country in the world. Table 11–7 shows the share for several selected countries. There are other factors at work in these figures—notably income—but packaging is an important contribution. Part of that contribution is the low proportion of food spoiled in commerce, as indicated in Table 11–8. Spoilage is dramatically less in the United States than in the former Soviet Union or in India, for example.

Federal Legislation for the Control of Solid Waste

Federal concern with solid waste originated with the Rivers and Harbors Act of 1899, which was the first attempt to control the dumping of refuse into surface waters. Section 13 was called the Refuse Act and prohibited discharge of solid refuse into navigable waters. The focus was to prevent interference with shipping rather than water quality, and these provisions had little impact on water quality at the time. This law was reinterpreted in the 1950s and 1960s as part of initial attempts to control some types of water pollution.

The first legislation that specifically recognized the role of solid waste in pollution was the 1965 amendments to the 1963 Clean Air Act, which became known as the Solid Waste Disposal Act of 1965. This legislation was the result of a 1964 congressional committee investigation where the concern was open burning at dumps, backyard burning of yard wastes, and low technology incinerators often found in apartment buildings. At the time, air pollution was the primary problem associated with solid waste. The act called for research to develop methods to avoid environmental contamination and began a series of surveys to develop a base of knowledge about the nature and magnitude of the problem. These surveys led to recognition both of a large potential for recovery and reuse of discarded material and of a problem with the disposal of toxic chemicals. The 1965 act was extended in the Resource Recovery Act of 1970, which was designed to foster the development of techniques for the reuse of waste material.

In 1976, Congress passed the Resource Conservation and Recovery Act (RCRA). Until this point, the federal approach had involved minimal intervention with waste management practices. RCRA took a more aggressive approach by initiating separation of hazardous waste from nonhazardous waste. RCRA also included a directive to close all open dumps and broadened the definitions of solid

TABLE 11–7   Food and Beverage Expenditures as a Percentage of Total Private Consumption

United States	12%
Japan	21%
Western Europe	23%
Former Soviet Union	38%
India	56%

Source: Based on data found in *Statistical Abstract of the United States, 1991.*

TABLE 11–8   Percentage of Food Spoilage in Commerce

United States	17%
Former Soviet Union	50%
India	70%

Source: Judd H. Alexander, *In Defense of Garbage* (Westport, CT.: Praeger, 1993), p. 69.

waste and of disposal to bring more of the problem under its jurisdiction. The act was amended in 1984 to address hazardous wastes from households, to require monitoring for groundwater contamination, and to require corrective action for active disposal sites that do not meet current standards. The effect was not only to reduce the prospects of landfills creating environmental problems but also to increase the costs of building and operating landfills.

EPA's Comprehensive Approach to Solid Waste

The EPA has proposed a hierarchical approach to solid waste disposal. The preferred solution is source reduction: generate less material that must be disposed of. The next preferred approach is recycling, followed by incineration, and last by landfill. Approaches that rank higher are always to be preferred to those that rank lower. Let's examine each of these approaches in turn to see if these preferences always hold.

Source Reduction

Source reduction means reducing the materials that must be discarded, with particular emphasis on reducing the use of toxic materials that can pose particular disposal problems. Source reduction techniques include producing or buying goods that last longer, reusing products instead of discarding them, using and discarding less material in production, and simply buying fewer goods.

By some measures, we have made some progress in source reduction in recent years. Between 1970 and 1988, solid waste discards of manufactured materials increased 43 percent. However, during the same period, real (inflation-adjusted) personal expenditures on goods increased 68 percent, and real personal consumption expenditures on services increased 86 percent. By these measures, it sounds as if we have been doing source reduction without even knowing it. The underlying reason is that source reduction is a natural by-product of economic competition. In a competitive market, there is an incentive to deliver the same product or service with less material and labor.

As long as source reduction is part of the natural drive for economic efficiency, it carries with it considerable benefits. When additional source reduction is mandated by law or regulation, however, several dangers emerge. The risk in regulating source reduction is in imposing the preferences of the regulators on the regulated. The population will likely have more diverse lifestyles, preferences, tastes, and income than the regulators. Mandating source reduction can have the effect of restricting consumer choice. The question is who decides which choices are restricted and in what ways. One person's frivolous luxury may be another person's necessity. Carried to an extreme, source reduction can mean fewer goods available to consumers, fewer conveniences, and fewer jobs. We thus need to avoid cures that are worse than the diseases. Note that recessions have been very effective means of source reduction.

Recycling

Recycling, which includes composting, is sending discarded materials to secondary markets rather than to municipal disposal sites. Composting is using aerobic (oxygen-using) bacteria to decompose organic waste. Large-scale municipal composting is used increasingly for lawn and yard waste. Composting requires separation of noncompostable materials, but can produce a valuable soil additive and conditioner. These resulting materials, however, are relatively low in nutrients and thus may not be useful for large-scale farming.

Composting may have fairly limited large-scale applicability, but recycling programs have spread throughout the United States and elsewhere in the world. Seattle is often cited by recycling proponents as a model to be emulated.[15] Seattle has curbside recycling at 170,000 homes. In 1992, however, the company that collected recycled glass in Seattle had a 6,000-ton surplus they could not sell. No one in the Seattle area wanted to buy it, and the transportation costs were too high to ship it anywhere else. Is this an aberration, or do some more basic questions about recycling need to be examined?

Let us look first at two propositions frequently put forward by recycling proponents. The first is that recycling is essential because landfill space is growing scarce. It is certainly true that in many parts of the country old landfills have been closing more rapidly than new ones have been opening. The perception we're running out of landfill space isn't true. The new dumps that have opened have been larger than the ones that have closed, so the country has more active dump space than ever before. The landfill crisis was popularized by the wandering garbage barge in 1987, which went up and down the East Coast looking for a place to dump its garbage. Playing on that, the disposal industry's own trade association furthered the notion of a shortage, and as a result, landfills found that they could increase the rates they had been charging.

The second proposition put forth by recycling proponents is that throwing things out is wasteful, so recycling makes inherent economic sense. Throwing things out may indeed be wasteful, but recycling is anything but costless. Waste Management, Inc., says that it costs an average of $175 per ton to collect and sort recyclable material. A 1991 New Jersey study found some recycling programs cost as much as $200 per ton, far greater than the cost of putting the material in landfills. The sorted material can then be sold for $44, a price that has been steadily declining since the late 1980s. Collection centers in the Midwest and Northeast have been buried in old newspapers, green wine and beer bottles, and plastic milk jugs that no one seems to want.

These sorts of cost figures suggest that recycling programs are poorly conceived and should be abandoned, but such a conclusion would be premature. Part of the problem faced by recycling programs is that recycled material has to compete with virgin material on the basis of price. If virgin materials are underpriced, then they may have an unfair advantage. Many virgin materials probably are underpriced. Logging, for example, can damage or destroy forest ecosystems and create severe erosion that harms streams and rivers. Making paper from trees can result in both water and air pollution. Mining can leave extensive damage on the surface, and producing metal from ore can also result in air and water pollution. If these environmental costs are not borne by the producers of virgin material and therefore reflected in the price, then virgin materials may have too low a price from society's viewpoint. It would be unfair to expect recycled materials to compete with these environmentally subsidized virgin material prices. In addition, these figures reflect all recycled materials. It may well be the case that some materials can be recycled profitably without public subsidy.

To examine recycling, first consider what recycling processors want. First, they need dependable, long-term supplies so that they can strike and fulfill long-term contracts with users of recycled material. Second, they need clean, contaminant-free material so that they can assure consistent quality to users. Finally, they would prefer a fairly homogeneous stream of materials so that their sorting and processing costs are kept low. One implication of these needs is that recycling would be easier for industry than for households because the waste streams are likely to be much more homogeneous. A second implication is that recycling would be easier in large population centers than in small ones. Large population centers provide a larger and more dependable supply of recyclable materials and a greater likelihood that customers for recycled materials are available locally, thereby keeping transportation costs down.

Recycling is further encouraged by a willingness of households to sort materials and place them in separate containers for curbside collection at no cost. The preference shown by governments, some businesses, and some consumers for recycled material, even when it is of inferior quality and more costly, also encourages recycling. Whether this preference will stand up over time, particularly among governments faced with increasing budget pressure, is open to question. Finally, rising costs of solid waste disposal make recycling a more attractive alternative because of the savings in tipping fees.[16]

The economic attractiveness of recycling depends on three main factors: technology, labor costs, and materials costs. The role of technology can be illustrated by considering environmental concerns in the early 1970s about abandoned cars. During that period, it generally cost consumers money to have their cars disposed of. To avoid these costs, many people simply abandoned their cars. At the time, many were concerned that we would soon be awash in abandoned junk cars. Two developments removed that concern. The first was the introduction of the electric arc steel furnace, the so-called mini-mills. This steelmaking technology used scrap steel to make new steel, whereas the previous technology had used only a small amount of scrap to supplement iron ore. The second development was the shredder that could shred cars to make separation of steel from the other materials easier. The result was that old car hulks could be profitably recycled into new steel and the concern about abandoned cars diminished.

Auto recycling had two important characteristics that are critical to the economics of recycling. The first was low collection costs because there was a large amount of steel per old car and because the steel could be easily separated from the other materials by shredding and magnetic separation. The second characteristic was that there was a strong demand for the final product, steel. Technology is not static, and the economics of auto recycling may be becoming less favorable. For one thing, the proportion of plastic in cars has increased from only about 2 percent in 1960 to about 12 percent now. That, coupled with auto downsizing, has meant that there is less steel per car and therefore less return for recycling. Second, it is now more expensive to handle the potentially dangerous wastes such as oil, gasoline, hydraulic fluid, and antifreeze that are found in cars. Thus, shredding has become more expensive. Perhaps in response to these changes, steel from electric arc furnaces, which had grown steadily as a percent of total steel from the mid-1960s to the mid-1980s, has been declining in importance in recent years.

Labor costs are another important factor in the economics of recycling. Until recently, recycling had shown a fairly steady downward trend because labor costs have risen faster than raw material costs. It has become cheaper to substitute the raw materials for the increasingly more expensive labor. At hospitals, rising labor costs lead to substituting disposable bedding for washing sheets. Returnable soft drink bottles are increasingly replaced by one-way plastic or glass bottles or aluminum cans. Moreover, virgin raw materials often have more consistent quality, easing production. Recycling has been made more attractive by the increasing costs of disposal that result from tighter environmental standards for landfills and incinerators. However, working conditions and labor standards at recycling plants have been largely overlooked. In general, sorting at such plants is done by low-paid or immigrant labor, and the work is dirty and often dangerous. If these conditions are not allowed to persist and labor standards rise, the cost of recycling will rise as well.

Recycling can be somewhat insulated from rising labor costs as long as consumers are willing to do much of the sorting of materials. The more consumers are willing to sort, the lower the sorting costs to processors. In one Japanese city, consumers sort their wastes into 32 different categories. In the United States, however, there is evidence that mandatory separation results in more contamination than voluntary separation, suggesting that there may be limits to how much sorting can be achieved. In addition, the greater the number of categories into which waste is sorted, the greater the collection expense for maintaining this separation until the material reaches the reprocessing center. Collection trucks with several separate compartments are more expensive both to buy and to operate than trucks with a single compartment. The difference is especially pronounced if the single-compartment truck compacts the waste as it is collected.

The economics of recycling are strongly affected by the materials costs of the principal competitor: virgin raw materials. Virgin raw materials prices often fluctuate. When they drop, prices for recycled material drop as well. In March 1993, for example, aluminum companies cut the used beverage can price by two cents per pound, a cut prompted by and mirroring the drop in the price of virgin aluminum. In 1988, 90 percent of the lead in car batteries was recycled, but the amount dropped to 80 percent the next year. The reason for the drop—a fall in the price of lead reduced the incentive to recycle. To the extent that virgin raw materials costs do not reflect their full social or environmental costs or are subsidized by government policies that encourage exploration and development, then recycled materials will suffer an unfair disadvantage. Partly because of dropping virgin raw materials prices and partly because a recent growth in recycling has increased the supply of recycled materials, the average price per ton for recycled materials has dropped 50 percent since 1988. Note that this figure is an average for all recycled materials; not all individual materials had the same fall in prices.

Clearly, a key factor in the economics of recycling is the market for recycled material. Recycling is pointless without a market because the material just ends up in a landfill, albeit perhaps a more distant one. The higher collection and processing costs are then wasted. Lack of a market is the current main constraint to recycling programs. Part of the reason is technology: most plants are geared more to processing virgin materials than to processing recycled materials. Most of the reason, though, is specific to the material being recycled. To understand recycling, we need to consider the characteristics of and markets for specific materials being recycled.

Aluminum.   Aluminum is the success story of recycling. In the United States, over 40 percent of all aluminum is recycled, and nearly two-thirds of aluminum beverage cans are recycled. Sweden uses a deposit system for aluminum cans, with the result that 70 percent are recycled. In the rest of Europe and in Japan, aluminum is not as widely used and recycling rates are lower. Recycling aluminum is attractive because making new aluminum from recycled aluminum requires only one-fifth the energy of making aluminum from bauxite ore. As a result, aluminum-recycling programs are profitable without government subsidy. Aluminum, however, makes up only about 1 percent of municipal solid waste by weight, so recycling programs have little impact on reducing the demands on landfills.

Paper.   An average American disposes of 540 pounds of old newspapers annually. It takes 150 acres of spruce and poplar just to provide the paper for a single edition of the Sunday *New York Times.* Not surprisingly, paper is a major component of landfills, and there is growing emphasis on recycling paper. But until recently, paper recycling had been declining. The percentage of paper recycled fell from 40 percent in 1945 to about 20 percent in the early 1980s. Paper comes in a wide variety of forms, and unfortunately newsprint, one of the largest components of municipal solid waste, has a very low recycled value. Germany has made recycling newsprint mandatory, and newsprint recycling has been growing in popularity in the United States. The result was a glut in the market for recycled paper and a collapse of prices. Increasingly, recycled newsprint has been sent to international markets. In 1970, the United States exported only about 3 percent of recovered waste paper, but by 1987, the figure had grown to 18 percent. Of these exports, 60 percent went to Taiwan, Mexico, and South Korea because these countries have a combination of low labor costs and relatively new and efficient paper mills for making recycled paper products. More recently, recycled newsprint has found new uses, such as using shredded newsprint for insulation, recycled newsprint prices have increased.

In addition to easing the load on municipal landfills, a common argument in favor of recycling paper is that by doing so, we can save both energy and trees. While such arguments are intuitively appealing, they do not always stand up to careful scrutiny. Both paper recycling and making virgin paper require energy. In the case of recycled paper, the energy comes mostly from fossil fuel. In the case of virgin paper, the energy comes from burning the by-products of the papermaking process. Indeed, many paper mills generate more energy than they use in production and sell surplus electricity to electric utilities. Thus, in terms of fossil fuel, making virgin paper requires less than recycled paper.

It is often cited that recycling a stack of newspaper only 3 feet high could save one living spruce or pine. Here again, while the argument may be correct, the situation is not as simple as it might at first appear. First, we need to put the notion of saving trees in context. In 1986, U.S. forests grew 27 billion cubic feet of wood. Of this, 16 billion cubic feet were harvested, and 4 billion cubic feet were lost to natural causes. Thus, U.S. forests experienced a net increase of 7 billion cubic feet in a single year. Overall, in 1987, the United States had 10 percent more forest land with 24 percent more cubic feet of wood than it had in 1952. Over the last half of the 1980s, an average of 5 million acres were planted with trees annually—an area about the size of Massachusetts. The concerns about logging on federal lands in the Pacific Northwest and about old growth forests are not fundamentally about paper. Federal lands account for about 20 percent of the annual forest products harvest, but that is harvested mostly for lumber rather than for paper. Indeed, nearly 70 percent of the wood pulp used for paper comes from the South. Pulp comes from the lowest-value timber—small or crooked trees or scrap from thinning commercial forests and from cottonwood. In the United States, the wood used for paper is grown much like a farm crop. Recycling paper may save trees, but these are trees that were planted for the purpose of making paper, not towering old-growth forests.

Plastics.   Plastics recycling is an industry that is still in its infancy. Technically, most plastics can be recycled, but only about 1 percent are currently recycled in the United States and hardly any are recycled in the United Kingdom. Plastics recycling has been started largely in response to public criticism and concern, and the underlying economics are unclear. It takes more energy to recycle plastics than to make plastics from virgin material, but energy conservation is not the only measure by which recycling programs should be judged. One problem is that plastics are light in weight and bulky so that collection costs are high.

A second problem is multi-resin plastics. In many applications, particularly food packaging, films of different plastics are bonded together to create a package suitable for the specific application. Separating these multi-resin plastics is very difficult, and considerable research is in progress to find ways to do this. Currently the most common use of recycled multi-resin plastics is to make plastic timber as a replacement for wood and other building material. Benches and picnic tables are often made from such material. In this application, recycled plastics are different from other recycled materials in that the recycled use is not a substitute for virgin material but a totally different application. Other plastics can be recycled to substitute for virgin material. Patagonia, the outdoor clothing supplier, pioneered selling some outdoor wear made largely from recycled plastic drink bottles as a substitute for virgin plastic and other suppliers have followed suit.

Glass.   Technically, glass can easily be recycled, but there are some practical difficulties. For one thing, glass is both heavy and bulky to ship. The bulk can be reduced by crushing the glass before shipment, but then neither the color purity nor the freedom from contaminants can be verified by the glass recycler receiving the shipment. Contaminants such as pieces of pottery can result in defective recycled products or in some cases can even damage the glass furnaces. Color purity is important because clear glass is worth between $45 and $60 per ton at the factory, but green glass has little or no value. Few furnaces in the United States are designed to take green glass, and because of foreign imports of beer and wine, more green glass is discarded here than is manufactured. An alternative is to use crushed old glass as a substitute for other materials, such as aggregate in paving material. In New York, for example, by mixing 20 percent glass with the other paving aggregate material, 38,000 tons of glass were used as paving aggregate in 1991.

The German Recycling Experience.   When the underlying economics do not result in recycling programs, one approach is for the government to mandate such programs. The most extensive government mandates are in Germany, where companies have a legal obligation to take back and recycle their products at the ends of the products' lives. The initial application of this legal obligation was started in 1991, for packaging. Manufacturers and packagers must pick up wrappings used in transport from retailers. They also have set up a dual collection system for household packaging. The packaging must be recycled, and incineration, even with energy recovery, is not considered recycling under the German program.

The costs of this program are borne both by consumers and by companies. Consumers must wash materials to be recycled and sort them into one of four bins. Heavy fines can be levied for placing materials in the wrong bins. Companies are charged a levy on each package. The package must be approved by the government, and approved packages carry a green spot. Retailers are reluctant to carry products without the green spot packaging because then the recycling burden falls on them. The overall costs of the program are high and amount to between $1.20 and $3.00 per individual plastic package. There is mounting pressure in Germany to apply similar programs to other goods, including automobiles. A similar but more modest program has been started in France and the European Commission announced a modest program to be phased in throughout Europe. The benefits of such a program are hard to assess. To be sure, pressure on landfills is reduced, but the cost to consumers in the form of higher prices and more obligations is high. The program also erects a substantial barrier to foreign companies wishing to do business in Germany. Thus, in an era of supposed opening of trade within Europe, Germany has managed to provide substantial protection of its companies on environmental grounds.

Germany is not alone in intermingling environmental and trade protectionist policies. Denmark banned nonrefillable drink containers. The European Commission brought suit against Denmark in the European Court, charging that this policy was a barrier to free trade. The European Court ruled that such environmental policy could take precedence over free trade. After that ruling, Germany followed suit, and the effect was protection of small bottlers of beer and soft drinks in politically sensitive regions of Germany. Germany also put a mandatory deposit on plastic bottles, which crippled the market for mineral waters from France and Belgium. As these examples illustrate, environmental policies can have effects far beyond simply protecting the environment.

As a result of the mandatory recycling program, Germany is collecting much more material than it has the capacity to recycle within its borders. For example, Germany has the capacity to reprocess about 60,000 tons of plastic but expects to collect 200,000 tons. The result has been a flood of recyclable material sent abroad, often accompanied with payments to accept it. Unsubsidized recycling programs in the receiving countries have little chance of standing up against the subsidized material from Germany.

Incineration

EPA's third preferred method, behind source reduction and recycling, is incineration. It is preferred to using landfills because it is far less land intensive, an important consideration in areas with high population densities and high land costs. In a sense, incineration leads to much faster degradation than other methods, and EPA forecasts that incineration will increase its share of municipal solid waste disposal from 14 percent in 1988 to 23 percent in 1995.

It is important not to confuse modern incineration with the old open burning that was common before the mid-1960s. Incineration takes place at controlled high temperatures that remove atmospheric pollutants. The heat from incineration can be recovered and is often used to generate electricity. The resulting ash is usually disposed of in landfills, often specially constructed and dedicated for incinerator ash because it can contain toxic substances. Incineration, even with ash disposal, uses less land than landfills but is more expensive. Less separation is required than for recycling, but concerns remain about emissions if temperatures are not carefully controlled. Used batteries are a problem for incineration because they are a major source of heavy metals in the environment. Used automobile batteries are routinely recycled, but household batteries are not and most of them contain mercury. If included in a stream of waste destined for an incinerator, the mercury can create environmental problems. Rechargeable nickel-cadmium batteries are also a problem as they are often difficult to remove from appliances. Some toxic substances, such as PCBs, can be destroyed by incineration. Other toxics remain concentrated in the ash. Disposing of ash containing toxics has become an increasing impediment to incineration.

Landfill

EPA's least preferred method of disposal is to place municipal solid waste in a sanitary landfill. With growth in the other three disposal methods, EPA predicts the share of municipal solid waste placed in landfills will decrease from 73 percent in the late 1980s to 53 percent by 1995. A sanitary landfill is much different from the open dumps of past years. A landfill begins with a lining of either clay or thick, high-density polyethylene, depending on the surface soils. A concern with landfills is that liquids will leach out and contaminate groundwater, and the lining prevents that from happening. When waste is put in the landfill, it is compacted and periodically covered with a layer of soil. These layers prevent odors from escaping the landfill and keep it from attracting birds and animals. Thus a landfill is built up with alternating layers of compacted waste and soil. When the landfill is full, it is covered with an even thicker layer of soil. Because of this compacting and layering, closed landfills can be turned into parks, recreational facilities, or other uses. A drawback with landfills is that they require large land areas, which can be a problem in highly urbanized locales. If the subsoils are permeable, leachate can be a serious problem, and decomposition in landfills can produce methane. Landfill use varies widely, with between 70 and 90 percent of solid waste in the United States going to landfills whereas only about 20 percent of waste goes to landfills in Europe.

Pickup and Collection. Pickup and collection are the major cost components of solid waste management. On average, two-thirds of waste management cost is collection, and only one-third is disposal. In most communities, household solid waste collection is done on a weekly basis and is free. Of course, it is not really free, but it is paid for by taxes, usually local property taxes. But to consumers it appears to be free because it does not cost them any more in weeks when they put large quantities out for collection than in weeks when they put out small quantities. In economic terms, collection is provided to households at zero marginal cost. Thus, in these communities, households do not really face the costs of disposing of their solid waste. To change this situation, some communities have started charging households for each bag or can of waste they have collected. It is fairly common for communities that charge by the bag for waste disposal also to provide free collection of sorted recyclable material. Some communities also require that yard waste be disposed of separately so that it can be composed rather than placed in a landfill.

When households are faced with by-the-bag charges for waste disposal, their incentives change. Typically the volume of waste collected drops, partly because households dispose of less, partly because they have more incentive to recycle, and partly because they do more compacting themselves to get more in each bag. Separation of yard waste combined with charges for it both enables large-scale community composting and encourages more households to compost. All of these things can reduce landfill costs and extend the life of existing landfills.

Landfill Space. The concern about running out of landfill space in the United States needs to be kept in perspective. Landfills fill up and close all the time, and the concern about where new landfills will be located is not new. For each of the last four decades, 50 percent of the then existing landfills were due to close within five years. Although a landfill may appear large when one first sees it, in total, landfills do not take up much space. Landfills are typically constructed to be small and deep rather than large and shallow. A small, deep landfill has less rain falling on it than does a large, shallow one of similar capacity. Reducing the rainfall eases the leachate problem.

Furthermore, finding locations for landfills with suitable geology is not difficult. The concern is not a lack of suitable geological sites but the growth of the NIMBY syndrome. While siting may be more difficult in some areas than in the past, is it really impossible? Consider what has happened to tipping fees. In response to the federal environmental regulations that stopped disposal at open dumps, a large number of such dumps closed quickly. As a result, the supply of dump space dropped quickly while demand continued to increase. The saga of New York's wandering garbage barge heightened awareness of the problem. In response to these circumstances, tipping fees increased and, by 1991, averaged $64.76 in the Northeast and $40.75 in the Middle Atlantic states.

Since the summer of 1992, however, the trend has reversed. When Boston renewed its disposal contracts, it found that tipping fees had dropped by 40 percent. Philadelphia and Cleveland found fees dropped by 20 percent. The high prices of the late 1980s had provoked the usual response from the market. The cost of building and operating a landfill rarely amounts to more than $30 per ton. With tipping fees substantially above that, private waste management firms began to acquire land and get the necessary permits. The process took some time, but by 1992, additional facilities had begun to come on line, increasing the supply and causing tipping fees to fall.

SUMMARY

We are faced with a wide variety of environmental problems, only a few of which have been described in this chapter. Some problems are more serious than they appear at first glance, while others pose fewer threats than is widely believed. If progress is to be made in solving the most serious environmental problems, the first step is to abandon preconceived notions about the environment and examine each of these problems, as well as proposed solutions, as objectively as possible.

DISCUSSION QUESTIONS

1. Under the Clean Air Act, how are new sources of pollution treated in comparison with old sources of pollutioon? Why? What are the principal effluents that have been the fo-

cus of public policy concerns about air pollution? What have been the trends in each of these effluents both before and after the passage of the Clean Air Act?

2. Under the Federal Water Pollution Control Act (and its amendments), how does the National Pollutant Discharge Elimination System (NPDES) work and what does it accomplish? What have been the trends in water quality following passage of the Federal Water Pollution Control Act?

3. Evaluate the accuracy of each of these statements. Your evaluation should be based on specific evidence and empirical data rather than on broad generalizations.

   "Recycling is essential because dump space is growing scarce"
   "Throwing things out is wasteful, so recycling makes inherent economic sense."

4. What are the four principal issues around which the debate on global warming seems to center? What is the evidence on each of these issues?

SUGGESTED READINGS

Frances Cairncross, *Costing the Earth* (Boston: Harvard Business School Press, 1993).
Robert Dorfman and Nancy S. Dorfman, editors, *Economics of the Environment: Selected Readings* (New York: W.W. Norton: 1993).
Kent E. Portney, *Controversial Issues in Environmental Policy* (Newbury Park: Sage, 1992).
Theodore D. Goldfarb, *Taking Sides: Clashing Views on Controversial Environmental Issues* (Guilford, Connecticut: The Dushkin Publishing Group, Inc., 1991).
S. Fred Singer, "Environmental Strategies with Uncertain Science," *Regulation,* Winter 1990, pages 65–71.

NOTES

1. Peter Brinblecombe, *The Big Smoke* (New York: Methuen & Co., 1987), 3.
2. Brinblecombe, 1987, 9.
3. A. R. Meethan, *Atmospheric Pollution: Its History, Origins and Prevention* (New York: Pergamon, 1981), 3.
4. Christopher Hamlin, *What Becomes of Pollution?* (New York: Garland, 1987) 15.
5. Hannah Bradby (ed.), *Dirty Words: Writings on the History and Culture of Pollution* (Earthscan, 1990), 52.
6. Joseph Alcamo, "Emergency Care Needed in Central and Eastern Europe," *Environment* 34, no. 3 (1992): 44.
7. Hillary F. French, "Eastern Europe's Clean Break with the Past," *Worldwatch,* March–April 1991, 23.
8. French, 1991, 23.
9. Hillary F. French, "Industrial Wasteland," *Worldwatch,* November–December 1988, 22.
10. French, 1988, 41.
11. French, 1988, 46.
12. French, 1988, 45.
13. Alcamo, 1992, 44.
14. Oliver S. Owen, *Natural Resource Conservation: An Ecological Approach* (New York: Macmillan, 1985) chap. 15.
15. Lester R. Brown, *State of the World 1991* (New York: W.W. Norton & Company, 1991) p. 51. Brown, in talking about recycling says, "Perhaps the best known and most successful program is in Seattle."
16. *Tipping fee* is the term used in the solid waste industry for the fee charged by landfills to those who dispose of their waste there. Tipping fees are usually stated in terms of cost per ton of waste.

12

Crime and Punishment in the United States

Crime and punishment: the stuff of tabloids, TV news, and sensationalist journalism. As a topic of general conversation, crime "sells." Indeed, the more lurid and bizarre the story, the easier it is to feed public curiosity and anger. The result can be loss of clarity at precisely the time that it is most needed. Penetrating the smokescreen of hype and hysteria in media reporting is difficult. In view of current levels of public anger over either perceived or actual upturns in crimes against people and property, how can sensible people sort through the truth of the crime and punishment problem in the United States?

A beginning is to recognize that the criminal justice business is now booming. Fed by media coverage of sometimes glamorous crimes of violence—often involving guns—and a growing sophistication of organized criminals supplied with the proceeds from the drug trade, the criminal justice business has become big business on both sides of the law. Police forces now appear understaffed but growing. Courts and prosecutors are busy, the prisons are full. Indeed, a massive prison building effort at all levels of government has now managed to imprison 1.4 million persons, the largest *proportion* of a nation's population kept behind bars in the world. Public policy threatens to expand the prison business even further with new "get tough on crime" laws—such as the "three-strikes-and-you're-out" proposal, which mandates life sentences for three-time felons—and expanded funding for federal prisons and state and local prison construction and maintenance.

A large crime-fighting industry has arisen, offering a dazzling array of smart weapons, futuristic vehicles, and assorted gadgets.[1] The development of criminal justice technology is sustained by the scramble to convert the military-industrial complex to peacetime conditions. Thus, the marketplace now offers "smart guns" that fire only for the owner, "smart cars" that hook computers to police mainframe computers in order to allow speedy booking of prisoners and other rapid exchanges of information, ultra high tech listening devices, noninjurious, incapacitating foams to be sprayed on threatening suspects, and retractable spiked barrier strips to be unfurled around fleeing vehicles. The list is nearly endless and growing.

Beyond the hyperbole, a serious and nonsensational puzzle confronts all civilized societies. Survival of civility and public order requires peaceful and lawful behavior by citizens in two respects: on the *civil side*, in the manner in which citizens interact with respect to commerce, contracts, understandings, and general dealings; on the *criminal side*, in the extent to which physical or material injury violates a moral code for which punishment is lawfully meted out to the guilty. The two puzzles apply as much to international communities and nations as to states and communities, although our concern here is with behavior *within* societies rather than *between* societies.

Of the two problems, crime represents a particular threat because criminal acts go beyond inflicting inappropriate costs and risks on other members of society. Crime destroys society. At its root, unchecked crime threatens the existence of civilized society by destroying the code by which all agree to live. Thus, failure to convict and punish the guilty is not only offensive to victims, criminal justice failure undermines the capacity of law to keep the promise of a rule of law. In short, an unpunished infraction means two infractions.[2] Absent law and order, life in any society threatens to become, in the words of the 17th-century English philosopher Thomas Hobbes, "Nasty, brutish and short." Policy analyst James Q. Wilson puts the same idea in a more modern context:

> Predatory crime does not merely victimize individuals, it impedes and, in the extreme case, even prevents the formation and maintenance of community. By disrupting the delicate nexus of ties, formal and informal, by which we are linked with our neighbors, crime atomizes society and makes of its members mere individual calculators estimating their own advantage, especially their own chances for survival amidst their fellows.[3]

How does society respond when the criminal code is broken? Civilized society must find the nerve and the means to deal with criminal activity that, in its definition, is not civilized and lies outside the rule of law. Thus, society must have a means by which behavior can be called to account, grievances redressed, and if necessary, punishment meted out. Criminal *justice* systems, then, are comprised of police, prosecutors, criminal courts, and prisons whose jobs are to prevent and deter crime, process allegations of criminality, and punish the criminal who is apprehended, tried, and convicted.

Although just punishment of criminal behavior seems a theoretically clear goal, the production of criminal justice is, in fact, made difficult by two classes of problems. One class is the conviction issue, whereby a person formally charged with having committed a crime—that is, arraigned by a court to answer an indictment—is found to have been either guilty or innocent. The second is the sentencing issue and concerns the application of punishment to convicted transgressors. Both issues involve high stakes judgments in circumstances where the protagonists have enormous incentives to misrepresent the "truth" and thus mislead the processing of criminal cases.

With respect to the conviction issue, two types of errors can occur. One is the *type I error*—the false positive—in which innocent people are wrongfully punished. The 1993 Oscar-winning movie, *In the Name of the Father,* serves as only one vivid reminder of how painful and unjust are mistaken convictions of innocent people. One study of the prospects for capital punishment's being inflicted on innocent people since 1900 found 250 errors in an examination of capital or potential capital cases punishable by death of which 23 were erroneously executed.[4] Moreover, the cases of erroneous execution were distributed throughout the 20th century and not concentrated in the earlier part of a crime-ridden century as some might suspect.

Current public discussion focuses on the case of Barry Lee Fairchild, an African American convicted in the 1983 rape and murder of Marjore "Greta" Mason.[5] Since August of 1983, Fairchild has been waiting on death row in an Arkansas penitentiary for the outcome of a continuous appeals process reviewing arguments on his behalf that his wrongful conviction was based on shaky evidence and coerced testimony. At this writing, Mr. Fairchild continues to wait for the outcome of the appellate process and is beginning to conclude that, if he is ultimately going to die in prison, he might as well get it over with rather than languish in jail for the rest of his life.

A second mistake is the *type II error*, the false negative, in which guilty people escape conviction and therefore punishment. There are many ways for type II mistakes to be made, including: the absence of the so-called "smoking gun" that clearly establishes guilt; confusion about the intent of the perpetrator, from which can be established the severity of the crime (e.g., Was the murder cold-blooded and premeditated or an unintentional crime of passion?); and the simple requirement that the burden of proof "beyond a reasonable doubt" falls on the plaintiff, which can raise the legal bar to conviction high enough that the prosecution cannot clear the hurdle and must allow guilty persons to escape a just conviction. Yet victims and policy makers have a clear interest in reducing the chance of a type II error brought about in cases where guilty persons are not charged for crimes committed and, if charged, are not convicted for the full severity of the crime.

A second broad goal of criminal justice systems is to match punishment to the crime committed. In the United States, the constitutional injunction (Eighth Amendment) proscribes "cruel and unusual punishment," but it does not say what might constitute proper punishment. A lighthearted formulation of the problem is presented in the Gilbert and Sullivan musical *The Mikado*, where a "humane" emperor—a bemused Mikado—punctuates his description of his Victorian philosophy with paroxyms of giggling:

> My object all sublime
> I shall achieve in time—
> To let the punishment fit the crime,
> The punishment fit the crime;
> And make each prisoner sent
> Unwillingly represent
> A source of innocent merriment,
> Of innocent merriment.
> All prosy dull society sinners,
> Who chatter and bleat and bore,
> Are sent to hear sermons
> From mystical Germans
> Who preach from ten till four.
> The amateur tenor, whose vocal villainies
> All desire to shirk,

Shall, during off-hours,
Exhibit his powers
To Madame Tussaud's waxwork.

How does society make punishment fit the crime? Mistakes can be made here as well. A punishment too great can be cruel and unusual, while one that is too light is both offensive to the victims and potentially of little use in deterring future crime. Readers can develop their own lists of crimes for which appropriate remedies and punishments might be debated simply to test the difficulty of assigning punishment even in cases where guilt is presumed known and certain. A sampling might include the following:

Premeditated murder	Rape by an acquaintance
Manslaughter	Grand larceny
Aggravated assault	Drug dealing
Car theft	Embezzlement
Bicycle theft	Credit card fraud
Robbery	Tax fraud
	Blowing up a federal building

The list can be extended simply to illustrate the further complexities for which systems of punishment must be developed. For example, discussion of punishment is often swayed by circumstances, such as whether the crime was an emotional response to an earlier incident, or whether the judged intent, the cumulative record, and the age of criminal merit special consideration.

THE GENERAL PROBLEM

The crime and punishment problem can be generally defined as a search for justice where the goal is that the guilty are caught, tried, convicted, and sent to an appropriate punishment, while the innocent are either undisturbed or quickly discharged from unjust custody. Although easy to define, the goal is difficult to achieve in practical terms. The essence of the problem involves two components: the *perpetrator*, who commits a crime, and the *victim*—consisting of an individual, a group, or society at large—who is criminally injured by the perpetrator in violation of laws against homocide, robbery, theft, and other forms of mayhem. Motives can establish an intent to commit crime, but the question of thoughts, speech, and motives is secondary to the fundamental fact that *unlawful behavior* is at issue and not thought or expression (for which the First Amendment to the Constitution serves as a bulwark).

All criminal justice systems operate on a basic logic: for law and public policy to worry about crime, there must be an official complaint charging criminal behavior. The standard is the criminal code that represents society's moral judgments about proper and improper behavior. Thus, murder, robbery, and theft are simple and obvious cases found in the criminal codes of all societies. On the other hand, spitting on the streets and use of soft drugs have different standings in different societies. Spitting, for example, is subject to fine and imprisonment in places such as Singapore, but not in other countries. The Netherlands has deliberately decriminalized soft drugs, such as marijuana, as a strategy simultaneously to keep track of drug use and to remove profits from the drug trade.

On the basis of the complaint, a plaintiff's claims are tested against the claims of the alleged perpetrator (i.e., the defendant) in order to determine whether charges should be brought and, if brought, whether there is basis for trial, and, if tried, whether conviction is justified, and what the appropriate sentence might be. Theoretically, the battle over guilt or innocence is fought in an adversarial arena in which the rules of the courtroom prevail: representatives of the accusers and representatives of the defendants test the strength of the charge and the prosecution on the presumption that the stronger argument and the right side will win in an arena in which fair rules of procedure and evidence prevail. This is sometimes referred to as the *fight theory* of justice.

Thus, the heart of the crime and punishment problem is revealed. Society decrees that convicted offenses be punished. Punishment is meted out, however, not for reasons of vengeance or denunciation—both emotional reasons—but because retributive punishment is a "penalty imposed in fulfillment of a legal requirement that it should be imposed on those who have infringed a rule."[6] In short, for the law to be effective its promises must be kept.

A corollary implication is also clear: without formal complaint or corpses whose death is suspicious, knowledge about the existence of crime is shaky. Thus, all crime data are suspect in the sense that most crime data measure *official* actions. But whether little *reported* crime implies the absence of a criminal justice problem is not clear. Crime-ridden societies can find it inconvenient to report true crime levels; alternatively, they may even decriminalize activities—drug use, for instance—considered obnoxious and offensive in other societies. Moreover, victims can find themselves in situations—such as in cases of rape, physical abuse, and organized crime—where they are unwilling to report crimes and charge perpetrators whom they may know intimately. Thus, it is possible for low rates of crime to be reported for societies that are, in fact, crime ridden.

Nor is it difficult, in contrast, to envision the presence of large amounts of reported crime derived from a basically lawful society as seen, for example, in societies where citizens are secure about reporting their complaints to the police and demanding service, namely that perpetrators be charged, tried, and, if convicted, punished. High-reporting societies therefore can appear statistically unruly even if other observers might conclude that general conditions of good will and civility predominate. We will shortly return to the question of drawing inferences from available crime data.

The Criminal Justice System

Complaints set the criminal justice machinery in motion, but three institutional processes—the police, the courts, and the prison system—make up the heart of what might be referred to as the criminal justice system. Police work involves crime prevention, investigating complaints, apprehending and detaining possible criminals, collecting evidence, and preserving the factual basis for prosecution, adjudication, and sentencing. The task of courts is to provide a fair decision arena and procedures to decide guilt or innocence and to adjudicate the conditions under which pleas of those accused will be bargained with prosecutors; in addition, courts interpret the law with respect to sentence, probation, and possible parole. Finally, the prison system executes the decisions of courts with respect to fines, punishment—even capital punishment—and parole.

Taken together, the elements of the criminal justice system influence, in part, the amount of original crime likely to occur in society and the likelihood that justice is achieved. As will be seen, however, the mistakes that can be made in criminal justice systems are not entirely independent but are linked to other parts of society. For example, what happens to justice if the court system becomes so clogged that full dockets prevent a speedy or impartial trial? Is justice served if the prisons are filled to capacity such that the incarceration of one more prisoner means necessarily that someone already in prison must be released? When and how can society avoid the two classes of errors in arriving at decisions about crime and punishment? For example, is it necessarily the case (as it would appear) that the avoidance of the type I error is achieved at the expense of a type II error?

Some Fundamental Issues

Clearly, many criminal justice decisions have already been made in advance of any specific crime being committed, for any society must think through its basic posture about how it will approach the question of crime and punishment. For example, some of the key U.S. concepts and constraints are clearly set forth in the Constitution. The most obvious constraint placed on the U.S. criminal justice system is the presumption of innocence given all citizens, where the burden of proving criminal behavior rests with prosecutors rather than with the defendant. The aim is to avoid a type I error: punishing innocent persons charged with a crime. Thus, a social choice has been made: society would rather endure the injustice of letting some guilty parties go free—the type II error—than to punish wrongly those who are innocent—the type I error. Not only would it appear difficult to avoid simultaneously both type I and type II errors, but U.S. criminal justice ethics are clearly tilted in favor of type II over type I.

A second constraint lies in safeguards placed on the accumulation and use of evidence. For example, the Fourth Amendment protects citizens from arbitrary "fishing expeditions" by police and prosecutors:

> The right of the people to be secure in their persons, houses, papers, and effects, against unreasonable searches and seizures . . . no Warrants shall issue, but upon probable cause, supported by Oath or affirmation, and particularly describing the place to be searched, and the persons or things to be seized.

But how far should public policy carry what has been known since 1914 as the exclusionary rule?[7] Does the exclusionary rule handcuff police and prosecutors and allow criminals to go free? Perhaps, as some observers argue, the rule does two things: first, it protects citizens from police misconduct and an overzealousness in clearing crime files; second, it actually improves police performance because misconduct is punished by denying police the reward of convicting guilty defendants and placing them behind bars.[8]

A third condition placed upon the criminal justice system consists of multiple safeguards to prevent the law from becoming capricious. For example, accused persons are entitled to the assistance of legal counsel for their defense (Sixth Amendment). But whether paupers were entitled to representation was decided only in 1963 in the celebrated case of *Gideon v. Wainright,* one of the most dramatic Supreme Court decisions on the civic right to legal representation.[9]

A fourth safeguard lies in the constitutional requirement for due process in the processing of judgments about guilt and innocence, as seen in the guarantee that accused persons cannot be required to testify against themselves. The Fifth Amendment sets the requirement as follows:

> No person shall be held to answer for a capital, or otherwise infamous crime, unless on a presentment or indictment of a Grand Jury . . . nor shall any person be subject for the same offence to be twice put in jeopardy of life or limb; nor shall be compelled in any criminal case to be a witness against himself, nor be deprived of life, liberty, or property, without due process of law.

Once again, controversy lurks. Must the police actively advise citizens of their Fifth Amendment rights, or are such rights to be regarded as tacitly understood? The Supreme Court has stepped into the discussion and defined current policy following its 1966 ruling in *Miranda v. Arizona*. In his majority opinion, Chief Justice Earl Warren concluded that the police must advise suspects of the Fifth Amendment protection against self-incrimination; and the result was the famous Miranda warning, which nearly every schoolchild can quote from memory:

> Prior to any questioning, the person must be warned that he has a right to remain silent, that any statement he does make may be used against him, and that he has a right to the presence of an attorney, either retained or appointed.

A fifth safeguard is that, under the Sixth Amendment, the nature of criminal proceedings is defined as follows:

> The accused shall enjoy the right to a speedy and public trial, by an impartial jury of the State and district wherein the crime shall have been committed, which district shall have been previously ascertained by law, and to be informed of the nature and cause of the accusation; to be confronted with the witnesses against him; to have compulsory process for obtaining witnesses in his favor, and to have the Assistance of Counsel for his defence.

Thus, there cannot be secret trials with secret information used to convict an accused person. Specifically, in the Anglo-Saxon fight theory, the court is an open arena in which each charge is publicly brought. The judge then presides over a public duel between prosecution and defense to determine beyond a reasonable doubt whether the accused person is guilty of a crime as charged.

Finally, limits are placed on punishment. Cruel and unusual punishment is proscribed by the Eighth Amendment, which also notes: "Excessive bail shall not be required, nor excessive fines imposed." In summary, then, the ideal criminal justice system consists of a logical, swift, and fair sorting through the criminal justice process and, in the end, produces justice in both judgment and punishment. Whether it can do so either in theory or in practice remains to be considered and is discussed below.

THE U.S. PROBLEM

Is the United States a crime-plagued society? If crime levels are too high, do we have justice? These questions are not entirely theoretical. Crime and the United States have been indissolubly linked in the global media and in the minds of many people who worry about crime and safety issues. Furthermore, there is some evidence that justice in the U.S. system has been hard to achieve.[10] Recent surveys tell part of the story.

Public Opinion Surveys

For all of the recent treatment of crime in the mass media, hard data that capture the extent to which the public actively worries about serious crime are not plentiful. Thus, polling organizations, such as the Gallup Polls, periodically sample public opinion about their fear of crime, but the results pertain to a cross-section of public opinion taken at a single time. One polling series—Gallup Polls—does sample public opinion over time about the extent to which people feel that crime is the most important public problem. The results, summarized in Figure 12–1, suggest that from 1980 until 1990 the proportion of the population who thought crime "is the most important problem" was relatively low, only between 1 and 6 percent.

From 1990 to the present, however, a decided upward trend in the extent of public worry about crime could be detected. As Figure 12–1 shows, those who thought that crime was the most important problem grew from 2 percent in 1990 to 6 percent in 1991 to 9 percent in 1993. The strong suspicion exists that the issue continues to grow in salience; evidence is found in some of the more recent telephone polls that ask respondents to rank problems facing the country. An example is the New York Times CBS News Poll that interviewed 1,146 adults nationwide from January 15 to 17, 1994; respondents cited the following problems as "the most important facing the country:"[11]

Crime and violence (19%)
Health care (15%)
Economy (14%)
Unemployment (12%)
Federal deficit (5%)
Welfare (2%)
War and peace (1%)

Comparison with other surveys is difficult because the basis for telephone sampling is not designed to be comparable with either Gallup or Harris Polls and those with "no opinion" were not included in the percentages.

The worry does not end with a reporting of general public opinion trends. Public concern has most recently focused on violent crimes concentrated among poor people in high-crime sections of cities where populations have mushroomed.[12] In essence, a population explosion fueled by immigrants and baby boomers has created enormous increases in the numbers of preschoolers and elementary school students now being crowded into underfunded and underserved schools and neighborhoods. Worrisome is a secure demographic prediction that the numbers of teenagers 15 to 19 years old will increase by nearly 25 percent overall and in some neighborhoods by as much as 50 percent.[13] Demographic shifts alone will have an enormous impact on crime policy.

The predicted consequences for the criminal justice system are potentially profound. As a rule, men between the ages of 18 and 24 are particularly likely to commit violent crimes compared to men over 25. Indeed, during the past decade, homicide rates for 14- to 17-year-olds have risen to twice the adult levels.[14] Crime—

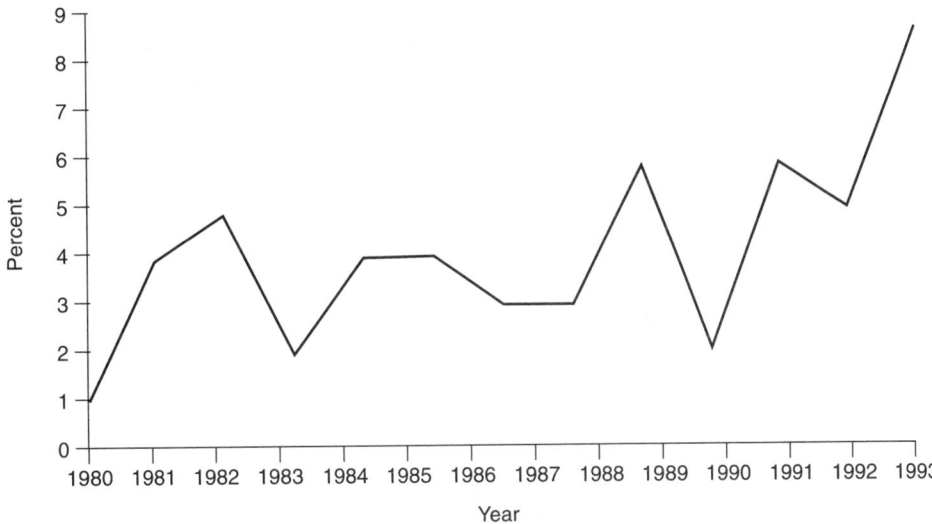

Figure 12–1   Percentage of Americans who think crime *is* the most important problem: 1980–1993

especially violent crime—is a young person's sport. Hence, the public worries about the effects of the approaching demographic tidal wave that will, over the next 10 years, fill in the spaces of urban areas most in need of services and most lacking in social programs. One midlevel administrator from an Upper Manhattan school district put the concern succinctly:

> All we need is 10 percent of those kids to grow up and decide it's all a crock and we've got a crime wave that will denude these communities of working and middle-class people. We're getting an overconcentration of much too young and much too educated people in one area where they can't do anything except tear each other apart.[15]

The policy implications of demographic change and crowding of the poor are profound. Whereas the bulk of public expenditures go to police and prisons, programs for children and teenagers are starved. Yet the logic of prevention would suggest that rather than spend $26 billion per year on police and prisons and only $2 billion on young people, the proportions should be reversed. Whether such a recommendation makes sense, however, depends on one's assessment of overall crime patterns.

Domestic Data on Crime

A review of the major felonies recorded by local police departments and reported to the Federal Bureau of Investigation (FBI), which reports summary statistics in the form of a Uniform Crime Report (UCR),[16] reveals that *reported crime* is booming! Conclusions are reached based on a reporting of felonies, which are serious crimes with mandatory incarceration in secure institutions upon conviction. Misdemeanors, by contrast, are misdeeds and minor offenses taking the form of nuisance crimes handled locally under low-security arrangements. The report of serious crimes forms a crime index aggregated from the following classification system:

Violent crime, crimes against people, including:

1. Murder: willful, felonious attempts on life
2. Forcible rape
3. Robbery: theft in which people are threatened
4. Aggravated assault: assaults intending to kill or inflict severe bodily injury

Property crime, including:

1. Buglary, especially breaking and entering crimes
2. Larceny, especially major theft
3. Motor vehicle theft

The UCR makes the United States appear to be a seething cauldron of crime for which more police, prisons, and courts are required simply to keep the system moving. Part of this is shown in Figure 12–2, which displays trends in major property crime. Thus, larceny and auto theft marched steadily up over the last 20 years, from nearly 2,100 and 454 thefts, respectively, per 100,000 inhabitants in 1970 to over 3,100 and 631 per 100,000 in 1992. Only the buglary rate moved up during the 1970s and then down during the 1980s, leaving a mystery about why the one countertrend existed. Is the burglar population aging and therefore less effective in its ability to vault fences and climb in and out of second-story windows? Have burglars moved on to more lucrative and violent crimes? Or is some other change under way only now dimly perceived and understood?

Trends in violent crimes against people parallel property crime trends, principally aggravated assault, robbery, forcible rape, and murder involving non-negli-

Figure 12–2   Index of reported property crime: 1970–1992

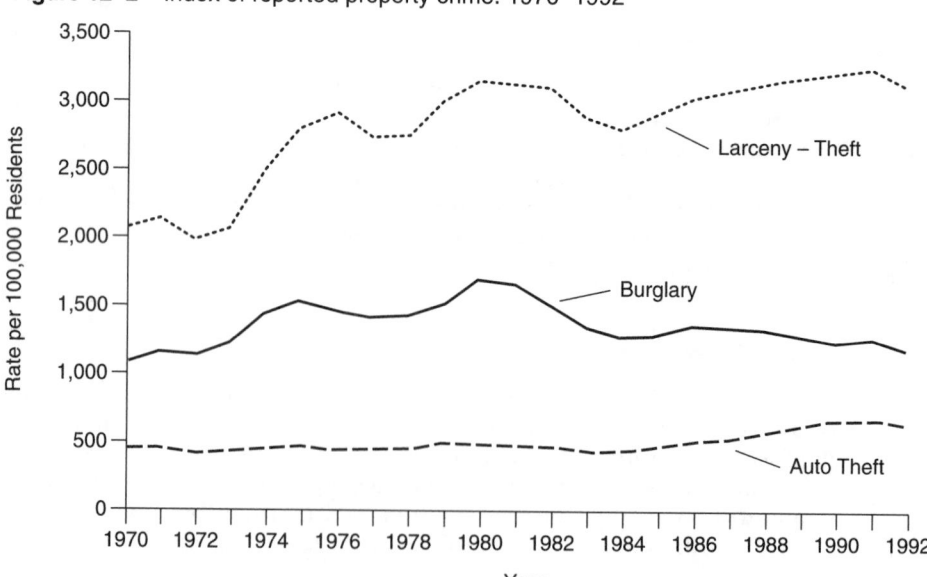

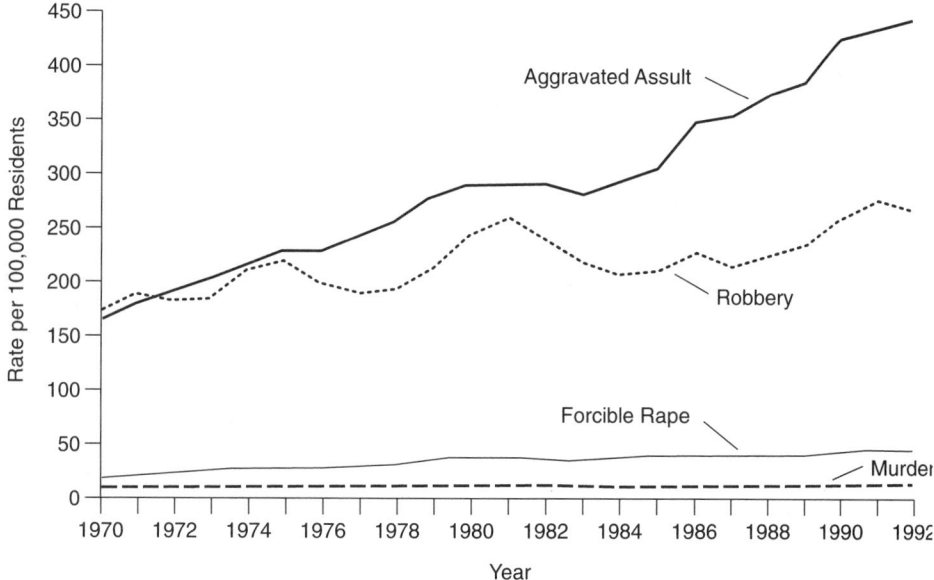

Figure 12-3   Index of reported violent crime: 1970–1992

gent manslaughter. These results are reported in Figure 12–3. By the test of reported crime, violence is increasing. For instance, murder increased from 7.8 per 100,000 inhabitants in 1970 to 9.3 per 100,000 in 1992; forcible rape increased from 18.3 per 100,000 in 1970 to 42.8 per 100,000 in 1992; and robbery increased from 172 per 100,000 in 1970 to 264 per 100,000 in 1992. Finally, aggravated assault leaped from 162 per 100,000 in 1970 to 442 per 100,000 in 1992. On what grounds can one assert that we are not an increasingly criminal society, especially where violent crime is concerned?

There are, however, other pieces to the puzzle. One is an estimate of the extent to which reported crime accurately captures the criminal state of the society, for reported crime is only one part of the puzzle. Indeed, it is entirely possible that what is displayed by the UCR is the increasing efficiency with which local police have been recording and reporting the amount of crime (if not capturing the criminal) quite independently of whether real crime rates are rising or falling. For example, *reported* crime could increase simply because people either trust the police more or are less timid about reporting the crime that does exist. An alternative explanation is that reported crime increases could simply be an artifact of automated record keeping; thus, by lowering the costs of record keeping, more records are kept.

The extent to which real crime exists in society has been a subject of a high-stakes debate among scholars and practitioners, with public policy and public program spending hanging in the balance. An alternative strategy exists for answering the question "How much crime is really out there?" and that is to survey the population. The result of this strategy is revealed by the National Crime Victimization Survey (NCVS), which estimates all crime—reported and unreported. The findings of the NCVS contradict the picture presented by the UCR. Citizen surveys reveal that the absolute amount of crime has not only *not* been rising, it has actually been declining in the area of property crime since the early 1980s. When viewed as a rate per 1,000 persons, violent crime changes very little from year to year, and property crime has actually declined over the last six years. These results are shown in Figure 12–4, which reports the surveyed victimization rate per 1,000 from 1973 to 1991.

The results are only partly comforting. All crime—crimes against both property and people—has been steadily declining since about 1977. Thus, all crime peaked at over 130 crimes per 1,000 in 1977 and has declined to just over 92 per 1,000 in 1991. The decline, however, has been due to declines in property crime, rather than violent crimes against people. Violent crime, by contrast, has maintained a steady rate, peaking in 1980 at just over 35 crimes per 1,000 persons, declining to nearly 27 per 1,000 in 1990, and rising during the years following 1990.

What is going on? Public hysteria is growing (see opinion survey data) at a time when the extent of all crime—both reported and unreported—is most certainly *not* growing and, according to crime surveys, is actually declining. Public opinion is moving in precisely the opposite direction to the facts about the condition of crime in the United States. The result is a complex pattern:

* Public fear and worry about crime are up.
* Reported serious crime is up.
* Real total crime is down.

The findings are correct in that they reveal a piece of the criminal justice mosaic in the United States. Yes, the public worries about crime with some substantial proportion admitting to real fear of victiminzation. Yes, the local police appear to be more efficient in recording an increasing proportion of all crimes committed.

Figure 12–4   U.S. criminal victimization rate: 1973–1991

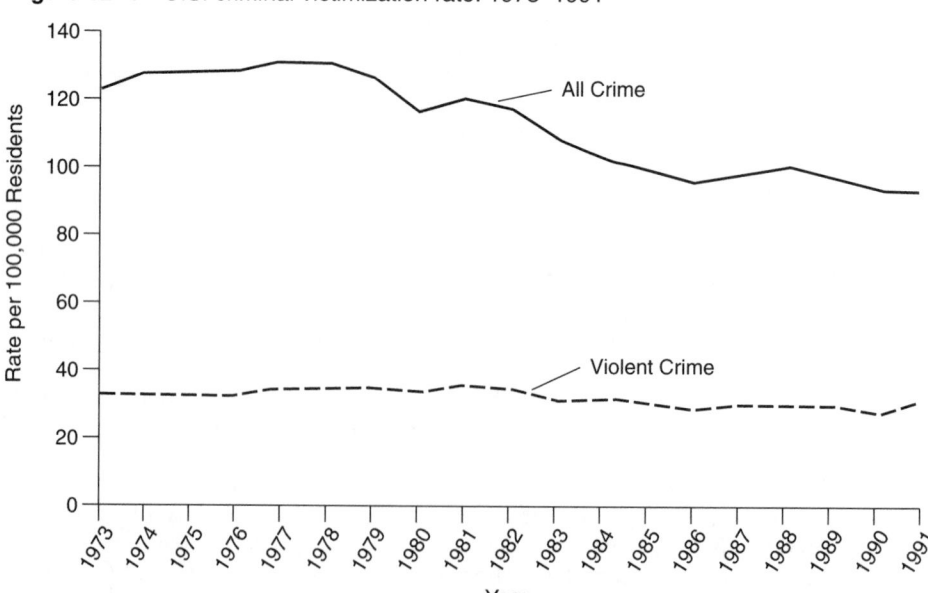

Finally, the base level of reported crime in the United States appears to be extraordinarily high, particularly in the area of violent crime. For example, aggravated assault rates of 442 per 100,000, robbery rates of 264 per 100,000, forcible rape rates of 43 per 100,000, and murder (including non-negligent manslaughter) rates of over 9 per 100,000 are not trivial risks.

Not surprisingly, the U.S. prison population mirrors the level of reported criminal activity. In short, the prison system is large, and the prison population is growing as Figure 12–4 clearly reveals. For example, in 1990, more than 4 million adults (juveniles excluded) were under *correctional supervision* by either federal or state courts, meaning they were either incarcerated, on probation from prison sentence (approximately 2.5 million cases), or paroled from prison. Over recent years, the prisons have filled and are bursting at the seams. The federal and state prison population has more than doubled from 1980 to 1990, rising from 330,000 prisoners in 1980 to over 774,000 inmates in 1990, and the vast majority of cases involve sentences of more than one year. Furthermore, an incarceration rate of nearly 300 per 100,000 population means that *hard time* in jail is not an uncommon feature of American life.

THE SYSTEM IS THE PUNISHMENT

How, then, does the criminal justice system work in the United States? In essence, four sets of actors are involved, each of which exercises important responsibilities, starting with civic and community groups that serve both as the front line of defense against criminal activity and as the ultimate recipients of those discharged by the criminal justice system at the end of the process.

Citizens and communities: prevention and reporting
Police: prevention, reporting, detection, investigation, arraignment
Courts: prosecution, grand jury, plea bargaining, trial, sentencing
Prisons: imprisonment, programming, parole, or discharge
Citizens and communities: transition from prison to community and work

There is more to the story, however. The actual process is exceedingly messy in the lower courts and at street level. One study, which surveyed over 1,600 criminal cases processed in New Haven, Connecticut, found a number of operational realities:[17]

- Although all defendants have a right to trial by jury, not one insisted on one.
- Even though indigent arrestees have a right to court-appointed counsel, only one-half had an attorney, including 20 percent of those charged with felonies and one-third of those receiving jail sentences.
- Even in those cases in which counsel was present, the contributions to a defense were questionable, marked by quick, furtive exchanges in the corridor and little independent investigation.
- Twice as many people are sent to jail before trial and detained until disposition of the case as are sent to jail after trial; although the type I error was found to have occurred in only 10 percent of all cases—90 percent were released before trial—the effect is substantial, given court caseloads.
- Although the Sixth Amendment to the Constitution guarantees the right to a speedy trial, seemingly simple cases characterized by no trial, no witnesses, no formal motions,

no pretrial involvement from the bench, and no presentence investigation still required as many as eight or ten different appearances spread over six months.

- Many complex cases were cut short because the accused had agreed to plead guilty at arraignment after the prosecutor advised him or her to "be smart and get it over with today."

- Despite elaborate state statutory classification of the seriousness of the crime and the penalties to be imposed under the law, there was no measurable relationship between seriousness of the charge and severity of the sentence. Those with previous records did not fare significantly worse than first offenders; in effect, sentences could not be correlated with standard expectations about either seriousness of the charge or a previous record.

Such a pattern exists, in part, because recidivism is the dominant pattern for predatory crime. The vast majority of the persons arrested for serious crime have been arrested before. Such a pattern changes the function of the courts, as noted by James Q. Wilson.

> In theory, the function of the courts is to determine the guilt or innocence of the accused. In fact, it is to decide what to do with persons whose guilt or innocence is not at issue. Our judiciary is organized around the assumption that its theoretical function is its actual one—hence the emphasis on the adversary system, the rules of evidence, and the procedures and standards for testimony. In some jurisdictions . . . the courts will act that way some of the time. But most of the time, for most of the cases in our busier courts, the important decision concerns the sentence, not conviction or acquittal.[18]

What does public policy do about the problem? Clearly, there is more to criminal justice policy making than invoking a flow chart of logically sequenced processes to be analytically sorted and managed to produce justice. The reality is far messier. Indeed, American public policy has been torn among a welter of criminal justice objectives. In the words of one analyst:

> Historically, Americans . . . have wanted a criminal justice system that apprehends and visits harm upon the guilty (punishment); makes offenders more virtuous, or at least more law abiding (rehabilitation); dissuades would-be offenders from criminal pursuits (deterrence); protects innocent citizens from being victimized by convicted criminals (incapacitation); and invites most convicted criminals to return as productive citizens to the bosom of the free community (reintegration). They want the criminal justice system to achieve these multiple, vague, and contradictory public goals without violating the public conscience (humane treatment), jeopardizing the public law (constitutional rights), emptying the public purse (cost containment), or weakening the tradition of state and local public administration (federalism). Thus, for example, Americans have wanted more prisons without additional corrections spending or sites for prison construction, jobs for prisoners without any loss of jobs to free workers, stern treatment of prisoners without any damage to prisoners' rights, and reintegration of offenders into the community without any threat to public safety.[19]

The reality, then, is that no analyst thinks that it is possible to achieve simultaneously all of the goals that might drive a criminal justice system. Instead, policy makers and managers have tended to react to public mood swings from liberal and conservative approaches based, respectively, on whether the aim was to attack the root causes of crime or to wage war against criminals.

Thus, between 1967 and 1992, the federal government waged two wars against crime. The first, fought between 1967 to 1980, was a war against poverty and the social conditions that produce crime; the aims of liberal strategists emphasized offender rehabilitation, reintegration, humane treatment, and constitutional rights of those accused. The second war, fought between 1980 and 1992, targeted criminals and emphasized punishment, deterrence, cost-effective incarceration and treatment, and intergovernmental cooperation.[20] Not surprisingly, the first war envisioned a large role for the federal government, which would use financial assistance to state and local government to strengthen poverty programs and enhance the local capacity to deal with crime sensibly and humanely. The second war, by contrast, constrained the federal role and sought to throw state and local governments into the breach; "The federal government would sound the charge, but the states and localities would have to do most of the actual fighting—and spending."[21]

What has been the result? A telling portrait is the *crime funnel*, which depicts the dominant crime pattern for the country. It shows the processing of all crime committed in the United States, beginning with a large opening through which all crimes are poured and ending with the narrow end through which convicted felons are sent to prison. The basic structure of the funnel at present involves a very wide mouth and a sharp narrowing of the funnel that then gradually becomes more narrow until the trickle at the stem is reached;[22]

- Thirty-five million crimes are committed in the United States each year, of which twenty-five million are serious, involving violence or sizable property losses.
- Only 15 million crimes, or 43 percent, are brought to the attention of the police.
- The police solve only 3.15 million reported crimes, or 21 percent, thus sending 3.2 million defendants to the courts for prosecution for the most serious crimes involving homicides, rapes, robberies, aggravated assaults, burglaries, larcenies, and auto thefts.
- Of the 3.2 million persons arrested and charged, only 2.59 million, or 81 percent, are actually prosecuted.
- Of the 2.59 million prosecuted, only 1.9 million, or 73 percent, are convicted; in essence, only 59 percent of those arrested for serious crimes are convicted.
- Of the 1.9 million persons per year convicted of serious crimes (minor crimes have been settled before a full court trial is required), about 500,000 persons, or 26 percent, were actually sent to prison.

Criminal justice analysts are fond of pointing out that a person committing a crime has only about a 5 percent chance of being charged and convicted and a 1 percent chance of going to jail! In some criminal matters, therefore, crime actually pays, particularly when the stakes are high and the risks of successful prosecution are low. This misapplication of statistics is often used to justify a "get tough" approach to crime, involving enormous expenditures to hire more police, criminal lawyers, and judges and to build more prisons to which convicted felons would go.

In actuality, however, the picture is far more complicated and ambiguous.[23] Of the 35 million crimes, only about 25 million are serious, involving violence or sizable property loss, but only 15 million come to the attention of the police. That is only the first narrowing of the funnel, for of the 15 million most serious crimes, only 3.2 million charged criminals are turned over to the courts for prosecution. Why does only one crime in five lead to an arrest? In millions of cases, arrests occur and are disposed of as misdeameanors. Many other cases are remanded to the juvenile justice system to be handled by "boys' and girls' schools" and by psychiatrists and social workers. Moreover, millions of burglaries and auto thefts are reported for insurance purposes and not because anyone expects an overwhelmed police force to make an arrest. There are many reasons why the linkages between crime, its reporting, and its disposition are loose.

VIOLENT CRIME AND GUNS

Compared to other countries, the United States is unique in one dramatic respect: the extent of gun distribution in the population and the frequency of gun use. Statistical data reported for 1992 by the U.S. Department of Justice show a number of alarming results.[24] First, the number of crimes committed with handguns approached one million, a record rate, over the previous five years. Thus, there were 917,500 nonfatal crimes committed with handguns in 1992, 50 percent above the average for the previous five years. In addition, handguns were used in 55.6 percent of the year's 23,760 murders, adding another 13,200 handgun homicides—24 percent more than the previous five-year average—to the handgun crime list.

This pattern of extensive handgun involvement with crime is consistent with an overall pattern of gun ownership and use. For example, the Bureau of Justice statistics reports additional findings for the period 1987 through 1992:

- Firearms were stolen in an estimated 340,000 crimes each year.
- An average of 62,000 people per year—about one percent of all violent crime victims—defended themselves with a firearm.
- About 21,000 victims a year were wounded, accounting for about 3 percent of nonfatal handgun crimes.
- Offenders fired their weapons in 17 percent of all nonfatal handgun crimes, thus missing the victim over four out of five times.

The extensive pattern of firearm possession and use sustains the international reputation of the United States as a country preoccupied with savagery and violence. The contrast is particularly stark in the case of the United Kingdom, a country one-fifth the size of the United States, where in Britain alone (thus, excluding Scotland, Wales, and Northern Ireland) the number of crimes involving a gun does not exceed one percent.[25] Furthermore, the British murder *rate* is one-fifteenth that found in the United States, and the murder rate involving handguns is nearly nonexistent—33 handgun murders were recorded in 1992.[26]

Clearly, regulation and control of guns in Britain and a lack of regulation in the United States have something to do with patterns of violence found in different societies. For example, in Britain, where all guns are tightly controlled, the number of persons registered as owning a shotgun, handgun, or rifle numbers 900,000, and the registration covers 5 million guns. An estimated 50 million gun owners maintain arsenals in the United States, estimated to include 220 million guns with little to no registration and certification.[27]

The differences among countries are clearly tied to different public tolerances for guns and gun use. Britain moved early in 1920 to regulate gun use—initially, in the cases of rifles and handguns—and has tightened its regulation at every wave of public panic over gun-related crime. Thus, after robbers brandished shotguns during a 1960s heist, Parliament added shotguns to the list of firearms for which licensing would be required. After Michael Ryan employed his arsenal, consisting of registered pistols and semiautomatic rifles including the Russian-made Kalashnikov AK-47, to shoot and kill his mother, a policeman, and 14 other people, the conservative government of Margaret Thatcher moved to tighten firearms control even further, including outlawing all semiautomatic weapons. The result is a nationally required but locally administered firearms law requiring a license consisting of the following steps:

1. A person completes an application explaining why and where he or she plans to use the gun (sport is acceptable, but self-protection is not) and pays a fee, estimated at about $25 for shotgun applications.
2. The applicant submits a letter from a doctor or other qualified professional attesting to the applicant's sound state of mind.
3. The applicant must possess or construct a burglarproof cabinet for storage.

After the qualifying steps have been completed, the local police superintendent can reject the application, leaving the applicant with only the option of going to court to reverse the judgment. Not surprisingly, when the Thatcher government's rules took effect in 1989, the number of Britons holding gun certificates declined 10 percent.[28]

In the United States, by contrast, a different set of expectations prevails. Even after the worst gun massacre in U.S. history, involving the killing of 23 persons at a Luby's restaurant in Killeen, Texas, in 1991, neither the Bush administration nor Congress even entertained regulation, let alone licensing and control. The only serious proposal that has escaped with congressional approval has been the Brady bill, discussed in the next section.

THE FUTURE OF CRIME POLICY

The entire strategy for dealing with crime is again on the policy table for discussion. One set of debates aims at identifying the part of the crime funnel that requires the greatest attention. Current policy discussions are focused on the end of the pipe in the form of "get tough" provisions aimed at sending more people to jail to serve longer sentences for committing serious crime. Thus, the recent anticrime legislation that has passed the U.S. Senate and the House of Representatives embodies the basic logic of an overall Clinton crime-fighting plan. Among the key provisions being worked out in conference committee are the following:[29]

• Put more police on the streets and create a police corps program that would authorize college scholarships for students who agreed to serve as police officers for at least four years.

• Finance a prison expansion program to house violent criminals and criminal aliens.

• Authorize the death penalty for several dozen federal crimes, including treason, genocide, causing death through a train wreck, and mailing explosives; also included could be gun murders committed during the course of another federal crime or murders involving a gun that had crossed state lines. As guns are made in only a few locations and therefore almost always cross state lines, the effect is to federalize many state and local crimes and potentially to apply the death penalty even in states that do not allow capital punishment.

• Ban the manufacture, sale, and possession of certain semiautomatic guns known as assault weapons.

• Create new federal penalties or stiffer sentences for crimes involving guns, in effect federalizing many violent crimes, for reasons noted above.

• Require mandatory sentencing. The most common version is the "three strikes and you're out" proposal, which requires life imprisonment for someone convicted of a third violent felony. The first two offenses could be state offenses, while the last would have to be a federal violent felony charge.

• Require adult trials for juveniles 13 years old or older for certain violent crimes if the crime involved the use of a gun.

• Introduce strong, new federal penalties for gang violence.

There are, of course, many variations on the "get tough" theme, but they all are nothing if not expensive. The target of the legislation is the end of the crime funnel rather than the opening. This means building more expensive prisons with high operating costs, after a decade of prison expansion. The effect will be to achieve a slight increase in the proportion of incarcerations applied to those offenses successfully prosecuted.

Another, very different strategy is to narrow the opening of the mouth of the funnel rather than enlarging the spigot at the end.[30] The thrust of this strategy is crime prevention and control. One illustration is found in proposals that emphasize the reduction of crime by inserting large numbers of police officers into community-policing roles; the police would enter into partnerships with people in communities to construct joint attacks on crime. For example, in cases where landlords profiteer by renting to drug dealers, the traditional response of dispatching police never works, as more dealers quickly move in. Yet pressuring landlords to evict the dealers can be achieved in many ways, including getting neighbors to challenge landlords in court, lodging complaints with a city housing agency or fire department, or even picketing landlords' homes in wealthy suburbs.

In addition, there are other crime prevention measures, including the following:

- Drug treatment programs for prisoners
- Job training, education, and counseling programs for convicted felons who might be granted probation in exchange for education and community service
- Community programming, including educational, sports, and cultural programs in schools and community facilities
- Innovations in the intermediate sanctions associated with probated sentences. Thus, the use of electronic monitoring, boot camps for youth, drug testing, and treatment all permit intervention and some social control in nonprison environments and provide some hope of preventing the recidivism that drives up both crime and prison populations.

Finally, criminal justice strategists must evaluate the Brady Handgun Violence Prevention Act (Public Law 103-159), which was signed into law on 30 November, 1993 and is notable as the first federal attempt to regulate and control the sale of handguns. The act provides for a waiting period before the purchase of a handgun and for a national system to check a criminal's background instantly; firearms dealers must contact the system before the transfer of any handgun to a purchaser. The act was named in honor of James Brady, who had been partially paralyzed from a gunshot to his head during the 1981 assassination attempt against President Ronald Reagan. Brady, once a press secretary for Reagan, and Sarah Brady, his wife, had long lobbied for the bill's passage.

The act regulates the conditions of handgun sales and, in so doing, attempts to reduce the number of guns placed in the hands of people likely to use handguns in the commission of crimes. It requires dealers, manufacturers, and importers to be licensed and to comply with the federal mandate that no handguns—defined as short stock firearms designed to be held and fired by the use of a single hand—be sold without checking the criminal and mental health record of the gun applicant. A five-day waiting period is designated by the act as the period during which applications are processed and background checks are conducted.

The ultimate effect of the act cannot be known at present. Compared to gun control laws in other countries, such as Great Britain, the regulatory power of the Brady bill appears modest. Only handguns are involved, thus excluding rifles, shotguns, and other rapid action firearms. Among the questions is whether such an act can curb the violent use of guns in a nation already possessing enough guns to arm every citizen with at least one gun and traditionally selling two million handguns, one million rifles, and over 500,000 shotguns per year.[31] The act appears to offer very little control for a large number of guns.

In addition, the Brady act has been subject to serious legal challenge in the form of a 16 May 1994 federal district court decision of Judge Charles C. Lovell of Missoula, Montana, who concluded that the act is unconstitutional. The issue was not, however, the "right to bear arms" clause of the Second Amendment. It was, instead, the Tenth Amendment that reserves to the states and the people all powers not assigned to the federal government.[32] In effect, Judge Lovell concluded that the federal government was not justified in adding an unfunded and unpopular mandate to the burdens carried by state and local governments. More specifically, the judge ruled that the federal government had overreached itself when it had, in effect, told Ravalli County Sheriff Jay Printz that he had to divert 16 officers and 13 support staff at his disposal to conduct background checks on Montana gun buyers. If allowed to stand, the task would have required the sheriff's department to chase down records, some located hundreds of miles away, in addition to providing sheriff services for 30,000 residents scattered through rugged territory in a large western Montana county. The decision will almost certainly be appealed.

The final lesson, then, is that although crime is widely perceived to be a serious problem, public policy recommendations must be affordable and workable. To be affordable, decision makers must at least ask whether the benefits to be derived from policy action justify the marginal costs even as they also ask whether justice is increased or decreased. To be workable, public policy must recognize the operating realities that define current criminal justice policy and then seek to design effective public action.

SUMMARY

Crime and punishment in the U.S. present a confusing pattern. Casual observation and sampling of newspapers suggest that the U.S. confronts a crime wave for which serious and large-scale public policy action appears to be justified. Thus, opinion surveys of public fear of crime and police reports indicate a growing crime problem exists. Victimization studies, on the other hand, show that the incidence of real crime is declining. Trends only tell part of the story, however, for the sheer size of the prison population and the comparisons with other countries of violent crime rates—particularly those involving guns—suggests that regardless of recent trends, crime remains a serious problem.

Strategies for dealing with crime vary in several ways. One is the decision about whether to focus resources on the front end or the back end of the crime funnel. Front end strategies attempt to prevent criminal activity in the first place by treating the social circumstance that give rise to crime or by deploying police and community resources in preventive postures. "End-of-the-pipe" solutions aim to improve criminal justice processing and incarceration of those crimes that are committed. Another decision rests with the kinds of crime that should receive the most attention, and it is in this context that gun control debates aim to curb the use of guns and therefore the wrongful deaths and injuries associated with guns. A third decision involves the assignment of roles to the many levels of government and police agencies that can be thrown into the crime battle.

DISCUSSION QUESTIONS

1. Is crime in the U.S. a crisis or simply a complex problem? What sorts of crime should now be most worrisome to policy makers (make a rank ordered list and discuss)?
2. Do U.S. policy makers need to rethink the constitutional rules that constrain the criminal justice system's attempts to deal with the crime problem? Should the system, for example, attempt to rebalance the likelihood of committing type I and type II errors?
3. What improvements should be made in the operation of the U.S. criminal justice system? Where should new public money be spent?
4. Should the U.S. adopt a British style gun control law?

SUGGESTIONS FOR FURTHER READING

Alfred Blumstein, Jacueline Cohen, Jeffrey Roth, and Christie Visher, *Criminal Careers and "Career Criminals"* (Washington, D. C.: National Academy Press, 1986).

Joel A. Devine and James D. Wright, *The Greatest of Evils: Urban Poverty and the American Underclass* (Hawthorne, N.Y.: Aldine de Gruyter, 1993).

Michael R. Gottfredson and Travis Hirschi, *A General Theory of Crime* (Stanford, Calif.: Stanford University Press, 1990).

Michael Lipsky, *Street-Level Bureaucrats* (New York: Russell Sage Foundations, 1980).

Robert J. Sampson and John H. Laub, *Crime in the Making: Pathways and Turning Points Through Life* (Cambridge, Mass.: Harvard University Press, 1993).

Wesley G. Skogan, *Disorder and Decline* (New York: Free Press, 1990).

Tom R. Tyler, *Why People Obey the Law* (New Haven: Yale University Press, 1990).

James Q. Wilson and Richard J. Hernstein, *Crime and Human Nature* (New York: Simon and Schuster, 1985).

Marvin E. Wolfgang, Terence P. Thornberry, and Robert M. Figlio, *From Boy to Man, from Delinquency to Crime* (Chicago: University of Chicago Press, 1987).

NOTES

1. Paulette Thomas, "Triangle of Interests Creates Infrastructure to Fight Lawlessness," *Wall Street Journal*, 12, May 1994, p. A1.
2. John Kaplan and Robert Weisberg, *Criminal Law: Cases and Materials* (Boston: Little, Brown & Co., 1991), 27.
3. James Q. Wilson, *Thinking about Crime* (New York: Basic Books, 1975), 21.
4. Hugo Adam Bedau and Michael L. Radelet, "Miscarriages of Justice in Potentially Capital Cases," *Stanford Law Review* 40 (1987): 21, 22–25, 31–36, 38–39, 72–75, 83–90. For a critique of the study and its implications, see: Steven J. Markman and Paul G. Cassell, "Protecting the Innocent: A Response to the Bedau-Radelet Study," *Stanford Law Review* 41 (1988): 121–123, 145–160.
5. Lynne Duke, "A Matter of Law and Death," *Washington Post*, 31 January–6 February 1994, national weekly ed., pp. 6–8.
6. Kaplan and Weisberg, 1991, 27.

7. The Supreme Court applied the exclusionary rule to federal proceedings in *Weeks v. United States* (1914). However, it was not until 1961 and *Mapp v. Ohio* that the Supreme Court affirmed the expanded constraint on the due process proceedings of state and local governments by holding that "all evidence obtained by searches and seizures in violation of the Constitution is, by that same authority, inadmissible in a state court."
8. Samuel Walker, *Sense and Nonsense about Crime: A Policy Guide,* 2d ed. (Pacific Grove, Calif.: Brooks-Cole, 1989), 118–119.
9. Anthony Lewis, *Gideon's Trumpet* (New York: Random House, 1964).
10. Malcolm M. Feeley, *The Process Is the Punishment: Handling Cases in a Lower Criminal Court* (New York: Russell Sage Foundation, 1979).
11. Richard L. Berke, "Tides That Brought Democrats to G.O.P. Have Turned," *New York Times,* Sunday, 20, February 1994, p. E3.
12. Malcolm Gladwell, "Baby Boom's Urban Cradle Braces for Future Rocked by Crime," *Washington Post,* May 26, 1994, pp. A25, 29.
13. Gladwell, 1994, p. A25.
14. Gladwell, 1994, p. A25.
15. Gladwell, 1994, p. A25.
16. U.S. Federal Bureau of Investigation, *Crime in the United States,* (Washington, D.C.: published annually by U.S. Government Printing Office).
17. Feeley, 1979, 9–10.
18. Wilson, 1975, 163.
19. John J. DiIulio, Jr., "Crime," in *Setting Domestic Priorities: What Can Government Do?* ed. Henry J. Aaron and Charles L. Schultze (Washington, D.C.: Brookings Institution, 1992), 105.
20. DiIulio, 1992, 106.
21. DiIulio, 1992, 110.
22. David C. Anderson, "The Crime Funnel," *New York Times Magazine,* Sunday, 12 June 1994, pp. 56–58.
23. Anderson, 1994, p. 57.
24. Michael J. Sniffen, "Handgun Crimes Hit Record Rate in 1992, U.S. Says," *Courier-Journal,* (Louisville, KY), 16 May 1994, p. A1.
25. Kevin Helliker, "As Gun Crimes Rise, Britain Is Considering Cutting Legal Arsenal," *Wall Street Journal,* 19 April 1994, p. A1.
26. Helliker, 1994, p. A10.
27. Helliker, 1994, p. A10.
28. Helliker, 1994, p. A10.
29. "Anti-Crime Bills Compared," *Congressional Quarterly,* 7 May 1994, 1147–1154.
30. Anderson, 1994, p. 58.
31. *New York Times,* Sunday, 15 August 1993, p. E1.
32. David Broder, "Law of Unintended Consequences Follows Passage of the Brady Bill," syndicated editorial, *The Herald-Times,* (Bloomington, IN), 1, June 1994, p. A8.

13

Agriculture Policy

Almost no one is happy with agricultural policy in the United States. Many believe that not enough is being done for the U.S. farmer. Congressional hearings, television documentaries, and benefit concerts tell a story of the loss of family farms; the rise of large, impersonal corporate agriculture; and the end of a way of life that is an integral part of our nation. These changes threaten both independent farmers and the economic vitality of the rural communities that depend on agriculture. Agricultural policy is also faulted by those concerned with the environment, who decry the loss of soil to erosion as well as the growing use of chemical fertilizers and pesticides whose runoff can cause problems.

Others see agricultural policy as a prime example of government programs that are at once horribly expensive and remarkably ineffective. The average annual cost of U.S. agricultural policy amounts to about $400 per nonfarm family. In addition to these direct costs, consumers also face higher prices for food in the stores as a result of these policies. Moreover, there are numerous examples of seemingly wasteful behavior in response to these policies. The government purchases grain from farmers, pays to store the grain, and then lets it rot. The U.S. Department of Agriculture (USDA) has programs to boost the income of tobacco farmers at the same time that other government agencies are trying to discourage smoking. Some farmers are paid to destroy their cattle and leave the dairy business, while others are paid subsidies of over $1 million per year per farm to produce dairy products.

In the 1980s, the Payment-in-Kind (PIK) program was used to convince farmers not to grow crops by paying them off with the same crops the government had bought from them in previous years. The PIK program gave farmers more than $10 billion worth of commodities in return for idling enough farmland to cover the entire states of Ohio and Indiana and half of Illinois. As one author put it,

"The effect was sort of like getting your slow-witted brother to buy a hound dog from you, then convincing him to give it back later because it was so obnoxious to keep, and besides he didn't want you to bring another one of those troublesome things home."[1] Fertilizer, farm equipment, and seed dealers were hurt, and some were driven out of business, when their sales were cut by 50 percent. According to one estimate, PIK-related losses to agriculture businesses totaled $4 billion. PIK also cost poultry, egg, pork, and cattle producers up to $7 billion because of higher feed grain costs. PIK is estimated to have cost the country 250,000 jobs and reduced gross national product (GNP) by 0.5 percent. Nonetheless, the agriculture secretary declared in 1983, "Never in the history of agriculture has there been a farm program more successful than PIK."[2]

We begin this chapter with a look at some of the recent trends in U.S. agriculture. Our focus will be to identify when these trends began and to understand the underlying forces behind them. To understand U.S. agriculture, we will have to understand agriculture and agricultural policy in other countries. As in so many other public policy areas, U.S. agricultural policy cannot be examined in isolation. Next we turn to the goals of agriculture in both the United States and elsewhere. We then examine the policy instruments governments use to try to achieve these goals. We look at the effects of agricultural policy, both in terms of costs to consumers and impacts on farmers. The chapter next takes a closer look at U.S. policies and their effects in several specific areas: sugar, dairy products, peanuts, and honey. Finally, the sum of the impacts of agriculture on the environment are discussed. While the focus of the chapter is on the United States, where possible we try to compare U.S. policy with the often more extreme policies elsewhere in the world. We find throughout that although these policies may have been developed with good intentions, the actual effects are often much different from policy makers' expectations.

TRENDS IN U.S. AGRICULTURE

As is evident in Figure 13–1, the number of farms in the United States has been declining steadily since the mid-1930s. From a peak in 1935 of over 6.8 million farms, the number had declined by two-thirds by the early 1990s. The drop in the number of farms, however, has been accompanied by an increase in the average size of farms. Figure 13–2 indicates that over the same period, the average size of farms has more than tripled. Thus, there has been relatively little change in the total acreage devoted to farming.

The origins of concerns about the loss of the family farm and the rise of large-scale corporate farming are easy to see in the figures. The story is clearly one of consolidating a large number of small farms into a smaller number of larger farms. This consolidation began in the 1930s because of the economic conditions of the Great Depression, coupled with a drop in exports as a result of recently enacted high tariffs. The average price received by farmers for products declined over 50 percent between 1929 and 1932. Farm income dropped sharply, and bankruptcies and foreclosures became common.

Land policies of the late-nineteenth century set the stage for this consolidation. Government decisions with respect to the pricing and distribution of public land favored family farms rather than large landholders. Under the Homestead Act of 1862, settlers were given the opportunity to obtain free land, provided they

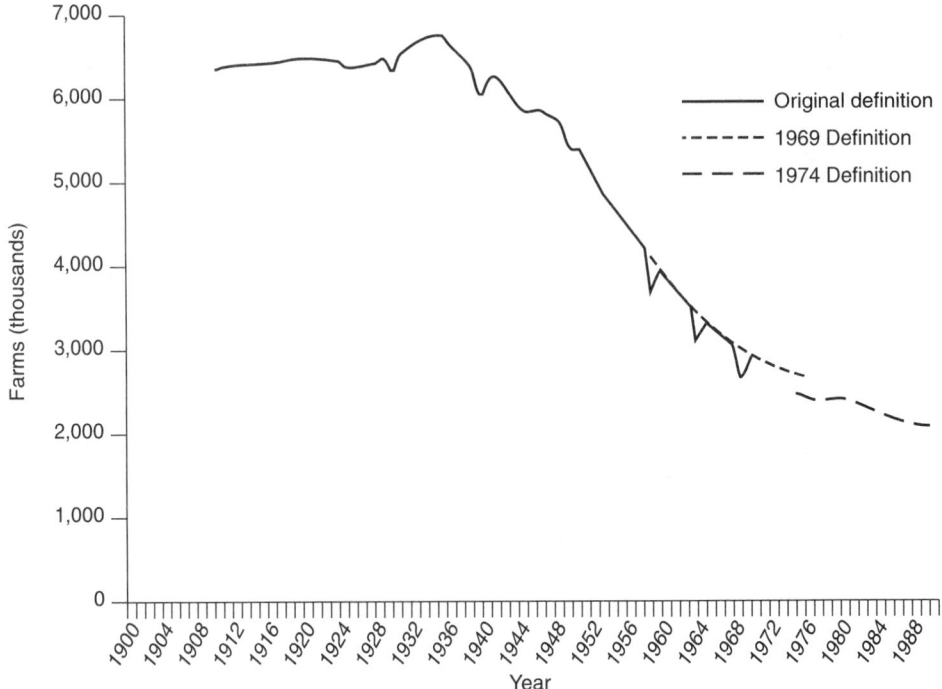

Figure 13–1   Number of farms in the United States

Source: Author's calculations based on U.S. Department of Agriculture Data.

lived on the land and farmed it for five years. These farms were initially limited to 160 acres, although that limit was later lifted in areas where rainfall was lower and more variable. Even before this act, farmers who had settled illegally were granted ownership rights retroactively and were permitted to purchase a minimum acreage at modest prices. The result of these and other supporting policies was that the U.S. agriculture sector entered the Depression with a larger number of smaller farms than might otherwise have been the case.

The Great Depression may have triggered a trend toward farm consolidation, but the trend continued long after the end of the Depression and has persisted through periods of economic prosperity and recession. The driving force behind this consolidation has been continuously improving farm productivity—that is, farms have become more productive by using less labor on the same amount of land or even less. Government policy has played a role in improved productivity through sponsored research in improved seeds and methods and by informing farmers of these improvements though extension services.

An important impact of improved productivity can be seen in Figure 13–3. Farm employment has declined almost since the turn of the century, with some-what sharper declines since the mid-1930s. This decline in employment while out-put was increasing indicates an improvement in labor productivity. As in other industries, productivity has improved in part because of better techniques and in part because of a substitution of capital for labor. Farm laborers have been given

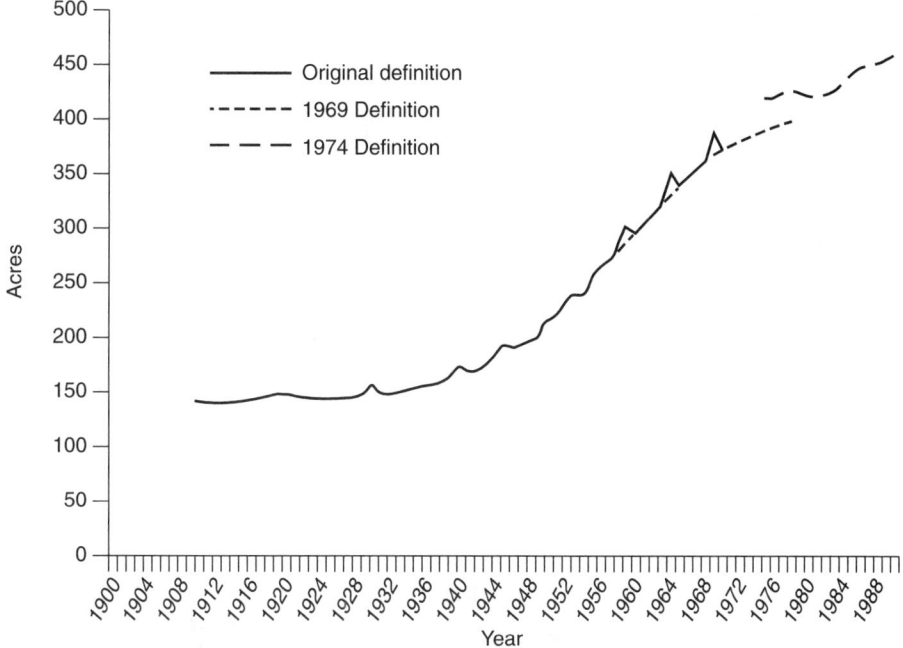

Figure 13–2   Average acres per farm

Source: Author's calculations based on U.S. Department of Agriculture data.

progressively better equipment with which to work and, as a result, have been able to produce more per person. For example, the number of tractors per 1,000 farm workers has increased from 667 in 1955 to 1,476 in 1986, an increase of over 120 percent in about 30 years. More generally, farming has become a very capital-intensive enterprise. In 1986, total capital investment per farm worker in the United States, not including investment in land and buildings, was $46,000—over 30 percent more than the $35,200 per worker found in U.S. manufacturing that same year. Thus, farming has become more capital intensive than manufacturing in the United States.

These productivity gains continued through the 1960s and 1970s. Between 1960 and 1980, agricultural output per worker grew 200 percent. Agricultural land per worker grew 111 percent. Machinery horsepower per worker, a rough indicator of the amount of equipment available, grew 267 percent. Fertilizer per worker grew 475 percent, although as we will see later in this chapter, fertilizer use in the United States is still far below that typically found in other developed countries.

The drop in farm employment is viewed as a problem by some and as a necessity by others. Those who view it as a problem point out that as labor productivity improves so that fewer workers can produce the same amount, more people often want to work on the farm than are needed. When that happens, the wages paid farm workers will drop. For farmers with their own small farms, the money they can earn farming may not pay their costs. That same land, if integrated into a bigger farm, may again become profitable to farm. It may simply not be possible to take as much advantage of productivity-improving equipment on a small farm as

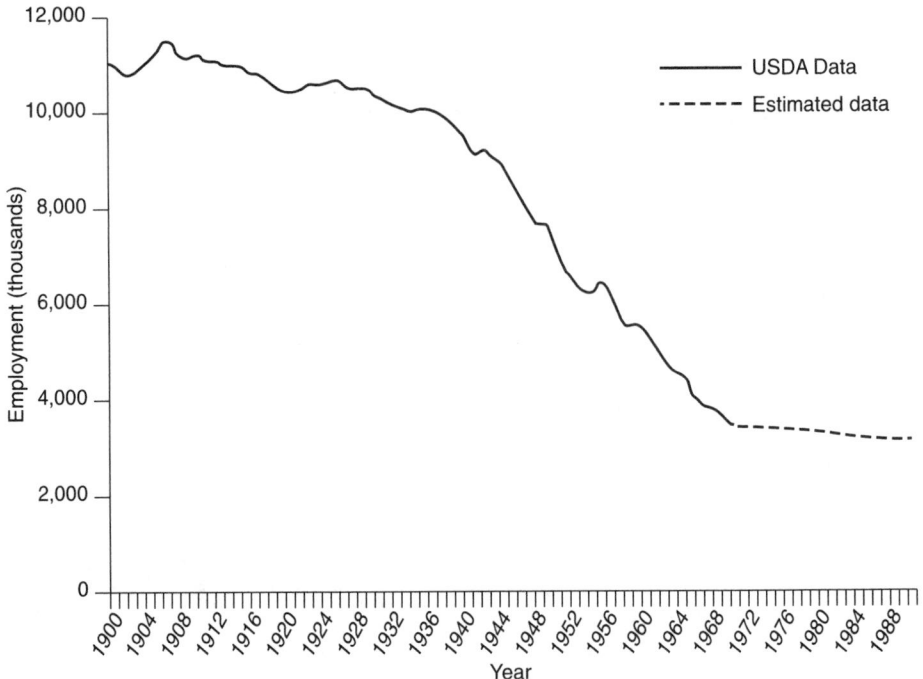

Figure 13–3 Civilian farm employment

Source: Author's calculations based on U.S. Department of Agriculture data.

on a large farm. In such cases, the hired hand may find that wages are better in some other industry, or the small farm owner may find that selling the farm and going to work in another industry may yield a higher income. In a sense, the improved productivity has forced the farmer off the land—some farmers find better opportunities off the farm than on. These transitions can be difficult for the people involved and likely involve relocating from a rural area to an urban one and changing to a different occupation. In many cases, farms that had been part of a family for several generations may have to be sold to a larger operation.

While it is important to recognize the hardship this may pose on families, the growth in manufacturing and other industries in the United States and throughout the world could not have occurred without the supply of labor released from farming through improved labor productivity. Without this labor supply, the growth of manufacturing, with its accompanying rise in the standard of living, would have been much slower.

In addition to labor productivity, the productivity of the land has also improved, as seen in Figure 13–4. Crop production per acre in the United States has climbed steadily since the mid-1930s. Productivity improvements have shown little indication of slowing in recent years. Between 1960 and 1980, productivity grew 40 percent, and the growth has continued through the 1980s. Much of the productivity gain is in response to government-sponsored research into more effective agriculture techniques. Some of the gain is the result of other government policies that have encouraged farmers to remove some of the least productive

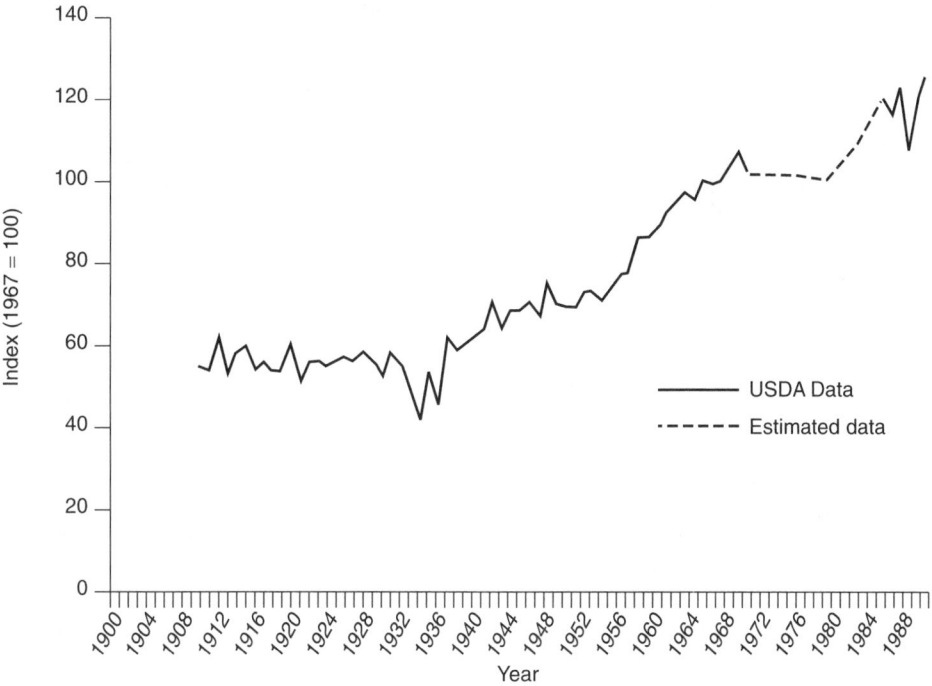

Figure 13–4   Crop production per acre

land from production and to concentrate their efforts on fewer more productive acres.

As a result of the consolidation of small farms into larger farms, by 1985 the farm economy of the United States looked as depicted in Table 13–1. Of the 2.2 million farms in the economy, over half have sales of less than $10,000. As a group, these farms lost money and had to rely on nonfarming sources of income. The situation was not much better for the 21 percent of farms with sales of between $10,000 and $39,999. These farms also lost money and had to rely on off-farm sources. Thus over 70 percent of U.S. farms were unprofitable. These farms, however, accounted for only about 10 percent of gross receipts. Farms with between $40,000 and $99,999 in sales were, as a group, profitable but relied on off-farm sources for about a third of their income. These farms accounted for 16 percent of gross receipts. In summary, about 85 percent of farms in the United States rely on off-farm sources for all or a substantial portion of their net income.

Looking at the bottom two lines of the table, one can see that a total of 14 percent of farms with over $100,000 in sales account for 74 percent of gross receipts. Moreover, these are clearly full-time farms with very little of their net income from off-farm sources. The very largest 1 percent of the farms account for nearly one-third of all farm gross receipts. It would appear from this table that the small family farm is no longer a dominant or even an important economic factor in U.S. agriculture.

Much of the rhetoric surrounding U.S. agricultural policy has been directed at the goal of saving the family farm and increasing economic returns to farming.

TABLE 13–1   Distribution of Farm Size, 1985

Sales Class	Number of Farms (Thousands)	Percentage of Farms	Percentage of Gross Receipts	Percentage of Total Net Income from Off-Farm Sources
Under $10,000	1,164	51	3	a
$10,000–$39,999	473	21	7	a
$40,000–$99,999	323	14	16	34
$100,000–$499,999	287	13	42	6
$500,000 and over	27	1	32	b
Totals	2,274	100	100	

a = Net loss from farming for this group.
b = Less than 1 percent.

Source: Kenneth L. Robinson, *Farm and Food Policies and their Consequences,* (Englewood Cliffs, NJ: Prentice-Hall, 1989), table 3.1, p. 37.

We will examine some of these policies as we look at agricultural policy goals and instruments in the next section. In examining how these policies have been implemented, we will also look at some of their effects, both intended and unintended.

GOALS OF AGRICULTURAL POLICY

Agricultural policy seems to have three principal goals throughout the world: (1) to keep prices stable; (2) to increase farm incomes and avoid loss of farm employment; and (3) to guarantee supplies of food. Different countries place different emphasis on these goals. Countries that import a substantial portion of their food, such as Japan, care most about guaranteeing supplies of food. Maintaining rural communities and increasing farm income, particularly of small farmers, have greater priority in the United States and Europe. In addition, farm policies may be intended to help maintain the health of rural communities and, in some cases, to reduce balance of payments difficulties.

Price Stability

The argument that farm prices are inherently less stable than other product prices is based on several factors. Farmers must base their production decisions not on current demand for their product but on what they expect that demand to be when that product is ready for market. Many crops operate on an annual cycle so that if too much is produced and prices fall or if too little is produced and prices rise, farmers cannot adjust their output until the following year. In addition, farm output is subject to added variability from weather and disease. Price stability is difficult to achieve, and government policies throughout the world have not been demonstrably successful in increasing price stability.

In one study of worldwide food prices, the authors developed an index of world food prices over the period 1900 to 1987.[3] This study noted two important features during this period. First, the trend in food prices has been generally downward, declining by an average of about 0.5 percent per year. Second, food prices have been quite volatile, and this volatility seems to have increased since the

1930s when efforts to stabilize prices began in earnest. Thus, it appears the efforts to stabilize food prices have not been successful. The overall fall in food prices points to a difficulty in achieving the second goal of maintaining or increasing farm incomes and avoiding loss of farm employment.

Farm Incomes and Employment

A wide variety of studies has consistently shown that on average, farm incomes are lower than incomes in the rest of the U.S. economy. As a result, it is widely perceived that there is a farm income problem. It is true that over 70 percent of U.S. farms have sales below $40,000 per year. But these farms derive less than 1 percent of their income from farming and must be regarded as at most part-time farms. Nor is this situation unique to the United States. For the smallest 40 percent of Japan's farms, only 2 percent of income comes from agriculture. When all income sources are taken into account, household incomes of U.S. farmers have generally been above average nonfarm incomes for the past 20 years. Full-time farmers have done even better: a full-time farmer's income in 1989 was about twice the national average and that full-time farmer was about 10 times wealthier, with roughly $700,000 in assets. Maintaining farm employment in the face of improving productivity and a slowly growing market is at best difficult and more likely nearly impossible. More than 3 percent of farmers and farm workers have left the land each year since 1950.

Guaranteed Food Supply

Food shortages in Japan and Europe during and immediately following World War II helped shape agricultural policy throughout the 1950s and 1960s, and more recently, images of famine in Africa and elsewhere continue to influence public policy. However, self-sufficiency in food production, where a country is able to grow all of the food its citizens need, is not the same as food security, where a country can obtain all of the food its citizens need. To obtain self-sufficiency means to have not only the productive capacity to grow the food but also the ability to produce the stream of energy, fertilizer, seeds, pesticides, machinery, spare parts, and so forth to keep the agriculture sector functioning. Self-sufficiency is an ambitious and costly goal.

An alternative is food security based on storage of food stocks and on international trade. With modern transportation, food can be delivered to most parts of the world within weeks. Over the past 50 years, world output of food has varied little even though there have been changes in harvests in particular regions. While crops have failed in some countries, there have been bumper harvests in others.

In the name of guaranteeing food supplies, agricultural policy may also seek to protect a nation's farmers from foreign competition. One justification can be that farmers of a particular country or region have some particular disadvantage that results in higher costs compared to those who farm elsewhere. Without protection, these low-cost (foreign) farmers would drive the nation's high-cost farmers out of business, and the country would lose the capability of growing that product or products. A second reason used to justify protection from foreign competition is that world market prices for farm products are affected by subsidies and policies of the host countries and do not reflect the real cost of production. In the face of such unfair competition, a country may believe it cannot open its markets to imports for fear of having its domestic producers driven from business by unfair subsidized competition. A third concern is that international prices are highly variable, and it would be unreasonable to subject either domestic consumers or producers to such variability in prices for major food products.

INSTRUMENTS OF AGRICULTURAL POLICY

A complete description of the wide array of instruments used in agricultural policy is far beyond the scope of this chapter. The basic approaches, however, can be described and their effects examined. One of the principal concerns of government policy makers is controlling the price of agricultural products. In the United States, the usual concern is keeping the price high to increase the income received by the farmer. The price can be controlled, or at least influenced, in four basic ways: (1) price supports enforced by purchases or loans; (2) limitation of output; (3) deficiency payments, a subsidy equal to the difference between the market price and some specified price; and (4) control over or influence on imports or exports. These approaches are not mutually exclusive and can be used in combination. Indeed, as will be seen, some of these approaches must be used in combination with others to be effective.

Price support programs have been the dominant U.S. policy since the mid-1930s. These programs are expensive and controversial. Should the government try to increase farm prices? If so, for what commodities and by how much? In the United States, about half the total value of agricultural output receives significant support and protection. The crops that have received almost continuous protection since the 1930s include wheat, corn, cotton, rice, peanuts, wool, sugar, tobacco, and dairy products. Other products have been supported intermittently and still others supported not at all. Other countries, such as Japan, Switzerland, and the European Community, support and protect a higher proportion of agricultural output. A few countries such as Australia and New Zealand support a lower proportion.

All of the methods used to support prices rely on the simple economics of supply and demand. When sellers try to offer their product at a particular price, three things can happen. If they try to charge too high a price, consumers will not want to buy as much of the product as suppliers want to sell. Sellers begin to see that they are going to have some of the product left over. To avoid that, they will lower the price so as to encourage greater sales in two ways: by encouraging people who had not previously bought any of their product to buy some of it and by encouraging people who had been buying some of the product to buy more of it. However, if the price they start to charge is too low, people will want to buy more than the sellers have. To avoid running out and to receive the most they can for the amount they have to sell, they will raise the price. Only when the price is right will the amount the sellers have to sell be the same as the amount the buyers want to buy at that price.

To be sure, in the real world these price adjustments do not work smoothly or perfectly. But in general, if the price is raised, consumers will want to buy less of that good, and if the price is lowered, they will want to buy more. Think of your own behavior when you walk into a restaurant. If you like both pizza and hamburgers, your choice will depend on what you feel like having at the time. However, if there is a half-price special on pizza, you may decide to substitute the lower-priced pizza for the regularly priced hamburger. The price of the pizza might even influence how much you choose to eat. Think about how people often behave at all-you-can-eat buffets. If the half-price pizza special is advertised, it might even encourage people to go to that restaurant who might otherwise not have done so that night. The point is that the price of a good, particularly in comparison with the prices of other goods that might be substitutes, can influence what people buy and how much they buy.

Much of the government's effort in agriculture policy is directed at increasing the prices farmers receive for their output. The notion is that if prices can be raised without an accompanying decrease in the amount that a farmer produces, the farmer's income will be increased. If a farmer tried to raise prices unilaterally, consumers would just buy from other farmers whose prices had not been raised. In the view of proponents of agriculture policy, the government must step in to raise prices or keep them high and thus insure that farm income is sufficient.

Purchases and Loans

One approach for the government to raise prices is for it to buy some of the commodity. If the government were to set a target price, it could make sure the farmers received that price by simply buying any surplus that consumers did not want. The difficulty with making purchases is in knowing how much to buy from which farmers. A principal way of accomplishing these purchases has been through the nonrecourse loan. With this system the farmer gets a loan from the Commodity Credit Corporation and uses the crop about to be grown as collateral for the loan. The purpose of collateral is to give the lender something of value to take if the borrower cannot pay back the loan. When the farmer puts up the crop for collateral, the Commodity Credit Corporation places a value on the crop equal to the size of the crop times the target price. The farmer has the option of either paying back the loan with cash from the sale of the crop or delivering the crop to the Commodity Credit Corporation. If the market price of the crop is above the target price, the farmer sells the crop and pays back the loan in cash. If the market price is below the target price, the farmer delivers the collateral. The amount of grain the government finally takes delivery of depends on the target price, the market price, and the number of farmers participating in the loan program.

Limiting Output

Another approach to increasing the price of a product without direct government purchases is to reduce the amount of the product produced. If less is offered for sale, that which is sold will be sold at a higher price. In principle, output can be limited by reducing any of the inputs for production—for example, labor, land, seeds, fertilizer. In the United States, the emphasis has been on limiting the amount of land used in production. Although there has been considerable variation in the details of the programs, acreage limits have been applied to wheat, cotton, feed grains, peanuts, rice, sugar, and tobacco. In some cases, the price support loans described previously have been used in conjunction with acreage limitations, with the limitations a requirement for participation in the loan program. Indeed, without output controls such as acreage limits, the cost of price support loan programs can become very large. Acreage can be limited either by having compulsory acreage allotments or by paying farmers for voluntarily keeping land idle.

While acreage restrictions are relatively simple to administer and enforce, focusing on only one factor of production limits their effectiveness. For example, reducing the acreage planted in a certain crop by 10 percent is unlikely to result in a 10 percent reduction in the amount of crop produced. For one thing, all land is not equally productive, and a farmer withdrawing 10 percent of the farmland from production is likely to withdraw the least productive land. Second, the farmer can increase production on the remaining land by cultivating it more intensely through the use of more fertilizer and pesticides or a more expensive and higher-yield hybrid seed.

Deficiency Payments

Another approach to increasing farm incomes is to make up the difference between the market price and the target or support price with a direct payment from the government. Deficiency payments allow the government to avoid the costs of transporting and storing the product and allow consumers the benefits of purchasing the product at the low market price. A deficiency payment program without limits, however, can become quite expensive: it gives farmers an incentive to increase production. These costs can be limited by paying farmers only for a specified quantity of product or by limiting the maximum payment that can be made to a large producer.

Imports and Exports

Keeping domestic prices high almost always requires some sort of import restriction. Limiting acreage to reduce the amount offered for sale is futile if imports of similar quality are offered for sale alongside the domestic product. Similarly, unrestricted, low-cost imports drive down the market price, thereby increasing the amount of deficiency payments needed. With nonrecourse loans or similar price support programs, the cost of the government can become astronomical if imports are permitted to drive most domestic production into the government's hands. Of course, limiting imports either through quotas or import duties is not well received by other countries. Another approach to boosting farm income is to subsidize exports. By encouraging exports through paying a subsidy to farmers for exported products, the amount of product left for domestic consumption is reduced, thereby driving up domestic prices. The problem, of course, is that what to one country is an export subsidy is dumping to the country receiving the export.

Other Programs

In addition to those programs designed to increase the prices received by farmers for their products, most countries have a wide variety of other programs to benefit agriculture. Many governments, including the United States, conduct or sponsor research and provide farmers with advisory and extension services. Subsidies for inputs and for investment in buildings and machinery are common. In many parts of the United States, irrigation water is provided to farmers at prices far below production and transportation costs. These programs reduce the cost of farming and in doing so, provide an incentive for increased production. Thus, to some degree, they can work at cross-purposes to the various price support programs outlined earlier.

EFFECTS OF AGRICULTURE POLICY

By 1985, U.S. agriculture subsidy programs of various forms cost $33.9 billion, and by 1991 U.S. farmers were receiving about 30 percent of their income in subsidies. Thus, for every $2.00 a farmer received from farming, the farmer received nearly $1.00 additional in subsidy from the government. While this might seem high, it is actually relatively low in comparison with most other developed countries in the world, as Table 13–2 indicates. Virtually all of Europe is dramatically higher than the United States, with European Community (EC) farmers averaging about half of their income from agriculture subsidies. In Japan, the figure is about two-thirds. In other words, in Japan a farmer receives on average $2.00 in subsidy for each $1.00 earned in farming. Among the countries in the table, only farmers in Australia and New Zealand receive a smaller proportion of their income from subsidy than do U.S. farmers.

In light of the high proportion of farm income from subsidy shown in Table 13–2, it is not surprising that the cost of agricultural support for nonfarm households is high. As seen in Table 13–3, agricultural support costs each nonfarm household in the United States about $400 per year. Moreover, these subsidies are not a particularly efficient way of transferring money from consumers and taxpayers to farmers. In the case of the United States, consumers and taxpayers pay $1.26 for every $1.00 received by farmers. Remarkably, subsidy costs for nonfarm households are dramatically higher in some other parts of the world than in the United States. In Japan, for example, subsidy costs are nearly six times higher than in the United States, and in the EFTA-5 countries (Austria, Finland, Norway, Sweden, and Switzerland) they are seven times higher. In the European Community (EC-12),

TABLE 13–2   Agriculture Subsidies

Country or Region	Subsidy as a Percentage of Income
United States	30
Canada	45
Japan	66
European Community	49
Switzerland	80
Finland	71
Norway	77
Sweden	59
Austria	52
Australia	15
New Zealand	4

Source: Derived from data contained in Organization for Economic Co-Operation and Development, *Agricultural Policies, Markets and Trade: Monitoring and Outlook 1992* (Paris: OECD, 1992) ANNEX, Tables III.2–III.23.

TABLE 13–3   Cost of Agricultural Support per Nonfarm Household, 1990

	Transfers from Consumers and Taxpayers	
	Per Nonfarm Household	Per Dollar Gained by Producers
United States	$400	$1.26
Japan	$2,290	$1.74
EC-12	$1,130	$1.25
EFTA-5	$2,800	$1.17

EC-12 includes Belgium, Denmark, West Germany, France, Greece, Ireland, Italy, Luxembourg, the Netherlands, Portugal, Spain, and the United Kingdom.

EFTA-5 includes Austria, Finland, Norway, Sweden, and Switzerland.

Source: Organization for Economic Co-Operation and Development, as reported in *The Economist*, 12, December 1992.

per-household subsidy costs are nearly three times higher than in the United States. The EC countries represented in the table are Belgium, Denmark, West Germany, France, Greece, Ireland, Italy, Luxembourg, the Netherlands, Portugal, Spain, and the United Kingdom.

Averages, of course, can conceal a great deal of variation. In the case of U.S. farm subsidies, there is considerable variation in which farmers receive which amounts of subsidy. Table 13–4 shows the distribution of farm income and government payments for various size categories of farms. The table also shows the average payment per farm for one category of subsidy program, direct payments per farm. The sales class categories are a collapsed version of those presented in Table 13–1. As is evident from Table 13–4, 13 percent of government payments go to the largest 1 percent of farms, and 68 percent of government payments go the largest 14 percent of farms, those with annual income from farm operations of over $100,000 that already earn 74 percent of their gross receipts from farming. At the other end of the distribution, 72 percent of the farms get only 10 percent of government payments and get direct payments averaging less than $500 per year. This is in contrast with the over $37,000 per year average payment to large farms earning over $500,000 in cash farm income. It appears from this table that the current system of government payments in the United States targets very little money at

TABLE 13–4   Distribution of Farms, Gross Cash Farm Income, and Government Payments

Sales Class	Percentage of Farms	Percentage of Cash Farm Income	Percentage of Government Payments	Average Direct Payment
Less than $40,000	72	10	10	$447
$40,000–$100,000	14	16	22	$5,193
$100,000–$500,000	13	42	55	$14,902
Over $500,000	1	32	13	$37,399

Source: Kenneth L. Robinson, *Farm and Food Policies and their Consequences*, (Englewood Cliffs, NJ: Prentice Hall, 1989), table 5.1, p. 72.

small, struggling family farms. Instead, well over half the payments go to farms that already have substantial income from farm operations.

U.S. agricultural policy did not start out with the goal of making large subsidy payments to large farms that already earn substantial revenue from farming activities. The policies have evolved slowly, and for the most part unintentionally, to produce that result. To understand how policies could produce such unintended consequences, it is instructive to consider the case of some specific commodities in more detail.

SUGAR POLICY

Sugar cane and sugar beets each account for roughly 50 percent of total U.S. sugar production. Sugar cane is grown largely in warmer climates with Florida, Hawaii, Louisiana, and Texas as the major-producing states. Sugar beets are grown more widely, and Minnesota, California, Idaho, North Dakota, and Michigan are the major-producing states. Sugar cane tends to be grown on very large farms compared to the average for other crops, whereas sugar beets tend to be grown on farms closer to the average size. U.S. consumption of sugar from cane and beets reached a peak of 11.5 million tons in 1972 before declining. By 1986, consumption had dropped 26 percent to 8.6 million tons with per capita consumption dropping 30 percent during this period. The drop in sugar consumption was not due to changing consumer tastes or the rise of low-calorie substitutes. Indeed, total consumption of caloric sweeteners increased 22 percent over the same period. The growth in sweetener came largely from rapid growth in the use of corn products such as high-fructose corn syrup, glucose, and dextrose. In fact, by 1986 corn sweeteners surpassed the combined total of cane and beet sugar.

The federal government's attempts to influence sugar prices date back to the nation's first tariff in 1789, which imposed duties on sugar. At that time, almost all the nation's sugar was imported, so this tariff raised the price of sugar to domestic users by about the amount of the duty. It also had the effect of raising the price the few domestic producers could charge for their sugar. These early tariffs were purportedly designed to raise tax revenue for the government rather than to help domestic producers, but they did both. The import duties on sugar were dropped in 1890 when there was a surplus in the federal treasury. This lapse in import duties was quickly followed by an influx of cheap imports from Europe, resulting in a drop in sugar prices below the cost of production of many U.S. producers. In 1894, a tariff was again levied on sugar imports, this time to protect local industry rather than to raise revenue. The pattern was set. Domestic producers gained from the import duties, and consumers paid higher prices. With the exception of a brief period in the 1890s, the United States has gradually increased duties on imported sugar since the inception of the duties.

The Jones-Costigan Act of 1934 added sugar beets and sugar cane to the list of crops to which acreage restriction and benefit payment programs applied. An important feature of this act was to place sugar import quotas on foreign nations— at a time when U.S. posture was to promote free trade. The Sugar Act of 1948 increased import restrictions. It was allowed to expire in 1974 in the belief that a sugar program was no longer needed. Sugar surpluses quickly developed, and prices dropped sharply, prompting Congress to include new sugar legislation in the Food and Agriculture Act of 1977. Before 1956, Cuba and the Philippines together accounted for about 96 percent of U.S. sugar imports. Following Castro's takeover, Cuba lost its import allocation, and its quotas were dispersed to other nations. By this point, imports were strictly limited, and domestic sugar prices were isolated from world market conditions. The U.S. Department of Agriculture controlled domestic production through acreage restrictions, established import quotas, and generally set sugar prices through the use of nonrecourse loans. Import quotas have become valuable commodities.

Because of these programs, U.S. consumers have paid higher sugar prices than have much of the rest of the world throughout most of the nation's history. However, the difference between the U.S. retail price and world market prices has grown since the early 1980s. By 1991, U.S. consumers were paying nearly twice the prevailing world price for sugar. In effect, U.S. agricultural policy had imposed the equivalent of a 92 percent tax on sugar consumption. Table 13–5 lists the equivalent tax on sugar caused by import restrictions and tariffs in several other countries. Remarkably, similar policies in other developed countries have resulted in even greater equivalent taxes on their sugar consumers. Policies vary but have similar results. In the United States the primary effect is that increasingly strict import quotas prevent cheap foreign sugar from flooding the market. In 1973, more than 5 million tons of sugar were permitted to enter the United States under the quota system. By 1986, imports had been reduced to 1.7 million tons.

The Philippines, Brazil, Australia, Taiwan, Fiji, Haiti, the Dominican Republic, Mauritius, Thailand, and South Africa are among the countries that have been granted sugar quotas in the past. These countries have been able to earn more from sugar sold in the United States than they could have earned by selling sugar at world market prices. Thus, the U.S. sugar program has been a vehicle for selectively aiding certain countries. The total import quota and the allocation among suppliers have been strongly influenced by political considerations. Domestic producers of both sugar beets and sugar cane want to restrict imports and gain a larger share of the total market. In return for protection, U.S. producers have had to accept acreage restrictions. Production rights have been allocated to certain states. When sugar production is profitable, members of Congress and senators vie with each other to obtain an allotment for their district or state or to increase their prior allotment. One way to increase the domestic allotment is to decrease the import allotment. When Cuba's quota was removed, part was reallocated to other countries, and part was reallocated to domestic producers.

TABLE 13–5   Equivalent Tax on Sugar, 1991

	Equivalent Tax Rate
Japan	354%
European Community	156%
Switzerland	132%
Sweden	108%
United States	92%
Australia	81%
Canada	10%
New Zealand	0%

Source: Organization for Economic Co-Operation and Development, as reported in *The Economist,* 12, December 1992.

Because of the value of import quotas and state allotments, lobbyists have played a major role representing the interests of both U.S. sugar producers and those of foreign countries. Competition has been intense, and there have been charges that various congressional committee members have accepted favors in exchange for support of a position. Foreign policy considerations have inevitably played a role in determining who gets a quota and how large it will be. The Philippines, for example, was guaranteed a quota as part of the treaty granting independence. The Irish lobby in the United States succeeded at one time in getting a small quota for Ireland. Australia retains a quota partly because it has been a reliable ally. Some members of Congress have tried to use sugar quotas as leverage to achieve other objectives. Members of the congressional black caucus, for example, have on several occasions attempted to reduce or eliminate the sugar quota given to South Africa.

In the United States, each sugar grower earns from subsidies alone twice the nation's average family income. The average Minnesota sugar beet grower got almost four times the financial return from growing sugar in 1982 that he would have received from growing corn. A Louisiana farmer received almost seven times as much per acre for growing sugarcane as would have been received from growing soybeans. As with other agriculture programs, production is concentrated in relatively few farms, and the subsidy benefits are concentrated among few recipients. In the sugar beet industry, 11 processors receive 40 percent of federal subsidies while the balance is divided among about 10,000 farmers. In the sugar cane industry, 5 corporations produce 98 percent of the Hawaiian crop, with fewer than 250 farmers producing the remaining 2 percent, and 2 corporations produce over half the Florida crop, with about 125 producing the rest.

A 1988 Department of Commerce study estimated that the sugar program is costing consumers up to $3 billion a year—more than $45 per year for the average family of four. Because food is a necessity, it commands a large share of the poor family's budget. Moreover, because healthy eating is expensive, there is a good chance that the poor are the greatest consumers of sugar and, therefore, the greatest contributors to the sugar programs. The mechanism that takes money from the poor and gives it to the rich is most extreme in Japan and Europe where the equivalent tax rates are highest, but it operates in the United States as well.

The effects of sugar policy do not end with an income transfer from consumers to producers. Those who make sugar substitutes have been major beneficiaries. Artificially high sugar prices have provided an opportunity for producers of substitutes, most notably, corn sweeteners. Indeed, soft drink manufacturers have switched almost entirely to high-fructose corn syrup or noncaloric sweeteners. Largely overlooked in the 1986 marketing furor over Coca-Cola's attempt to change its classic formula was the fact that the formula did quietly change from sugar to high-fructose corn syrup. The corn sweetener industry has also been helped by government subsidies to make ethanol from corn. Sugar now accounts for less than half of the U.S. market of caloric sweeteners. One study estimates that the corporations that make nonsugar sweeteners gain almost as much from sugar programs as do the sugar growers themselves. Thus, the corn sweetener lobby has become a powerful advocate of the sugar program.

High sugar prices have also increased the importation of sugar-containing products. Such products do not bear import tariffs or restrictions. This has become a problem for U.S. processors of products such as candy. Candy companies that can operate both in the United States and in countries such as Canada, which does not support the price of sugar, have had a substantial competitive advantage. In the early 1980s, when U.S. sugar prices were seven times higher than world prices, some entrepreneurs imported high sugar content products such as iced tea mix, sifted the sugar from the mix, and sold the sugar at high domestic prices. The government responded by banning all imported foods containing sugar. Commerce was disrupted as hundreds of private contracts were nullified and a wide variety of foods, including pizzas and noodles with less than 1 percent sugar, were impounded. With such a price differential, sugar smuggling became potentially more profitable, and the Justice Department caught 20 sugar bootleggers in Operation Bittersweet.

Import restrictions also have an adverse impact on the countries who produce sugar cheaply, but do not have a share of the U.S. quota. This group includes countries such as Ivory Coast and Tanzania. They are among the world's poorest nations, and farmers are among their poorest citizens. One study indicated that worldwide liberalization of trade would lead to $7.5 billion in extra exports from low-and middle-income developing countries. As it is, sugar policies help to keep these countries poor and sugar growers in developed countries rich.

DAIRY POLICY

Like many other farm price support programs, the origins of the dairy program predate the New Deal legislation of the 1930s. Cartelized dairy marketing was assisted by passage of the Capper-Volstead Act in 1922 that exempted farm cooperative-marketing organizations from some antitrust provisions. Dairy cooperatives were negotiating prices, weighing and testing milk for butterfat and bacteria count, and representing the political interests of the cooperative, as well as processing cheese, butter, and other products. Milk production cartels were given another boost in the early 1930s when milk was included in the commodities eligible for price supports in the Agricultural Adjustment Act of 1933. Although milk was included, no method comparable to the acreage reduction program for crops was provided for restricting milk supplies.

The major program for milk price enhancement was established with the Agricultural Marketing Agreement Act of 1937. The act established the basic structure of the current milk marketing orders at a time when the road transportation network and refrigeration technology were yet to be developed. The goal was to make each small geographic area self-sufficient in milk. Milk is required to be classified according to its final use, such as fluid, processed milk in products such as cheese or ice cream, and dried milk. The country is divided into 44 marketing regions, and minimum and uniform prices are set by the Department of Agriculture in each region. The price of Class 1 milk, fluid milk, is set at a higher level than other classes, which often results in excess production of this class. Since drinking milk is highly perishable and heavy, little is shipped from one market to another. Consequently, local dairy farmers can exercise considerable power over the price of Class 1 milk in each of the local markets. The market power exercised by the cooperatives is greater and the price of milk generally higher in those markets where a single cooperative controls a major portion of the supply.

Although the Agricultural Marketing Agreement Act contained no specific method for controlling supply, its provisions have been used for supply control purposes. The most important of the supply control features are classifying milk and setting minimum prices for each class. The minimum price of Class 1 milk is generally negotiated at well above cost of production, and the quantity not sold as fluid milk goes into manufactured milk products. The fluid milk price thus usually exceeds the competitive price level.

State and local regulations ostensibly designed to protect public health by assuring high-quality drinking milk were frequently used to limit the free flow of milk from low-cost to high-cost producing areas. The Agricultural Marketing Agreement Act specifically prohibits any marketing order from limiting the marketing of U.S.-produced milk or milk products. Nevertheless, factors such as alleged faulty labeling, reluctance to grant permits, different sanitation requirements, costs of sanitation permits, and state trade practice regulations often function as barriers to entry. These barriers are seldom necessary for the maintenance of high-quality milk and are used primarily to aid local producers in restricting supplies and maintaining higher prices.

Restrictions on the use of reconstituted milk also limit the interregional movements of dairy products. Milk produced where costs are low can easily be dried, shipped to areas where costs are high, and reconstituted. Neither consumer taste testers nor lab chemists can distinguish ordinary fresh milk from a blend of 70 percent reconstituted milk and 30 percent fresh milk. However, federal milk-marketing orders require that milk used in a drinking product must be sold at the Class 1 price. If the processor purchases powdered milk at cost and then adds water, the difference between Class 1 and Class 2 price must be paid into a pool to be distributed to dairy farmers. Thus consumers pay the same price, and the supplier of the dried-milk mixture makes no additional profit. The advantage of this potential for a lower-cost milk product is denied consumers.

Supply control of dairy products at the national level has consisted largely of import quotas. Quotas have been imposed on imports of dairy products since 1953. Nonfat dry milk and butter imports are banned. Cheese imports are limited to a small percentage of annual U.S. consumption, less than 2 percent. Such quotas keep lower-priced foreign dairy products out of the United States and thereby increase the cost of such products to consumers.

With dairy products, as with other agricultural products, prices set by the government at above-market levels provide incentive for increased production and concurrently add to consumer costs, thus reducing the quantity demanded. The Agricultural Act of 1949 made support prices mandatory not only on Class 1 milk but also on all milk and milk products. By agreeing to purchase all milk that cannot be sold in the market at the federally established support price, the government has maintained the price of milk at or above market levels each year since supports began. In some years, the support price and the market price were close, and only a small quantity of dairy product had to be purchased by the government. In other years, support prices were far above market prices, and as much as 10 to 12 percent of total production had to be purchased by the government. In 1980, the USDA purchased two billion pounds of surplus dairy products. By 1981, federal spending on dairy subsidies had increased sixfold in two years, and the government had a $3 billion surplus in storage. The Commodity Credit Corporation was buying nonfat dry milk at 94 cents a pound and selling it for 55 cents a pound to help provide hogs with their minimum daily calcium intake. By 1983, the USDA was spending more than a quarter of a million dollars *an hour* buying surplus dairy products and spending more than a million dollars *a day* to store them. Throughout the period from 1981 to 1985, the government spent an average of $2.2 billion per year to remove surplus dairy products. More recently, the USDA bought butter from American farmers at $3,000 a ton and sold it overseas for $1,000 per ton. Dairy price supports alone cost each household in the United States about $30 per year in taxes. In addition, consumers pay a higher price for dairy products than they would without the program.

In 1983, Congress created a"guaranteed one time only" solution to the dairy surplus by paying farmers not to produce milk and to kill their cows. The buyout was started in November 1983 but paid farmers for any reduction in milk production since 1982, thereby paying farmers for actions they had already taken for other reasons. While the government paid some farmers to reduce their milk production, other dairy farmers were not prevented from increasing their production. At the end of the program, after $995 million had been spent, there were only 10,000 fewer dairy cows in the United States than there had been in the beginning. The USDA had paid the equivalent of about $100,000 for each net cow reduction. A used dairy cow normally sells for about $1,000. After the program ended, dairy farmers adjusted their herds, and soon the nation had 11.2 million cows, the largest herd since 1975.

In 1986 and 1987, the USDA ran a "guaranteed second time only" dairy buyout, again to pay farmers to kill or export their cows. Under this Dairy Termination Program, 144 dairy owners received a million dollars each, and one California producer received $10 million. New Mexico State University received $314,000 for selling 280 cows it had used for research. The USDA gave one farmer $585,000 to leave the dairy business even though his partner, a son-in-law, stayed in the business and kept the farm. The USDA ruled that a farmer could take the Dairy Termination Program money and invest in another dairy farm. The USDA paid up to $22.50 a hundredweight to reduce milk production at a time when milk was selling for $11 a hundredweight. In examining the program, the General Accounting Office (GAO) found that 26 percent of the recipients reported that they "probably or definitely would have quit dairy operations without the program." The GAO also noted that "total milk production did not decrease because nonparticipating farmers increased their production during the program period."[4]

As with many other agricultural support programs, payments tend to be concentrated among a relatively small number of farms. Between January 1984 and April 1985, in the five largest milk-producing states, 42,000 producers were paid approximately $955 million, or about $22,700 each, in return for diverting up to 30 percent of their production from the market. However, about one-fourth of the recipients received over 60 percent of the total payment. These recipients were paid an average of $57,100 each. The highest-paid 95 percent of Florida recipients (177 farmers) got an average of $226,000, and the highest-paid 87 percent of California recipients (608 farmers) got an average of $142,200 each.

Despite these programs, the number of commercial dairy producers has fallen from 600,000 to fewer than 130,000 since 1952. The number of dairy farmers has decreased by an average of 4,800 every year since 1970.

PEANUT POLICY

In 1933, Congress began supporting peanut prices by buying farmers' peanuts at very generous prices. Not surprisingly, farmers responded to the high prices by boosting production. Congress responded to large peanut surpluses in 1941 by placing mandatory controls on peanut farmers and prohibiting any citizen from growing peanuts commercially without a federal license, which specified to the hundredth of an acre how much land could be cultivated. The right to grow peanuts in the future was based on the number of acres of peanuts farmers had grown in the past. Almost all peanut imports were prohibited.

Congress set peanut price supports very high over the years, thereby encouraging farmers to maximize production on their limited acreage. Relatively high peanut prices mandated by the government repressed peanut consumption, and the result was perpetual surpluses. Congress, in an attempt to drive up domestic peanut prices, changed the peanut license system from a base of acres to a base of pounds, allowing the USDA tighter control over production. The federal government has reduced the domestic peanut supply since 1975, causing an artificial peanut shortage and shifting the cost of the peanut program from the government (actually the taxpayer) to the consumer.

Congress keeps the peanut licenses, or *quota allotments,* in the same congressional districts. Quota allotments cannot be rented outside the county in which they were originally allocated in 1941. Peanuts cause a depletion of soil nutrients, and as a result, peanut yields in parts of Texas have long been declining. Although many acres with yields below 1,000 pounds have quotas, over a million acres with potential yields of 2,500 to 5,000 pounds or more may not be used to produce peanuts for domestic consumption.

In 1981, Congress decided that farmers without quota licenses would be allowed to grow peanuts, but with no real price guarantees from the government and only if the peanuts were not consumed within the United States. Georgia farmers are profitably growing peanuts for export at $325 a ton at the same time that the USDA maintains a support price of $615.85 a ton. Thus, foreigners can buy U.S. peanuts for half the price Americans can.

The American Peanut Product Manufacturers Institute estimates that net returns to peanut farmers are four to ten times higher than are returns from competing crops. Twelve peanut growers each received benefits exceeding $250,000 from the program. The bankruptcy rate among peanut farmers is far lower than the bankruptcy rate among all farmers. The USDA estimates that the peanut program boosts peanut butter prices 13.5 percent and costs consumers $300 million to $500 million a year.

In 1930, U.S. farmers planted 1.1 million acres each of peanuts and soybeans. In 1933, Congress decided to protect peanuts and leave soybeans to the marketplace. By 1980, U.S. farmers were growing 1.4 million acres of peanuts and 68 million acres of soybeans. The peanut crop was worth about $500 million, while the soybean crop was worth more than $13 billion.

HONEY PROGRAM

The honey program cost taxpayers $100 million in 1988, almost equal to the market value of all U.S. honey production. Yet less than 6 percent of the nation's 200,000 beekeepers received benefits from the government, while several beekeepers received over $1 million a year from the government for their surplus honey.

Until 1949, honey production was not subject to government price supports. During World War II, honey production was increased to compensate for a temporary sugar shortage. When the war ended, a honey glut occurred, and a price support program was instituted. Until the early 1970s, the cost of the price support program was small because the support price was below world market prices. However, between 1982 and 1984, honey price supports increased 370 percent to far above world prices. Congress scaled back the price supports in 1985, but they remain about 50 percent above world market prices.

Unlike many other price-supported crops, honey is not subject to acreage limitations or their equivalent, nor is imported honey subject to high import tariffs. Thus, when the support price for honey is high, low-priced foreign imports of honey increase. U.S. beekeepers increase production in response to the government price signal, and the government ends up buying more U.S.-produced honey. In 1985, the USDA bought about 130 million pounds of domestically produced honey in an attempt to increase honey prices, while Mexico, Argentina, China, and other countries sold 138 million pounds of honey to U.S. customers, thereby negating USDA'S efforts.

Some U.S. processors in 1984 were reportedly buying foreign honey at 40 cents a pound and selling it to the USDA for 59 cents a pound. As the GAO said in a report, "USDA generally does not perform tests on honey used for loan collateral to ensure that the honey is not imported or adulterated with corn syrup." At the same time the government works to protect honey, there is no federal support program for molasses or maple syrup.

AGRICULTURE AND THE ENVIRONMENT

There is increasing recognition that major environmental impacts result from agricultural practices and, more importantly, that the design of agricultural policy can greatly affect the environment. Unfortunately, this second realization has been slow in coming, and much of the agricultural policy in this country has actually encouraged environmental degradation.

Agriculture can cause three basic categories of potentially adverse environmental impacts off the farm: (1) pollution of surface water by eroded sediment from cropland, nitrates from livestock manure, and runoffs from fertilizer, herbicide, and pesticide; (2) pollution of groundwater from many of the same runoffs that can pollute surface water; and (3) loss of wildlife habitat when wetlands are converted to agricultural use. In addition, aquifers depleted by agricultural irrigation cannot provide water for other uses. Erosion, the depletion of soil nutrients, and the use of fertilizers, herbicides, and pesticides can also have adverse impacts on the farm itself, but presumably the farmer takes account of these effects in selecting agricultural practices. Thus, it is the off-farm effects that are of greatest concern for public policy.

These effects can be large. The Department of the Interior estimates that conversion to agricultural use accounted for 87 percent of wetland loss from the mid-1950s to the mid-1970s. For the most part, however, we know very little about the environmental impacts of agriculture. We know there is surface water pollution, but the full effects of that pollution are just beginning to be recognized and assessed. Similarly, we know there is groundwater pollution from agriculture, but we know very little about how much or even where the pollution is worst.

Some of agriculture's productivity gains have come from the use of pesticides, herbicides, and fertilizer. Pesticide use doubled between 1970 and 1980. Some of the increased use of these chemicals is the direct, although unintended, result of agricultural policies. High crop support prices encourage farmers to increase their output, but the often accompanying acreage limitations restrict the amount of land they can use. The resulting incentive is to farm the existing land more intensely, and as noted at the beginning of the chapter, crop production per acre has been increasing impressively. A common way to get this increase, however, is to use more fertilizer and pesticide. Programs that base this year's permissible production on last year's production also discourage crop rotation, thereby increasing the depletion of soil nutrients. These problems are not unique to the United States, nor are they even most severe here. The European Community, South Korea, and Japan, for example, use far more fertilizer per acre than does the United States. Of course, Canada, New Zealand, and Australia all use less.

Environmental degradation is not the intent of these agricultural policies, but it has been the widespread result. The unintended consequences of agricultural policy, both environmental and otherwise, illustrate two essential points in public policy. First, policies formulated to address problems in one area will inevitably have consequences in other areas. Thus, effective public policy cannot be formulated if one looks only at the narrow sector where the issue first arises. One must consider far more than agriculture when formulating agricultural policy. Second, it is critical that policy makers consider the incentives, and especially the economic incentives, they are creating for people with their policies. Farmers' behavior in response to these various programs is easily understood and can be readily predicted if one pays attention to the incentives these programs give farmers. To the extent that some of these policies have failed, the failure to consider the incentives is to blame.

SUMMARY

It seems clear that agriculture policy, as practiced in the United States, is helping neither consumers nor small family farmers. These policies cost taxpayers a great deal and push up the prices of many farm products. However, these policies have been very difficult to change. The beneficiaries of these policies, the large farms who receive the bulk of the subsidies, are well organized and have been effective at lobbying Congress. Those who pay the price, consumers and taxpayers, are not nearly so well organized nor are many informed of the true character of some of these policies. Thus, these policies have persisted with little real change for over 50 years.

Congressional reluctance to tackle agriculture policy may be changing, however. As concern about budget deficits increases and as a wide variety of government programs are viewed with increased scrutiny, the costs and effects of U.S. agriculture policy are coming under attack from an increasingly wide array of interests. Members of Congress who have expressed little interest in challenging agriculture interests in the past seem increasingly willing at least to raise questions about these policies. Perhaps agriculture policy will emerge with little change from these closer examinations. Perhaps, however, the growing pressure for reexamination of these policies will result in dramatic changes similar to those described earlier in transportation and other policy areas.

DISCUSSION QUESTIONS

1. What are the principal goals of agriculture policy? For each of these goals and provide specific evidence about the extent to which public policy has been successful in achieving the goal. Use evidence from both the United States and throughout the world.
2. What are the principal instruments of agriculture policy in the United States? How does each work and what goal is each used to achieve?
3. What are the principal barriers to making major changes in agriculture policy in the United States?
4. Which of the current agriculture policies do you think would be easiest to change? Which policies do you think would be hardest to change?
5. Why do you think the agriculture lobby is so powerful in the United States and elsewhere in the world? Based on the proportion of the population involved in agriculture, would you expect it to be so powerful?

SUGGESTED READINGS

U.S. General Accounting Office, *Peanut Program: Changes Are Needed to Make the Program Responsive to Market Forces*, (Washington, DC: Government Printing Office, 1993).

Dennis T. Avery, *Global Food Progress 1991* (Indianapolis, IN: Hudson Institute, 1991).

Clifton B. Luttrell, *The High Cost of Farm Welfare* (Washington, DC: The Cato Institute, 1989).

Kenneth L. Robinson, *Farm and Food Policies and their Consequences* (Englewood Cliffs, NJ: Prentice Hall, 1989)

US General Accounting Office, *Dairy Termination Program: A Perspective on its Participants and Milk Production* (Washington, DC: Government Printing Office, May 1988).

NOTES

1. Clifton B. Luttrell, *The High Cost of Farm Welfare* (Washington, D.C.: Cato Institute, 1989).
2. John Block, *The PIK Program—An Assessment* (Washington, D.C.: USDA Press Office, 1983), 2.
3. Rod Tyers and Kym Anderson, *Disarray in World Food Markets* (Cambridge: Cambridge University Press, 1992), p. 20.
4. U.S. General Accounting Office, *Dairy Termination Program: A Perspective on its Participants and Milk Production* (Washington, D.C.: U.S. Government Printing Office, 1988).

14

Foreign and National Security Policy

A HISTORY OF ISOLATIONISM AND INTERVENTION

U.S. foreign policy has mostly been dominated by the desire to avoid the types of foreign entanglements that had plagued European countries for hundreds of years.[1] The founding fathers were also skeptical about the use of force in the solution of international disagreements, thinking it caused more problems than it solved. In the 18th century, Alexander Hamilton professed astonishment "with how much precipitancy and levity nations still rush to arms with each other . . . after the experience of its having deluged the world with calamities for so many ages." Even the Monroe Doctrine (1823), which warned Europeans against encroachments in the western hemisphere, implied no commitment to the security or freedom of any other state.

Because of this history, which was bolstered by being separated from most world conflicts by two oceans, the United States had the luxury of being able to define its interests primarily in terms of its own part of the world. This attitude characterized U.S. diplomacy into the 20th century. If the United States went to war, it was for its own reasons and for its own security. It was not until its entry into World War I that a new internationalist attitude took hold in the United States. President Woodrow Wilson saw the war as a way to ensure a balance of power favorable to the United States and to "make the world safe for democracy." Although Wilson was attacked by Henry Cabot Lodge and others for his shift in traditional U.S. policy and lost the vote in Congress to ratify the League of Nations treaty, the fundamental concept took root in some quarters despite strong isolationist sentiments that again dominated U.S. foreign policy after the war.

The dominance of isolationism continued in the United States until the country was attacked by the Japanese and entered World War II. As recently as a few weeks before the attack, President Franklin D. Roosevelt was vowing publicly to keep the United States out of the conflict in Europe and Asia and even had to hide the U.S. contributions to Great Britain's military with the ruse that the United States was only lending Britain equipment. The war changed U.S. foreign policy permanently. President Roosevelt later verbalized this shift in attitude when he said, "We must live like men and not ostriches."[2] He and Winston Churchill, the British prime minister, put the change into policy when they signed the Atlantic Charter in 1941. The charter, later incorporated into the United Nations Charter, listed the freedoms guaranteed to the peoples of the world. These included the right to choose their own governments, freedom of religion, freedom of the press, and the right to engage freely in international commerce.

Public opinion polls in the United States during that period supported the international initiatives of the United States and Great Britain, by a large majority. These initiatives included setting up the United Nations (UN) and enacting the Marshall Plan to restore wartorn Europe. With the activation of the Cold War with the Soviet Union in the late 1940s, the United States even discarded its old reluctance to engage in foreign alliances and entanglements and established, with its allies in Western Europe, the North Atlantic Treaty Organization (NATO) in 1949. NATO's intent was to provide Cold War security to the United States and the Western European alliance, and other military alliances in other parts of the world (e.g., SEATO in Southeast Asia) soon followed.

The Cold War, and the policy of Soviet containment, dominated U.S. foreign policy until the early 1990s, although there was by no means a consistent approach throughout this period. In 1950 the United States (under President Harry S Truman) responded to the invasion of the southern peninsula of Korea by the communist regime of North Korea. The conflict lasted until 1953 when President Dwight D. Eisenhower arrived at a truce with the North Koreans and their Chinese allies, who had entered the war when U.S. forces moved close to the Korea-China border. In the early 1960s, under President John F. Kennedy, the nation had a confrontation with the Soviet Union over the stationing of ballistic nuclear missiles in Cuba, just 90 miles south of Miami. At that time, the United States also initiated action in Vietnam to aid the democratic south in its civil war with the communist north.

The Vietnam conflict, initiated under Kennedy and waged during the tenure of three presidents, resulted in bringing down Lyndon Johnson's presidency in his first elected term following President Kennedy's assassination. The Vietnam War divided the country as no other war had in modern times and rekindled isolationism in the nation. Those supporting the war did so on the basis of containing communism and argued that other nations in Southeast Asia would fall like dominoes unless the North Vietnamese were stopped. Their opponents believed that what happened in Vietnam was of little concern to the United States, certainly not of sufficient concern to sacrifice the lives of young American soldiers in an attempt to influence events there. The eventual resolution, after many U.S. casualties and great national conflict, occurred with the withdrawal of U.S. forces and the victory of North Vietnam. Afterward, the United States retreated from its foreign intervention policy that had marked the 1950s and 1960s.

President Richard M. Nixon, reflecting this altered view of the world, stated in 1969, "We cannot—and will not—conceive all the plans, design all the programs, and undertake all the defense of the free nations of the world. We will help where it makes a difference, and is considered in our interests." Nixon even opened the door to Red China, which had been closed to the West virtually since the end of World War II, after the Communists had forced the Nationalists to retreat to Taiwan. Nixon also initiated steps to try to arrive at a détente with the Russians, by using the rivalry that had built up between the Chinese and Russian Communists after the war.

President Jimmy Carter continued the policy of reluctance to intervene militarily in other parts of the world that had characterized the Nixon administration. His primary contribution to foreign policy was the very successful brokering of the Egyptian-Israeli Camp David Peace Accord. Carter also tried to lend moral support to Soviet dissidents of that time, such as Andrei Sakharov. Carter was severely criticized by many people, however, for his unwillingness to help the Shah of Iran keep Islamic fundamentalists from gaining power in Iran.

President Ronald Reagan entered office with a belligerent attitude toward the Soviets, even referring to them in an early speech as the "evil empire." He launched the largest military buildup since the Vietnam War and initiated the Strategic Defense Initiative (SDI) to develop an antiballistic missile defense system. Many believe this buildup and the SDI were the final blow to the Soviets, who found themselves increasingly unable to continue a Cold War in which they were spending an unsustainable percentage of their gross domestic product (GDP) for defense. Reagan also showed less reluctance than had other presidents to mount military incursions; he initiated successful interventions in Panama, Grenada, and Libya. In his second term, Reagan was eventually able to establish a reasonable relationship with Mikhail Sergeyevich Gorbachev, president of the Soviet Union, while at the same time subsidizing insurgents in several Third World communist countries.

President George Bush reaped the benefits of Soviet internal pressures and problems: the fall of the Berlin Wall in 1989 signaled the beginning of the end of the Soviet empire. Bush also propelled the coalition that pushed Iraq out of Kuwait, which Iraq had invaded in the summer of 1990. The events culminating in the Gulf War, combined with the elimination of the Soviet threat, led some to wonder whether the United States was going to return to the interventionist role it had played until the war in Vietnam. But Bush's unwillingness to push the Gulf War to a conclusion that would have required the United States to take a direct hand in politically stabilizing Iraq, and his subsequent defeat in the 1992 presidential election, seemed to imply that the United States was, after all, not interested in being the world's police department.

THE UNITED STATES IN A NEW WORLD ORDER

With the collapse of the Soviet Union and the Warsaw Pact in 1991, and the conversion of former U.S. adversaries into new friends (or at least friendly associates), the United States is now in the process of redefining its foreign policy fundamentals. That is what President Bush tried to do when he referred to the "new world order" and what President Bill Clinton and his advisers struggled with in the first years of new administration. The precise definition of this new order, however, is still awaiting elaboration, not to mention public understanding. The government continues to try to settle the particulars of how the United States will fit into this new environment, and the president must be able to convince the public to support these new foreign policy objectives and programs.

After considerable criticism for the lack of foreign policy direction in the first half-year of his term, President Clinton and his advisers attempted to explain their vision of post-Cold War foreign policy. They strongly rejected isolationism in favor of engagement. The United States would engage in multilateral actions on a pragmatic basis. The policy of containment of the Soviet threat would be replaced by "enlargement of market democracy" as a major principle of U.S. foreign policy. This policy would be accomplished by "strengthening the rich democracies; by helping countries which were making the transition to pluralistic politics and market economies; by countering the troublesome "backlash states" that opposed such changes, and by providing humanitarian relief where it could do the most good."[3]

In October 1993, Warren Christopher, the secretary of state, listed six foreign policy goals: economic security, reform in Russia, a new framework for NATO, trade relations with the Far East, Middle Eastern affairs, and nuclear nonproliferation.

One of Clinton's congressional leaders, Lee Hamilton (D, Indiana), then chairman of the House Foreign Relations Committee, suggested a further clarification of the intervention question. He said the United States needs to be mindful of the importance of national sovereignty and should therefore consider intervention only when a situation poses a clear threat to international peace; when officials in suffering countries refuse or block assistance; or when decisions to intervene are made multinationally, preferably by the UN Security Council.

Others argue that U.S. relations with the rest of the world should be guided by the need and opportunity to build democracies and free markets in the former communist countries and parts of the developing world.[4] Since democracies do not usually fight each other (a generality not true in Eastern Europe) promoting democracy is an investment in our own national security. The United States, through its example of an open society where minorities are protected and respected, should also consciously and actively serve as an example to emerging democracies of how to conduct a multicultural society. Harlan Cleveland, a distinguished scholar and a former U.S. ambassador to the UN, stated at a 1993 Washington, D.C., meeting of the National Academy of Public Administration, "For Americans, our preference for diversity may be our biggest foreign policy asset."

Another argument concerns the degree to which U.S. foreign policy leadership takes a back seat to the multinationalism of the UN. As an example, there was considerable negative reaction among some observers to the Clinton administration's decision to agree that any first use of NATO planes in the Bosnian conflict must be authorized by the UN secretary general. As suggested by columnist George Will, "Americans will support or forgive much that is done in the name of nationalism. They will not forgive subordinating U.S. policy to people who pledge allegiance to the United Nation's blue flag."[5]

Paul Wolfowitz, dean of the Nitze School of International Studies at Johns Hopkins University, writes that President Clinton needs to be cautious in "embracing" both multilateralism and peacekeeping: "Successful foreign policy depends upon a clear definition of national interests, but also depends on a clear understanding of how to pursue those interests."[6] He goes on to argue: "The U.S. should not engage its forces and put its personnel at risk except on behalf of important national interests, as determined by the American people and their elected leaders."[7]

George Kennan, a primary architect of the post-World War II policy of Soviet containment, and the first U.S. ambassador to the Soviet Union, argues for "a very modest and restrained foreign policy, directed to the curtailment of external undertakings and involvements wherever this is in any way possible, and to the avoidance of any assumption of new ones. This means a policy far less pretentious in word and deed than the ones we have been following in recent years. It means, in particular, a rejection of the tempting but fatuous assumption that we can find, in our relations with other countries or other parts of the world, relief from the painful domestic confrontation with ourselves."[8]

The debate goes on. We are all witnesses to a fundamental change in U.S. foreign policy. It is truly an interesting and historic time to observe this process of redefinition. Irrespective of the answers to these questions, however, there are three key principles upon which U.S. foreign policy will be based. These principles are perhaps a good starting place for an assessment of U.S. foreign policy as the end of the 20th century approaches. We can then try to appraise the forces, factors, and policy issues that will influence how the United States responds to the new international environment that is evolving. The rest of this chapter examines the three primary purposes of U.S. foreign policy:

1. To advance U.S. influence over world affairs and improve the predictability of events
2. To promote U.S. economic interests
3. To preserve national security[9]

MAKING THE WORLD MORE PREDICTABLE

The 40-year Cold War between the West and the Soviet Union was obviously a difficult and expensive time for the United States. However, if there was a positive aspect of that period, it was that at least the nation had a relatively stable and predictable threat toward which it could direct its foreign policy. Modern economic systems depend on a stable environment and an open trading system, so that stability is important. The disintegration of the Soviet empire ended that stability and inaugurated a period of international uncertainty to which the United States is still trying to adapt.

President Bush's "new world order" imagery meant to convey the idea that the loss by the United States and Europe of a common strategic opponent has resulted in the need for *a new organizing principle* for the next stage of international politics. Both the United States and its allies are now attempting to determine just what will be this organizing principle and how U.S. relationships, common threats, and institutional responses will evolve.

One possible way to approach the redefinition of U.S. foreign policy is to focus on what must be involved in making the international environment more predictable than it has been, in other words, moving the "new world" farther along the path of "order." This process entails (1) looking at situations in the world that create uncertainty and the possibility of instability and chaos; (2) reviewing how these situations affect national interests; (3) considering the options for controlling these situations; (4) assessing the U.S. power to support democratic principles that may improve these areas' stability and predictability; and (5) determining what existing or new institutional arrangements and alliances can help with this task.

Potential Regions of Instability

It does not take an international expert to spot the current regions of potential instability in the world:[10]

The Middle East and North Africa.   A major source of political instability in this region stems from the continuing conflict and animosity between Israel and its Arab neighbors. The origins of the conflict include the three wars over the establishment of Israel following World War II and the religious and cultural differences in the region. The signing of the peace treaty between Israel and the Palestine Liberation Organization (PLO) on the White House lawn in October 1993 marked what many observers hope will be the beginning of the end of that conflict.

The agreement means that the PLO must accept the existence of Israel as a permanent fact of life in the Middle East and that Israel must recognize the PLO as the legitimate representative of the Palestinian people. In addition, as a first step in trying to arrive at a comprehensive peace settlement, the Israelis agreed to withdraw their military and police forces from Jericho and the Gaza Strip and to turn the administration of those territories over to the PLO. (See Figure 14–1 for a map of the region and Figure 14–2 for the text letters exchanged by Israeli Prime Minister Yitzhak Rabin and PLO Chairman Yasser Arafat, detailing their mutual recognition.) The Palestinians and the Israelis formally signed the agreement in October 1994.

The Israelis also initiated negotiations with both Jordan and Syria to settle their territorial and political disputes. The peace agreement with Jordan was concluded in the fall of 1994 and signed in a memorable ceremony in what was once a no man's land between the two countries. The agreement effectively provides Israel with a 200-mile buffer zone to the east, greatly enhancing its national security. For the Arabs, Israel has forgone the dream of early Zionists to extend its territory from the Mediterranean Sea to the Jordan River.

At this writing, negotiations continue with Syria, with no agreement yet reached on the disposition of the Golan Heights captured by the Israelis from the Syrians in the 1967 War. Syria regards the return of the Golan Heights as non-negotiable, while many Israelis are reluctant to totally withdraw from a region that was used to attack Israeli villages in the 1967 War, and where Israeli settlers now reside.

The implementation of peace agreements such as these are often more difficult than reaching an agreement to settle old disputes, but it now seems that the Arab leadership has accepted the fact of Israel and that the Israelis have reached a point where they are willing to trade land for peace. There is, therefore, for the first time in almost 50 years, a chance for a pragmatic resolution of the territorial, governance, and security disputes that have continuously plagued the region and caused instability in many other parts of the world.

Of course there is no reason to be too Pollyannaish about the resolution of any conflict as basic and complicated as the Arab-Israeli confrontation. Yet there are clear grounds for hope. The Israeli-Palestinian-Jordanian agreements were the result of pragmatic pressures on all parties. The PLO had fallen on hard financial times, as support was withdrawn by the Gulf states irritated at the PLO for its support of Saddam Hussein during the Gulf War. The PLO had also lost a patron when the Soviet Union collapsed. On the Israeli side, the government had not been able to provide internal security to its citizens; public opinion had swung toward trying to reach a settlement with the Palestinians; and the Israeli leaders and the Jordanians saw their future role in the world handicapped as long as the conflict continued. They were also concerned about the rise of terrorism and conflict in the region, as the PLO was unable to make progress in moving toward a homeland for the Palestinian people.

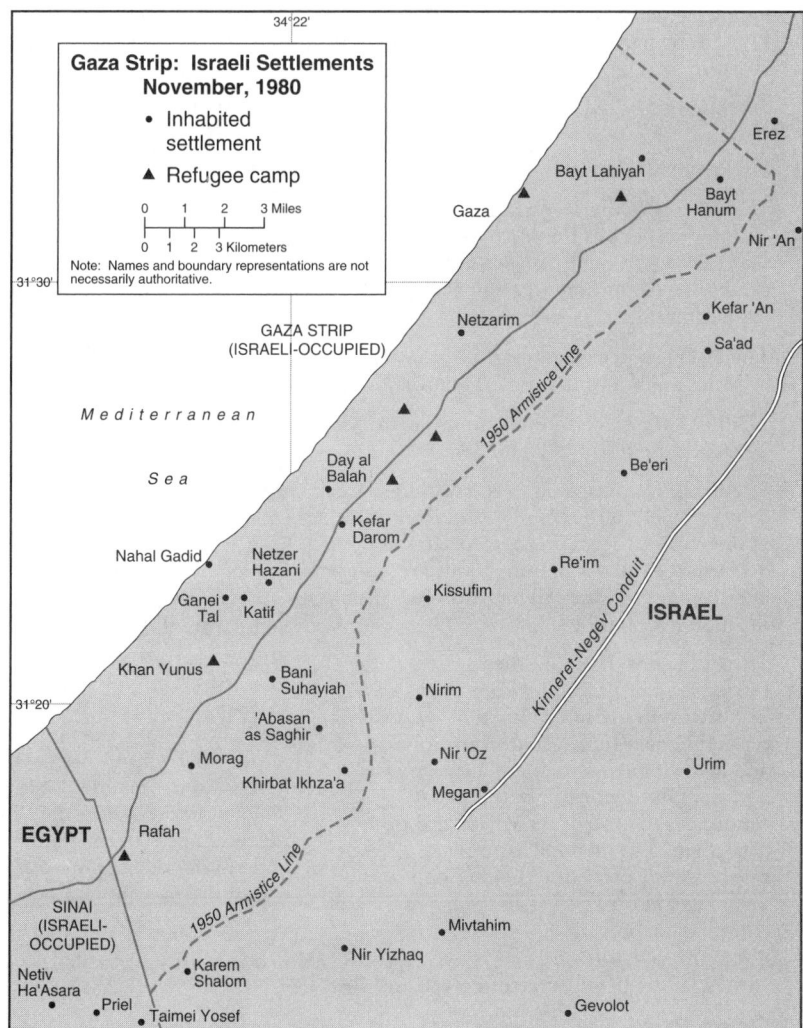

Figure 14–1   Gaza Strip: Israeli settlements, November 1980

Note: Names and boundary representations are not necessarily authoritative.

If for no other reason, a successful implementation of the peace agreements has the potential of setting the stage for the economic advancement of the entire region, an outcome that would certainly improve stability and predictability of events. It is therefore clearly in U.S. interests to support this process in any way possible. Unfortunately, terrorist attacks from those in opposition to the peace agreements, and to any rapprochement attempted by Israel and the Arab countries, continue to threaten the peace process.

For the moment, Iraq's threat to regional tranquillity has been sidelined by the 1991 Gulf War and the Desert Storm onslaught of the United States and its allies. The Middle East, however, continues to be a potential threat. The oil-rich Gulf

Following is the text of letters exchanged between Israeli Prime Minister Yitzhak Rabin and PLO Chairman Yasser Arafat detailing their mutual recognition.

September 9, 1993

Mr. Prime Minister,

The signing of the Declaration of Principles marks a new era in the history of the Middle East. In firm conviction thereof, I would like to confirm the following PLO commitments:

The PLO recognizes the right of the State of Israel to exist in peace and security.

The PLO accepts United Nations Security Council Resolution 242 and 338.

The PLO commits itself to the Middle East peace process, and to a peaceful resolution of the conflict between the two sides and declares that all outstanding issues relating to permanent status will be resolved through negotiations.

The PLO considers that the signing of the Declaration of Principles constitutes a historic event, inaugurating a new epoch of peaceful coexistence, free from violence and all other acts which endanger peace and stability. Accordingly, the PLO renounces the use of terrorism and other acts of violence and will assume responsibility over all PLO elements and personnel in order to assure their compliance, prevent violations and discipline violators.

In view of the promise of a new era and the

signing of the Declaration of Principles and based on Palestinian acceptance of Security Council Resolutions 242 and 338, the PLO affirms that those articles of the Palestine Covenant which deny Israel's right to exist, and the provisions of the Covenant which are inconsistent with the commitments of this letter are now inoperative and no longer valid. Consequently, the PLO undertakes to submit to the Palestinian National Council for formal approval the necessary changes in regard to the Palestinian Covenant.

Sincerely,
Yasser Arafat
Chairman
The Palestine Liberation Organization

September 9, 1993

Mr. Chairman,

In response to your letter of September 9, 1993, I wish to confirm to you that, in light of the PLO commitments included in your letter, the Government of Israel has decided to recognize the PLO as the representative of the Palestinian people and commence negotiations with the PLO within the middle East peace process.

Yitzhak Rabin
Prime Minister of Israel

Figure 14–2   The historic accord

Source: Wall Street Journal, 10 September 1993, p. A1. Reprinted by permission of the *Wall Street Journal,* 1993 Dow Jones & Company, Inc. All Rights Reserved Worldwide.

states of Saudi Arabia, Kuwait, Qatar, Bahrain, Oman, and the United Arab Emirates are still tempting, vulnerable targets. The anti-West regime of Iran continues, the Iraqis and Iranians are still mortal enemies, and the turmoil caused by the presence of the ethnic Kurds in Iraq, Iran, and Turkey continues to beg a permanent solution.

Militant religious fundamentalism is another potential source of instability in the Middle East and North Africa. An important reason for this problem is that many of those with this orientation make no separation between church and state. They therefore create conflict in strategic parts of the world with people of other religious, cultural, or ethnic backgrounds by imposing their dogmatic and doctrinaire views. The appeal of fundamentalism is strengthened by the poverty and high levels of unemployment in some of the countries in the Middle East and North African region, in particular Egypt, Algeria, the Sudan, Yemen, Lebanon, and Jordan. Assistance in the economic development of the region is one important way in which the United States can support stability and peaceful modernization.

The United States also faces the problem of finding itself allied here with what are essentially absolute monarchies, or at least nondemocratic governments with little, if any, political representation for the people of the country. The policy dilemma for America in those instances, then, is whether to support those governments and risk an anti-U.S. situation such as that of the Shah of Iran's overthrow, or whether the United States should use its influence to encourage a transition to more open and democratic societies in those nations. On the other hand, those opposed to a U.S.-led attempt to democratize the Middle East and North Africa argue: "The pressure for premature democratization can fatally weaken existing regimes, with all their flaws, and lead to their overthrow, not by democratic opposition, but by other forces that then proceed to establish a more ferocious and determined dictatorship."[11] The goal according to this view is that the United States should promote human rights in the region, not elections.

Eastern and Central Europe. This region will continue to present stability problems until it completes a successful transition to market economies and democratic societies (Figure 14–3). Ethnic and nationalistic issues also are potential sources of instability, such as the present conflict in the Bosnian region of the former Yugoslavia. As a young German diplomat commented shortly after the fall of the Berlin Wall, "It is as if the Eastern Europeans were frozen in ice in 1945. When they thawed out in 1991, they had the same religious, ethnic, and nationalistic prejudices as when they were frozen."[12] Meanwhile, the Western European countries had settled old disputes and were on the way to economic, and perhaps ultimately political, union. To date, the Central European states, in particular Hungary and the Czech Republic, have made the most economic progress. The Slovak regions of Eastern Europe are lagging behind, although Poland, and particularly Slovenia, are showing signs of economic vitality. In 1993, Poland's GDP grew 4 percent, and inflation was at its lowest rate in seven years. But unemployment was still high at 15.7 percent.

Potential trouble spots other than Bosnia in the Balkan region of Europe also could cause significant instability that could spill over into the rest of Europe. For example, some Albanians look at the success of the Serbs in creating a greater Serbia out of the turmoil in Bosnia. They wonder why they cannot add the two million ethnic Albanians in the Kosova province of Serbia, the 430,000 Albanians in Macedonia, and the 200,000 Albanians in northern Greece to create a Greater Albania of close to six million people.[13] Of course, actions by the Albanians to initiate such a course could result in a war involving Serbia, Greece, and maybe even Turkey, which could decide to come to the aid of the largely Muslim Albanians.

Hungary could have similar problems if ultranationalists gain power. There are currently 15 million Hungarians living in Central and Eastern Europe, but only 10.5 million of them live in Hungary. The others live primarily in the province of Vojvodina in Serbia, in the Transylvanian region of Romania, in Slovakia, and in the Transcarpathian region of the Ukraine.[14] To date, the Hungarian government

Figure 14–3   Eastern and Central Europe

has focused only on trying to see a framework established in Europe for minority rights. But should any of the nations with significant minority Hungarian populations abuse these groups or attempt the type of ethnic cleansing implemented by the Serbs, it would not be unreasonable to expect the Hungarians to take stronger action.

Even the Germans are potentially involved in the messiness of the dispersion of ethnic minorities in Central and Eastern Europe. There are estimated to be 3.5 million ethnic Germans now living in Eastern Europe and the former Soviet Union.[15] Over one million live in Poland, the Czech Republic, Slovakia, and Hungary, with the balance in the former Soviet republics. The German government has expressed interest in the welfare of these people and, needless to say, right-wing groups in Germany are even more vocal on the issue.

William Pfaff, a syndicated columnist for the *International Herald Tribune* (Paris), suggests that the ethnic disputes that are occurring in Eastern Europe are a product of political imagination, not 14th century hatreds. These disputes, he argues, result from 19th century "romanticism, the emergence of the modern nation state after the French revolution, (and) the collapse of the Hapsburg and Ottoman empires."[16] He points out that Yugoslavia did not even exist until 1918, furthermore, no nation in Europe is ethnically pure but is a result of successive migrations over the centuries. For example, there are no distinct physical, anthropological, or language differences between the Bosnian Serbs and the Bosnian Muslims. Their problems stem instead from somewhat different historical experiences—the urban Muslims in Bosnia-Herzegovina converted to Islam when they were overrun by the Turks in the 15th century, and the Serb peasants in the rural areas remained Orthodox Christian. In fact, the Hungarians—who arrived in the region from Central Asia in the 9th century and who have a language distinctive in Central and Eastern Europe—are the only people in Eastern Europe who can make a serious claim to be a "race."

Russia.   Russia and the newly independent states that once made up the Soviet Union continue to be very worrisome. The former Soviet republics are in a shambles, and it will be a long time before they complete a transition to modern economies and democratic societies. Many also suffer from some of the same ethnic and religious animosities found in Bosnia, the Middle East, Africa, and the Balkan states. Armed conflict has existed within Georgia and between Azerbaijan and Armenia for several years. To make matters worse, many are still well armed with the remnants of the Soviet military machine, including nuclear armaments which remained in the present states of Ukraine, Kazakhstan, and the Russian Federation. Although there is an agreement to destroy or turn the nuclear weapons over for storage in Russia, the fragile political situation in all of these countries can lead to policy changes on short notice.

Sixteen million Russians are living in other nations in Europe, (of which about eleven million are in. Ukraine and another ten million in central Asia. These Russians are increasingly militant about their situation and their relationship to their motherland, and the political attractiveness of defending their rights has not been lost on the politicians in Moscow. There are particularly serious problems brewing in the Crimean region of Ukraine where Russians constitute a majority of the population; they succeeded in electing an ethnic Russian as the president of Ukraine in 1994. The Crimea was given to the Ukraine only in 1954, by Nikita Khrushchev, a former Soviet premier. Russian separatists also set up their own administration in Moldavia, in 1993.

The Russian Federation itself is in danger of splintering; some of its diverse ethnic and religious states are pushing for more autonomy and in some cases independence. The 1994–95 conflict between the Russian army and independence-minded Chechnyan Muslim partisans in the Caucasus Mountains is a case in point. The rebels received moral, if not material, support from other Muslim areas of the Federation.

In the Baltic States of Latvia, Lithuania, and Estonia, there are also large Russian populations with the potential to cause trouble. In Tallinn, the capital of Estonia, about half the population is Russian, and Russian speakers account for roughly 40 percent of the population of the country. As early as 1940, Russians made up 25 percent of the population of Latvia, and Lithuania has large numbers of both Russian and Polish citizens.

A consensus is building in the United States that it and its industrial allies need to be actively supporting the transition of these former Soviet societies to democracy and open-market economies. The decisions of the Group of Seven (G-7) (Chapter 6), at their Tokyo meeting in mid-1993, to lend additional financial support to Russia were significant. On the political front, the support of President Boris Yeltsin in his constitutional (and eventually military) confrontation with the former Russian parliament enhanced the political and economic stability of the region. But in the aftermath of Yeltsin's victory and subsequent parliamentary elections, some of the old nationalistic, anti-West sentiments emerged, and it is increasingly unclear to many analysts whether Russia will ultimately be a friend or foe to the Western Alliance.

Senator Richard Lugar (R, Indiana) argued in a speech in early 1994 that the Russians are "tough rivals, not partners."[17] He described two conflicting "prominent schools of thought" with regard to our foreign policy approach to Russia.

1. Russia is a partner of the United States and could and should help combat problems such as global terrorism, nuclear proliferation, and general political instability.
2. Russia's interests are basically incompatible with those of the United States, and a policy focusing on cooperation is misguided.

Senator Lugar thinks that neither of these approaches is adequate, because "neither meets our national interests, nor do they foster the kind of Russia we want to see develop. Many Russians are suspicious of our assistance efforts precisely because they cannot see how such assistance benefits American national interests." Everyone hopes Russia and the United States can "achieve harmony in the preservation of peace and the increase of human freedom," but the senator argues that the United States now must perfect the General Agreement on Tariffs and Trade (GATT) and NATO and seek hardheaded arrangements with the Russians in which mutual advantage is evident and spelled out. The United States should not hesitate to offer advice on building democratic institutions, enlarging human rights, and expanding market economic arrangements that may be helpful, nor be shocked if the United States is rarely heard. "We should be prepared to explore with them the cooperative or mutual aspects of that relationship as well as to promote and defend U.S. interests when our positions diverge."[18]

China.   Winston Churchill once referred to the Soviet Union as a riddle wrapped in an enigma. The phrase *also surely* applies to China. With nearly one-fourth of the world's population and a potential market that could dwarf both Europe and North America, it will clearly increasingly be a player in the new international order. China has made amazing progress in the restructuring of its economy since the dark days of the Cultural Revolution. The Chinese economy is now far ahead of the remnants of the Soviet empire. Parts of the country, particularly in the south (near Hong Kong), are aggressively converting to market economies. Expatriate Chinese, outstanding businesspeople and entrepreneurs, are showing new interest in expanding business opportunities in and with the mainland. In 1993 there were approximately 50,000 foreign investors operating in the Guangzhou (formerly Canton) region. Improved relations with Taiwan, and the acquisition of Hong Kong in 1997, will have a major impact on incorporating the Chinese economy into the world-trading system.

Some have suggested that future historians may conclude that the most significant development of this time was the emergence of a vigorous market economy—and army—in China, the most populous country in the world.[19] According to World Bank projections, China's net imports in 2202 will be $639 billion, compared to $521 billion for Japan. China's GDP in the same year will reach $9.8 trillion, compared to $9.7 trillion for the United States.[20] This economy is fueling, and will continue to fuel, an expanded demand for raw materials and resources; will generate potentially threatening acid-rain and global-warming environmental problems; and will finance a growing military force that will increasingly expand its influence in Asia and elsewhere.

China is now entering what will be a defining period in its history. The old guard, left from the revolutionary days, is being replaced with a younger generation. How far this generation will move from communist dogma toward a market economy is still to be demonstrated, but it appears that is its course. It is also unclear if the new generation will gradually relax the authoritative nature of government institutions, permitting even closer collaboration with the western industrialized world. On the downside of this situation, the spring 1994 debate between the Chinese government and the U.S. State Department over human rights issues in China, and the U.S. threat to withdraw most-favored-nation trading status, seemed to accomplish little but to irritate the Chinese.

The U.S. stance in this situation is delicate. The United States must do what it can to help China in this transition, without appearing to condone either the repressive nature of its society or its contributions to world instability through the support of groups like the Khmer Rouge (Cambodia) or the North Koreans and through the sale of weapons to unstable and authoritative regimes in other parts of the world. The participation of the Chinese prime minister in the Asia/Pacific Economic Cooperation (APEC) (discussed in the next section) meetings in November 1993 in Seattle, Washington, was a step in the direction of including China as a full partner in the developing Asia–Pacific trading region.

As was put by Lee Kuan Yu, former prime minister of Singapore, "The size of China's displacement of the world balance is such that the world must find a new balance in 30 to 40 years. It is not possible to pretend that this is just another big player. This is the biggest player in the history of man."

North Korea.   The major Asian trouble spot of the mid-1990s is North Korea. The country is dominated by an authoritative communist regime that is a relic of the 1950s. Its combination of tight political control, isolation from other countries, paranoia about what it sees as its enemies, and a well-armed and large military establishment make North Korea a true loose cannon on the deck of the modern world. This situation is made even more dangerous by the likelihood that it has been able to develop and construct a limited number of nuclear weapons. The North Koreans have been reluctant to allow international inspection of their nuclear facilities and have test-launched ballistic missiles capable of reaching nations as far away as Japan.

The danger of the North Koreans' being willing to use these weapons against their neighbors in Asia, and perhaps eventually to supply nuclear arms to other loose cannons in the world, creates a situation where the United States cannot simply sit by and let events take their course. The agreement reached between the United States and North Korea in the fall of 1994, wherein the Koreans agreed not to develop nuclear weapons and to eventually permit international inspection of their nuclear facilities in exchange for advanced nuclear power technology and improved relations with America, is a start in defusing a potentially dangerous situation.

Sub-Saharan Africa. This area seems trapped in a downward spiral. The roots of the problem are the political instability brought about by colonialism, wars, and dictatorial regimes and the resulting poverty. The situation is getting worse, not better. The annual rate of population growth is 3.1 percent per year, the highest in the world. Almost one-half of the 480 million population lives in poverty, and per capita incomes fell 2.8 percent per year during the 1980s, leaving most countries worse off economically than they were under colonial rule.

The U.S.-led Operation Rescue in 1993–1994, meant to save the people of Somalia from starvation, ended in a fiasco when the mission evolved into an attempt at nation building. This experience, which also injured the reputation of the United Nations, makes it even more unlikely that the U.S. public would support another such rescue mission, let alone extensive involvement in the political or economic affairs of southern Africa. The policy dilemma, therefore, is how to aid half a continent containing almost half a billion people in its entry into modern society.

South Africa. This country has great resources and potential, but is still struggling to put together an integrated society from the shambles left by its apartheid policies. It is also plagued by tribal warfare and ethnic animosities left from the last century. On the one hand, the country can still tilt toward great instability and civil war, which would have negative repercussions throughout the continent and the rest of the world. On the other hand, now that apartheid has been officially ended and the Western boycott of its economy is over, South Africa has the opportunity to establish a model for the rest of Africa and the economic potential to help lead the continent into the modern world. The 1994 election of a government led by Nelson Mandela brings new hope to many concerned about the stability of the region, but it is still too early to predict success.

The end of the Cold War offers the United States and its allies a new opportunity to try to stabilize the African continent by making dictatorial regimes more difficult to sustain, by supporting democratization movements, and by launching a major effort to rebuild agriculture and to construct modern economies in the region.

South and Central America, the Caribbean, and Mexico. These countries have made major progress over the past few years. There are now more democratic regimes in Latin America than at any time in history. Cuba is the only dictatorship left in the western hemisphere, now that President Jean-Bertrand Aristede has been restored to power in Haiti. Several of the economies in the region are making major changes based on privatization, slashing inflation, cutting tariffs, opening the doors to foreign investment, and pursuing free trade agreements. The results have been extremely positive.

The major sources of instability in Latin America are the wide differences in income distribution and the accompanying poverty among a large share of the population in some countries. Much of the population has so far shared few benefits of the current expansion in the region's economies, a situation that must be remedied to ensure political stability and economic growth for the whole hemisphere.

The Bush and Clinton administrations set the U.S. goals for this region to be continuing support and encouragement of democratic governments and economic reform and aid in opening freer trade in the region. The North American Free Trade Agreement (NAFTA) offers a major opportunity to get this process underway. An expanding free trade bloc that extends NAFTA to the whole South American continent and the Caribbean basin will be the next important U.S. initiative in this region. The policy confrontation in the United States will come from those interests that believe an open trading system in the western hemisphere will disadvantage U.S. workers and hurt the economy. Those on the other side of the issue argue that U.S. technology, productivity, and expanding markets in Latin America will more than make up for U.S. jobs lost as a result of lower wages in other countries.

INSTITUTIONS RELEVANT TO U.S. FOREIGN POLICY RESPONSE

U.S. Agency for International Development

Between 1961 and 1993, the U.S. Agency for International Development (USAID) delivered more than $180 billion in foreign assistance to 153 countries. In 1991, the USAID budget was $17.3 billion.[21] This amount was distributed as indicated in the map in Figure 14–4. U.S. foreign aid amounted to about 0.2 percent of its GDP, compared to Norway's 1.2 percent and Japan's 0.3 percent ($11.1 billion) (see Figure 14–5). In 1993, USAID had 105 overseas offices. The 1993 (General Accounting Office GAO) report on the foreign assistance program argued that the program was spread too thin from both a management and a program basis and needed major overhaul.

The post-Cold War scheme by which the United States distributes foreign aid is under review. A major objective of the U.S. foreign aid program during the Cold War was to help contain the Soviet Union. The United States now needs to shift resources to help stabilize its former adversaries and to contribute to stability and predictability in other regions of the world that will be increasingly crucial to U.S. interests.

During the 1992 campaign, President Clinton called for the United States to aid the emerging democracies in Eastern Europe and the former Soviet Union by organizing and leading a long-term strategy of "engagement for democracy" in which food aid, technical assistance, open markets, and U.S. expertise in converting former defense industries would assist the Eastern European transition. President Bush had also endorsed further aid to Eastern Europe, and before leaving office, signed the Freedom Support Act to authorize additional aid.

In November 1993, the administrator of USAID announced that it would be reducing the number of recipients of its already limited assistance by about one-half. Israel and Egypt—the two countries that have been receiving about one-third of all U.S. foreign assistance—will no doubt also lose in this redesign of U.S. aid packages. The United States can help them by supporting and continuing to encourage the Middle East peace process and by assisting the economic development of the entire region. Other nations that were originally supported to keep them out of the Soviet orbit, like Greece, Turkey, and Portugal, have made good economic progress and will also probably decline in the USAID priority list.

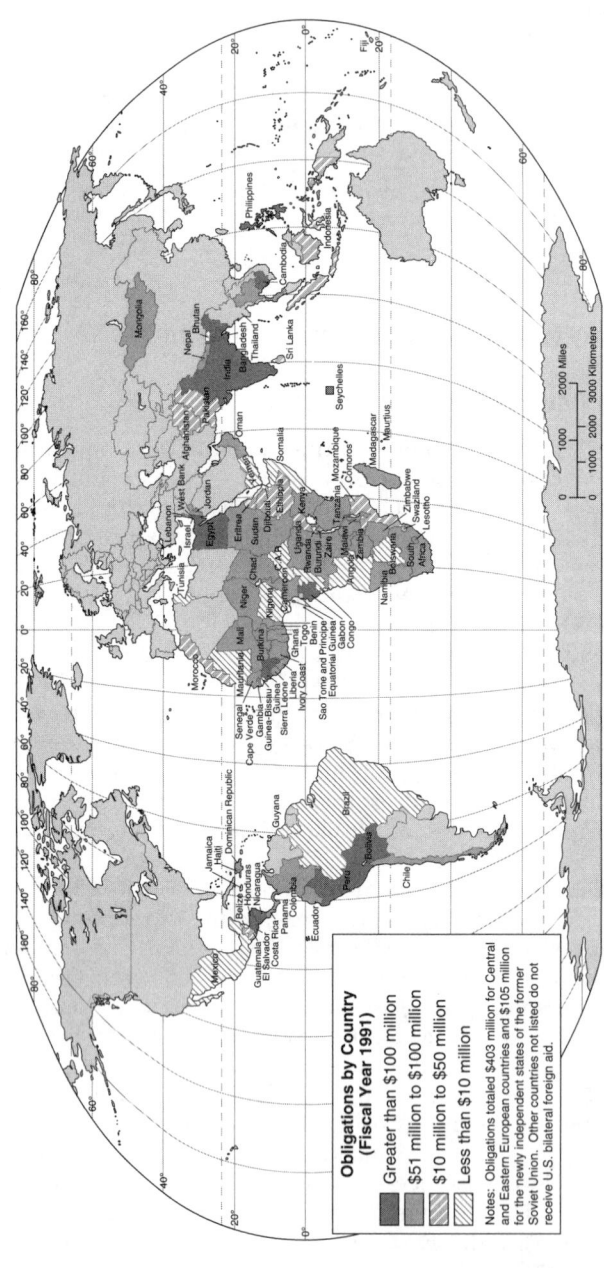

Figure 14–4 U.S. obligations by country (fiscal year 1991)

Notes: Obligations totaled $403 million for Central and Eastern European countries and $105 million for the newly independent states of the former Soviet Union. Other countries not listed do not receive U.S. bilateral foreign aid.

World map as of February 1992.

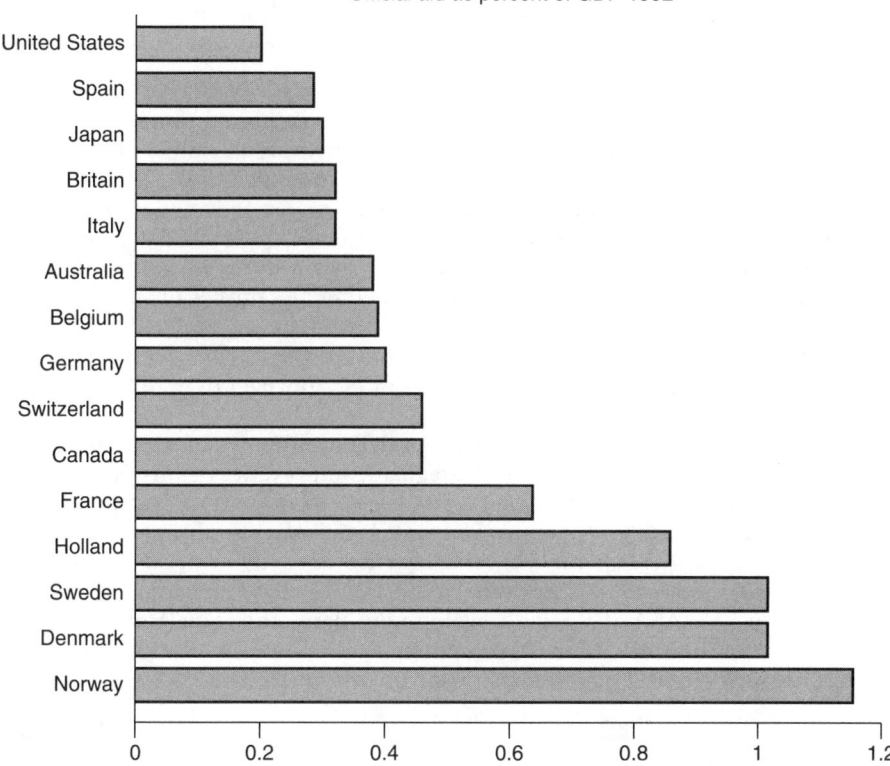

Figure 14–5   Official aid as percentage of GDP 1992

Source: OECD.

Instead of distributing funds principally to friendly countries, as it did during the Cold War, the United States will use foreign aid to advance such broad public policy goals as promoting democracy, encouraging free trade, and combating terrorism and nuclear proliferation.[22] The new program also proposes to bring all federal agencies with international programs into a coordinated assistance effort. The six policy objectives of the Clinton foreign policy overhaul are to:

1. Promote sustainable development by encouraging economic growth, population control, and protection of the environment;
2. Promote democracy by aiding new democracies, especially with training. Aid would be cut off to any nation where an elected government was overthrown by a military coup;
3. Promote peace by aiding regional defense groups and anti-drug efforts and rewarding nations that refrain from developing weapons of mass destruction;
4. Provide humanitarian assistance by creating an Emergency Refugee and Migration Assistance Fund that would allow the president to take money from other programs and agencies for emergency relief;
5. Promote growth through trade and investment by coordinating the work of the Export-Import Bank, the Overseas Private Investment Corporation, and other international development agencies with the aid program;
6. Advance diplomacy by specifying that the secretary of state direct policy for all U.S. in-

ternational programs, not just in USAID but in related agencies such as the Export-Import Bank and the Overseas Private Investment Corporation. It would be up to the secretary of state to decide whether the aid package for any country should include military assistance.

USAID, the World Bank, and other international donor agencies have also recently emphasized another programmatic approach that shows promise: using *nongovernmental* and *private voluntary organizations (NGOs* and *PVOs)* in the developing world to help set priorities, initiate self-support activities, and deliver social services. These types of organizations have the ability to involve people in their own development, to bypass the inefficient bureaucracies of many countries, and to generate new sources of development income. Examples of such organizations include agriculture and business cooperatives, nature and environmental conservancy organizations, and university programs. (NGOs are described in more detail in Chapter 16, as part of a discussion of new approaches to delivering government services.)

Another tool the United States will undoubtedly continue to use to increase the predictability of events of strategically important regions of the world are the *several alliances and institutional arrangements* in our orbit. The principal organizations in this category are the UN, the International Monetary Fund (IMF), the World Bank, NATO, the Organization for Security and Cooperation in Europe (OSCE), the Western European Union (WEU) the Association of Southeast Asian Nations (ASEAN), the Asian Development Bank, the Inter-American Development Bank, the Inter-American Development Bank, the Asian-Pacific Economic Cooperation group (APEC), and the European Union (EU).

The United Nations (UN)

The UN has gained new respectability under the leadership of Secretary-General Boutros Boutros-Ghali. The UN role during the Gulf War and subsequent dealings with the Iraqis in destroying their capability to use weapons of mass destruction has also altered the view of some previous critics about its usefulness in maintaining world stability. The U.S.–UN mission to avert mass starvation in Somalia must also be considered a success. Although Somalia still suffers from severe political instability and clan rivalries, the horror of mass starvation was averted by the U.S.-led UN intervention. While the UN has not been very successful in helping resolve the disputes in the former Yugoslavia, it has been more forceful and effective than any other institution, including the U.S. State Department and the European Union (EU).

The UN does have critics. Some are disappointed with its inability to successfully resolve several of the war and famine situations in the Sudan, Liberia, Angola, Rwanda, and Mozambique. They also criticize the general reluctance (or inability) of the UN to provide the financial support necessary to place enough forces on the ground to make a difference in some of the crisis situations.

There is also an ongoing debate about the role of the UN in the post-Cold War world, not dissimilar to that regarding U.S. foreign policy. Does the UN have the right to intervene, for humanitarian reasons, in a country's internal affairs without waiting for permission from the country to do so? As Peter Calvocoressi asked in a collection of essays on international intervention, "What do you do, what are you entitled to do, and what ought you do if you repeatedly hear your neighbors beating their children?"[23] To date, the UN has not gone into a country without at least the acquiescence of the country's officials.

The legal right of the UN to intervene in the internal affairs of a sovereign nation is fuzzy. The UN Charter (Article 2) states; "Nothing contained in the present Charter shall authorize the United Nations to intervene in matters which are essentially within the domestic jurisdiction of any state." However, it also states, "This principle shall not prejudice the application of enforcement measures under Chapter VII," which gives the UN Security Council the power to take actions ranging from economic sanctions to military action.[24]

It is clear that the debate is not finished. Arrayed against those who believe the UN should intervene more aggressively in chaotic situations are those who believe that the UN is merely a tool of the major powers and that their actions smack of neocolonialism. That said, if Mr. Boutros-Ghali is able to construct the rapid deployment force he has proposed for dealing with destabilizing conflicts in the world, if he can successfully reform the moribund UN bureaucracy, and if the Security Council structure of the UN, now dominated by the allies who won World War II, can be altered to be more representative of the 21st-century realities of economic and political power (e.g., by including Japan and Germany), the UN may eventually begin to live up to its original promise.

We have already discussed the IMF and the World Bank in Chapter 5. Clearly they are both important institutions in the stability of the world financial system and in the development of the Third World. The United States will continue to work closely with both organizations.

North Atlantic Treaty Organization (NATO).   At the end of 1993, barring some major change, it seemed that NATO faced the prospect of becoming an organization without a mission. As 1994 and 1995 unfolded, however, it appeared that it was making progress in redefining its role in the post-Cold War world. NATO's successful threat of using air strikes against the Serbs surrounding Sarajevo, its attack against Serb aircraft violating the no-fly zone, and its air attacks against Serb ethnic cleansers surrounding Gorazde strengthened both its self-confidence and its credibility. Under its new role, NATO has declared its right to undertake peacekeeping functions beyond its region and will operate joint task forces enabling units from several countries—including non-NATO nations—to work together in "coalitions of the willing" peacekeeping activities.

NATO was designed to confront the Soviet Union and its Warsaw Pact allies to prevent their invasion of Western Europe. Now that this is no longer a threat, the question is: What is NATO's role, if any? Some interests in Europe, led by the French, prefer to downplay NATO and have the OSCE and the Western European Union (WEU) and its 40,000 member *Eurocorps* take on the security role for Western Europe. Others, including some in both Europe and the United States, are concerned that such a move would break up the trans-Atlantic alliance that includes the United States and Canada and create an unhealthy chasm between North America and Europe. Some Europeans are also concerned about the major role that the newly unified Germany would have in a security system that does not include the United States and Canada.

The U.S. strategy, in contrast, is to endorse the WEU and OSCE security roles in general but to work to limit them in practice to relatively minor intra-European matters (such as small disputes). Thus NATO would have the broader role of the defense and stability of Western Europe. Whether NATO will eventually include any of the former Warsaw Pact countries is also an issue that remains to be resolved. Senator Richard Lugar (R, Indiana), a leading foreign policy opinion leader in congressional circles, argued that NATO should allow at least Poland, Hungary, and the Czech Republic to have intermediate membership, to promote democracy and bolster market economies in Eastern Europe. The Clinton administration appeared reluctant to take this step. Having its former Warsaw Pact allies join NATO is not regarded too kindly by Russia. The result was the initiation of a Partnership for Peace (PFP) relationship with the former Soviet bloc countries that would not include them in NATO but would provide for joint military exercises, training, and planning. Even this halfway step toward NATO membership was criticized by Russia, which is concerned about being isolated and targeted by such a NATO alliance. In spite of this reluctance, Russian joined the PFP in May 1995.

Ronald Asmus, Richard Kugler, and Stephen Larrabee argue that six steps are necessary to develop a new, NATO-based, transatlantic bargain between the United States and Europe.[25]

1. The United States needs to share the financial and military burden with its European allies.
2. A new understanding must be reached that harmonizes the interests of both the U.S. and Europe. Future U.S. involvement will be conditioned on Europe's willingness to bear its own share. The United States must be willing to accept a stronger European identity, including an identity in security affairs.
3. Germany must be a full partner in NATO and its affairs and relinquish its postwar aversion to sending troops outside of its own borders.
4. The Central European nations of Poland, Hungary, the Czech Republic, and Slovenia must be integrated into both the EU and NATO.
5. Russia must be helped to stabilize politically and economically. A strong security partnership with Russia will be one of the strongest guarantees of peace and stability in Europe. Therefore, as NATO moves eastward, it must expand its security dialogue with the Russians. But, "to hold the future of NATO hostage to the outcome of Russian politics is a recipe for the demise of the alliance."
6. The NATO alliance must be reorganized militarily because its current structure no longer matches Europe's new strategic challenges. NATO must develop the capability to conduct military operations beyond its borders and must maintain a Rapid Reaction Corps. It must also eventually expand its full security guarantees to allow it to deal with the spectrum of possible conflicts in Europe, ranging from small to large and from peacekeeping to combat operations.

Organization for Security and Cooperation in Europe (OSCE)

Formerly known as the Conference on Security & Cooperation in Europe (CSCE) the name was changed in 1995 to reflect its activities. The OSCE is more of a potential than a player in maintaining international stability. The organization, headquartered in Strasbourg, France, is composed of 53 countries, including the former Soviet Union and its Warsaw Pact allies and the United States. So far, its main role has been that of a convener and a forum for debate on matters related to human rights. Both the French and the Russians have periodically argued for a stronger OSCE role in maintaining peace and stability, but the consensus approach to decision making in the OSCE leads others to be skeptical that the organization could really take action—in the way that NATO could—in a crisis situation.

The Western European Union (WEU)

The WEU is often described as the European pillar of NATO. It was founded in 1948 (one year before NATO) and was reactivated in 1984. Its members include the 15 member countries of the European Union, plus Iceland, Norway, and Turkey. The WEU is designed to give Europe an independent military force to allow it to respond to situations in which the US and Canada cannot or do not wish to be involved. The WEU uses many of the same military assets as NATO.

Asian Development Bank, The Association of Southeast Asian Nations (ASEAN), and the Asian-Pacific Economic Cooperation (APEC) Organization

Of the three Asian organizations, ASEAN is mainly a Southeast Asian regional security organization, and the Asian Development Bank is a development-financing institution. The precise role of APEC in the new world order has not been determined as it was founded only in 1989. APEC is unique in the Asian region because it includes (as Pacific powers) the United States, Canada, Australia, and New Zealand. It is now focused on economic cooperation, but it has the potential for evolving into a forum for discussing security, political, trade, and economic integration issues. At its November 1993 meeting in Seattle, Washington, and its fall 1994 meeting in Indonesia, the 13 national leaders took preliminary steps that can convert it into a useful organization in the future. It is quite possible that it can eventually become the Asian-Pacific region's counterweight to the EU and the North American trading blocs.

The European Union (EU)

The EU, until 1993 known as the European Community (EC) and earlier the European Economic Community (EEC), was created in 1967 by merging the European Atomic Energy Community and the European Coal and Steel Community. The purpose of the EU has been both political and economic. Politically, it is driven by the desire to link the countries so tightly together that they will not degenerate into the kinds of conflict that Europe has endured for centuries and that led to the two world wars. Economically, the goal has been to break down barriers and to eventually develop a single market. For the past several years, the EU has had 12 member nations (Germany, France, Luxembourg, Italy, Great Britain, Denmark, the Netherlands, Ireland, Belgium, Spain, Portugal, and Greece). In the spring of 1994, Austria, Sweden, and Finland (effective January 1995) all joined the EU, bringing the total to fifteen member nations.

The EU is governed by a Council of Ministers; a Commission that is located in Brussels and provides a bureaucracy; the European Court of Justice, which is located in Luxembourg and has a mission similar to the U.S. Supreme Court; and an elected European Parliament that has offices in Brussels but meets in Strasbourg. The Council of Ministers, composed of the key cabinet ministers of the member countries, is the most powerful body in the EU at the moment.

In the years leading up to the early 1980s, there was an increasing concern in Europe that the EEC had lost its momentum and was losing economic ground to the United States and Japan. The leaders of the community decided that a new push was needed to restore momentum. In 1985, they determined to move much more aggressively to establish a true economic and political community. This move was signified by changing the name of the organization to the European Community, symbolizing a purpose that would be much more than purely economic.

Another key step that was taken was to allow decisions to be made on a so-called qualified majority basis, which gave the larger states (Germany, France, Italy and Great Britain) more votes and the ability to make decisions that previously had to be made unanimously. In 1990 the Council of Ministers then decided to take the following steps, which went into effect at the end of 1992:

> To eliminate physical barriers between the twelve nations; to eliminate tax and technical barriers so goods can travel from one border to another easily; to allow the free movement of workers and wage earners; to provide a common market for services as well as goods; to allow the free movement of capital among the countries; and to increase the cooperation of the European companies with each other.

At a meeting in Maastricht, the Netherlands, in 1991, the EC decided to move to a single currency and establish a common central bank (to be located in Germany) by 1999. This move created a great deal of controversy in some countries and is still not settled. The Maastricht Treaty went into effect on November 1, 1993, officially transforming the EC into the EU and awarding EU citizenship status to citizens of the 12 member states. Progress will be assessed on several aspects of European integration at a series of follow-up meetings (the Intergovernmental Conference) scheduled to begin in November 1996.

Two other important issues are yet to be resolved. The first is referred to as *deepening* the community. By this term, supporters of a federal Europe mean moving even further toward political integration, or a "United States of Europe." The second issue, *broadening*, concerns the membership of the EU (which must have unanimous approval to be expanded). With the disintegration of the Soviet bloc, the EU membership question has been elevated to a higher priority. Hungary, the Czech Republic, Switzerland, Poland, and Turkey have all expressed interest in joining the EU. Others are waiting in line (see Figure 14–6 for EU membership status).

If the EU moves in this broadening direction, it will undoubtedly make progress toward the deepening option less likely. The more countries involved in the discussion, the less likely they will be to reach an agreement on political issues. As indicated earlier, some members of the EU also believe the union should develop its own common foreign policy and security apparatus. As noted earlier in this chapter the WEU, led by Germany, France, and Great Britain, have formed a common 40,000-member military force, the Eurocorps. It was described by German Defense Minister Volker Rühe as "the central building stone for European defense. We are creating an instrument for a joint foreign and security policy of Europeans."[26] He suggested that, in case of war, the Eurocorps be placed under the command of NATO (assuming the latter continues to exist).

The completion on December 31, 1992 of the single market created a European trading bloc of 380 million people, with the largest GDP of any market in the

Figure 14–6   EU membership status

world. This market is obviously very important to the United States both as a market and as a competitor. The EU's foreign-defense policy is also of great interest to the United States and must be considered in rethinking US strategic international interests and foreign policy.

Summary

In summary, the effectiveness of U.S. foreign policy in reducing instability and achieving better predictability of factors bearing on critical U.S. interests will be determined by how well the United States recognizes the situation in crucial regions of the world and the success with which it manipulates the tools (such as foreign aid) at its disposal. The United States will also need to rely on the co-operation of a number of key institutions and allies in different parts of the world.

PROMOTING U.S. ECONOMIC INTERESTS

The second primary objective of U.S. foreign policy is to promote our economic interests. Many of these issues are discussed in Chapter 6 under the heading of international economic policy, and little more need be added to that discussion. In spite of the 1993 congressional battle over the NAFTA and the conflict with France over the conclusion of the Uruguay round of the GATT negotiations, the current consensus among key U.S. policy makers continues to support expanding free trade and opening markets. Protectionism results in reduced world trade and lower productivity and per capita income and eventually hurts all countries. Free trade can cause painful dislocations in some industries or regions that have enjoyed protection, but it is still in the interest of the country as a whole.

One of the key features of the world-trading environment that has emerged in the 1990s is the trend toward regional integration. The evolution and prospects of the EU are discussed in the previous section and also in Chapter 5, where it is observed that trading blocs imply reducing trade barriers *within* the bloc, not necessarily establishing barriers *between* blocs. The balance of the 20th century will see an expansion in both the number and size of regional trading organizations. The United States will seek to expand NAFTA to include other nations in Central and South America. The EU will predictably broaden to include at least some of the Central European countries hoping to join, and the Asians will solidify the APEC into a more-formalized agreement. The U.S. interests in this environment will be to prevent these organizations from imposing restrictive trading practices between the blocs, and all the organizations must work together to see that the developing nations of the southern hemisphere are not left out of the benefits that should flow from the resulting worldwide expansion of trade and economic development.

For the longer term, if the United States can help build new, modern economies in Eastern Europe and encourage countries such as India and China to open their economies and move toward more open societies, the size and value of the world market will grow exponentially. Here lies the opportunity for the next generation.

PRESERVING NATIONAL SECURITY

Providing for our national security is the third essential purpose of U.S. foreign policy. Although it may sound crass to say so, the use of military force is ultimately just another method of achieving foreign policy objectives.

The national security establishment of the United States is quite extensive and reaches much further than most people realize. Graham Allison and Greg Treverton, in their book, *Rethinking National Security,* offer a broad estimate of the various government activities involved in defense of the nation.[27] Their summary includes some components of agencies that would not ordinarily be thought of as part of the national security establishment (see Figure 14–7). They estimate that

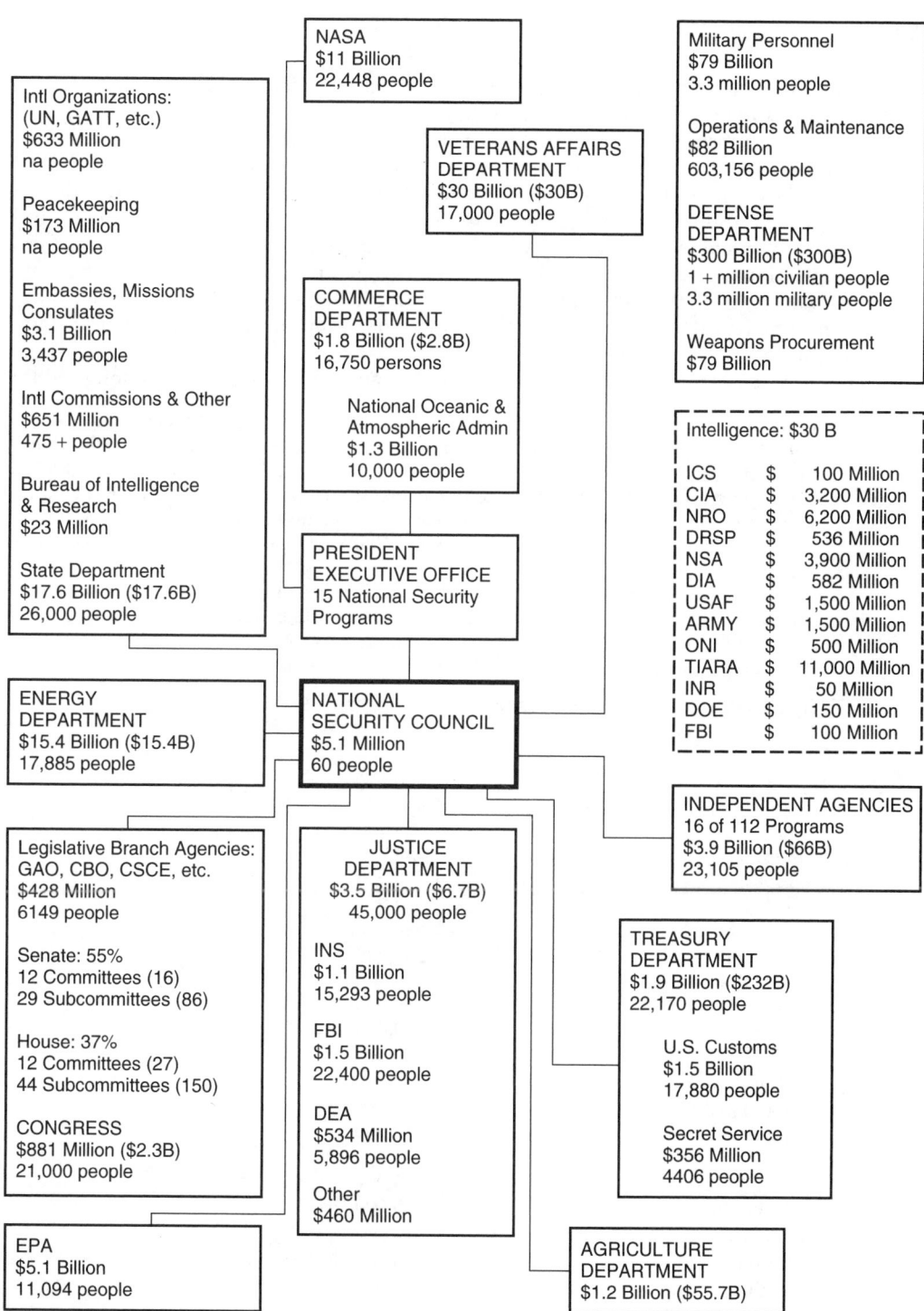

Figure 14–7 U.S. National Security Establishment (budget U.S. Government, fiscal year 1991)

NA = not available.
B = Billions of U.S. Dollars.

Source: Graham Allison and Greg Treverton, *op. cit.* (pg. 42).

the total number of people employed in U.S. national security activities in 1990 exceeded the population of New Jersey.

The portfolio of assets that are part of the national security apparatus includes strategic nuclear forces; advanced conventional forces; the weapons industrial base, including research and development (both civilian and military weapons support centers); an overseas basing structure; European alliances and arms; intelligence; energy security (including strategic oil reserves); and preventive diplomacy (e.g., the Arab-Israeli peace agreement, Gulf War coalition, Panama Canal Treaty).[28] With the end of the Cold War, each element of this portfolio is under review to determine its function, role, and relevance to the new world paradigm.

Since the late 1940s, U.S. military forces and alliances have been designed to:

1. Confront the presence of a large Warsaw Pact land army facing Western Europe, designed for a quick and massive attack into West Germany. At most, the United States would have had two-weeks' warning. As a result, the United States and its NATO allies maintained a large military presence in Germany, meant to slow a Soviet advance long enough to move an additional two divisions to Europe and to activate other U.S. forces. Table 14–1 shows that the United States had 350,000 troops in Western Europe (mainly West Germany) in 1989;[29]

2. Maintain open shipping lanes, protect U.S. trading partners, and present a sea-based strategic threat to the Soviets with U.S. 16-carrier battle groups and a fleet of nuclear submarines;

TABLE 14–1   U.S. Military Forces by Basing Location, 1989

Total, Worldwide	*2,100,000*
United States Territory	*1,600,000*
Continental United States	1,250,000
Alaska	25,000
Hawaii	50,000
Afloat	200,000
Other	75,000
Europe	*350,000*
Germany	250,000
United Kingdom	25,000
Italy	15,000
Spain	10,000
Afloat	20,000
Other	20,000
East Asia and Pacific	*130,000*
Japan	50,000
Korea	45,000
Philippines	15,000
Other and afloat	20,000
Rest of World	*45,000*
Panama	20,000
Saudi Arabia	10,000
Other and afloat	15,000

Totals may not add up because of rounding.

Source: Department of Defense.

3. Deter a Soviet strategic missile and aircraft nuclear threat to the United States and Western Europe by nuclear missile and long-range bomber forces.

The addition of the Reagan Strategic Defense Initiative (SDI) anti-missile program, though new and incomplete, added a fourth wild card factor to the confrontation and probably had something to do with the Soviet decision to move from a policy of confrontation with the West. The costs of keeping up with the United States in expenditures to counter this new technology must have been prohibitive.

The end of the Cold War made the U.S. military strategy obsolete. With the collapse of the Warsaw Pact, the key nations that had previously provided the geographic base for a confrontation with Western Europe are no longer in the Soviet orbit. East Germany is now part of the unified Germany, and Poland, Hungary, the Czech Republic, and Slovakia all have democratic governments and have essentially dismantled their offensive military forces. As noted earlier, some have even applied for admission to the EU and NATO. In addition, much of the army and navy of the former Soviet Union has been divided among the former member nations. For example, Ukraine retained about half of the Soviet fleet. In short, the Soviet military is no longer a threat to the West—at least for the foreseeable future.

As a result of these changes, the United States needs to reassess the national security component of its foreign policy with a view to what are the security threats facing it and the size and shape of the military needed to confront these threats. But even before the disintegration of the Soviet Union, Congress and the Bush administration had already decided to make substantial cuts in the nation's defense budget as a result of the improved relationship with the Soviets. Table 14–2 shows the composition and cost of the U.S. military establishment in 1989 and projects what at that time seemed to be a reasonable cutback in defense by the end of the 1990s.

With the end of the Cold War, there now truly is no global threat facing the United States. Charles Krauthammer, in his article "The Unipolar Moment," argues that instead of a multipolar world with several centers of power including Russia, Europe, and Japan, the United States has emerged as the only unchallenged power in the world.[30] All others are second-ranked powers. Krauthammer also suggests that this situation occurs at a time when there are renewed isolationist pressures in the United States, and new security threats have emerged from small weapons states, so-called because they are armed with weapons of mass destruction and have an increasing ability to deliver them.

Alternative Visions of the U.S. Role in a Post-Cold War World

The debate underway that will eventually shape the U.S. national security structure for the post-Cold War era also revolves around several competing visions of the future and of the most desirable role for the United States in these scenarios. Larry Korb, former assistant secretary of defense and director of the Center for Public Policy at the Brookings Institution, describes the four competing visions of the future U.S. international role as follows.[31]

Come Home, America.   This envisions a return to the traditional U.S. semi-isolationist view that the nation should not involve itself in the problems of Europe and the other trouble spots of the world. Instead, it should define its interests narrowly, bring U.S. troops home, and let the Europeans and the Japanese defend themselves.

It is interesting that this attitude is shared by both left- and right-wing politicians. It was George McGovern's view of the world in the 1970s when he ran for president during the Vietnam War, and the view was also embraced by Pat Buchanan in his 1992 primary bid for the Republican presidential nomination. The 1992 third-party presidential candidate Ross Perot also seemed to be sympathetic to this view of the world.

Pax Americana. This vision of U.S. foreign relations argues that the United States should use its power to protect its security, the security of its friends, and the

TABLE 14–2   Cost and Structure of U.S. Forces: Current Conditions and Future Alternatives

Forces		Fiscal 1989 Force Levels	Fiscal 1989 Cost per Year (Billions)
Army			
Active divisions		18	49.8
Independent brigades		8	7.9
Reserve divisions		10	13.0
Fixed costs		—	7.2
	TOTAL	36	77.9
Navy			
Surface combatants		373	53.5
SSNs		100	8.8
SSBNs		35	15.0
Other ships and crafts		283	4.0
Marine divisions		4.0	8.8
Fixed costs		—	6.3
	TOTAL	795	96.4
Air Force			
Tacair squadrons		78	31.3
Tacair support squadrons		44	10.8
Strategic bombers and support squadrons		37	18.7
ICBM squadrons		20	4.0
Aircraft-refueling squadrons		72	14.2
Reserve squadrons		149	13.3
Fixed costs		—	5.1
	TOTAL	400	94.4
Total			
Army, Navy, Air Force		—	271.7
OSD, JCS, other		—	18.6
Defensewide		—	0.7
Atomic energy		—	8.1
Defense-related		—	0.6
	TOTAL	—	299.7

Totals may not add up because of rounding.

Source: Department of Defense.

stability of the entire world by providing a police force for the world. This idea was floated as a trial balloon in the summer of 1992 by high-ranking officials in the Pentagon and the State Department. However, after negative reactions in the press and on Capitol Hill, the Bush Administration backed away from the proposal.

Regional and International Organization Reliance. Analysts who hold this view suggest that the United States should increasingly rely on both regional and international organizations like NATO, ASEAN, and the UN to provide world stability and security of U.S. interests. The United States should avoid direct unilateral action and cede the maintenance of world stability to these international organizations. The policy also would allow U.S. troops to serve under the direct command

Fiscal 1999 Force Levels	Fiscal 1999 Cost per Year (Billions)	Fiscal 1999 with Reduced Investment and Replacement Rates (Billions)	Fiscal 1999 with Reduced Investment and Replacement and O & S (Billions)
10	26.9	23.2	18.3
8	7.9	6.8	5.4
5.0	6.5	5.6	4.4
—	7.2	7.2	7.2
23	48.5	42.8	35.3
271	39.3	31.4	25.5
74	6.4	4.6	3.9
17	7.3	5.8	4.7
213	3.0	2.4	1.9
4.0	8.7	7.2	5.8
—	6.3	6.3	6.3
579	71.0	57.7	48.1
38	16.8	13.8	11.1
20	4.7	3.9	3.1
10	4.1	3.3	2.7
20	17.3	13.4	11.0
34	5.6	4.5	3.7
73	6.4	4.8	4.0
—	5.1	5.1	5.1
195	60.0	48.8	40.7
—	179.4	149.4	124.2
—	12.4	12.4	12.4
—	0.7	0.7	0.7
—	8.1	8.1	8.1
—	0.6	0.6	0.6
—	201.2	171.2	146.0

of these international bodies—a first for U.S. defense forces and an approach generally opposed by Congress and the defense establishment.

As recently as mid-1993, it appeared that the Clinton administration was indeed heading in this direction, as it deferred to NATO for a response to the war in Bosnia and to the UN to authorize, and later assume, the rescue mission in Somalia. Although the initial policy was to rely on these organizations for leadership in crisis response, the conflict with Somali warlords resulted in disillusionment about allowing U.S. troops to be commanded by a non-U.S. military leader. Some critics also argued that even under a UN flag, the presence of a U.S. commander, or U.S. troops, made the mission a de facto U.S. operation in the eyes of the world. They suggest that the United States cannot consider itself just one of the boys, when it is the only superpower left in the world.

Pragmatic Interventionism.   The premise in this argument is that if the United States comes home from Europe and Asia, a vacuum will be created that no other country is capable of filling. It is unrealistic to expect that a UN force can be made to work for serious security threats. As a result, without a strong U.S. presence, there can be a great deal of instability and potential for chaos in the international system. This situation would hurt U.S. economic and long-term political interests. The nation must therefore be prepared to intervene whenever international events demand.

Both Bush and Clinton seem to be in this camp. In Bush's vision of the future, alliances and institutions that won the Cold War would stay in place and gradually evolve to meet new circumstances. Bush would have continued to depend on NATO as a key institution and would have gradually strengthened the military power of the UN for some peacekeeping missions. Had he been re-elected, he would have tried to retain 150,000 troops in Europe. He also would have avoided using U.S. troops to control regional civil conflicts such as are now occurring in Eastern Europe.

During the 1992 presidential campaign, Clinton suggested he would move in the same general direction but would cut U.S. troop levels in Europe to between 75,000 and 100,000 soldiers. He also said he would be willing to turn over more police actions to a UN peacekeeping, rapid deployment force. The new president also stressed the need to reinforce democratic governments in the world as the best way to achieve stability in the long term.

U.S. Department of Defense Planning Guidelines, Threat Assessment, and Defense Strategy

The Department of Defense view of the altered security situation facing the United States is based on the considerations that follow.[32]

Planning for Uncertainty.   The United States is now facing the problem of putting together military forces for a future threat that it cannot precisely identify. The U.S. defense establishment, however, has *strategic depth:* the country is not threatened by anything in the short run that can affect its vital interests. There are adequate forces to deal with any problem that might arise in the future and sufficient time to prepare for any major threat that might develop in the long run.

The Defense Department is redefining the U.S. military presence abroad.

The new configuration will include combined exercises with U.S. allies (even including the Russians), new access and storage agreements, security and humanitarian assistance, port visits, military-to-military contacts, and periodic rotational troop deployments.

Attention is also being given to developing a capability to project military power in response to any crisis that may develop. This shift in priorities has led to a redefinition of how U.S. military forces are aligned, organized, staffed, and equipped to meet the demands of quick, flexible, and decisive action, if and when needed.

Shaping the Strategic Environment.   Deterring nuclear attack remains the top priority. The nation must retain strategic nuclear forces and a reliable warning system. As the only remaining superpower, the United States now also has the ability to shape political, economic, and defense strategies to further reduce potential threats to itself and the rest of the world. It can accomplish this through techniques such as nuclear disarmament and nonproliferation agreements with the Russians and a focus on Third World nuclear and biological weapons reduction and deterrence.

Utilizing Defense Technology.   Future U.S. military actions will be designed to reduce as much as possible the loss of any fighting men and women. One way to accomplish this, as was so well demonstrated in the Gulf War, is through the development and deployment of sophisticated military technology. In keeping with this political necessity, defense budgets of the future must be focused on retaining and enhancing the U.S. technological edge. The country cannot afford to lose its defense research and development capability. Meeting this objective will have a significant impact on the overall composition of the defense establishment and its assets and on its ability to do its job in the future.

Reconstitution.   As the defense industrial base is downsized to meet the reduced threat of the post-Cold War world, the United States must ensure that it has a *rational* builddown of its military forces that allows for stockpiling weapons and mothballing planes and ships. It is also important that the United States retain the ability to *reconstitute* its defense industrial base if needed in the future. It must find ways, in spite of budget cuts, to retain high-quality industrial and technical personnel and defense-industry capabilities.

This reconstitution capability also means being able to form, train, and field new fighting units from cadres, mobilizing previously trained or new personnel and maintaining experienced military personnel, technology, doctrine, training, and innovation necessary to retain the competitive edge in decisive areas of potential military competition.

Defense Strategy

On 2 August, 1990, President Bush outlined a new strategy for U.S. national security and a new concept of the *base force* levels needed to support that strategy. Unfortunately for the president, the speech that day was overshadowed by Iraq's invasion of Kuwait. The strategy was further spelled out by the defense secretary, Richard Cheney, in a speech in February 1991 (before the total collapse of Communism in August 1991). The key elements of that new (1991) Department of Defense strategy are, first, continued U.S. reliance on seven strategic alliances:

- NATO
- The Australia–New Zealand alliance (ANZUS)
- The United States–Japan Treaty of Mutual Cooperation and Security
- The Mutual Defense Treaty between the United States and South Korea
- The Mutual Defense Treaty with the Philippines
- The Southeast Asia Collective Defense Treaty
- The Inter-American Treaty of Reciprocal Assistance

These treaties are complemented by certain bilateral and informal agreements with countries such as Israel, Saudi Arabia, Egypt, Singapore, and Thailand.

The second key element is the continued importance of forward presence in key areas including Europe, Asia (Japan, Korea, Singapore), and the Middle East.

The third element is the need for force structure and mobility for crisis response. The United States needs to retain capability to deploy both heavy and light forces of significant size at great distances. This involves pre-positioning personnel and equipment on both land and sea, as well as air- and sea-lift capability and control of vital air and sea lanes. The five major choke points are the Panama Canal, the Straits of Gibraltar, the Suez Canal, the Straits of Malacca, and the Straits of Hormuz (through which 20 percent of U.S. oil consumption passes).

The fourth element is the ability to reconstitute U.S. forces against a renewed global threat. Force structure reductions are based on the premise of considerable warning time—in years, not months—before the United States would have to face a massive conventional threat. However, plans need to be made for a dramatic expansion of forces, if needed. Weapons systems capabilities and specialized, highly skilled personnel must also be retained.

The final element of the new strategy involves strategic deterrence through a balance of offensive and defensive capabilities. U.S. nuclear ballistic missile deterrent capability would be retained, and development of the SDI program would continue to guard against an accidental or terrorist launch of nuclear missiles against the United States. (This item was later deleted from the defense budget by the Clinton administration.)

In January 1992, the late representative (died in May 1995) Les Aspin, chair of the House Armed Services Committee, developed what he referred to as a "threat-driven analysis" for a new U.S. defense strategy. The representative proposed that the United States "systematically inventory the real world threats of the post-Soviet world, and . . . shape and size our forces for the 1990s to deal with these threats."[33] He argued that we "need a strategically sound, *bottom up* approach to determine what the country really needs militarily. Otherwise we will be drawn into a divisive political wrangle, which could produce a *defense budget by subtraction*. We would simply buy less of the same old Cold War forces."[34]

The use of the threat approach to structuring U.S. defense forces was not uniformly agreed to at that time. General Colin Powell, then chair of the Joint Chiefs of Staff, argued instead for a base force that is built on U.S. superpower status rather than imagined threats. Former secretary of defense Arthur Schlesinger agreed that the defense structure should be designed to maintain the "overall aura of American power."

Notwithstanding these reservations, when Les Aspin was appointed secretary of defense in the new Clinton administration, he proceeded to build a defense strategy and budget on the basis of his bottom-up review approach that he had advocated when he chaired the House Armed Services Committee. Secretary William Perry, who succeeded Secretary Aspin after one year, followed the Aspin approach. It is therefore worth reviewing that bottom-up process to achieve a better understanding of the underlying strategic thinking behind current national security policy. Irrespective of whether or not this bottom-up, building block approach is used in the future, it exemplifies the kind of thinking that has in the past gone, and continues to go, into designing a national security structure.[35]

The Aspin view of the changing security situation facing the United States is summarized in Table 14–3. When he compares the Old World security environment with the New World environment, the list of differences, in essence, reflects

TABLE 14–3   The Post-Cold War Changing Security Environment

Old World	New World
U.S. PERCEPTIONS	
Soviet military power	Spread of nuclear weapons
	Terrorism
	Regional thugs
	Drug traffickers
Deliberate Soviet attack	Instability in former Soviet Union
Economic power assumed	Japanese economic power
High defense budgets	Declining defense budgets
Global security concerns paramount	Domestic security concerns paramount
GEOPOLITICAL CONTEXT	
Bipolar rigidity	Multipolar complexity
Predictable	Uncertain
Communism	Nationalism and religious extremists
U.S. dominant western power	U.S. militarily no. 1 but not economically
Fixed alliances	Ad hoc coalitions
"Good guys and bad guys"	"Gray guys"
U.N. paralyzed	U.N. viable
THE THREAT	
Single (Soviet)	Diverse
Survival at stake	U.S. population and interests at stake
Known	Unknown
Deterrable	Nondeterrable
Strategic use of nukes	Terroristic use of nukes
Overt	Covert
Europe centered	Regional, ill-defined
High risk of escalation	Little risk of escalation
MILITARY FORCES	
Attrition warfare	Decisive attacks on key nodes
War by proxy	Direct involvement
High tech dominant	High, medium, low tech mix
Forward deployed	Power projection
Forward based	U.S. based
Host-nation support	Self-reliant

Source: House Armed Services Committee, U.S. Congress.

the situation facing U.S. defense organizations after the significant changes from a bipolar world to a unipolar world.

Chairman Aspin's assessment of the various threats facing the United States was explained in his 28 January, 1992 memo to his congressional colleagues. The United States must be prepared to:

1. Counter regional aggressors
   a) Middle East and Southwest Asia
   b) North Korea
   c) Elsewhere

2. Combat the spread of nuclear and other mass terror weapons
3. Fight terrorism
4. Restrict drug traffic
5. Keep the peace
6. Assist civilians

As a benchmark for future regional threats, Aspin used what he called an "Iraqi equivalent," that is, Iraq's offensive power before Operation Desert Storm decimated the Iraqi army. Before the war, Iraq had the world's fourth-largest army; it included 6000 tanks; battle-hardened, well-led troops; 700 military aircraft and a modern air defense system; capabilities for chemical and biological warfare; and theater ballistic missiles. By comparison, the force structures of current potential regional threats are presented in Table 14–4.

From the viewpoint of the United States, in Aspin's analysis, the minimum number of U.S. forces necessary to counter regional threats similar to that posed by Iraq in its invasion of Kuwait was defined as one "Desert Storm equivalent." This force level included six heavy army divisions; one light transportable division; one marine division on land and one at sea; 24 Air Force fighter bomber squadrons; 70 heavy bombers; two early-arriving carrier battle groups, later building to four (including AEGIS cruiser and destroyer defenses); and four battleships capable of launching cruise missiles. The Aspin defense strategy was heavily influenced by some of the lessons learned from the Gulf War, for example:[36]

TABLE 14–4   Current Force Structures of Selected Countries (Iraq-Equivalent Scale)

	Land	*Sea*	*Air*
Iraq (prewar)	1.0	1.0	1.0
Middle East, Southwest Asia			
Iraq (today)	.4	<.5	.5
Iran	.2	7	.4
Syria	.6	2	.8
Libya	.3	13	.7
Asia			
North Korea	.6	80	.6
China	1.4	90	2.6
Western Hemisphere			
Cuba	.2	5	.2

Source: Congressional Budget Office.

Unity of Command Was Great. Until the passage of the Goldwater-Nichols bill a few years ago, the United States had no unity of command in its military conflicts. In the war in Vietnam there was an air war commander (Admiral ELMO Zumwalt) headquartered in Hawaii and a ground war commander headquartered in Vietnam (General William Westmoreland). The chair of the Joint Chiefs of Staff had no real power, and the military services acted essentially independently of each other.

But the United States learned from the mistakes in Vietnam and in later incursions into Panama and Grenada. In the Gulf War, General H. Norman Schwarzkopf had full authority to run the war. He even fired a Navy admiral during the war, a previously unheard of act for a general. When the Navy complained, Colin Powell, the chair of the Joint Chiefs of Staff, backed up General Schwarzkopf. The lesson learned is that the United States can no longer tolerate traditional service rivalries and turf compromises. "Purple suits" are the wave of the future.[37]

Professional Military Fought the War. The U.S. armed forces in the Gulf War were older (average age of 28 versus 19 in Vietnam), knew their jobs, and were better trained than forces in Vietnam. The Gulf War emphasized the U.S. need to retain and build on its professional military capability.

Logistics Were Superb. The U.S. armed forces and their allies had time to prepare before the action started, and the technical representatives of the services did a superb job of keeping equipment operating in difficult circumstances. This support continued even as the military action progressed on both land and sea.

During the war it became apparent that U.S. air- and sea-lift capabilities need to be enhanced for future conflicts that may have less lead time than was the case in Iraq, and the United States cannot count on having forward staging bases in convenient locations near the front such as Saudi Arabia and Turkey.

Investment in High Tech Military Equipment under the Reagan Administration Paid Off. The newly developed *smart bombs* proved extremely successful. Stealth aircraft flew 80 percent of the combat sorties. The United States needs to retain this technology edge by maintaining its research and development and industrial base capabilities. High tech weapons will save lives in a future conflict.

Even though Saddam Hussein had a large army, the United States had a favorable match, mainly due to its ability to withdraw from Europe forces no longer needed to confront the Soviets. The United States will seldom have the luxury of a six-month buildup in future conflicts, with the ability to draw on a huge, well-trained force and with a predictable military matchup. The nation therefore needs to have available a rapid deployment capability of adequate forces.

As a result of these changes, the mission, size, composition, and shape of U.S. military forces need to be reconsidered. That process began during the first Clinton defense budget, but it is by no means complete. Most agree that it will not be adequate simply to cut all the services across the board. The United States needs not only a smaller military force but a different type of military force from that envisioned just a few years ago.

The military consensus that appears to be developing at this writing supports a force structure in which mobility and quick response will play a major role. In this scenario the Navy and Marine Corps play a much more prominent role, relatively speaking, than during the Cold War years when their major mission was to confront the Soviet Navy on the blue waters of the high seas and to launch nuclear weapons from our *boomer* submarines. Today the Navy is being reconfigured to project force to and through the brown waters, the littoral regions adjoining land masses.[38] At the same time the Navy will most likely be performing this mission with 300 ships rather than the 600-ship navy proposed, and almost delivered, by President Reagan. The Marine Corps, in contrast, is the only service branch maintaining, or perhaps even increasing, its budget.

Drawing on these lessons and potential threats, Secretary Aspin then translated the threats into what he called "building blocks for defense," shown in Figure 14–8. He then converted these into the alternative force structures shown in Table 14–5. Finally, he converted these forces into defense budget dollars.

The 1993 budget agreed to by the House and Senate Budget Conference Committee was $277 billion. By fiscal 1994 the defense budget had dropped to two hundred and sixty-seven billion. This would yield a fiscal 1996 budget of two hundred and forty-eight billion. Projections for the rest of this century are:

Fiscal 1997	$245 billion
Fiscal 1998	$254 billion
Fiscal 1999	$260 billion
Fiscal 2000	$273 billion
Fiscal 2001	$286 billion

In assessing the likelihood of future defense budget outcomes, it is useful to look at the history of U.S. expenditures for defense, at least one measure of how much the U.S. public is willing to devote to this sector of its economy. Figure 14–9 traces defense spending as a percentage of gross national product (GNP) since 1890. From this graph it is clear that, with the exception of World Wars I and II, the Korean War, and the Cold War years since 1950, U.S. defense expenditures have been consistently less than 5 percent of GNP. Since the Korean War, when defense consumed almost 15 percent of GNP, the ratio has been in a long-term decline.

The strategy underlining the above defense budget commitment is essentially what Secretary Aspin had referred to as Option C (Table 14–5) in his congressional memos. Military personnel would be reduced from 2 million in 1991 (during Desert Storm) to 1.6 million in 1995 and 1.2 million (or less) in 1997. The estimated base force structure consistent with these reductions is given in Table 14–6.

The "Hollow Military" Argument

There are those who are now arguing that the United States has already exceeded the safety level of defense budget cuts and has produced a military incapable of carrying out its duties and responsibilities in the world. Military leaders argue that the Gulf War was not typical of the kinds of conflicts for which the country needs military forces. They suggest that there are now "pockets of unreadiness" and question whether the United States could really fight two simultaneous regional wars. The U.S. Government Accounting Office has entered the debate with the argument that the Defense budget plan of $1.2 trillion over the period from 1995 to the end of the century will be $150 billion short. They suggest that this may result in the scrapping of several planned new weapons systems.

Others counter this argument with the observation that, in spite of the decreasing share of GDP the United States devotes to defense, it still spends more on defense than all of the other countries in the world combined.[39]

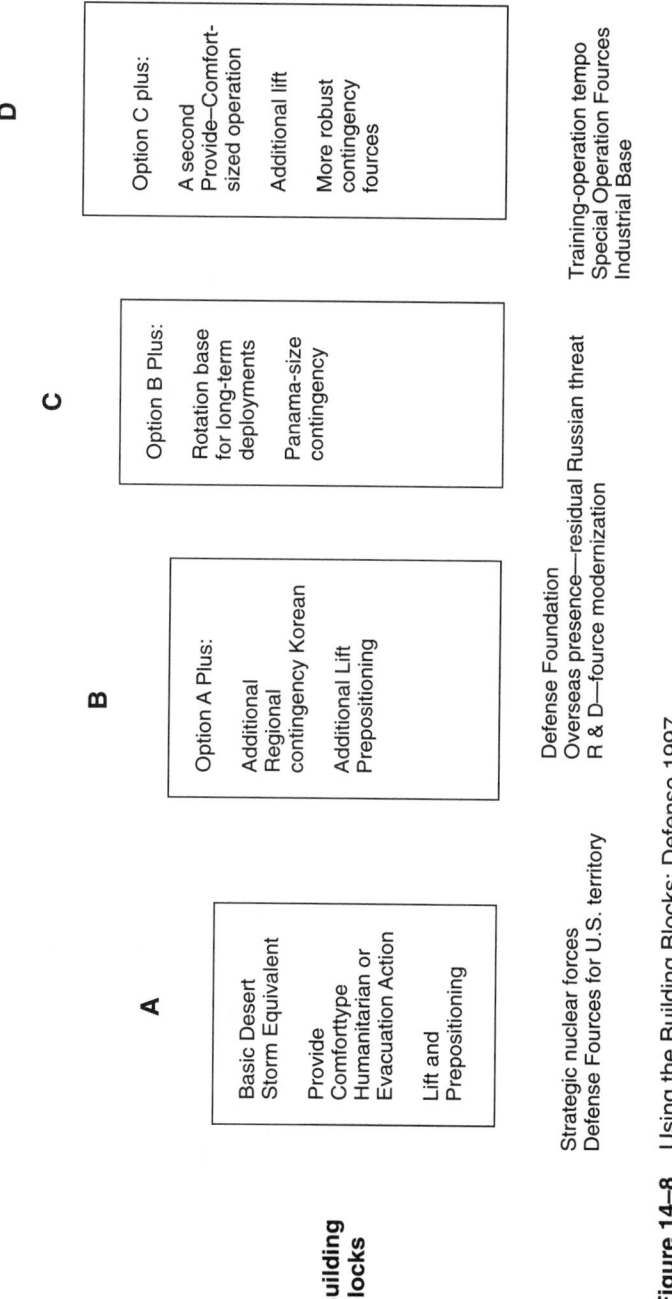

**Building
Blocks**

A

Basic Desert
Storm Equivalent

Provide
Comforttype
Humanitarian or
Evacuation Action

Lift and
Prepositioning

Strategic nuclear forces
Defense Fources for U.S. territory

B

Option A Plus:

Additional
Regional
contingency Korean

Additional Lift
Prepositioning

Defense Foundation
Overseas presence—residual Russian threat
R & D—fource modernization

C

Option B Plus:

Rotation base
for long-term
deployments

Panama-size
contingency

D

Option C plus:

A second
Provide–Comfort-
sized operation

Additional lift

More robust
contingency
fources

Training-operation tempo
Special Operation Fources
Industrial Base

Figure 14–8 Using the Building Blocks: Defense 1997

Source: Representative Les Aspin, Chair, House Armed Services Committee, February 1992.

TABLE 14–5 Comparison of Alternative Future Force Structures

	Force A	Force B	Force C	Force D	Base Force	End FY 9 Force
Army						
Active Divisions	8	8	9	10	12	16
Reserve Divisions	2	2	6	6	6	10
Cadre Divisions	0	0	0	0	2	0
Marine Corps						
Active Divisions	2	2	2	3	$2\,^1/_3$	3
Reserve Divisions						
Air Force						
Active Wings	6	8	10	11	15	22
Reserve Wings	4	6	8	9	11	12
Navy						
Ships (Total)	220	290	340	430	450	528
Carriers	6	8	12	15	13	15
SSNs	20	40	40	50	80	87
Assault Ships	50	50	50	82	50	65
Sealift						
Fast Sealift Ships	16	24	24	24	8	8
Afloat Prepositioning Ships	20	24	24	24	8	8

Source: Representative Les Aspin, Chair, House Armed Services Committee, February 1992.

Figure 14–9 Defense spending as a percentage of GNP, 1890–2000

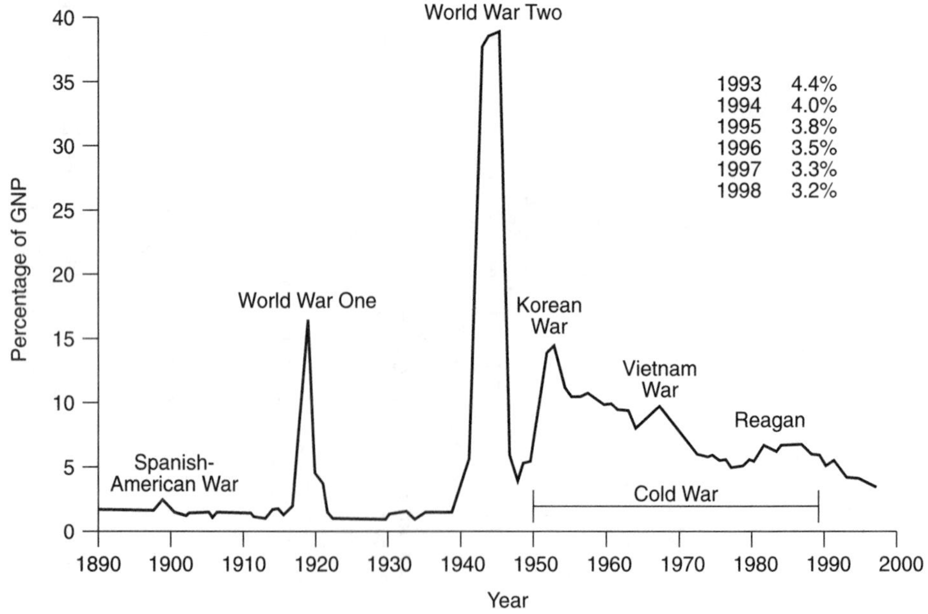

Source: Dr. Loren B. Thompson, Georgetown University.

TABLE 14–6   Base Force Structure, 1990–1995

	FY 1990	FY 1991	FY 1992	FY 1993	FY 1994	FY 1995
Army Division						
Active	18	16	14	14	14	12
Reserve	10	10	10	8	8	6*
Aircraft Carriers						
Active	15	15	14	13	13	12
Training	1	1	1	1	1	1
Carrier Air Wings						
Active	13	13	12	11	11	11
Reserve	2	2	2	2	2	2
Battle Force Ships	546	526	464	447	434	429
Tactical Fighter Wings						
Active	24	22	16	16	15	15
Reserve	12	13	12	12	12	11
Strategic Bombers	268	228	209	169	172	176

*Excludes 2 cadre divisions.

Source: House Armed Services Committee.

Where Is All This Heading?

The factors that will influence the choices—the judgment calls—that eventually emerge from the debate over the future size and shape of U.S. military forces and the industrial base to back it up were included in Secretary Aspin's analysis. These factors include questions and tentative answers about the following issues:

- The adequacy of forces to meet regional threats
    How large a threat does the United States anticipate?
    Must it prepare for simultaneous threats?
    How much can the nation depend on its military reserve forces?
- What are the proper amounts and types of overseas presence necessary to U.S. security interests?
- What type, and how much, of U.S. defense industrial capability can the nation afford to retain? Will this be adequate if it needs to reconstitute its defense forces in the future?
- How much can be saved in the U.S. defense budget by the end of this century without impairing the nation's ability to defend its interests? Is this amount of savings consistent with the need to reduce the federal budget deficit?
- What long-term costs has the United States incurred in past and current budget years that will inhibit its ability to shift defense priorities? Can any of these costs be eliminated?

It is clear that the United States is still a long way from reaching a consensus on the shape and size of the defense structure for the post-Cold War era. However, the analysis initiated by former Secretary Aspin and the debate it generated can only be considered a healthy approach for reaching rational conclusions about this important dimension of U.S. public policy.

The government is moving toward a consensus on defense that will provide for the unknown contingencies facing the United States in its role as the only de-

fense superpower left in the world, while at the same time freeing enough resources to begin to better position the nation to expand global economic competition. As this process unfolds, the country must avoid the same mistakes of
isolationism and dismantling of defense capability made in the past. These mistakes have invited foreign adventurism, instability, and conflicts affecting vital U.S.
interests and have cost the country more in the long run than had it retained an
active international security role with an adequate defense capability.

There are also a number of important political decisions that both the
United States and its industrial nation partners need to make if the nation is to enjoy the benefits of a stable and nonchaotic world in the future. It is essential that
the western democracies and Japan not be penurious in their approach to helping
the members of the former Soviet bloc and the developing nations of the world to
improve their economies and move toward democratic governments.

This approach will require opening both U.S. purses and markets. It is the
only way in which these countries will eventually reach the economic and political
stability that is key to the world of the future. At the same time, as cautioned by
Senator Richard Lugar of Indiana, the United States must appreciate that the Russians are "rivals, not partners," who have their own set of national interests and priorities. This does not mean the two great landmass nations cannot work together
in their mutual interests. It simply means that the United States must understand
the relationship and act pragmatically and in a sophisticated manner as this new
relationship develops.

DISCUSSION QUESTIONS

1. How has the national security situation of the United States changed with the end of the
   Cold War? What questions must be answered and what choices made as the nation reori-
   ents its military forces to deal with the new environment?
2. Both President Bush and President Clinton have attempted to define the *new world order*
   following the end of the Cold War. How are U.S. foreign policy goals changing to reflect
   this new order, and what tools does the country have to help reach those goals?
3. Which of the competing alternative visions of the U.S. role in the post-Cold War world
   would you support? Why?
4. What should be the posture of the United States in assisting the developing countries of
   the world? Why?
5. With the demise of the Soviet threat in Europe, some critics of U.S. foreign policy believe the nation should withdraw from NATO and let the Europeans handle their own security needs. Explain why you agree, or disagree, with this proposition.
6. Does the bottom-up review approach to building a defense budget make sense? What are
   its advantages and shortcomings?

SUGGESTED READINGS

Graham Allison and Gregory F. Treverton, *Rethinking America's Security: Beyond Cold War to
    New World Order*, W.W. Norton & Company, New York, London, 1992.
Agenda 1994: Critical Issues in Foreign Policy, Council on Foreign Relations, New York, 1994.
Joseph J. Romm, *Defining National Security: The non-military aspects*, Council on Foreign Rela-
    tions Press, New York, 1994.

Ann Markusen and Joel Yudken, *Dismantling the Cold War Economy*, Basic Books, 1992.
Murray Weidenbaum, *Small Wars-Big Defense*, Oxford University Press, New York, 1992.

NOTES

1. For a more detailed exposition of this topic, see the excellent discussion by David C. Henderson, "The End of American History: American Security, The National Purpose, and the New World Order," in *Rethinking America's Security*, ed. Graham Allison and Gregory F. Treverton (New York: W. W. Norton, 1992).
2. For more detail on this change in policy, see "Otherwise Engaged," *The Economist*, 30 October 1993, 21–24.
3. *Economist*, 1993.
4. Henry R. Nau, *The Myth of America's Decline* (New York: Oxford University Press, 1990).
5. George F. Will, "Surrendering the Stars and Stripes," *Washington Post*, 2 September 1993, p. 27.
6. Paul Wolfowitz, "Clinton's First Year," *Foreign Affairs: Agenda 1994*, (New York: Council on Foreign Relations, 1994), 9.
7. Wolfowitz, 1994, 11.
8. George Kennan, *Around the Cragged Hill* (New York and London: W. W. Norton, 1993), 183.
9. Clarke E. Cochran, Lawrence C. Mayer, T. R. Carr, and N. Joseph Cayer, *An Introduction to American Public Policy* (New York: St. Martin's, 1990), 443.
10. In this section I look at potential foreign policy problems on the basis of regions of the world that appear to be particularly tumultuous at this time. Another approach is suggested by Samuel Harrington in an article in *Foreign Affairs: Agenda 1994* (New York: Council on Foreign Relations, 1994), 120, where he argues that the world is moving away from the traditional rivalry between nation states and toward a "Clash of Civilizations." These, he suggests, are Western, Confucian, Japanese, Islamic, Hindu, Slavic-Orthodox, Latin American, and possibly African. "The most important conflicts of the future will occur along the cultural fault lines separating these civilizations from one another."
11. Bernard Lewis, as quoted in "The Challenge of Radical Islam," *Foreign Affairs: Agenda 1994* (New York: Council on Foreign Relations, 1994), 183.
12. Comment made to Dr. Bonser during a meeting in Paris at l'École nationale d'administration, June 1992.
13. For a discussion of this situation, see *The Economist*, 25 December, 1993, 17–20.
14. *Economist*, 25 December 1993.
15. *Economist*, 25 December, 1993, 20.
16. William Pfaff, "Invitation to War: Ethnic Conflict in the Balkans," *Foreign Affairs: Agenda 1994* (New York: Council on Foreign Relations, 1994), 43.
17. Richard G. Lugar, "The Russians Are Rivals, Not Partners," speech to the *American Spectator* Washington Dinner Club, 7 March, 1994.
18. Lugar, 1994.
19. Lugar, 1994, 75.
20. Nicholas D. Kristof, "The Rise of China," *Foreign Affairs:Agenda 1994*, (New York: Council on Foreign Relations, 1994), 73.
21. General Accounting Office, "Foreign Assistance," Report to the Congress (Washington, D.C.: U.S. General Accounting Office, 1993).
22. Jeffrey R. Smith, "Clinton Moves to Ease Pakistan Nuclear Curb: New Bill Would Allow Waiver on Aid Cutoff," *Washington Post*, 25 November, 1993, p. A59.
23. Peter Calvocorcssi, "Foreign Policy Ea la carte? European Union," *The Economist*, 26 December 1992–8 January, 1993, 58.

24. *Economist,* 1992–1993.
25. Ronald D. Asmus, Richard L. Kugler, and F. Stephen Larrabee, "Building a New NATO," *Foreign Affairs: Agenda 1994* (New York: Council on Foreign Relations, 1994), 205.
26. Mark M. Nelson, "Joint Army Unveiled in Bid for EC Unity," *Wall Street Journal,* 8 November, 1993, p. 11.
27. *Rethinking National Security: Beyond Cold War to New World Order,* ed. Graham Allison and Greg Treverton (New York: W. W. Norton, 1992).
28. Allison and Treverton, 1992, 51–56.
29. Allison and Treverton, 1992, 49.
30. Charles Krauthammer, "The Unipolar Moment," *Foreign Affairs* 70, No. 1 (1990–1991): 24–33.
31. Dr. Larry Korb, speech at the Crane Division of the Naval Surface Warfare Center, Washington, D.C., June 1991.
32. Department of Defense releases, "National Security Strategy of the United States" (Washington, D.C.: U.S. Government Printing Office, 1993).
33. Memorandum from Les Aspin to the House Armed Services Committee.
34. Memorandum from Les Aspin to the House Armed Services Committee, January 1992.
35. President John F. Kennedy's approach was that the United States needed to be capable of fighting two large wars and a "brushfire" war at the same time. President Richard Nixon cut this requirement to one and a half large wars and a smaller conflict.
36. This formulation was developed by Dr. Larry Korb of the Brookings Institution.
37. A term conveying the change to a more generic military—that is, moving away from the khaki of the army and the blues of the air force and navy to the "purple suits" of a common service.
38. For a more detailed discussion of this strategy, see Department of the Navy, "From the Sea: Preparing the Navy for the 21st Century" (Washington, D.C.: U.S. Government Printing Office).
39. An observation made to the authors by Dr. Larry Korb of the Brookings Institution.

15

Governmental Reform: A Work in Progress

A HISTORY OF REINVENTION

There is presently a considerable amount of ferment and change in public management at all three levels of government in the United States. A simplistic answer as to why this is the case in the United States in the 1990s is that the electorate has become increasingly dissatisfied with the performance of government and wants more for its money. The result has been a search for new ways of doing things, both in terms of management performance and in terms of who does what in the implementation of public policy and the delivery of public services.

Indeed, this dissatisfaction with government was a persistent theme in the 1992 presidential election and in the congressional elections of 1994, which resulted in a Republican takeover of both the House of Representatives and the Senate and in victories in most states where a governor was being elected. The scramble among candidates to revamp the way government does business in this country continues into the 1996 national campaigns.

In this chapter we review the attempts to transform the what and how of the management of government at various periods in history; we explore some of the reasons behind the current move to *reinvent* U.S. government; we look at the issue of the role of the professional public service; and we examine the inherent problems of measuring government performance and attempting to link such measurement to the budget process through changes in the management system. The discussion in this chapter sets the stage for Chapter 16, where we examine in some detail current attempts at governmental reform.

MAJOR GOVERNMENTAL REORIENTATIONS IN U.S. HISTORY

As John DiIulio, Gerald Garvey, and Donald Kettl point out, the idea of reinventing the U.S. government is not new.[1] In fact, the metaphor arose from the nation's founding fathers' "preoccupation with Newtonian mechanisms." Thomas Jefferson once suggested the nation should abolish the structures of our government and reinvent them every 20th Independence Day. The major periods of reinvention during U.S. history are perhaps open to interpretation, but it is possible to identify at least four, and possibly five, reinventions that have taken place since the founding of the republic.

In the first instance, when President Andrew Jackson took office in 1828, the leadership powers of the presidency had not been fully utilized by any of his predecessors. Jackson established a direct link to the people of the country with the slogan "Let the people rule." On taking office, he said: "The federal constitution must be obeyed, state rights preserved, our national debt paid [which he did], direct taxes and loans avoided, and the federal union preserved." In carrying out this pledge, he challenged the Supreme Court and the Congress, and he vetoed more legislation than had all the presidents before him. As a result, he changed the political order and relationships among political parties, Congress, and the presidency.

The second major reorientation of the federal government came with the election of Abraham Lincoln and the nation's involvement in the Civil War. As discussed earlier in this book, the country's founders had very modest goals in mind for the new government. In fact, a major purpose of the government, in their view, was to protect the liberty of the citizens from the government.

Although the original battle cry of the Civil War was to restore the Union, Lincoln's Emancipation Proclamation freeing the slaves produced a new view of the role of government. The war became a crusade, in Lincoln's words, "for a new rebirth of freedom." Before the war, the federal government was quite small and had little impact on the lives of most people. At the end of the Civil War, the number of federal employees had grown to 53,000, and the government had a much more activist view of itself. This was particularly true about its new role in the economic development of the nation.

The end of the Civil War saw a need for reconstruction in the South, expansion to the West, and a push for economic development throughout the country. The government, for the first time, was actively involved in all phases of this development movement. It found itself engaged in a myriad of economic activities even beyond the establishment of tariffs, a banking system, and currency management. It also encouraged immigration to expand the labor force, set up land grants to develop the West; established a system of land grant colleges; and issued bonds for the development of a rail system and other public development projects.

The third reinvention of government came later in the 19th century with the reformists, led by President Theodore Roosevelt and a future president, Woodrow Wilson. When Roosevelt was first elected in 1901, he took on the railroad barons, monopolists, land speculators, and other major corporations. During his administration, Congress passed laws to regulate railroads, to protect the public from harmful food and drugs and to conserve the nation's forests and other natural resources. In doing so, Roosevelt, who acquired the nickname "Trust Buster," established the economic regulatory role of U.S. government.

With his election as president in 1913, Wilson took major steps to strengthen the operation of the U.S. economy by establishing the Federal Reserve System (FRS) and having Congress improve international trade by reducing tariffs. Wilson also was able to introduce organizational reform legislation, including the establishment of the Federal Trade Commission (FTC) and the Department of Labor; and he promoted the passage of the Clayton Anti-Trust Act, which increased the power of the federal government to police unfair practices of big business. On the political front, Wilson should receive the major credit for the enactment of the constitutional amendment that provides for the direct election of U.S. senators rather than for election by state legislators, as well as for the passage of the 19th Amendment to the Constitution, which gives women the right to vote.

The reformists of the 1870s and 1880s had earlier redefined the relationship between politics and the administration of government. In the *Federalist Paper* 72, Alexander Hamilton stated, "The administration of government, in its largest sense, comprehends all of the operation of the body politic, whether legislative, executive, or judiciary." Wilson challenged this view when he articulated the basic outlines of the U.S. system of governmental management in his classic article, "The Study of Administration," published in the *Political Science Quarterly* in June 1887. Wilson defined the policy administration dichotomy when he wrote: "The field of administration is a field of business. . . . It is a part of political life only as the methods of the counting-house are a part of the life of the society. . . . Administrative questions are not political questions."[2]

Wilson aided in the implementation of this philosophy during his presidential administration (1913–1921), and reforms designed to continue to professionalize the management of government continued throughout the 1920s and 1930s. These reform steps included the development of civil service merit systems, rational budget systems, and other steps designed to depoliticize the management of government.

The late 1800s had also produced governmental reform at the state and local levels.[3] Theodore Roosevelt urged delegates at the first Annual Conference for Good Government in 1884 to find ways to streamline and improve government. Municipal reformers defined the elements of good government as public programs that benefit all citizens equally; budget controls to make sure public services were delivered at the lowest cost; politics separate from day-to-day administrative services; professional managers in government; and the principle of scientific management, as practiced in business. Reformers also fought to loosen state control over cities and promoted the strong mayor form of local government. In 1913, the National Municipal League proposed that governmental reforms include a professional city manager. By 1928, the city manager form of local government had been instituted in 324 cities.[4]

The fourth reinvention came with the Great Depression of the 1930s and the election of Franklin Delano Roosevelt as president.[5] The Depression began in 1929 with a stock market collapse, which was a traumatic event in the lives of all who witnessed it, and which still affects U.S. national character. Thirty-four billion dollars of security values vanished almost overnight. Corporations went bankrupt; banks closed before people could get their money out (there was no Federal Deposit Insurance Corporation then to back up depositors' claims on banks); and farm prices collapsed. High tariffs on imported goods resulting from the protectionist legislation of the Smoot-Hawley Bill led to retaliatory measures by foreign trading partners, which further exacerbated the depression.

When Roosevelt was elected in 1932, unemployment in the country was close to 25 percent of the labor force. Roosevelt's campaign stressed an activist role for government in getting the country moving again—what he called a New Deal for the people. With his inauguration in March 1933, he began to initiate action on several fronts, including the following:[6]

1. restoring confidence in the banking system;
2. reforming the currency;
3. initiating federal expenditures to stimulate the economy, such as public works projects;
4. introducing unemployment and old age assistance;
5. bringing aid to the beleaguered agricultural sector;
6. helping sustain the nation's railroad system;
7. arranging collection of some of the outstanding debts owed the United States by its World War I allies;
8. reforming the national debt;
9. working with U.S.'s international trading partners to reform the system of tariffs that had strangled international trade;
10. gearing up militarily and diplomatically to deal with the Fascist threat to international stability that was developing in Europe and the Far East.

Roosevelt was elected to four terms of office (he died before completing the fourth). His presidency transformed the U.S. government from having a passive to an active role in serving the everyday welfare of the citizens of the nation. Programs taken for granted today, such as the Social Security system, the welfare system, farm price supports, the federal insurance of bank deposits, and unemployment insurance, all had their origins in this period. Today, federal, state, and local governments combined have expenditures amounting to almost 40 percent of total national economic output, with programs and regulations touching virtually every aspect of life.

The fifth and present reinvention began in the late 1970s. President Jimmy Carter was elected in 1976 on what many observers would describe as an anti-Washington, antigovernment platform. In 1978, Proposition 13 was passed in the state of California, rolling back property taxes and severely limiting the growth of government programs. Similar, though less drastic, government backlashes occurred in other parts of the country.

In 1980, President Ronald Reagan was elected after arguing that government was not the solution to the nation's problems; government was the problem. The Reagan tax cuts, and the president's inability to move congress to achieve comparable real domestic budget cuts at the same time as defense spending was substantially expanded, led to the high level of federal deficits that are still unresolved. President Reagan also shifted many responsibilities of the national government to the state and local governments. In doing so, many believe, he, intentionally or not, rejuvenated the federal system as states took on the new responsibilities with a new latitude of operation.

Several reasons have been advanced as to why the U.S. public supported such actions at this time: the rapid growth in taxes as a percentage of real family income; the public's increasing annoyance with government interference in their lives; the Watergate, Iran-Contra, and other scandals; and the general dissatisfaction with government that lingered as a result of the war in Vietnam.

A 1992 report of the National Academy of Public Administration suggested the following possible reasons for the shift in public attitudes toward government:

- Adequate supply of services: people were generally satisfied with services they were receiving and were not inclined to pay for more.
- Excess capacity in government: voters saw government as too big.
- Outmoded machinery of government: the bureaucracy was unable to supply effective and efficient services.
- Inadequate performance. A slower economy reduced government's ability to provide added services without taxing real income gains. (This was particularly evident following the Arab oil embargoes of 1974 and 1978.)
- Morally bankrupt leadership: indicators were Watergate, and other political, financial, and moral scandals.
- More effective political opposition to governmental involvement in society.

Whatever the reasons, it seems clear that the public was ready for another reinvention of government in the late 1970s.

PROBLEMS IN THE FEDERAL SYSTEM

The late Charles Levine, Professor of Public Administration and researcher for the Congressional Research Service, commented that not only are there issues of what government should do and how it should do it, there is also the matter of who should do it. These issues deal partly with matters of involvement of the private sector in public service delivery and partly with which level of government should perform which functions.

Until the New Deal of the 1930s, the national government was not much involved in the country's daily life. Whatever the public service or support functions that government performed, they were performed by local and sometimes state governments. President Roosevelt initiated the involvement of the federal government in people's lives to a much greater extent than had been the case previously, and the degree of this involvement has ebbed and flowed ever since.

From a management standpoint, there has periodically been support for both centralization and decentralization of public service provision. Until the first administration of Richard Nixon (1969–1972), the trend had been increasingly toward centralization of government services. This approach culminated in the Great Society programs of President Lyndon Johnson. Nixon criticized Johnson's approach and took steps to disengage the federal government from direct service provision. Congress enacted revenue-sharing programs that collapsed many of the Great Society programs, while continuing to provide state and local governments with the funds, under both functional bloc and general revenue grants, to enable the localities to continue to provide many of the public services through federal support and local management. This approach of federal financing, with local government program management, continued until the Reagan administration in 1980. President Reagan ended the federal revenue-sharing program as well as several of the programs they financed. The result was that states and localities would have to pay for the programs themselves, if they were to be offered.

The change was traumatic for many of the states and cities of the nation, but there has been virtually no political support for a recentralization of the federal government's direct involvement in these types of programs. Even concerted attempts by state and local interest groups to revive the federal revenue-sharing programs of President Nixon failed easily in Congress (no doubt spurred by the problems with the federal budget deficit). At the same time, however, there was an increase in the number of mandates the federal government imposed on states, particularly in such areas as health, welfare, and the environment, which in effect increasingly moved the federal-state relationship from one of cooperation toward one of coercion.[7] Against this backdrop, one of the key features of the 1994 Republican Contract with America was a vow to end unfunded federal mandates to state and local government. Upon assuming office in January, the Republican Congress introduced this ban as one of their first orders of business.

The trend under Presidents George Bush and Bill Clinton has been to continue the movement toward greater decentralization of government service provision as a means of achieving better program productivity and success. Even at the local level, support for centralization of government services through means such as instituting metropolitan government is being challenged by those who favor program management at the village or neighborhood level as a means of achieving greater efficiency and public support. The U.S. Advisory Commission on Intergovernmental Relations studies suggest that "a diversity of local governments can foster key values of democratic government-efficiency, equity, responsiveness, accountability, and self-governance."[8] This decentralization movement is very much a part of contemporary management thinking exemplified in both total quality management and in reinventing-government proposals described in Chapter 16.

In 1992, Alice Rivlin, then with the Brookings Institution (and later Director of President Clinton's Office of Management and Budget), argued for a "reopening of the 200 year old question of the desirable division of responsibilities between the states and the federal government."[9] Her vision would involve three major changes:

1. The federal government would broaden its social insurance responsibilities to include basic health insurance for everyone (as President Clinton later proposed)
2. States would take primary responsibility for a "productivity agenda" involving education, workforce skills, and public infrastructure, while the federal government would withdraw from those areas
3. A new system of common shared taxes—including a value-added tax (a broad-based form of sales tax)—would replace state retail taxes in order to put the states on a firmer financial basis

Rivlin's proposal essentially recognized the desirability of the decentralization of such "people programs" as education, crime control, drug-use control, housing, and community development. Such social service and infrastructure projects that require direct community involvement and commitment to make them truly effective. At the same time, the federal government would be free to do those things it is better equipped to do than are the states: for example, provide for international relations and defense and offer those public services that clearly spill over state lines, such as scientific research, food and drug regulation, Social Security, national transportation safety (e.g., airlines, railways, and highways), environmental protection, and regulation of the economy and commerce.

PRESSURES FOR CHANGE IN PUBLIC MANAGEMENT

In addition to the pressure for change in the role of government in the lives of the U.S. public, there was (and is) a coincident considerable amount of criticism about how government carries out the business of the people. As a result, there have been numerous attempts to overhaul the management of the federal government in this century. Figure 15–1 lists the major management-study commissions established by the executive branch of the U.S. government since 1905. It is worthwhile noting, however, that some scholars have pointed out the *pendulum* nature of public satisfaction or dissatisfaction with both the public and private sectors of our society. In the 1930s, the level of confidence in these sectors was exactly the inverse of what it is in the 1990s.[10]

Almost every president has seen the need for such management reform efforts. It would be an overstatement to refer to them as reinventions, but most reforms made important incremental improvements in how the government carries out the public's business. The latest effort at management improvement has come from the Clinton administration. In the summer of 1993, the report of the government task force on the National Performance Review (otherwise known as the

Figure 15–1   PRESSURES for change in public management (major commissions to improve the executive branch, 1905–1993)

Keep Commission (1905–1909)
   Studied personnel management, government contracting, information management
President's Commission on Economy Efficiency (1910–1913)
   Made a case for a national executive budget
Joint Committee on Reorganization (1921–1924)
   Studied methods of redistributing executive functions along the departments
President's Committee on Administrative Management (1936–1937)
   Recommended creation of the Executive Office of the President; founded on substantial academic theory.
First Hoover Commission (1947–1949)
   Reviewed the organization and function of the executive branch; built on task force reports.
Second Hoover Commission (1953–1955)
   Followed up the first Hoover commission; focused more on policy problems than on organizational structure
Study Commissions on Executive Reorganization (1953–1988)
   Iniated series of low-key reforms that produced quiet but important changes
Ash Council (1969–1971)
   Proposed a fundamental restructuring of the executive branch, including creation of four new super departments.
Carter Reorganization Effort (1977–1979)
   Suggested botytom-up, process-based effort to reorganize government; mostly ended in failure; new cabinet departments created
Grace Commission (1982–1984)
   Attempted a large-scaled effort to determine how government could be operated for less money
National Performance Review (1993)
   Attempted to reinvent government to improve its performance

Source: Ronald C. Moe, *Reorganizing the Executive Branch in the Twentieth Century: Landmark Commissions,* Report 92–293 GOV (Washington, D.C.: Congressional Research Service, March 1992).

NPR, or the Gore Report) was released. We will review the recommendations of that report in Chapter 16, but at this point it is worth noting some of the views of the task force about the current state of public opinion with regard to the management of the federal government and the consequent need for a major overhaul in public management.[11] The NPR reports that the average person believes that 48 cents out of every federal tax dollar is wasted and that only 20 percent of people trust the federal government to do the right thing most of the time, down from 76 percent 30 years ago. It should be pointed out, however, that some believe views such as these are primarily ideological rather than managerial and are used to support a particular point of view about government and its role in society.[12]

Other indicators of problems pointed to by the NPR are many. The Defense Department owns more than $40 billion in unnecessary supplies; a century after farming has been replaced by industry as the principal employer, the nation still operates 12,000 agricultural field service offices; ineffective regulation of the financial industry produced the savings and loan debacle of the early 1990s; ineffective welfare and housing programs undermine families and cities; the government funds 150 different employment and training programs, yet the average person has no idea where to get job training, and the skills of the workforce fall further behind those of U.S.'s competitors.

The issue, in the view of the NPR, is not lazy or incompetent government employees. "It is red tape and regulations so suffocating that they stifle every ounce of creativity. . . . The federal government is filled with good people trapped in bad systems: budget systems, personnel systems, procurement systems, financial management systems, information systems." The NPR suggests that the root problem is that government organizations are "designed for an environment that no longer exists—bureaucracies that are so big and wasteful they can no longer serve the American people."[13]

DiIulio, Garvey, and Kettl argue that the functional specialization of government that has evolved in the United States (e.g., agencies established to deal with specific problems such as agriculture, defense, and commerce) was meant to offer efficiency in achieving public goals but has instead caused efficiency problems as government becomes increasingly differentiated and complex.[14] In addition, as agencies have been created to mirror particular constituencies, industries, and policy areas, the result has often been the type of *iron triangle*-issue power coalitions discussed in Chapter 2.

This organizational design situation is made more complex by the fact that many federal agencies are monopolies and , as such, have few incentives to innovate or improve. In addition, given the political nature of the government and the political risks of poor program performance, elaborate control systems are used to minimize the risk of scandal. Tasks are spelled out in detail, and audit systems make sure performance details are adhered to. As the Gore Report puts it: "In Washington, the greatest risk is not that a program will perform poorly, but that a scandal will erupt. . . . The result is a culture of fear and resignation. [Employees] follow the rules, pass the buck, and keep their heads down."[15] In 1986, Charles Levine[16] wrote that the loss of confidence in government that has been apparent in the country since at least the late 1970s stems from the following issues:

1. The disappointing results of attempts to shape the future through government
2. A corresponding change in public attitudes about the desirability of government action

3. The success of the Reagan administration in stimulating public discussion and debate over the three main dimensions of the "administrative state": what the government should do; how it should do it; and who should do it

It makes sense to add the following to that list:

4. The rapid expansion of entitlement programs, coupled with the unwillingness of the public to pay a much larger share of their income to government, resulting in fiscal crises at all levels of government and added pressure on governments to do more with less
5. The end of the Cold War and the shift to new public priorities, which will eventually result in a total restructuring of a large part of the federal service
6. The competitive pressures of a developing global economy, coupled with the possibilities for innovation introduced by new technology in everything from information processing to telecommunications to transportation, resulting in the need for virtually all organizations—including governments—to revisit the way in which they are conceived, organized, and function

David Osborne[17] argues that the public sector has an outmoded way of doing business. Government runs by monopoly and takes its customers—the citizens of the country—for granted. He also thinks that modern technology has affected the public's view of government by bringing it into living rooms and by providing the public with the ability to compare government's monopolistic, single-vendor service delivery with consumers' increasingly varied choices of private-sector goods and services. The contrast between the delivery of public services by large, centralized bureaucracies and the market-segmented, flexible manufacturing methods of the private sector has become increasingly stark in recent years.

Other critics elaborate on these systemic problems of management in the federal government. William Gadsby, former director of government-business operations issues for the General Accounting Office (GAO), suggests that federal governmental management in the past has suffered from three fundamental problems, which have created substantial and serious performance difficulties:[18]

1. A short-term mentality on the part of key managers and policy makers in the federal government
2. A governmental structure that inhibits results
3. A lack of accountability for results

SHORT-TERM MENTALITY

The problems of short-term mentality in the federal government stem from several factors that have become ingrained in the way the government does business. Gadsby cites the current federal-budgeting process as a prime example. The federal budget is now set by Congress on an annual basis, with little attention paid to the long-run implications of budget decisions. Furthermore, the basic approach to the development of the budget is incremental; that is, when decisions are made about how much to spend for a particular government program in a given year, the starting point of the discussion is How much was spent last year? Congress then decides on the budget in terms of an increment to be added to or subtracted from last year's budget. An alternative or at least supplementary approach would be basing the decision primarily on a program basis, that is, what the government wants to accomplish with a program and how much it must spend to reach its objectives. Attempts to take this approach to budgeting in the federal government, however, have not been very successful.

Another condition that contributes to a short-term, rather than long-term, approach to decision making is the high turnover of the top policy makers in the government. The experience of the Clinton administration may be different from those of its predecessors, but to date the average tenure of political appointees in high-level federal government policy-making jobs has been 2.6 years. For example, until Dr. Otis Bowen's three-year term as secretary of Health and Human Services (HHS) in the second Reagan administration, no HHS secretary in the past several administrations had lasted more than about 18 months in the job. The record for key deputies in the major government departments has been even less impressive: an average of 1.7 years. Clearly, with such a short time horizon, it is difficult for any department head to accomplish much. Established goals and objectives tend to be short term and limited, and it is next to impossible to measure the impact any government leader in his or her area of responsibility.

At present, there are approximately 3,000 federal political appointees. The Volker Commission on the Public Service argued that the government needs no more than 2,000 to meet the policy objectives of a particular presidential administration. Critics of the present system believe the constant turnover of such a large number of executive positions in the government "robs agencies of continuity and subjects the career work force to enormous uncertainty."[19] As a result, the career leadership of the government is compromised by the limitation of executive opportunities for career civil servants, encouraging them to leave government when they are at the top of their abilities and still have a great deal to contribute.

Another factor that contributes to the short-term mentality of the government is the publicity focus by the media on the policy-making side of government. Political appointees are, after all, politicians who are concerned with achieving favorable publicity for themselves and for their president (or governor) and his or her administration. Policy-making is glamorous and attracts media attention. Good management, although it may make a more important contribution to the long-term public good, is seldom as newsworthy, and its benefits are likely to be more visible in the long run rather than the short run.

GOVERNMENT STRUCTURE INHIBITS RESULTS

One of Gadsby's criticisms of federal government management is that it is too centrally controlled. In a concern over abuse by the bureaucracy, several presidential administrations have established processes that require advance clearance by the Office of Management and Budget (OMB) for the issuance of regulations and for information collection and testimony before congressional committees; and OMB has retained tight financial management and budgeting control over the agencies.

Congress also has micromanagement tendencies that compound the lack of management discretion by the agencies responsible for implementing the policies of the government and delivering public services. Indeed, some have suggested that federal agencies are in essence co-managed by the executive branch and the Congress.[20] Thus federal managers' ability to deal with unanticipated problems is reduced, and management creativity is inhibited. Indeed the organization of Congress itself is a management problem: competing congressional committees may oversee a particular government program and place considerable oversight burden on the bureaucratic agency responsible for program administration. The result is that agency executives spend an inordinate amount of time testifying before, and otherwise interacting with, Congress.

As earlier mentioned, federal government (and most state governments, which typically mirror the federal structure) evolved over the years as a complex of functional area organizations. This evolution resulted in a situation where agencies created to deal with specific problems or opportunities often find themselves stepping on each other's toes as lines between past problems and responsibilities become increasingly blurred and as new issues appear on the public agenda. For example, when the Environmental Protection Agency (EPA) was created, it merged a number of programs that had existed in other departments and agencies. The merger was far from smooth, and there are still environmental program areas that overlap other departments such as agriculture, interior, commerce, and even defense.

As DiIulio, Garvey, and Kettl put it: "Today, overlapping jurisdictions create endless jockeying for lead-agency status on high profile problems. . . . Because many agencies have a stake in, but no clear responsibility for other problems, solutions fall through the cracks. . . . Incoherence in policymaking and confusion in implementation have resulted."[21] In addition to the coordination problems between potentially competing federal agencies and congressional committees, boundary problems also exist between federal, state, and local governments and between the public and private sectors; these all make life difficult for public managers and result in less than optimal government performance.

Lack of Accountability for Results

The structural and systemic characteristics of the federal government, and many state governments as well, almost inevitably lead to other results that further impede the ability of government to function as a modern, adaptive organization capable of meeting the public's expectations of what government should do for it and for the country. If it is difficult to pin down precisely who is in charge of what, how can anyone be held accountable for results?

Gadsby suggests that one manifestation of this situation is an absence of a clearly stated, results-oriented organizational vision in the responsible agencies and departments. Good financial and program information is seldom available to program managers, and performance incentives in the organizations are not usually based on results.

The rules orientation of the government has led to silly and nonproductive regulations that many understand but few have attempted to change. For example, the annual budget cycle, with its disallowance of departmental carryover funds from one budget year to the next, gives program managers the incentive to spend their entire budget in the appropriated fiscal year rather than to lose the unspent funds, with the added implication that they were overfunded in the first place. This situation leads to the well-known (to grant seekers at least) scramble to allocate unspent funds as the October end of the fiscal year approaches. The centrally operated, rule-driven personnel system of the federal government has made it difficult for the operating (as opposed to support) agencies to recruit to meet their current and future program needs and almost impossible for program managers to reward high-quality performance with pay raises and promotion. The byzantine, rule-based procurement system has resulted in multiple fiascoes ranging from excessive costs when purchasing the simplest of goods, to wasted money on items such as Department of Defenses infamous $500 toilet seats, to millions of dollars in cost overruns on major weapons systems.

A simple example of the results of the mindless, rule-driven process comes from the Gore Report and conveys the gist of the problem:

> In Atlanta, after federal Marshals seize drug dealers' homes, they are allowed to sell them and use the money to continue their efforts to control drug trafficking. To do that they, of course, need to keep the homes presentable, including keeping the lawns mowed. But procurement regulations of the government require the Marshals to bid out all work competitively, and neighborhood teenagers don't compete for lawn maintenance contracts. The result is that the teenagers miss an opportunity to make money, and the federal government winds up paying an average of $40 per lawn cutting, instead of the $10 the teenagers would have cost.[22]

CIVIL SERVICE REFORM ISSUES

Including the uniformed services, the postal service, and the legislative and judicial branches, the combined federal workforce numbered about six million employees in 1991. Contrary to popular belief, the federal workforce has declined in relationship to total government employment over the past 30 years. Federal employment, as a percentage of total government employment, dropped from 28.1 percent in 1960 to 16.7 percent in 1990.

As discussed earlier, presidents have been expressing their dissatisfaction with government for many years. But seldom have any of the nation's chief executives directly criticized the abilities or dedication of federal employees. In the 1992 presidential campaign, President Bush said he would "right-size" government by "redirecting current funding away from bureaucracies and towards people" and would change the organization of government.[23]

Bill Clinton called for a "revolution in government" by "taking away power from the entrenched bureaucracies and special interests that dominate Washington." He said he would radically change the way government operates and "shift from top down bureaucracy to an entrepreneurial government that empowers citizens and communities to change our country from the bottom up." Part of this change was to be the elimination of 100,000 "unnecessary" federal government positions (which later grew to 272,000).

Ross Perot argued for returning government to the people. He was the only candidate who said anything complimentary about the public service during the 1992 presidential campaign. "Public service is a sacred trust. Being an elected, appointed, or career public servant is a noble calling." He also said, "We need to restore pride in the federal service so that our employees will smile every day at the office and be polite," and he argued for "reducing civil service restrictions to allow more discretion so that federal employees can be more responsive. . . . We need fewer employees and more rewards." But then he went on to rail against lobbyists and former federal employees who sell their services to special interests when they leave office and demanded a "tough ethics code for private citizens who serve as consultants and advisors to government."[24]

In their book, *Reinventing Government,* David Osborne and Ted Gaebler are more concerned with the how than with the what or who of government. They state that U.S. governments are in deep trouble. But they go on to say, "The people who work in government are not the problem; the systems in which they work are the problem. . . . Our intention is to bash bureaucracies, not bureaucrats."[25] Others point out, however, that it is not that easy to separate bureaucracies from bureaucrats, and that "they all get bashed together."

A New Look at the Merit Principles

The professional public service in the United States was developed in the late 1800s by progressives whose primary purpose was to reform government. One of their goals was to stop the practice of politicians' using jobs in the public service to pay off their political supporters. With the passage of the Pendelton Act in 1883, the reformers created the civil service system of the United States. The key features of the merit principles that have guided the U.S. civil service since the 19th century include (1) fair and open competition for federal jobs, (2) admission to the competitive service only on the basis of neutral examinations, (3) protection of those in the civil service from political influence and coercion, and (4) noninvolvement in political activities by the members of the civil service.

The Hatch Acts of 1939 and 1940 codified the no-political-involvement restrictions for the federal government and for state and local employees who are at least partly funded by the federal government. The Hatch Act provisions have been upheld several times by the Supreme Court. In 1993, the Hatch Act was liberalized to the extent that career employees can be somewhat more involved in political activities, but the act retains the provisions restricting government employees from running for office or conducting political activities at their place of work.

In 1970, and again in 1978, the Civil Service Commission restated the merit principles for the record. Their elaboration of the original principles added topics such as the need for training, more specificity about equal opportunity and diversity in the federal workforce, equal pay for equal work, and protection for public employee whistle-blowers who reveal wrongdoing in government. These changes by the Civil Service Commission increased the number of merit principles to nine and added to their complexity.

The thesis of Osborne and Gaebler and other critics of the civil service reformers is that, while the reformers were successful in ridding the government of many of its tawdry aspects, in the process they developed organizations that can no longer function effectively in today's society. The system that evolved from the original merit principles has grown enormously in complexity, and many believe it needs substantial overhaul. As Osborne and Gaebler put it, "In their zeal to control the inputs, integrity, and open access to government, the reformers ignored the outputs."[26] Patricia Ingraham and David Rosenbloom remark that although President Jimmy Carter declared there is "no merit in the merit system," others argue there is no system in the merit system.[27]

Incremental laws and procedures accumulating over a one-hundred-year period have created a jerry-built set of rules and regulations whose primary emphasis is on negative control of federal personnel, rather than on a positive affirmation of merit and quality in the public service. The many restrictive components of the contemporary merit system severely inhibit the long-term effectiveness of the federal government. Merit has come to signify a narrow and negative focus on positions and jobs, rather than competence, accountability, and effective public service.

Thus critics argue that the civil service reform movement has been very successful in eliminating fraud and dishonesty from government service, but the result is a government that is slow, inefficient, and impersonal. This situation may be acceptable even in today's high tech world, but for many public services that require innovative, high-quality delivery (e.g., education, health care, housing, defense), the bureaucratic model is no longer appropriate. In the modern age of information technology, global markets, and employee empowerment, traditional bureaucracies no longer can function effectively in complex settings. They are not capable of responding to their customers' needs in a timely and efficient manner, of offering choices of nonstandard services, and of giving their employees a sense of meaning, control, and ownership.

In recent years there has been a great deal of discussion within the professional public administration community, practitioners and academics, about the loss of confidence in government. Looking at it from its own world, the professional public administration community has sometimes portrayed the phenomenon as a crisis in the public service. And indeed the complaints about government have damaged the morale of the professional public servants and no doubt further reduced their effectiveness.

As previously noted, Charles Levine mentions that opinion surveys found serious morale problems among career civil servants. He warned that this could have important repercussions in the recruitment of talented young people into government positions at a time when their skills are increasingly needed. He proposed that people free themselves from the endless arguments and complaints about government and focus on finding clearer answers to the questions of what government should do, how it should do it, and who should be doing it.

THE 1978 REFORM ACT

The general dissatisfaction with how the federal bureaucracy is working has led to several attempts to change the system. In 1978, Congress enacted the first major change to the Pendleton Act when it passed the Civil Service Reform Act (CSRA). This new legislation was an attempt to deal with what many considered to be fundamental problems with the federal civil service. The act provided for the following:

- Dividing the Civil Service Commission into the Office of Personnel Management (OPM), the Merit Systems Protection Board, and the Federal Labor Relations Authority
- Creating the Senior Executive Service (SES) to replace the "supergrades" GS-16 through GS-18 (10 percent of which may be political appointees)
- Introducing pay for performance (annual merit pay based on performance appraisals) for mid-level managers (GS-13 through GS-15)
- Giving the newly created OPM the authority to approve up to 10 agency personnel experiments at a time. Some of the subsequent experiments have been extremely useful in identifying the value of possible future changes in the federal personnel system

One of the purposes of the organizational changes was to avoid the problems associated with the Civil Service Commission's acting as both a central management and a regulatory agency—both judge and jury. The SES was intended to offer the 7,500 managers and technical specialists in the federal service opportunities for mobility among agencies, special training, and bonuses for outstanding performance. The implementation of the act by the Reagan administration took a different direction when Don Devine, the head of OPM in the first Reagan administration, expressed a negative view of the changes just passed by the Carter administration. This in turn fueled disaffection among the career civil servants and a four-year war between Devine and the federal bureaucracy.

WORKER DISSATISFACTION

Another major issue of concern in the federal service in the late 1980s was the lack of comparability of pay between similar jobs in the public and private sectors. Part of the problem was that congressional pay was tied to executive branch pay, and Congress would not increase the pay of the professional bureaucracy without increasing its own pay—a politically difficult task. In 1990 the pay differential with the private sector was 22–32 percent for low-skill, entry-level jobs and 39–55 percent for mid-and upper-level managers. These disparities increasingly irritated government workers, had a negative effect on morale and performance, and hindered the ability of the government to hire highly qualified persons. Changes made in the pay structure in 1991 significantly improved this situation, but there is still a great deal of dissatisfaction in the higher levels of the federal service.

Some observers suggested that as many as 1,000 senior executives would leave the government through early retirement during the period from 1993 to 1995. In 1987 the GAO conducted a survey, asking the SES members who had left government the previous year to rank their reasons for taking early retirement. The top eight reasons were:

1. dissatisfaction with top management;
2. unfair distribution of performance bonuses;
3. frustration with actual and proposed changes to compensation;
4. dissatisfaction with political appointees;
5. frustration with criticism of federal workers by the press, politicians, or the public;
6. unfair distribution of rank awards;
7. limited availability of bonuses;
8. dissatisfaction with agency management practices (i.e., amount of freedom given to manage their jobs).[28]

This study also showed "a growing perception among federal employees that they are unappreciated and under rewarded, which is affecting the morale and quality of the federal work force at the entry level, among shortage groups, and at senior levels."[29]

Public servant dissatisfaction may manifest itself in a variety of ways. Rather than leave the public sector, civil servants may choose to voice their objections to changes in policy that accompany a new administration. For instance, employees may argue or try to persuade political appointees to take an alternative policy direction. They may join forces with others in the agency and attempt to sway an administrator through collective action. Employees may attempt to sabotage the efforts of the administration by either leaking delicate information to outside parties or inhibiting the processes of the agency as they relate to the objectives of the administration. Finally, unhappy employees may choose to simply ride it out and wait for the administration to change; hardly an effective way to conduct the government's business.[30]

Some observers believe the stringent ethics requirements placed on federal employees have negative effects on the ability of the federal government to attract highly qualified persons for both short- and long-term service. These requirements may affect their job prospects when they leave the federal service, such as revolving-door provisions that restrict later employment opportunities, and impose pre-employment requisites such as open disclosure of financial interests to deter conflict-of-interest situations and divestiture of certain assets (causing tax difficulties).

PAY, DECENTRALIZATION, DEREGULATION

Charles Levine and Rosslyn Kleeman identify "two over-arching" questions involved in the debate about the civil service:[31]

1. Should the pay, benefits, and responsibilities of civil service jobs be competitive in all respects with comparable jobs in the private sector?
2. Should the civil service be a unitary entity or be splintered into many different systems of pay, benefits, and other conditions of work based on markets for different occupations and localities?

The consensus answer to date to question 1 appears to be "Sort of," and to question 2, "Cases can be made both ways." The professional personnel in government are split between those who favor a centrally driven system continuing to be run by the OPM and those who favor a more decentralized system controlled predominantly by agencies and those in the field. It seems that those favoring decentralization are gaining ground in the policy argument. That is certainly the direction chosen by the Gore commission in the NPR (to be discussed in Chapter 16). But it is also interesting to note that a recent Merit Systems Protection Board survey of personnel specialists in government found that "whereas 83 percent of respondents believe that delegation of personnel management authority from the central OPM to agency personnel offices can lead to improved personnel management, only 60 percent think the same is true of delegation from agency personnel offices to line (and field) management."[32] These remarks sound like another case of "where you stand depends upon where you sit."

There does seem to be widespread agreement that the complex of rules and regulations that define the composition and work of the civil service begs deregulation. Constance Horner, director of OPM in the second Reagan administration, stated in 1987:

> The size of the government work force could be substantially reduced if public managers had more flexibility in making basic personnel and purchasing decisions, and if lower paperwork requirements freed them to focus more on the services they are supposed to provide. . . . It would be much better if senior managers could get their appropriated budgets and decide how many people to hire, at what pay levels, to get the job done.

However, critics of all-out deregulation stress that caution must be used in such changes to make sure that more operating agency flexibility and less oversight do not invite corruption. As DiIulio, Garvey, and Kettl argue, "The solutions lie in an incremental move toward flexibility, decentralization, and deregulation guided by a consciously worked-out public personnel philosophy."[33] While it is important that the relaxation of personnel system rules and procedures continues, the Executive Office of the President, probably through the Office of Personnel Management, should retain active involvement in setting the tone and overall personnel policy for the government, in monitoring agency personnel management performance, and in conducting long-range workforce planning for the government as a whole.

The result of the current situation is that there continues to be very strong support for the principle of merit in government service but widespread dissatisfaction with the merit system as it now operates. In the survey of agency personnel directors in the federal government reported by Ingraham and Rosenbloom, most analysts believe the basic design of the present merit system is not appropriate for either current or future recruiting and hiring needs. DiIulio and co-workers argue that there is indeed a mismatch between the federal workforce recruited and hired on the basis of civil service norms and the wholesale orientation of its current mission. A smaller proportion of federal workers is now involved in delivering goods and services than was once the case. "Federal employees instead supervise a vast network of contractors, state and local governments, and other agents—the retailers who actually deliver the programs that the federal government funds."[34] To date, insufficient attempts have been made to attract the kinds of people to the federal service that are capable of such activities as contract negotiating, auditing, and performance analysis.

THE PROBLEM OF MEASURING GOVERNMENT PERFORMANCE

Over the years, one of the major obstacles to reform of the government has been that measuring the performance of government is a complicated and difficult matter.[35] In the private sector, companies have their ultimate overall measure in their profit and loss statement, the so-called bottom line. The greater the profitability of the company over time,the more successful it has been in meeting its objectives. But public agencies do not have the luxury of such an easy and convenient measure to keep them posted on their progress toward goal accomplishment. As a result, governments have instead focused on measuring inputs and outputs: the resources used in producing the government good or service and the activities performed by the government agency.

Public-budgeting systems add to the problem. The typical governmental budget is constructed on a line-item basis. These budgets show how much the chief executive expects to spend on each program and how the money should be allocated among the program components. But this type of budget does not offer a link to anticipated program results; instead it shows how money should be spent rather than what should be accomplished with the funds.

In order to truly measure the performance of government at any level, it is necessary to measure outcomes, or the broader results of the government program. Such a measure in itself presents a number of difficulties. First, it is necessary to clarify the goals of a government program before attempting to measure its results. The problem is, however, that there are many actors involved in establishing and overseeing governmental programs—for example, the legislative body, the executive branch of government, sometimes the courts, special interest groups, and the general public. These actors do not always agree on just what are the goals of the program.

Even within a given organization there may be differences of opinion about the goals of the program. For example, one person may believe the primary goal of a government-training program is to remove people from the welfare roles at the lowest-possible cost to the government. Another may believe the main goal of the program is to educate a workforce for the 21st century. Unless the priorities are clearly specified, the different goals can result in vastly different approaches to training and education and different measures of success. President Clinton's proposals to reform the nation's health care system offer an example of different— and multiple—program goals. For instance, one goal is to extend health care coverage to include all citizens. Another goal is health care cost containment. Which goal takes precedence, and how does government measure success?

The problem is complicated even if the goals are clearly understood and agreed upon. Government agencies are usually capable of describing and measuring their outputs, their activities. But outcome measures are harder to come by. They are also usually impossible to translate into monetary values because there are no markets for most government activities. For example, how does government measure the success of the defense establishment in preventing war (an outcome)? What is the value of providing financial security to the nation's seniors through the Old Age and Survivors Insurance program (Social Security) or the public housing programs? How do people measure the value of protecting endangered species?

Of course, many government programs are primarily concerned with delivering public services; for such programs it is possible to design outcome measures once the goal has been agreed upon. These kinds of programs are more likely to be offered at the state and local level than at the federal level of government. The limited geography of local government also makes performance measurement easier. Table 15–1 offers some examples of the differences between output and outcome measures for selected public services.

Several attempts have been made by government reformers to incorporate performance measurement into government operations. Many of these attempts have focused on trying to use performance measurement in budget allocation, but such an approach presents another difficulty. It is virtually impossible to establish common denominators of performance among the disparate activities of government. For example, how can government compare the results of programs in health, land-use planning, education, and defense? Budgetary tradeoffs among these priority areas are, like beauty, in the eyes of the beholder. Performance measures may be useful within the categories in comparing alternative approaches to a specific goal, but not in making choices between the basic policy areas.

ATTEMPTS TO LINK PERFORMANCE WITH BUDGETS

Since 1947, three approaches to performance budgeting have been tried.[36] The first was proposed by the first Hoover Commission in 1949, when it suggested that performance budgeting be used to help managers develop measures of workload and cost-effectiveness. The focus was on management concerns for the purpose of improving government efficiency rather than for a tool to help the government do a better job of making tradeoffs between competing budget options. The idea was to direct attention to the work to be done, not to the usefulness of the objectives. The proposal was never adopted in any consistent way, but it did introduce to government the concept of linking program information with budgeting.

TABLE 15–1 Government Performance Measure Examples

Output Measures	Outcome Measures
Elementary and secondary education	
Student days	Test score results
Students graduated	Percentage of graduates employed
Dropout rate	
Hospitals	
Patient-days	Mortality rates
Average length of stay	Patient survey results
Admissions	Readmission rates
Mass transit	
Vehicle miles	Population served (percentage)
Number of passengers	Late trips (percentage)
Police	
Hours of patrol	Rates at which cases are cleared
Crimes investigated	Response time
Number of arrests	Citizen satisfaction
Public welfare	
Programs	
Number of requests	Applications processed in 45 days
Amount of assistance	Payment error rates
Road maintenance	
Miles resurfaced	Lane-miles improved (percentage)

Source: Congressional Budget Office, *Using Performance Measures in the Federal Budget Process.*

A second attempt to introduce performance measurement in the federal government came in the Johnson administration in the mid-1960s, when secretary of Defense Robert McNamara put his Planning, Programming, Budgeting System (PPBS) into practice in the Department of Defense. President Lyndon Johnson ordered the system to be put in place throughout the federal government in 1965. While somewhat successful in the Department of Defense, it was never incorporated to the same degree into other agencies. Ultimately, the system could not change the federal budget process so as to focus on major program changes rather than on the incremental, marginal, line-item budgeting that was traditional in the federal government. The GAO cites this failure as resulting mainly from introduction without adequate preparation; political opposition (particularly in Congress) to rational budgeting approaches; the shortage of adequate data and analysts; and disagreement about the main assumption that efficiency was the primary value to be considered in evaluating the usefulness of a public program.

A third attempt at linking performance with budget reform came with the zero-based budgeting (ZBB) recommendations of the Carter administration in 1976. Under the ZBB system, all programs are evaluated each year instead of dealing only with annual changes at the margin. The essence of the concept is to start at base zero for every program and examine whether or not, and for how much, the program can be justified. As readers can imagine, for a budget system the size of the federal government, this task is truly daunting. But the system was never fully introduced. Instead, agencies were asked to rank their programs within budget limits, setting priorities on the basis of alternative funding levels. The approach, however, was criticized as being excessively time consuming and unrealistic, and President Reagan abandoned ZBB when he took office in 1981.

The GAO analysis of these attempts at management reform suggests that all three approaches had common themes that ultimately spelled their demise:

1. These rational budget systems were antithetical to those who had a stake in the budget approach that already existed. Budgeting is inherently a political process, and the political system that deals best with budgetary schemes reduces, not increases, conflict
2. Although the systems were all top down, they suffered from a lack of clear agreement between superiors and subordinates about goals and objectives
3. There was a general inability to gain the support of the management of the agencies, many of whom felt threatened by the possibility of being punished for nonperformance of their programs
4. The performance-measurement approaches all had an overwhelming need for data in order to survive, and in many ways, they died of their own weight[37]

On the positive side, each of the systems had the largely unintended consequences of increasing the demand for analysis, expanding the capability of those able to carry out performance research, and emphasizing the importance of using data in analyzing public policy problems. These are all important to the new wave of government reform that has been precipitated by the privatization, quality management, and market systems approaches to government that have emerged in the 1990s and that are discussed in Chapter 16.

The most recent major effort at performance measurement did not come until the first year of the Clinton Administration. As part of the implementation of the NPR report of the Gore Commission, Congress passed the Government Performance and Results Act of 1993. The stated purpose of the act was to "provide for the establishment, testing, and evaluation of strategic planning and performance measurement in the Federal Government, and for other purposes."[38] The act requires the president, beginning in 1999, to submit an overall federal government annual performance plan along with the budget, derived from agency performance plans.[39] Thus will begin an explicit link between expected results and budgeted expenditures. The act also requires that there be two-year pilot projects in performance budgeting in at least five federal programs, and beginning in 1998 all federal agencies must develop strategic plans and measure outcomes. The act then calls for a report from the Office of Management and Budget on the test results, along with recommendations on whether the entire budget ought to be cast in those terms. New legislation is required for full implementation of performance budgeting throughout the federal government.

SUMMARY

This chapter has examined some of the reasons behind dissatisfaction with the operation of U.S. government at various times in history and has reviewed several of the major attempts to address these concerns. Much of the problem has to do with matters and issues inherent in the structure of the democratic system and with the multiple goals and objectives that are natural features of the system. In spite of this situation, numerous incremental changes have been made over the years and have led to vast improvements in government's ability to perform its functions of implementing public policy and delivering public services.

Many people would defend the effectiveness and performance of U.S. government officials throughout history. In fact, the U.S. public has been served quite well by its various governments. As the world moves toward the 21st century, however, the U.S. concern is not past history, valuable though it has been. The United States, along with much of the rest of the world, has moved into a new environment defined by rapid economic, technological, social, and political change. The organizational models in both the public and private sectors that once served well may no longer be appropriate. If that is indeed the case, what is the *post-bureaucratic* model that will take its place? That is the issue that is now on the public agenda and to which we turn in Chapter 16.

DISCUSSION QUESTIONS

1. Discuss what seem to be the principle reasons for public dissatisfaction and loss of confidence in our government. Are these criticisms justified?
2. Does the structure of the U.S. government inhibit efficient public policy implementation? Why? What could be done to improve the situation?
3. Are the governmental reforms proposed in Chapter 15 likely to improve the public's satisfaction with government?
4. Chapter 15 described a series of "reinventions" that have taken place in the U.S. government since the early 19th century. Is this process likely to continue in the future? What, if any, will be the focus of the next reinvention?

SUGGESTED READINGS

B. Guy Peters, *The Politics of Bureaucracy,* Longman Publishers, White Plains, N.Y., 1995.

Alice Rivlin, *Reviving the American Dream,* The Brookings Institution, Washington, D.C., 1992.

Patricia W. Ingraham and Donald Kettl, eds., *Agenda for Excellence: Public Service in America,* Chatham House Publishers, Inc., Chatham, N.J., 1992.

Robert Higgs, *Crisis and Leviathan,: Critical Epsiodes in the Growth of American Government,* Oxford University Press, New York and London, 1987.

NOTES

1. John J. DiIulio, Jr., Gerald Garvey, and Donald F. Kettl, *Improving Government Performance: An Owner's Manual* (Washington, D.C.: Brookings Institution, 1993).
2. David Rosenbloom, editor of the *Public Administration Review,* pointed out this difference in an editorial in the December 1993 issue, in the course of suggesting that David Osborne and Ted Gaebler's reinventing-government thesis, discussed in this chapter, is a throwback to Wilson's view, which he does not believe was tenable then or now.
3. Dennis R. Judd, *The Politics of American Cities: Private Power and Public Policy* (Glenview, Ill.: Scott, Foresman, 1988), 95–109.
4. Judd, 1988, 106.
5. For an excellent discussion of the details of the New Deal under President Roosevelt, see Charles Hurd, *When the New Deal Was Young and Gay* (New York: Hawthorn, 1965).
6. Hurd, 1965.
7. Andrew E. Reeves, "Enhancing Local Self-Government and State Capabilities: The U.S. Advisory Commission of Intergovernmental Relations Program," *Public Administration Review,* vol. 52 (July 1992): 401.
8. Reeves, 1992.

9. Alice M. Rivlin, "A New Vision of American Federalism," *Public Administration Review* 52 (July 1992): p. 315.

10. For example, Herbert Kaufman, *The Limits of Organizational Change* (University of Alabama Press, 1971); and Albert O. Hirschman, *Shifting Involvements: Private Interest and Public Action* (Princeton, N.J.: Princeton University Press, 1982).

11. "From Red Tape to Results: Creating a Government That Works Better and Costs Less: Executive Summary, Report of the National Performance Review," *The Review* (Washington, D.C.: U.S. Government Printing Office, 1993).

12. See for example Craig W. Thomas, "Reorganizing Public Organizations: Alternatives, Objectives, and Evidence," *Journal of Public Research and Theory* 4, no. 4 (October 1993). Also John T. Tierney, *Postal Reorganization: Managing the Public's Business* (Boston: Auburn, 1981) suggests the problems of organizations like the Postal Service have more to do with politics than with management.

13. Thomas, 1993, 2.

14. DiIulio, Garvey, and Kettl, 1993, 29.

15. "From Red Tape to Results," 1993.

16. A special report prepared for the National Academy of Public Administrations, Washington, D.C., 1986.

17. David Osborne in a speech to National Academy of Public Administration, attents of Gov. June, 1992, at the Jimmy Carter Presidential Library.

18. Lecture, Indiana University public policy class, November 1992.

19. "From Red Tape to Results," 1993, 57.

20. Robert S. Gilmour and Alexis A. Haley, *Who Makes Public Policy: The Struggle for Control between Congress and the Executive* (Chatham, N.J.: Chatham House Publishers, Inc., 1994).

21. DiIulio, Garvey, and Kettl, 1993, 16.

22. "From Red Tape to Results," 1993, 4.

23. "Blueprints for Cutting the U.S. Work Force," *Washington Post*, 26 October 1992, p. 19.

24. "Blueprints for Cutting the U.S. Work Force," 1992, p. 19.

25. David Osborne and Ted Gaebler, *Reinventing Government* (Reading, Mass.: Addison-Wesley Publishing Co., 1992), preface p. xviii.

26. Osborne and Gaebler, 1992, 14.

27. Patricia W. Ingraham and David H. Rosenbloom, "The State of Merit in the Federal Government," in *Agenda for Excellence: Public Service in America*, ed. Patricia W. Ingraham and Donald F. Kettl (Chatham, N.J.: Chatham House Publishers, Inc., 1992), 275.

28. Charles H. Levine and Rosslyn S. Kleeman, "The Quiet Crisis in the American Public Service," in *Agenda for Excellence: Public Service in America*, ed. Patricia W. Ingraham and Donald F. Kettl (Chatham, N.J.: Chatham House Publishers, Inc., 1992), 231.

29. Levine and Kpeeman, 1992.

30. Marissa Martino Golden, "Exit, Voice, Loyalty, and Neglect: Bureaucratic Responses to Presidential Control During the Reagan Administration," *Journal of Public Administration Research and Theory* 2, no. 1 (January 1992): 29–63.

31. Golden, 1992, 263.

32. Ingraham and Rosenbloom, 1992, 293.

33. DiIulio, Garvey, and Kettl, 1993, 70.

34. DiIulio, Garvey, and Kettl, 1993, 66.

35. The primary resource for the concepts in this section was a special study by the Congressional Budget Office, *Using Performance Measures in the Federal Budget Process* (Washington, D.C.: Congress of the United States, U.S. Government Printing Office, July 1993).

36. Congressional Budget Office, 1993, 23.

37. Congressional Budget Office, 1993, 25–26.

38. U.S. Senate, *Report of the Committee on Governmental Affairs*, Report 103–58 (Washington, D.C.: U.S. Government Printing Office, 16 June 1993).

39. U.S. Senate, 1993, 18–19.

16

Managing Government in the 21st Century

In Chapter 15 we discussed some of the reasons behind the current high level of interest in searching for new ways of managing the public's business. We also reviewed previous attempts at governmental reform and speculated about the reasons for both the success and failure of those initiatives. As the end of the 20th century approaches, U.S. government, including the professional public service bureaucracy, has much of which to be proud. For over 50 years both management systems and public servants have, by and large, successfully adapted to a rapidly changing set of demands and accommodated new policy initiatives and institutions.

It is equally obvious, however, that the forces that have led to the current reexamination of public policy implementation and public service delivery systems are continuing to pressure government's ability to carry out its responsibilities; management systems are under stress and are in the process of significant change. The political success of the Republican Contract with America[1] in the fall 1994 congressional campaign offers further evidence that the U.S. public supports fundamental change in the way government conducts the public business.

The types of fundamental changes in government currently being discussed will require the approach to the management of the nation's public organizations to undergo substantial transformation, or frame-breaking change. As suggested in Chapter 15, this situation is occurring because of changes in the political and economic environment, in values, and in information technology. All of these are forcing change in the mission, function, and in some ways, the purpose of U.S. government organizations.[2] This type of organizational transformation involves simultaneous and sharp shifts in strategy, power, and structure and will be painful, difficult, and resisted by those wedded to the traditional ways.

Three important interrelated approaches to public management are currently attracting considerable attention among those interested in inducing governmental transformation in society: (1) privatization of public functions, (2) private-sector quality management applications to government operations, and (3) the set of market-based approaches to public service delivery made popular in the 1992 book *Reinventing Government,* by David Osborne and Ted Gaebler, and subsequently adopted by the Clinton administration in its report of the management task force headed by Vice President Albert Gore, The National Performance Review (NPR). In this chapter we review the logic of these approaches, examine the extent to which they are being implemented in the federal, state, and local governments, and consider some of the criticisms they have generated among thoughtful observers. We conclude with observations on what seems to be the future of this current generation of management innovations for public service delivery and the implementation of public policy.

PRIVATIZATION OF GOVERNMENT PROGRAMS

In the 1960s and 1970s there was considerable international activity in the nationalization of many industries and in expanding government enterprise in general. The prevalent view was that, with regard to performance, it did not matter whether the private or the public sector owned a commercial or industrial activity. Indeed, public enterprises were the organizational choice for many countries. The result was that everything from banks to airlines to mining and manufacturing companies was owned and operated by governments. However, as the years passed, it became increasingly apparent that the economic performance of most of these activities was dismal. Government treasuries were drained by inefficient and noncompetitive performance, and corruption in some countries led to disillusionment about governments trying to act like businesses. The dissolution of the Communist countries of Europe and the economic reforms of Latin America and other regions have accelerated this move away from government ownership of productive assets.

The privatization movement, which began to attract considerable attention with the sale of British Telecom in Great Britain in 1984, has become a worldwide phenomenon in the past few years. In 1993, it was estimated that $69 billion worth of state-owned companies passed into private hands, making the total public-to-private transfer $328 billion since 1985.[3] Some observers believe this figure could more than double by the year 2000.

The Economist suggests that there are essentially two overriding aims of the current privatization movement: to shrink the size of the state in the interest of greater efficiency and to raise cash to aid troubled public budgets. Emanuel Savas, in his definitive book on privatization, describes his view of the forces behind the increasing tendency to shift the delivery of public services from the government to the private sector.[4] He believes this change results from the desire for more efficient and cost-effective public services, from ideological arguments that government is too large, from business groups interested in strengthening the viability of and opportunities for private companies, and from the populist view that people should have more choices in their consumption of public services.

The mix of activities chosen for privatization varies widely from country to country and has included everything from trash collection to banks. In 1993, the French parliament passed legislation privatizing 21 large companies, including the National Bank of Paris, the Renault auto manufacturer, Air France, and the huge oil company Aquitaine. Italy privatized businesses in the oil, telecommunications, energy, engineering, and insurance industries. Other countries with major privatizing efforts have included Finland, Spain, Sweden, Egypt, Malaysia, Japan, Australia, New Zealand, Mexico, Chile, Peru, Venezuela, Argentina, and of course, the Eastern European nations now in the process of getting rid of their state-dominated economies.

A 1992 World Bank study of privatization efforts in Britain, Malaysia, Mexico, and Chile found that in 11 of 12 cases examined, there were big economic gains as a result of the privatizations.[5] The Bank suggested that, depending on the company's particular situation, higher investment, managerial innovation, better pricing, and loss of surplus workers were all factors in the improvements after privatization.

Although the United States has not had the same level of public enterprise as have many other parts of the world, it still has many opportunities for privatization, and the trend to do so has been accelerating. In 1988 the White House received a report from the President's Commission on Privatization that contained a series of recommendations about federal government opportunities for privatizing various public functions.[6] They ranged from housing finance to air traffic control to prisons. Most of the recommendations were not pursued at that time, but many are still under discussion and some, such as the privatization of the air traffic control system, were recommended in the Clinton administration's NPR.

The Reason Foundation estimates that potential privatization sales in the United States could amount to as much as $200 billion. In May 1992, President George Bush's executive order removed many of the barriers to the privatization of city- and state-owned infrastructure developed with federal assistance. Since then, many states and localities have been privatizing a host of enterprises and government activities. In addition to local services such as trash collection, recycling, snowplowing, and street resurfacing, likely candidates include airports, toll roads, museums, convention centers, and sports centers. A 1992 study by the Heartland Institute estimated that the city of Detroit could save $337 million per year (14 percent of its budget) by privatizing a variety of public services and facilities.[7]

Two of the municipal leaders in the privatization movement have been Newark, New Jersey, which contracts out to the private sector 18 services in the public works area alone, and Indianapolis, Indiana, which has established a separate commission to "inventory every government service and asset, to move these functions into the marketplace, and to distinguish areas in which the private sector has a competitive advantage from those in which it does not.[8] As of 1994, privatization recommendations in Indianapolis have ranged from city golf courses and skating rinks to contracting out microfilming, sewer billing and collections, to selling city-owned surplus properties.

PUBLIC SERVICE-DELIVERY OPTIONS

We indicated in Chapter 1 that there are several different ways in which a government can provide a public service if it so chooses. The most important are the following.[9]

- *Government service.* Delivery of a service is provided by a government agency, using its own employees. Government acts as both the service arranger and the service producer (paid for from either the general tax system or user taxes).
- *Government vending.* An individual or company can arrange to buy goods or services from a government agency, for example, rights to water, pasture, minerals, and timber. Also, a private agency can arrange to buy police services for specific facilities, such as a sports arena.
- *Intergovernmental agreement.* A government can hire or pay another government to supply a service. For example, a city government can sell subsidized bus services to a county government. States often contract with local governments to provide local social services.

- *Contracts.* Governments can contract with private companies to provide a public service. These contracts can be for such diverse purposes as ambulance services, road repairs, trash pickup, sewage treatment, and recycling. At the federal level, most military equipment is provided by government contractors. The Department of Defense now even hires private companies (known as government contractors, or "go-cos") to manage military installations.
- *Franchises.* Exclusive franchises are an award of monopoly privileges to a private company to supply a particular service, usually with price regulation by the government. Examples include airport and park management and utilities such as electric power, natural gas, water, and cable television. Multiple franchises are also awarded to private companies for public mass transportation, taxis, and vehicle-towing services.
- *Government-sponsored enterprise.* Government can create enterprises necessary to carry out public work in cases where no provider of services can be found. It can also create enterprises in the private and not-for-profit sectors through multiple systems of authorization and partial financing. Enterprises can be based on various strategies that blend fee income with public subsidy where enterprise goals are either strictly commercial or public goods creating. Examples of these enterprises are the Postal Service and the newly proposed Air Traffic Control corporation.
- *Self-service.* Government can encourage citizens to serve themselves by providing voluntary association and self-service arrangements for such needs as housing, food distribution, child care, community crime watch, and private security. Government may also provide the information to enhance informed and productive consumption by individual citizens.
- *Private markets.* Government can rely on private markets to supply services that it requires. Thus citizens can be required to contract for their own garbage disposal, automotive emission control, inoculations, and landscaping.
- *Grants.* Public and private goods whose consumption is to be subsidized can be supported by the provision of both grants and vouchers. Under a grant system, subsidies are given directly to the private producer of the good or service. This can come either in the form of cash transfers or by providing tax credits, low-cost loans, or loan guarantees to the producer. Examples include agricultural subsidies to farmers, low-cost housing support to home builders, construction grants to hospitals and universities, and subsidized mass transit.
- *Vouchers.* These are designed to encourage consumption by a particular class of consumers. Examples include housing-purchase and rent certificates and food stamps. Forms of vouchers have also been used for child day care, drug treatment, and recreation services. A Medicare or Medicaid enrollment card can be viewed as a voucher. There has recently been increased interest among educational reformers in the idea of issuing educational tuition vouchers to all citizens in a community; these would allow them to purchase primary and secondary education services from alternative public and private schools.

Governments also often utilize both the public and the private sectors at the same time by mixing responsibility for the three functional areas of good or service provision: ownership, management, and operations. For example, a government can utilize a management contract with a private company to manage a bus company where the equipment is owned by the government and the employees are public employees. Or it can manage a publicly owned hospital with privately hired employees.

Savas identifies the factors affecting whether and how a particular public good or service can successfully be privatized as including:[10]

- *The nature of the good.* In the terms of Chapter 5, is the exclusion principle operative? In other words, can those who do not choose to pay for the public good or service be excluded from receiving its benefits? If so, the provision of that service may lend itself to privatization.

- *Service specificity.* Some services can be much more precisely defined than others. For example, it is much easier to identify goals and estimate costs in street paving than it is in education.
- *Availability of producers.* In the case of certain kinds of specialized goods and services there may not be sufficient producers to permit the government to rely on the private sector to meet the needs of the public. For instance, it is conceivable that the nation needs certain defense weapons that cannot support a private-sector supplier. In that case the government will have to produce the good itself.
- *Efficiency and effectiveness.* If efficiency and effectiveness are primary considerations in the delivery of a particular public good or service, then an obvious factor in the selection of a delivery mode is the extent to which competition among possible public or private providers is present or can be introduced. This is a major argument being made by those in favor of issuing tuition vouchers to provide educational choice.
- *Scale.* Is the scale of operations sufficient for the government to deliver the service itself, or would it be more cost-effective to rely on other public or private providers?
- *Benefit-cost Relationships.* "Efficiency is enhanced if there is a direct link between paying for the service and realizing its benefits, and the consumer has an economic incentive to shop wisely."[11] This link exists only for private and toll goods.
- *Responsiveness to consumers.* The closer the link between the service provider and the consumer and the more control the consumer has over the service choice, the more susceptible is the service to privatization.
- *Susceptibility to fraud.* Some might argue that contracts, vouchers, and franchises are particularly vulnerable to collusion, bribery, and extortion, but Savas notes that these approaches to service delivery have no monopoly on corruption.
- *Economic equity.* Do the alternative arrangements provide services to consumers in a fair and equitable manner? If not, are there income enhancement options available that compensate for the equity impact?
- *Equity for minorities.* Does the privatization alternative offer equal treatment without discrimination? Does it offer equal contract and employment opportunity?
- *Responsiveness to other public priorities.* What is the differential impact, if any, on other public priorities such as economic development and neighborhood renewal?

Of course, privatization has not always proceeded smoothly, nor has it been without controversy. In Savas's research, the principal debates and arguments about privatization occur when:

1. the program shifts from government provision to contract, grant, voucher, or other form of nondirect provision;
2. grants are eliminated in favor of direct consumer subsidies;
3. government enterprises and other assets are denationalized;
4. user charges are levied for previously generally provided programs;
5. franchises are eliminated and services are deregulated to permit the market to respond.

Other arguments offered in opposition to privatization center around the issues of a possible decline in accountability and privatization's possible distorting effect on public choice and quality of service. Dennis Palumbo for example, warns that privatizing such public responsibilities as prisons may result in neglecting complicated management, constitutional, and ethical issues in the interest of efficiency and profit making.[12] The same argument, or an even stronger one, arises when the function being privatized is the national defense industrial base. Some express concern that an agency may be so depleted of staff that it is incapable of conducting effective oversight of private contracts and the process of privatization.[13] The wrenching cutbacks underway in the defense budget in the 1990s certainly leave the door open for problems of this sort.

H. George Frederickson argues that, in the long run, these problems with privatization make its processes just as difficult to control as those of the bureaucracy. But irrespective of these difficulties, it seems clear that the trend toward more privatization of public services and public enterprises is destined to continue and expand. As suggested earlier, the twin motives of relieving public budget pressure and achieving efficiencies and productivity improvements that have escaped the public sector's attempts will by themselves undoubtedly continue to drive this movement on a worldwide basis.

Privatization is not best interpreted as an ideological framework, even though some support it for ideological reasons. Privatization is essentially a management technique, available to public officials along with other possible ways of delivering a public service or program. The Privatization Council speaks of it as "a variety of techniques and activities to get more involvement of the private sector in providing traditional government or public services. It enables each party to do what it does best and results in a win-win solution to providing public services."[14]

THE ROLE OF NONGOVERNMENTAL ORGANIZATIONS

At first blush, the implicit assumption of most observers of the privatization movement is most likely that the sole alternative to direct governmental ownership or operations or both is the for-profit private sector. In fact, the United States has quite a sizable *third sector,* which performs many functions in the public arena that are neither private for profit nor governmental. This third sector, nongovernmental organizations (NGOs), includes those organizations sometimes known as private voluntary organizations (PVOs) and sometimes simply not-for-profits. They are distinguished by the fact that they are constitutionally separate from government, are not primarily profit seeking in purpose, have independent processes for self-governance, and are created and organized to serve a public purpose.[15]

These NGOs include a diversity of organizations of many sizes, types, and purposes. For instance, local economic development corporations, the American Red Cross, the National Audubon Society, the United Way, NSF International (a public health–environment standards development and assessment organization), and many different educational–public service–public welfare enterprises are NGOs each serving a public purpose. At the national level, NGOs are more likely to be of the advocacy type of organization, while at the local level they typically function as service providers. Those NGOs operating primarily as service providers, in particular, offer another alternative to the direct ownership of productive assets and the provision of public services by governments, and they have historically played a very important role throughout the world.

NGOs theoretically exist because of "inherent failures or limitations of both the market and the government in providing public goods."[16] The market cannot meet the demand for certain goods and services because of the inoperability of the exclusion principle (described in Chapter 5). As noted earlier, people choosing not to pay for a public good or service cannot be completely excluded from receiving the benefits. At the same time, there may be inadequate political support for the goods to be offered by government action. Thus the third sector, the NGO, steps into the vacuum. Sometimes the NGOs function in direct cooperation with, if not sponsorship of, the government, and sometimes they operate at arm's length.

The relationships between NGOs and their host governments vary considerably. In many countries, for example, NGOs function as the service deliverer of choice for both governments and international donor agencies. They are even occasionally instigated and organized by their host government. In other cases the NGOs have a de facto adversarial relationship with their host government and indeed in some instances regard themselves as almost shadow governments.

Complications in the NGO-government relationship sometimes occur because of the functions both perform.[17] NGOs have service functions, social functions, and constituent representation functions. Governments have finance, regulatory, and service functions. Therefore, an NGO can have one type of relationship with government with respect, for example, to its service functions and another with respect to its representation or advocacy functions. Complicated situations can result when an NGO is at odds with the government on a policy issue at the same time as it relies on government for financial support for some of its other functions. Governments, in turn, can find themselves in situations where they are enforcing regulatory restrictions on organizations that are needed to carry out public missions.

Benjamin Gidron, Ralph Kramer, and Lestor Salamon identify four basic models in their typology of the government-NGO relationship.[18] These are:

1. The government-dominant model, in which the government plays the major role in both financing and delivery of public services
2. The third-sector-dominant model, in which the NGO plays the dominant role in both financing and delivery of public services
3. The dual model, where finance and delivery of public services are shared between the sectors, but each works within its own sphere
4. The collaborative model, where the sectors work together rather than separately

The collaborative model (most typical in the United States) usually means that government provides the finances and the NGO delivers the service. The NGO may simply function as an agent of the government, with little discretion of its own, as a "collaborative vendor," or it may retain considerable discretion in the development and management of the programs, as a "collaborative partner."

Examples of collaborative NGOs are often found at the local level of government. For instance, an NGO established at the instigation of a city to recycle waste for a larger geographic area may be categorized as a collaborative-vendor NGO, as are the privately managed correction facilities springing up in some parts of the country. In essence, their policies are controlled by the local governments in the region in which they operate. A local example of the more independent collaborative-partnership NGO may be a local economic-development corporation that works closely with the local region, receives some of its funds from local, state, and federal sources, yet is relatively independent in its policies and program management.

Whatever the NGO-government relationship, NGOs in the United States and other countries have played a significant role historically in the delivery of public services, and they continue to do so. In fact, given the decentralization of government efforts discussed later in this chapter, it can safely be assumed that NGOs will play an even more important role in the future, particularly as they are able to fill the gap between what governments cannot do well and what the private sector will not do at all.

THE QUALITY MANAGEMENT REVOLUTION

Another important force now having a considerable impact on the management of public affairs in the United States has grown out of the so-called total quality management (TQM) movement that originated in the manufacturing sector of the economy in the early 1980s. Many observers believe it to be a fundamental change in management philosophy and style particularly suited to the conditions, customers (and constituents in the case of government), and workers of today's society. It is arguably the most significant development in management thinking since Frederick Taylor's introduction of *scientific management* in the 1920s and the introduction of modern management approaches to government that began with Woodrow Wilson in the late 19th century. TQM changes scientific management's focus on planning, organizing, staffing, directing, and controlling work and workers to decentralization, continuous process improvement, worker empowerment, and primary attention to the needs of the customer.

The U.S. Department of Commerce recognized the quality management movement when it established the Malcolm Baldridge National Quality Award in 1987, to be awarded to U.S. companies that excel in quality achievement and quality management. During the same period, the President's Award for Quality was instituted for public-sector quality excellence, and the Federal Quality Institute was established. Companies that have won the Baldridge Award include Xerox, Motorola, Westinghouse, American Express, the Ritz-Carlton Hotel group, and the United Services Automobile Association (USAA), a comprehensive insurance and financial services corporation. Federal government agencies that have won the President's Award include the Naval Air Systems Command, the NASA Lewis Research Center, and the Internal Revenue Service.

The U.S. Navy defines total quality management (or total quality leadership, in Navy terms) as the combination of quantitative methods, human resources, and management techniques used to assess and improve (1) all materials and services supplied to the organization; (2) all significant processes within the organization; and (3) all systems of the organization applied to meeting customer needs, now and in the future. TQM also requires the involvement of an organization's entire workforce in improving quality.

The Federal Quality Institute cites the three principles of total quality management as:

1. Focusing on achieving customer satisfaction
2. Seeking continuous improvement in all work processes and systems
3. Involving fully the entire workforce

There are several individuals who, over the past three decades or more, have been responsible for developing and promoting the quality management philosophy that is rapidly winning converts in both the public and private sectors of our society. The late W. Edwards Deming is the best known of the quality management gurus. Most of the quality management discussion in this chapter focuses on his approach, which is used more than other approaches in government circles because of its strong emphasis on management and leadership philosophy as compared to engineering and physical production. Other leaders in the quality management movement include J.M. Juran, Phillip Crosby, Armand V. Feigenbaum, and Kaoru Ishikawa. Both Juran and Ishikawa, like Deming, came to prominence from their involvement in helping the country of Japan overcome a negative quality image that prevailed after World War II. A brief description of these three approaches to quality management demonstrates the similarities among the researchers.

J.M. Juran

J. M. Juran has been working in the quality management field since the early post-World War II period.[19] He, like Deming, had early contacts with the Japanese and offered quality production seminars for their manufacturers in 1954. His first book on the topic was published in 1978 (*Upper Management and Quality*). Juran's approach to quality management comes from the engineering discipline. He defined quality as "fitness for use,"—the users of a product or service must be able to depend on that product or service for whatever purpose they had in mind. His fitness for use included quality of design, quality of conformance, availability, safety, and field use. To achieve this status over the life cycle of the good or service, Juran developed the concept of the "Juran Trilogy":

Quality planning

1. Determine who the customers are
2. Determine the needs of the customers
3. Develop product features that respond to the customers
4. Develop processes that are able to produce those product features
5. Transfer the resulting plans to the operating force

Quality control

1. Evaluate actual quality performance
2. Compare actual performance to quality goals
3. Act on the differences

Quality improvement

1. Establish the infrastructure to secure annual quality improvement
2. Identify the specific needs for improving the improvement projects
3. For each project, establish a project team with clear responsibility for bringing the project to a successful conclusion
4. Provide the resources, motivation, and training needed by the teams to diagnose the causes, stimulate establishment of a remedy, and establish controls to hold the gains

Juran's book then examines these points in some detail and offers management and statistical tools for quality improvement.

Kaoru Ishikawa

Ishikawa entered the quality management field about the same time as did Deming and Juran and acted as a quality control consultant to U.S. companies in the early 1960s. The Ishikawa approach describes the essence of quality control as:[20]

1. Knowing the requirements of the consumers
2. Knowing what the consumers will buy
3. Knowing the cost in order to define quality
4. Anticipating potential defects and complaints
5. Accompanying quality control by action
6. Achieving an ideal state of quality control where inspection is no longer needed

Ishikawa describes the character of quality assurance as follows:

1. quality must be built in at each design and each process. It cannot be created through inspection;
2. quality control that emphasizes inspection is not useful;
3. the basic notion behind control is prevention of errors;
4. the very essence of total quality control is in the quality control and quality assurance of new product development;
5. the cause, the basic cause, and not the symptoms, of quality failure must be removed;
6. when all of a company's new products succeed and consumers say, "We can buy their new products gladly with confidence," then that company's quality control has truly come of age.

Ishikawa's book is readable, useful in its discussion of techniques and applications, and recommended to those interested in learning more about the roots and operational detail of the quality management movement.

W. Edwards Deming and Total Quality Management

Deming was trained as a statistician, and his thinking about how to improve quality production was very much influenced by the concept of statistical dispersion central to the thinking of statisticians. He saw the basic issue of quality as distinguishing output variation that could indicate problems with an organization's systems. To improve the system, "common-problem causes" had to be removed.

Deming's work on quality management first came to prominence in 1950 when he was a visiting American lecturer at a seminar of the Union of Japanese Scientists and Engineers (JUSE). In the seminar he talked about the use of the cycle of plan-do-check-action to enhance quality (some refer to this as "ready, fire, aim"); the importance of having a feel for dispersion in statistics (as companies try to enhance quality); and the use of control charts for process control.

The Japanese government and manufacturers were enamored with Deming's philosophy and adopted it as their own. He was greatly honored by the Japanese and is credited with much of the success of Japanese manufacturing in the 1970s and 1980s. A Deming Award was established by the Japanese government to recognize outstanding Japanese manufacturers, and Emperor Hirohito awarded Deming one of the nation's highest honors, the Medal of the Sacred Treasury, in 1960. It was 30 years after Deming's introduction of quality management concepts to Japan, however, before U.S. businesses responded to Deming's message. He was over 90 years old when he died in late 1993 and was still lecturing to large crowds of corporate and government disciples about using his quality management approach to achieving organizational transformation.

As suggested earlier, Deming's approach to quality management is preferred by many in government circles because it focuses more on the cultural and leadership dimensions of total quality management and integrates process improvement methods with new methods of leading people. It requires top-down leadership that focuses on quality, user needs, and user requirements in the design and development of new products and services. It is a bottom-line approach to assess and improve continually the processes by which an organization conducts its business.

Deming maintained that if U.S. manufacturing is to regain its competitive position in the world, and indeed even to stay where it is, the U.S. style of management must be transformed. He argued that our leaders need to take a long-term view of profitability rather than using the short-term profit-and-loss statement approach prevalent in U.S. business for too many years. Deming asked, "Where do you want to be five years from now?" and "By what methods do you plan to reach this goal?" In Deming's words, "Innovation, the foundation of the future, cannot thrive unless the top management has declared unshakable commitment to quality and productivity." The journey is long term and involves a fundamental cultural change in most organizations. It is a "journey, not a destination."[21]

As pointed out earlier, Deming's approach to quality management is not now limited to manufacturing or other private-sector business organizations. Nineteen federal government agencies began a TQM program in 1988. Many more now have active programs under development. At last count, 36 states had quality management programs underway. President Bill Clinton uses many of the TQM concepts in his speeches, illustrating his support of the quality management movement. As will be discussed later in this chapter, the NPR uses many of the quality management concepts in its recommendations for public management improvement.

Deming's Recommendations

Deming often focused on the "deadly diseases" in many U.S. organizations and the obstacles to improving them. His approach to organizational transformation revolves around 14 strategic points that, he believed, organizations must accept as their basic management philosophy. The diseases about which he was concerned are:

- lack of constancy of purpose,
- emphasis on short-term profits (or results),
- performance evaluation,
- running the organization on the basis of visible numbers alone, and
- the job mobility of many U.S. managers.

The 14 points that he argues organizations must adopt can be grouped into three basic elements: (1) quality; (2) a scientific approach founded on processes (not people) and data-based decisions; and (3) the team concept. A summary of his 14 principles follows; for more detail, consult Deming's seminal book, *Out of the Crisis.*[22]

Principle 1: Create Constancy of Purpose. This principle argues for hard thinking about the future and for an organization's abandoning the quest for quick results and profits. The purpose of an organization is not to make a profit but to stay in business and provide jobs. To achieve this goal, an organization needs an unshakable, constant commitment to quality and productivity and an understanding that the consumer is the most important part of the production line. Some obstacles to achieving such constancy are neglect of long-term planning, false starts, and a culture of management job hopping.

Customers, suppliers, and employees need a leader's long-term attention. Management job hopping, which has become part of the U.S. organizational culture, "annihilates teamwork and constancy. . . . How can anyone be committed to quality and productivity when his tenure is only a few years, in and out?"[23]

Principles 2 and 3: Adopt the New Philosophy, Cease Dependency on Inspection. The United States can no longer live with an organizational culture of commonly accepted levels of delays, mistakes, defective materials, and defective workmanship. Inspection following production of goods and services and simply acceptable quality levels are insufficient methods of improving quality.

Inspection to improve quality comes too late. Instead, the focus should be on building quality into the product in the first place. "Do it right the first time" is often a meaningless slogan. Quality comes from improving the process, not evaluating the output after the fact. Leaders need to provide the tools and processes and then delegate the correction of the special causes of poor quality. This need also extends to other organizations with which the subject organization works. Management has the responsibility to work with its suppliers to get its input right. Once again, the concept is not to rely on inspection and discard incoming goods that do not meet the company's needs, but to work with suppliers in a close, cooperative manner to improve their quality processes and production.

Principle 4: Do Not Award Business on the Basis of Price, but Concentrate on Minimizing Total Costs. Too many business and government organizations select their suppliers totally on the basis of the lowest bid on a project. But price has no meaning without a complete measure of long-term quality. The entire package of goods and services must be considered, including factors such as delivery time, condition and quality of the good or service delivered, longevity of the product's usefulness, and the variability of the goods or services over time.

Deming argued for the development of long-term supplier relationships in an atmosphere of cooperation and mutual confidence. The goal should be to receive the lowest cost per hour of usage, not to receive the lowest bid. The attitude should be to "make a partner of every vendor."

In Japan, production contracts are usually long term (often as long as six years) and may include requirements for product design and testing. The contracts also contain other demanding requirements, including exceptional quality, just-in-time delivery, exact quantities, and continuous productivity improvements by the supplier, which result in reduced costs.

Principle 5: Improve Production and Service Systems Constantly and Forever. This Will Improve Quality and Productivity and Will Decrease Costs. This is a key principle of TQM. It means that management and workers alike have a responsibility to work constantly on improving the processes of the organization. Quality should be built in at the design stage and attention directed to reducing the variability of the organization's output to meet customer quality requirements. The result will be a continual reduction of waste and continual improvement of the quality of every activity in the organization. Deming identified two means of process improvement: (1) working on the "common causes" that are systemic and (2) removing the "special causes" that result in nonrandom variation in the organization's systems. Common causes include problems such as poor product or service design, inferior materials or services from suppliers, poor facilities, and improper operating systems and processes. Special causes include lack of needed knowledge or skills within the organization; worker sloppiness or inattention to detail; or failure by the workers to identify poor inputs to their work. In Deming's view, management is responsible for common causes of poor quality, which account for 85 percent of all quality problems. Workers are responsible for the 15 percent accounted for by special causes.

Principle 6: Institute On-the-Job Training for All Employees.   Too often managers blame workers for quality problems, when the real culprit is a lack of training and inadequate design of the production (or service) system. Both of these are the responsibility of management, not the workers. Management must eliminate process and training problems that prevent employees from doing their job with satisfaction. "It is the manager's responsibility to gather, tabulate, classify, and scientifically reduce information to principles, laws, rules, and formulas that can be taught to and used by workers as guides to better performance. Managers, not workers, are responsible for scientifically selecting, training, teaching, and developing each employee to achieve his or her maximum potential."[24]

Principle 7 and Principle 8: Institute Leadership, Drive Out Fear.   The main job of management throughout the organization is leadership, not supervision. The role of a leader is to help people do a better job. A leader must function as a colleague and a coach, not a judge. The primary focus of leadership should be process improvement, not evaluating outcomes. The leader needs to strive to remove barriers to pride of workmanship in the organization.

Leadership must function in a helping, not authoritarian, relationship. Workers cannot perform at their best unless they feel secure in their work. Fears of punishment, layoff, or discipline ensure that workers will lack the security necessary for high performance. Workers in an organization must feel free to express opinions and ask questions. There is room for all to succeed in a quality organization, without fear of zero-sum games. In other words, one person's gain is not necessarily another's loss. The prime motivators in an organization are those that appeal to and recognize self-pride and self-esteem.

Principle 9: Break Down Barriers.   Organizational barriers and work processes that separate people, disciplines, and departments must be dissolved. Workers in diverse fields such as research, design, production, and sales (or constituent relations in the case of government), must work together as a team to foresee the problems of production and use that may be encountered with the product or service. There must be a free flow of information and open cooperation, both vertically and horizontally, within the organization.

It is the responsibility of leaders to connect specialists and help them communicate. Internal conflicts must be eliminated and teamwork instituted. All members need to focus on constituent-customer needs for the organization's good or service. Organizational goals are established to "coordinate all units toward a successful integrated unity." If necessary, the organizational structure must be changed to accommodate the need for teamwork.

Principle 10: Eliminate Slogans and Targets.   Slogans do not help people do a better job. They are directed toward the wrong people. Targets without methods are ineffective. How can someone "do it right the first time" if the incoming material is off-gauge, off-color, or otherwise defective; if a machine is not in good order; or if the measuring instruments are not trustworthy? Slogan campaigns eventually are recognized as hoaxes. They only create adversarial relationships between the management and the workers. Low-quality output results from an inadequate system and lies beyond the power of the workers. Again, the systems are the responsibility of the managers.

Principle 11: Eliminate Work Standards and Quotas. Stop Management by Objective. Eliminate Management by Numbers. Deming argued against the use of numerical standards and quotas by which worker output is judged. "Quotas do not help people do a job. Replace standards with knowledge, intelligence, and leadership." Performance figures must be used to help people improve, not to rank them. "The intent of a work standard is noble; to establish a ceiling on costs. But the actual cost is to double the cost of operation and to stifle pride of workmanship." Piecework and incentive pay are even more devastating than are work standards. Workers soon learn that they get paid for making defective items and scrap. Where is pride of workmanship? Work standards, incentive pay, and piecework are manifestations of an inability on the part of managers to understand and provide appropriate supervision. Bonuses for extra achievement backfire and burn out. Managers must replace performance standards with intelligent supervision.

Deming was also opposed to the use of the once popular "management by objective" (MBO) approach to leadership and regarded it as inconsistent with process improvement. "If you have a stable system, there is no use to specify internal goals. A stable system will deliver whatever the system is capable of delivering. A goal beyond the capability of the system will not be reached."[25]

Principle 12: Remove Barriers That Rob People of Their Right to Pride of Workmanship. Annual performance or merit ratings are management by fear. They nourish short-term performance and ruin long-term planning. They hurt teamwork and joint activities and lead to rivalries and politics. They reward people for not rocking the boat. They leave people bruised and battered. They are also imperfect, random ways of distributing rewards. With a focus on the end product rather than on process improvement, the organization loses.

Failure to make a good grade in the annual performance rating system leads a person to look for better opportunities elsewhere. It is not unusual for one's strongest competitor to be someone who left the organization upon failure to receive a promotion. Give the workforce a chance to work with pride, and the 3 percent who do not care will erode itself by peer pressure.

Principle 13: Institute a Vigorous Program of Education and Self-Improvement. People need ever-broadening opportunities. It is inevitable that some improvements to the organization's systems may displace workers. The organization therefore needs a program of cross-training so the talents of displaced employees can be used. Prepare the workers in advance for possible changes in production processes and technology.

Principle 14: The Transformation Is Everybody's Job. All Must Be Involved. Every activity, every job in the organization is part of the production process. A critical mass of leaders must understand and accept the importance of the organizational quality transformation being proposed. Leaders need to explain why change is necessary and that change must involve everyone in the organization.

Ongoing consumer research is crucial to process improvement. Each organizational component (team) has a customer. The attitude in the organization should be, "Here is what I can do for you, here is what you can do for me." All stages of the production process work together toward delivering the quality output that will satisfy—indeed exceed—the expectations of the ultimate customer. Quality transformation of an organization will not happen by itself. An organization needs to be created to guide the transformation process and to focus on continued improvement.

Leaders communicate their involvement by planning, educating, choosing teams; working on organizational processes; setting examples through how they spend their time, the questions they ask, their reactions to critical situations, and the behaviors they reward. They need to be aware of these points at all times, and act accordingly.

TQM Implementation

The implementation of TQM in any organization is far from a simple matter. Deming's admonitions that everyone in the organization must be involved and that the top leadership needs to be absolutely committed to the transformation are crucial. It is also essential that all understand that quality management is a "journey, not a destination," and that it is naive to expect quick results.

A typical approach to introducing TQM involves establishing small groups with various assignments in the subject organization. The key units of this structure are "quality management boards," which oversee the effort, are multilevel in their composition, and provide informal lateral and vertical communication within the organization about the transformation project. The principal operating units are usually known as "process action teams." As expected, these units focus on process improvement at their particular level in the organization.

Most TQM implementation consultants provide measurement systems and techniques that assist the action teams in identifying improvement needs, including which quality problems result from common causes and which from special causes. These techniques include tools such as control charts—statistical plots designed to detect so-called process drift by displaying the changes in variation of a characteristic over time; parieto charts—bar graphs that rank causes of process variation by the degree of their impact on quality; and cause and effect ("fishbone") diagrams—tools for analyzing which causes lead to which effects.

Experience has shown that a transformation to TQM in an organization, public or private, requires the following components:

1. A commitment on the part of the leadership of the organization to see the change through. Top management must play a visible role in the implementation of TQM
2. A supportive organizational structure
3. The development of appropriate analytical tools and processes that reflect and measure the organization's important characteristics
4. Top-down-driven educational programs that prepare the workforce for both the process improvement effort and the cultural change embodied in TQM
5. Appropriate reward strategies in the organization that reflect the philosophy of quality management
6. Complete and regular communication about the transformation effort and an appreciation that it takes time and a disciplined approach to understand the processes of the organization

The Federal Quality Management Institute, in one of its reports on quality management in the federal government, states its belief that the adoption of TQM in an organization results in "a profound change in the overall culture and atmosphere of the organization."[26] Some of the ways in which TQM organizations differ from more traditional organizations are listed in Table 16–1.

Summary Comments on TQM

There is no mistaking the fact that the quality management revolution has occurred in both the private and public sectors of society. This is not just a new management technique that is likely to go the way of other trendy developments. Quality management, by whatever name it goes, is a cultural change in organizations that is becoming a worldwide phenomenon. Its principles are even being incorporated into supplier requirements that demand quality systems be in place in order for companies to participate in international business networks.[27] Its key concepts are also evolving into new generations of management thinking under such themes as organizational re-engineering and the development of the virtual organization.

In government, TQM has been implemented in a wide variety of organizations ranging from hospitals to weapons producers to motor vehicle agencies. The implementation of TQM has not always been easy, smooth, or successful. But its coverage of government agencies has grown enormously and continues to expand.

Some criticisms of the application of TQM and other recent approaches to

TABLE: 16–1   Characteristics of a Quality Organization

Traditional Way of Managing	TQM Approach
The organizational structure is hierarchical and has rigid lines of authority and responsibility.	The organizational structure becomes flatter, more flexible, and less hierarchical.
Focus is on maintaining the status quo (don't fix it if it ain't broke).	Focus shifts to continuous improvement in systems and processes (continue to improve it even if it ain't broke).
Workers perceive supervisors as bosses or cops.	Workers perceive supervisors as coaches and facilitators. The manager is seen as a leader.
Supervisor subordinate relationships are characterized by dependency, fear, and control.	Supervisor subordinate relationships shift to interdependency, trust, and mutual commitment.
The focus of employee efforts is on individual effort; workers view themselves as competitors.	The focus of employee efforts shifts to team effort; workers see themselves as teammates.
Management perceives labor and training as costs.	Management perceives labor as an asset and training as an investment.
Management determines what quality is and whether it is being provided.	The organization asks customers to define quality and develops measures to determine whether customers' requirements are met.
Primary basis for decisions is on gut feeling or instinct.	Primary basis for decisions shifts to facts and systems.

public management are reviewed later in this chapter. Notwithstanding those criticisms, quality management is an integral part of the reinventing-government movement that is rapidly gaining support at all three levels of government in the United States as well as many other countries in the world.

MARKET-BASED APPROACHES TO PUBLIC POLICY IMPLEMENTATION AND THE DELIVERY OF PUBLIC SERVICES

As the nation entered the 1990s, the influence of the privatization and TQM movements began to be realized in new thinking about how public officials go about the business of implementing public policy and delivering public services. These new attitudes implied that there was nothing sacred about traditional bureaucratic delivery organizations and mechanisms and that it was time to consider new, perhaps radical, approaches.

Many of these new approaches are based on the work of microeconomic theorists and so-called rational choice political scientists. Given well-defined goals and sufficient decentralized latitude in decision-making discretion, individuals and organizations will develop methods of work and systems that enable them to minimize their costs and maximize their output and, consequently, their gain. To achieve this change within government, officials "must promote . . . a culture that values a proactive, problem-solving attitude to replace the reactive, problem-avoiding attitude that too often dominates the federal bureaucracy."[28] The result will be improved productivity, lower costs, and better service for the public.

The reinventing-government proposals espoused by David Osborne and Ted Gaebler draw on many of the same concepts used by those who argue for privatization.[29] On the other hand, Osborne and Gaebler do not regard privatization as a panacea. Instead, they approach the provision of public services from a pragmatic, rather than ideological, frame of reference. They say, "The task is not about making government smaller, or weaker. The task is to make government stronger, by making it work again. . . . We don't need more government, we need better governance." They define governance as the act of collectively solving problems. "Government is the instrument we use. The instrument is outdated, and it is time to remake it."[30]

Like other institutions in today's society, "Governments must learn to discard the old bureaucratic ways, with elaborate rules and regulations and hierarchical chains of command, and become flexible, adaptable, and innovative. They must search constantly for new ways to improve services and heighten productivity."[31] In other words, they need to learn to operate like successful business in today's highly competitive economic environment. (Those who do not continuously improve and innovate, die!)

According to Osborne and Gaebler, governments must adopt a series of new principles that define what they refer to as entrepreneurial, decentralized government. They suggest, "For the last 50 years, political debate has centered on the questions of ends; what government should do, and for whom. We believe such debates are secondary today, because we simply do not have the means to achieve the new ends we seek. . . . The central failure of government today is one of means, not ends."[32] The principles the authors propose as necessary for moving government to this new approach to public affairs follow.

Catalytic government. Governments must steer rather than row. They must attempt to leverage private-sector actions to solve public problems. For example, the redevelopment of the Indianapolis central city was accomplished by public-private cooperation. Twenty years ago, the political leadership of the city developed the vision that rejuvenated the city, resulting in such facilities as the Hoosier Dome, Market Square Arena, the Indiana University–Purdue University joint campus in Indianapolis, and the historic Union Station. The same leadership developed an urban mall in the center of the city (opened in September 1995) and the White River Urban Park. A new task force is also underway to redefine the next generations vision for the city's future. None of this could have happened if the city had tried to do it all itself. But the combination of the city steering the plan and the private sector participating in its financing and implementation made it work.

Community-owned government. Entrepreneurial public organizations empower families, neighborhoods, and communities to solve their own problems. Examples include home instruction for preschool children, home health service provision and education, and neighborhood crime-watch programs. In a way this principle simply advocates a return to the traditional type of voluntary activity that was a mainstay of community social systems for many years.

Competitive government. In traditional governments, "Monopoly is the American way." Osborne and Gaebler argue that more productivity and innovation in public services require introducing the discipline of competition into government programs. In Bloomington, Indiana, both the city and Indiana University operate bus services. Some argue otherwise, but Osborne and Gaebler would probably praise such competition. Other examples of introducing competition into public service delivery include school voucher systems, competitive bidding between government service providers (e.g., trash hauling) and private contractors, and competitive health providers. This concept is important to several health care cost-containment proposals under discussion in the 1990s.

Mission-driven government. The best example of this principle is the need for government to provide adequate housing for all people. Government can achieve this aim by providing public housing, as it has since the 1930s, or by simply giving people money (housing certificates) and allowing them to buy or rent their own housing on the open market. Osborne and Gaebler clearly opt for the latter approach.

Results-oriented government. Traditional public institutions focus too much on the inputs and not enough on the outputs(or better yet, the outcomes). For example, educators measure student credit-hour production and call it output. In fact, of course, it is an input; what the student learns is the output. Other examples of focusing on inputs are measuring public safety by the number of police officers hired rather than the impact on crime and deciding the amounts to be spent on roads and streets rather than specifying objectives and results. Entrepreneurial governments measure outcomes and reward success.

Customer-driven government. To best assure that the objective of a service is met most efficiently and productively, the customer must always be the focus of any good or service provider. Osborne and Gaebler argue that the best way of assuring this in government is to give the resources, whenever practical, directly to the customer and allow the recipient of the service in question to choose the provider, thus both forcing competition and giving the customer a choice. Food stamps, housing certificates, school vouchers, and college Pell grants are all excellent examples of this philosophy.

Enterprising government. The profit motive can be effectively turned to public use. For example, the state government of Rhode Island developed a software system and markets it to the private sector. Many cities use private-sector sponsors to support locally run athletic competition. The city of Indianapolis has purchased the old L. S. Ayres Department Store building and will lease it to private businesses as part of an urban mall development. In Orlando, Florida, the new city hall was built without the use of general revenues; the mayor asked developers to compete for contracts in exchange for the right to build two office towers next door. Rents from the towers are programmed to pay off the city's bonds for the project, and the city will receive 20 percent of net rental proceeds from the office buildings, plus 20 percent of any sale or refinancing. Another example of enterprising government is the increased use of budgetary cost centers (sometimes known as "responsibility center budgeting"), which try to combine business profit-center concepts with public budgeting.

Anticipatory government. Here, the concept is prevention rather than cure. Classic examples are public health programs to avoid costly medical treatments (e.g., drug-abuse and AIDS awareness and antismoking campaigns); fire prevention codes and inspection; agricultural and economic development programs for developing nations; recycling of waste; and environmental and safety regulations. Many of these programs typically use incentives of one kind or another to be effective.

Decentralized government. According to this principle, those closest to the problem are most able to develop appropriate responses, design the most useful programs, and make the best decisions. Direct employee involvement in decision making, one of Deming's recommendations, results in more flexibility, innovation, and higher organizational morale. Decentralization also recognizes what many people regard as the need for better labor-management cooperation if public organizations are to meet public needs.

Market-oriented government. This principle uses market incentives to accomplish public purposes; for example, incentives (or disincentives) to encourage environmental cleanup and pollution prevention. The 1990 Clean Air Act includes provisions for emissions trading that encourages coal-burning power plants to shift to cleaner fuels or better scrubbers. Tax incentives for hiring and training hard-core unemployed people; impact fees paid to local city governments by developers of new housing to cover impact costs of schools, parks, streets, sidewalks, and other local public services—these are all examples of market-oriented government.

Osborne and Gaebler also approach the question of who should do what in the provision of public services and the implementation of public policy. They provide a categorization of the strengths and weaknesses of public- and private-sector providers of goods and services with these arguments:

- Public service institutions are best at policy management, regulation, equity ensurance, prevention of discrimination or exploitation, maintenance of continuity and stability of services, and ensuring social cohesion (e.g., racial integration programs)
- Private-sector providers are better at performing complex tasks, replicating the successes of other organizations, delivering services that require rapid adjustment, delivering services to diverse populations, and delivering services that become obsolete quickly
- The third (not-for-profit, NGO, or voluntary) sector is best at tasks that generate little or no profit or margin and require compassion and commitment to other humans, a comprehensive approach, extensive trust on the part of customers, and hands-on personal attention to social services

THE NATIONAL PERFORMANCE REVIEW (NPR)

David Osborne was a speechwriter for Bill Clinton in the 1992 presidential campaign, and Clinton was well versed in concepts of reinventing government. Not surprisingly, soon after taking office President Clinton asked Vice President Albert Gore to head a task force examining federal government operations, seeking to get rid of "useless bureaucracy and waste, and free the government of red tape and senseless rules." In his charge to the vice president announcing the National Performance Review (NPR), the president said: "Our goal is to make the federal government both less expensive and more efficient, and to change the culture of our national bureaucracy away from complacency and entitlement, toward initiative and empowerment. We intend to redesign, to reinvent, to reinvigorate the entire national government."[33]

Six months later (7 September, 1993), the vice president delivered the report, "From Red Tape to Results: Creating a Government That Works Better and Costs Less" (also known as the NPR).[34] The recommendations of the NPR closely parallel the philosophy of Osborne and Gaebler's thesis for reinventing government. The report contains four chapters, the subheadings of which are indicative of the direction of the task force recommendations. Below are the list of recommendations and brief explanatory comments about the report.

Chapter One: Cutting Red Tape

Step 1. Streamline the budget process by budgeting on a two-year basis (biennial budget); give managers more discretion in using funds; minimize congressional budgetary restrictions; and allow agencies to carry over one-half of unspent amounts into the next fiscal year, rather than having the funds revert to the general fund for reappropriation as now.

Step 2. Decentralize personnel policy to the operating agencies, and simplify the job classification system of the federal government.

Step 3. Streamline the federal procurement process. Rely more on the commercial marketplace and less on uniquely designed government specifications.

Step 4. Reorient the inspectors general of the various agencies away from auditing and investigating their agencies and toward helping managers evaluate their management control systems.

Step 5. Eliminate regulatory overkill.

Step 6. Empower state and local governments by reducing red tape and regulation on federal programs and reducing the number of unfunded mandates that Washington imposes on state and local government.

Chapter Two: Putting Customers First

Step 1. Give customers a voice and a choice.

Step 2. Make service organizations compete.

Step 3. Create market dynamics by a variety of actions, such as converting the air traffic-control system into a corporation; involving the private sector in the management of governmental rental properties and mortgage loans to the private sector; and managing federal assets to optimize returns for taxpayers.

Step 4. Use market mechanisms to solve problems such as environmental protection, public housing, and worker health and safety.

Chapter Three: Empowering Employees to Get Results

Step 1. Decentralize decision-making power and deregulate management discretion.

Step 2. Hold all federal employees accountable for results by requiring measurable objectives, clarifying the objectives of federal programs, and measuring outcome.

Step 3. Give federal workers the tools they need for their jobs. Grant agencies the flexibility to train their workers, upgrade technological training for all federal employees, and create a coherent financial management system and a strategic plan for using information technology throughout the federal government.

Step 4. Enhance the quality of work life in the federal government.

Step 5. Form a labor-management partnership.

Step 6. Take steps to strengthen leadership at all levels of government, and launch quality management basic training for all employees.

Chapter Four: Getting Back to Basics

Step 1. Eliminate what government does not need. Give the president a line-item budget veto; close unneeded federal facilities; streamline regional and overseas offices; and make a special effort to eliminate program duplication and special interest privileges.

Step 2. Collect more revenue by expanding user charges, collecting outstanding debts, and eliminating fraud.

Step 3. Invest in greater productivity by encouraging innovation and long-term investments.

Step 4. Reengineer programs to cut costs.

President Clinton assured the nation that the NPR "will not just gather dust in some warehouse." Vice President Gore stated, "How we proceed is just as important as what we have done to date. . . . We must actively involve government leaders at all levels . . . [and] seek the guidance of those who have successfully transformed large organizations in both the private and public sectors."

The announced implementation plans included steps such as establishing "reinvention teams and labs," asking the Cabinet to develop "performance agreements," establishing a "management council" to monitor change and provide guidance and resources to those working to accomplish the goals of the NPR, and launching future reviews of the federal government targeted at specific problems. The report concludes by stating:

> Over time, it will become increasingly obvious that people are not the problem. As old ways of thinking and acting are replaced by a culture that promotes reinvention and quality, a new face of government will appear—the face of employees newly empowered and newly motivated, and of customers newly satisfied.[35]

THE REPORT OF THE WINTER COMMISSION

At about the same time the NPR was underway, another group, the National Commission on the State and Local Public Service (known colloquially as the Winter Commission), was also at work on similar issues as they affect state and local government. The commission, established in 1991 with the support of several private foundations, was chaired by William F. Winter, the former governor of Mississippi; Frank Thompson, dean of the Graduate School of Public Affairs at the State University of New York, served as executive director. The commission presented its first report, "Hard Truths/Tough Choices," to President Clinton in June 1993.[36]

The report stated: "There is a growing consensus among both citizens and public officials that state and local institutions of government need to drastically improve their capacity and performance if we are to meet the challenges of our rapidly changing economic and social systems." It then offered a series of proposals that would "constitute a significant change in how our more than 15 million state and local employees perform their duties."[37]

The proposals are organized under the five following themes:

1. Remove the barriers to strong executive leadership by reducing the number of independently elected cabinet-level officials (e.g., some states elect the superintendent of education and the attorney general), strengthening executive authority, and consolidating overlapping governmental units. Managers would act as coaches and facilitators rather than supervisors and controllers.

2. Remove the barriers to lean, responsive government by reducing the number of management layers, and deregulate government by reforming the civil service, streamlining the procurement process, and increasing the flexibility of the budget process.
3. Remove the barriers to a high-performance workforce by expanding education and training, basing pay increases on skills, and encouraging a new approach to labor-management communication. Emphasize skills such as team building, negotiation, communication, employee involvement, cultural awareness, and quality performance.
4. Remove the barriers to citizen involvement by opening the books on campaign finance and lobbying, limiting the time for political fundraising, and encouraging citizens to solve problems by experimenting with citizen liaison offices and establishing a national service corps.
5. Reduce fiscal uncertainty by dealing with the financing crisis in health care.

Frank Thompson, commenting on the recommendations, indicated that this report is merely the first of what is expected to be an ongoing effort. He went on to say:

> Many of our agencies were created to solve tough problems, but are now too rule-bound and slow-footed to move with the times. Many of our public employees are motivated by undertaking challenging work and accomplishing something worthwhile, but are not offered the skills to do either or the decision-making authority to make it worth their while. Many of the unions that represent those employees want to share in constructive change, but feel that they have been shut-out because of a management knows-best mentality that pervades government. Many citizens have the potential to participate in solving their own problems, but have been discouraged and frustrated by government and government systems. . . . But governments can change, and citizen action is possible.[38]

Although the Winter Commission report is not as directly tied to the reinventing-government recommendations as is the NPR, it can be considered a first cousin. The report has met with some criticism, but in general has been well received by the public administration community.

One interesting reaction to the report occurred in the academic community, where a task force of public administration faculty suggested that the report was a "call for a new kind of public service which will require radical [public administration] curricular transformation." The task force suggested that "the report challenges programs of public affairs and administration to equip students with the knowledge and abilities to be catalysts for change, rather than guardians of the status quo.[39] Academic programs must thus increase their emphasis on skills such as team building, negotiation, communication inside and outside the organization, employee involvement, cultural awareness, and achieving program quality.

OTHER POINTS OF VIEW

As might be expected, the reactions of the professional public administration community to the movement represented by the management directions discussed in the previous sections have not been uniformly favorable. The criticisms essentially fall into two categories: (1) those who do not support the fundamental ideas of TQM, privatization, or the use of market principles in government and (2) those who believe the NPR and similar implementation efforts are mistaken or will be ineffective.

CRITICISMS OF THE USE OF TQM IN GOVERNMENT

As discussed earlier, one of the key features of the quality management movement is the primacy of the consumer, that is, government must grow more consumer oriented. H. George Frederickson, a long-time scholar and creative thinker in the field of public administration, argues that citizens are the owners, not the customers, of government.[40] The job of government managers is to execute the law, not transfer power to either bureaucrats or citizens in such a way as to undermine the democratic process. If government is more responsive to customers, will the most fortunate and vocal have their needs best served, to the detriment of the less fortunate and less organized? Will decentralizing decisions to citizens result in a lack of uniformity in public policy making?

DiIulio and coworkers point out that responding to citizens as service recipients is not the only goal of government. Government agencies operate under principles of democracy and are creatures of legislative bodies, subject to the review of the judicial system. These overseers expect and are due financial and programmatic accountability, which takes precedence over "paying attention to citizens as service recipients. . . . The emphasis on efficiency typically applies to those programs citizens do not themselves receive. When they are the focus of a program, no expenditure can seem enough, as reformers in health and education policy have discovered."[41]

James Swiss argues that there are four problems with adapting TQM, as practiced in the private sector, to government.[42] The customer-taxpayer ambiguity discussed earlier is one. He also argues that the compromise between quality and cost that allows consumers to optimize for themselves the quality-cost trade-off for a product does not work in government because the buyer of a government service (the taxpayer) is not always the same as the consumer. Further, the application of TQM to services is problematic because services are more labor intensive and can lack a uniformity of output; consumers evaluate services not only by results but also by the behavior and even the appearance of the persons delivering them. Finally, Swiss argues that the TQM focus on process improvement will cause goal displacement within the public service. Given the natural tendencies of the bureaucracy, the service goals of the government agencies would be replaced by an emphasis on containing taxpayer costs and on implementing procedural rules.

This later point may recall Deming's view about quality in government service.

> In most governmental services, there is no market to capture. In place of capture of the market, a governmental agency should deliver economically the service prescribed by law or regulation. The aim should be distinction in service. Continual improvement in government service would earn appreciation of the American public and would hold jobs in the service, and help industry to create more jobs.[43]

Swiss does believe that adapting TQM to government holds promise, assuming appropriate adaptations that take these kinds of objections into account. As DiIulio and colleagues point out: "Emphasizing client feedback, defining, measuring, and tracking performance, seeking continuous improvement, and encouraging worker participation can all promote better performance."[44] They therefore recommend that the OMB should promote the adaptation of TQM within the federal government.

CRITICISM OF THE REINVENTING-GOVERNMENT THEMES: CAN GOVERNMENT REALLY BE MADE BETTER BY MAKING IT MORE LIKE THE PRIVATE SECTOR?

In H. George Frederickson's view, the reinventors have gone after the wrong set of problems.[45] He contends that the real problem with government has little to do with public management, which he thinks is done rather well, by and large. Instead, he argues that the primary problems of government have to do with the failure of political will, the power of interest groups and lobbyists, and weakness in the conduct of statecraft by our elected leaders. With his tongue at least partially in his cheek, he proposes the seven following principles of "total quality politics" that, if implemented along with TQM, would vastly improve the present situation.

1. Avoid the "wrong problems problem": do not blame management for a policy failure.
2. Practice citizen-centered government: nurture participation and recognize that not all citizens are capable of voicing and defending their needs.
3. Engage in "transformational politics": focus on the greater good rather than self-interest.
4. Exercise candor and courage regarding costs: do not assign or mandate programs to lower levels of government without providing the funds to support the programs.
5. Be fair and equitable to all, regardless of education, race, wealth, or talent.
6. Respect the public service: do not make invidious comparisons with the private sector or imply that one is more capable or worthy than the other.
7. Cautiously sustain the free enterprise system: reach a balance between the needs of the capitalist economy on the one hand and fairness, equity, and consumer protection on the other.

Other critics have added to the discussion about the appropriateness of the reinventing-government proposals of Osborne and Gaebler and the NPR. Comments from the professional public administration community include the following:[46]

- It should be remembered that government managers should not be empowered beyond the restraints of law and due process
- Can the 10 reinventing-government principles be applied to all public administration cases?
- The major problem is not that the government does not know how to administer programs. The problem is that the public demands more in service and benefits than it is willing to pay for
- When public service is completely subjected to market forces, it is much easier for the conduct of public managers to be less responsible
- To think that American society is going to be able to deal effectively with a wide variety of public problems by creating organizational arrangements that allow public administrators to become entrepreneurs is first-order political naïveté
- Legislators and high-level executive branch officials are unlikely to give up control of policy formulation and development prerogatives to independently functioning entrepreneurs.

David H. Rosenbloom, editor of the *Public Administration Review,* wrote in an editorial in late 1993;

> We need a full-fledged discussion of the political impact of the would-be-reformers prescriptions. For surely the day is long past when proponents of change can act as if there are no trade-offs, collective action problems, or fundamental disagreements over the means and ends of government.

Osborne and Gaebler would transform citizens in a political community into customers of government in simulated markets. DiIulio, Garvey, and Kettl display no qualms about letting Congress know how to spend the public's money, how many political executives and appointees there should be, how to go about closing and consolidating federal field offices, and how to strengthen the president's reorganization authority. But as Dwight Waldo has so clearly demonstrated, administrative theory is political theory and so, too, administrative prescription is political prescription. This is an old lesson: those who want better government better talk politics.

Professor Charles Goodsell, a long-time public administration scholar, summarizes what appears to be the view of many of those concerned about the prominence and apparent ready acceptance of the reinventing-government thesis:[47]

- Through their elected representatives, the people are in charge of U.S. government, not the entrepreneurs.
- Government is intended to serve the public interest, not create unspent reserves or feed entrepreneurial egos.
- Government must operate according to the Constitution and the laws of the land, not niche mission statements.
- Government should be flexible and innovative, but also act as steward of the public's money and be financially and programmatically accountable.
- In government, private managerial conduct must comply to the nonprivate ideals of equal opportunity and open scrutiny.

Frank Sherwood, another pillar of the public administration scholarly community, raises the specter that "everyone loves decentralization until they get it. Then as the primacy of the center is threatened, the revisions begin to appear." In fact, "We ought to understand that real delegation means abdication." Sherwood does support the NPR concept of franchising and focusing on the needs of line managers, injecting competition, finding market instead of administrative solutions, and fostering excellence. But he warns that "this will not be an easy process. The idea of applying market incentives to internal federal services is revolutionary to those who have practiced in the 100 year monopoly tradition."[48]

John DiIulio suggests that looking to the state and local governments for reform ideas (as did the NPR when it relied heavily on Osborne and Gaebler's work) is looking in the wrong place. He thinks that studies of what federal bureaucrats do indicate that their tasks are unlike the tasks of state and local officials and private-sector managers. "State and local civil servants provide direct services to citizens. They fight fires, handle troubled children, process welfare checks. Most federal workers supervise a vast network of contractors. . . . Only about 6 percent of the non-defense federal budget goes into the direct administration of anything." He also believes TQM will be of limited use to federal government. "The kinds of changes the NPR seeks to make will take not four months or four years but more like a generation."[49]

On a more cynical note, Gerald Caiden offers this view: "The reformers want to change the over-regulated and over-bureaucratized culture of American public administration to a more entrepreneurial and energetic one. . . . Unfortunately, [they] do not tell us how they will overcome a prevailing political (and administrative) culture of self-serving, of exploiting public office and public purse for self-interest, in which politicians, lobbyists, contractors, and public employees, too, participate unmindful of the consequences for the country. Whatever happened to the virtues of public interest, guardianship, integrity, merit, accountability, responsibility, and truth?"[50]

Ronald Moe of the Congressional Research Service has been particularly critical of reinventing-government proposals. Moe believes "the net result of the Gore Report. . . . will be a government much less accountable to the citizens for its performance. . . . The root cause of the problems afflicting the federal government today will not be solved by the 'four bedrock principles' of entrepreneurial management or 'cascading' behavioral modification sessions. . . . The problem is fundamentally an institutional and legal problem and must be addressed at that level."[51]

IMPLEMENTATION ISSUES

In December 1993, in response to requests from several members of Congress, the U.S. Government Accounting Office (GAO) released a detailed report commenting on the NPR recommendations for each of 38 government agencies.[52] The GAO report agreed with most of the recommendations and believes that their successful implementation "can make an important contribution in addressing the federal government's management and programmatic problems." The report went on to say however, that the ultimate success of the NPR will depend on the implementation strategies and actions used, and these, in turn, will depend on the administration's forging "a strong, coordinated partnership with Congress to develop these strategies." It will also require improving agencies' management capabilities so they can assume the additional authority and responsibility contemplated by the NPR and be held accountable for programmatic outcomes. These comments reflect the GAO's long-standing interest in the type of performance budgeting and measurement required in the Government Performance and Results Act of 1993 (discussed in Chapter 15).

There are others who support many, if not all, of the NPR recommendations but who are concerned about whether and how they are to be implemented. Much of the concern is focused on the recognition that Congress will need to take action on well over half of the recommendations. It is therefore necessary that the executive branch and congressional leadership work closely to move the recommendations forward. Given the other policy demands on both branches of government, not to mention political division between the White House and the Congress in the second half of the Clinton Administration, such cooperation will not be easy. There is also the concern that the NPR will be seen primarily as simply a way to cut the federal budget rather than a basic reorientation of public management. The fundamental concept should be that the NPR is a first step in building a process and capacity for continuous improvement of the federal government.

The board of trustees of the National Academy of Public Administration (NAPA), in an attempt to move the process of reform forward, suggested in early 1994 that the NPR was "in danger of becoming mired in unproductive discussions about its role in deficit reduction; dismembered through piecemeal consideration; and lost in traditional dueling between the branches (of government)." The trustees, while noting they did not agree with every NPR recommendation, regarded the NPR as an "important first step in a long-term process of continuous change that can help counter cynicism about the public sector by significantly improving the federal government's delivery of benefits and services to Americans."[53] In order to "bring serious reform to its operations, and to institute the needed cultural change, the federal government must discard its business-as-usual approach." The NAPA Trustees suggested a process to help this situation:[54]

1. An annual bipartisan gathering of congressional and executive branch leaders should be held to assess the progress of the NPR and to select reform targets for the upcoming year
2. A fast-track procedure, similar to that used for trade agreements, should be used by Congress for up-or-down votes on omnibus legislation to reform government
3. Administrative authority to waive federal mandates should be allowed for innovative approaches to achieve selected outcomes on the part of state and local governments and the independent (the third or NGO) sector
4. A grass-roots effort to educate government workers and the public about not only how the NPR's new culture and processes will generate a more responsive federal government, but how it will also better inform them about their roles in the governance system.

As part of the effort to keep the reform initiative alive, NAPA is also the prime mover behind the Alliance for Redesigning Government and, with the support of several private foundations as well as some government agencies, is actively conducting research and developing demonstration projects in which Osborne and Gaebler's principles are prominent.

In March 1994 the NPR newsletter, "The Reinvention Roundtable," reported that 80 percent of the 384 recommendations were already being implemented. The president had signed 18 implementation directives, 50 bills were pending before Congress, 155 of the recommendations appeared in the budget, and "another 38 will appear in individual agency budget justification documents to be sent to Congress in the coming weeks." The newsletter also announced that "over 130 Reinvention Labs are cutting red tape and improving customer service." Later that year the president announced that he would cut 272,000 federal jobs by 1998 and save the federal treasury $40 billion over five years.

In his 1995 State of the Union address, President Clinton announced that he and Vice-President Gore were moving ahead with phase two of the National Performance Review. David Osborne suggested that phase two should eliminate not just programs but subsidies that favor special interests and distort the market. Many of these were proposed for elimination in NPR One, but were vetoed by the president. He also argued for a major effort to make government more effective by reinventing programs like education, welfare, job training, and public housing to expand opportunity and empower individuals.[55]

SUMMARY: WHAT NOW? THE FACE OF GOVERNMENT IN THE 21ST CENTURY

It is not easy to appraise the several trends explored in this and the preceding chapter in order to draw conclusions about the likely future shape of U.S. government. No one is prescient, and readers will ultimately have to draw their own conclusions. It is clearly a time of turmoil and change in utilizing government structures and personnel to implement public policy and to deliver public services. It is also true, as some critics point out, that it does not make sense to speak of government generically. Instead, government does and should take several shapes. Moving into the 21st century and trying to deal with the changing demands and the vastly altered world environment, government must have more variety and more flexibility in its options.

Nevertheless, appropriate compromises will be found, and the United States will continue to move gradually in the direction of a new management paradigm appropriate to the informational, technological, political, and behavioral environment of the 21st century. It seems that this paradigm will include some of what has proven most useful from the management and political heritage that helped to operate the U.S. government over the past 50 years. For some tasks, indeed, the traditional hierarchical bureaucratic structures may, after all, be the best delivery mechanism, particularly given other governmental objectives. At the same time, it seems clear that 21st-century governments will necessarily also incorporate those new concepts and techniques of governance that have evolved in recent years and for which there is certainly opportunity and need.

Osborne and Gaebler's thesis is that current government is designed for an environment that no longer exists. In fact, it is probable that the reinventing-government advocates would agree, upon some reflection, that neither does the current government about which they speak truly exist. There are numerous versions of "government" at all levels of the federal system, most unalike and virtually all in various stages of transition and evolution most of the time. The management reform movement has been underway for over 100 years, and most of the bursts of innovation at various times have added positively, at the margin, to government's ability to do the public's business.

There are certainly many problems in implementing public policy and delivering public services that need addressing, and the current reform wave of privatizers, quality managers, and reinventors has a great deal to contribute to the improvement of that situation. There is nothing wrong with trying to encourage an internal (to government) and external consumer (or constituent) orientation on the part of public servants. Many of the other philosophical principles of the TQM advocates are similarly difficult to argue against. How can good managers be opposed to focusing more on long-term objectives, developing workers in a positive atmosphere, measuring performance, and continuously working to improve the quality output of the organization? In good organizations, of which there are plenty in government, many of these concepts have long been practiced. However, it is worth keeping in mind, as is commonly observed in the public administration community, while there are indeed many similarities between business administration and public administration, most of them are trivial. Just because a particular approach worked well in the private sector does not necessarily mean it is appropriate for the public sector.

The arguments of the NPR that concern changes in the system such as decentralizing personnel management to the working agencies, reducing micromanagement by the Office of Management and Budget and Congress, and clearing up ambiguities among agency responsibilities are by and large positive changes that have been advocated by many professionals in the federal government for years. If the NPR gives these reforms a positive boost, why not?

It is easy to make a case for many of the other changes that flow from these interrelated concepts. Despite the enthusiasm that typifies reform movements, however, people must recognize that the reformers can also be criticized if they pursue a one-size-fits-all approach. In fact, as suggested, government is quite diverse in what it is asked to do and in how it approaches and carries out its tasks. It certainly cannot be thought of generically.

The answer, then, is that the reform movement, whether it be privatization, quality management, re-engineering, or reinvention, has much to contribute to many of the functions and goals of government. The task is to determine where the contributions can be most profitably pursued and not to get lost in the maze by trying to force these changes where they simply do not make sense. As the critics have also pointed out, several of the most difficult management problems facing public administrators are the resultant externalities of the structure and operation of our constitutional and political system of governance. Although some of these externalities can perhaps be ameliorated, it will not be easy (or necessarily correct) to eliminate incremental budgets, the high turnover of political appointees at the executive level, and the oversight burden of the Congress nor to realign responsibilities among the units of government in the federal system.

The title of Chapter 15 of this book, "Government Reform: A Work in Progress," aptly describes the true nature of the ongoing and long-standing attempts to continuously improve the U.S. system of implementing public policy and delivering public services. As this evolutionary reform process continues, people must be mindful of the complications and nuances of the multilayered system of governance and avoid simplistic changes that are inappropriate to government and incompatible with the fundamental goals of a democratic society.

DISCUSSION QUESTIONS

1. The reinvention of government, as proposed in the Gore Report, has both its supporters and detractors. Where are you on this issue and why?
2. How would you judge the usefulness of the Osborne/Gaebler reinvention proposals for a place like the state of Indiana? For Indianapolis?
3. Discuss the key principles of total quality management. Can such a system really be utilized to improve government?
4. Why are some observers concerned that such new directions as those proposed in the Gore report (the National Performance Review) will result in a government that is less accountable to the people of the nation? Do they have a point?

SUGGESTED READINGS

David Osborne and Ted Gaebler, *Reinventing Government,* Addison-Wesley Publishing Company, Inc., New York, 1992.

E.S. Savas, *Privatization: The Key to Better Government,* Chatham House Publishers, Inc., Chatham, N.J., 1987.

Privatization: Toward More Effective Government, Report of the President's Commission on Privatization, U.S. Government Printing Office, 1988.

Albert Gore, *Creating a Government That Works Better and Costs Less: Report of the National Performance Review,* U.S. Government Printing Office, Wash. D.C., also available from the Penguin Group, New York, 1993.

Warren Schmidt and Jerome P. Finnigan, *The Race Without a Finish Line: America's Quest for Total Quality,* Josey-Bass Publishers, San Francisco, 1992.

NOTES

1. The contract included promises to introduce legislation dealing with welfare reform, tax reductions for middle-class families, a balanced budget constitutional amendment,

congressional term limits, reductions in congressional staff and budgets, elimination of unfunded state mandates, and imposing on Congress the same laws that everyone else is subject to.

2. For a discussion of organizational transformation in the private sector, see Ralph H. Kilmann (ed.), *Corporate Transformation: Revitalizing Organizations for a Competitive World* (San Francisco, Calif.: Teresa Joyce Covin and Associates, 1988).

3. "Selling the State: Privatization," *The Economist*, 21, August 1993, p. 18.

4. Emanuel S. Savas, *Privatization: The Key to Better Government* (Chatham, N.J.: Chatham House Publishers, Inc., 1987), 5.

5. Ahmed Galal, Leroy Jones, Pankaj Tandon, and Igo Vogelsang, "Welfare Consequences of Selling Public Enterprises," *The Economist*, 13, June 1992.

6. The White House, "Privatization: Toward More Effective Government," *Report of the President's Commission on Privatization* (Washington, D.C.: U.S. Government Printing Office, March 1988).

7. Michael Mills, Charles D. Van Eaton, and Robert Daddow, *Revitalizing the American City: A Market Perspective for Detroit* (Detroit, Mich.: The Heartland Institute, 1992).

8. Stephen Goldsmith, "When Cities Turn to Privatization; Indianapolis Competition," *Wall Street Journal*, 3, December 1992, p. 14.

9. Savas, 1987, 84–85.

10. See Savas, 1987, for much more detail on privatization options. This section is based primarily on his ideas.

11. Savas, 1987, 98.

12. Dennis Palumbo, "Privatization and Corrections Policy," *Policy Studies Review* 5, no. 3 (1986): 598–605.

13. H. Brinton Milward and Keith Provan, "The Hollow State: Private Provision of Public Services," in *Public Policy for Democracy*, ed. Helen Ingram and Steven Rathgeb Smith Washington, D.C.: (Brookings Institution, 1994).

14. *The Privatization Review*, published by the Privatization Council, April 1992, 18.

15. Benjamin Gidron, Ralph M. Kramer, and Lester M. Salamon (eds.), *Government and the Third Sector* (San Francisco, Calif.: Jossey-Bass, 1992), 5.

16. Gidron et al., 1992, 7.

17. Gidron et al., 1992, 11.

18. Gidron et al., 1992, 19.

19. See J. M. Juran, *Juran on Leadership for Quality* (New York:Free Press, 1989).

20. See Kaoru Ishikawa, *What Is Total Quality Control?* (Englewood Cliffs, N.J.: Prentice Hall, 1985); translation of the original Japanese edition.

21. W. Edwards Deming, *Out of the Crisis* (Cambridge, Mass.: MIT Press, 1986).

22. Deming, 1986.

23. Deming, 1986.

24. Deming, 1986.

25. Deming, 1986.

26. *Introduction to Total Quality Management in the Federal Government* (Washington, D.C.: Federal Quality Institute, 1991).

27. The ISO 9000 requirements of the International Standards Organization are rapidly being adopted by most major corporations in Europe and the United States. In essence this set of standards requires the suppliers of these corporations to be certified that they have quality management systems in place.

28. John J. DiIulio, Jr., Gerald Garvey, and Donald Kettl, *Improving Government Performance:An Owner's Manual* (Washington, D.C.: Brookings Institution, 1993).

29. David Osborne and Ted Gaebler, *Reinventing Government* (Reading, Mass.: Addison-Wesley Publishing Co., 1992). The following discussion is based on their work.

30. David Osborne, "Government That Means Business," *New York Times Magazine*, 1, March 1992, pp. 20–28.

31. Osborne and Gaebler, 1992.

32. Osborne and Gaebler, 1992.

33. Quote from President Clinton's speech announcing the NPR, Washington, D.C., March 1993.

34. "From Red Tape to Results: Creating a Government that Works Better and Costs Less: Executive Summary, Report of the National Performance Review," *The Review* (Washington, D.C.:U.S. Government Printing Office, 1993).

35. "From Red Tape to Results," 1993.

36. "Hard Truths/Tough Choices" (Washington, D.C.: Winter Commission, June 1993).

37. "Hard Truths/Tough Choices," 1993.

38. "Hard Truths/Tough Choices," 1993.

39. Delmer D. Dunn, "Public Affairs, Administrative Faculty and the Winter Commission Report," *Public Administration Review* (March–April 1994).

40. H. George Frederickson, "Painting Bull's Eyes around Bullet Holes," *Governing* 6 (October 1992): 13.

41. DiIulio et al., 1993, 50.

42. James E. Swiss, "Adapting Total Quality Management to Government," *Public Administration Review* 52 (July–August, 1994): 356.

43. Deming, 1986, 6.

44. DiIulio et al., 1993, 54.

45. H. George Frederickson, "George and the Case of the Government Reinventors," *PA Times* 17, no. 1 (1, January 1994).

46. "ASPA on Governmental Reform" (Washington, D.C.: American Society for Public Administration); Reprints of author, title, dates from *PA Times* and *Public Administration*.

47. Charles T. Goodsell, "Reinvent Government or Rediscover It?" *Public Administration Review* (January–February, 1993).

48. Frank Sherwood, speech at the University of Southern California, October 1993; published in the *PA Times* (November 1993).

49. John J. DiIulio, Jr., "Reinventing Government or the Wheel?" *Washington Post Weekly*, 5, September 1993, p. 23.

50. Gerald E. Caiden, "Administrative Reform—American Style," *Public Administration Review* (March–April 1994): 134.

51. Ronald Moe, "The Reinventing Government Exercise: Misinterpreting the Problem, Misjudging the Consequences," *Public Administration Review* (March–April 1994).

52. General Accounting Office, "Management Reform: The GAO's Comments on the National Performance Review's Recommendations" (Washington, D.C.: U.S. Government Printing Office, December 1993).

53. National Academy of Public Administration, "A Year From Day One: An Update on the National Performance Review" (Washington, D.C.: 18, February 1994).

54. National Academy of Public Administrßation, 1994.

55. David Osborne, "Can this President Be Saved?" *Washington Post Magazine*, 8, January 1995, pp. 28–29.

Appendix: A Quick Guide to Public Affairs Information

Students of public affairs need to know how to find and use information and statistics relevant to public issues. Most students understand that the *Public Affairs Information Service* and the *Reader's Guide to Periodical Literature* are standard guides to magazines and newspapers, but in many cases the information needed is more specialized. This appendix summarizes some of the leading categories of public affairs information that can make obscure sources accessible. In some cases, sources cited will be available in the local public library. Virtually all sources, however, should be found in the large university libraries serving as repositories for public documents.

The guide is not comprehensive. It does not include, for instance, listings of books, periodicals, and journal articles. Moreover, it does not begin to capture the enormous changes in the distribution of information, including rapidly expanding uses of compact disks, electronic networks, and computerized indexing services. However, it does show how access to a wealth of information can be achieved quickly and easily through indexes, catalogs, and search services. For the most part, this appendix is a compilation of selected data sources frequently used by students in the general area of public affairs as well as by those with special interests in public policy and public management.[1]

BASIC SOURCES: U.S. GOVERNMENT

Students are not always aware that one of government's main functions is the collection, processing, and dissemination of data and information about all aspects of public life. Thus, every public agency has important responsibilities for managing public information, particularly the federal government that often plays a co-ordinative role with other parts of society. Listed here is merely a sampling of the major central compilations from which students can branch out into specialized areas.

General Federal Sources

The *United States Government Manual,* published annually by the General Services Administration, is the basic handbook for the federal government. It lists all agencies of the legislative, judicial, and executive branches, including all official and quasi-official boards, commissions, regulatory bodies, independent agencies, and government corporations. This volume provides agency descriptions, legislative authorization, policy purposes and main work activities, organization charts, and names, addresses, and phone numbers of top officials.

The *Monthly Catalog of United States Government Publications* is the official printed card catalog of the U.S. Government Printing Office, listing publications of executive, congressional, judicial, and independent agencies. Documents are indexed by author, agency, title, key word, subject, and publication number. Three retrospective indexes to the *Monthly Catalog* simplify the search for early periods or long time spans: *Cumulative Subject Index to the Monthly Catalog, 1900–1971; United States Government Publications Monthly Catalog: Cumulative Index;* and *Cumulative Title Index to United States Public Documents 1789–1976.*

The *Index to U.S. Government Periodicals,* published quarterly and cumulated annually, provides author and subject access to articles in 171 titles issued by more than 100 agencies. This commercially published index constitutes the only systematic guide to federal government periodicals.

Congressional Quarterly's *Washington Information Directory,* published every year, is a comprehensive guidebook to official and unofficial Washington, D.C. It provides a wealth of ready reference information on members of Congress and the executive agencies, important individuals and organizations in the media and the private sectors, foreign embassies and diplomats, and lobbying groups in all aspects of public life. Headings include economics and business, energy, equal rights, health and consumer affairs, national security, and a dozen more.

Federal Executive Branch Sources

The *Weekly Compilation of Presidential Documents* is the official record of all statements, speeches, press conferences, executive orders, dedications, and nominations made by the president. It is indexed each week, with cumulations issued quarterly and annually.

The *Budget of the United States Government* is the primary document detailing the annual revenues and expenditures of the federal government. Before the Bush administration, it was supplemented by three additional volumes: *The Budget in Brief,* which provides an overview of the budget in summary form; *Special Analyses,* which presents analytic reports for selected policy areas; and the massive *Appendix to the Budget,* which gives line item spending levels and authorizations of all departments, agencies, and other federal government bodies. The format of the budget changed during the Bush administration and was issued in a single, fat "Sears catalog" format. Currently, the Clinton administration budget is organized in four volumes: *Budget of the United States Government; Analytical Perspectives; Historical Tables;* and *Appendix.*

The *Federal Register* is the document published every weekday to announce all administrative rules and regulations, proposed rules, legal notices, meetings, and orders issued by the executive agencies including the office of the president. It is arranged by subject matter and updated annually in the *Code of Federal Regulations.*

The *Catalog of Federal Domestic Assistance* is a comprehensive guide to federal grant programs. The 1982 edition catalogs funding, eligibility, and contact information for 988 programs administered by 52 federal agencies and offices. Program areas include community development and services, alcohol and drug abuse, health and social services, and many other areas of public concern. It is indexed by subject, function, agency programs, and applicant eligibility.

Students of federalism and intergovernmental relations should become familiar with the publications of the Advisory Commission on Intergovernmental Relations (ACIR), an independent commission created in 1959 by Congress to study the U.S. federal system and to recommend improvements. ACIR publishes annual reports on federal, state, and local finance as well as special reports on government structure and functions, including substate regionalism and the intergovernmental grant system.

An important source of digested information on the federal government can be found in the *National Journal,* a reporting service specializing in analytical articles on politics and government with an emphasis on the executive branch. It is issued weekly by the Government Research Corporation and constitutes an independent source of nonpartisan journalism covering Washington's policy-making machinery.

Congressional Sources

The *Congressional Record* is the daily publication of the proceedings of the floor debates in Congress, including the complete text of speeches and bill introductions and any supplementary material that members of the House and the Senate insert into the "Extensions of Remarks." For current access to information in the *Record,* one may consult the "Daily Digest" in each issue, which summarizes the contents of that day's activities.

The *Congressional Information Service Index to Congressional Publications (CIS)* is an indexing and abstracting service to all publications of the Congress except the *Record.* The coverage of *CIS* includes publications issued by the approximately 300 House and Senate committees, subcommittees, joint committees, and special offices of the Congress. These working papers of the Congress, which currently amount to over 850,000 pages each year, include committee hearings, committee prints, House and Senate reports and documents, and publications of the Office of Technology Assessment and the Congressional Budget Office.

CIS is issued in two parts, indexes and abstracts, which are published monthly with quarterly cumulations of the indexes and annual cumulations of both parts. The indexes provide detailed cross-referencing by subject matter, agencies, names of committee witnesses, organizations, titles, and bill numbers. The abstracts present analytic summaries of testimony, identify witnesses by name and affiliation, and list supplementary material and written testimony submitted for the record. Complete bibliographic information is included: titles, dates, paging, report and document numbers, and Superintendent of Documents classification numbers.

The *Congressional Index* is a loose-leaf service published by Commerce Clearing House, giving the most up-to-date information readily available on all bills and resolutions introduced in the House and the Senate. Detailed indexing by subject matter and names of members of Congress provides access to pending legislation. Bills and resolutions are arranged in numerical order, and status tables indicate what action, if any, has been taken on particular bills. Currency is usually within two to three weeks of action. Special features include names, addresses, and biographies of all current members of Congress, voting records, and maps of current districts for the House of Representatives.

The laws enacted by Congress are published by year in the order in which they were passed in the *United States Statutes at Large* and are codified into 50 broad subject areas, or titles, in the *United States Code.* Since the *Statutes* are issued two years or more after enactment, a more timely, although unofficial, publication of the laws of Congress can be found in the *U.S. Code Congressional Administrative News,* published by West Publishing Company of St. Paul, Minnesota.

The *Congressional Directory* and the *Congressional Staff Directory,* both published annually, are valuable sources of information on members of Congress and their staffs. The former provides biographies, committee assignments, and statistical data on all members as well as information on state delegations, executive departments and independent agencies, the judiciary, diplomatic representatives, and members of the print, broadcasting, and wire services covering the Capitol. The *Staff Directory* presents information on the staffs of the senators, representatives, officers, committees, and subcommittees. Special features include biographies of approximately 3,000 staff members and their job titles and room and phone numbers; key personnel of the executive departments and agencies; and congressional districts and representatives of 9,900 cities and towns.

The General Accounting Office (GAO) is the auditing and investigative arm of the Congress. Students of the congressional process should be aware of the wealth of information contained in GAO reports and legislative analyses. The *Monthly List of GAO Reports* provides a capsule summary of reports issued each month in diverse areas such as national defense, energy, personnel management, natural resources and environment, social services and community development, transportation, and general government operations. Two important directories issued by the GAO are *Federal Program Evaluations* and *Federal Information Sources and Systems.*

The *Congressional Quarterly Weekly Report* is a weekly compilation of major activities of Congress, including in-depth analyses of House and Senate processes, tables of pending legislation, roll calls of key votes, and profiles of senators and representatives. Special issues are devoted to committee assignments, campaign and election activities, the full text of inaugural addresses, major political speeches, and party convention proceedings and platforms.

Congressional Quarterly, Inc. (CQ) also publishes a variety of other reference works on the federal government. The *CQ Almanac* provides an annual summary of congressional operations and actions as well as a discussion and chart of legislative procedural flow and a glossary of terms. The *CQ Guide to the Supreme Court* (1979) gives historical background on the Court and the justices, summarizes major cases and decisions, and analyzes current trends in the judicial branch.

Other CQ titles include *Guide to Congress, Guide to U.S. Elections, Congressional Roll Call,* and *Guide to Current American Government.*

BASIC SOURCES: STATE AND LOCAL GOVERNMENT

The *Monthly Checklist of State Publications* is issued by the Library of Congress as a compilation of all state government publications received by the library during that month. Documents are listed alphabetically by state and agency and are indexed annually. There is also a semiannual listing of periodicals in June. The *Monthly Checklist* is a systematic guide to what is being published by state governments, although the materials themselves are frequently difficult to obtain.

Index to Current Urban Documents, published by Greenwood Press of Westport, Connecticut, since 1972, lists publications of selected U.S. and Canadian cities and towns; coverage includes documents issued by the 272 largest municipal governments, special districts and authorities, and regional councils and agencies. The *Book of the States,* published every other year by the Council of State Governments, is a guide to state government organizations, finances, processes, activities, and intergovernmental relations. In addition to narrative and statistical data on these areas, there are tables providing capsule information on a variety of subjects, allowing at-a-glance comparisons of the 50 states on topics such as gun control legislation, age of majority for various activities, and participation in uniform state laws.

The *Almanac of American Politics,* published every other year, is a ready reference source of information on the 50 states, including narrative and tabular presentations of the political environment of each state. Voting records, districts, and photos of all U.S. senators and representatives and all 50 governors are provided along with census data, election results, and profiles of the voting constituencies. A unique feature is found in the "Group Ratings" for each politician from such diverse political and social organizations as the Americans for Democratic Action, the Americans for Constitutional Action, the National Taxpayers Union, the Consumer's Federation of America, and the National Associated Businessmen.

U.S. STATISTICAL DATA

American Statistics Index

The best place to begin a search for statistical information on the United States is the *American Statistics Index* (*ASI*). This is an indexing and abstracting service that covers virtually all statistical publications of over 300 federal agencies, boards, commissions, committees, regulatory bodies, and independent government corporations. It excludes only classified material, highly technical data, and congressional publications that contain no substantial statistical information. The *ASI* is published in monthly issues, with quarterly cumulated indexes and annual cumulations. The 1974 edition contains retrospective coverage of some materials dating back to 1960. Both the annual and monthly issues are divided into index and abstracts volumes. The index volume directs the searcher to the abstracts volume to find a brief description of the publication containing the desired information. The abstract also provides the call number of the publication and the specific pages for particular statistical tables. The "User Guide" in the front of the annual volume gives detailed instructions for using *ASI*.

General Statistical Sources

Several other federal statistical compilations and guides are basic to any statistical research. These include the annual *Statistical Abstract of the United States, Historical Statistics of the United States,* and *Statistical Services of the United States Government.*

The *Statistical Abstract* has been issued every year since 1878 by the Census Bureau and contains many kinds of aggregated data on U.S. population, government, economy, and numerous categories of resources. Data are reported on the following topics:

Agriculture
Banking, finance, and insurance
Business enterprise
Communications
Comparative international statistics
Construction and housing
Domestic trade and services
Education
Elections
Energy and science
Federal government finances and
  employment
Fisheries
Foreign commerce and aid
Forests and forest products
Geography and environment
Health and nutrition
Immigration and naturalization

Income, expenditures, and wealth
Labor force, employment, and earnings
Law enforcement, federal courts,
  prisons
Manufacturers
Mining and mineral products
National defense and veterans' affairs
Outlying areas under the jurisdiction
  of the United States
Population
Prices
Public lands, parks, recreation,
  and travel
Recent trends
Social insurance and welfare services
Transportation: land, air, and water
Vital statistics

The *Historical Statistics of the United States: Colonial Times to 1970* provides statistical tables covering the first two centuries of U.S. national life. This two-volume set is particularly useful for presenting statistical trends over a number of years. The subjects covered include many of the basic social, economic, and governmental statistics detailed in the *Abstracts* as well as a section entitled "Colonial and Pre-federal Statistics." The explanatory texts preceding the tables in each section are particularly valuable for identifying existing source materials for that topic.

Statistical Services of the United States Government, published by the Office of Management and Budget, is a descriptive and analytical study of the decentralized system of the federal government. It presents an overview of the system, briefly discusses the major economic and social statistical series, and describes the statistical responsibilities and titles of each agency. It has been updated every five to seven years since 1959.

Census Bureau

No guide to federal statistics would be complete without a review of the major series of the Census Bureau. These statistical reports include the massive decennial census of population and housing, the subject censuses taken every fifth year detailing all sectors of the economy, and a variety of annual surveys and reports.

Decennial Censuses.   The activity most often associated with the Census Bureau is the enumeration of the entire U.S. population at the beginning of each decade. Since 1940, the population census has incorporated the decennial housing census. Together these volumes provide data on social, demographic, educational, and economic characteristics of the population as well as statistics on housing quality, value, density, occupancy, and plumbing. The tables provide data for geographic levels from national and regional to state and local—including even some statistics for single city blocks in urbanized areas of 50,000 or more. The smaller the geographic unit, the less detailed is the information available, however, due to concern for privacy.

Economic Censuses.   The five-year economic censuses are taken in years ending in 2 and 7 to avoid the peak activity period of the decennial census. Through 1940, parts of the economic censuses were included in the decennial census. These publications include the following: Agriculture; Business; Construction; Industries; Governments; Manufacturers; Mineral Industries; Transportation.

Current Surveys.   The Census Bureau conducts an ongoing series of surveys, which are issued annually or more frequently. The most important of these reports are the following: *Annual Survey of Manufacturers; County Business Patterns; Current Housing Reports; Current Industrial Reports; Current Population Reports; Current Trade Reports; Government Employment; Government Finances in the United States; State and Local Government Special Studies; World Population.*

STATE AND LOCAL STATISTICAL DATA

The *ASI, SRI, Statistical Abstract, Historical Statistics,* and Census Bureau series not mentioned above contain a wealth of statistical data on states and municipalities. In addition to these sources, there are many specialized titles for research on state and local governments. The *Book of the States,* described earlier, publishes a wide variety of statistical information on state governments. Most states publish their own statistical abstracts or yearbooks, which provide data on state economies, demographics, and politics.

Two additional sources of state and local area statistics can be found in the Census Bureau's *County and City Data Book* and the *State and Metropolitan Area Data Book.* The former has been published roughly every five years since 1947. In addition, the *Municipal Year Book,* published annually for nearly half a century by the International City Management Association (ICMA), is an invaluable reference source of narrative and tabular information for these local government units. The seven chapters cover profiles of individual cities (PICs) for all cities of 10,000 or more residents; intergovernmental relations and problems; local government management style and structure; management issues and trends; directories of elected and appointed officials, associations, and councils; references and guides to further sources of information.

Three Census Bureau series already mentioned—the quinquennial *Census of Governments,* the annual *Government Employment,* and the annual *Government Finances in the United States*—provide statistical information on current and historical characteristics of governmental units at all levels in the United States. The *Census of Governments* is a comprehensive accounting of government organization and structure, elected officials, government employment and payrolls, property valuation and tax assessment, revenues and expenditures, and selected topical studies for national, state, and local governments.

INTERNATIONAL, FOREIGN, AND COMPARATIVE DATA

International Sources

A rapidly growing number of important international and foreign publications can be found. In addition, cross-national compilations of statistical data are increasing as global comparisons are being developed for all areas of public affairs. Some of the major international governmental organizations are introduced here along with a few of the primary statistical series from each.

United Nations

The United Nations (UN) is the basic source for much of the world's economic and demographic statistical data. Most UN publications, both statistical and non-statistical, are indexed in the *UN Documents Index,* the *UNDEX,* and the *UNDOC: Current Index.* A good place to get an overview of the statistical services and series of the UN, its specialized and regional agencies, and a variety of other international organizations is the *Directory of International Statistics,* first issued in 1975 and reissued in updated form in 1982. These volumes, published by the UN Statistical Office, constitute an important guide to international statistical sources, standards, and more recently, computerized data banks.

The UN issues regional statistical bulletins for Africa, Asia and the Far East, Europe, Latin America, and most other areas of the world. In addition to these regional bulletins, the UN publishes the following titles: *World Economic Survey; Demographic Yearbook; Statistical Yearbook; Yearbook of National Accounts; Yearbook of International Trade; Monthly Bulletin of Statistics.*

International Finance

The International Bank for Reconstruction and Development (IBRD), better known as the World Bank, is another vital source of world economic and financial information. The bank and its affiliated institution, the International Monetary Fund (IMF), publish several important series providing statistics on both the developed and the developing worlds. These publications include the following: *World Development Report* (IBRD); *World Tables* (IBRD); *International Financial Statistics* (monthly, IMF); *Balance of Payments Yearbook* (IMF); *Government Finances Statistical Yearbook* (IMF); *World Economic Outlook* (IMF).

Industrialized Nations

The European Community (EC) and the Organization for Economic Cooperation and Development (OECD) are regional intergovernmental organizations representing European and other industrialized countries. Both organizations publish ongoing statistical series on agriculture, energy, foreign trade, industrial production, labor force, and social indicators. The EC Statistical Office issues over 100 statistical titles. The following major sources of data are available from these two international bodies: *Basic Statistics of the Community* (EC); *Eurostatistics* (EC); *Economic Survey of OECD Member Countries* (OECD); *OECD Economic Outlook* (OECD); *Main Economic Indicators* (monthly, OECD); *OECD Statistical Bulletin: Foreign Trade* (monthly), including *Overall Trade by Countries, Analytical Abstracts,* and *Commodity Trade.*

Developing Nations

Developing nations of the Third World have established a number of intergovernmental associations with statistical reporting systems of their own. These regions are represented by the statistical bulletins of the UN regional commissions noted earlier, but these independent organizations also issue many significant statistical documents. Major organizations and their publications include the following: Organization of American States (OAS), *Statistical Bulletin of the OAS;* Caribbean Community (CARICOM), *Digest of Trade Statistics* and *National Accounts Statistics;* Asian Development Bank (ADB), *Key Indicators of Developing Member Countries of ADB;* Organization of Petroleum Exporting Countries (OPEC), *Annual Statistical Bulletin.*

Social Statistics

Although most of the international publications listed here deal with economic, financial, and trade data, a number of international organizations issue social, demographic, and cultural statistics, including quality of life measures such as health, crime, labor, communications, and educational attainment. Some significant organizations and their publications are as follows: World Health Organization (WHO), *World Health Statistics Annual;* International Criminal Police Organization (INTERPOL), *International Crime Statistics;* International Labor Organization (ILO), *Yearbook of Labor Statistics;* International Telecommunication Union (ITU), *Yearbook of Common Carrier Telecommunication Statistics;* United Nations Educational, Scientific, and Cultural Organization (UNESCO), *Statistical Yearbook* and *Statistical Digest.*

Index to International Statistics

Two factors hampering the timely and effective use of many international statistical publications have been the lack of awareness of their existence and the absence of a comprehensive cataloging and indexing system. Both of these problems have been answered by the *Index to International Statistics* (*IIS*), a master guide to international statistical publications. The *IIS,* which began publication in 1983, is published by the producer of the *CMF, ASI,* and *SRI* already described. The organization and format of the *IIS* is similar to that of the other three systems. Monthly index and abstract volumes catalog, index, and summarize the commissions as well as the EC, OECD, OAS, and about 30 other intergovernmental organizations. Indexing provides access by subject, title, and geographical area.

Foreign Yearbooks

Sources of foreign and comparative international statistical data issued by foreign governments are too numerous to list. Researchers needing to find foreign statistical data should remember that foreign government publications are normally in the language of the country, although many nations do issue English translations or multilingual versions of their national statistical abstracts. Frequently, a foreign language yearbook is fairly simple to interpret with the aid of a dictionary or a basic knowledge of the language as the data are presented in Arabic numerals and the table headings are typically single words or short phrases.

Foreign Censuses

Censuses of foreign nations can be particularly valuable sources of basic national information. The *International Population Census Bibliography,* a project of the Population Research Center of the University of Texas, is a master guide to national population censuses. Six volumes cover Latin America, Africa, Oceania, North America, Asia, and Europe. Each volume is arranged alphabetically by country and chronologically by year of census. Bibliographic citations follow each entry identifying and describing published population reports from the earliest verified census in each country to 1967. Another volume, the *International Population Census Bibliography: Revision and Update, 1945–1977,* brings the project up-to-date and provides additional citations for the period from 1945 to 1967.

U.S. Sources

The U.S. government publishes a vast range of statistical information on foreign countries, dealing with trade, economics, politics, demographics, agriculture, arms and disarmament, and social statistics. A few of the more important series and titles are listed now along with their issuing agencies.

Agriculture.   The Foreign Agricultural Service (FAS) and the Economic Research Service (ERS) of the U.S. Agriculture Department issue a number of documents detailing world agricultural conditions and markets. Among these publications are the following: *Foreign Agriculture* (monthly, FAS); *FAS Report: Weekly Roundup of World Production and Trade* (FAS); *World Agricultural Production and Trade Statistical Report* (FAS), superseded by *World Agricultural Supply and Demand Estimates* (FAS); *World Crop Production* (FAS); *Foreign Agricultural Trade of the United States* (ERS).

Commerce.   The Commerce Department also produces numerous studies and reports on world trade and commercial activities and conditions in various countries. A sampling of titles includes: *Global Market Surveys* (for commodity groups); *Overseas Business Reports; Foreign Economic Trends and Their Implications for the United States; U.S. Direct Investment Abroad.*

Demography.   The Census Bureau has an active international statistics program. Its publications include statistical summaries of selected foreign countries and projections of global population: *Country Demographic Profiles; Illustrative Projections of World Populations to the 21st Century* (1979); *World Population.*

Intelligence.   The Central Intelligence Agency (CIA) is the source of many publications giving vital information about foreign countries. The CIA publishes maps, directories, analytical reports, and statistical compilations on many nations. Major titles include the following: *World Factbook,* formerly *National Basic Intelligence Factbook; Chiefs of State and Cabinet Members of Foreign Governments; Handbook of Economic Statistics; International Economic and Energy Statistical Review.*

Diplomacy and Foreign Relations.   The State Department publishes many series, studies, newsletters, and other documents dealing with all aspects of U.S. relations with foreign nations. Several of the more useful reference publications are as follows: *Background Notes; Diplomatic List; U.S. Overseas Loans and Grants; The Planetary Product* (global GNP estimates); and *Post Reports* (of foreign service posts).

Disarmament.   The Arms Control and Disarmament Agency (ACDA) publishes a variety of documents, reprints of speeches, analytical pamphlets, and a statistical compilation of the global trade in arms. Two significant ACDA titles are the following: *Documents on Disarmament* and *World Military Expenditures.*

Human Services.   The agencies concerned with social and human services also issue international and foreign studies and statistics. The Departments of Education, of Health and Human Services, of Housing and Urban Development, and of Labor issue the following titles respectively: *Education around the World* (The educational systems of specific countries); *Syncrisis: The Dynamics of Health; HUD International Country Profiles;* and *Country Labor Profiles.*

Army Area Handbooks.   Finally, the most comprehensive studies done on foreign countries by the U.S. government are the *Area Handbooks,* researched by the Foreign Area Studies of the American University in Washington, D.C., and published by the Department of the Army. These volumes are designed to aid foreign service and military personnel assigned to overseas posts, but their broad scope and authoritative coverage make them valuable for academic research as well. The *Area Handbooks* contain historical, geographical, political, social, cultural, economic, and statistical information for about 100 countries. Extensive bibliographies allow researchers to find additional reference material on the country. The only drawback lies in the infrequency of the revisions. Handbooks for some countries are eight to ten years old before a new edition is published.

International and Foreign Yearbooks

The *Europa Year Book,* published since 1926, is one of the most useful compilations of international and foreign data. In two volumes, the *Europa* presents a wide variety of narrative, statistical, and directory information on hundreds of international organizations, approximately 220 nations and territories, and cross-country comparisons. Background information on countries includes recent history, government, economy, industry, mining, finance, trade, education, transportation, and communications. Names of officials and addresses of organizations are listed for government, diplomacy, business, publishing, religion, and other categories.

The *Statesman's Year-Book,* published annually for over a century, is a world survey of international organizations and over 300 countries, territories, and states, including the 50 U.S. states. The format is similar to the *Europa,* but this is a much more compact volume. Special features include comparative statistical tables on major agricultural commodities, petroleum, territorial sea limits, and an index of products.

The *International Yearbook and Statesmen's Who's Who,* published since 1953 in the United Kingdom, is another authoritative source of national and international information updated each year. The first half contains descriptive essays of major international organizations, organizational charts of the foreign ministries of the five great powers, and narrative and statistical surveys of all countries, territories, and states. The second half gives biographical sketches of world leaders in government, business, industry, publishing, media, education, and religion.

PUBLIC OPINION, ELECTIONS, AND GROUPS

Students can also find several cumulative printed indexes to public opinion polls. The U.S. guide includes *The Gallup Opinion Index* (1965–1981), which was followed by its continuation in *The Gallup Report* (1981 to the present). Foreign public opinion data are collected in two volumes: *The Gallup International Public Opinion Polls, Great Britain,* 1937–1975; and *The Gallup International Public Opinion Polls, France,* 1939 and 1944–1975.

Several additional reference works and indexes on public opinion include: *The Harris Survey Yearbook of Public Opinion,* 1970–1973; *Current Opinion,* 1973–1978; and *Public Opinion Quarterly,* 1937 to present. Moreover, several titles are published by Congressional Quarterly, Inc., and provide detailed statistical data on elections, voting records of national politicians, and political processes.

Finally, there is some information about interest groups and associations. One compilation is Frederick G. Ruffner and Margaret Fisk (eds.), *Encyclopedia of Associations,* 15th ed. (Detroit: Gale Research Company), published annually. One compilation of public-sector interest groups is found in Roy Jumper and Steve Gutnayer, *What's What in Public Sector Professional Associations: A National Guide* (Bloomington, Ind.: Midwest Intergovernmental Training Committee, 1977). Finally, many associations conduct their own surveys and collect data of interest to their memberships; an example is the International City Managers Association's Municipal Data Service (MDS).

SOCIAL AND SCIENTIFIC INDICATORS

Social Indicators

One of the newer areas of policy analysis is the study of social indicators—data describing the noneconomic dimensions of national quality of life such as health, culture, safety, environment, education, employment, Social Security, and mobility. The Office of Management and Budget published *Social Indicators 1973,* the first volume of a series later continued by the Census Bureau. *Social Indicators 1976* expanded the first version, adding several chapters, including "Social Mobility and Participation." *Social Indicators III,* published in 1980, is the volume of the series adding material on transportation and environmental concerns. The second and third reports provide international statistical comparisons as well as attitudinal measures of public perception. In general, the data are presented in an objective, noninterpretive manner. The latest volume includes two appendices: "Principal Sources and Quality of the Data" and "Glossary of Terms."

Scientific Indicators

Another field of growing importance is the study of scientific indicators. The lead agency in this area has been the National Science Foundation (NSF). Every other year since 1972, the annual reports issued by the National Science Board of the NSF have been titled *Science Indicators.* These volumes present narrative and statistical data on a wide range of scientific and technological activities, finances, and personnel at the national and international levels. A series of related reports by the NSF include the following: *Science and Engineering Personnel: A National Overview; National Patterns of Science and Technology Resources; Academic Science: R & D Funds;* and *Annual Science and Technology Report to Congress.*

Several other agencies also publish recurring titles describing various aspects of the state of science and technology in the United States. The Department of Energy issues a *National Survey of Compensation Paid Scientists and Engineers in R & D Activities.* The National Aeronautics and Space Administration (NASA) is the source of many technical reports and surveys of scientific progress. Notable among these are the *Aeronautics and Space Report of the President* and *Spinoff: An Annual Report.* This last report is a full-color review of new technology generated by NASA programs with beneficial applications in industry, energy, health, safety, and many other areas outside the aerospace field.

ENERGY AND ENVIRONMENTAL SOURCES

A great deal of public policy analysis and formulation concerns the public and private use of renewable and nonrenewable natural resources. In particular, the consumption of vegetable and mineral resources for energy generation leads directly or indirectly to many environmental problems. Thus, the areas of energy and environmental protection are inextricably woven together. Nowhere is this fact more graphically demonstrated than in the *Global 2000 Report to the President,* a joint effort of the Council on Environmental Quality and the State Department. Commissioned by President Jimmy Carter in 1977 and published in 1980, this three-volume study is the most comprehensive and detailed attempt yet in print for forecasting in quantitative and qualitative terms the state of humankind and the planet in 2000. Projections are made for population, income, climate, agriculture and fisheries, forestry, water, energy, fuel and nonfuel minerals, and the environmental consequences likely to accompany all of these anticipated changes.

Energy Sources

The following indexes, abstracts, and reference works provide a good starting point for researching energy and energy-related information; reports and indexes are issued on an annual basis except where noted: *The Energy Index; Energy and Technology Review; Energy Abstracts for Policy Analysis; Energy: A Continuing Bibliography with Indexes; Energy Information Directory; Energy Information, Quarterly Report to Congress;*

Energy Insider; Energy Research Abstracts; EIA Publications—New Releases (monthly); *Energy: A Guide to Organizations and Information Sources in the U.S.; McGraw-Hill Encyclopedia of Energy.*

Environmental Sources

The following indexes, abstracts, and other reference works on environmental science constitute only a partial list of available guides in the field: *Environment Index; Environment Abstracts; Pollution Abstracts; EPA Publications Bibliography: Quarterly Abstract Bulletin; EPA Journal; Environment Midwest; Environment Health Perspectives; Environmental Quality* (CEQ Annual Report); *102 Monitor; Congress and the Nation's Environment; McGraw-Hill Encyclopedia of Environmental Science.* In addition, students interested in researching international environmental problems should also consult the publications of the UN Environment Programme and many other intergovernmental organizations.

LABOR AND EMPLOYMENT, EARNINGS AND PRICES

Labor and Occupational Information

The Bureau of Labor Statistics (BLS) of the U.S. Labor Department is the primary source for statistics, directories, and analytical studies of the U.S. labor market. Two monthly BLS periodicals, *Monthly Labor Review* and *Employment and Earnings,* provide detailed and up-to-date labor force information in statistical and narrative form.

The *Monthly Labor Review* contains historical studies, analytical articles on current labor issues, and reports on trends in employment and unemployment. It has a statistical supplement presenting summary labor statistics for preceding months and years. *Employment and Earnings* consists almost entirely of statistical tables detailing household and establishment data, employment and unemployment characteristics, and average earnings by states, cities, industries, and occupations.

The *Occupational Outlook Handbook* is a guide to career information on about 250 occupations grouped into 20 broad categories. This is a comprehensive source of current information on job descriptions, working conditions, areas of employment, earnings, educational requirements, training and advancement, and the future outlook for each occupation. A related title is the *Occupational Outlook Quarterly,* which reports on current vocational trends, presents in-depth articles on selected job areas, and highlights new or unusual work opportunities. Both are published by the BLS.

The categories used in the *Handbook* are based on the *Standard Occupational Classification Manual,* compiled by the Office of Federal Statistical Policy and Standards. A related publication, issued by the Employment and Training Administration of the Labor Department, is the *Dictionary of Occupational Titles.* This volume, now in its fourth edition, provides detailed definitions for about 20,000 jobs. These job descriptions are organized into a nine-digit numbering system, which groups occupations together into broad categories and then into more specific divisions and groups.

Consumer and Producer Prices

The rate of inflation in the United States is based in large part on the federal government's measurement of increases or decreases in consumer and producer prices. Several periodicals published by the BLS comprise the official accounting of monthly price changes. These include: the *Consumer Price Index;* the *CPI Detailed Report;* and the *Producer Price Indexes.* The *Consumer Price Index* is used as a monthly newsletter, presenting summary price information for major commodity groups and consumer expenditure categories, such as housing, food, health care, utilities, transportation, and miscellaneous items; while some data are provided for major cities, most of the statistics are nationwide. The *CPI Detailed Report* is a much more comprehensive monthly accounting of average price changes broken down by expenditure categories, commodity and service groups, consumer categories, regions, and major metropolitan areas. Tables present price changes for current and preceding months and indicate both unadjusted and seasonally adjusted data.

The *Producer Price Indexes,* also in newsletter format, give a similar account of price changes at the producer and wholesale trade level. This is the successor to the *Wholesale Price Index,* reflecting changes at three stages of processing: crude, intermediate, and finished goods. Many economists regard this as a more accurate measure of inflationary trends.

A nongovernmental source of consumer price information can be found in the *Inter-City Cost of Living Indicators,* published by the U.S. Chamber of Commerce Researcher's Association. This quarterly report provides indexes and prices for detailed commodities by city. It publishes the results of a survey of over 200 U.S. cities and presents comparisons among all cities responding to the survey. Data are reported in three sections: (1) All-Cities Index, (2) Metropolitan Cities Index, and (3) Price Report.

HISTORICAL AND CURRENT PROBLEMS

It is frequently necessary to know the dates or sequences of important events or the facts about historical and current events. Five publications are particularly helpful. The largest is the *Annual Register of Historical Events,* a British digest that has been published annually since 1758. Second, *Keesing's Contemporary Archives* is a weekly, comprehensive, worldwide reporting service, which tends to emphasize British and Commonwealth affairs, like the *Annual Register.* Third, *Facts on File* is a weekly publication produced in the United States and therefore presents a U.S. point of view. Fourth, speeches by leaders in government and diplomacy, business and industry, education, economics, media, and other public affairs fields are reprinted in a bimonthly publication called *Vital Speeches of the Day;* an annual publication that reprints major speeches delivered in the United States is *Representative American Speeches.*

Finally, researchers interested in current social and political problems from a legal point of view should be aware of the three major publishers of loose-leaf reports: Commerce Clearing House (CCH), Bureau of National Affairs (BNA), and Prentice Hall. These take the form of large ring binders in which updated reports can be inserted weekly or even daily to keep up with rapidly changing problem areas such as environmental law, labor relations, tax policy, and pending legislation. The three reporting services also issue a variety of special studies.

PERIODICALS AND PERIODICAL INDEXES

Major Periodical Indexes

There are four main periodical indexes for public affairs literature. One of the most basic and comprehensive is the *Public Affairs Information Service (PAIS)*, which has been indexing public affairs literature since 1915. *PAIS* covers almost 1,400 journals as well as many books, bibliographies, directories, and government documents.

The *Social Sciences Citation Index (SSCI)* is a second indexing service that provides extensive coverage of the social science literature, including reviews, editorials, proceedings, and over 2,000 journals. *SSCI* is referred to as "an international interdisciplinary index to the literature of the social, behavioral, and related sciences." Coverage began in 1966, with a five-year cumulative edition for 1966 to 1970. It is issued annually thereafter. In addition to the more familiar author and subject indexes, *SSCI* has a unique feature called the citation index in which authors cited in other publications are arranged alphabetically, followed by references to the articles in which they are cited. Thus researchers can locate all places in which an author has appeared in a footnote in another article or publication, and can also identify and locate related social science materials.

The third and fourth series consist of the *Reader's Guide to Periodical Literature,* which generally covers popular magazines from 1900 to the present, and its companion publication, the *International Index to Periodicals.* The *International Index* is more scholarly and cites many foreign and specialized journal articles. Historians should note that in 1965 the name changed to the *Social Sciences and Humanities Index,* which, in 1974, was separated into *Social Sciences Index* and *Humanities Index.*

Newspaper Indexes

Many major newspapers also publish indexes of which the following major newspaper indexes are particularly important guides to the contents of some of the nation's most important newspapers, including: the *Baltimore Sun; Chicago Tribune; Christian Science Monitor; Dallas Times; The Los Angeles Times; The National Observer; The New York Times; Philadelphia Inquirer; The Times* (London); *The Wall Street Journal;* the *Washington Post.* The most-read newspapers are significant both for the news they originate as well as the weight of the editorial interpretations they provide. Because of the quality and originality of articles and editorials, their staff reporters and editorial writers are often syndicated throughout the newspaper publishing world.

QUICK GUIDE TO THE INTERNET

Cruising on the information highway can be fun and productive if the traveler knows what he or she is doing and is prepared for the constantly changing array of on- and off-ramps, detours, roadblocks, and limited access side roads characteristic of information age infrastructure. Once one understands the logic and constantly changing character of this new transportation system, including the fact that both the maps and the structures to which the maps refer are constantly changing, the prospects for productive use of a powerful new information tool can more readily be appreciated.

Definitions

Metaphors are used to characterize the structures, processes, and activities involving information technology. Thus, some are fond of fishing in a "vast and expanding ocean" in which there are waves of technology and change; here it becomes important to stay afloat and navigate. Alternatively, others invoke images of physical infrastructure, as in the Information Superhighway, for which there are maps, roadways, and access ramps negotiated with varying speeds to move from origin to destination.

The Internet is the precursor of what will eventually become the Information Superhighway.[2] It is a loosely linked collection of nearly 2.5 million mainframe and personal computers around the world involving an estimated 50 million users. The Internet exists as a network or networks and thus as a *virtual* network; it has the appearance of a network even though its foundation is unplanned and unmanaged. This feature presents a source both of great confusion and great potential. The Internet provides two kinds of communication services: interactive conversation and access information stored in libraries. Conversation can occur in several forms, including e-mail (i.e., real-time conversation) and bulletins. The possibilities for conversational connections are literally worldwide and provide for unedited discussions on any subject with anyone willing to respond. Bulletin boards are another conversational device, where thousands of messages and announcements organized by subject are posted by people who either know something and want to share or do not know something and seek help on a specific subject.

The Internet is also a massive library, consisting of stock information, classic novels, pornography, electronic newstands, book reviews, and databases of every shape and size. Sorting through such a massive set of possibilities and accessing the information that is desired poses a major challenge: how does one wade through a sea of junk in order to find a few nuggets of desired information? The problem involves finding ways to *browse* through the list of possibilities, *search* for relevant information, and *fetch* desired data and information. Expertise in these tasks can involve a learning curve that comes from simply getting on the net and learning to navigate in cyberspace. Happily, some tools are available to assist the Internet surfer.

University students will be pleased to discover that on most campuses they do not have to spend the equivalent of a $1,000 to $1,500 to buy a computer and software fast and large enough to access the highway, as well as a communication device, specialized software, phone connection, and access to a gateway that lets the user on the highway. Fortunately, the public access sites on many campuses are already configured with hardware, software, and connections that allow students to operate some of the major Internet tools, such as Archie, Gopher, MUD, Veronica, WAIS (swais), World Wide Web (with point and shoot graphical software, such as Mosaic or Netscape), HYTELNET, WHOIS, CNIDR, and LEXIS-NEXIS. The list of browse, search, and fetch engines is growing constantly.

Illustrative Uses

The only way to appreciate the actual and potential applications of the Internet is to log on and start pushing buttons in response to specific information needs. Students are encouraged to spend a little time just fiddling with the systems to see what is out there. However, the time allocated to idle exploration should be controlled by one's schedule and patience. Students and ordinary citizens will want to be able to connect with key public affairs sources without leaving the comforts of hearth and computer. This access is easily achieved by linking with major university gateways and thus to a large number of search and browse engines. Alternately, sources can be approached directly by means of the universal resource locator (URL) that provides the end user with a direct connection. Among the most prominent URLs in the public sector are World Wide Web nodes and Gopher addresses; the former act merely as computer server nodes in an electronic spider web, and the latter appear as end-point addresses in a "gopher tunnel."

World Wide Web
National Performance Review: http://www.npr.gov/
U.S. Census Information Server: http://www.census.gov/
U.S. Legislative Branch Resources: http://lcweb.loc.gov/global/congress.html
U.S. Executive Branch Resources: http://lcweb.loc.gov/global/executive.html
White House: http://www/whitehouse.gov/
Social Security Administration: http://www.ssa.gov/
Federal technical information: http://www.fedworld.gov/

Gopher
Government Information Sources: gopher://gopher.oar.net
North American Free Trade Agreement: gopher://wiretap.spies.com Or gopher://gopher.scs.unr.edu
U.S. Department of Urban Development: gopher://gopher.hud.gov
Congressional Quarterly: gopher://gopher.cqalert.com
Congress: gopher://marvel.loc.gov
President's Economic Plan: gopher://wiretap.spies.com

Users should note that the URLs and addresses are *case sensitive.* Users should also note the enormous size of the internet which in some estimates doubles in size every few months.

NOTES

1. Adapted from Eugene B. McGregor, Jr., and Nels Gunderson, *Lazy Person's Guide to Public Affairs Statistics and Information Sources: The Third Generation* (Bloomington, Ind.: School of Public and Environmental Affairs, August 1992).

2. The classic introduction to the Internet is Adam Engst's best-selling *Internet Starter Kit,* 2d edition. Another concise introduction is Paul Gilster, *Finding It on the Internet* (New York: John Wiley & Sons, Inc. 1994). A succinct depiction of a broad array of on-line services can be found in: Dylan Tweney, *The Traveler's Guide to the Information Highway* (Emeryville, Calif.: Ziff-Davis, 1994). In addition, new books appear practically every month; for example, see: Bruce Maxwell, *Washington Online: How to Access the Federal Government on the Internet 1995* (Washington, D.C.: Congressional Quarterly, 1995).

Glossary

Absolute poverty   A statistical measure of poverty that uses a fixed benchmark, such as money income, to identify a poverty line. Distinguished from relative poverty, below which people are said to be poor.

Act to Regulate Commerce of 1887   The federal law that gave rise to the Interstate Commerce Commission in response to monopoly practices of the railroads.

Aid to Families with Dependent Children (AFDC)   As the cornerstone of the U.S. welfare system, AFDC, created by the Social Security Act (1935), provides cash benefits to assist needy families with children under the age of 18. Paid by federal-state contract in which the federal government pays a 50 to 66 percent share of the program costs.

America 2000   The Bush Administration's precursor to Goals 2000.

American Federation of Labor-Congress of Industrial Organizations (AFL-CIO) A voluntary federation of over 100 national and international unions operating in the United States. The AFL-CIO was created to represent the affiliated unions in the creation and execution of broad national and international policies and in coordinating a wide range of joint activities.

Arrow's Paradox   The demonstration by economist Kenneth Arrow that the rules of democracy, particularly the principles of majority rule and equality of voting, do not necessarily produce logically consistent policy choices. Indeed, policy contradictions can occur when as few as three people or factions each have different policy preferences and each person's preference ordering counts the same. A process of political decision making is required to break the intellectual deadlock.

Asia Pacific Economic Cooperation Group (APEC)   Established in 1989 to encourage economic cooperation in Asia/Pacific region. Includes 18 nations bordering the region, including the United States, Canada, Australia, New Zealand, Mexico, and Chile.

Asian Development Bank   A multilateral development bank whose primary aims are to promote economic and social development in the Asian and Pacific region by lending funds and providing technical cooperation to countries in the region.

Association of South East Asian Nations (ASEAN)   A regional alliance of countries located in South East Asia whose mission is to foster economic growth, social progress, and cultural development in the region.

Brady Handgun Violence Prevention Act   Popularly known as the Brady Bill, it is designed as a first step to register all handguns bought and sold in the United States.

Brown v. Board of Education (1954)   Landmark Supreme Court decision holding that the separation of children by race in public schools is unconstitutional, violating the equal protection clause of the Fourteenth Amendment.

Budget deficit   An excess of expenditure flow over income flow.

Capitalism   An economic system that permits the private ownership of the means of production.

Categorical logic   A welfare policy logic where a government action may be invoked when an accredited government agency must first find that a client belongs to a category eligible for government service or assistance, such as being poor, disabled, unemployed, or elderly, before receiving public assistance.

Charter schools   An institutional arrangement designed to break the monopoly power held by educational authorities by allowing more than one organization to offer public education in the community.

Checks and Balances   Constitutional doctrine that provides for each of the three branches of government to exercise powers granted to the other two branches, such as when a president (chief executive) vetoes legislation or nominates judges to serve in the district, appellate, and supreme courts.

Chlorofluorocarbons (CFCOs)   Chemical compound that is believed to deplete the layer of ozone in the upper atmosphere.

Citistates   Geographic clusters of related industries, supported by networks of local world-class research institutes, specialized business services, a work force with specialized skills, and demanding and knowledgeable local consumers who set the pace for global markets.

Clayton Act of 1914   The federal law that extended the Sherman Act's prohibition against monopolies and price discrimination. Further, it exempted labor unions from antitrust laws and limited the jurisdiction of courts in issuing injunctions against labor organizations.

Clean Air Act   A federal statute to protect public health and welfare from the effects of air pollution. Through this act national air quality standards and specific automobile emission standards were established.

Clean Water Act   A federal statute on restoring and maintaining the chemical, physical, and biological integrity of the nation's waters.

Communism   An economic system that is based on public ownership of all productive wealth and much consumption wealth.

Community Action Programs (CAP)   War on Poverty programs to develop centers of community leadership and civic participation in poor communities.

Comparative advantage   A general principle explaining the condition under which mutually profitable trade between two economic regions can occur.

Council of Economic Advisors (CEA)   As a part of the Executive Office of the President, this council consists of three economists, appointed by the president with the advice and consent of the senate, who assist in making fiscal policy.

Current account balance   The portion of a nation's balance of payments that is a record of all trade (exports and imports) between a nation and the rest of the world.

Democracy   A form of government in which rule is by the people, implying that elections are held to determine the popular will.

Depression   An extended period of economic restructuring and institutional change that is marked by stagnant growth or decline (unemployment levels are usually higher and the inflation rates lower than in a recession).

Design standard   A pollution standard in which the polluter must use a particular pollution abatement device in a given facility.

Earned Income Tax Credit (EITC)   Federal legislation permitting payroll tax reduction for the working poor, who are allowed to pay lower taxes (a tax credit) as a result of income level and family size. Amended several times since 1975 as a means of providing federal cash assistance to persons whose income falls below the poverty line.

Economy of scale   The reduction in average unit cost associated with the increase in the size of plant or activity up to a point and thereafter an increase in such cost.

Environmental Protection Agency (EPA)   Federal agency created to permit coordinated and effective governmental action on behalf of the environment. The primary mission of the EPA is to abate and control pollution systematically by proper integration of a variety of research, monitoring, standard setting, and enforcement activities.

Equal Employment and Opportunity Commission (EEOC)   Created by Title VII of the Civil Rights Act of 1964, the EEOC's mission is to end discrimination based on race, color, religion, sex, or national origin in hiring, promotion, firing, wages, testing, training, apprenticeship, and all other conditions of employment and to promote voluntary action programs by employers, unions, and community organizations to make equal employment opportunity an actuality.

European Community (EC)   A forerunner of the European Union (see below).

European Monetary System (EMS)   A voluntary system of semifixed exchange rates between several of the member countries of the European Union.

European Union (EU)   An organization of 15 Western European nations designed to foster economic cooperation and common development, with the eventual aim of economic and monetary union together with a measure of political unity.

Exchange rate   The price of one currency in terms of another currency.

Exports   The goods and services sold to citizens of another country plus the services furnished to the citizens of the foreign country in shipping, financing, and otherwise facilitating the export.

Externalities   Economically, externalities are costs or benefits not taken into account in a transaction or system of transactions.

Family and Medical Leave Act of 1993   Federal legislation granting the right of unpaid leave to employed persons confronting emergencies of family care.

Family Support Act of 1988   Sweeping federal legislation designed to support families in the administration of welfare programs, including attaching the wages of "deadbeat dads" and permitting experimental changes by states in merging welfare programs with employment and training programs.

Federal Aviation Administration (FAA)   A federal administration housed within the Department of Transportation whose primary mission is to regulate air commerce in ways that best promote its development and safety.

Federal Bureau of Investigations (FBI)   As principle investigative arm of the U.S. Department of Justice, the FBI is charged with gathering and reporting facts, locating witnesses, and compiling evidence in matters in which the federal government is, or may be, a party of interest.

Federal Communications Commission (FCC)   Federal agency that regulates interstate and foreign communications by radio, television, wire, and cable.

Federal Deposit Insurance Corporation (FDIC)   Federal body established to promote and preserve public confidence in banks and to protect the money supply through the provision of insurance coverage for bank deposits.

Federal Emergency Management Agency (FEMA)   Federal agency that is accountable for emergency preparedness and response for all levels of government and for all types of emergencies (natural, manmade, and nuclear).

Federal Energy Regulatory Commission   An independent five-member commission within the Department of Energy that sets the rates and charges for the transportation and sale of natural gas and electricity, and oversees the licensing of hydroelectric projects.

Federal Home Loan Bank Board   Federal body that supervises and regulates savings and loan organizations.

Federal Maritime Commission   Federal agency that regulates the waterborne foreign and domestic offshore commerce of the United States, assures that U.S. international trade is open to all nations on fair and equitable terms, and guards against unauthorized monopoly in the waterborne commerce of the United States.

Federal Reserve System   The central bank of the United States charged with administering and making policy for the nation's credit and monetary affairs. The system includes twelve Federal Reserve Banks, 25 branches, and several committees.

Federal Savings & Loan Insurance Corporation (FSLIC)   Run by the Federal Home Loan Bank Board, the FSLIC protects the savings of Americans with savings accounts in FSLIC-insured savings and loan associations.

Federal Trade Commission (FTC)   An independent federal agency run by a five-member commission that is charged by Congress with preventing unfair and deceptive business activities and monopoly practices that inhibit competition.

Federalism   A mode of political organization that divides power among general and constituent governments in a manner designed to protect the existence and authority of both national and subnational political systems, such as states, enabling all to share in a decision-making and policy execution.

The Federalist   The pamphlets written under the pseudonym "Publius" produced by John Jay, Alexander Hamilton and James Madison following the Constitutional Convention of 1787. The papers explained why the Constitution should be adopted.

Fiscal policy The portion of government policy concerned with raising revenue through taxation and other means and deciding on the level and pattern of expenditure. Through this policy the government has some control over the level of aggregate demand in the economy and, thus, over the rate of new job creation and, to some extent, the rate of inflation.

Food and Drug Administration (FDA) The federal agency that aims to protect the health of U.S. citizens against impure and unsafe foods, drugs, and cosmetics.

Frictional unemployment Unemployment resulting from the time lags involved in the redeployment of labor.

Full employment An economic situation in which all those who want to work are able to find employment. Full employment levels usually entail unemployment rates between 3 to 6 percent, since frictional unemployment and structural unemployment (see below) always exist.

Full Employment Act of 1946 An Act of the U.S. Congress that mandated the government to use all practicable means to achieve maximum employment, production, and purchasing power. Created the Council of Economic Advisors.

General Agreement on Tariffs and Trade (GATT) A multilateral trade agreement containing guidelines for conduct of international trade based on three basic principles: nondiscriminatory treatment of all signatories in trade matters; eventual elimination of tariff and nontariff barriers to trade; and resolution through consultation of conflicts or damages arising from trade actions of another signatory.

Gerrymander The intentional design of political boundaries of noncontiguous districts to ensure that a majority of a given political party exists within the boundary.

G.I. Bill Serviceman's Readjustment Act of 1944 that pays for college education for returning veterans.

Goals 2000 Federal strategy of education reform passed by the Educate America Act of 1994 that aims to create a "World-Class Education for Every Child" through a series of goals and standards.

Government A social institution empowered to make decisions for a whole society or community.

Grant Sometimes referred to as a grant-in-aid. Producer subsidy financed with government financial assistance. May be targeted through categorical grants or distributed as a block grant covering a wide spectrum of needs.

Gross Domestic Product (GDP) The money value of all final goods and services produced in an economy during a given time period. GDP is considered a measure of aggregate production of the economy during that time period.

Gross National Product (GNP) GNP plus the production of U.S. citizens or companies that occurs outside of the United States.

Group of Seven (G-7) Composed of the heads of state of the seven major industrialized nations who meet periodically to coordinate economic policy. Includes the United States, France, Germany, Great Britain, Canada, Italy, and Japan.

Health Maintenance Organization (HMO) A health organization that maintains clinics and hospitals and supplies physician and health care specialist care and medication based on a fixed annual fee per person (capitation financing).

Homestead Act of 1862   Granted public land to settlers on condition that they live on the land and make it productive. While the first homestead law was signed by President Lincoln in 1862, homestead laws were used to settle the West.

Human Capital   A concept that views human workers as assets in the same sense as financial capital rather than simply as costs to be minimized.

Human Resource Capitalism   The public policy strategy for economic growth that emphasizes investing heavily in the education and training of people as the basis for securing a competitive economic position.

Ideology   The combined doctrines, assertions, and intentions with which a social or political group justifies its behavior.

Import quota   The fixed amount of goods that may be imported.

Imports   Commodities or services bought from foreign countries.

Inflation   A period when purchasing power of a monetary unit is falling.

Institutional agenda   The composite of public policy issues that, at any particular time, have reached the action stage of consideration by government.

Internal Revenue Service (IRS)   Federal agency within the Treasury Department that is responsible for administering and enforcing the internal revenue laws, except those relating to alcohol, tobacco, firearms, and explosives.

International Monetary Fund (IMF)   Established by the Bretton Woods (1944) conference, this fund was designed to meet the requirements of international monetary cooperation.

Interstate Commerce Commission (ICC)   Federal commission that regulates interstate surface transportation, including trains, trucks, buses, inland waterway and coastal shipping, freight forwarders, and express companies.

Iron Law   Every act of government creates winners and losers within the competitive sector of the economy.

Iron Triangle   A public policy coalition of institutions and individuals that is more or less fixed in its membership and focus.

Issue attention cycle   The phases through which a public policy issue passes as it moves toward public visibility and prominence.

Laissez-faire   Term that generally refers to the lack of governmental interference in the economy.

Land Ordinance of 1785   The first national K-12 education policy that under the Articles of Confederation required that land surveyed in the Northwest Territories be parceled out with a fixed amount of land allocated to the support of public education.

Medicaid   Federal-state program that pays for medical care for the poor.

Medicare   The U.S. federal program that pays for health care services for the elderly and the disabled.

Monetary policy   Government policy efforts to manage the money supply in the economy in the pursuit of macro economic goals, such as low inflation, low unemployment, and high rates of economic growth.

Monopoly   A market situation in which there is only one producer/seller of a good or service.

Morrill Act of 1860   Federal education legislation that established the land-grant system of colleges and universities in which Congress gave land to states for the support of programs in agriculture and mechanical arts.

National Academy of Public Administration (NAPA)   Organization of distinguished practitioners and scholars in public administration dedicated to improving public management in the United States.

National Aeronautics and Space Administration (NASA)   A federal agency whose main function is to conduct research and development on the problems of flight within and outside the earth's atmosphere and to explore outer space.

National Defense Education Act   A 1958 act to strengthen national defense and to encourage and assist the expansion and improvement of higher education programs in science, technology, mathematics, and modern foreign languages.

National Institutes of Health (NIH)   The principal biomedical research agency of the U.S. federal government. It's mission is to employ science in the pursuit of knowledge to improve human health conditions.

National Labor Relations Board (NLRB)   Federal agency that administers the nation's laws relating to labor relations in the private and nonprofit sectors.

National Oceanographic and Atmospheric Administration (NOAA)   A federal administration whose primary mission is to explore, map, and study the world's oceans and atmosphere.

National Performance Review (NPR)   A program established by the Clinton Administration to strengthen the delivery of public services at all levels of government. The first report of the program was published in 1993.

Non Governmental Organizations (NGOs)   Private, not-for-profit organizations of a charitable, public service, research, or educational nature concerned with problems of a global, national, or local scale.

North American Free Trade Agreement (NAFTA)   A trade agreement removing trade barriers between the United States, Canada, and Mexico.

North Atlantic Treaty Organization (NATO)   A mutual defense alliance formed in 1949 whose purpose was to provide for the collective defense of the member states against the perceived threat of the Soviet Bloc.

Northwest Territory   Land governed by surveying practices of the Land Ordinance of 1785 covering the current states of Ohio, Indiana, Illinois, Michigan, Wisconsin, and parts of Minnesota.

Occupation Safety and Health Administration (OSHA)   Federal body that develops regulations and standards relating to occupational health and safety issues.

Office of Management and Budget (OMB)   An office in the executive branch of the federal government that is designed to help the president prepare the fiscal budget and manage the government.

Old Age Survivors Disability Insurance (OASDI)   Federal program created by the Social Security Act of 1935 that taxes both workers and employers to pay benefits to retired and disabled people, their dependents, widows, widowers, and children of deceased workers.

Opportunity cost   The highest valued alternative given up to pursue an activity.

Organization of Petroleum Exporting Countries (OPEC)   Oil producing countries that are net exporters of crude oil and petroleum-based products.

Palestine Liberation Organization (PLO)   A representative organization of the Palestinian people.

Per capita income   The mean income for every man, woman, and child in a particular group.

Performance standard   Pollution standard in which the polluter must meet a specific level of performance in pollution abatement, but the method used to achieve that performance is left up to the polluter.

Popular agenda   The policy issues that are considered important by the general public at any particular time.

Pork barrel   A term used to refer to expenditure authorizations that are included in a government's budget to benefit a particular constituency or special interest group.

Post-industrial economy   An economy where the primary focus is on the production of services, rather than goods. Characteristics of a post-industrial economy include the pre-eminence of a professional and technical class, the centrality of theoretical knowledge as the source of innovation and policy making, and the emphasis on the creation of intellectual technology.

Predatory pricing   Selling below purchase price or cost of production except in the case of seasonal or perishable goods. The objective of predatory pricing is to drive competitors out of business.

Privatization   The conversion of publicly delivered services into private-sector provision of the same service.

Productivity   A measure of output for a given level of input.

Protectionism   Actions taken by a government to limit foreign economic competition to its domestic enterprises.

Real value   Value measured in dollars of a constant purchasing power or adjusted by some index serving the same purpose.

Recession   A real (actual adjusted for price changes) decline in GDP for two consecutive quarters.

Regulation   The rule-making process of those administrative agencies charged with the official interpretation of a statue.

Regulatory barrier   This type of trade barrier—sometimes known as nontariff barriers—includes regulations and product standards that imported products must satisfy.

Relative poverty   A measure of poverty that is indexed in terms of the well-being enjoyed by everyone else in the society, rather than defined as a fixed benchmark that constitutes absolute poverty.

San Antonio Independent School District v. Rodriquez (1973)   The Supreme Court decision that examined the constitutionality of the Texas school finance structure and, by a narrow majority, refused to extend the "equal protection" clause of the Fourteenth Amendment to cover state school finance plans.

Securities and Exchange Commission (SEC)   Federal Commission that seeks the fullest possible disclosure to the investing public and seeks to protect the interests of the public and investors against malpractice in the securities and financial markets.

Separation of Powers   Constitutional doctrine that divides government power into three independently tenured branches granted legislative, executive, and judicial power.

Sherman Act (1890)   Federal statute that held "every contract, combination in the form of trust or otherwise, or conspiracy, in restraint of trade or commerce . . . is hereby declared to be illegal." While the statute was directed at industrial monopolies, the courts used the act punitively against the budding union movement. Subsequent legislation (The Clayton Act of 1914) exempted unions from the Sherman prohibitions on the restraint of trade.

Social Security   Otherwise known as the Old Age Survivors Disability Insurance program (OASDI), created during the Great Depression in 1935 to provide income support for dependent populations without the means of self support.

Social Security Administration (SSA)   U.S. government agency, originally part of the Department of Health and Human Services, that administers the natinal program of contributory social insurance whereby employees, employers, and the self-employed pay contributions that are pooled in special trust funds used to provide income to those eligible for Social Security.

Socialism   An economic system that would have the government or guilds of workers own and operate all means of production thus restricting, if not entirely eliminating, private enterprise.

Strategic Defense Initiative (SDI)   A program of the U.S. Department of Defense designed to create an air defense shield against ballistic missiles.

Structural unemployment   Unemployment that is a result of a basic change in the economic circumstances and work skills required in a region or nation that leaves some without jobs or the long-term prospects of finding full-time, paid employment.

Subsidy   A payment by a government agency to producers of goods, intended to make prices lower than they otherwise would be.

Supplemental Security Income (SSI)   Federal program that assures a minimum monthly income to especially needy people with limited income and resources who are 65 or older, blind, or disabled.

Tariff   Tax imposed on imports. Generally, tariffs are used for the purpose of protecting domestically produced goods.

The Poverty Line   Federal statistical measurement device used to record levels of absolute poverty in the United States. Defined as a basic food budget multiplied by three and indexed for inflation. First developed in the early 1960s.

Total Quality Management (TQM)   A management system that focuses on improving the overall quality of a good or service produced by an organization.

Trade deficit   The money total by which imports exceed the money total of exports.

Transfer payments   Payments by government made to individuals who provide no goods or services in return.

Type I error   An inferential error that occurs when attempting to generalize about reality based on examination of sample evidence or data. In statistics, the type I case involves a false-positive judgment, meaning that test results suggest significant association among variables where none in fact exists; thus, the researcher incorrectly accepts the false research hypothesis and rejects a true null hypothesis of no predictive association among variables. In practical terms, the type I error occurs whenever an innocent person is erroneously judged to be guilty and punished or when a patient tests positive and is treated for an illness he or she does not have. Attempts to reduce type I errors often increase type II errors.

Type II error   An inferential error that occurs when attempting to generalize about reality based on examination of sample evidence or data. In statistics, the type II case involves a false-negative result, meaning that test results suggest insignificant association among variables where a significant association does in fact exist; thus, the researcher incorrectly rejects the true research hypothesis and accepts the false null hypothesis of no predictive association among variables. In practical terms, the type II error occurs whenever a guilty person is erroneously judged to be innocent and is set free or whenever a sick patient is erroneously judged free of disease based on test results and not treated. Attempts to reduce type II errors often increase type I errors.

U.S. Agency for International Development (USAID)   Unit of the U.S. government that carries out assistance programs designed to help the people of less developed countries develop their human and economic resources, increase productive capacities, and improve the quality of life.

U.S. Department of Commerce (DOC)   Cabinet level department of the federal government that encourages, serves, and promotes the nation's economic development and technological advancement.

U.S. Department of Defense (DOD)   Federal agency responsible for providing the military forces needed to deter war and protect U.S. security.

U.S. Department of Health and Human Services (DHHS)   Cabinet level department of the federal government most concerned with health, welfare, and income security plans, policies and programs. Formerly titled the Department of Health, Education and Welfare.

U.S. Department of Housing and Urban Development (HUD)   Main federal agency responsible for programs concerned with housing needs and improving and developing the nation's communities.

U.S. Department of Justice (DOJ)   Cabinet level department of the U.S. federal government that represents the citizens of the United States in enforcing the law in the public interest.

U.S. Department of Labor (DOL)   Federal agency whose purpose is to foster, promote, and develop the welfare of the workforce of the United States, to improve their working conditions, and to advance their opportunities for profitable employment.

U.S. Department of Transportation (DOT)   Cabinet level department of the federal government that establishes the nation's overall transportation policies.

Unemployment Insurance (UI)   Federal legislation that established programs designed to provide cash benefits to once regularly employed members of the labor force who become involuntarily unemployed and who are able and willing to accept suitable jobs. Created by the Social Security Act of 1935.

United Nations (UN)   An association of independent countries from all over the world with the aim of promoting international peace, security, and cooperation.

Voucher   Consumer subsidy in which consumers exercise choice in purchasing publicly funded services.

War on Poverty   A services-based strategy for dealing with problems of poverty in the United States. Promoted by the Johnson Administration in the mid-1960s.

World Bank   A multilateral development agency formed to provide loans and technical assistance to the less developed countries of the world.

Index

A

Abrams v. United States (U.S. Supreme Court), 15–16
Act to Regulate Commerce (1887), 62, 219
Africa, 152, 345
  North, 368–369
  South, 352, 374
  sub-Saharan, 147, 374
Age and poverty, 171–172
Agriculture, 338–359
  employment in, 340, 342, 345
  environment and, 358–359
  farm income from, 343, 344, 345
  policy goals for, 344–346
  price stability for, 344–345, 347–348. *See also*
    Dairy policy; Honey program; Peanut
    policy; Sugar policy
  subsidies for, 17–18, 138, 348–351
  U.S. trends in, 339–344
Agriculture policy:
  effects of, 349–351
  food and, 345–346
  instruments of, 346–349
Aid to Families with Dependent Children
  (AFDC), 38, 173–174, 176–177, 474
Airline industry, 220–222, 223–232
  fares and, 226–228
  safety and, 228–232
  service and, 228

Aluminum, recycling of, 311
America 2000, 260, 261
American Civil War, 12, 96, 404
American Federation of Labor-Congress of
  Industrial Organizations (AFL-CIO), 474
American Revolution, 96
American Society for Testing and Materials
  (ASTM), 72
Anarchy, 13
Appendix on education, 272–275
Arabs, 247, 366–367
Arrow, Kenneth, 18
Arrow's paradox, 18–20, 474
Asia Pacific Economic Cooperation Group
  (APEC), 153, 161n.22, 373, 381, 474–475
Asian Development Bank, 381, 475
Asmus, Ronald, 380
Aspin, Les, 392–394
Association of South East Asian Nations
  (ASEAN), 381, 475
Automobile import-restraint agreement (U.S.
  and Japan), 61

B

Balkan states, 369, 370, 371
Banfield, Edward, 179–180
Basic Education Opportunity Grant, 176–177
Becker, Carl, 15

Body politic, 14
Bosnia, 369, 370, 371, 378, 379
Brady Handgun Violence Prevention Act (1993), 334–335, 475
Broder, David, 42
Brown v. Board of Education of Topeka (U.S. Supreme Court), 268–269, 475
Bureaucracy(ies), 24–25
   vested interests of, 39
Bush, George, 153, 363, 375, 391, 408, 427

C

Caiden, Gerald, 449
Canada, 85, 148, 153, 256
   agriculture in, 349, 353–354, 359
   environment and, 293, 294, 299. *See also* Great Lakes
   government outlays in, 74, 377
   health care in, 196, 197, 203
   trade with, 132–133, 153–154
Cantril, Hadley, 2
Capital gains tax, 113
Capitalism, 475
Carnegie Commission (National Commission on Excellence in Education), 245–246, 248
Carter, Jimmy, 363, 406, 421
Categorical logic, 174–175, 475
Census Bureau, statistical data by, 461–462
Charter schools, 266–267
Checks and balances, 22, 32
China, 136, 300, 358, 362, 363, 372–373
Chlorofluorocarbons (CFCs), 284–285
Citizens, 14
Civil Aeronautics Board (CAB), 220–222, 223–224
Civil service, 414–419
   reform of, 414–416
Civil Service Reform Act (1978), 416–417
Civil War (U.S.), 12, 96, 404
Clayton Act (1914), 475
Clean Air Act, 286–287, 475
Clean Water Act, 287–289
Clinton administration, 111–112, 113, 119, 124, 136, 153, 156, 187, 207
   education and, 260–261
   foreign policy of, 363–364, 375, 377–378, 380
   government reform and, 408, 409–410, 426
   national security and, 392–393
Clinton, Bill, 2, 443, 451
Commodity Credit Corporation, 347, 355
Communism, 475
Communitarian perspective on society, 27, 28, 29

Community Action Programs (CAPs), 180
Comparative advantage, 58–59, 138, 139
Comprehensive Environmental Response, Compensation, and Liability Act (CERCLA), 290–291
Conference on Security and Cooperation in Europe (CSCE), 378, 379–380. *See also* Organization for Security and Cooperation in Europe [OSCE]
Congress
   103rd, 129, 137, 153, 333
   104th, 5, 124, 385
   source information for, 458–460
   trade and, 135, 136
Conservative view, 40
Constitution (U.S.), 15, 22, 23, 26, 36–37, 112, 268–269
   commerce clause of, 56
   Eighth Amendment to, 323
   Fifth Amendment to, 268, 323
   First Amendment to, 15, 268, 320
   Fourteenth Amendment to, 268–269
   Fourth Amendment to, 322
   Nineteenth Amendment to, 405
   Preamble to, 26
   Sixth Amendment to, 322, 323
   Tenth Amendment to, 36, 335
Consumer and producer price indexes, 470
Contract with America, 2–5, 92, 112, 408
Corporate Average Fuel Economy (CAFE) standard, 59–60, 61
Council of Economic Advisors (CEA), 99, 476
Crime, 317–335
   data on, 325–329
   guns and, 332–333, 334–335
   issues of, 322–323, 336n.7
   policy for, 333–335
   problem of, 320–323
   public opinion surveys of, 324–325
   punishment and, 329–331
   U.S., 323–329
Criminal justice system(s), 318–319, 321–322
Criticism and analysis, 15
Culture and government, 42–43
Currency exchange, 138, 156–158
Current account balance, 476
Czech Republic, 142, 150, 369, 370, 380, 382, 387

D

Dairy policy, 354–356
Day Care (Title XX Social Security Act), 176–177
Deming, W. Edwards, 434–439

Democracy, 13–14, 20
  attributes of, 14
  laboratories of, 24, 35n.25
  parliamentary, 20
  presidential, 20–21
  U.S. form of, 20–26
    chief executive in, 24–25
    complexities with, 24–26
Democratic party, 40, 41
Demographics and government, 37, 325
Depression, economic, 476
Design standard in pollution abatement, 283
DiIulio, John, 410, 413, 418, 419, 447, 449
Division of powers, 22, 32
Drucker, Peter, 26

E

e pluribus unum problem, 18
Earned Income Tax Credit (EITC), 184–185
Economic policy
  domestic, 96–126
  fiscal policy in, 115, 477–478
  foreign policy and, 384
  international, 128–159
  monetary policy in, 116, 479
  objectives of, 105–119
  policy issues for, 124–125
Economy
  assessment of, 119, 123–124
  government in, 97–99
    allocation by, 98
    income distribution by, 98–99
    stabilization by, 99
  growth of, 99, 103–114
  information sources for, 465, 470
  measurement of, 99–103
    growth and, 103–105
  price supports and, 346–348
  stabilization of, 99, 114–119
Economy of scale, 476
Education, 245–271, 272–275. *See also*
    Schools
  academic achievement and, 254–256
  communities and, 264
  condition of, 250–257
  expenditure rates for, 253–254
  funding for, 267–270
  "high-performance" standards and, 273–274
  "innovation process" and, 274
  labor market and, 248, 249, 258–259,
    264–265
  "moving foundations" for, 272–273
  performance standards for, 263
  the problem of, 246–250

reinvention of, 259–260
  school-to-work programs and, 264
  standards for, 257–258, 272–275
  strategies for, 258–267, 272–275
  technology and, 246, 248, 258
  values training and, 259
  vocational, 264
  vouchers and, 265–266
Egypt, 110, 367, 369, 375, 392
Eighth Amendment, 323
Employment. *See also* Unemployment insurance
  on farms, 340, 342, 345
  in government, 7, 9
  information sources on, 464, 469
  training and, 264, 265, 272–275
Energy information sources, 468–469
Entrepreneurship, 10
Environment
  agriculture and, 358–359
  information sources on, 468, 469
Environmental policy, 278–315
  approaches to, 281–283
  costs and benefits with, 282
  early problems in, 279–280
  global warming and, 294–298
  laws embodying, 285–291, 306–307
  radon and, 298–300
  science in, 283–285
  solid waste and, 300–315
  standards with, 282–283
  toxic chemicals and, 291–294
Environmental Protection Agency (EPA), 44,
    62, 286, 288, 289, 290, 291, 314, 385,
    476
  solid waste disposal and, 307
Equal Employment and Opportunity
    Commission (EEOC), 476
Equity, 185–186. *See also* Earned Income Tax
    Credit (EITC)
Eurocorps, 379, 382
Europe
  Central, 142, 369–371
  Eastern, 279–280, 369–371, 375
European Community (EC), 150, 157
  agriculture in, 346, 349, 350, 359
  statistical sources by, 463–464
European Monetary System (EMS), 156–157
European Union (EU), 131, 150, 151
  security policy and, 381–383
  trade and, 137, 138, 149, 150
Exchange rate, 476
Excise taxes, 75, 83–85, 94
Exclusionary rule, 322, 336n.7
Exports, 476
Externalities, 50, 65–66, 281

F

Family and Medical Leave Act (1993), 183–184
Family Support Act (1988), 182–183
Federal Aviation Administration (FAA), 228, 477
Federal Bureau of Investigation (FBI), 325, 477
Federal Communications Commission (FCC), 477
Federal Deposit Insurance Corporation (FDIC), 477
Federal Emergency Management Agency (FEMA), 477
Federal Energy Regulatory Commission (FERC), 477
Federal executive branch, source information for, 457–458
Federal Home Loan Bank Board, 477
Federal Maritime Commission, 477
Federal Quality Institute, 432
Federal Reserve Board ("Fed"), 56, 116–117, 118–119, 123, 130–131, 405, 477
Federal Savings and Loan Insurance Corporation (FSLIC), 477
Federal Trade Commission (FTC), 477
Federalism, 22–24, 477
  problems in, 407–408
The Federalist Papers, 10, 21, 405, 477
Fifth Amendment, 268, 323
Firearms and crime, 332–333
First Amendment, 15, 268, 320
Fiscal policy, 115, 477–478
Food, 345–346
Food and Drug Administration (FDA), 67, 207, 478
Food stamps, 176–177
Foreign policy, 361–384
  economic policy and, 384
  information sources for, 464–467
  institutions of, 375, 377–384
  world order and, 365–375, 401n.10
Fourteenth Amendment, 268–269
Fourth Amendment, 322
France, 148, 150, 157, 381, 382, 383
  agriculture in, 350
  government outlays in, 74, 377
  health care in, 196, 197
  security policy in, 379, 380, 382
Frederickson, H. George, 447, 448
Free, Lloyd A., 2
Freedom of expression, 14–15, 34n.17
  limiting of, 16
Frictional unemployment, 478
Full employment, 478
Full Employment Act (1946), 99

G

Gadsby, William, 411, 413
Gaebler, Ted, 42, 414–415, 426, 441–443
Garvey, Gerald, 410, 413, 418, 419, 447
GATT (General Agreement on Tariffs and Trade), 137–138, 148–150, 151–152, 478
Gaza Strip, 367
GDP (gross domestic product), 99–100, 101, 103, 104–105, 120
General Agreement on Tariffs and Trade (GATT), 137–138, 148–150, 151–152, 478
Germany, 148, 150, 157, 159, 370, 380, 381, 382, 386, 387
  education in, 250, 264
  environment in, 280, 311, 312–313
  government outlays in, 74, 377
  health care in, 197, 203–204
  security policy in, 379, 382
Gerrymander, 478
G.I. Bill (Serviceman's Readjustment Act), 251
Glass, recycling of, 312
Global warming, 294–298
Glossary of terms, 474–483
Goals 2000, 260–262
Goods and services
  classification of, 27, 28
  consumption and, 27, 28
  exclusion and, 27, 28
Goodsell, Charles, 449
Gore, Albert, 294, 443, 444, 445
Government, 12–13, 26, 32
  American attitudes toward, 10
  competition within, 25. *See also* Power(s)
  culture and, 42–43
  direct action by, 30–31
  domestic economy and, 97–99
  employment in, 6, 7
  environmental intervention of, 282–283
  federal, 6, 7, 8, 9, 23, 24–25, 37
    budget deficit of, 107–108, 109, 110–112, 475
    budget for, 411, 420–422
    management reform in, 409–411, 448–450
    problems under, 407–408
    short-term mentality in, 411–412
    source information for, 456–460
  financing of, 74–95
  forms of, 13–14
  goals of, 26, 32, 419–420
    actions and, 26–32
  growth of, 7, 8–9
  laissez-faire, 29–30, 97, 479

local, 6, 7, 8, 9, 24, 37
    source information for, 460, 462–463
performance by, 51–52, 412–414, 419–422
    accountability and, 413–414
    budgeting and, 420–422
    civil service and, 414–416
    Congress and, 412–413
    measurement of, 419–420
    structure of and, 412–414
private market solutions by, 31–32
privatization and, 67, 426–427, 448–450
quality management and, 432–441, 447
reform of, 403–423, 425–453
republican form of, 14, 21–22
revenues of, 8
services by, 30–31, 37–41, 427–430, 441–443
    demographic change and, 37
    income per capita and, 38
    income redistribution and, 38
    inefficiency in, 39–41
    population and, 38
    risk aversion and, 38
    vested interests in, 38–39
special purpose units of, 6, 10
state, 6, 7, 8, 9, 23, 24, 37
    source information for, 460, 462–463
table of, 6
21st century and, 425–453
worker dissatisfaction with, 417–418
Grant, 478
Great Britain, 146, 148, 150, 157, 362, 381, 382,
    383, 386
    agriculture in, 350
    environment in, 279, 301–302
    form of government in, 13
    government outlays in, 74, 377
    guns and, 332–333
    health care in, 196, 197, 203, 212
    security policy in, 382
Great Depression, 135, 163, 173, 339, 340, 405
Great Lakes, 291–294
Greece, 150, 350, 369, 370, 375, 381
    early democracy in, 13
Greenhouse effect, 296–297
Gridlock, 26
Gross domestic income (GDI), 100–101, 103
Gross domestic product (GDP), 99–100, 101,
    103, 104–105, 120
Gross national product (GNP), 100
Group of Seven (G-7), 131, 148, 372

H

Hamilton, Alexander, 361, 405
Harrington, Michael, 178–179, 180

Harrington, Samuel, 401n.10
Health care, 191–213
    access and, 194–195, 204, 207
    catastrophic insurance and, 211
    context for, 191–200
    cost of, 195, 207–208
    delivery mechanisms and, 204–205
    government planning and management of,
        205, 206–207
    indicators for, 195–200
    national health service and, 212
    national insurance and, 211
    policy choices for, 207–212
        present system and, 209–210
    quality of, 195
    rationing of, 197
    regulation and, 208, 210
    restructuring of, 212
    technology and, 205–206
Health care industry
    alternatives for, 203–207
    assessment of, 200–203
    institutional arrangements of, 202–203
    organized interests of, 201–202
    U.S. indicators of, 195–200
Health insurance, 192–193
    catastrophic, 211
    national, 211
    pre-existent conditions and, 192, 214n.5
Health maintenance organizations (HMOs),
    208–209, 478
Health security (*see* Health care)
Highways, 238
Historical and current data sources, 470
"Hollow military," 396
Holmes, Oliver Wendell, 15–16
Homelessness, 169, 171
Homestead Act (1862), 478
Honey program, 357–358
Horner, Constance, 418
Houghton, Richard, 294
Human capital, 478–479
Human resource capitalism (HRC), 262–265, 479
Hungary, 142, 150, 369–370, 371, 380, 382, 387

I

Ideology, 479
Immigration, 106, 107
Import quota, 479
Imports, 479
Income
    farm, 344, 345
    government services and, 38
    redistribution of, 38

Income tax
   corporate, 75, 82–83, 94
   personal, 74–75, 80–82, 94
Individual rights, 37, 40
Individualistic view of society, 28–29, 175, 178, 180
Industrial policy, 113–114
Inflation, 117–119, 479
Infrastructure, 37
Institutional agenda, 45–48, 479
Interest(s)
   private, 17–18, 21
   public, 12–13, 18
Intergovernmental grants, 75, 90–91
Intergovernmental mandates, 91
Internal Revenue Service (IRS), 479
International Bank for Reconstruction and
     Development (World Bank), 146, 147–148, 378
   statistical sources by, 463
International Institute of Economics (IIE), 145, 155–156
International Monetary Fund (IMF), 146, 147–148
   statistical sources by, 463
International statistical sources, 463–467
Internet information, 471–473
Interstate Commerce Commission (ICC), 56, 62, 219, 232–233, 234, 235–236, 479
Iran, 247, 363, 368
Iraq, 44, 363, 367–368, 378, 394, 395
Iron Law of regulation, 57–62
Iron triangle(s), 25, 47, 479
Ishikawa, Kaoru, 433–434
Israel, 110, 247, 366–367, 375, 392
Issue attention cycle, 44, 479
Issue coalitions, 46, 47

J

Jackson, Andrew, 404
Japan, 148, 159, 386
   agriculture in, 345, 346, 359
     subsidies and, 349, 350
   education in, 250, 252, 264
   environment in, 301
   government outlays in, 74, 375, 377
   health care in, 196, 197, 203
   industry in, 248
   trade and, 61, 131, 132–133, 136, 154–156
   U.S. security and, 392
Jefferson, Thomas, 16
Job Training Partnership Act, 176–177, 181
Johnson, Lyndon, 180, 362, 407, 421

Johnson, William, 43–44
Jordan, 366, 369
Juran, J.M., 433

K

Kazakhstan, 371
Kettl, Donald, 410, 413, 418, 419, 447
Korb, Larry, 387–390
Korea
   North, 362, 373–374, 394
   South, 250, 256, 311, 359, 386, 392
Krauthammer, Charles, 387
Kugler, Richard, 380

L

Labor statistics sources, 469
Land Ordinance (1785), 250, 479
Larrabee, Stephen, 380
Latin America, 374–375
   trade with, 124, 131, 135, 136, 137, 154
Law, environmental, 285–291, 306–307
Layer cake metaphor, 23
Lee Kuan Yu, 373
Legislature, 25
Levine, Charles, 410–411, 416
Liberal political view, 40
Libya, 363
Licensing fees, 75, 89
Lincoln, Abraham, 404
Lindzen, Richard, 294
Lugar, Richard, 154, 372, 380

M

Madison, James, 21
Mandates, intergovernmental, 91
Market intervention and environmental policy, 281–283
Marriage and poverty, 172–173
Marshall, Ray, 249, 260, 262–263
Mass transit. *See* Public transit
McCulloch v. Maryland (U.S. Supreme Court), 11
McNamara, Robert, 421
Medicaid, 176–177, 201, 479
Medical Information Bureau, 202, 214n.5
Medicare, 176–177, 201, 479
Mencken, H.L., 29
Merit good, 98
Mexico, 118, 153, 358, 374–375
   trade with, 137, 142, 153–154, 311
Middle East, 118, 152, 364, 366–369, 392, 394

Mieklejohn, Alexander, 16–17
Mill, John Stuart, 15
Models, 49
Moe, Ronald, 450
Monarchy, 13
Monetary policy, 116, 479
Monopoly(ies), 39, 62–65, 479
    artificial, 64
    natural, 63–64
    regulation and, 67–69
Morrill Act (1860), 251
Mortality and income, 187
Musgrave, Richard, 97–98

N

National Academy of Public Administration
    (NAPA), 407, 450–451, 479
National Aeronautics and Space Administration
    (NASA), 479–480
National Commission on Excellence in
    Education (Carnegie Commission),
    245–246, 248
National Commission on the State and Local
    Public Service (Winter Commission),
    445–446
National Defense Education Act (1958), 251
National health service, 212
National income accounts, 99–103
National Institutes of Health (NIH), 197–198,
    480
National Labor Relations Board (NLRB), 480
National Oceanic and Atmospheric
    Administration (NOAA), 480
National Performance Review (NPR), 409–410,
    422, 426, 443–445, 450–451
National security policy, 384–400
    defense strategy and, 391–400
    foreign security organizations and, 379,
        380–381, 382
    post-Cold War era and, 387–391
"New world order," 363–365
NIMBY (not in my backyard), 301
Nineteenth Amendment, 405
Nixon, Richard, 362–363, 407
Nongovernmental organizations (NGOs), 378,
    430–432, 480
North Africa, 368–369
North American Free Trade Agreement
    (NAFTA), 129, 136, 137, 153–154,
    375
North Atlantic Treaty Organization (NATO),
    362, 379–380, 392, 480
    U.S. view of, 390

Northwest Territory, 480
NSF International, 72, 430

O

Occupational Safety and Health Administration
    (OSHA), 56, 67, 69, 480
Office of Management and Budget (OMB),
    412, 480
Officials of government, 14
Old Age Survivors Disability Insurance (Social
    Security), 174, 176–177, 480
O'Lessker, Karl, 112–113
Oligarchy, 13
Opportunity cost, 480
Organization for Economic Cooperation and
    Development (OECD), 134, 135
    statistical sources by, 463, 464
Organization for Security and Cooperation in
    Europe (OSCE), 380–381
Organization of Petroleum Exporting
    Countries (OPEC), 132–133, 247, 480
Osborne, David, 42, 411, 414–415, 426,
    441–443, 451
Ozone depletion, 284–285

P

Palestine Liberation Organization (PLO), 366,
    368, 480
Palumbo, Dennis, 429
Paper, recycling of, 311–312
Parliamentary systems, 20
Payment-in-Kind (PIK) program, 338–339
Peanut policy, 356–357
Pentagon Papers, 16, 34n.17
Per capita income, 480
Performance standard in pollution abatement,
    283
Periodical indexes, 471
Perry, William, 393
Pfaff, William, 371
Pierce, Neal, 42
Plastics, recycling of, 312
Poland, 142, 369, 370, 380, 382, 387
    environment in, 279–280
    form of government formerly in, 13
Policy analysis, 15, 48–53
    framework for, 52
Policy choices, framework for, 48–53
Policy networks, 25
Population and government, 38
Pork barrel projects, 38–39
Portugal, 150, 350, 375, 381, 383

Post-Cold War world, 387–390
Post-industrial economy, 481
Poverty, 163, 164–173
 absolute, 164, 165–168, 474
 age and, 171–172
 alternatives for, 175, 178–187
 marriage and, 172–173
 race and, 171, 172
 relative, 164, 168–169, 171
Poverty Line, the, 482
Powell, Colin, 392, 395
Power(s)
 checks and balances to, 22, 32
 division of, 22, 32
 separation of, 21, 22, 32, 40
Predatory pricing, 481
Price stability, 117–119
Prisons, 317
Productivity, 103, 107
Property tax, 75, 86–89, 94
Protectionism, 481
Protectionism. See also Trade, protectionism
 and
Public affairs information
 periodicals on, 11, 471
 source and statistical data for, 456–473
Public good, 13, 26, 98
Public housing, 176–177
Public interest, 12
Public-interest groups, 39
Public opinion poll sources, 467
Public policy, 36
 agenda of, 43–48
 action on, 47–48
 admission to, 40, 43–46
 institutional, 45–48
 ordering of, 40
 political parties and, 41
 popular, 43–45
 analysis of, 15, 48–53
 externalities in, 50, 359
 development of, 36–53
 government services and, 37–38, 39–41
 pre-policy process and, 43–50
 process of, 43–47
 vested interests and, 38–39
 education and, 250–257
 implementation of, 40–43, 51, 441–443
 evaluation of, 51–52
 market-based approaches to, 441–443
 monitoring of, 51–52
Public responsibility, 10
Public service. See Civil service
Public transit, 238–240

Q

Quotas in trade, 137

R

Race and poverty, 171, 172
Radon, 298–300
Railroad industry, 218, 219, 232–235
Raspberry, William, 42
Reagan, Ronald, 2, 363, 406, 407
Real value, 481
Recession, 481
Regional trade organizations, 150, 153–155
Regulation, 30, 55–73, 481
 environment and, 282–283, 286–291
 growth of, 55–56
 health care and, 208, 210
 information with, 66–67
 Iron Law of, 57–62
 issues with, 67–71
 monopoly and, 67–69, 219
 reasons for, 56–57, 62–67
 standard setting with, 69–71
 trade barriers and, 137–138
 of transportation, 218–224
Reich, Robert, 125
Religious fundamentalism, 368–369
Republican party, 2–4, 5, 40, 41, 92, 113
Resource Conservation and Recovery Act
 (RCRA), 289–290, 306–307
Revolution (1776), 96
Ricardo, David, 138–139
Rights of individuals, 37, 40
Risk aversion in government, 38
Rivlin, Alice, 408
Roosevelt, Franklin Delano, 362, 405, 406, 407
Roosevelt, Theodore, 404, 405
Rosenbloom, David H., 448–449
Ruhe, Volker, 382
Russia, 110, 148, 159, 370, 371–372, 387
 security policy in, 380
 U.S. interest with, 364, 372, 375, 380

S

Sachs, Jeffrey, 147–148
Sales taxes, 75, 83, 84, 85, 94
San Antonio Independent School District v. Rodriguez
 (U.S. Supreme Court), 269
Savas, Emanuel, 42, 428–429
School lunch program, 176–177
Schools, 245–246, 247, 248–271. See also
 Education
 charter, 266–267

completion rates for, 253
condition of, 250–257
enrollment in, 252–253
expenditure rates for, 253–254
funding for, 267–270
goals of, 257–258
strategies for, 258–267, 272–275
values training and, 259
Science
environmental policy and, 283–285
selected sources for, 468
Section 8 program, 176–177
Securities and Exchange Commission (SEC),
481
Self-government, 15, 16–17
Separation of powers, 21, 22, 32, 40
Serbia, 369, 370
Serviceman's Readjustment Act (G.I. Bill), 251
Shaw v. Reno (U.S. Supreme Court), 481
Sherman Act (1890), 481–482
Sixth Amendment, 322, 323
Sizer, Theodore, 260
Slovenia, 369, 370, 380
Smith, Adam, 97, 138
Smoot-Hawley legislation, 135
Social Darwinism, 12, 34n.11
Social good, 98
Social indicator sources, 467–468
Social Security (Old Age Survivors Disability
Insurance), 174, 176–177, 482
Social Security Administration (SSA), 165,
482
Social welfare, 37
Socialism, 482
Solid waste disposal, 300–315
federal legislation for, 306–307
incineration in, 313–314
landfills and, 303, 305, 308, 314–315
recycling and, 308–313
costs of, 308–310
source reduction for, 307–308
Solid Waste Disposal Act (1965), 306
South Africa, 352, 374
Special interests, 38–39
Spencer, Herbert, 178
Standard(s)
design pollution, 283
performance pollution, 283
voluntary consensus, 69–70, 71–72
State lotteries, 89, 90
Strategic Defense Initiative (SDI), 363, 387
Structural unemployment, 482
Subsidies in trade, 138
Sugar policy, 351–354
Superfund, 290–291

Supplemental Security Income (SSI), 174,
176–177, 482
Sweden, 150, 153, 299, 311, 370, 381, 383
agriculture in, 349, 350
government outlays in, 74, 377
health care in, 196, 197, 204
labor market in, 264, 265
Swiss, James, 447
Syria, 366

T

Tariffs, 136, 144, 482
Taxes, 74–75, 76–89, 92–94, 113–114
bases for levying of, 76–78
consumption, 93
equity in, 78–79
flat, 92–93
reform efforts for, 92–93
types of, 79–89
Technology and education, 246, 248, 258
Tenth Amendment, 36, 335
Thompson, Frank, 445, 446
Thurow, Lester, 249–250
Tipping fee, 316n.16
Total quality management (TQM), 432,
434–441, 447
Toxic chemicals, 291–294
Trade, 128–159
currency exchange barriers in, 138
deficits in, 482
export subsidies in, 138, 348
free, 138–145
international organizations in, 146–155
Japan and, 61, 131, 132–133, 136, 154–156
protectionism and, 17, 136–139, 140–145,
313
agriculture under, 345–346, 348
political support for, 140
regulatory barriers in, 137–138, 313
U.S. policy for, 130–131, 134–136
Transfer payments, 482
Transportation policy, 215–243
competition and, 222–224
control of monopoly and, 219
deregulation in, 223–224
industrial adequacy and, 219–222
promotion with, 217–219
Trucking industry, 219, 220, 235–237
Tuberculosis (TB), 193–194
Tucker, Marc, 249, 260, 262–263
Turkey, 368, 369, 370, 375, 381, 382
21st century, 425–453
Type I error, 482
Type II error, 482–483

U

Ukraine, 370, 371, 387
Underwriters Laboratories (UL), 72
Unemployment insurance, 174, 176–177
Unemployment Insurance Act (UI), 483
United Kingdom. *See* Great Britain
United Nations (UN), 362, 378–379
    statistical sources by, 463
    U.S. view of, 390
United States, statistical sources on, 460–463
Urban transportation, 238–240
U.S. Agency for International Development
    (USAID), 375, 377–378, 483
U.S. Department of Agriculture (USDA),
    338–339, 385
U.S. Department of Commerce (DOC), 483
U.S. Department of Defense, 385, 386, 388,
    390–391, 421
U.S. Department of Health and Human
    Services (DHHS), 483
U.S. Department of Housing and Urban
    Development (HUD), 483
U.S. Department of Justice (DOJ), 483
U.S. Department of Labor (DOL), 483
U.S. Department of the Interior, 358

U.S. Department of Transportation (DOT), 483
U.S. General Accounting Office (GAO), 450
User charges, 89

V

Value-added tax (VAT), 85–86, 94
Vested interests, 38–39
Voltaire, François Marie Arouet, 15

W

War on Poverty, 483
Welfare, 173–175
    alternatives for, 175, 178–187
    social, 37
Western European Union (WEU), 379–80, 381
Wilson, James Q., 1, 318, 330
Wilson, Woodrow, 361, 405
Winter Commission, 445–446
Wolfowitz, Paul, 364
Women, Infants, and Children (WIC), 176–177
World Bank, 146, 147–148, 378
    statistical sources by, 463
World Trade Organization (WTO), 147–150